Using Quattro®

by
David P. Gobel

Que™ Corporation
Carmel, Indiana

Library of Congress Catalog No.: 88-60444
ISBN 0-88022-334-8

91 90 89 88 8 7 6 5 4 3 2

Interpretation of the printing code: the rightmost double-digit number is the year of the book's printing; the rightmost single-digit number, the number of the book's printing. For example, a printing code of 89-1 shows that the first printing of the book occurred in 1989.

Using Quattro is based on Quattro Version 1.0.

Dedication

To moms and dads
everywhere . . .

especially Maria and Elsie

Publishing Director
Scott Flanders

Senior Editor
Lloyd J. Short

Editors
Sandra Blackthorn
Kelly Currie
Jeannine Freudenberger, M.A.
Steven L. Wiggins

Product Supervisor
David Maguiness

Technical Editor
Karen A. Bluestein

Editorial Assistant
Debra S. Reahard

Book Design and Production
Dan Armstrong
Sharon Hilgenberg
Carrie Torres Marshall
Jennifer Matthews
Cindy L. Phipps
Dennis Sheehan
Peter Tocco

Composed in Garamond and American Typewriter
by Que Corporation

About the Author

David P. Gobel

David P. Gobel is the president of Office Systems Services, a Springfield, Virginia, firm that specializes in consulting and programming services for IBM microcomputers. He has 14 years of experience in the office automation industry at IBM and other concerns. As Director of Computer Products Development for one of *INC. Magazine*'s 500 fastest growing companies and later as vice president of a local programming and consulting firm, he was a forerunner in the use of microcomputers in information systems management, service, support, and training.

Mr. Gobel lectures extensively on advanced microcomputer topics and has trained more than 4,000 corporation managers and PC coordinators. He is the author of *Using Lotus® HAL™*, published by Que Corporation.

Contents at a Glance

Part I Using the Quattro Spreadsheet

Uno-Dos-Tres . . . Quattro! An Overview 7
Getting Started 31
Learning Spreadsheet Basics 49
Working with the Menu Commands 75
Formatting Cell Contents 135
Using Basic Spreadsheet Functions: The Heart of Quattro 155
Using Advanced Spreadsheet Functions 227

Part II Managing Quattro Files, Reports, and Graphs

Managing Files in Quattro 297
Printing Professional Reports 331
Graphing with Quattro 367

Part III Managing Data with Quattro

Data Management 419
Quattro's Advanced Data Analysis Commands 465

Part IV Customizing Quattro: Menus, Macros, and Add-In Programs

How To Make Quattro Look and Work the Way You Want... 491
Working with Add-In Programs 523
Using Macros in Quattro 547
Quattro Macro Command Reference 571
Making the Best Use of Quattro's Macro Debugger 621

Appendix A: Command Reference Tables 637
Appendix B: Installation 645
Index 649

Table of Contents

Introduction 1

Who Should Buy This Book? 1
How To Get the Most Benefit from This Book 2
What's in This Book 2

I Using the Quattro Spreadsheet

1 Uno-Dos-Tres . . . Quattro! An Overview 7

What is Quattro? 8
The Quattro "Electronic" Spreadsheet 8
Formulas 10
What-If Analysis 12
Functions 13
- Mathematical Functions 13
- Financial Functions 13
- Statistical Functions 13
- String Functions 14
- Date and Time Functions 14
- Special Functions 14

Spreadsheet Commands 15
- Formatting the Worksheet 15
- International Formats 16
- Naming Blocks 16
- Copying Cell Entries 16
- Recalculating the Worksheet 17
- Quattro File Commands 18
- Protecting Cells and Files 18
- Password Protection 19
- Printing the Worksheet 19

Quattro Graphics 19
- Performing What-If with Graphics 20
- Printing Graphics 20

Quattro Database Management 21
- Advanced Commands and Functions 22
  - The /Advanced What-If Command 23
  - Multiple Regression and Simultaneous Equations 23

Keyboard Macros and the Macro Commands 23
Quattro Software and Hardware Requirements and Options 24
The Quattro Disks 25
Quattro on the IBM PC and PS/2 25
Hardware Requirements and Extras 26
Quattro's Use of Memory 27
Operating Speed of Quattro 29
Add-In Software 29
Chapter Summary 30

2 Getting Started 31

Starting Up and Exiting Quattro 32
Learning the Quattro Keyboard 33
The Alphanumeric Keys 35
The Numeric Keypad and the Cursor-Movement Keys 36
The Function Keys 37
Learning the Quattro Screen Display 39
The Input Line 40
The Descriptor Line 40
The Mode Indicators 40
The Lock Key Indicators 41
Other Indicators 41
The Error Messages Area 43
Using the Quattro Help Features 43
Finding On-Screen Help 43
Making Quattro Act Like 1-2-3 45
Taking the Quattro Tutorial 47
Chapter Summary 47

3 Learning Spreadsheet Basics 49

Entering Data into the Worksheet 50
Entering Numbers 50
Entering Formulas 51
Using Operators in Formulas 53
Correcting Errors in Formulas 54
Using Functions 55
Entering Labels 56
Editing Data in the Worksheet 59
Using the Search and Replace Commands 62
Moving around the Spreadsheet 67
Using the Basic Cursor-Movement Keys 69
Using the End Key for Cursor Movement 70
Jumping to a Cell 72
Chapter Summary 73

4 Working with the Menu Commands 75

Selecting Commands from Command Menus 76
Viewing Expanded Menus 78
Assigning Accelerator Keys to Menu Commands 80
Using the Primary Spreadsheet Commands 82
Using Blocks in the Worksheet 82
Naming Blocks 84
Using Block Names To Streamline Your Work 86
Deleting Block Names 89
Erasing Blocks 89
Getting a List of Block Names 89
Creating a Table of Block Names 91
Copying the Contents of Cells 91
Addressing Cells 97
Referencing Cells with Relative Addressing 97
Mixing Relative and Absolute Addressing 98
Using the F4 (Abs) Key To Set Absolute and Relative References 103
Converting Formulas to Values with the /Block Advanced Values Command (/BAV) 106
Transposing Rows and Columns with the /Block Advanced Transpose Command (/BAT) 106
Moving the Contents of Cells 108
Using the Expanding Cell Pointer for Pointing to Blocks 111
Using the End Key for Pointing to Blocks 113
Filling Blocks with Numbers 114
Protecting Cell Contents and Areas of the Worksheet 118
Managing Columns and Rows 119
Setting Column Widths 119
Hiding Columns 120
Inserting Rows and Columns 122
Deleting Rows and Columns 122
Erasing the Worksheet from Memory 127
Erasing the Worksheet 127
Laying Out the Spreadsheet 128
Freezing Titles on the Screen 128
Splitting the Screen 131
Saving Your File before You /Quit 133
Chapter Summary 134

5 Formatting Cell Contents 135

Setting Block and Default Formats 136
General Format 138
Fixed Format 139
Scientific Format 140

Currency Format 141
Financial (Comma) Format 142
The +/- Format 142
Percent Format 142
Date and Time Formats 143
Text Format 145
Hidden Format 146
The Reset Format Command 146
International Formats 146
Using the /Block Reformat Command for Formatting Text 147
Using Conditional Cell Colors 150
Dealing with Formatting Problems 151
Chapter Summary 153

6 Using Basic Spreadsheet Functions: The Heart of Quattro 155

Function Syntax 156
Quick Function Entry Aid 158
Math Operators 159
Comparison Operators 159
Precedence 160
Editing and Debugging Functions and Formulas 160
Gobel's First Law 161
The Acid Test for Debugging Formulas 161
Using /**B**lock **R**eformat To Compile and Decompile Formulas ... 162
Gobel's Second Law 167
A Summary 169
Statistical Functions 169
Basic Statistical Functions 171
@SUM 171
@AVG 171
@COUNT 173
@MAX 174
@MIN 178
Advanced Statistical Functions 180
@STD 180
@VAR 184
Mathematical Functions for General Use 184
@ROUND 184
@INT 185
@MOD 186
@RAND 187
@ABS 191
Logical Functions 191

@IF 191
Multiple Conditional Tests 193
Nested @IF Functions 193
Testing Transactions with @IF 195
Other Logical Functions 197
@ISSTRING 197
@ISNUMBER 197
@TRUE 197
@FALSE 198
@ISNA 198
@ISERR 198
Error Suppression 199
Financial Functions 199
@NPV 201
@IRR 203
@PV 205
@FV 206
@PMT 207
@RATE 209
@TERM 210
@CTERM 211
@SLN 212
@SYD 213
@DDB 214
Date and Time Functions 214
@DATE 216
@DATEVALUE 217
@DAY 218
@MONTH 219
@YEAR 220
@TODAY 220
@NOW 221
@TIME 223
@TIMEVALUE 223
@SECOND 224
@MINUTE 224
@HOUR 225
Chapter Summary 226

7 Using Advanced Spreadsheet Functions ... 227

Table and Array-Handling Functions 227
@CHOOSE 228
@VLOOKUP 230
@HLOOKUP 232
Text Lookups 235

@INDEX 238
@@ 240
Database Statistical Functions 243
@DSUM 245
@DAVG 246
@DCOUNT 248
@DMAX 248
@DMIN 249
@DSTD 249
@DVAR 250
Text Functions 250
@FIND 251
@MID 254
@LEFT and @RIGHT 257
@EXACT 258
@REPLACE 259
@LENGTH 259
@LOWER, @UPPER, and @PROPER 263
@REPEAT 264
@N and @S 267
@STRING 269
@VALUE 270
@TRIM 271
@CLEAN 272
@CHAR 272
@CODE 274
Macro-Related Special Functions 274
@CELL and @CELLPOINTER 276
@CELLINDEX 278
@NA and @ERR 279
@ROWS and @COLS 280
@CURVALUE 281
@FILEEXISTS 282
@MEMAVAIL and @MEMEMSAVAIL 284
Engineering and Trigonometric Functions 285
@SQRT 285
@PI 287
@SIN, @COS, and @TAN 287
@ASIN, @ACOS, @ATAN, and @ATAN2 288
@DEGREES 289
@RADIANS 289
@EXP 290
@LN 290
@LOG 290
Programmers' Functions 291
@HEXTONUM 291
@NUMTOHEX 291
Chapter Summary 293

II Managing Quattro Files, Reports, and Graphs

8 Managing Files in Quattro 297

A General Description of Quattro Files 298
Saving Files 299
Naming a New File.. 299
Saving Later Versions 301
Retrieving Files.. 302
Using Wild Cards for File Retrieval.......................... 304
Retrieving Files from Subdirectories 304
Translating Files 306
Using Password Protection.. 310
Deleting Files 313
Specifying Drives and Directories 313
Using Advanced File Handling Commands 314
Combining Files 314
Extracting Files 318
Accessing DOS from Quattro.. 320
Using !SQZ! To Compress Files.. 321
Importing Files 323
Parsing To Make Import Files Usable.......................... 325
The /File Parse Command 325
Cautions about Using /File Parse.......................... 330
Chapter Summary.. 330

9 Printing Professional Reports............... 331

Setting Up Your Reports.. 332
Printing Basic Draft-Quality Reports.......................... 333
Using the Sample Cash-Flow Projector Spreadsheet.............. 333
Quickly Printing One Screenful of Data (PrtSc).................. 336
Printing Draft-Quality Reports on One Page or Less 337
Printing Reports Longer than One Page.......................... 338
Hiding Segments within the Designated Print Block 342
Excluding Rows.. 342
Excluding Columns.. 343
Excluding Blocks.. 344
Controlling Paper Movement 345
Using the Print Menu's Line, Page, and Align Options.......... 345
Setting Page Breaks within the Spreadsheet.................. 346
Changing the Print Options.. 347
Headers and Footers 348
Left Headings and Top Headings 350

Setup Strings 353
Page-Break Characters 356
Page Layout: Margins and Page Length 356
Printing a Listing of Cell Contents 357
Resetting the Print Options 358
Preparing Output for Acceptance by Other Programs 359
Managing Printer Settings 360
Current Printer Hardware Settings 360
Default Hardware Text_Printer Options 361
Page-Layout Options 363
Page-Layout Setup Strings 364
Chapter Summary 364

10 Graphing with Quattro 367

Reducing Data "Noise" with Graphs 368
Basic Requirements for Creating a Graph 368
Hardware and Software Setup 369
Selecting a Graph Type 371
Specifying a Worksheet Data Block 372
Constructing a Combined Lines and Markers Graph 374
Enhancing the Appearance of a Basic Graph 375
Adding Descriptive Labels and Numbers 376
Using the Titles Option 376
Entering Labels within a Graph 379
Entering Labels below the X-Axis 381
Using the Legend Option 382
Altering the Default Graph Display 384
Setting a Background Grid 385
Changing the X- and Y-Axis Scale Settings 386
Spacing Display of X-Axis Labels 389
Overriding Graph Types 390
Working with Multiple Graphs 391
Creating Graph Specifications for Reuse 391
Resetting the Current Graph 392
Choosing the Right Graph 392
Selecting an Appropriate Graph Type 392
Building Graph Types 395
Combined-Lines-and-Markers Graphs 395
Stacked-Bar Graphs 397
Area Graphs 399
Bar, 3-Dimensional-Bar, and Rotated-Bar Graphs 400
Pie Graphs 405
XY Graphs 406
Quattro's Graph Output 410
Selecting and Setting Up Printers 411
Adjusting Graph Layout 414

Setting the Current Graph for Printing........................ 414
Chapter Summary... 416

III Managing Data with Quattro

11 Data Management 419

What Is a Database?.. 420
What Can You Do with a Quattro Database?........................ 421
Creating a Database.. 423
Setting Up a Database.. 424
Entering Field Names and Formatting a Database.................. 425
Entering Data.. 426
Using the Form Input Command.................................... 427
Modifying a Database... 429
Sorting Database Records....................................... 431
Adjusting the Sort Order....................................... 432
Using a One-Key Sort... 433
Sorting on Two or More Keys.................................... 435
Restoring the Presort Order.................................... 437
Searching for Records.. 439
Setting Minimum Search Requirements............................ 440
Defining the Search Block...................................... 442
Defining the Criteria Table.................................... 442
Issuing the Locate Command..................................... 443
Using the Formula Criterion Command............................. 444
Listing All Specified Records with the Extract Command......... 447
Defining the Output Block...................................... 447
Executing the Extract Command.................................. 448
Using More Complicated Criteria................................ 451
Wild Cards in Criteria Tables.................................. 451
Formulas for Searching Numeric Fields.......................... 452
Compound Conditions in a Criteria Table........................ 454
String Searches.. 459
Special Operators.. 459
Performing Other Types of Searches............................. 461
Searching for Unique Records................................... 461
Deleting Specified Records..................................... 462
Chapter Summary.. 464

12 Quattro's Advanced Data Analysis Commands 465

Table Building 470
  Advanced Database Output Using What-If Tables 476
  Frequency Distributions 481
The /Advanced Regression Command 484
The /Advanced Matrix Command 486
Chapter Summary 488

IV Customizing Quattro: Menus, Macros, and Add-In Programs

13 How To Make Quattro Look and Work the Way You Want 491

Modifying Hardware-Related Defaults 492
  Retaining Modifications to Defaults 492
  Modifying Hardware Screen Settings 493
Modifying Default Color Choices 494
  Choosing Palettes 496
  Selecting Menu Colors 497
  Selecting Spreadsheet Colors 498
  Setting Conditional Cell Colors 499
  Changing the Help Screen Colors 501
Internationalizing Quattro 502
Controlling Quattro's Formats 503
  Standardizing Display Formats 504
  Setting Label Alignment 504
  Suppressing the Display of Zeros 504
  Setting a Spreadsheet's Global Width of Column 505
  Modifying the Clock's Look 505
Setting Default Directories 506
Recalculating the Worksheet 507
  Choosing a Recalculation Mode: Automatic or Manual 508
  Choosing the Order of Recalculation:
    Columnwise or Rowwise 509
  Recalculating the Worksheet in Natural Order 511
  Using Iterative Recalculation 511
Protecting Your Spreadsheets 514
Defining Startup Defaults 514
  The Autoload File and Auto-Execute Macros 515
  Consequences of Changing the Default Extension 516

The Beep Default 516
Help Access Method 518
Default Add-Ins 518
The Menu Tree Defaults 518
The Compatibility Options 519
Chapter Summary 521

14 Working with Add-In Programs 523

Using Add-In Programs 524
Loading, Running, and Removing Add-Ins 524
Setting Up a Default Add-In 525
Using the Menu Builder Add-In 527
Adding a Macro to the Main Menu 527
Inserting a New Command 532
Using the Transcript Add-In 537
Working with Transcript 538
Recovering a Spreadsheet Block with Transcript 540
Using Transcript To Undo Errors 545
Chapter Summary 545

15 Using Macros in Quattro 547

Understanding Basic Macro Concepts 548
Creating Macros 552
Locating Macros 552
Planning and Typing Macros 553
Recording Macros 554
Starting Macros 559
Pauses for Input 562
Automatic Macro Execution 564
Designing Reliable Macros 565

16 Quattro Macro Command Reference 571

The Elements of Macro Commands 572
Macro Command Syntax 572
Flow Control Commands 573
The BRANCH Command 574
The DISPATCH Command 575
The FOR Command 576
The FORBREAK Command 578
The IF Command 578
The ONERROR Command 582

The QUIT Command 584
Subroutines 584
The RESTART Command 586
The RETURN Command 587
The STEPON and STEPOFF Commands 588
The WAIT Command 589
Variable Management Commands 590
The BLANK Command 591
The CONTENTS Command 592
The DEFINE Command 594
The LET Command 595
The PUT Command 598
The RECALC and RECALCCOL Command 600
User Interface Commands 601
The BEEP Command 602
The BREAKOFF and BREAKON Commands 602
The GET Command 603
The GETLABEL Command 605
The GETNUMBER Command 606
The INDICATE Command 607
The LOOK Command 607
The MENUBRANCH Command 608
The MENUCALL Command 611
The PANELOFF and PANELON Commands 612
The WINDOWSOFF and WINDOWSON Commands 612
File Manipulation Commands 613
The OPEN Command 614
The CLOSE Command 615
The READ Command 616
The READLN Command 617
The WRITE Command 618
The WRITELN Command 618
The SETPOS Command 619
The GETPOS Command 620
The FILESIZE Command 620
Chapter Summary 620

17 Making the Best Use of Quattro's Macro Debugger 621

Stepping through a Macro 622
Editing a Macro in DEBUG Mode 626
Inserting Macro Breakpoints 630
Testing the Results of Conditional Formulas 633
Keeping Track of Specific Cells 634
Chapter Summary 635

A **Command Reference Tables** 637

B **Installation** 645

Index 649

Acknowledgments

Primarily, I want to thank Debbie Gobel for her many important content suggestions and her continual support in the book's creation.

Second, thanks to Tye Gaither, Tony Korkolis, Doug Daniel, and Tommy Rice for their help and friendship.

Third, thanks to the staff at Que, who worked hard to ensure that this book is the best Quattro book available, especially Pegg Kennedy, Dave Maguiness, and Scott Flanders.

Trademark Acknowledgments

Que Corporation has made every effort to supply trademark information about company names, products, and services mentioned in this book. Trademarks indicated below were derived from various sources. Que Corporation cannot attest to the accuracy of this information.

Above Board is a trademark of Intel Corporation.

COMPAQ and COMPAQ 386 are registered trademarks of COMPAQ Computer Corporation.

dBASE, dBASE II, dBASE III, and dBASE III Plus are registered trademarks of Ashton-Tate Corporation.

EPSON is a registered trademark of Epson Corporation.

Hercules Graphics Card is a trademark of Hercules Computer Technology.

IBM is a registered trademark and OS/2, PC XT, Proprinter, and PS/2 are trademarks of International Business Machines Corporation.

LaserWriter is a registered trademark of Apple Computer, Inc.

Lotus, Symphony, VisiCalc, and 1-2-3 are registered trademarks of Lotus Development Corporation.

Microsoft is a registered trademark of Microsoft Corporation.

Paradox is a trademark of Ansa Corporation.

PFS:FILE is a registered trademark of Software Publishing Corporation.

PostScript is a registered trademark of Adobe Systems Incorporated.

Quattro is a registered trademark of Borland International, Inc.

Rampage is a registered trademark of AST Research, Inc.

SQZ! and Turner Hall are trademarks of Turner Hall Publishing.

SuperCalc is a registered trademark of Computer Associates International, Inc.

WordPerfect is a registered trademark of WordPerfect Corporation.

WordStar is a registered trademark of MicroPro International Corporation.

Conventions Used in This Book

The conventions used in this book have been established to help you learn to use the program quickly and easily. As much as possible, the conventions correspond with those used in the Quattro documentation.

In commands and menu options, the letter you press to choose that command is printed in boldface type; if a command has more than one word an underscore connects the words: /**B**lock **A**dvanced **M**ake_Table.

Spreadsheet cells are designated by the letter of the column and the number of the row: F10. A block of cells is listed as A3..D5.

Block names are written in all capital letters: DEPT.

Keys are written as they appear on the IBM keyboard. Function keys often include the name of the Quattro function: F1 (Help). Keystroke combinations are connected by a hyphen: Alt-F1.

Introduction

Quattro®: The Professional Spreadsheet has been a best-seller since its release. This new spreadsheet has full compatibility with 1-2-3®, the spreadsheet standard in the field of spreadsheets. Wisely, the designers of Quattro did not try to reinvent the wheel—they did not try to make an entirely new spreadsheet. Instead, they created a spreadsheet that is fully compatible with 1-2-3 but incorporates many improvements over 1-2-3 Release 2.0.

Using Quattro is a complete introduction to this amazing new product. This book provides everything you need to know to use Quattro efficiently.

Who Should Buy This Book?

If you use or are considering using Quattro, you should buy this book because *Using Quattro*

- Gets you up to speed quickly through the use of real-world spreadsheet applications
- Goes beyond the scope of the documentation or of other books about Quattro
- Explains not only how to use the features in Quattro but also how to make them work together so that you work less

In this book, you get more than syntax descriptions or command procedures. You see when to use certain commands or functions and when to avoid them. Because you get the benefit of the author's decade of business use of spreadsheet programs, you can take advantage of little-known techniques that can make a real difference to you as a user of Quattro.

If you are a new or infrequent user of Quattro, *Using Quattro* will show you how to become productive quickly. If you are an experienced spreadsheet user, the advanced techniques, shortcuts, and extensive function and macro reference sections will be indispensable. If you are a corporate trainer or PC coordinator, *Using Quattro* is the textbook to choose for training new or infrequent Quattro users.

How To Get the Most Benefit from This Book

The four-part organization of *Using Quattro* makes it convenient for use by readers with different purposes and levels of experience. Because each part treats a major component of the program, you can easily home in on the area of the program that interests you at any moment.

If you are a new user of spreadsheets, you will find significant help in the first part of the book. Part 1 helps you understand the basics of building a Quattro spreadsheet and provides a general overview of the program's functions. Most users also will benefit from the comprehensive function-reference chapters in this part.

All users can benefit from Part 2 because it deals with the enhancements Quattro brings to the spreadsheet standard. Part 2 concentrates on how to generate output from Quattro in terms of saving files and creating reports and graphs.

Intermediate and advanced users will find Part 3 particularly valuable. Part 3 concentrates on the data management capabilities of Quattro, including database management and statistics.

Finally, Part 4 shows you how you can customize Quattro through add-in programs, macros, and menu creation. Included in Part 4 is a complete reference chapter on Quattro's macro command language with example macros.

What's in This Book

As already pointed out, *Using Quattro* is organized into four parts. This organization makes the book convenient to use.

Part 1 provides a foundation for new users. In this part, you learn about spreadsheets in general and Quattro in particular. When you finish Part 1, you will know how to create a spreadsheet and use it for most basic spreadsheet activities.

Specifically, Chapter 1, "Uno-Dos-Tres . . . Quattro! An Overview" introduces you to electronic spreadsheets, describes the basic features of Quattro, and explains the open-software architecture, which lets you add programs to the central Quattro program.

In Chapter 2, "Getting Started," you learn how to start and leave Quattro. This chapter also describes how Quattro affects the keyboard and screen display and tells you how to access the program's Help systems.

You start building a spreadsheet in Chapter 3, "Learning Spreadsheet Basics." You learn to move the cell selector around the worksheet and to enter and edit data and formulas. The powerful Search and Replace commands, which automate cell editing, also are described.

Chapter 4, "Working with the Menu Commands," teaches you how to use the command menus and how to use named *blocks* (rectangular groups of cells, called *ranges* in 1-2-3). This chapter provides a comprehensive tutorial and reference source for the Block, Default, Column, Row, and Quit commands.

In Chapter 5, "Formatting Cell Contents," you learn how to change the way data is displayed in the worksheet (for example, currency, percentages, dates, or scientific notation).

"Using Basic Spreadsheet Functions," Chapter 6, and Chapter 7, "Using Advanced Spreadsheet Functions," provide an extensive tutorial for using Quattro's built-in formulas, the @functions. These functions are really the "heart" of Quattro. The functions can be learned and referenced according to the following groups: statistical, mathematical, logical, financial, date and time, table and array, database, text, special, engineering/scientific, and programming.

You learn the basics of saving, retrieving, and protecting your Quattro files in Chapter 8, "Managing Files." You also learn how to extract and combine data from portions of files. The chapter shows you how to use DOS subdirectories with Quattro and how to manage resource, definition, and program files. This chapter also explains how to use the superior file-translation capability of Quattro and how to prepare and save a file for use with dBASE® and other programs.

Part 2 emphasizes the new elements in Quattro. You learn in these chapters how to produce high-quality, professional-looking reports and graphs.

Chapter 9, "Printing Professional Reports," shows you how to print draft-quality reports from your Quattro spreadsheets and how to use a variety of print options to enhance the appearance of your printed reports. The chapter also shows you how to tailor Quattro to your specific hardware and printing needs.

In Chapter 10, "Graphing with Quattro," you learn how to take advantage of Quattro's extensive graphics capabilities. The text details how to create various graph types and how to print graphs.

Part 3 concentrates on Quattro's database capabilities, from simple data sorts to advanced mathematical and statistical analyses.

Chapter 11, "Working with Databases," teaches you how to manage data in Quattro. The material explains how you sort your data. In addition, you are shown how to set up a database input screen and how to make inquiries of the database to answer specific questions.

You find in Chapter 12, "Quattro's Advanced Databases," a survey of the advanced commands that allow you to do statistical analysis, such as linear regression, matrix analysis, and frequency analysis.

Part 4 shows you how to do the out-of-the-ordinary with Quattro. You learn to use macros, the Quattro command language, and special add-in programs.

Chapter 13, "How To Make Quattro Look and Work the Way You Want," shows how to set Quattro's default settings to control color, layout, and keyboard actions. In addition, you see how to set up certain cells so that they change color, based on the entry in the cell (for example, red for "over budget").

In Chapter 14, "Working with Add-in Programs," you learn to add programs to Quattro by using the Add-Ins section of the Macro menu. You see how to use the Quattro Menu Builder and the powerful Transcript add-in programs.

"Macro Fundamentals," Chapter 15, is an introduction to macros, with emphasis on quickly getting up to speed in creating macros. You are shown how macros automate repetitive operations and speed your work.

Chapter 16, "Quattro Command Language Reference," is a comprehensive reference chapter detailing the powerful command programming language in Quattro. You are shown how the commands work and when to use them. Each command is explained fully with appropriate examples.

Finally, in Chapter 17, "Making the Best Use of Quattro's Macro Debugger," you are introduced to the new debugging module of Quattro. You see how easily you can use the debugger to fix macros. You learn how to use the debugger to step through macros in slow motion and trace the action of a macro on various cells.

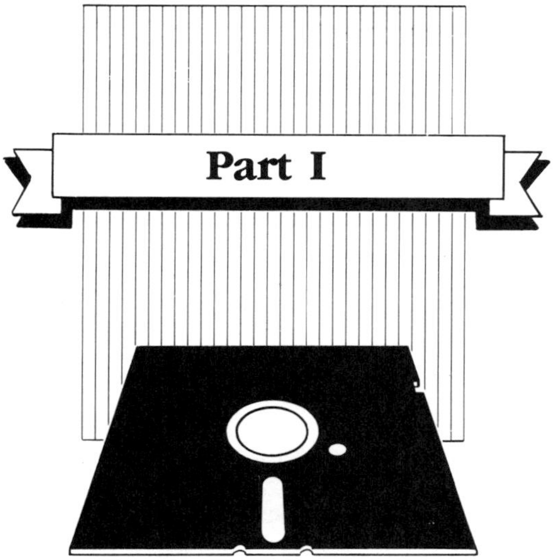

Using the Quattro Spreadsheet

Includes

Uno-Dos-Tres . . . Quattro! An Overview

Getting Started

Learning Spreadsheet Basics

Working with the Menu Commands

Formatting Cell Contents

Using Basic Spreadsheet Functions:
The Heart of Quattro

Using Advanced Spreadsheet Functions

CHAPTER

1

Uno-Dos-Tres . . . Quattro! An Overview

When the people at Borland International first decided to create a spreadsheet, they realized that 1-2-3® from Lotus® was the heavily entrenched standard in the field of professional spreadsheets. Instead of trying to reinvent what a spreadsheet is and how it should act, they decided to follow the standard with complete compatibility and provide improvements wherever possible. The result is Quattro®: The Professional Spreadsheet.

Quattro succeeds because it significantly improves on the standard that 1-2-3 established while maintaining complete compatibility. Also, Quattro is *not* copy protected. Even more impressive, Quattro is less than half the price of 1-2-3, and discounted versions are available.

These factors have led to phenomenal sales for Quattro. In the first month after the product shipped, Quattro sold nearly 100,000 copies. Quattro has continued to be a best-seller since then.

Despite the impressive start, this is just the beginning for Quattro. The next release of Quattro will provide support for OS/2™ and will maintain compatibility with 1-2-3 Release 3.0. Thus, Quattro and 1-2-3 will coexist in the office for years to come.

This chapter introduces you to the power of Quattro. You will learn about the basic design and features that classify Quattro as a world-class spreadsheet program and about the special features that set Quattro apart from its competition. This overview will help prepare you for applying Quattro to your business tasks.

What is Quattro?

What makes Quattro such an impressive spreadsheet program? Quattro integrates display graphics, output graphics, and data management with a first-rate spreadsheet. Quattro's overall design, built-in functions, and commands are based on the conventions used by early spreadsheet programs such as VisiCalc® and SuperCalc®; more importantly, they are completely compatible with 1-2-3. This compatibility means that if you know 1-2-3, you can use Quattro with almost no learning curve. Later, you can begin to use the impressive features that make Quattro a unique spreadsheet program.

Quattro uses several conventions that make it an excellent spreadsheet program. First, Quattro is designed as an "electronic" replacement for the accountant's columnar pad, pencil, and calculator. Second, Quattro understands relationships among all the numbers and formulas in a single application, and automatically updates values whenever a change occurs. Third, Quattro's commands simplify and automate the procedures for creating, changing, updating, printing, and graphing spreadsheet data.

The Quattro "Electronic" Spreadsheet

Quattro is essentially an electronic spreadsheet—an electronic replacement for the traditional financial modeling tools: the accountant's columnar pad, pencil, and calculator. In some ways, spreadsheet programs are to those tools what word processors are to typewriters. Spreadsheets offer dramatic improvements in ease of creating, editing, and using financial models.

The electronic spreadsheet is the foundation of the Quattro program. The framework of this spreadsheet contains the graphics and data-management elements of the program. Graphics are produced through the use of spreadsheet commands. Data management occurs in the standard row-column spreadsheet layout.

The importance of the spreadsheet as the basis for the whole product cannot be overemphasized. The spreadsheet commands and all the commands for related features are initiated from the same main command menu, and all the commands are in the same style. (For a complete listing of Quattro's commands and 1-2-3's equivalent commands, see Appendix A, "Command Reference Tables.") All of Quattro's special features originate from the spreadsheet. For instance, in data management, the database consists of records that are cell entries in a spreadsheet. Similarly, macros and macro commands are statements placed in adjacent cells in out-of-the-way sections of a spreadsheet. And all the commands for displaying graphs use spreadsheet entries to draw graphs on the screen.

The typical electronic spreadsheet formats a computer's on-screen appearance to resemble an accountant's columnar pad. Because this "pad" exists in the dynamic world of the computer's memory, the pad is different from paper pads in some important ways. For one thing, electronic spreadsheets are much larger than their paper counterparts. Quattro has 8,192 rows and 256 columns!

Each row in Quattro is assigned a number, from 1 to 8,192, and each column a letter, from A for the first column to IV for the last. The intersections of the rows and columns are called cells. Cells are identified by their row-column coordinates. For example, the cell located at the intersection of column A and row 15 is called A15. The cell at the intersection of column X and row 55 is called X55. Cells can accept three kinds of information: numbers; mathematical formulas, including special spreadsheet functions; and text (also called labels).

A *cell selector* allows you to enter information into the cells much as a pencil lets you write on a piece of paper. In Quattro, as in most spreadsheets, the cell selector looks like a bright rectangle on the computer's screen. The cell selector typically is one row high and one column wide.

With 8,192 rows and 256 columns, the Quattro worksheet contains more than 2,000,000 cells. A good way to visualize the worksheet is as one giant sheet of grid paper that is about 21 feet wide and 171 feet high!

There are some limitations to using the entire sheet, however. If you store just one character in each of the 2,097,152 available cells, your worksheet becomes far larger than the 640K maximum random-access memory (RAM) of an IBM® PC.

The Quattro program alone requires 343K of RAM. Quattro needs this much RAM because the program remembers cell formats, worksheet and command blocks, print options, hardware setup, and graph settings in RAM. Table 1.1 lists Quattro's specifications.

Because the Quattro grid is so large, the entire spreadsheet cannot be viewed on the screen at one time. The screen thus serves as a window onto the worksheet. To view other parts of the sheet, you *scroll* the cell selector across and down (or up) the worksheet with the arrow keys (and other *cursor-*

Table 1.1
Quattro at a Glance

Published by:
    Borland International

Minimum system requirements:
    IBM PC or compatible
    Display: color or monochrome
    Minimum disk drives: two 360K double-sided disk drives
    Minimum RAM memory size: 512K
    Maximum usable memory size: 640K plus 500K expanded memory (practical useful limit)
    Operating system: PC DOS Version 2.0 or above, or OS/2

Other hardware:
    color/graphics adapter, printer, plotter, expanded memory (to the computer's limit of 4M), 8087/80287/80387 coprocessors, hard disk

Also available for:
    IBM Personal Computer AT and compatibles
    IBM PS/2™ Computers
    IBM 3270 PC

movement keys; see Chapter 3). When the cell selector reaches the edge of the current window, the window shifts to follow the cell selector around the worksheet.

To illustrate the window concept, imagine cutting a hole one inch square in a piece of cardboard. If you placed the cardboard over this page, you would be able to see only a one-inch square section of text. Naturally, the rest of the text is still on the page; it is simply hidden from view. When you move the cardboard around the page (much as the window moves when you use the cursor-movement keys), different parts of the page become visible.

Figure 1.1 gives you an idea of the vast scope of the Quattro spreadsheet. If a Quattro worksheet uses the default column width of 9 characters, only 20 rows and 8 columns appear on-screen at one time.

Formulas

Electronic spreadsheets allow mathematical relationships between cells to be created. For example, if the cell named C1 contains the formula

```
+A1+B1
```

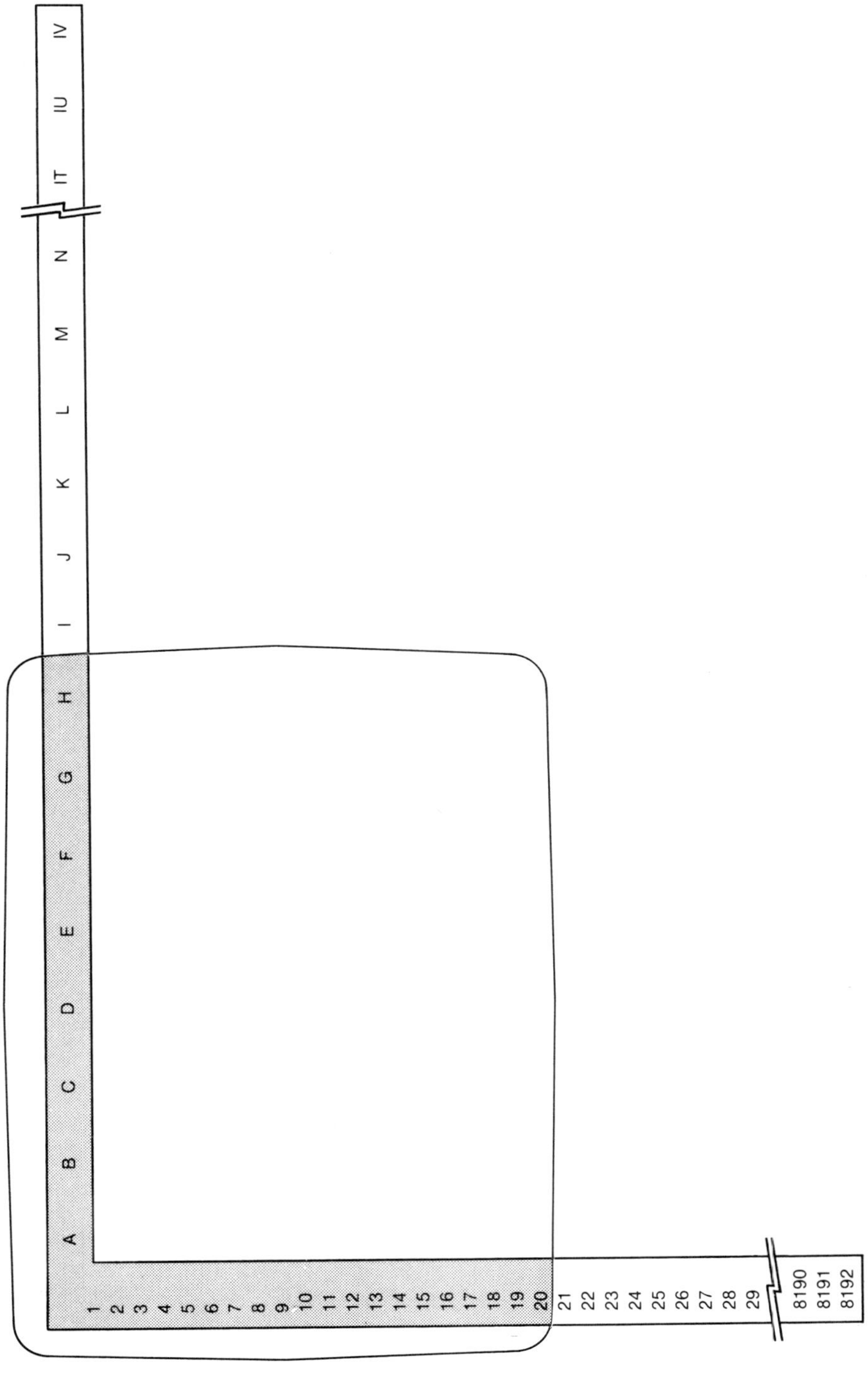

Fig. 1.1. The Quattro spreadsheet, showing the on-screen portion.

then C1 displays the sum of the contents of cells A1 and B1. (The + sign before A1 tells Quattro that this is a formula, not text.) The cell references serve as variables in the equation. No matter what numbers are entered in A1 and B1, cell C1 always returns their sum. For example, if cell A1 contains the number 5 and cell B1 contains the number 10, the formula in cell C1 returns the value 15. If you change the number in cell A1 to 4, then C1 changes to 14. Of course, spreadsheet formulas can be much more complex than this simple example. A cell can be added to, subtracted from, multiplied by, or divided by any other cell.

What-If Analysis

Through formulas, Quattro maintains the relationships between cells. Until you decide to change the relationships, every sum, product, division, subtraction, average, and net present value remains the same. Each time you enter data into the model, Quattro makes calculations at your command with no extra effort from you. Quattro calculates all these computations correctly, if you entered the correct data and instructions; spreadsheets don't make math errors. And next month, if you decide to use the same model again, the formulas will still be in place, ready to calculate at your command.

Even more important, spreadsheet software allows you to play what-if with your model. After you build a set of mathematical relationships into the worksheet, you can recalculate the worksheet with amazing speed, using different sets of assumptions. If you use only paper, a pencil, and a calculator to build your models, every change to the model requires recalculating every relationship within the model. If the model has 100 formulas and you change the first one, you must make 100 calculations so that the change flows through the entire model. However, if you use a spreadsheet, the same change requires pressing only a few keys; the program does the rest. This capability permits extensive what-if analysis.

For example, suppose that you build a financial projection for your business for the years 1988 through 1992. In building this forecast, you assume that your sales will grow at an annual rate of 10 percent. But what happens to your projections if the growth rate is only 3 percent? What if the rate is 15 percent? It might take hours to compute the effects of these changes using a pencil and calculator. With Quattro or other electronic spreadsheets, all you need to do is change the growth rate you entered in the sheet and strike one key to recompute. The calculations take just seconds.

As your models become more complex, this capability becomes more and more valuable.

Functions

As explained previously, you can create simple formulas involving only a few cells by entering cell addresses with the appropriate operator (+, -, /, *). To create complex formulas, you use Quattro functions. Functions are shortcuts that help you perform common mathematical computations with a minimum of typing. Functions are like abbreviations for otherwise long and cumbersome formulas. You use an @ symbol to signal Quattro that an expression is a function. For instance, the SUM function in Quattro is written as @SUM(A1..C1).

Quattro offers all the spreadsheet functions you would expect to find in a powerful spreadsheet program—and then some. The functions available in Quattro go beyond the standard set by 1-2-3 and cover a wide range of application needs, from financial to statistical to string functions. As illustrated in Chapter 16, combining Quattro's set of functions with the program's macro commands provides the capabilities available in high-level programming languages.

Mathematical Functions

Quattro offers a complete set of mathematical functions, not only for use in business, but also for engineering and scientific use. Quattro includes such common mathematical functions as @LOG, @EXP, @SQRT, @INT, and @ABS; a complete set of common trigonometric functions; a random-number-generator function; and functions for rounding and determining remainders.

Financial Functions

Quattro has a wealth of financial functions. In addition to the basic financial functions for net present value and internal rate of return calculations, the program includes a complete set of functions for annuity and compound growth rate calculations. Quattro even has functions for calculating depreciation by several common methods—straight line, sum of the years digits, and double declining balance.

Statistical Functions

Quattro offers basic statistical functions to calculate the sum, average, minimum, maximum, count, variance, and standard deviation of a block of values. These functions provide the worksheet's basic statistical capabilities. Corresponding database statistical functions perform the same calculations on those rows of a Quattro database that meet specified selection criteria.

For those who need greater statistical capabilities, Quattro also includes a multiple regression command (not a function) that can perform a regression with up to 16 independent variables.

String Functions

Quattro's string (or text handling) functions give you the power to manipulate strings in much the same way you manipulate numbers in a spreadsheet. The @FIND function, for example, allows you to locate the starting position of one string within another string. With the @MID, @LEFT, and @RIGHT functions, you can extract one string from another. Quattro includes several other string functions that provide a complete capability for manipulating alphanumeric data. These functions significantly enhance the integration of Quattro's spreadsheet and database capabilities.

Date and Time Functions

The Quattro date and time functions give you tremendous flexibility for manipulating dates and times in your worksheets. With the basic @NOW function, you can capture the current date and time from your system clock. The @DATE and @DATEVALUE functions allow you to enter dates in numeric or string formats, whereas @TIME and @TIMEVALUE give you the same capability for times.

Once dates and times are stored as date serial numbers in the worksheet, you can use ordinary mathematical commands to perform date and time arithmetic. A complete set of functions lets you extract the second, minute, hour, day, month, and year from a date serial number. Quattro also has a variety of formats for displaying date serial numbers as dates and times in the worksheet.

Quattro even has a special keystroke (Ctrl-D) to allow you to enter dates directly into the spreadsheet without having to reformat them later. Just press Ctrl-D, and enter a date such as 10-DEC-88. Quattro takes care of the format and conversion details.

Special Functions

Special Quattro functions include those to change numeric entries to strings (and vice versa) and others that help you manage both numbers and strings in your worksheets. Another special function, @FILEEXISTS, allows a macro to test whether a file is in the current directory before the macro tries to combine the file with another file. Other special functions are @@ (the indirect addressing function) and @CELL.

@CELL provides information about the contents of spreadsheet cells. If, for example, you enter @CELL("width",b12..b12), Quattro returns the width of column B as viewed in the current window. In addition to indicating width, the @CELL function can indicate a cell's address, data type, label prefix, format, or row and column number.

Spreadsheet Commands

Quattro includes several important commands that manipulate the worksheet in various ways. For example, all electronic spreadsheets include a command (or commands) to format the appearance of the contents of cells in the sheet. These commands can alter the display to make numbers appear in a variety of forms. You activate commands by pressing the slash key (/). After you type the slash, a menu of commands appears on the screen. You then select the command to be implemented.

Spreadsheet commands can be used at every phase of building and using a model. Because a spreadsheet holds a model in the computer's memory while you build it, you are not bound by the physical limitations of the printed page. Are some of your formulas repeated in different sections of your model? Use the spreadsheet's copy feature to quickly project your assumptions from one cell to another. Did you forget a row or a column? Simply insert the row or column at the appropriate point.

Quattro has many commands that allow you to perform a number of tasks in the spreadsheet. Commands are available to format the worksheet, name blocks, erase and copy data, perform calculations, store files, protect worksheet cells, protect files with passwords, and print your graphs and spreadsheets.

Formatting the Worksheet

Quattro offers a wide variety of formats for numeric entries. These formats include displaying or printing numbers with embedded commas, dollar signs, parentheses, or percent signs, and specifying the number of digits to display to the right of the decimal. For example, Quattro can format the number 12345 to look like $12,345.00, 12,345, 1.2345+4E, or 12345; the number -12345 to look like ($12,345.00) or -12,345; and the number .45 to look like 45% or $.45. (The details of Quattro's cell formats are covered in Chapter 5.)

These formatting features allow users to create finished reports and financial statements directly from analyses. Numbers can appear as you would expect them to in a formal document, and eye-pleasing spacing can be achieved by varying column widths.

Quattro always assigns formats to a block of cells. In fact, the format command is an option of a higher level command called /**B**lock. A block in Quattro can be as small as a single cell or as large as the entire worksheet. When you assign a format, the program prompts you to designate the appropriate block for that format by pointing to its limits with the cell selector.

International Formats

Through the /**D**efault **I**nternational command, you can change **C**urrency, **P**unctuation, **D**ate, and **T**ime formats to International defaults. The **C**urrency option, for example, enables you to change the default dollar sign ($) to a foreign currency sign such as the British pound (£) if you plan to use that format regularly throughout your worksheet.

Naming Blocks

Quattro also allows you to assign a name to a block. This feature lets you label an area for use in formulas or as the block for a command. For example, if a part of your worksheet is named SUMMARY, you can tell Quattro to print the section of the sheet called SUMMARY (see fig. 1.2). Quattro will print only the cells contained in that region. Similarly, if you have created a temporary area called SCRATCH, you can use that name with Quattro's /BE (for /**B**lock **E**rase) command to blank that part of the screen. (This exciting feature is discussed in Chapter 4.)

Copying Cell Entries

Quattro uses a /**B**lock **C**opy command to make replicas of values, labels, or formulas in other cells. This replication allows you to develop a model quickly by building a few key relationships and replicating them over the entire workspace.

Quattro allows cell references to be defined as relative or absolute at the time the cell is defined. Relative cell references are entered in the normal way. Absolute references are entered with a dollar sign ($) preceding the reference. For example, in the formula

+A1+$A2+A$3+A4

the reference to cell A1 is relative. The references to cells A2 and A3 are mixed (relative in one direction and absolute in the other). The reference to A4 is absolute in both directions.

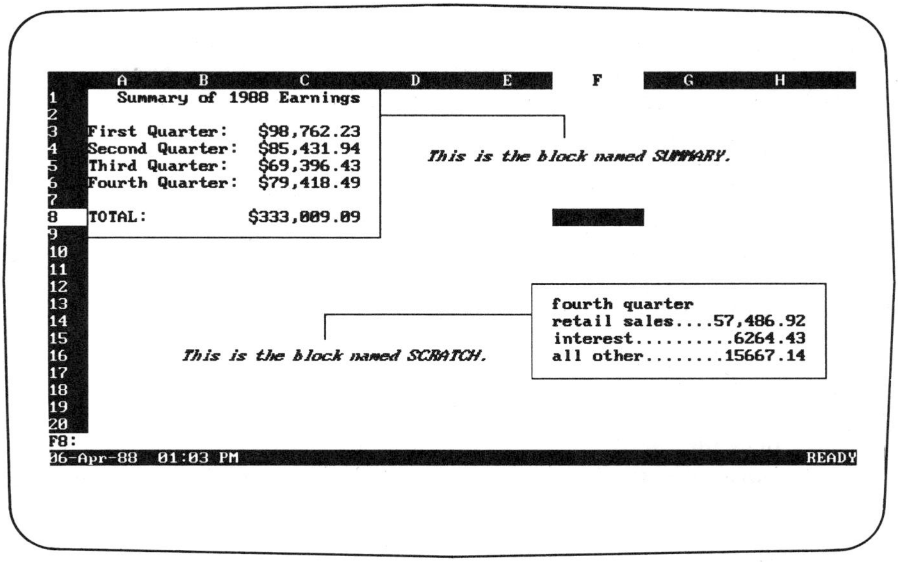

Fig. 1.2. Using block names in Quattro.

This method of determining absolute and relative references has some interesting advantages. For example, you can /**B**lock **C**opy a single cell into a block of cells without making complicated formula adjustments. (See Chapter 4 for complete details of this important feature.)

Recalculating the Worksheet

Quattro is a thoroughly modern spreadsheet. Unlike 1-2-3's method of recalculating spreadsheets, Quattro updates only cells that need updating. Thus, if you enter text, Quattro recognizes that the text probably has nothing to do with a budget calculation. If you accidentally press F9 (Calc), Quattro spends a fraction of a second to recognize the key, but no recalculation occurs. Other spreadsheets recalculate completely, even though nothing needs updating. With a large spreadsheet application, this unnecessary calculation can take precious time away from your work.

In addition to this "minimal recalculation," Quattro offers a *natural* order of recalculation. Natural recalculation begins by discerning the most fundamental cell in the worksheet (that is, the cell on which most other cells are based). Quattro evaluates this cell first. Next, the program searches for the second most basic formula in the worksheet and evaluates that cell. This process continues until Quattro recomputes the entire worksheet.

Accompanying natural recalculation is the capability to perform iterative calculations. In Quattro, the user can specify the number of passes the program should make through the same worksheet each time the program recalculates the worksheet. Iterative calculation helps to relieve the problem of circular references.

These features simplify the design and use of complex spreadsheets. With Quattro, you do not have to be as careful about planning the locations of the various model sections. Instead, the computer can manage the order of recalculation, regardless of section locations. (More details on recalculation are provided in Chapter 3.)

Quattro File Commands

Quattro offers the basic file loading and saving commands found in other electronic spreadsheets. Three types of Quattro files can be created: normal spreadsheet files (.WKQ), text files (.PRN), and graph files (.PIC). In addition, the program has the capacity to import a text file created by another program, including WordStar®, WordPerfect®, Microsoft® Word, and other word-processing files. This feature allows you to import information from other sources into Quattro.

More importantly, Quattro can directly retrieve and save files created by 1-2-3, Symphony®, dBASE III® Plus, Paradox™, Reflex, and files used with !SQZ!—the spreadsheet file compressor. Database translations appear in standard Quattro database format, with each row representing a record and each column representing a field. (Chapter 8, "Managing Files," covers in detail the use of Quattro's storage commands.)

Protecting Cells and Files

Quattro allows you to protect cells in a worksheet so that unintentional changes cannot be made—for example, in cells that contain important formulas. To protect your worksheet, you use two commands: the /**D**efault **P**rotection **E**nable command and the /**B**lock **A**dvanced **P**rotect command. These commands prevent someone from erasing, moving, or changing the cells even though the cell contents appear on-screen. /**D**efault **P**rotection **E**nable protects the entire worksheet, and /**B**lock **A**dvanced **P**rotect protects a cell or a block.

You also can hide blocks of cells and use passwords to protect your worksheets when you save them on disk. If you want to prevent the display of cell contents on-screen, you can use the /**B**lock **D**isplay Format **H**idden command.

Password Protection

Quattro's /File Save command also lets you password protect your worksheet files when you save them. A password-protected file is encrypted and cannot be examined or retrieved without the password. Confidential or sensitive data is protected from use by anyone who does not have the correct password. This encrypted password is even more secure and tougher to decode than the password system in 1-2-3 and is thus more secure for a corporate environment.

Printing the Worksheet

Quattro has more printing flexibility than most other spreadsheets that work with DOS. You have the choice of printing the entire worksheet or any part of the worksheet. In addition, you can alter the left, right, top, and bottom margins on the page; change the page length and width; insert page headers and footers, which can even contain the date and page number; and send setup codes to the printer to alter the type size and style used to print. (For more information on printing, see Chapter 9.)

Quattro Graphics

The spreadsheet alone makes Quattro a powerful program with all the capabilities needed by many users. Graphics added to Quattro's spreadsheet extend Quattro as a tool for presenting data and conducting what-if analysis. Quattro's graphics capability is also remarkably versatile and easy to use. It even allows you to do what-if analysis with graphs. Unlike other spreadsheets, Quattro allows you to set up and print graphs to *hard copy* (paper) without leaving the program—a significant improvement over 1-2-3.

Quattro has 10 basic graph types: bar, stacked bar, line, scatter, pie, 3-D bar, area, horizontal bar, marker, and combined line and marker. A single graph can include up to six blocks of data (except for pie and scatter graphs). For example, you can create a line graph with six different lines.

Graphs are created by using Quattro's /Graph command. Although the program has a number of options, you need to specify only a graph type and a single data block. After providing the required information, you simply type *v*, for View. This option plots the graph to the screen. If the computer has both a color and a monochrome display, the graph appears on the color screen while the spreadsheet remains on the monochrome monitor. If the computer has a color monitor only, the graph replaces the spreadsheet on the display until you press a key.

Quattro gives you an exceptional amount of flexibility in formatting graphs. You can display as many colors as your graphics hardware supports. On a black-and-white monitor, you can choose different shading patterns. The *color legend*, which defines the color or pattern for each data block, also can be displayed on the screen.

You can format graphs in many other ways as well. Labels can be inserted in graphs by referencing a list in the worksheet. Although Quattro automatically scales the X- and Y-axes to fit the data being plotted, users are free to adjust the scaling to suit their tastes. A grid can be placed over the worksheet. You can specify a title and a subtitle for each graph, as well as labels for both the vertical and horizontal axes. In line and scatter graphs, you have the option of selecting the type of symbol to represent the data on the graph and connecting the data points with a line.

Because Quattro lets you name graphs after creating them, you can replot these graphs by typing /gnd (for /**G**raph **N**ame **D**isplay) and supplying the graphs' names. With this feature, you can create a slide show of graphs that are recalled, one after another, and plotted to the screen, a printer, or a plotter.

Performing What-If with Graphics

The most exciting aspect of Quattro's graphics is not the variety of graphs but the degree to which the graphics and spreadsheet elements are interrelated. With Quattro, you can design and alter graphs quickly as worksheet data changes. This capability means that Quattro can change graphs almost as fast as it recalculates the data.

True graphics what-if analysis can be performed with Quattro. In fact, the F10 function key allows you to replot a graph after making changes to the worksheet, without having to redefine the graph with the /G command. This replotting immediately shows the effects of changes on the current graph.

Printing Graphics

One of Quattro's strengths is that it can print graphs from within the main program. This capability does away with the need to quit the program and load another specialized graph program. In addition, you can specify different types of graphic output devices. You can select a printer if you want to print a graph quickly, or a plotter if you want to produce a high-quality color graph. If you are in too big a hurry to wait for your graph to print, you can send it to a network laser printer or simply "park" it in a graph file.

Quattro makes it easy to create graphs for desktop publishing. You can create a PostScript® graphics file, for output to a laser printer, or a .PIC file, Lotus's popular graph file format.

The professional results that the graph printing commands can obtain are another indication of the overall high quality of the Quattro program. The user friendliness of Quattro's graphics capability is also important.

With previous graphics software, the time and trouble involved in creating and changing graphs often outweighed the benefits. Quattro graphs, however, can be created and changed quickly and easily. With Quattro, managers can use graphs more frequently both to increase their own understanding and to communicate their analyses to others.

Quattro Database Management

The column-row structure used to store data in a spreadsheet program is similar to the structure of a relational database. The similarity between a database and a spreadsheet is demonstrated by the expanded lookup capabilities of the spreadsheet programs developed before and at the same time as Quattro. Quattro provides true database-management commands and functions so that you can sort, query, extract, and perform statistical analysis on data. One important advantage of Quattro's database manager over independent database programs is that its commands are similar to the other commands used in the Quattro program. You can therefore learn how to use the Quattro database manager along with the rest of the Quattro program.

Advanced Commands and Functions

Once a database has been constructed in Quattro (which is no different from constructing any other spreadsheet table), a variety of functions can be performed on the database. Some of the tasks you will want to perform on a Quattro database can be accomplished with standard Quattro commands. For example, you can add records to a database with the /RI (/**R**ow **I**nsert) command. You can add fields with the /CI (/**C**olumn **I**nsert) command. Editing the contents of a database cell is as easy as editing any other cell; you simply move the cursor to that location, press F2 to call up the editor, and start typing.

Data can also be sorted. Sorts can be done with both a primary and a secondary key, on up to five sorting keys, in ascending or descending order, using alphabetic or numeric keys. In addition, various kinds of mathematical analyses can be performed on a field of data over a specified block of records. For example, you can count the number of items in a database that match a set of criteria; compute a mean, variance, or standard deviation; and find the maximum or minimum value within the block. The capacity to perform statistical analysis on a database is an advanced feature for database management systems on a microcomputer.

These and other database operations require database commands, such as /ADQU (/**A**dvanced **D**atabase **Q**uery **U**nique) and /ADQL (/**A**dvanced **D**atabase **Q**uery **L**ocate). You can query a Quattro database in several ways. After specifying the criteria on which you are basing your search, you can ask the program to point to each selected record in turn, or to extract the selected records to a separate area of the spreadsheet. You also can ask the program to delete records that fit your specified criteria.

Several commands help the user make inquiries and remove duplicate data. All of these commands are subcommands of the /ADQ (/**A**dvanced **D**atabase **Q**uery) command. These commands require that the user specify one or more criteria for searching the database. The criteria refer to a field or fields in the database and set the conditions that data must meet in order to be selected.

Quattro allows a great deal of latitude in defining criteria. As many as 32 cells across, each containing multiple criteria, can be included in the criteria block. Criteria can include complex formulas as well as simple numbers and text entries. Two or more criteria in the same row are considered to be joined with an *and*. Criteria in different rows are assumed to be combined with an *or*. Criteria also can include *wild-card* characters: characters such as # and ? that stand for other characters.

Quattro also has a special set of statistical functions that operate only on information stored in the database. Like the query commands, the statistical functions use criteria to determine which records to operate on.

Quattro supports the following database functions: @DCOUNT, @DSUM, @DAVG, @DVAR, @DSTD, @DMAX, and @DMIN. These functions perform essentially the same tasks as their spreadsheet counterparts. For example, @DMIN finds the minimum number in a given block. @DCOUNT counts all of the nonblank entries in a block. @DSTD computes the standard deviation of the items in the block.

The combination of these functions and Quattro's database commands makes this program a capable data manager. Quattro's data management capabilities, however, do not put the program in competition with more sophisticated database packages such as Paradox or dBASE III Plus. Both these programs use a database language to translate the user's requests to the computer. By comparison, Quattro's data management is fairly simple.

When compared to less powerful data managers, however, such as PFS®:FILE, Quattro looks good. Quattro is fast and has adequate capacity (at 8,192 records) for most simple data management tasks. Because Quattro's data management uses the same basic command structure as the rest of Quattro, the program is easy to learn. In summary, the database function of Quattro is valuable and sets Quattro apart from the generic spreadsheet. (Quattro's data management capabilities are covered in detail in Chapters 11 and 12.)

The /Advanced What-If Command

One of the most useful, but most misunderstood, commands in Quattro's menu is the /Advanced What-If command. A *what-if* table is simply a way to look at all the outcomes of a set of conditions without having to enter each condition manually into the equation. The command simply allows you to build a table that defines the formula you wish to evaluate and that contains all the values you want to test. A what-if table is similar to the X-Y decision grids you probably constructed as a math student in high school.

The /Advanced What-If command can be used to structure a variety of what-if problems. It also can be combined with Quattro's database and statistical functions to solve far more complex problems. (Chapters 11 and 12 explain in detail the /Advanced What-If command and give examples to help you master this powerful tool.)

Multiple Regression and Simultaneous Equations

Quattro's multiple regression command significantly expands the program's capabilities for statistical analysis. If you use regression analysis, the regression command could save you the cost of a stand-alone statistical package. For business applications, the /Advanced **R**egression command probably meets all your regression analysis needs.

An /Advanced **M**atrix command can be used to solve systems of simultaneous equations. This capability is likely to be of interest mostly to scientific and engineering users.

Keyboard Macros and the Macro Commands

One of Quattro's most exciting features is its macro and macro command capabilities, which allow you to automate and customize Quattro for your special applications. Quattro's macros and macro commands allow you to create, inside the Quattro spreadsheet, user-defined programs that you can use for a variety of purposes. At the simplest level, these programs can reduce, from many to two, the number of keystrokes needed for a Quattro operation.

At a more complex level, Quattro's macro commands give you full-featured programming capability.

Whether you use Quattro's programming capability as a typing alternative or as a programming language, you'll find that it can simplify and automate many of your Quattro applications. When you create typing-alternative macros, you group together and name a series of normal Quattro commands, text, or numbers. Once you have named a macro or macro command program, you can activate its series of commands and input data by pressing two keys—the Alt key and a letter key—or by pressing F8 (Macro).

The applications for such typing-alternative macros are limited only by Quattro's capabilities. For example, typing the names of months as column headings is a task frequently performed in creating a budget spreadsheet. You can easily turn this task into a Quattro macro, thereby reducing multiple keystrokes to a two-keystroke combination—the Alt key and a letter key. You also can structure an Alt sequence in Quattro to make decisions when the sequence is executed. These decisions can be based either on values found in the spreadsheet or on input from the user when the sequence is executed. By combining the typing-alternative features of Quattro's macro capability with the macro commands, you can cause the program to prompt the user and pause for input.

In addition to keystroke and command macros, Quattro has a macro learn mode that allows you to record your keystrokes in the spreadsheet automatically. These recordings can then be played back any number of times.

When you begin to use Quattro's sophisticated macro commands, you'll discover the power available for your special applications. For the application developer, the macro commands are much like a programming language (such as BASIC), but the programming process is simplified significantly by the powerful features of Quattro's spreadsheet, database, and graphics commands. If you want to use Quattro to create typing-alternative macros or programs, Chapters 15 and 16 give you the information you need to get started.

Quattro Software and Hardware Requirements and Options

Understanding the operation of the Quattro spreadsheet, the types of commands and functions, and the program's advanced features is the first step to becoming a proficient Quattro user. But learning how to benefit most from Quattro's capabilities also involves understanding Quattro's capabilities in reference to specific software and hardware capabilities. How much memory does Quattro require to run? How much memory do Quattro worksheet applications use? What additional software or hardware can be used with Quattro beyond what's minimally required? How do additional software and hardware expand Quattro's capabilities? The following sections answer these questions and discuss the specific software and hardware requirements and options available with Quattro.

The Quattro Disks

From the moment you open the package, it is obvious that Quattro is a formidable product. The program is so large that it is distributed on four 5 1/4-inch floppy disks for IBM PC and compatible systems. Quattro is distributed on two 3 1/2-inch microfloppy disks for IBM PS/2 computers.

Quattro on the IBM PC and PS/2

The IBM PC and PS/2 computers, with their memory capabilities and video displays, enable Quattro to be a true business tool, capable of performing tasks that at one time were possible only on mini- and mainframe computers. Many corporations and individuals have found the IBM-plus-spreadsheet combination to be a terrific investment, saving time and effort while improving analysis.

Quattro uses virtually every key on the PC keyboard, including all the function keys, the delete (Del) key, and the alternate (Alt) key. The function keys serve several purposes. For instance, the F1 key activates Quattro's on-line help facility. F2 activates the program's editor. The F10 key replots graphics. In addition, the PgUp key jumps the cell selector up one screen, and the PgDn key moves the cell selector down one screen. The Home key returns the cell selector to cell A1.

The standard PC keyboard layout poses one problem, however. Because the numeric keypad doubles as a cursor-movement keypad, using these keys both for entering numbers and for moving the cell selector can be quite cumbersome.

The Enhanced Keyboard of IBM PS/2 and some other computers solves this numeric keypad problem. Because the Enhanced Keyboard has a separate cursor-movement keypad as well as a numeric keypad, users no longer need to press the Num Lock key to switch from one function to the other on the numeric keypad. (See Chapter 2 for more information on how Quattro uses keys on different IBM keyboards.)

Hardware Requirements and Extras

At one time, a considerable investment in hardware would have been required to make full use of a spreadsheet's capabilities. Today, with the availability (and lower costs) of computers equipped with at least 512K of memory, that investment is smaller. In fact, many new Quattro users and businesses are able to purchase computer equipment that is more powerful than the minimum equipment required to run Quattro. To run Quattro, you must have at least 384K of random-access memory (RAM) and at least two double-sided disk drives. However, a computer with one floppy and one hard disk drive is recommended.

An added enhancement that users and PC coordinators will appreciate is Quattro's capability to automatically sense the hardware it is installed on, and to configure itself to best use that hardware. This capability means that when you first load Quattro from the box, it will run without needing to go through a special installation process.

If you have a monochrome (one-color) monitor, you will be able to see the spreadsheet and database parts of Quattro and print graphs. To view your graphs in black and white on your monochrome monitor, you need a Hercules Graphics Card™ (or another Quattro-compatible monochrome graphics adapter) or a PS/2 computer with a monochrome monitor. Graphics cards such as the Hercules Graphics Card can generate raster graphs on a monochrome monitor, which cannot normally display graphics. A color monitor is required if you want to use Quattro's color graphics capability.

For maximum use of Quattro's capabilities, you need appropriate hardware. If you are considering buying new equipment, investigate the COMPAQ 386® family of computers, or the IBM PS/2 Model 50, 60, or 80 to determine which is best suited for your business needs—today and in the future. With any of these machines, all of which allow you to add an 80287 or 80387 math coprocessor and which come with support for graphics, you can take immediate advantage of Quattro's speed, memory, and VGA graphics capabilities.

If you currently have an IBM PC, PC AT, PS/2 or compatible computer, you may want to invest in the following additional hardware:

- Additional RAM memory, up to 640K
- 500K of expanded memory
- An 8087, 80287, or 80387 coprocessor chip

These hardware extras greatly expand the practical size of Quattro's spreadsheet and speed up calculations.

You also need a printer with graphics capabilities (such as an EPSON® FX or LQ series printer) or a plotter to produce printed graphs. For professional-quality graphs and reports, Quattro supports a number of laser printers, including PostScript printers. A versatile choice that gives you draft or near-letter quality printouts, graphics, and color graphics is Hewlett-Packard Company's 3630A color ink jet printer. It can take the place of a dot-matrix printer, plotter, letter quality printer, and (slow) laser printer.

Quattro's Use of Memory

Quattro offers 256 columns by 8,192 rows, or more than 2,000,000 cells. To take advantage of all of that space, you'll need much more than the 384K of RAM memory required to run the program. Quattro can accommodate up to 640K of RAM memory plus up to 4M of expanded memory. (Remember that Quattro can effectively use 500K of expanded memory but can "see" 4M.)

There is no simple way to equate the number of active cells in a worksheet to its RAM requirements, because the contents of cells can vary greatly. Perhaps the best way to get a realistic notion of the potential size of a worksheet is to conduct two simple tests. In the first, we'll relate the size of the worksheet to the number of standard 8 1/2-inch-by-11-inch pages that can fit into it. In the second, we'll experiment—using Quattro's /**B**lock **C**opy command to fill cells in the worksheet to see when we run out of main memory. From these two tests, we can draw conclusions about worksheet size.

To begin the first test, we'll use 640K of RAM—the maximum configuration possible for Quattro without an expanded memory card. After subtracting 343K for the Quattro program and about 55K for DOS, about 230K of usable memory remains, depending on your version of DOS. If we divide this amount by the number of pica type characters on a standard 8 1/2-inch-by-11-inch page (66 lines by 80 characters = 5,280 total characters), we get approximately 43 pages. Although this is a rough measure, it points out the considerable capacity of the Quattro worksheet.

For the second test, we'll again use a system with 640K of main memory. This time we make various types of entries in cell A1 and copy the entries to other cells until the worksheet is full. Table 1.2 shows the result.

As the table shows, the maximum number of nonblank cells in the Quattro spreadsheet depends on the kinds of entries made in those cells. Integer numbers require the least memory per entry; therefore, a spreadsheet containing integer numbers can have many more entries than a spreadsheet containing formulas or long labels. In practice, a worksheet for a business application contains entries of different types, and the maximum number of nonblank

Table 1.2
Spreadsheet Capacity To Hold Various Types of Entries

Type of Entry	*Maximum Number of Cells*
Integer (the number 1)	39,519
Real Number (the number 1.1)	16,384
10-Character Label (ABCDEFGHIJ)	9,359
50-Character Label (ABCDEFGHIJKLMNOPQRSTUVWXYZabcdefghijklmnopqrstuvwx)	3,504
Small Formula (+B1+B2)	3,212

cells will be somewhere between the value for all integers and the value for formulas or long labels.

In a few situations, the size of your worksheet will exceed memory, unless your system is configured at substantially less than 640K. If you have an application that exceeds the capacity of your system's main memory, Quattro has the capacity to use special expanded memory boards such as Intel's Above Board™ or the AST Rampage® board to add up to 4M of expanded memory to the 640K maximum main memory.

Quattro uses the expanded memory to store real numbers, formulas, and labels in the worksheet. Integer numbers are still stored in the main memory, and a selector is stored in the main memory for each item stored in expanded memory. This expanded memory increases the spreadsheet capacity for any type of entry to the number of integers that can be stored in your system's main memory.

One application that may require large amounts of memory is database management. To handle larger databases (greater than 1,000 records), you need to invest in an expanded memory card.

All other things being equal, too much memory is better than too little. Because RAM is relatively inexpensive (and is getting even more so) and is important to increasing your productivity with Quattro, it makes sense to buy as much RAM as your system can support.

Remember, though, that an application that requires 4M of expanded memory also requires about the same amount of storage on disk. Large spreadsheets or databases that require expanded memory are practical only if you have a hard disk installed in your computer. Fortunately, Quattro comes with a file compression utility—!SQZ!—that can compress Quattro files by up to 95%. Thus a 100K file can be compressed down to just 5K. The only penalty to using the !SQZ! utility is that it takes a little extra time to save and retrieve squeezed files.

Quattro has an advanced memory management scheme that allots main or expanded memory space only to cells with entries. Blank, unformatted cells use no memory space. Earlier spreadsheet programs use memory space for every cell in the active worksheet area (defined as the smallest rectangle that contains all cells with entries). For example, in Quattro an entry in cell IV8192 (the cell in the lower right corner of the worksheet) takes up no more space than an entry in cell A1. In 1-2-3 Release 1A, however, an attempt to enter a value in cell IV2048 (the lower right corner of 1A's worksheet) results in the error message `Memory Full`.

When you delete part of a worksheet, Quattro reclaims some of the main memory; you can reuse that memory immediately. This capability is in contrast to earlier spreadsheet programs. After you deleted part of the worksheet in these early spreadsheets, you had to save and retrieve the worksheet to reclaim memory.

Operating Speed of Quattro

Given the staggering size of the Quattro spreadsheet, you might expect the program to be a bit slow. Happily, this is not the case. Quattro's spreadsheet is one of the fastest spreadsheet programs available today—particularly when used with computers containing an 80286 or 80386 microprocessor and 80287 or 80387 coprocessor chip.

Quattro is written in assembly programming language. The program is well designed, and Quattro retains its advantage in speed over competing spreadsheets and integrated packages.

Add-In Software

As Quattro users have become more experienced, so too has the need to provide them with additional features not available within the Quattro program itself. Recognizing this need, Borland has responded by supporting (and developing its own) supplementary software programs that you can use with or in addition to Quattro.

Quattro add-in programs become a part of Quattro; loaded into your computer's memory along with Quattro, these programs remain in memory as you use Quattro. Whenever you want to use the add-in, simply use the /**M**acro **L**oad and /**M**acro **R**un commands to access the feature. Some add-ins operate while the worksheet remains in view; others allow you to leave the worksheet momentarily and then return as soon as you have completed an operation. You can use the supplied Transcript program to automatically record a transcript of your keystrokes to disk. Another add-in program is Menu Builder, which lets you modify the standard Quattro menus or design your own menus.

Chapter Summary

Quattro is becoming a popular program for many reasons. First, it combines several sought-after functions into one program. Second, and more important, the program is "done right." Quattro is one of the few microcomputer programs that is not filled with compromises. Third, Quattro is faster than most spreadsheets. And perhaps most important, the program is fun to use, especially for those who have used 1-2-3; Quattro maintains compatibility with 1-2-3, but also adds important features.

CHAPTER

2

Getting Started

This chapter helps you begin using Quattro. The information contained here is useful if you have little familiarity with computers or with Quattro. If you find this introductory material too basic and want to begin using the Quattro spreadsheet immediately, turn to Chapter 3.

The last section in this chapter shows you how to use the various learning aids that Borland includes in the Quattro package. Many first-time users find these aids a helpful introduction to Quattro. You may want to use the aids with this book during the early stages of learning the program.

The following topics are covered:

- How to start up and exit from Quattro
- How Quattro uses the computer keyboard
- How Quattro uses the screen display
- How to make Quattro act like 1-2-3
- How to use the Novice menu system
- How to use the Quattro learning aids

Starting Up and Exiting Quattro

Starting up Quattro requires only two or three steps. If Quattro is installed on your hard disk, the program is located in a subdirectory called *QUATTRO*.

To start up Quattro on a hard disk system, do the following:

1. Change to the directory called QUATTRO by typing *cd\quattro* at the C> prompt and pressing Enter.
2. Start Quattro by typing *q* and pressing Enter.

If you have a two floppy disk system or a two microfloppy disk system, the start-up procedure is slightly different. Note that in this book, the term *microfloppy* is used to designate the 3 1/2-inch disks enclosed in a hard-plastic case that are used by the IBM PC Convertible and the IBM PS/2 family of computers.

To start up Quattro on a two floppy disk system or two microfloppy disk system, do the following:

1. Place the Quattro System/Resource disk into drive A.
2. If the A> prompt is not displayed, type *a:* and press Enter.
3. Start Quattro by typing *q* at the A> system prompt and pressing Enter.

After a few seconds, the spreadsheet appears and you're ready to start using Quattro.

To exit Quattro, you must use the Quattro main command menu. Quattro commands and their menus are explained extensively throughout the book. At this point, however, you need to know only how to access the main menu and to use one of two easy commands.

To access the command menu, press the slash (/) key. A menu containing 12 options appears on the right side of the worksheet (see fig. 2.1). Select **Quit** to exit the worksheet.

/**Quit** exits the worksheet and the Quattro program. Type *q* or use the pointer to select this option; then press Enter. If you have changed your spreadsheet since the last time you saved the file, you are asked to verify this choice before you exit. Your data is lost if you then quit Quattro without saving your file. To verify that you want to exit, type *y* to select **Yes** or move the pointer to **Yes** and then press Enter. If your file already is saved safely to disk, Quattro does not ask you to save the file again.

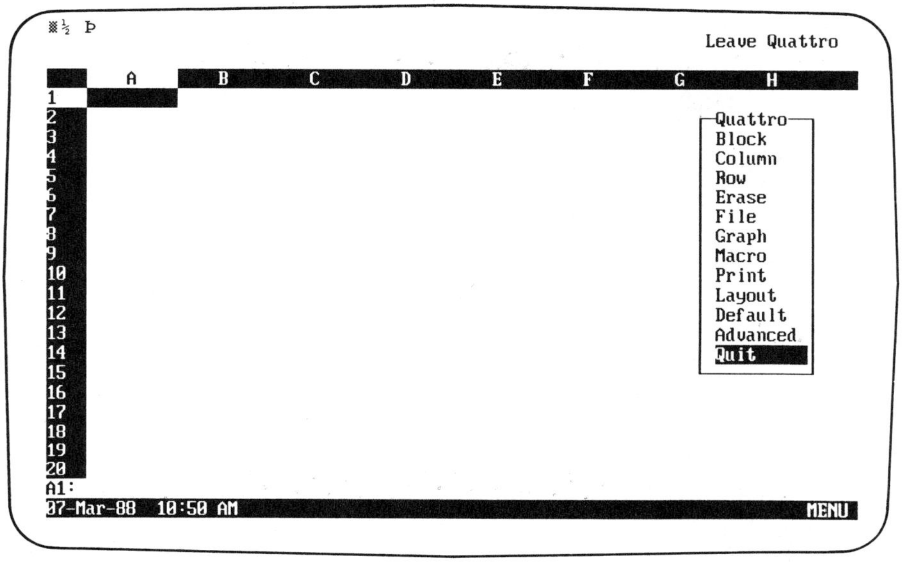

Fig. 2.1. The Quattro main command menu.

Learning the Quattro Keyboard

The three most commonly used keyboards on IBM and IBM-compatible personal computers are shown in figures 2.2, 2.3, and 2.4. The keyboards are divided into three sections: the alphanumeric keyboard in the center, the numeric keypad on the right, and the function key section on the left or across the top. The enhanced keyboard, which is used by the IBM Personal System/2 family, the IBM PC AT, and some compatibles, also has a separate grouping of cursor-movement keys.

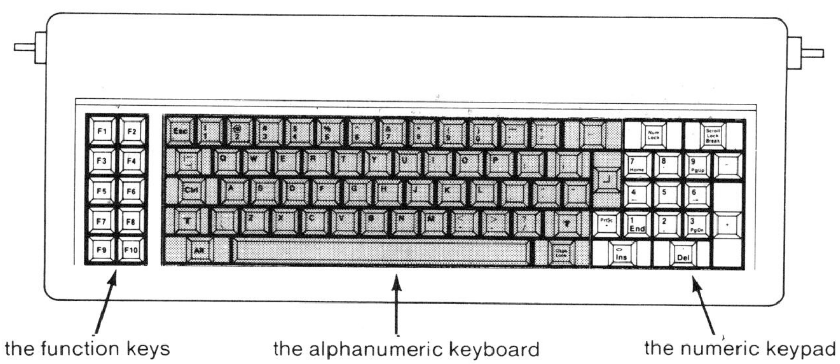

Fig. 2.2. The keyboard of the IBM PC.

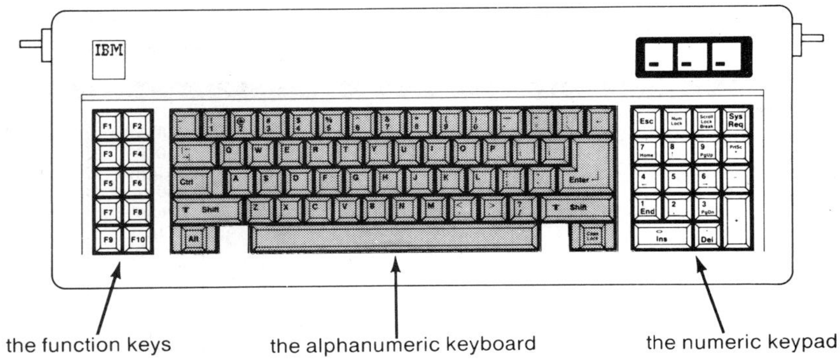

Fig. 2.3. The keyboard of the IBM Personal Computer AT.

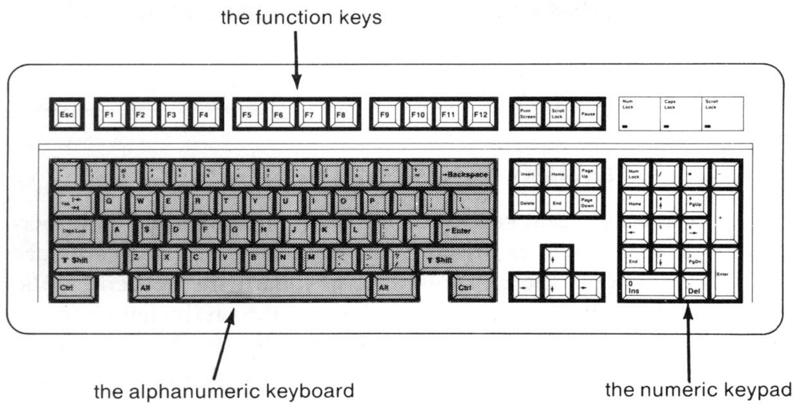

Fig. 2.4. The IBM enhanced keyboard.

Most of the keys in the alphanumeric section at the center of the keyboard resemble those found on a typewriter. And most of these keys maintain their normal functions in Quattro. Several keys, however, take on new and unique functions or are not found on typewriter keyboards. These keys are Esc, Tab, Shift, and Alt.

The numeric keypad on the right-hand side of the keyboard normally is used for entering numbers in most programs on IBM personal computers. In Quattro, however, the main purpose of the numeric keypad is for cursor movement. An exception is on the enhanced keyboard. The enhanced keyboard has separate cursor keys; the numeric keypad of this keyboard also can be used for cursor movement, but the keyboard ordinarily is used only for entering numbers.

The function keys are designed for special purposes that range from getting help to drawing graphs. These keys are located across the top of the enhanced keyboard and on the left-hand side of the standard keyboards.

The Alphanumeric Keys

Although most of the alphanumeric keys shown in figures 2.2, 2.3, and 2.4 have the same functions as on a typewriter, several keys have special functions in Quattro. These keys and their functions are listed in table 2.1. If some of the functions do not make much sense the first time through, don't worry. The functions' meanings become clearer as you read this book.

Table 2.1
Alphanumeric Key Operation

Key	*Function*
⇆ (Tab)	Moves the cursor one screen to the right when used alone and one screen to the left when used with the Shift key
Alt	When used simultaneously with other individual alpha keys, invokes keyboard macros and macro commands. Used to extend function keys.
⇧ (Shift)	Changes the central section of the keyboard to uppercase letters and characters. It also allows you to key in numbers, using the numeric keypad on the right (equivalent of a temporary Num Lock). Used with function keys to access additional functions.
← (Backspace)	During cell definition, erases the previous character in a cell
/ (Slash)	Starts a command; calls up the command menu. It also is used in its normal mathematical function as a division sign.

Key	*Function*
. (Period)	Separates cell addresses when blocks of cells are defined and, in a different manner, anchors cell addresses during the pointing procedure. It also is used as a decimal point.

The Numeric Keypad and the Cursor-Movement Keys

The keys in the numeric keypad on the right-hand side of the IBM PC- and AT-style keyboards are used mainly for cursor movement (refer to figs. 2.2 and 2.3). The enhanced keyboard has separate keys for cursor movement (see fig. 2.4). The functions of the cursor-movement keys are explained in Chapter 3; the other keys on the numeric keypad are listed in table 2.2.

Table 2.2
Numeric Key Operation

Key	*Function*
Num Lock	Activates the numeric characters of the keys in the numeric keypad instead of activating the directional/movement keys
Esc	Escapes from a command menu and moves to the previous menu, erases current entry when specifying a command line or block, or returns from a Help screen
Del	Deletes the character above the cursor during the process of editing command lines. Also deletes the current cell when in READY mode. Use this key with caution.
Scroll Lock/Break	In the Break position, used with Ctrl to return Quattro to READY mode or to halt execution of a macro

When you want to use the numeric keypad to enter numbers rather than to position the cursor (on the PC- or AT-style keyboard), you can do one of two things. First, you can press the Num Lock key before entering numbers and press the key again when you are done. (This method is used in most IBM personal computer software.) The second way is to hold down the Shift key while pressing the number keys.

Neither way is ideal because you have to worry about switching back and forth between using the keypad for entering numbers and using it for cursor movement. This worry is removed if you have an enhanced keyboard. Because you have a separate set of cursor-movement keys, you can reserve the numeric keypad for entering numbers.

If you don't have an enhanced keyboard, you can solve the problem by using a macro. You can create a macro to enter numbers down a column of cells without having to press the Num Lock key or hold down the Shift key. You easily can apply the macro to entering numbers in any direction.

The Function Keys

The function keys, F1 through F10 (refer to figs. 2.2, 2.3, and 2.4), are used for special situations in Quattro. Notice the difference in location of the function keys on the two types of keyboard; the keys are on the far left of the PC and AT keyboards but across the top of the enhanced keyboard.

Borland provides a plastic function-key template that fits over the function keys of IBM personal computers, compatibles, and the PS/2 family. Unfortunately, the template does not give you adequate information when you first start out. For help in early sessions until you memorize the functions, look at table 2.3, which lists the function keys and an explanation of what each key does.

Table 2.3
Function Key Operation

Key	*Function*
F1 (Help)	Accesses the Quattro on-line help system
Alt-F1 (Previous)	Returns to the previous Help screen
F2 (Edit)	Shifts Quattro from READY mode into EDIT mode. Allows the contents of cells to be altered without retyping the entire contents.
F3 (Names)	Displays a list of the block names in the current worksheet. Press the + key on the numeric keypad to see the block name coordinates.

Key	*Function*
Alt-F3 (Functions)	Opens a box listing Quattro functions. Press the + key on the numeric keypad to see abridged syntax. Move the cursor to the desired function and press Enter to copy the function to the input line.
Shift-F3 (Macros)	Opens a box listing Quattro macro commands. Press the + key on the numeric keypad to see abridged syntax. Move the cursor to the desired command and press Enter to copy the function to the input line.
F4 (Abs)	When used in VALUE mode, changes a relative cell address into an absolute or mixed address
F5 (GoTo)	Prompts for a cell address or block name and jumps there immediately after the Enter key is pressed
F6 (Window)	Moves the cursor to the other side of a split screen
F7 (Query)	Repeats the most recent /**D**atabase **Q**uery operation
Alt-F7 (Table)	Repeats the most recent What-if operation
Shift-F7 (Add-in)	Repeats the most recent Add-In operation
F8 (Macro)	Opens a box of block names that can be selected in order to start a macro. All block names are displayed whether or not they start a macro.
Alt-F8 (Record)	Starts the macro recorder. All keys pressed are saved to the spreadsheet. Press Alt-F8 again to turn off the recording.
Shift-F8 (Debug)	Turns on the macro debugging environment
F9 (Calc)	Recalculates the spreadsheet
F10 (Graph)	Redraws the graph defined by the current graph settings

Learning the Quattro Screen Display

The main Quattro display is divided into several parts; some of the parts are the input line at the top of the screen, the descriptor line and the status line at the bottom of the screen, and the worksheet area itself (see fig. 2.5). A reverse-video border separates these areas. This border contains the letters and numbers that mark columns and rows. The reverse video in the border is "blacked out" on the row number and column letter that correspond to the cell selector's position. Thus, you are given a quick visual point of reference when you want to know in what cell the selector is located.

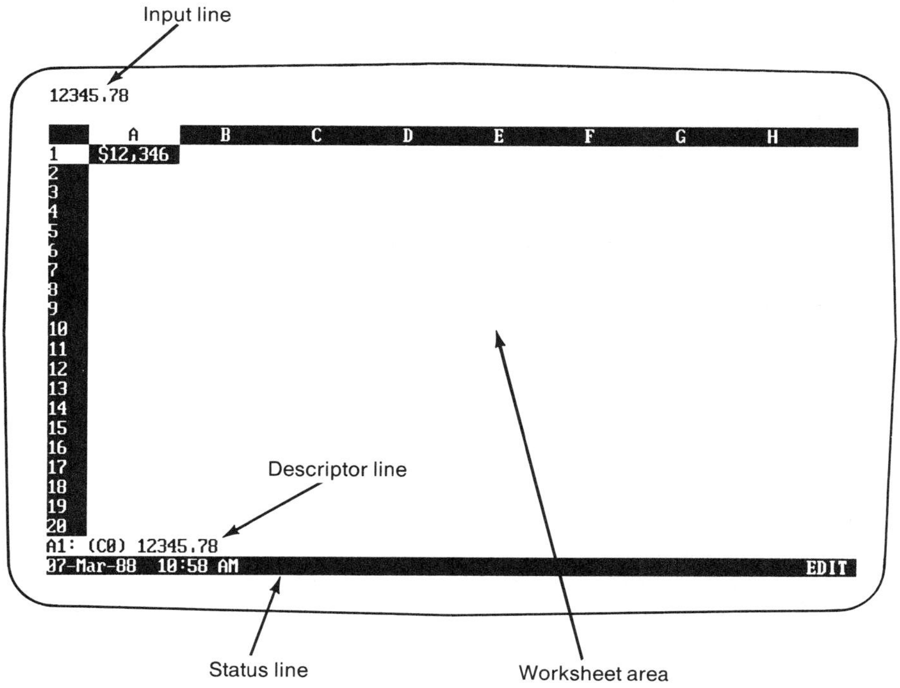

Fig. 2.5. The Quattro display.

Other important areas of the screen are the mode indicators (lower right corner), the lock key indicator (lower middle), and the message area in the lower right corner. The message area shows an error message when certain kinds of errors are made.

The Input Line

The input line is the area above the reverse-video border.

The input line contains the characters that are being entered or edited. When the menu is active, the same area contains explanations of the current command-menu item. As you move the pointer from one item to the next in a command menu, the explanation on the line changes. If a command menu is not in effect, this line is blank.

The Descriptor Line

The descriptor line contains all the information about the current cell. A *current cell* is the cell where the cell pointer currently is located. The first item in the line is the address of the cell. The second item is the display format, which always is displayed in parentheses. (Display formats are covered in detail in Chapter 5.) The last item in the descriptor line is the actual contents of the current cell. The first line also may contain items that explain protection status (PR or U) and column width ([Wxx]). Both column width and protection status are explained in Chapter 4.

The Mode Indicators

One of Quattro's different modes is always in effect, depending on what you are doing. The mode indicator, located in the lower right corner of the screen, always shows which mode Quattro is in. The mode indicators and descriptions of the functions are listed in table 2.4.

Table 2.4
Mode Indicators and Descriptions

Mode	*Description*
READY	Quattro is waiting for you to enter a command or make a cell entry.
VALUE	A number or formula is being entered.
LABEL	A label is being entered.
EDIT	A cell entry is being edited.
POINT	A block is being pointed to.
FILES	Quattro is waiting for you to select a file name from the list of file names.

Mode	*Description*
NAMES	Quattro is waiting for you to select a block name from the list of block names.
MENU	A menu item is being selected.
HELP	Quattro is displaying a Help screen.
ERROR	An error has occurred, and Quattro is waiting for you to press Esc or Enter to acknowledge the error.
WAIT	Quattro is in the middle of a command and cannot respond to other commands. Flashes on and off.
FIND	Quattro is in the middle of an /**A**dvanced **D**atabase **Q**uery operation and cannot respond to commands.
REP	The entry you make will replace the current entry.
FRMT	Display while editing the /**F**ile **P**arse format line.
DEBUG	A keyboard macro or macro command is in single-step excecution.

The Lock Key Indicators

IBM personal computers have "lock" keys: Num Lock and Caps Lock. (Unlike 1-2-3, Quattro does not support the Scroll Lock key.) In Quattro, you always know the status of these keys because a special area of the screen is set aside to show that information. Each key has its own reverse-video indicator that appears in the lower middle of the screen when the key is activated (see fig. 2.6).

Other Indicators

Other indicators in Quattro also appear at the bottom of the screen. These indicators, which display the status of certain keys and special situations, are listed in table 2.5.

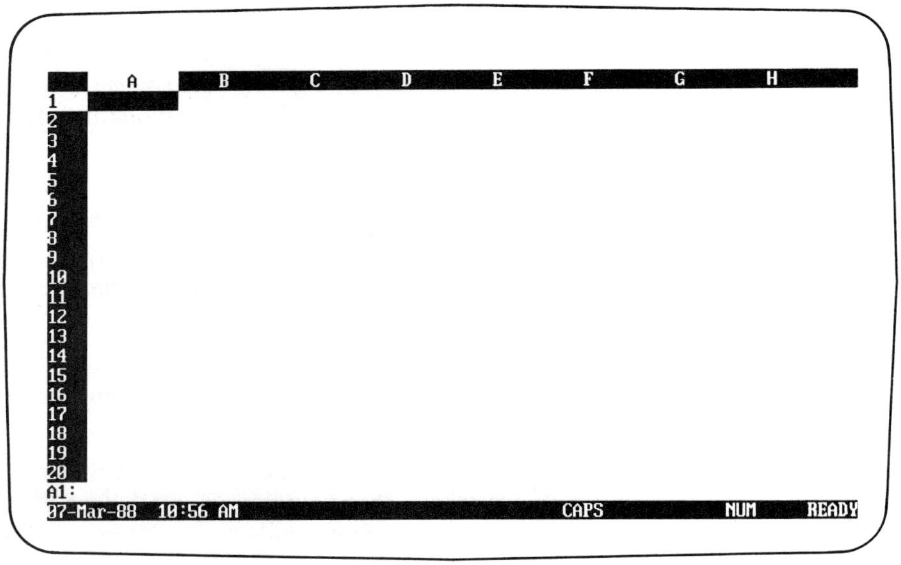

Fig. 2.6. The Quattro display showing the lock key indicators in the lower middle of the screen.

Table 2.5
Status Indicators and Descriptions

Indicator	*Description*
NUM	The Num Lock key has been pressed; pressing the number keys on the numeric keypad produces numbers.
CAPS	The Caps Lock key has been pressed; pressing the letter keys on the alphanumeric keyboard produces capital letters.
END	The End key has been pressed and is now active.
OVR	The Insert key has been pressed, and Quattro is now in typeover mode.
CALC	The worksheet has not been recalculated since the last change to the cell contents.
CIRC	A circular reference has been found in the worksheet.
MEM	Random-access memory is almost exhausted. Flashes on and off.

The Error Messages Area

When an error occurs in Quattro, a message appears in the lower right corner of the screen. Errors may occur for many reasons; perhaps the disk to which you are trying to save a file is full, or perhaps no files of the type you want are on disk.

To clear the error and return to READY mode, you must press Esc or Enter. If you don't press one of these keys, the message does not clear.

Using the Quattro Help Features

One of the biggest selling points of Quattro is its user friendliness. Borland obviously went to a great deal of trouble to ensure that the spreadsheet is easy to learn and use.

The most conspicuous user-friendly feature of Quattro is the support that Borland provides for new users who are learning the program. Borland provides context-sensitive help screens. And in the *Getting Started with Quattro* manual is a self-paced instructional tutorial that leads you through a series of actual Quattro worksheets that use important features of the program.

Finding On-Screen Help

Another user-friendly feature of Quattro is its extensive series of interconnected Help screens. By pressing the F1 (Help) key, you can gain access to the Help Topics screen, which is shown in figure 2.7. This screen has headings that can connect you to Help screens that cover every aspect of the program's operation (see fig. 2.8).

Each Help screen contains information about a single topic as well as names of other topics; these names are positioned at the foot of the screen. To move to another topic, use the cursor-movement keys to move the cursor to the name of that topic; then press Enter. To return to the Help Topics screen, move the cursor to `Help Topics [F1]` and press Enter or press F1.

One of the best features of the on-screen help facility is that you can press the F1 key at any time during a Quattro session, even while issuing a command or defining a cell. The F1 key is context sensitive; if you are using a particular command when you press F1, Quattro gives you a screenful of help on that command. Once you have the information, you return to Quattro by pressing the Esc key.

One enhancement in Quattro's help system is the capability to remember which Help screen you accessed the last time you used it. This feature gives

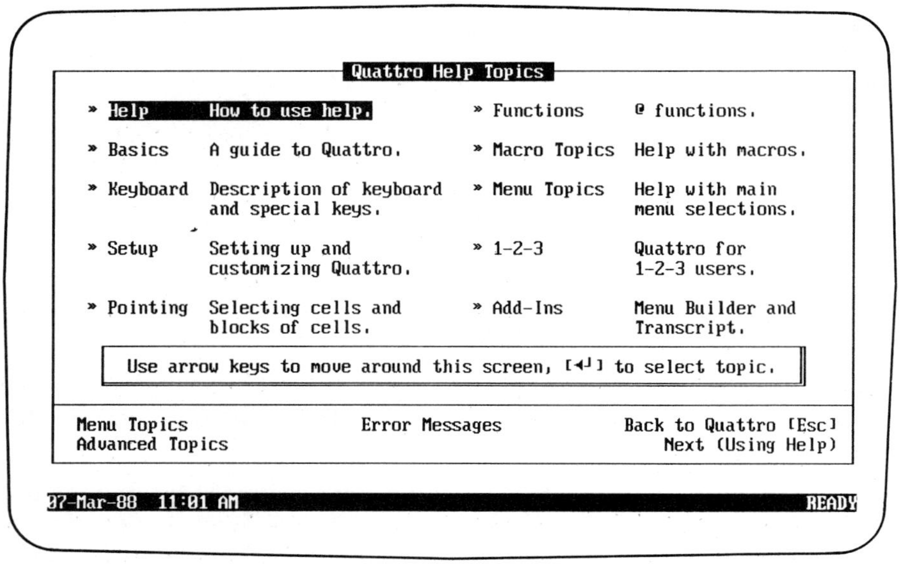

Fig. 2.7. The screen that appears when you press F1 (Help).

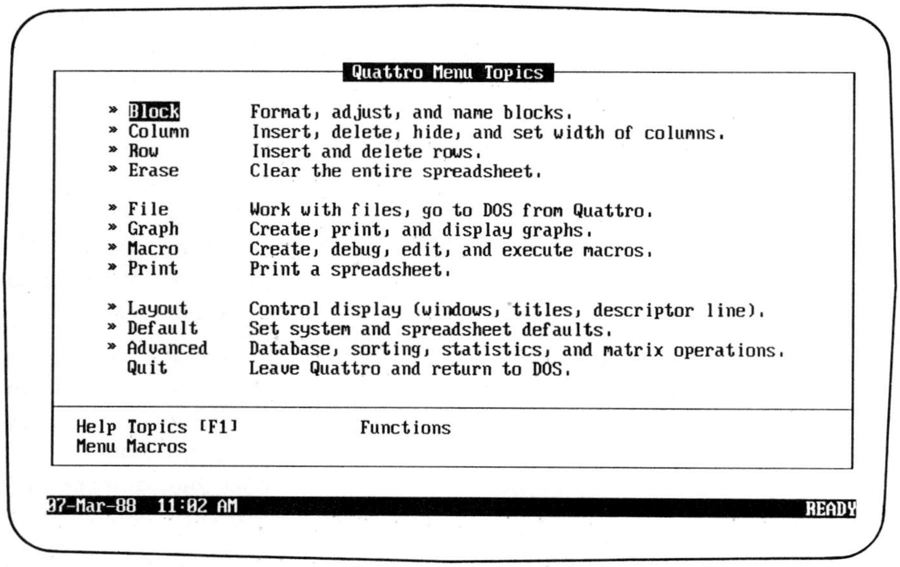

Fig. 2.8. A second-level Help screen.

you the ability to toggle between the spreadsheet and a specific help page if you don't have total recall.

You also can use the PgUp key in the help system to move back to previously viewed screens. This key is helpful if you find yourself in the right neighborhood of help but in the wrong spot; instead of starting over at the beginning of the Help screens, press PgUp until you get to the screen that meets your needs.

Making Quattro Act Like 1-2-3

If you are a user of 1-2-3 and are starting to work with Quattro, you may want to use the familiar 1-2-3 menu. Or you may want to use macros that were created in 1-2-3 and are dependent on its menu commands.

These activities are possible in Quattro; the menu interface and other Quattro defaults are incorporated into the main program as modules instead of being "hard coded" into the spreadsheet. The menu is therefore a removable/replaceable part like an oil filter on a car. Quattro as shipped comes with three main menu files named QUATTRO.RSC, 123.RSC, and NOVICE.RSC. These three files hold the menu structures that can be added to Quattro as the main menu.

When you receive Quattro, the QUATTRO.RSC menu has been preinstalled. If you want to use the 1-2-3 compatible menu system, make sure that you are in the QUATTRO directory; then, at the DOS prompt, type the following:

Q/DQC123.DEF (for a color system)

or

Q/DQM123.DEF (for a monochrome system)

Quattro loads the 1-2-3 menu system and sets up the spreadsheet to appear and be as compatible with 1-2-3 as possible.

Figures 2.9 and 2.10 show how Quattro looks with its own menu system and worksheet layout and how Quattro looks in 1-2-3 compatibility mode. Notice the difference in the commands on the main menu.

You can toggle back and forth between the standard Quattro menu and another menu such as the 1-2-3 menu system; use a second menu controlling option, the **/D**efaults **S**tartup **M**enu_Tree **A**lternate_Menu command, to select another optional menu, 123.ALT. When you have made the selection, you must leave Quattro and reload the program before you can access the alternate menu. Once you have set up the alternate menu, you can use the **/D**efaults **S**tartup **M**enu_Tree **S**witch_Menus command to use the alternate 1-2-3 menu.

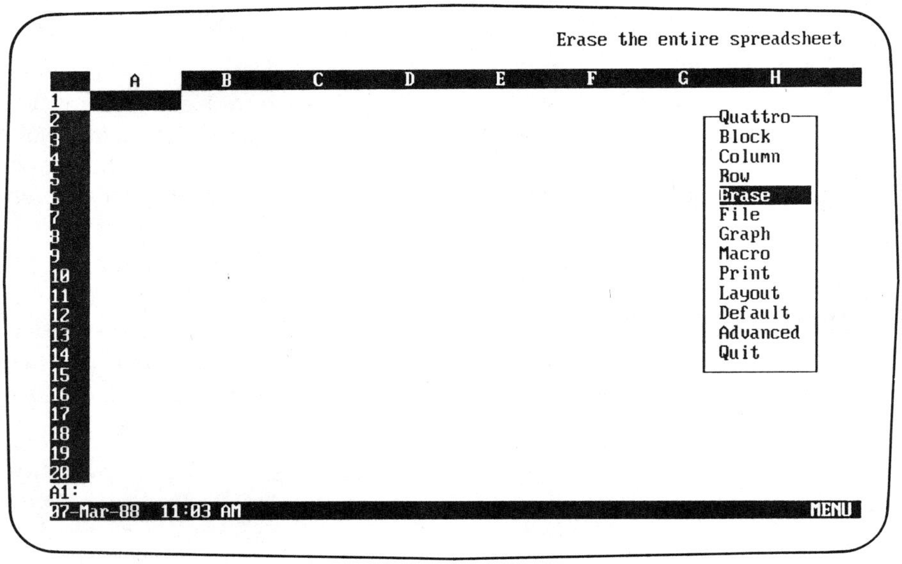

Fig. 2.9. The default Quattro menu and status line display.

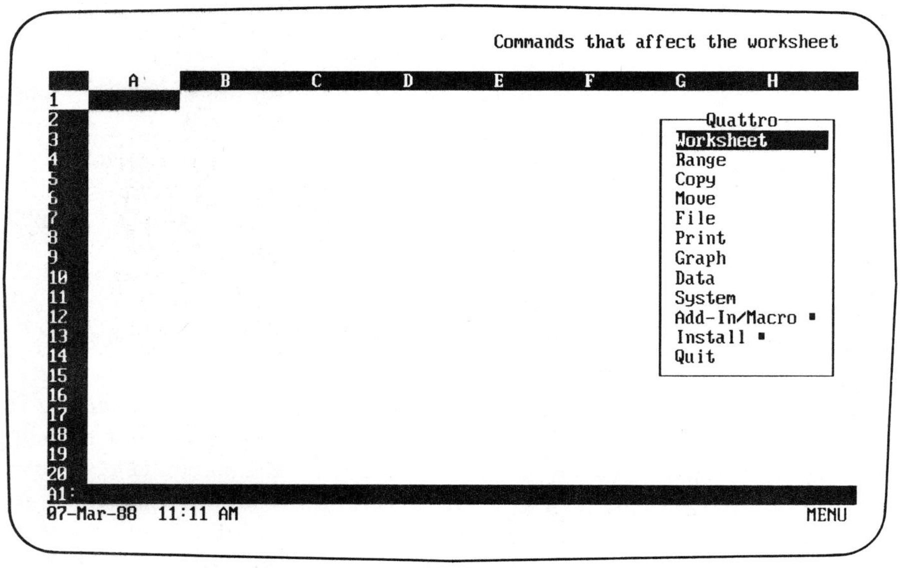

Fig. 2.10. Quattro's 1-2-3 compatible menu and status line display.

Taking the Quattro Tutorial

Another learning resource from Borland is the *Getting Started with Quattro* manual, a book that comes with the documentation. The tutorial in the *Getting Started with Quattro* manual provides a self-paced guide to learning Quattro. The tutorial goes through a series of lessons on Quattro in a step-by-step fashion. The lessons are arranged in order of increasing difficulty and build on each other. The tutorial does not cover all of Quattro's functions and commands but covers enough to give you a basic understanding of the program.

The tutorial begins by providing complete instructions for starting up your computer with Quattro, moving the cursor around the worksheet, and accessing the Quattro command menu.

The tutorial then progresses through lessons on basic worksheet skills, more advanced worksheet skills, printing reports from the worksheet, printing graphs by using the database functions, and using Quattro macros to simplify and automate your Quattro applications.

Borland designed the tutorial to take as little of your time as possible, but you will not be able to complete the tutorial in one sitting. The tutorial is divided into six chapters with several lessons in each chapter. Do one or two lessons at a time. You can go back later to different lessons in order to refresh your memory.

The *Getting Started with Quattro* manual contains a useful chapter describing some of the features and usage techniques for users of Quattro.

If you are comfortable with basic spreadsheet skills and want to learn about a more specialized topic, such as database skills or macros, the lessons in the tutorial are organized so that you can work through only those lessons that cover the topic of interest.

For more information on Quattro functions and commands, refer to the *Reference Manual*, to the appropriate sections of this book, and to Appendix A at the back of this book.

Chapter Summary

In this chapter, you learned how to begin using Quattro. The chapter also explained how the computer keyboard is adapted for use with Quattro and how Quattro uses the screen display to convey important status information to the user. And you were introduced to the tutorial in the *Getting Started with Quattro* manual.

The next step in learning Quattro is to start working with the Quattro spreadsheet. Chapter 3 shows you how to enter and edit data in the worksheet, how to move the cursor around the worksheet, and how to start using the power of Quattro by entering and using formulas.

CHAPTER

3

Learning Spreadsheet Basics

If you are new to spreadsheet software, this chapter introduces you to the features that make an electronic spreadsheet a powerful tool of data analysis. If you are familiar with spreadsheets but are new to Quattro, you will learn the conventions and features that are unique to this program.

The fundamental power of the Quattro spreadsheet is its capability to store and manipulate large amounts of information. The first step in accessing that power is to enter data into the cells of the worksheet. This chapter shows you how to enter data and how to modify, or edit, that data.

If you are like most people, you're using Quattro because you work with quantifiable information, such as inventories, schedules, budgets, financial analyses, work plans, or production forecasts. Whatever kind of data you work with, you will want to know how to enter numbers and how to start manipulating numbers. The sections on using formulas, operators, and functions help you start using Quattro to meet your needs.

Computers love numbers, but the human mind needs a mixture of numbers and language. To organize and keep track of the numeric data in the worksheet, you need titles, headings, names, comments, descriptions, and a variety of other English-language entries. Quattro calls all these entries *labels* and handles them in a slightly different way than numbers. The section on entering labels shows you how to use labels in the worksheet.

Because of the worksheet's size, you need to learn quick, easy ways to move around in it. Moving the cell pointer is a skill and an art, learned mostly by practice. This chapter shows you the available tools and how to use them.

You will learn how to do the following:

- Enter data into the worksheet
- Enter formulas, operators, and functions
- Enter labels
- Edit data in the worksheet
- Move the cell selector around the worksheet

Entering Data into the Worksheet

You enter data into a cell simply by highlighting the cell with the cell selector, using the cursor-movement keys, and then typing the entry. To complete the entry, press Enter or any of the cursor-movement keys discussed later in this chapter.

If you enter data into a cell that already contains information, the new data replaces the earlier entry. This procedure is one way to change information in a cell; the other way, which involves the F2 (Edit) key, is explained in this chapter's "Editing Data in the Worksheet" section.

Two types of cell entries are available: values and labels. Values can be either numbers or formulas (including functions, which Quattro treats as built-in formulas). From the first character that you enter, Quattro determines which type of cell entry you are making. If you start with one of the following characters, Quattro treats your entry as a value (a number or a formula):

0 1 2 3 4 5 6 7 8 9 + - . (@ # $

If you begin by entering a character other than one of the preceding characters, Quattro treats your entry as a label.

Entering Numbers

The rules for entering numbers are simple:

1. A number cannot begin with any character except 0 through 9, a decimal point, a minus sign (-), or a dollar sign ($). Numbers

also can begin with a plus sign (+) or can be entered in parentheses, but the + and the ( ) do not appear in the cell.

2. You can end a number with a percent sign (%), which tells Quattro to divide by 100 the number that precedes the sign.

3. A number cannot have more than one decimal point.

4. You can enter a number in scientific notation—what Quattro calls the **Scientific** format (for example, 1.234E+06).

5. You cannot enter numbers containing commas.

If you do not follow these rules, Quattro beeps when you press Enter while trying to enter the number into the spreadsheet, and Quattro automatically shifts to EDIT mode just as if you had pressed F2. (The "Editing Data in the Worksheet" section later in this chapter explains how to respond.)

Entering Formulas

In addition to simple numbers, formulas also can be entered into cells. You can enter formulas in two ways: type the formula into the cell or combine typing with moving the cell pointer.

Suppose that you want to create a formula that adds a row of numbers. For example, suppose that you want to add the amounts in cells B1, C1, D1, and E1 and place the result in cell F1 (see fig. 3.1).

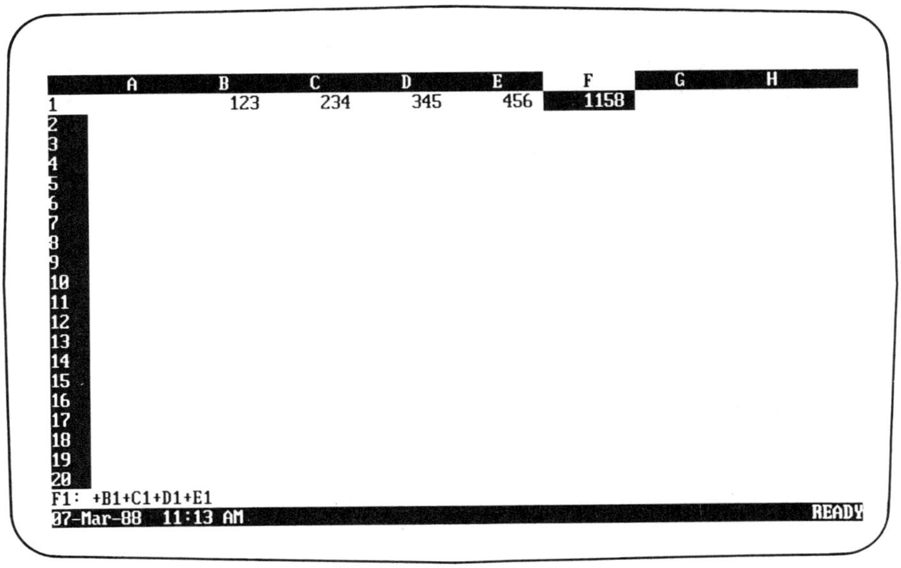

Fig. 3.1. A simple addition formula.

One formula that performs the addition is +B1+C1+D1+E1. You can place the result of the addition into cell F1 simply by typing this formula into cell F1. Notice the + sign at the beginning of the formula. For Quattro to recognize the formula as a formula and not as a label, the formula must begin with one of the following characters:

0 1 2 3 4 5 6 7 8 9 . + - (@ # $

Because you started with +, Quattro recognizes your entry as a formula and switches to VALUE mode, the appropriate mode for entering numbers and formulas.

Remember that two methods can be used to enter a formula that contains a cell address: typing and pointing. Both methods accomplish the same result, and you can mix and match the two techniques within the same formula. Pointing to cell addresses requires some explanation.

For example, to enter the formula shown in figure 3.1 by pointing, begin by using the cell selector to highlight cell F1 and enter the first plus sign into cell F1; then move the cell selector to B1. The mode indicator in the lower right corner of the screen shifts from VALUE to POINT mode as you move the cell selector to cell B1. Notice that the address for the cell appears after the plus sign in the descriptor line—that is, +B1.

To continue to the next address in the formula, keep the cell selector in cell B1 and type another plus sign. The cursor moves immediately from cell B1 to the cell at which it was located when you began entering the formula—in this case, cell F1. Also, the mode indicator shifts back to VALUE mode. Now move the cell selector to cell C1 and type another plus sign. Continue this sequence of pointing and entering plus signs until you have the formula you want. Then press Enter to complete the operation.

In Chapter 4, you will be introduced to the concept of block names. A block name can be assigned to any cell or groups of cells. During formula creation, you have the option of pressing the F3 (Names) key. When you press the key, a box appears that contains the currently available block names. While in POINT mode, you can select one of these block names to include the cell named in the formula you are creating.

Remember that you may use a combination of pointing and typing. Use whatever method works best for you. Usually, the easiest method is to point at cells that are close to the cell you are defining and to type references to distant cells. Another benefit of pointing is that you can verify visually that you actually are using the cell you meant to use and have not made an error.

Using Operators in Formulas

Operators indicate arithmetic operations in formulas. Operators can be separated into two types: mathematical and logical. The logical operators are covered in Chapter 6, in connection with the logical functions. Here are the mathematical operators in order of precedence:

Operator	*Meaning*
^	Exponentiation
+, -	Positive, Negative
*, /	Multiplication, Division
+, -	Addition, Subtraction
&	String addition

An important part of understanding operators is knowing their order of precedence. Operators that are higher on the list are evaluated prior to operators that are lower on the list. Operators with equal precedence are on the same line in the table; in these cases, the operators are evaluated from left to right.

The first operator that is evaluated in a formula is *exponentiation*—the power of a number. In the formula 8+2^3, for example, 2^3 (2 to the power of 3) is evaluated before the addition. The answer is 16 (8+8), not 1000 (10 to the power of 3).

The next set of operators to be evaluated indicates the sign of a value (whether the value is positive or negative). Notice that Quattro knows the difference between a + or - sign that indicates positive or negative value and a + or - sign that indicates addition or subtraction. Used as a sign, these operators are evaluated before multiplication and division; used as indicators of addition and subtraction, the operators are evaluated after multiplication and division. For example, 5+4/-2 is evaluated as 5+(-2), giving 3 as the answer. Notice that Quattro first recognizes that the - sign indicates that 2 is negative; then Quattro divides 4 by -2, which gives an intermediate answer of -2, and finally adds the -2 to 5, giving the answer of 3.

You always can use parentheses to override the order of precedence. In the list of formulas that follows, consider the order of precedence, where B3=2, C3=3, and D3=4, and see if you get the same answers. In the first two formulas, notice particularly how parentheses affect the order of precedence and, ultimately, the answer.

Formula	*Evaluation*	*Answer*
+C3-D3/B3	3-(4/2)	1
(C3-D3)/B3	(3-4)/2	-0.5
+D3*C3-B3^C3	(4*3)-(2^3)	4
+D3*C3*B3/B3^C3-25/5	((4*3*2)/(2^3)-(25/5))	-2

Correcting Errors in Formulas

Errors are easy to make when entering formulas. The more complex the formula you are trying to use, the more likely you are to confirm the saying "Whatever can go wrong, will." Quattro provides ways to help you discover and correct the inevitable errors.

If you attempt to enter a formula that contains a logical or mathematical error, the program beeps, changes to EDIT mode, and moves the cursor to the section of the formula where the problem most likely exists. You then can correct the problem and continue.

Quattro has the capability to show you all 240 characters that can be included in a formula. If the formula exceeds the screen's width when in EDIT mode, the formula wraps around and down to the next one or two lines so that you can see all of the formula without having to scroll to the right.

If you don't know what is causing the error message, you can buy some think time by converting the formula to a label: press the Home key and then enter an apostrophe (') at the beginning of the formula. Then use the /**B**lock **C**opy command (discussed in Chapter 4) to copy the label-formula to another section of the worksheet for debugging and testing. When you discover the problem, correct the original formula and remove the apostrophe.

If your formula is long and complex, try breaking it into logical segments and testing each segment separately. Using smaller segments is not only an aid in debugging but also may be necessary in order for the program to accept the formula. Quattro limits cell entries to 240 characters. If your formula length exceeds the limit, you must use smaller segments.

Some common errors are open parentheses and commas that are missing from built-in formulas (see the extensive section on advanced function debugging methods, covered in Chapter 6). What appears to be a logical error may be merely a missing punctuation mark. When Quattro beeps to indicate a formula error, check the formula for a missing parenthesis or comma at the cursor position.

The program also provides two commands to help you examine and analyze your formulas. Until you are familiar with the use of commands, keep these debugging methods in mind. Commands are discussed extensively in the next chapter.

The /**P**rint **F**ormat **C**ell-Formulas command prints a list of all the formulas in your worksheet. The /**D**efault **F**ormats **D**isplay **T**ext command produces a screen display that shows all your formulas in their spreadsheet locations. To make your analysis easier, use both commands to get a complete view of your formulas.

Using Functions

Like most electronic spreadsheets, Quattro includes built-in functions. These functions are of three basic types:

- Simple abbreviations for long or complex mathematical formulas (these functions are considered formulas by Quattro)
- Nonmathematical "string" functions that work with alphanumeric data (these functions manipulate labels)
- Special functions that provide information or perform other specialized spreadsheet tasks

All three types of functions are considered values by Quattro, and all three types are entered in the same way.

Functions consist of three parts: the @ sign, a function name, and in most cases, an argument or block. The @ sign signals to Quattro that a function is coming. The name indicates which function is being used. The argument or block is the data required by Quattro to perform the function; the argument always is placed within parentheses.

Before you learn about functions in detail (in Chapter 6), you need to learn about several other topics, such as the concept of blocks. The following example, however, helps you begin to understand Quattro functions.

In figure 3.1, you needed to refer individually to four cells to create the desired formula. You could, however, use the @SUM function to sum the numbers in the example. The concept of blocks is important to the @SUM function. (Blocks are covered in detail in Chapter 4.) For now, simply think of a block as a rectangular group of cells.

The equivalent to the +B1+C1+D1+E1 formula, using the @SUM function, is @SUM(B1..E1). The only difference between the two formulas is one of convenience. If you had several other entries extending down the row, the @SUM function would change only slightly to use the address of the last cell to be summed. For example, @SUM(B1..Z1) sums the contents of the first row all the way from B to Z.

To make full use of formulas, you need to understand relative, absolute, and mixed addressing. These concepts are covered extensively in the "Copying the Contents of Cells" section of Chapter 4.

Entering Labels

The third type of data that can be entered into a cell consists of labels. Labels, commonly used for row and column headings and a variety of other purposes, can be up to 240 characters long and may contain any string of characters and numbers. A label that is too long for the width of a cell overlaps (for display purposes) the cells to the right, as long as the neighboring cells contain no other entries (see fig. 3.2).

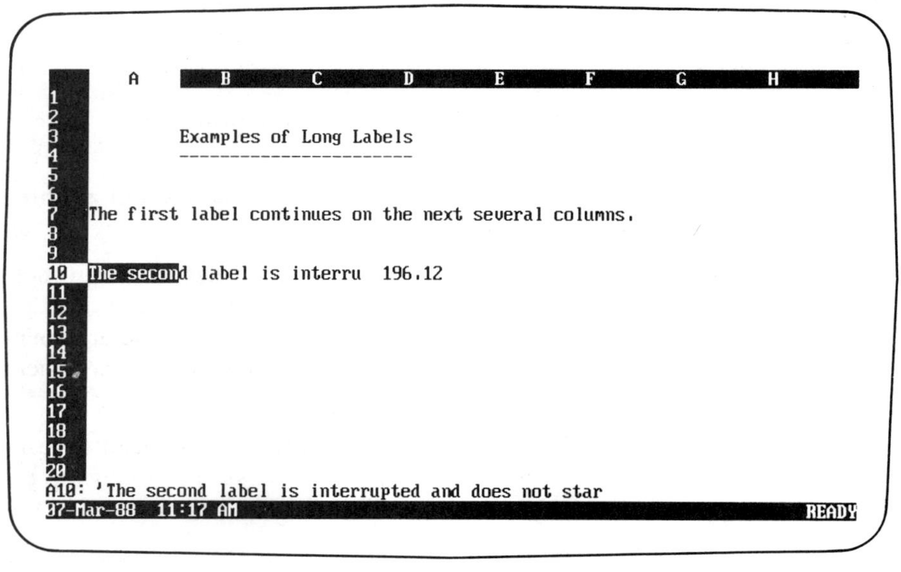

Fig. 3.2. A label continuing across cells.

When you make an entry into a cell and the first character is not a number or an indicator for entering numbers and formulas, Quattro assumes that you are entering a label. As you type the first character, Quattro shifts from READY mode to LABEL mode.

One advantage of Quattro is that you can left-justify, center, or right-justify labels when you display them (see fig. 3.3). To determine a label's position, you must begin the label with one of the following label-prefix characters:

Label Prefix	*Action*
'	Left-justifies
^	Centers
"	Right-justifies
\	Repeats

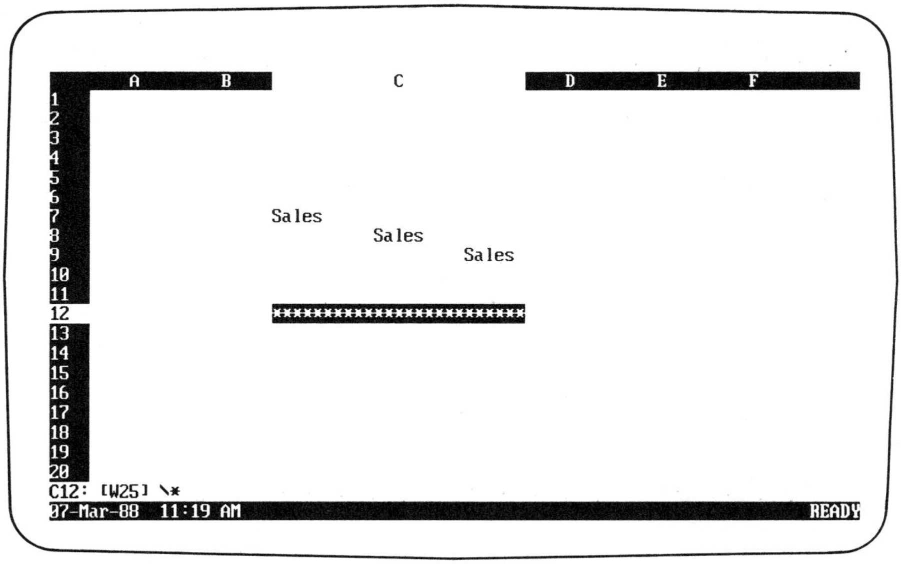

Fig. 3.3. Examples of left-justified, centered, right-justified, and repeated labels.

The default for displaying labels is left justification. You don't have to enter the label prefix in this case because Quattro automatically supplies the prefix for you. If you want, however, you can enter the ' label prefix just as you can enter any other label prefixes.

What You Enter	*What Quattro Stores*
Net Income	'Net Income

The one exception for all types of alignment occurs when the first character of the label is a number or an indicator of a number or formula (see the list in the "Entering Formulas" section of this chapter). For example, suppose that you want to enter the number 1989 as a label. If you type *1989*, Quattro assumes that you are entering a value. You need some way to signal that you intend this numeric entry to be treated as text. You can indicate this distinction by using one of the label-prefix characters. In this case, you could enter 1989 as a centered label by typing *^1989*.

The most unusual label prefix is the backslash (\), which is used for repetition. One of the most frequent uses of this prefix is to create a separator line.

The first step in creating a separator line is to enter * into the first cell (in fig. 3.3, cell C12). This entry causes asterisks to appear across the entire cell. Once you set up the first cell, you can use the /**B**lock **C**opy command to replicate the cell across the page. (For additional information about the /**B**lock **C**opy command and replication in general, see Chapter 4.)

Several ways are available to control label prefixes. For example, suppose that you entered a series of labels, using the standard default of left justification; then you decide that you would rather have the labels centered. You could change manually all the label prefixes, or, using the /**B**lock **L**abel_Align command, you could change the prefixes all at once.

From this point on in the book, you need to know how to use the Quattro command menus. Remember from Chapter 2 that you access the main command menu by pressing the slash (/) key. When the main command menu appears, you can choose any item on the menu, either by using the up- and down-arrow keys to point to the item and then pressing Enter or by typing the first letter of the item.

For example, **B**lock is an option on the main command menu. Either highlight this word by using the cursor-movement keys and then press Enter or simply type *b*. When you make this selection, the main menu disappears and the Block menu appears in its place. **L**abel_Align is an option on the Block menu; choose this option as you would choose an option from the main menu. As you work with Quattro, you probably will find that typing the initial letter is easier than using the pointing method.

This book uses the following convention when giving a command:

/**O**ption1 **O**ption2 **O**ption3 . . .

Notice that the first letter of the option is in boldface. This letter is the one to type to select the option. To help you follow the sometimes bewildering sequence of Quattro commands, look at the command reference tables in Appendix A.

Now, using whatever method you prefer, select the /**B**lock **L**abel_Align command. When you select this command, you are given the following choices:

Left
Right
Center

Each choice gives you the appropriate label prefix.

If you select **C**enter, Quattro asks you to designate a block of cells to change. When you specify a block and press Enter, the cells are displayed as centered.

Another option for changing label prefixes is to change the default setting for text justification. The command that changes the default setting is /**D**efault **F**ormats **A**lign. This command gives you the same options as the /**B**lock **L**abel_Align command. Previously entered cells, however, are not affected by the /**D**efault **F**ormats **A**lign command. Only subsequent entries show the change. In addition, cells that were set previously, using /**B**lock **L**abel_Align, maintain the alignment set by that command.

Editing Data in the Worksheet

When you start using Quattro, one of the first things you will want to do is modify the contents of cells without retyping the complete entry. This modification is quite easy to do. You begin by moving the cell pointer to the appropriate cell and pressing the F2 (Edit) key. An alternative is to press F2 when you are entering cell contents.

When you press F2, Quattro enters EDIT mode. Normally, Quattro is in READY mode. The main difference between the two modes is that some keys take on different meanings. Table 3.1 shows the functions of keys that are different in EDIT mode.

Table 3.1.
Key Action in EDIT Mode

Key	*Action*
←	Moves the cursor one position to the left
→	Moves the cursor one position to the right
→|(Tab) or Ctrl→	Moves the cursor five characters to the right
|←(Backtab) or Ctrl←	Moves the cursor five characters to the left. To use Backtab, you must hold down the Shift key when you press |←.

Key	*Action*
Home	Moves the cursor to the first character in the entry
End	Moves the cursor to the last character in the entry
Backspace	Deletes the character just to the left of the cursor
Ins	Toggles between INSERT and OVERTYPE modes
Del	Deletes the character above the cursor
Esc	Clears the input line but does not take you out of EDIT mode

After you press F2, the mode indicator in the lower right corner of the screen changes to EDIT. The contents of the cell are duplicated in the input line and are ready for editing.

To show how the various keys are used, consider two examples. First, suppose that you want to edit in cell E4 an entry that reads `Sales Comparisson`. After you highlight cell E4 with the cell selector, correct the misspelling of `Comparisson` by pressing the following keys:

Keys	*Input Line*	*Explanation*
F2	`'Sales Comparisson_`	The cursor always appears at the end of the input line when you press F2.
←	`'Sales Comparisson`	
←	`'Sales Comparisson`	
←	`'Sales Comparisson`	The cursor now appears below the errant `s`.
Del	`'Sales Comparison`	The Del key deletes the character above the cursor.
Enter	You press Enter to update the entry in the spreadsheet and return to READY mode.	

Now suppose that you want to modify a formula in cell G6 from +D4/H3*(Y5+4000) to +C4/H3*(Y5+4000). After you highlight cell G6 with the cell selector, press the following keys to change the formula:

Keys	*Input Line*	*Explanation*
F2	+D4/H3*(Y5+4000)_	Again, the cursor always appears at the end of the input line when you first press F2.
Home	+D4/H3*(Y5+4000)	The Home key takes you to the first position in the input line.
→	+D4/H3*(Y5+4000)	The → key moves the cursor one position to the right.
C	+CD4/H3*(Y5+4000)	When you enter a character in EDIT mode, the character normally is inserted to the left of the cursor. Entering a character never causes you to write over another, unless you have pressed the Ins key to toggle into OVERTYPE mode. Unwanted characters can be eliminated with the Del and Backspace keys.
Del	+C4/H3*(Y5+4000)	Use the Del key to delete the character above the cursor.
Enter	Again, press Enter to update the entry in the spreadsheet and return to READY mode.	

One thing to remember about using EDIT mode is that you can use EDIT mode when you enter data into a cell for the first time. If you make a mistake when you are in EDIT mode, you do not have to retype the entire entry.

Using the Search and Replace Commands

If you have a situation where several cell entries need to be edited in an identical fashion, you will be grateful for the inclusion of Quattro's global search and replace command. The command is found in the Block Search/Replace menu.

The spreadsheet in figure 3.4 is admittedly a small one. The spreadsheet really is a small sample of a much larger application. If many more than 50 employees were listed, you would need quite awhile to find the employee named Julia Kesler. For the sake of the illustration, the database was kept small.

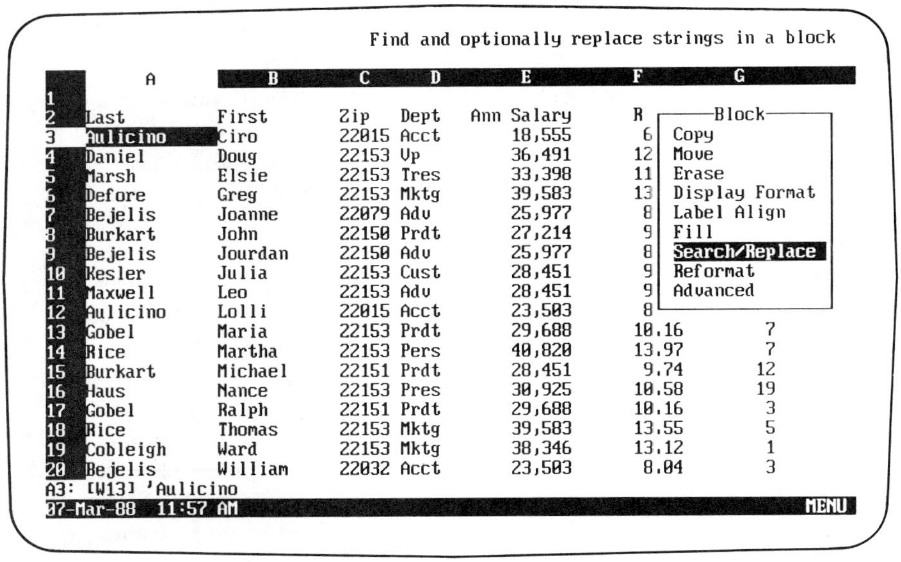

Find and optionally replace strings in a block

	A	B	C	D	E	F	G
1							
2	Last	First	Zip	Dept	Ann Salary	R	
3	Aulicino	Ciro	22015	Acct	18,555	6	
4	Daniel	Doug	22153	Vp	36,491	12	
5	Marsh	Elsie	22153	Tres	33,398	11	
6	Defore	Greg	22153	Mktg	39,583	13	
7	Bejelis	Joanne	22079	Adv	25,977	8	
8	Burkart	John	22150	Prdt	27,214	9	
9	Bejelis	Jourdan	22150	Adv	25,977	8	
10	Kesler	Julia	22153	Cust	28,451	9	
11	Maxwell	Leo	22153	Adv	28,451	9	
12	Aulicino	Lolli	22015	Acct	23,503	8	
13	Gobel	Maria	22153	Prdt	29,688	10.16	7
14	Rice	Martha	22153	Pers	40,820	13.97	7
15	Burkart	Michael	22151	Prdt	28,451	9.74	12
16	Haus	Nance	22153	Pres	30,925	10.58	19
17	Gobel	Ralph	22151	Prdt	29,688	10.16	3
18	Rice	Thomas	22153	Mktg	39,583	13.55	5
19	Cobleigh	Ward	22153	Mktg	38,346	13.12	1
20	Bejelis	William	22032	Acct	23,503	8.04	3

Block
Copy
Move
Erase
Display Format
Label Align
Fill
Search/Replace
Reformat
Advanced

A3: [W13] 'Aulicino
07-Mar-88 11:57 AM MENU

Fig. 3.4. Preparing to search for and replace an employee's name.

The reason you need to search for Julia Kesler is that she recently married Leo Maxwell and has decided to change her last name. Quattro has the capability to search quickly for text in any area of the spreadsheet. Figure 3.5 shows the Search/Replace menu that you will use to search for the label `Kesler`. Several options are on the Search/Replace menu. The following list explains for what purpose each choice is used.

Command	*Description*
Block	Limits the search/replace to the block of cells specified
Search String	Prompts you for the text/values that you want to find/replace
Replace String	Prompts you for the text/values to substitute for the current text/value
Go	Performs the operation based on the defined Block, Search String, and, optionally, Replace String

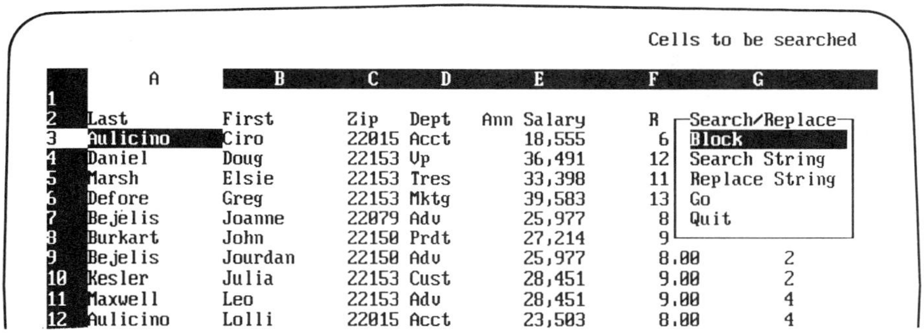

Fig. 3.5. The Search/Replace menu.

Figure 3.6 shows the entry `Kesler` in response to the search prompt after the block was defined for the search. Figure 3.7 shows the replace prompt and the entry `Maxwell`.

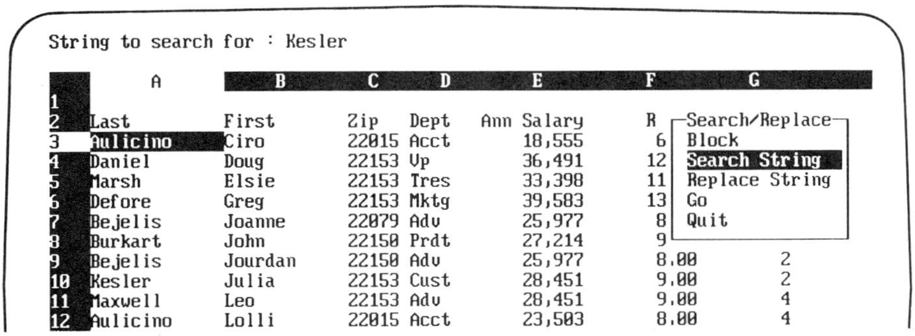

Fig. 3.6. Setting the Search String option.

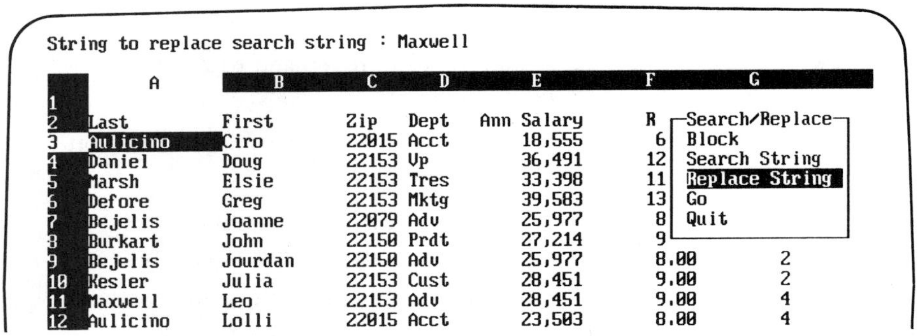

Fig. 3.7. Setting the Replace String option.

Once the Search String and Replace String options are set, press the **Go** option from the menu. If a match is found, a window is opened in the display; the window shows the location of the first match in the block and the character where the match begins. Figure 3.8 shows the result of choosing **Go**.

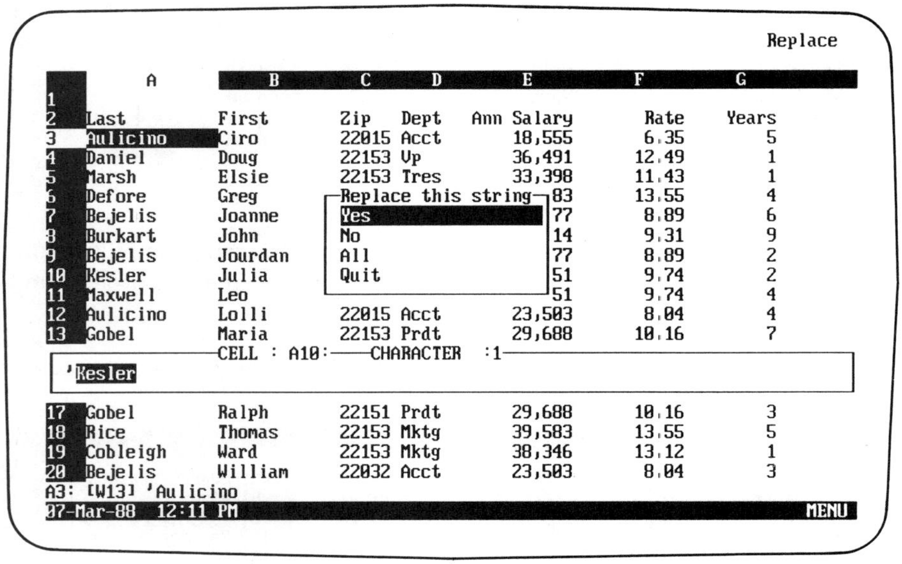

*Fig. 3.8. The menu box and window that appear after choosing **Go**.*

Next, a menu box is opened. The "Replace this string" menu box gives you the opportunity to decide whether or not to accept the replacement.

Caution: Even if you didn't specify a Replace String, the "Replace this string" option box still opens. If you accidentally choose **Yes** or **All** from the "Replace this string" menu, the text is replaced with nothing, thus erasing the text you wanted to find. The following list shows what the Replace options do.

Command	*Description*
Yes	Go ahead and replace only the text in the Replace window and then search for the next instance, if any, and redisplay the "Replace this string" options menu.
No	Don't replace the text in the Replace window; skip it and search for the next instance, if any.
All	Go ahead and replace all instances found without stopping for individual confirmation.

Quattro is especially clever when finding text, because it looks at a cell's entire contents, not just the starting characters.

In this example, Quattro actually is looking in the current block for any label that contains the text `Kesler`. If someone named Keslerson was listed earlier, Quattro would have found the cell containing that name.

All the rules described earlier remain true when you are looking for numbers or formulas in cells.

Figure 3.9 shows the result after the **Yes** choice was selected from the menu. Now Julia is officially a Maxwell.

	A	B	C	D	E	F	G
1							
2	Last	First	Zip	Dept	Ann Salary	Rate	Years
3	Aulicino	Ciro	22015	Acct	18,555	6.35	5
4	Daniel	Doug	22153	Vp	36,491	12.49	1
5	Marsh	Elsie	22153	Tres	33,398	11.43	1
6	Defore	Greg	22153	Mktg	39,583	13.55	4
7	Bejelis	Joanne	22079	Adv	25,977	8.89	6
8	Burkart	John	22150	Prdt	27,214	9.31	9
9	Bejelis	Jourdan	22150	Adv	25,977	8.89	2
10	Maxwell	Julia	22153	Cust	28,451	9.74	2
11	Maxwell	Leo	22153	Adv	28,451	9.74	4
12	Aulicino	Lolli	22015	Acct	23,503	8.04	4

Fig. 3.9. The result of choosing Yes from the "Replace this string" menu.

The next series of figures illustrates the use of the global replace operation (within the block specified). Figure 3.10 shows that the `Prdt` entries in the database will be replaced with the full word `Production`. Figure 3.11 illustrates the Search window that opens on the first instance of `Prdt` after you selected **Go**. Figure 3.12 shows the replacements after you use the **All** menu choice.

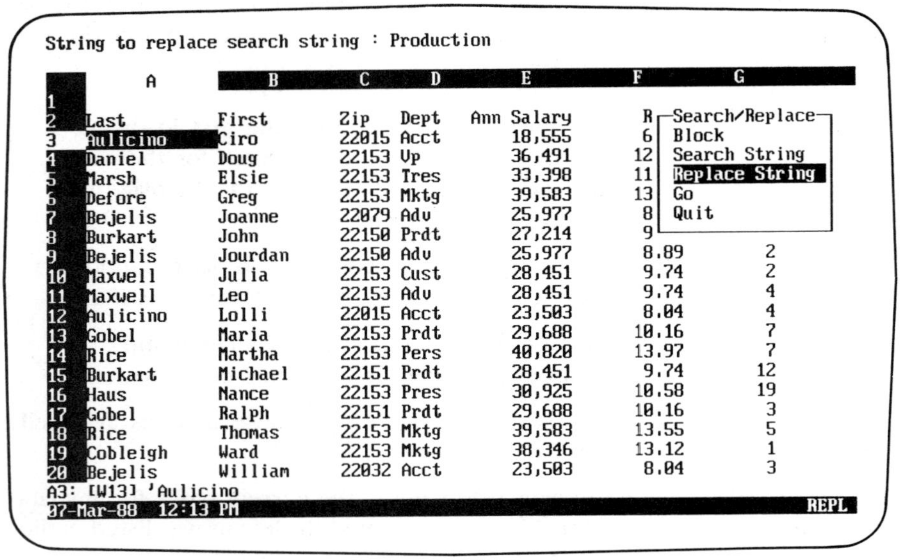

```
String to replace search string : Production

          A                B          C      D        E              F              G
 1
 2  Last            First         Zip    Dept   Ann Salary         R ┌Search/Replace─┐
 3  Aulicino        Ciro          22015  Acct       18,555         6 │ Block         │
 4  Daniel          Doug          22153  Vp         36,491        12 │ Search String │
 5  Marsh           Elsie         22153  Tres       33,398        11 │ Replace String│
 6  Defore          Greg          22153  Mktg       39,583        13 │ Go            │
 7  Bejelis         Joanne        22079  Adv        25,977         8 │ Quit          │
 8  Burkart         John          22150  Prdt       27,214         9 └───────────────┘
 9  Bejelis         Jourdan       22150  Adv        25,977      8.89           2
10  Maxwell         Julia         22153  Cust       28,451      9.74           2
11  Maxwell         Leo           22153  Adv        28,451      9.74           4
12  Aulicino        Lolli         22015  Acct       23,503      8.04           4
13  Gobel           Maria         22153  Prdt       29,688     10.16           7
14  Rice            Martha        22153  Pers       40,820     13.97           7
15  Burkart         Michael       22151  Prdt       28,451      9.74          12
16  Haus            Nance         22153  Pres       30,925     10.58          19
17  Gobel           Ralph         22151  Prdt       29,688     10.16           3
18  Rice            Thomas        22153  Mktg       39,583     13.55           5
19  Cobleigh        Ward          22153  Mktg       38,346     13.12           1
20  Bejelis         William       22032  Acct       23,503      8.04           3
A3: [W13] 'Aulicino
07-Mar-88  12:13 PM                                                          REPL
```

Fig. 3.10. Preparing to replace Prdt *with* Production.

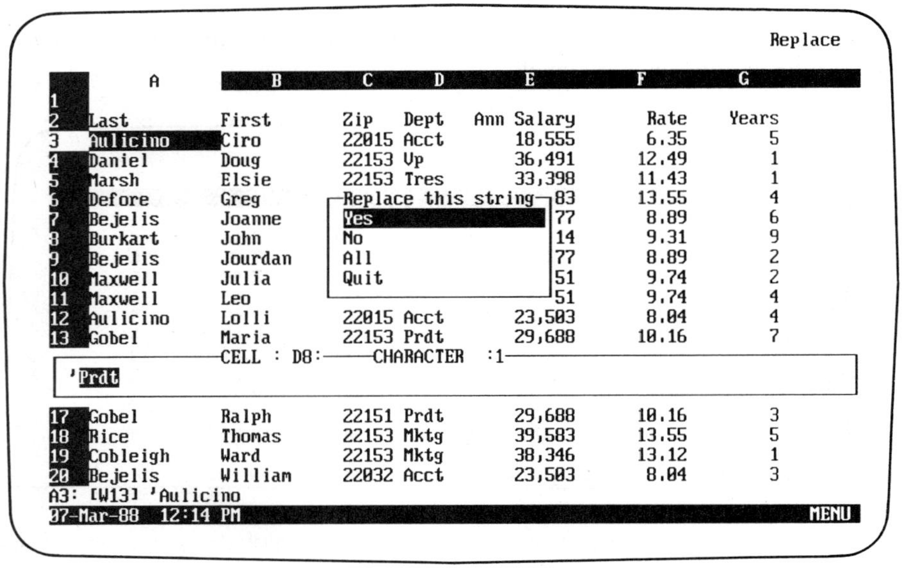

```
                                                                       Replace

          A                B          C      D        E              F              G
 1
 2  Last            First         Zip    Dept   Ann Salary         Rate      Years
 3  Aulicino        Ciro          22015  Acct       18,555         6.35          5
 4  Daniel          Doug          22153  Vp         36,491        12.49          1
 5  Marsh           Elsie         22153  Tres       33,398        11.43          1
 6  Defore          Greg         ┌Replace this string┐83         13.55          4
 7  Bejelis         Joanne       │Yes                │77          8.89          6
 8  Burkart         John         │No                 │14          9.31          9
 9  Bejelis         Jourdan      │All                │77          8.89          2
10  Maxwell         Julia        │Quit               │51          9.74          2
11  Maxwell         Leo          └───────────────────┘51          9.74          4
12  Aulicino        Lolli         22015  Acct       23,503         8.04          4
13  Gobel           Maria         22153  Prdt       29,688        10.16          7
┌──────────────────────────CELL : D8:────CHARACTER  :1─────────────────────────┐
│ 'Prdt                                                                         │
└───────────────────────────────────────────────────────────────────────────────┘
17  Gobel           Ralph         22151  Prdt       29,688        10.16          3
18  Rice            Thomas        22153  Mktg       39,583        13.55          5
19  Cobleigh        Ward          22153  Mktg       38,346        13.12          1
20  Bejelis         William       22032  Acct       23,503         8.04          3
A3: [W13] 'Aulicino
07-Mar-88  12:14 PM                                                          MENU
```

Fig. 3.11. The Search window that opens when the first match is found.

	A	B	C	D	E	F	G
1							
2	Last	First	Zip	Dept	Ann Salary	Rate	Years
3	Aulicino	Ciro	22015	Acct	18,555	6.35	5
4	Daniel	Doug	22153	Vp	36,491	12.49	1
5	Marsh	Elsie	22153	Tres	33,398	11.43	1
6	Defore	Greg	22153	Mktg	39,583	13.55	4
7	Bejelis	Joanne	22079	Adv	25,977	8.89	6
8	Burkart	John	22150	Production	27,214	9.31	9
9	Bejelis	Jourdan	22150	Adv	25,977	8.89	2
10	Maxwell	Julia	22153	Cust	28,451	9.74	2
11	Maxwell	Leo	22153	Adv	28,451	9.74	4
12	Aulicino	Lolli	22015	Acct	23,503	8.04	4
13	Gobel	Maria	22153	Production	29,688	10.16	7
14	Rice	Martha	22153	Pers	40,820	13.97	7
15	Burkart	Michael	22151	Production	28,451	9.74	12
16	Haus	Nance	22153	Pres	30,925	10.58	19
17	Gobel	Ralph	22151	Production	29,688	10.16	3
18	Rice	Thomas	22153	Mktg	39,583	13.55	5
19	Cobleigh	Ward	22153	Mktg	38,346	13.12	1
20	Bejelis	William	22032	Acct	23,503	8.04	3

A3: [W13] 'Aulicino

07-Mar-88 12:16 PM READY

*Fig. 3.12. The result of choosing **All** from the "Replace this string" menu.*

As a bonus, the Search and Replace commands in Quattro have the capability to modify formulas, functions, and values. This feature can save you untold amounts of time when you want to change a number, a block name, or cell address specification found in several cells. Without this command, you would have to locate and edit each cell individually, a dull "search and destroy" mission. If you make the changes manually, you almost always introduce mistakes to the application in the process.

In the database application, the records in the Rate column hold the formula (Annual salary/365.25)/8 to get the hourly rate for each individual. Rather than use 365.25, the accounting department wants to use 360 days. Figure 3.13 shows the number found within the first formula after the Search String was defined as 365.25. Figure 3.14 demonstrates the successful replacement in column F after the **All** option was selected from the Replace menu.

Moving around the Spreadsheet

Soon after you start entering data into your worksheet, you will find that you need some easy ways to move the cell selector quickly and accurately. Remember that the Quattro spreadsheet is immense—8,192 rows and 256 columns, or more than 2,000,000 cells. As your use of Quattro becomes more

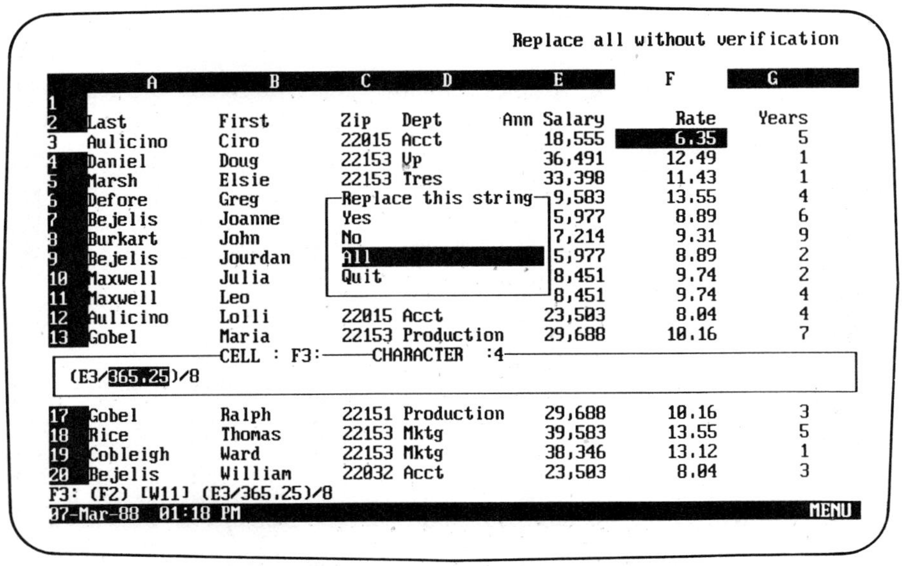

Fig. 3.13. The Search window opened on the first match found.

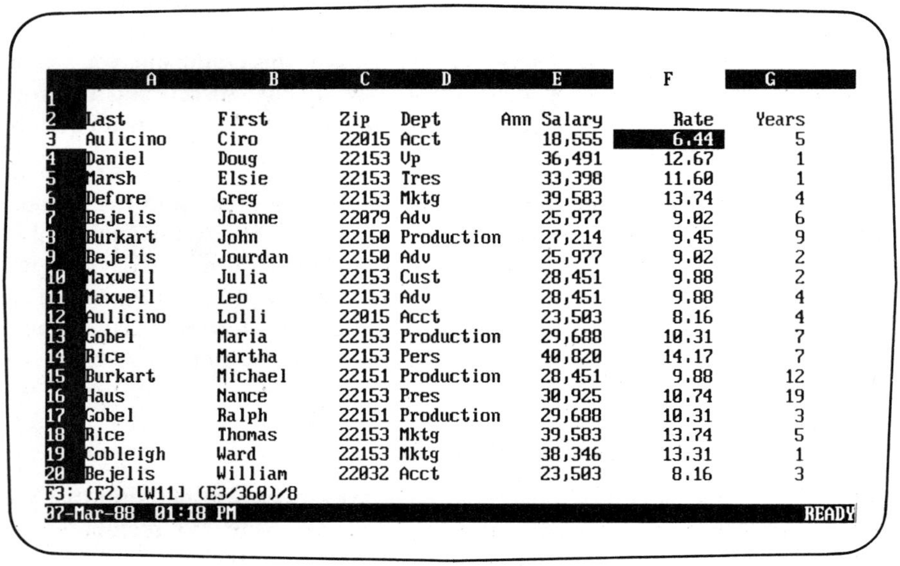

Fig. 3.14. The result of using the All option to make the replacement.

extensive, you may have blocks of data of various sizes in widely separated parts of the worksheet. The program provides several ways to move the cell selector quickly anywhere in the worksheet.

Remember that the cell selector is not the same as the cursor. The cell selector is the bright rectangle that highlights an entire cell. The cursor is the blinking line that is sometimes inside the cell selector and sometimes on the input line. The cursor indicates the position within a particular cell where your keyboard activity takes effect; the cell selector indicates the cell that is affected. Whenever you move the cell selector, the cursor inside the selector moves also. Thus, we sometimes talk about cursor-movement keys when we really mean keys that move the cell selector.

When Quattro is in READY mode, the cursor-movement keys are used to move the cell selector; when Quattro is in POINT mode, these keys are used to point out a block. The cursor-movement keys either cannot be used at all or have a different action when you are in EDIT mode, are making a cell entry, or are in the process of entering a Quattro command.

Using the Basic Cursor-Movement Keys

The arrow keys on the numeric keypad (or on a separate pad of the enhanced keyboard) are the basic keys for moving the cell selector. The cell selector moves in the direction of the arrow on a key as long as you hold down that key. When you reach the edge of the screen, the worksheet scrolls in the direction of the arrow.

You can scroll the worksheet one screenful at a time to the left or right by holding down the Ctrl key and pressing the left- or right-arrow key. You also can scroll the worksheet to the right with the Tab key and to the left with Shift-Tab (hold down the Shift key while you press Tab). These four keys and key combinations provide quick ways of "paging through" the worksheet.

To scroll up or down one screen at a time, use the PgUp and PgDn keys—not the up- and down-arrow keys.

The Home key provides a quick way to return to the beginning of the worksheet. From anywhere in the worksheet, pressing Home causes the cell selector to return to cell A1. Table 3.2 summarizes the action of the cursor-movement keys. Remember from the "Editing Data in the Worksheet" section earlier in this chapter that some keys, such as Home and End, have different actions in EDIT mode.

Table 3.2
Cursor-Movement Key Operation

Keys	*Function*
→	Positions the cell selector one column right
←	Positions the cell selector one column left
↑	Positions the cell selector one row up
↓	Positions the cell selector one row down
Ctrl→ or →|(Tab)	Moves the cell selector one screen to the right
Ctrl← or |←(Shift-Tab)	Moves the cell selector one screen to the left
PgUp	Moves the cell selector up an entire screen
PgDn	Moves the cell selector down an entire screen
Home	Returns the cell selector to cell A1 from any location in the worksheet. Also used after the End key to position the cell selector at the end of the active worksheet.
End	When entered prior to any of the arrow keys, positions the cell selector in the direction of the arrow key to the cell on the boundary of an empty and filled space
F5 (GoTo)	Moves the cell selector to the cell coordinates (or block name) provided

Using the End Key for Cursor Movement

Quattro uses the End key in a unique way. When you press an arrow key after you press and release the End key, the cell selector moves in the direction of the arrow key to the next boundary between a blank cell and a cell that contains data. For example, the indicator in the lower right corner of the screen in figure 3.15 shows that the End key has been pressed. If you press the right-arrow key, the cell selector jumps to the first boundary, as shown in figure 3.16.

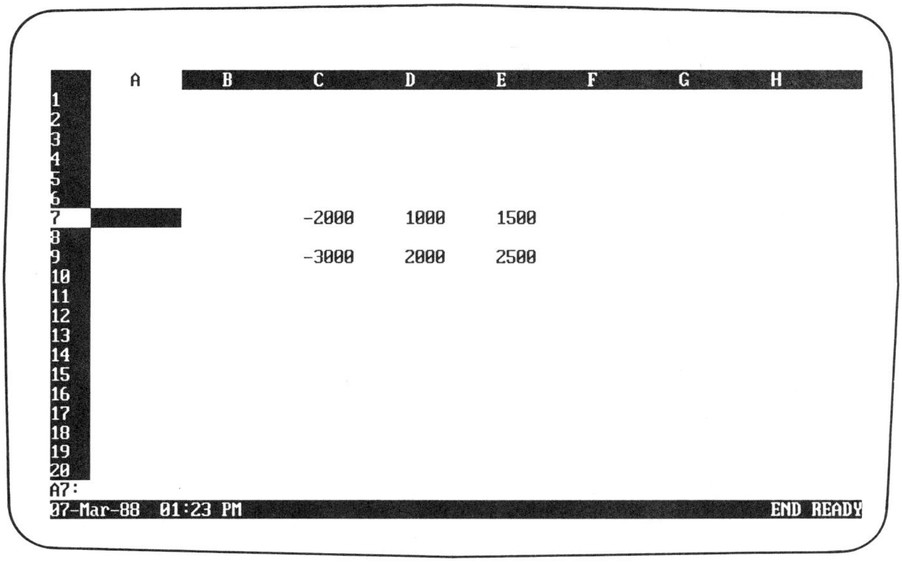

Fig. 3.15. Using the End key to move the cell selector.

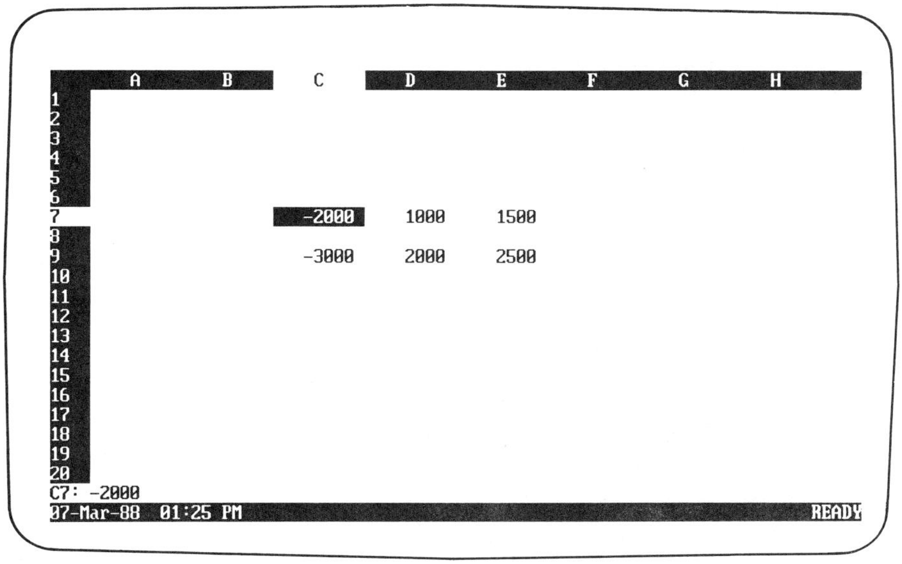

Fig. 3.16. Using the right-arrow key after pressing the End key.

If you again press the End key, followed by the right-arrow key, the cell selector jumps to the next boundary, cell E7, which contains the value 1500. If you repeat the process one more time, the cell selector jumps all the way to the right boundary of the spreadsheet, cell IV7. The End key works in a similar fashion with the other arrow keys.

You also can use the End key, followed by the Home key, to move the cell selector from any position on the spreadsheet to the lower right corner of your active worksheet. In figure 3.15, this corner is cell E9 and contains the value 2500. In a sense, the End-Home combination has the opposite effect of the Home key when used alone, because the Home key always moves the cell selector to cell A1, the upper left corner of every spreadsheet.

Using the End key for cursor movement may sound complex; in practice, though, using the End key is an easy and quick way to find the boundaries of blocks of data in your worksheet. Remember, however, that if gaps are in the blocks of data, the End key procedure probably will be less useful because the cell selector will go to the boundaries of each gap.

You will look at several interesting applications for the End key in following chapters.

Jumping to a Cell

The F5 (GoTo) key gives you a way to jump directly to a cell location. To move the cell selector to any cell on the spreadsheet, just press the F5 key. When Quattro asks you for the address to go to, type the cell address. Then press Enter.

Remember that every cell has an address, defined by the cell's row and column coordinates. The columns have alphabetic names, starting with A through Z, AA through AZ, and so on, up to IV. The rows have numeric names, running from 1 to 8192. The cell addresses are a combination of the alphabetic and numeric names, running from A1 through IV8192. When you press F5 and then type any one of the 2,097,152 addresses on the spreadsheet, the cell selector immediately jumps to that address.

Another nice feature of the F5 key is that you can combine the key with block names. Remember that a block is a rectangular block of cells; this block can be given a name—RATIOS, for example. When Quattro asks you for the address to go to after you press F5, you can enter *ratios* instead of an address such as *A94*. If you don't want to type the block name manually, press the F3 (Names) key and use the cursor-movement keys to select the block name from the list of block names presented in the box. This topic is covered in the "Naming Blocks" section of Chapter 4.

Chapter Summary

This chapter showed you the basics of entering and editing data in a worksheet. You learned how to enter and use formulas, as well as operators within formulas. You also learned that functions are built-in formulas that can be used for rapid, easy manipulation of data. And you learned how to move the cell selector quickly and easily to any part of the worksheet.

Chapter 4 discusses the next step toward mastering the Quattro spreadsheet—using commands. You had a brief introduction to commands in Chapter 2, where you learned to start up and exit Quattro. In Chapter 4, you start using the program's extensive command structure to accomplish a wide variety of spreadsheet tasks.

CHAPTER

4

Working with the Menu Commands

Using Quattro means using Quattro commands. Commands are the tools that the program provides for performing its tasks. If you want to rearrange the data on your worksheet, save the worksheet or access a different worksheet, print reports or create graphs based on the worksheet, or accomplish a wide variety of other tasks, you need to use commands.

This chapter teaches you the principles of using fundamental Quattro commands. If you have read Chapters 2 and 3, you already have been given a brief introduction to commands; because you will need to use them regularly from this point on, however, you now should learn thoroughly how to use commands.

To make sense of the command structure, you need to understand one preliminary concept: the concept of blocks. Some commands affect the entire worksheet, but other commands affect only certain cells or groups of cells. Quattro uses the term *block* for a rectangular group of cells and builds many highly useful actions around this concept. This chapter explains blocks and the group of commands that are designated as block commands.

The chapter also explains the commands that affect the entire worksheet. Commands that accomplish several other important spreadsheet tasks also are covered.

This chapter shows you how to do the following:

- Accelerate menu selections
- Use blocks in a worksheet
- Use /**B**lock commands
- Use the /**B**lock **C**opy and /**B**lock **M**ove commands to manage data within a worksheet
- Use relative and absolute cell referencing/addressing
- Use /**C**olumn and /**R**ow commands
- Save your worksheet before you /**Q**uit Quattro

Selecting Commands from Command Menus

If commands are the tools for performing Quattro tasks, command menus are the toolboxes. The menus display the commands that are available for use. In Quattro, the command menus are especially helpful for several reasons. First, Quattro lists the full command words (see fig. 4.1).

To display the main command menu shown in figure 4.1, press the slash (/) key. Remember to press the slash key while in READY mode whenever you want to activate any command.

A second feature of the command menus is illustrated on the top line of the display in figure 4.1. This line lists available choices from the command that is highlighted. In fact, as you point to the different items in the command menu by moving the cell selector down the list, new choices appear on the top line for each command-menu item. This feature is in every command menu.

A third friendly aspect of command menus relates to how a command is initiated. You can point to the option you want, or you can type the first letter of the command name.

To point to a command-menu item, use the up- and down-arrow keys on the right-hand side of the keyboard. When the cell selector is positioned on the proper item, press Enter. If you move the cursor to the last item in the list and then press the down-arrow key again, the cursor "rounds the horn" and reappears on the first item on the top of the list. Similarly, if the cell selector

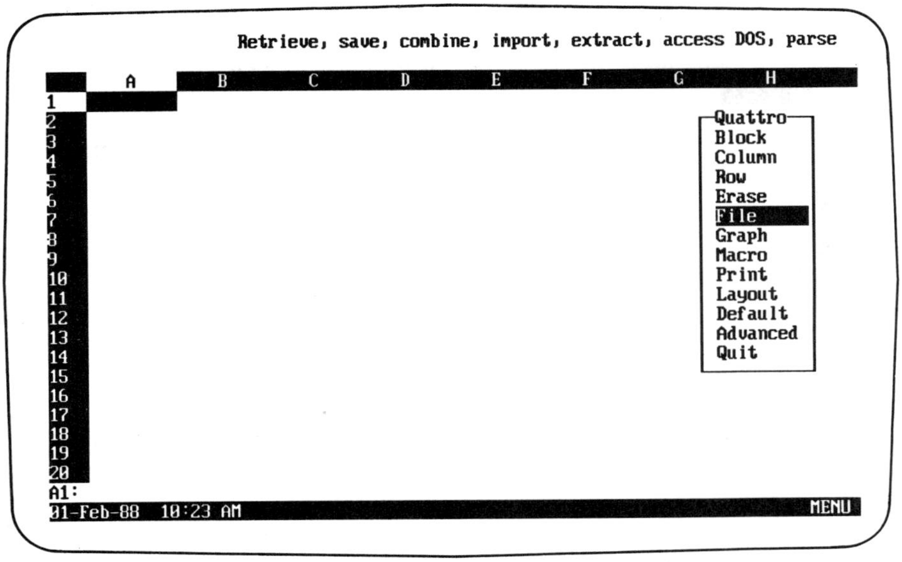

Fig. 4.1. The Quattro main menu.

is on the first item in the menu, press the up-arrow key to move the cursor to the last option. Note that you also can move the cursor to the end of the command menu by pressing the End key and to the beginning of the menu by pressing the Home key.

Typing the first letter of the command-menu item is the other way to select a command. For example, to select the /**D**efault **H**ardware command, which informs you of the status of several of Quattro's global parameters, type / to select the main command menu, followed by *d* to select **D**efault. At this point, another menu appears:

Hardware
Colors
International
Formats
Directories
Recalculation
Protection
Startup
Update
Quit

From this line, select **H**ardware by pressing the H key. A display similar to the one shown in figure 4.2 appears.

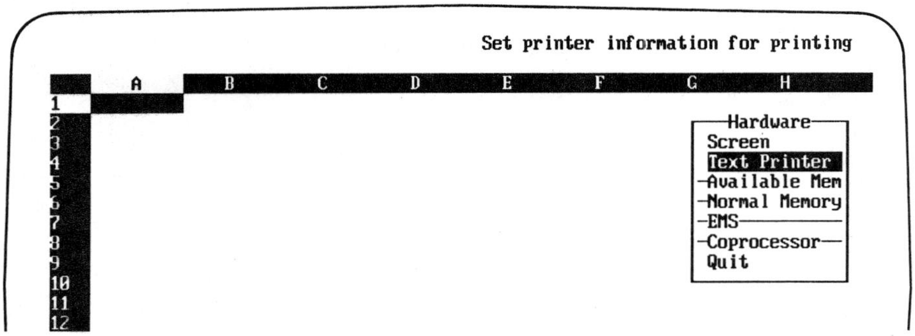

Fig. 4.2. The Default Hardware menu.

If you make the wrong command selection, you can press Esc at any time to return to the previous command menu. For instance, if you realize that you should have selected **C**olors, not **H**ardware, press Esc to return to the higher level menu. You can press Esc as many times as necessary to return to whatever point you want in the series of command menus, even out of MENU mode altogether. One alternative to pressing Esc repeatedly is to hold down the Ctrl (Control) key and then press the Break key. Doing so cancels the entire command and returns you to READY mode.

When using Quattro, the novice can point to the different commands and get a full explanation of each one, and the experienced user can enter at high speed a long series of commands, using the first-letter convention without reading the explanations. Thus, Quattro can grow with you as you become more experienced.

If you look at Quattro's main command menu, shown in figure 4.1, you can see the wide range of commands offered by Quattro. For a complete picture of the complexity of the command structure, look at the command reference tables in Appendix A.

Viewing Expanded Menus

Quattro's menus come in two sizes: regular and expanded. The regular or default width for the menus makes available only the choice portion while expanded menus provide both choices and status information (not all menus are expandable). For instance, the Default Hardware menu contains choices that let you modify the settings for the **S**creen and **T**ext_Printer. The regular menu size for this menu is shown in figure 4.2. If you press the gray + key on the right of the numeric keypad, the menu is expanded to present the additional information shown in figure 4.3. If you want to unexpand a menu, simply press the gray - (minus) key.

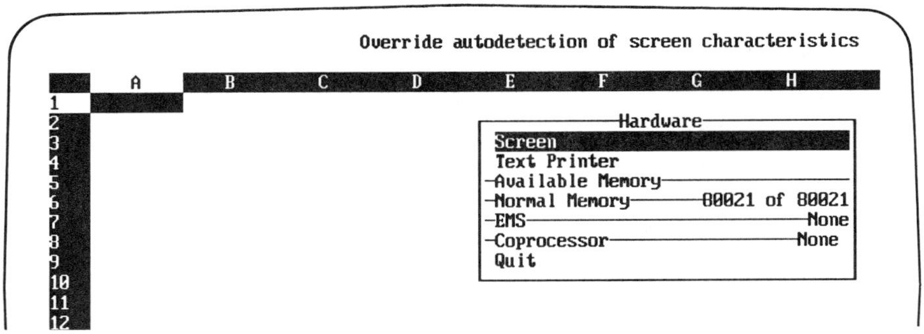

Fig. 4.3. The expanded Default Hardware menu.

You probably will agree that seeing all the information you can is better, and the only disadvantage to seeing the expanded version of menus is that the bigger menu hides more of the spreadsheet.

You can set up Quattro so that menus are always in their expanded form by selecting the /**D**efault **S**tartup **C**ompatibility_Options **K**eep_Wide command. This menu is shown in figure 4.4.

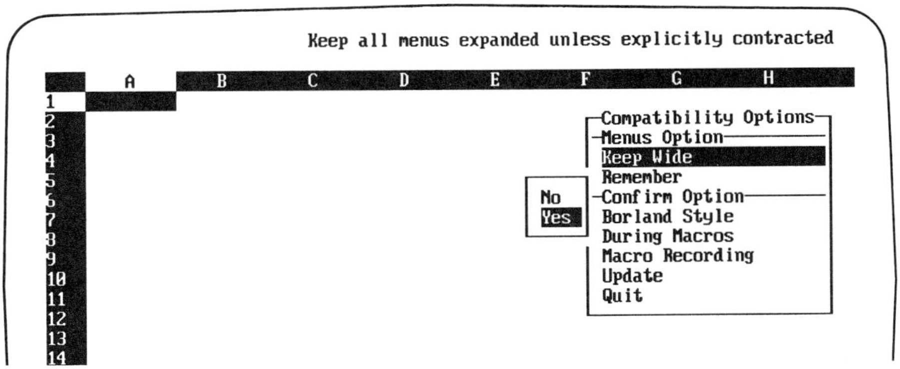

Fig. 4.4. Setting up Quattro to keep menus in expanded form.

You also can tell Quattro to remember what you selected from the menus the last time you used them. The **R**emember choice lets you set the menu system so that it positions the menu bar on the most recent series of menu choices. This setup is useful because menu operations tend to be repetitive in nature. For example, suppose that you perform a /**B**lock **D**isplay_Format **F**ixed command once; you are likely to need it again. If you have turned on menu memory, just press Enter three times on your second journey through the menu; the menu bar automatically highlights the previous choices.

The Confirm Options section of the menu tells Quattro how to treat the menu system if you want to maintain macro compatibility with 1-2-3. If you use the **B**orland_Style menu choice, confirmation menus only appear if they are needed.

For example, when you select /**Q**uit, 1-2-3 always prompts Yes/No, forcing you to verify that you want to leave the program. In Borland style (default), the prompt only appears in situations where you will lose data if you quit Quattro. For macro compatibility, you can set this choice to **N**o so that the 1-2-3 convention will be used. For complete macro compatibility with 1-2-3 during macro recording and playback, you should set the **D**uring_Macros and **M**acro_Recording choices to be compatible with 1-2-3.

Be sure to choose **U**pdate from the menu if you want to make the changes the new defaults.

Assigning Accelerator Keys to Menu Commands

With Quattro, you can assign a sequence of menu keystrokes to a single keystroke. The resulting keys are called accelerator keys.

To create an accelerated keystroke combination for a command such as /**F**ile **S**ave, bring up the menu to the last menu choice in the sequence and place the menu bar over the appropriate choice—in this case, the **S**ave command. Do not press Enter at this point.

Once the menu bar is in position, press Ctrl-Enter (press the Ctrl key and keep pressing it while briefly pressing the Enter key). Immediately, a prompt appears at the top left of the display; the prompt tells you to press a Ctrl-*key* combination. This prompt is shown in figure 4.5. When you press this combination, it invisibly enters the manual command-menu keystrokes. In the /**F**ile **S**ave example, you would press Ctrl-S (S for **S**ave). Now, you need only press Ctrl-S to process the /**F**ile **S**ave command. This sequence will be available no matter which spreadsheet you have on-screen.

Accelerator keys are discarded after a Quattro work session if they are not saved in the QUATTRO.DEF file by selecting /**D**efault **U**pdate.

Do not create accelerator keys lightly. They are difficult to remove after they are updated/added to the definition file QUATTRO.DEF, which is where Quattro stores most of its defaults. As a precaution, keep an original version of the QUATTRO.DEF file on your Quattro backup disks. That way, if you make a mistake with an accelerator key set, you can restore the definition file to its original state by copying the original QUATTRO.DEF file over the one you have modified.

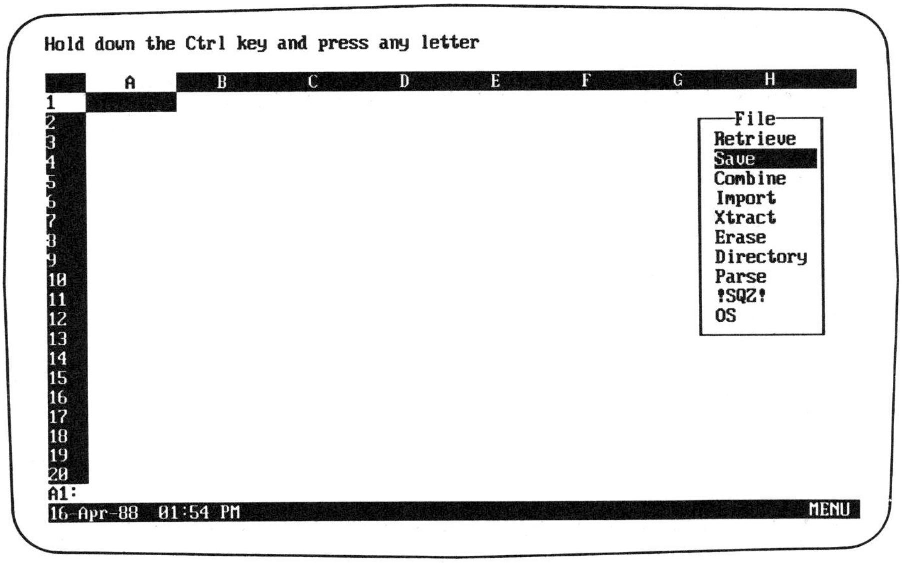

Fig. 4.5. Assigning an accelerator key to a menu command.

Here are five useful accelerator keys and their actions:

Keystroke:	*Accelerated Menu Commands*
Ctrl-Q	/**Q**uit
Ctrl-S	/**F**ile **S**ave
Ctrl-R	/**F**ile **R**etrieve
Ctrl-M	/**D**efault **S**tartup **M**enu_Tree **S**witch_Menus **M**ain_Menu
Ctrl-A	/**D**efault **S**tartup **M**enu_Tree **S**witch_Menus **A**lternate_Menu

You can use Ctrl-A and Ctrl-M to switch back and forth between the Quattro menu and the alternate 1-2-3 menu system. In order to use menu switching, you must set up the 123.ALT file as the alternate menu on the Menu_Tree submenu. Once you have updated the addition of this alternate menu, quit Quattro; then when you restart Quattro, you can press the accelerator keys to switch menu trees quickly.

Using the Primary Spreadsheet Commands

Now that you know more clearly how to make menu selections, you can investigate the power of the menu commands themselves.

Using Blocks in the Worksheet

Quattro's commands and functions often require that you deal with a *block*, a group of cells in aggregate. Before learning more about Quattro's commands, you need to learn a bit about blocks. Quattro's definition of a block is one or more cells in a rectangular group. With this definition, one cell is the smallest possible block, and the largest block is the entire worksheet. The use of blocks offers many advantages, making your work less tedious and more efficient. Giving names to blocks allows you to process blocks of cells in commands and formulas at the same time, by using the block name instead of cell addresses.

When to use blocks in Quattro depends to some degree on your personal preference. In many cases, such as in a formula or macro, you decide whether to provide blocks. In other cases, however, Quattro prompts you for blocks.

Blocks are rectangular in shape, as illustrated in figure 4.6. The expanding cell selector allows you to see the shape of blocks in Quattro. When you are using a Quattro command and are asked to designate a block, you can do so in one of three ways. You can enter the addresses of the cells in the block, use the cell selector to point to the cells in the block, or simply enter a name that you have assigned to the block.

When a block has been designated, the cells of the block show up in reverse video. Reverse video makes pointing an easy way to designate blocks, because the reverse-video rectangle expands as you move the cell selector (see fig. 4.7).

Blocks are specified by diagonally opposite corners, usually the upper left and lower right cells. The other set of corners, however, also may be used to identify the block. For example, the block shown in figure 4.7 could be identified as A1..D5, A5..D1, D5..A1, or D1..A5.

The usual custom is to separate by two periods the two cell addresses that specify the corners. Here are some examples:

A7..D10
AA1..AB20
J2..K4

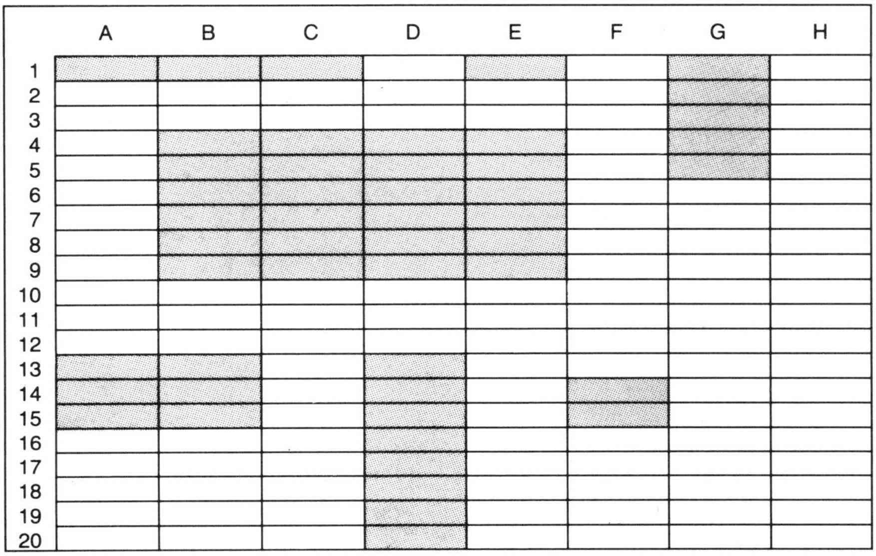

Fig. 4.6. A sample of Quattro blocks.

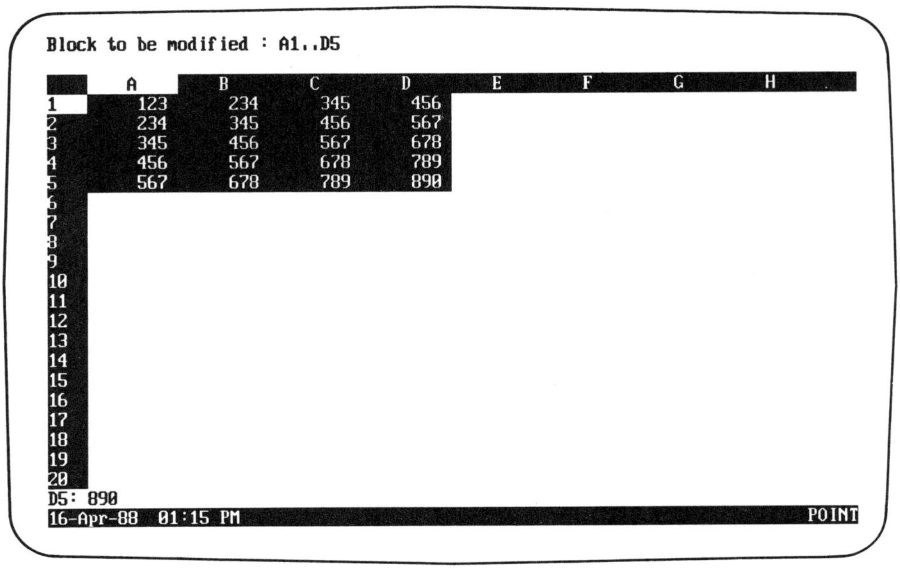

Fig. 4.7. A block highlighted by the expanding cell selector.

Naming Blocks

A name can be assigned to a block of cells. Block names can be up to 15 characters long and should be descriptive. The advantage of naming blocks is that block names are easier to understand than cell addresses and allow you to work more naturally. For example, the phrase *SALES_MODEL25* is a more understandable way than *A7..D10* to describe the sales for Model #25.

Block names are created with the /**B**lock **A**dvanced **C**reate and /**B**lock **A**dvanced **L**abels commands. Once names are established, they can be applied easily in both commands and formulas.

The /**B**lock **A**dvanced **C**reate command allows you to specify a name for any block—even as small as one cell. To access this command, first type a slash (/) from READY mode. At the main command menu, type a *b* to access the following **B**lock command menu:

Copy
Move
Erase
Display_Format
Label_Align
Fill
Search/Replace
Reformat
Advanced

This menu presents a set of commands that affect blocks. Select **A**dvanced by typing *a*. Then type *c* to select **C**reate. When the program asks you to `Enter Name to Create/Modify:`, type whatever block name you want and then press Enter. Don't use a name that could be confused with a cell address. For example, don't name a block *EX87*, even though Quattro allows the use of such a name. When you try to use this name in a command or formula, or with the F5 (GoTo) key, Quattro will take you to the cell located at EX87 rather than to the block EX87.

When you are asked to specify a block, such as when you are using a copy command, you can specify a block by one of two methods: typing the cell addresses or pointing. If you choose the pointing method, the cell selector expands as you use the arrow keys to designate the block.

/**B**lock **A**dvanced **C**reate can be used also to respecify a block if its location has changed. If minor changes occur to the block, such as a column or row of numbers being deleted from or added to the block, Quattro handles these changes internally without any respecification. If you delete a column or row that contains a corner of the block, however, the block specification is corrupted.

The /**B**lock **A**dvanced **L**abels command is similar to /**B**lock **A**dvanced **C**reate except that the names for blocks are taken directly from adjacent label entries. The adjacent entry must be a label; numeric entries and blank cells are ignored. Figure 4.8 illustrates one example of using the /**B**lock **A**dvanced **L**abels command to name a block.

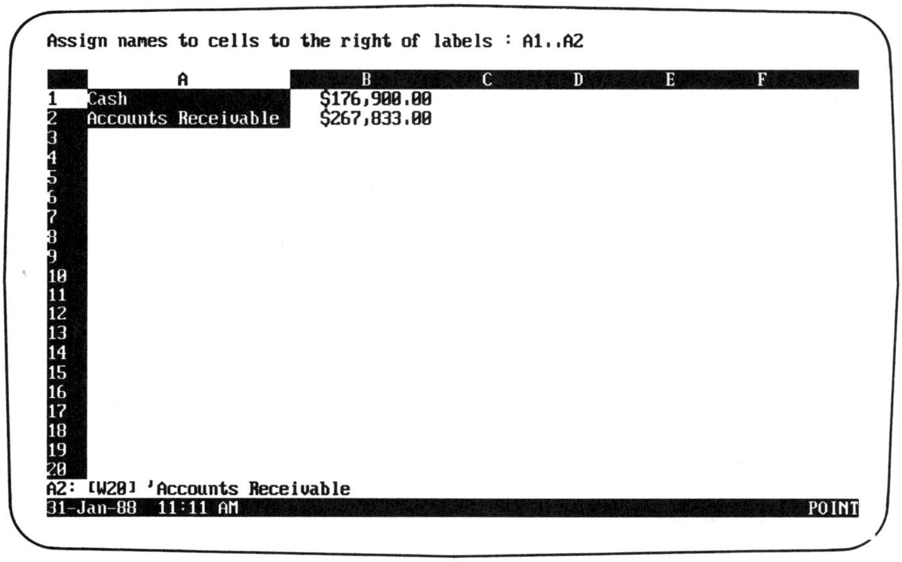

Fig. 4.8. Labels to be used in a /Block Advanced Labels command.

If you use the /**B**lock **A**dvanced **L**abels command and specify that the appropriate name for cell B1 is to the left in cell A1, you can assign the name CASH to the block B1. In this example, place the cell selector on cell A1, type /balr, and press Enter; the name CASH will be assigned to the one-cell block to the right—cell B1.

If you also use the /**B**lock **A**dvanced **L**abels command for ACCOUNTS RECEIVABLE, remember that a block name can be only 15 characters long. The resulting block name will be ACCOUNTS RECEIV. Another alternative would be to use the /**B**lock **A**dvanced **C**reate command to give cell B2 an appropriate name.

The /**B**lock **A**dvanced **C**reate and /**B**lock **A**dvanced **L**abels commands are different. When you create a name, you assign a name to a group of cells, perhaps as few as one cell but probably more. When you assign a label, you pick up a label from the spreadsheet and make that label the block name of a one-cell block above, below, to the left, or to the right of the label. You can assign more than one label at a time, but each label applies only to one adjacent cell.

The advantage of using /**B**lock **A**dvanced **C**reate is that you can give a name to a multicell block. Naming multicell blocks is important if you are using block names in functions and formulas or in move and copy operations. On the other hand, if you have a series of one-cell entries with adjacent labels or a series of columns or rows with headings, the /**B**lock **A**dvanced **L**abels command is a quick way to assign appropriate block names to the one-cell blocks or to the first entry of the column or row. The label method provides an easy way to find the column or row: press F5 (GoTo), enter the label (block name), and press Enter, and the cell selector jumps to the head of the column or row.

Block names are used also for naming macros. Although macros are covered in detail in Chapter 15, note here that macros can be named with the Macro commands; they also can be named with the same commands that name a block. You will learn that when you access a macro, you are jumping to the first entry in a block, because a macro name is actually a block name.

Using Block Names To Streamline Your Work

Block names can be useful tools for processing commands and generating formulas. In both cases, whenever a block must be designated, you can respond with a name instead of entering cell addresses or pointing to cell locations. For example, suppose that you had designated the block name SALES for the block A5..J5 in one of your worksheets. The simplest way to compute the sum of this block would be to use the function @SUM(SALES) rather than @SUM(A5..J5). Similarly, to determine the maximum value in the block, you could use the function @MAX(SALES). In functions and formulas, block names always can be used in place of cell addresses.

Notice that Quattro allows you to use multiple names for the same block. For example, a cell can be given the block names SALES_1987 and SALES_PREV_YR in the same worksheet. (Note that the underlines are part of the block names).

Still another advantage is that once a block name has been established, Quattro automatically uses that name throughout the worksheet in place of cell addresses. The following list shows the effect of assigning the name REVENUES to the block A5..J5.

Before Creating Block Name	*After Creating Block Name*
@SUM(A5..J5)	@SUM(REVENUES)
@MAX(A5..J5)	@MAX(REVENUES)

Figure 4.9 shows an example of a simple case of summing a block of values.

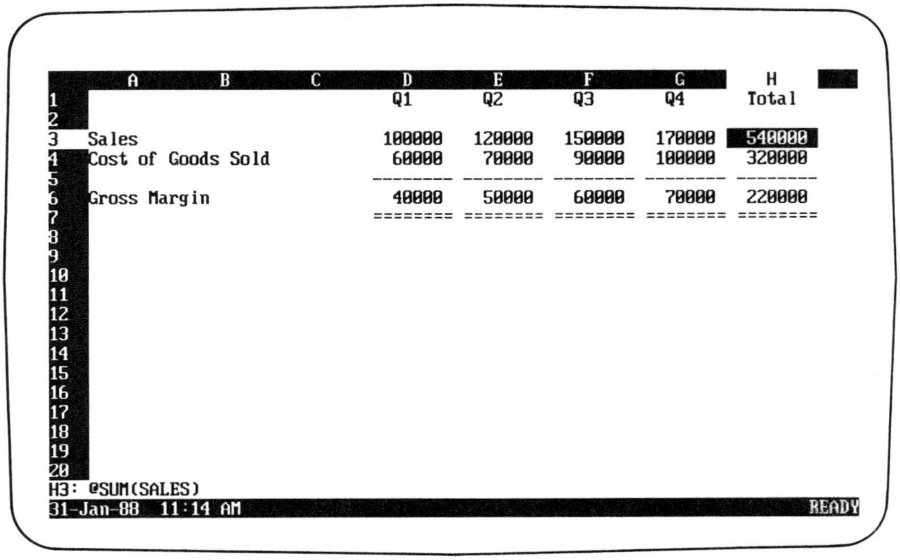

Fig. 4.9. Using block names in @SUM functions.

If the block name SALES is assigned to the block D3..G3 and the name CGS to block D4..G4, cell H3 can be defined with the formula

@SUM(SALES)

Similarly, cell H4 can be assigned the formula

@SUM(CGS)

Finally, cell H6 can contain the formula

@SUM(SALES)-@SUM(CGS)

The formulas in cells D6, E6, F6, and G6 cannot be defined in terms of the two blocks SALES and CGS, however; the reason is that these blocks refer to the two groups of cells that contain the values for all four quarters, not to the individual cells that contain the values for each quarter.

Another example uses names to designate the blocks of cells to be printed or extracted (using the /**F**ile **X**tract command) and saved to another worksheet. Suppose that you set up special names corresponding to different areas, and then you want to print, or extract and save to another worksheet, the corresponding portions of the current worksheet.

When Quattro prompts you for a block, you can enter a predefined name rather than actual cell addresses. For example, suppose that you were using the /**P**rint **B**lock command to print a portion of a worksheet. In response to `The block of the spreadsheet to print:` prompt, you could enter the block name PAGE_1 or the name PAGE_5.

A third example using block names involves the F5 (GoTo) key. You may recall that the F5 key allows you to move the cell selector directly to the cell you specify. Another alternative is to provide a block name instead of a cell address. For example, suppose that you use the block name INSTRUCT for a set of cells that includes a set of instructions. When you press F5 and enter *Instruct* in response to the prompt `Enter address to go to`, you get the results shown in figure 4.10. The GoTo instruction sent the cell selector to the upper left corner of the defined block.

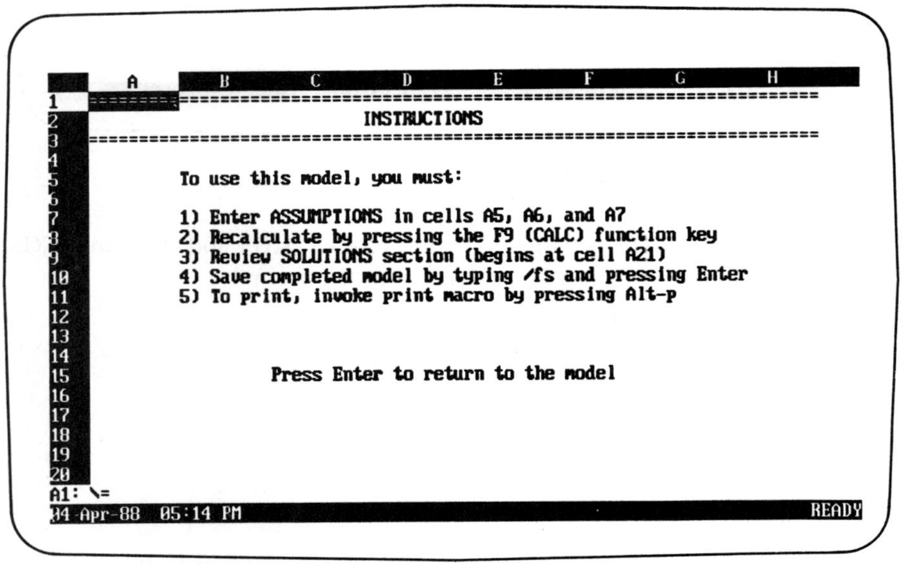

Fig. 4.10. A screen display of instructions.

Deleting Block Names

Block names can be deleted individually or all at once. The /**B**lock **A**dvanced **D**elete command allows you to delete a single block name, and the /**B**lock **A**dvanced **R**eset command causes all block names to be deleted. Because of its power, the latter command should be used with caution.

If a block name is deleted, Quattro no longer uses that name in formulas and reverts to cell addresses; for example, @SUM(REVENUES) returns to @SUM(A5..J5). The contents of the cells within the block, however, remain intact. To erase the contents of blocks, you use the /**B**lock **E**rase command, which is explained next.

Erasing Blocks

The /**B**lock **E**rase command allows you to erase sections of the worksheet. This command can operate on a block as small as a single cell or as large as the entire worksheet. For an example of this command, suppose that you created the simple block of cells shown in figure 4.11. Now suppose that you want to erase the block from A1 to C3. To remove this block, issue the /**B**lock **E**rase command. Quattro prompts you to supply a block to delete. Either by pointing or by entering the coordinates from the keyboard, you instruct Quattro to erase the block A1..C3. After you press Enter, Quattro immediately erases the block.

You can erase blocks more easily if you already have assigned names to them. Using the example in figure 4.9 again, suppose that you have assigned the name CGS to the block D4..G4. You can erase this portion of the worksheet by typing /**B**lock **E**rase and entering the block name *CGS* rather than the cell coordinates D4..G4.

An erased block cannot be recovered unless the Transcript add-in program is active or unless you saved the worksheet previously. You must reenter all the data to restore the block. For more information on Transcript, see Chapter 14.

Getting a List of Block Names

Using figure 4.9 again, suppose that you type the /**B**lock **E**rase command and then cannot remember the name of the block you want to erase. You could press the F3 (Names) key to produce an alphabetical list of the block names in the current worksheet. Figure 4.12 shows the screen at that point.

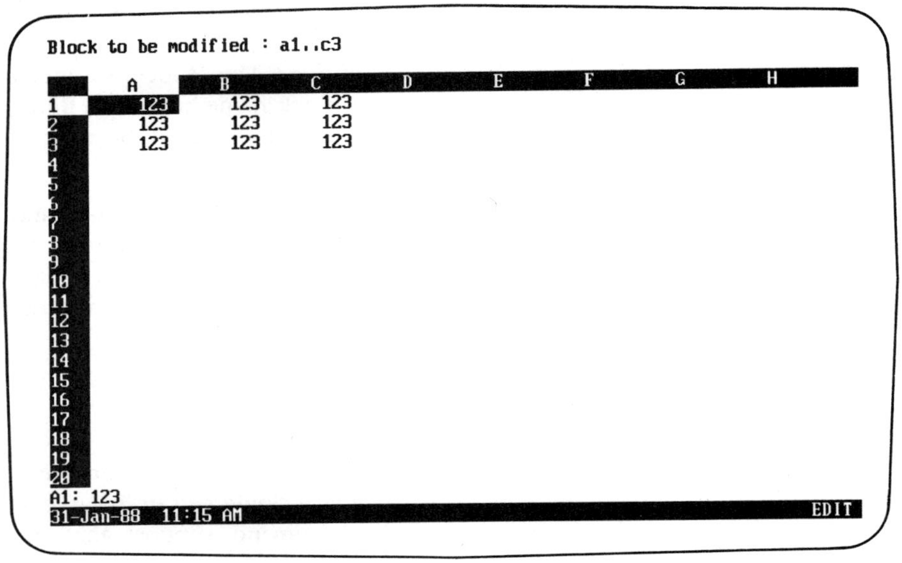

Fig. 4.11. A simple worksheet with values in cells A1..C3.

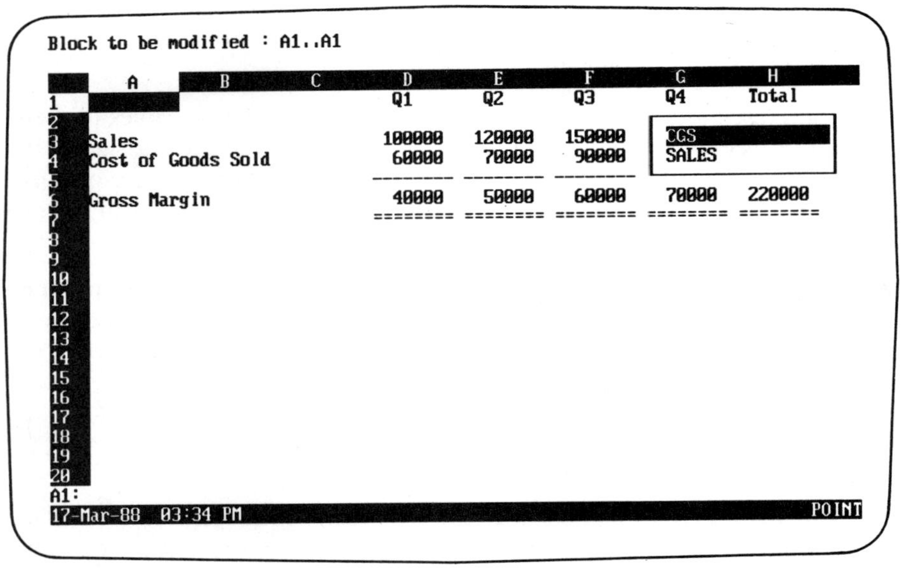

Fig. 4.12. The effect of using the F3 (Names) key during a /Block Erase command.

After the list appears, select CGS by pressing Enter. If you wanted to delete SALES, you would use the cell pointer to move down to `Sales` and select it by pressing Enter.

The F3 (Names) key can be used whenever the worksheet is in POINT mode or READY mode. You can print a copy of this list by holding down the Shift key and pressing the PrtSc (PrintScreen) key. On enhanced and extended keyboards, the Shift key is not necessary; just press the PrtSc key. (Using Shift-PrtSc while your printer is turned on and on-line prints whatever is on the screen.)

You can use the F3 (Names) key with the F5 (GoTo) key to select the name of a block to which you want to move the cell selector. If you press F5 and then press F3, an alphabetical list of the block names in your spreadsheet appears in a list box that can be used to designate the block you want to jump to. Select a name from the list by using the arrow keys. When you press Enter, the list disappears and the cell selector is positioned at the upper left corner of the selected block.

Creating a Table of Block Names

If you are using block names in a worksheet and have created several block names, you may want to document the names in a table in the worksheet. To perform this task, Quattro provides the /**B**lock **A**dvanced **M**ake_Table command. Creating a block name table is simple, but you must exercise care in your placement of the table. Make certain that your placement will not write the table over an important part of the worksheet.

To create the block name table, select the /**B**lock **A**dvanced **M**ake_Table command. When Quattro asks for the location for the table, indicate the cell where you want the upper left corner of the table to appear and then press Enter. Allow space for each block name to be itemized with cell addresses to be placed in cells to the right.

Quattro writes a table that consists of all your block names in a column, with the referenced blocks in the cells to the immediate right of each block name. Figure 4.13 shows a block name table containing several names and referenced blocks.

Copying the Contents of Cells

On many occasions, you will want to copy the contents of cells to other locations in a worksheet. These occasions can be separated into four categories.

First, you may want to copy from one cell to another. For example, in the worksheet shown in figure 4.14, you might want to copy the contents of cell A1 to cell A2.

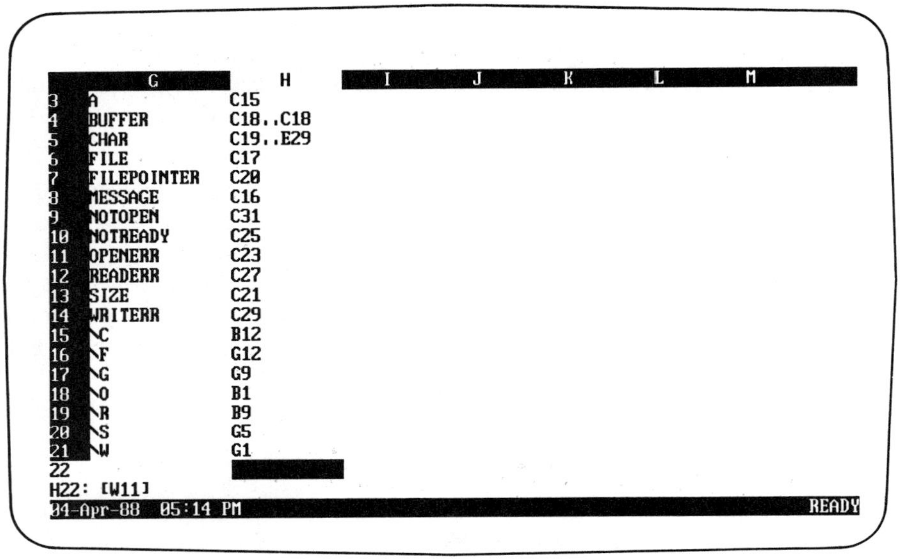

Fig. 4.13. A block name table created with the /Block Advanced Make_Table command.

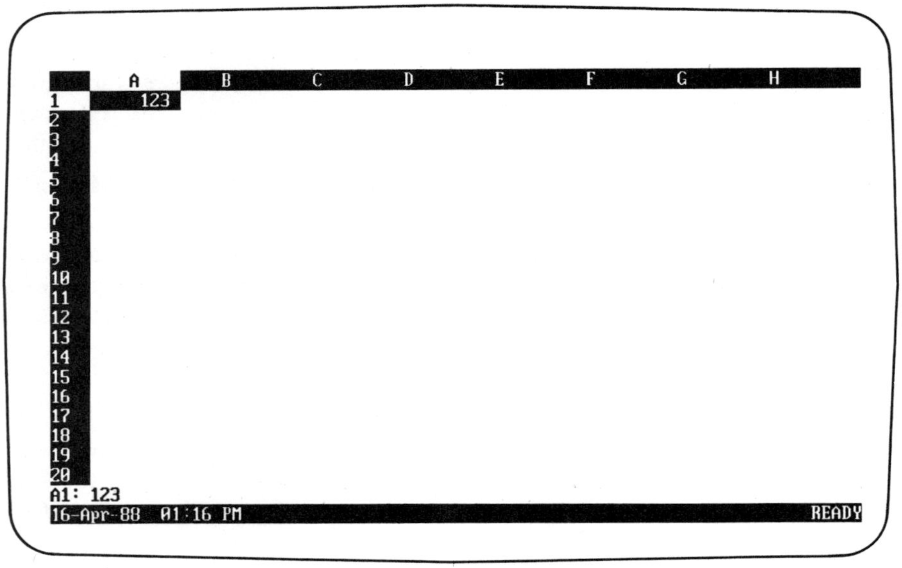

Fig. 4.14. The worksheet before using the /Block Copy command.

To do this task, issue the /**B**lock **C**opy command. Quattro then prompts you to supply a `Source block of cells:`. Because you want to copy from cell A1, enter *A1* in response to this message. (Because the cell pointer is on cell A1, you simply can press Enter.) Next, Quattro prompts for a `Destination for cells:`. Because you want to copy the contents of cell A1 to cell A2, enter *A2* as the destination block. Figure 4.15 shows the results of this operation.

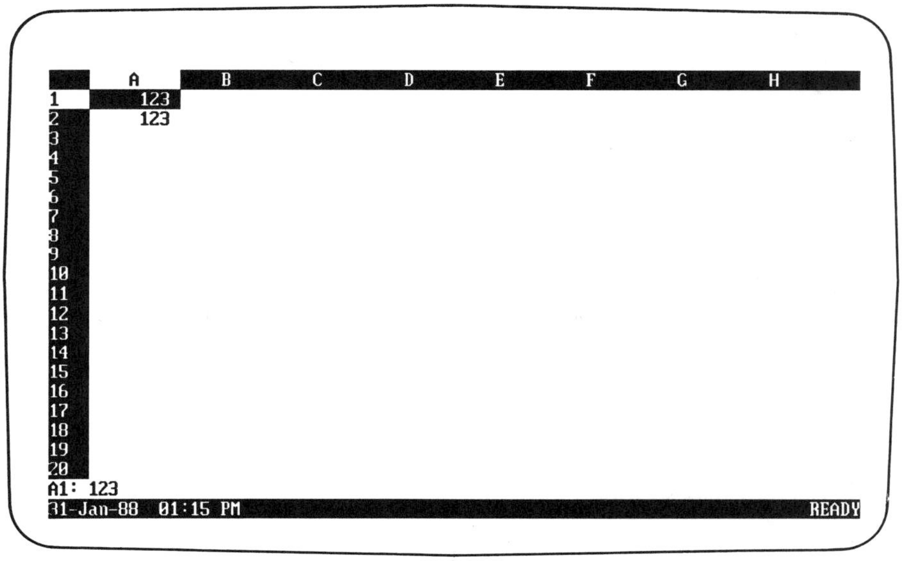

Fig. 4.15. The worksheet after using the /Block Copy command.

The steps required for all copy operations are basically the same as for this simple example: issue the /**B**lock **C**opy command, specify the source block, and then specify the destination block. The only things that change in the copying process are the size, shape, and locations of the source and destination blocks.

In the second type of copy operation, you copy from one cell to a block of cells. Suppose that you want to copy the contents of cell A1 (in the worksheet shown in fig. 4.14) into the block A1..H1. To do this task, issue the /**B**lock **C**opy command, specify A1 as the source block, and then specify A1..H1 as the destination block. Remember that you either can type the coordinates of the destination block from the keyboard or point to the block, using POINT mode, or type the block name as the source and/or destination. The results of this copy are shown in figure 4.16.

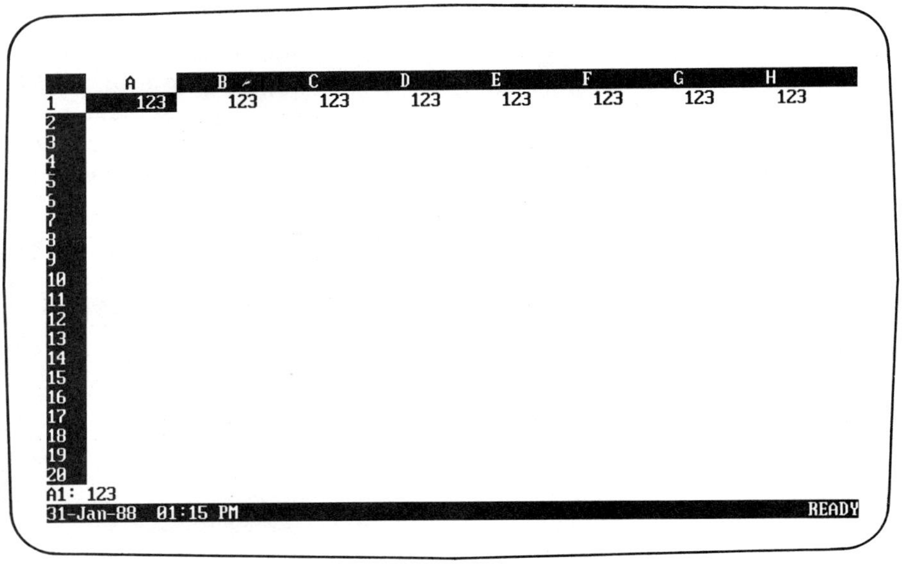

Fig. 4.16. The result of copying from a cell to a block.

The third type of copy operation is a little more complicated. You may want to copy a block of cells to another place in the worksheet. Using figure 4.16 as an example, suppose that you want to copy the block A1..H1 to the block A2..H2.

As always, begin by issuing the /**B**lock **C**opy command. Next, specify the source block—in this case, A1..H1. Remember that you either can type the coordinates or use the cursor keys to point to the block or type the block name as the source and/or destination. Next, specify the destination block. At this point, things get a bit tricky.

Even though you are copying into the block A2..H2, the destination block in this example will be the single cell A2. The results of this command are shown in figure 4.17.

Although this destination block does not seem to make sense, it is perfectly logical. Think about selecting the destination block this way: You want to /**B**lock **C**opy the eight-cell partial row A1..H1. Because the source block is an eight-cell partial row, the destination block also must be an eight-cell partial row. Because the destination block must be an eight-cell partial row, the first cell in that partial row is sufficient to indicate the destination for the block. Given a starting point of A2, the only possible destination for the rest of the block is A2..H2. Similarly, specifying the single cell H3 as the destination block

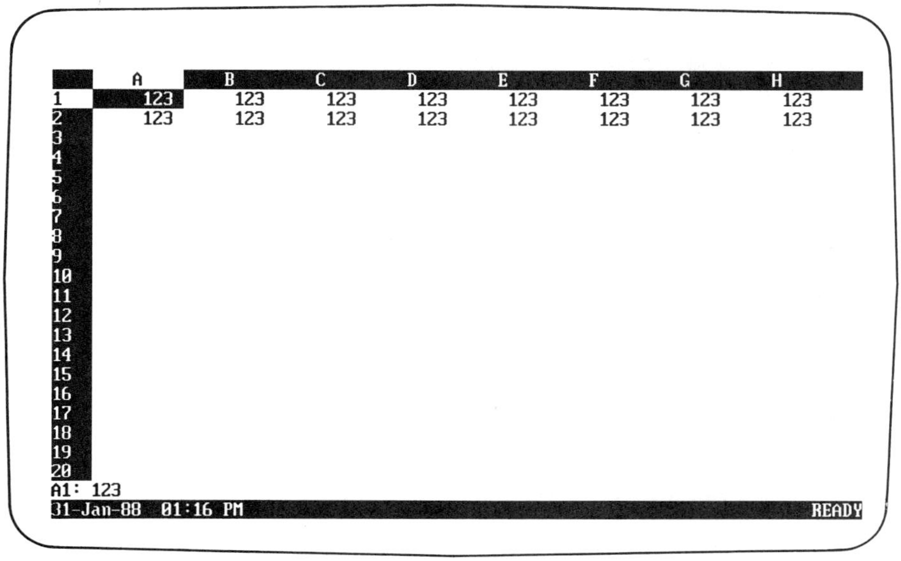

Fig. 4.17. The result of copying the partial row A1..H1 to A2.

would imply a destination of H3..O3. In other words, Quattro is smart enough to deduce the rest of the destination from the single cell provided as the starting point for the destination.

The same principle applies to copies of partial columns. For example, look back at figure 4.15, which shows the results of the first copy example, and suppose that you want to copy the block A1..A2 to the block B1..B2. The first two steps should be familiar by now: issue the /**B**lock **C**opy command and specify the source block A1..A2. What would the destination block be? Because you want to copy the two-cell partial column A1..A2 into the two-cell partial column B1..B2, you need supply only the starting point (B1) of the destination block to create figure 4.18.

Finally, you may want to copy a block of cells to an even larger block of cells somewhere else in the worksheet. Using figure 4.16 as an example, suppose that you want to copy the block A1..H1 into the rectangular block A2..H20. As before, issue the /**B**lock **C**opy command and define the source block as A1..H1. The destination block is A2..A20. Figure 4.19 shows the results of this copy.

Think of this type of copy as an extension of the previous type. In essence, the copy you made in figure 4.19 could have been created also by repeating the copy command 19 times and specifying 19 different single-row destination

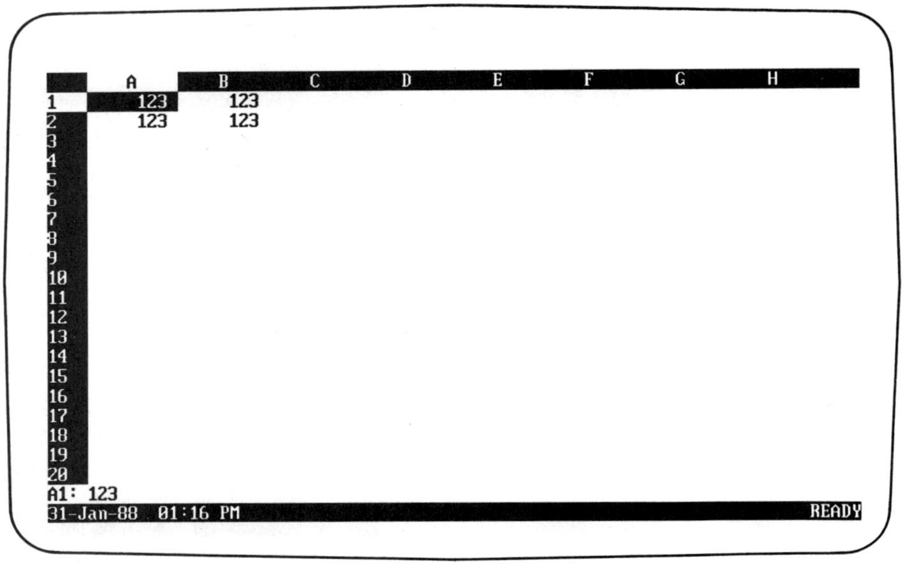

	A	B	C	D	E	F	G	H
1	123	123						
2	123	123						
3								
4								
5								
6								
7								
8								
9								
10								
11								
12								
13								
14								
15								
16								
17								
18								
19								
20								

A1: 123
31-Jan-88 01:16 PM READY

Fig. 4.18. The result of copying the partial column A1..A2 to B1.

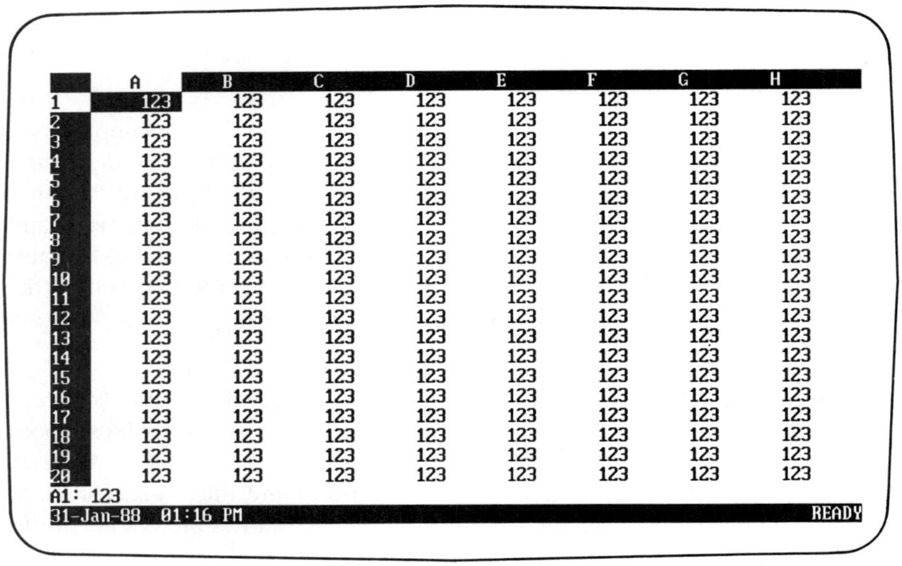

	A	B	C	D	E	F	G	H
1	123	123	123	123	123	123	123	123
2	123	123	123	123	123	123	123	123
3	123	123	123	123	123	123	123	123
4	123	123	123	123	123	123	123	123
5	123	123	123	123	123	123	123	123
6	123	123	123	123	123	123	123	123
7	123	123	123	123	123	123	123	123
8	123	123	123	123	123	123	123	123
9	123	123	123	123	123	123	123	123
10	123	123	123	123	123	123	123	123
11	123	123	123	123	123	123	123	123
12	123	123	123	123	123	123	123	123
13	123	123	123	123	123	123	123	123
14	123	123	123	123	123	123	123	123
15	123	123	123	123	123	123	123	123
16	123	123	123	123	123	123	123	123
17	123	123	123	123	123	123	123	123
18	123	123	123	123	123	123	123	123
19	123	123	123	123	123	123	123	123
20	123	123	123	123	123	123	123	123

A1: 123
31-Jan-88 01:16 PM READY

Fig. 4.19. The result of copying the block A1..H1 to the block A2..A20.

blocks. The first destination block would be A2, the second would be A3, the third A4, and so on. The results are the same for either method, but you can save a great deal of time by using the A2..A20 block as shown.

The concept of destination blocks is tricky. The best way to learn about the effects of using different destination and source blocks is to experiment on your own. After a while, the rules of copying will be second nature to you.

When you copy a cell, Quattro automatically copies the format of the cell with it. (See Chapter 5 for more information on formats.) This automatic format-copying feature saves you from having to preset the format for the destination for an entire block of cells before copying to them.

Addressing Cells

Two different methods of addressing cells can be used in replication: *relative* and *absolute*. These two methods of referencing cells are important for building formulas. In fact, talking about the two methods of addressing without treating both topics at once is difficult. The type of addressing you use when you reference cells in formulas can affect the results of the formulas when you copy or move those formulas to different locations in the worksheet.

Referencing Cells with Relative Addressing

Whenever you copy or move a formula, unless you specify otherwise, the addresses of the cells referred to in the formula are adjusted automatically to fit the new location. This process is known as relative addressing. A formula copied across a table of yearly information such as a budget model will address the month column that is appropriate for it. For example, January's net profit will be based on January's results, and when the formula for net profit is copied across the row, the new formulas will address the columns to which they apply. Quattro's default is relative addressing.

As a further example of relative addressing, suppose that you want to sum the contents of several columns of cells, but you don't want to enter the @SUM function over and over again. Figure 4.20 shows a sample worksheet with five columns of numbers. Only column C has been summed, using the formula @SUM(C5..C8) in cell C10.

You want to add the contents of the cells in columns D, E, F, and G in the same manner that you added the contents of the cells in column C. Use the /**B**lock **C**opy command, the command for replicating cells in Quattro.

To initiate the command, choose /**B**lock **C**opy from the main command menu. Quattro then asks for a source block of cells to copy. Enter *C10* and press

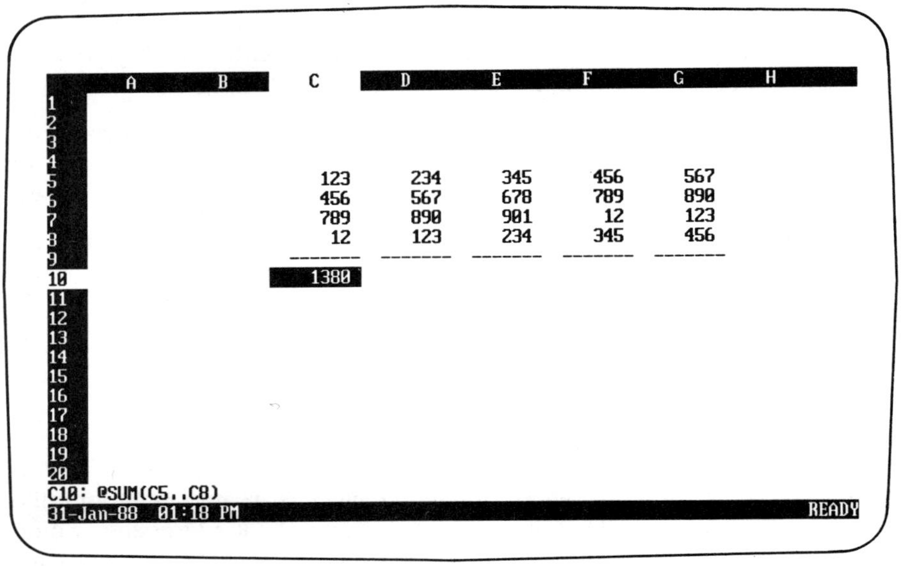

Fig. 4.20. A sample worksheet with one column summed.

Enter. Next, Quattro asks for the destination of this block of cells. Designate *D10..G10* by pointing or by entering the cell addresses. When you press Enter, Quattro replicates the @SUM formula in cell C10 to the other cells, as shown in figure 4.21.

Notice that the formula in the descriptor line contains the proper cell addresses for adding the cells in column F rather than column C. Quattro is smart enough to assume that you meant the relative addresses of the cells in column F, not their absolute addresses.

Mixing Relative and Absolute Addressing

In some cases, a formula has an important address that will not be changed automatically when the formula is copied. In Quattro, you can create an *absolute address*, an address that does not change at all as the address is copied. You also can create a *mixed address*, an address that sometimes changes, depending on the direction of the /**B**lock **C**opy. The following examples help clarify the concepts of absolute and mixed addresses.

Mixed cell-addressing refers to a combination of relative and absolute addressing. Because a cell address has two components—a column and a row—you can fix (make absolute) either component while leaving the other unfixed (relative). The best way to explain this capability is to use an example.

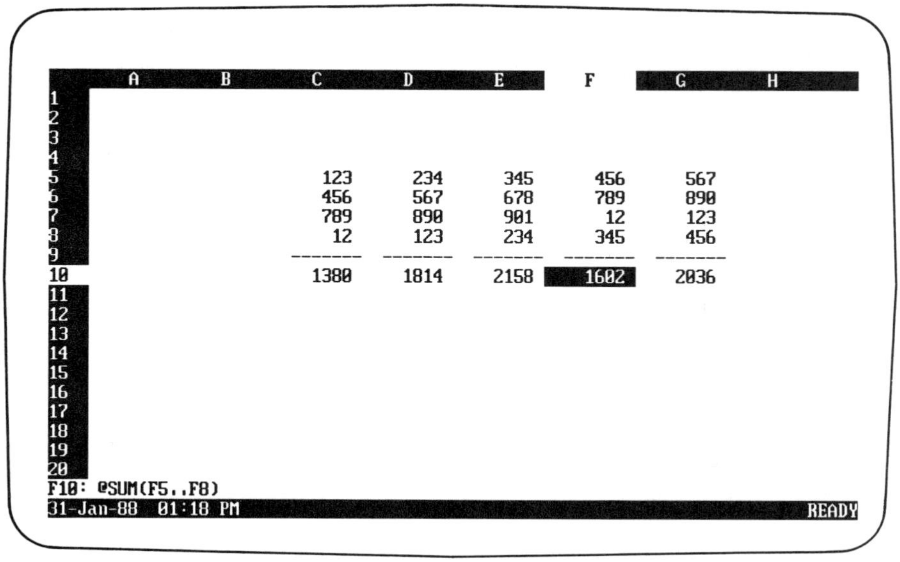

Fig. 4.21. Copied @SUM formulas with relative addressing.

Suppose that you want to create a projection of monthly sales in dollars for Product 1. In the first pass, you want to use a specific retail price, average discount rate, and unit volume for the projection. But later you will want to change these parameters to see what happens. Figure 4.22 shows how you might set up the projection.

Notice, in the descriptor line, the dollar signs in the formula for cell D10. These dollar signs signal Quattro to use absolute addressing on the column portion of the addresses. Because no dollar signs are in front of the row portion of the addresses, Quattro will use relative addressing there.

To see the importance of this type of referencing, /**B**lock **C**opy the contents of cell D10 into the block E10..H10. As before, first issue the /**B**lock **C**opy command and then designate the source block (D10) and the destination block (E10..H10). Figure 4.23 shows the results of the command.

Compare the formula in cell E10 with the original formula in cell D10:

E10 = `+$C7*(1-$C1)*E9`

D10 = `+$C7*(1-$C1)*D9`

Notice that the formulas are identical except for the last term. Quattro has held constant the addresses for C7 and C1. Only the reference to cell D9 has been altered. In essence, this formula says, "Using a constant price (C7) and

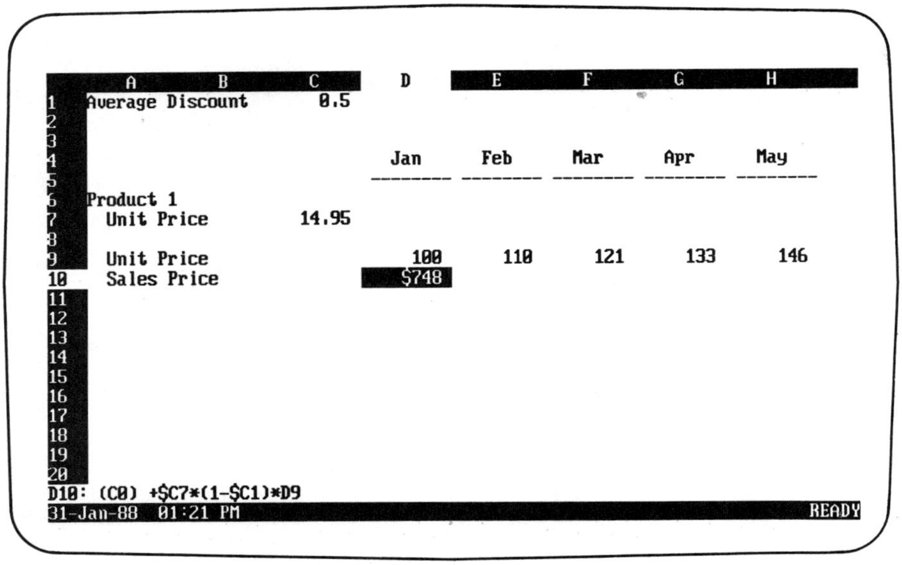

Fig. 4.22. A simple formula using mixed addressing.

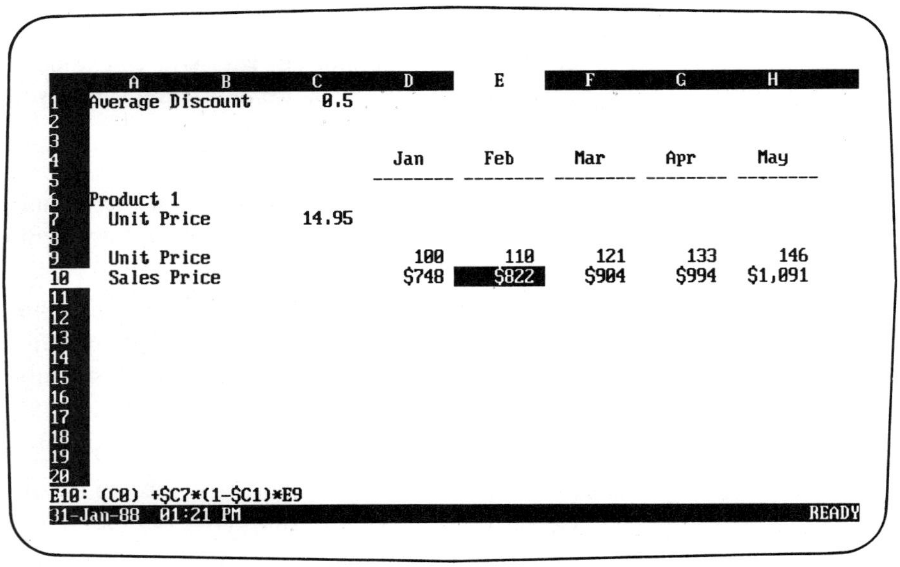

Fig. 4.23. The result of copying the mixed address formula.

a constant discount (C1), compute the dollar sales for Product 1 at each month's sales volume (D9..H9)."

Now suppose that you want to create a projection for a second product. You can create the projection by duplicating the labels in column A and changing the product name to Product 2. Finally, copy the contents of the block C7..H10 to the block C14..H17. Figure 4.24 shows the results of the copy operation.

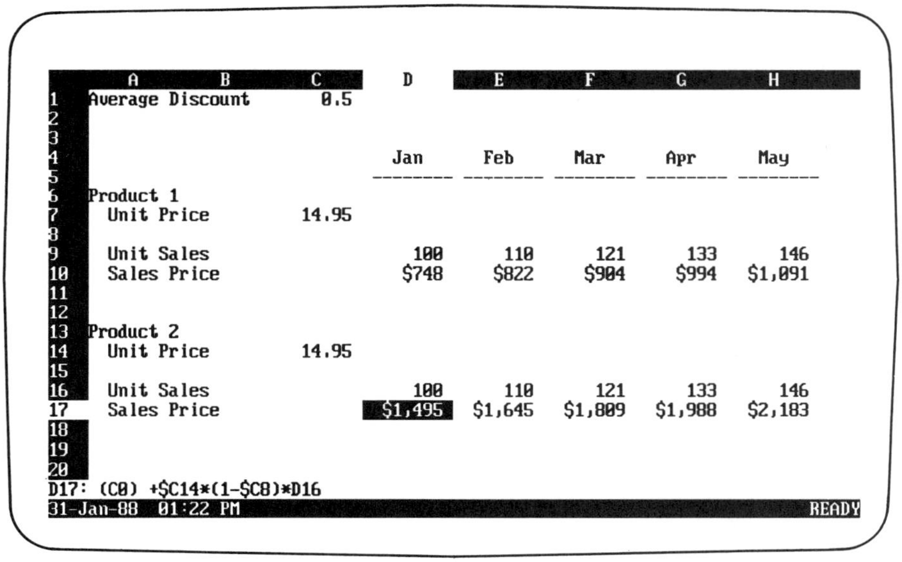

Fig. 4.24. The worksheet after copying from A7..H10 to A14.

Notice that the numbers in row 17 are not correct. Although you assigned the same price and unit sales volumes to Product 2, that product shows monthly dollar sales double those for Product 1. To figure out why, look at the formula in cell D17:

```
+$C14*(1-$C8)*D16
```

The references to cells C14 and D16 are correct. These cells contain the unit price and unit sales for Product 2. But notice that the reference to cell C1 has changed so that the cell refers to cell C8. This change occurred because the row designation in that address—8—was relative, not absolute. When you copied the formulas containing the address $C1 down the worksheet, Quattro assumed that you wanted to adjust the row component of the address.

You can correct the problem by changing the reference to cell C1 from a mixed reference to an absolute reference. Going back to the model in figure 4.22, edit cell D10 and change the formula to the following:

```
+$C7*(1-$C$1)*D9
```

The only difference between this formula and its predecessor is the addition of a $ in front of the 1 in the address C1. This added $ changes the address from mixed to absolute.

Now you must copy the new formula in cell D10 to the block E10..H10 so that all formulas in the row are the same. Then you can recopy the areas D10..H10 into the block D17..H17. Figure 4.25 illustrates the adjusted worksheet.

	A B	C	D	E	F	G	H
1	Average Discount	0.5					
2							
3							
4			Jan	Feb	Mar	Apr	May
5			--------	--------	--------	--------	--------
6	Product 1						
7	Unit Price	14.95					
8							
9	Unit Sales		100	110	121	133	146
10	Sales Price		$748	$822	$904	$994	$1,091
11							
12							
13	Product 2						
14	Unit Price	14.95					
15							
16	Unit Sales		100	110	121	133	146
17	Sales Price		$748	$822	$904	$994	$1,091
18							
19							
20							

D17: (C0) +$C14*(1-$C$1)*D16

31-Jan-88 01:23 PM READY

Fig. 4.25. A copied formula using an absolute address.

Notice that the numbers in cells D17..H17 are now correct. Look at the formula in cell D17:

```
+$C14*(1-$C$1)*D16
```

The reference to cell C1 remained fixed during the copy.

Remember that when you copy cells by using absolute addressing, you must prepare the cell to be copied before initiating the command. That is, you must enter dollar signs in the appropriate column and row designations during the initial or subsequent cell definition. If you forget to prepare the cell, you may get results you neither expected nor wanted.

Using the F4 (Abs) Key To Set Absolute and Relative References

Two ways are available to enter dollar signs in formulas: you can type the dollar signs as you enter the formula, or you can use the F4 (Abs) key to have Quattro automatically enter the dollar signs for you.

The list that follows shows what happens to a cell address when you press F4 after typing the address (but before pressing Enter or a cursor-movement key) or while in EDIT mode. (Note that for F4 to work, the cursor must be located under the cell address or directly after the cell address. If placed between the two addresses, the cursor will change the one that follows.)

First time	`$C$7`
Second	`C$7`
Third	`$C7`
Fourth	`C7`

Suppose that your typing or pointing (or both) results in `C7`, the first portion of the formula shown in the descriptor line of figure 4.22. To change to an absolute address, press the F4 key. The formula in the status line changes to `$C$7`. Pressing the F4 key again shifts the address to `C$7`. A third press of F4 changes the address to `$C7`, which is the desired result.

Notice that block names were not used in this example; the F4 key loses much of its power when used with block names. Most important, you cannot use F4 with a block name to set a mixed address. You can change from relative to absolute addresses by using F4, and from absolute to relative addresses, but not within the same edit operation. You cannot toggle back and forth without first ending the edit operation and starting a new one.

A second example of mixed cell-addressing appears in figure 4.26. Here is a table created for you to explore the effect of different interest rates and years to maturity on the monthly payment for a $100,000 mortgage. The general format of the Quattro @PMT function follows:

@PMT(principal,interest,term)

The object of this example is to use a single formula for the entire model and then to copy the formula by using mixed cell-addressing, as shown in figure 4.26.

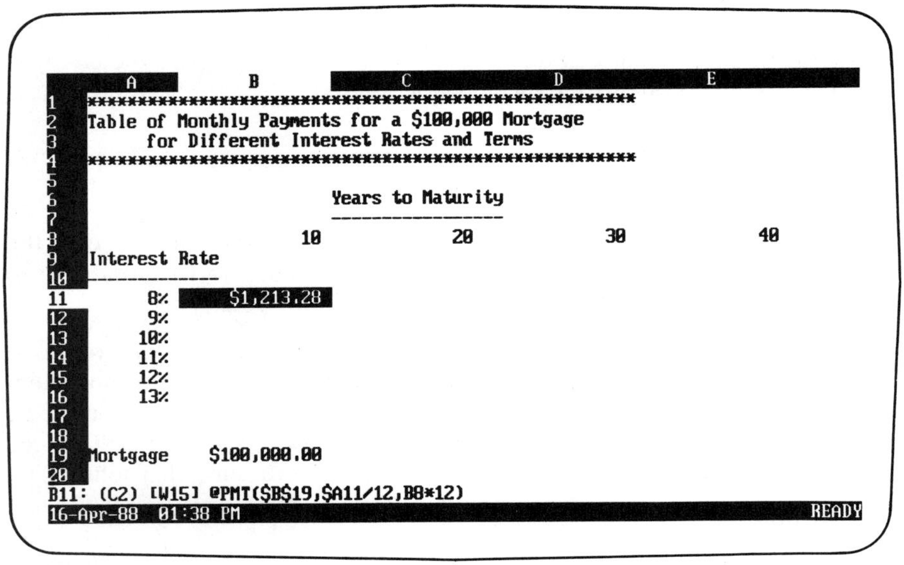

Fig. 4.26. Using a @PMT formula with mixed addresses.

Once again, if you look at the descriptor line, you see the special places at which dollar signs appear. The idea in this example is to use absolute addressing (B19) on the column portion of the interest-rate address and relative addressing on the row portion ($A15). Conversely, use relative addressing on the column portion of the years-to-maturity address and absolute addressing on the row portion (B$8).

Compare the formula for cell B11 in the descriptor line in figure 4.26 with the one for cell D15 in figure 4.27. Notice that column A for the interest rate and row 8 for the years to maturity have not changed, but the other portions of the addresses have.

A third way mixed cell-addressing can be used is to accumulate a running total across a row of numbers. In this example, you will use the formula @SUM(C5..C5) in cell C7 and copy the formula across cells D7 through G7. In figure 4.28, notice in the descriptor line that the formula for cell E7 has changed to @SUM(C5..E5); the relative address in the formula changed when you copied cell C7 to cell E7.

The best way to become comfortable with mixed cell-addressing is to experiment with it. Try several different examples.

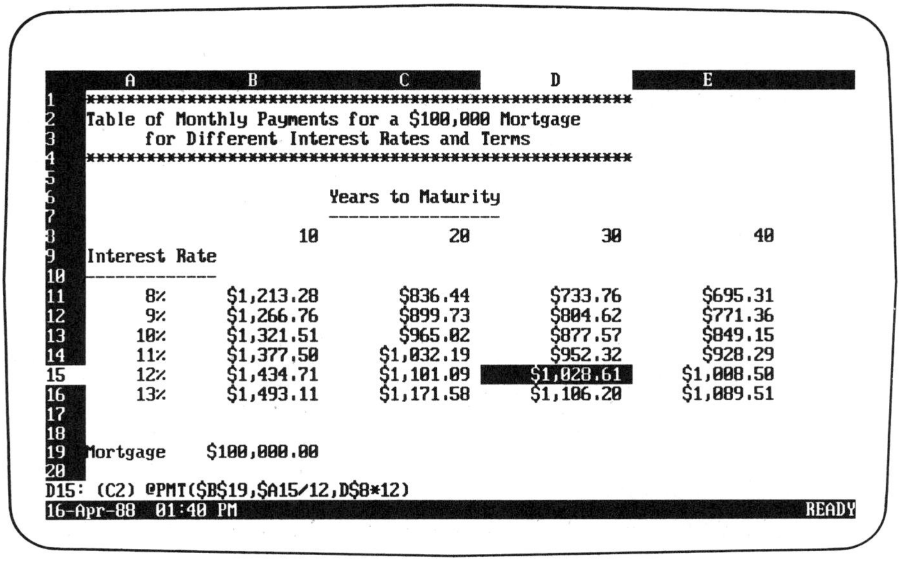

Fig. 4.27. The result of copying the @PMT formula.

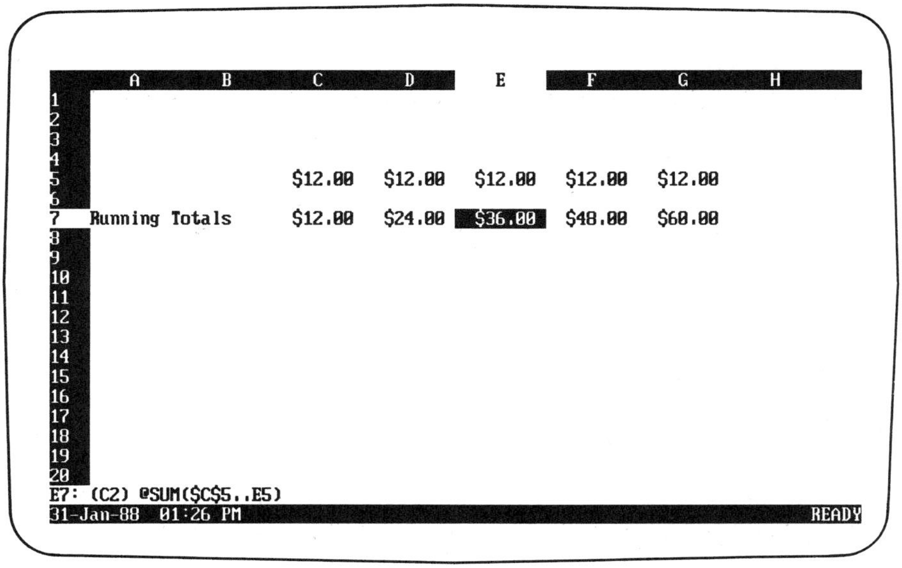

Fig. 4.28. Using absolute addressing to create a running total.

Converting Formulas to Values with the /Block Advanced Values Command (/BAV)

For copy operations beyond Quattro's normal copy commands, Quattro has two specialized copy commands: /**B**lock **A**dvanced **T**ranspose and /**B**lock **A**dvanced **V**alues. The /**B**lock **A**dvanced **T**ranspose command discussed in the next section copies columns into rows and rows into columns. The /**B**lock **A**dvanced **V**alues command copies the values (but not the formulas) from one block to another.

The /**B**lock **A**dvanced **V**alues command lets you copy the values (versus formulas) of the cells in one block to another block. This command is useful whenever you want to preserve the current values of a block of cells instead of having only the changed values after the worksheet has been updated. What is particularly important about the /**B**lock **A**dvanced **V**alues command is that it converts formulas to values. You don't have to worry, therefore, about formulas that depend on cell references (when using /**B**lock **A**dvanced **T**ranspose, for example).

Figure 4.29 shows a worksheet with a monthly income statement and a year-to-date total column. As you change the worksheet every month, the year-to-date (Y-T-D) totals also change. If, however, you want to save the Y-T-D totals to compare them with previous years or quarters, the /**B**lock **A**dvanced **V**alues command enables you to do so. When you use the command, the program asks for a source block to copy from and a destination block to copy to, just as the program does with the /**B**lock **C**opy command. In the example in figure 4.30, the Y-T-D totals in column G are being saved as values in column N.

Transposing Rows and Columns with the /Block Advanced Transpose Command (/BAT)

The /**B**lock **A**dvanced **T**ranspose command copies each row of the source block into the corresponding column of the destination block or each column of the source block into the corresponding row of the destination block. The result is a transposed copy of the source block. Figure 4.31 shows the result of using the /**B**lock **A**dvanced **T**ranspose command to transpose the block A1..D2 to the block A5..B8 and then the block A5..B8 to the block A11..D12.

When copying formulas, the /**B**lock **A**dvanced **T**ranspose command behaves just like the /**B**lock **C**opy command. When a block is transposed, cell references in the transposed block are adjusted, just as references are adjusted in a normal /**B**lock **C**opy command.

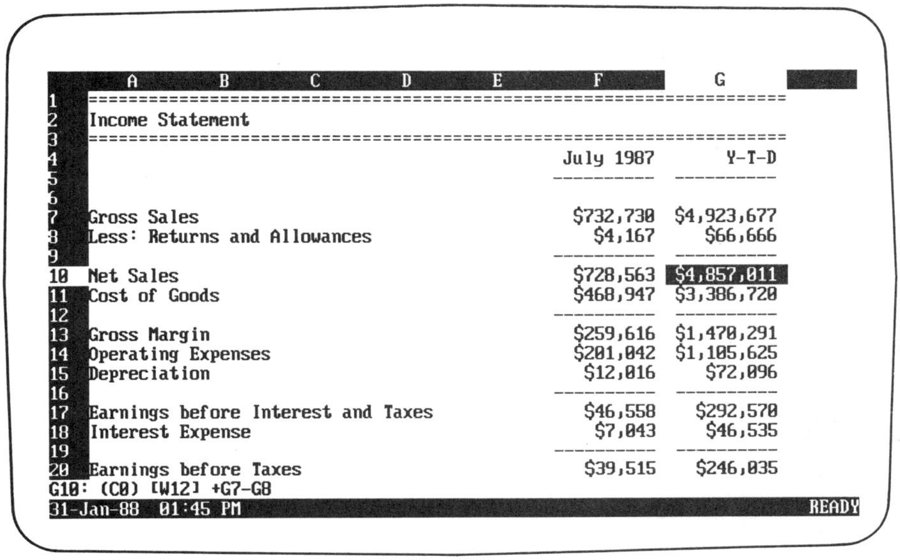

Fig. 4.29. The worksheet with a monthly and a year-to-date income column.

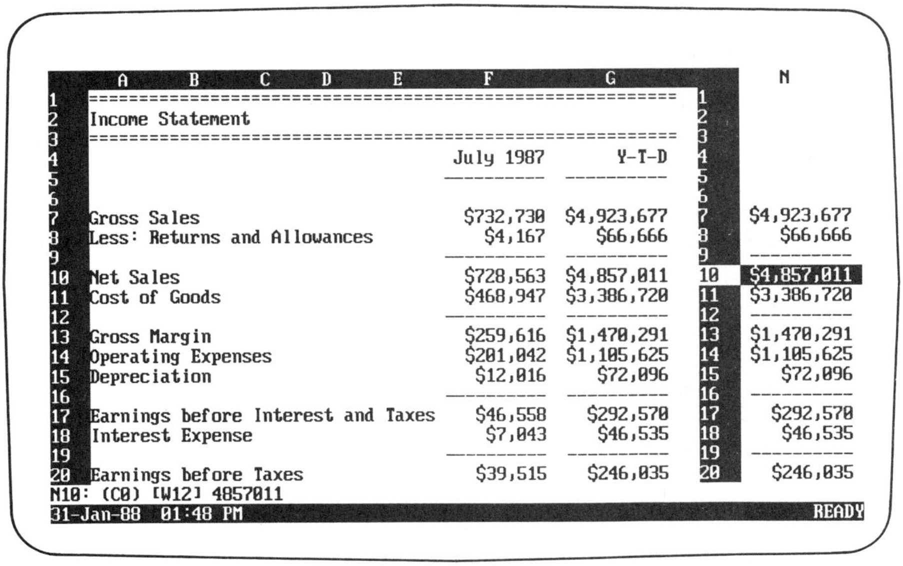

Fig. 4.30. Saving the year-to-date values with /Block Advanced Values.

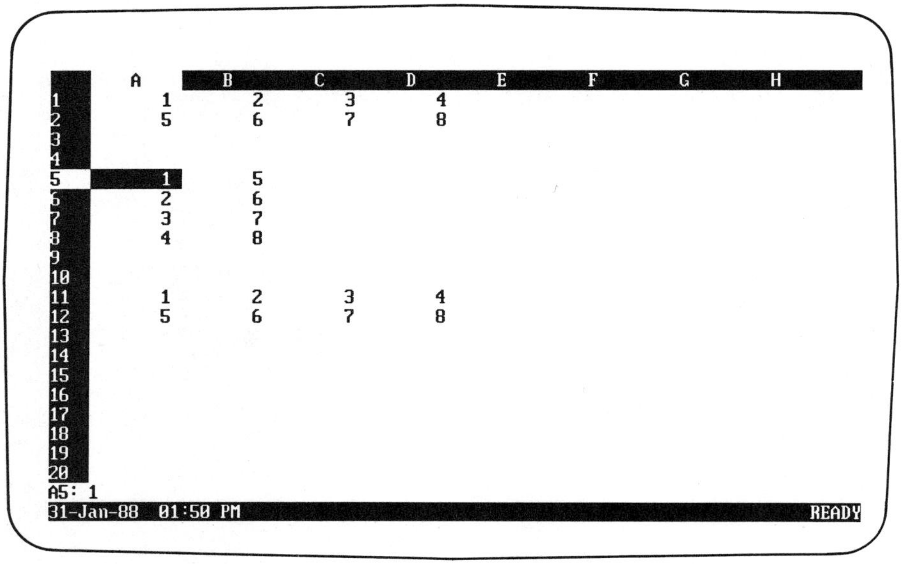

Fig. 4.31. Transposing blocks.

This adjustment of cell references can lead to serious trouble when you use the /**B**lock **A**dvanced **T**ranspose command to transpose a block containing formulas. The transposed formulas will be incorrect; the values, however, will remain in the same order. Because the cell references are not transposed, the relative and mixed cell references in the transposed block will refer to unintended locations after the transposition.

You can avoid the problem of incorrect cell references in transposed blocks by converting the formulas in the source block to values before transposing. The /**B**lock **A**dvanced **V**alues command is a convenient way to convert a block of formulas to values.

Moving the Contents of Cells

In the days of manual spreadsheets, the process of moving data around on the page was called *cutting and pasting* because scissors and glue were used to move sections of the spreadsheet. Quattro lets you cut and paste automatically.

The /**B**lock **M**ove and /**B**lock **C**opy commands allow you to move and copy the contents of cells and blocks of cells from one part of the worksheet to another. The difference between moving and copying is that data which is *moved* from one cell to another disappears from the first cell and data that is *copied* appears in both cells.

For an example of moving data, suppose that you created the sample worksheet shown in figure 4.32. Suppose further that you want to move the contents of block C1..D3 to the block E1..F3. After you enter /**B**lock **M**ove, Quattro responds with the message `Source block of cells:`. Notice that a default block already is specified after the prompt. If the cell selector was at cell D7 when you started, the block specified is D7..D7. Quattro always tries to stay one step ahead in helping you designate blocks.

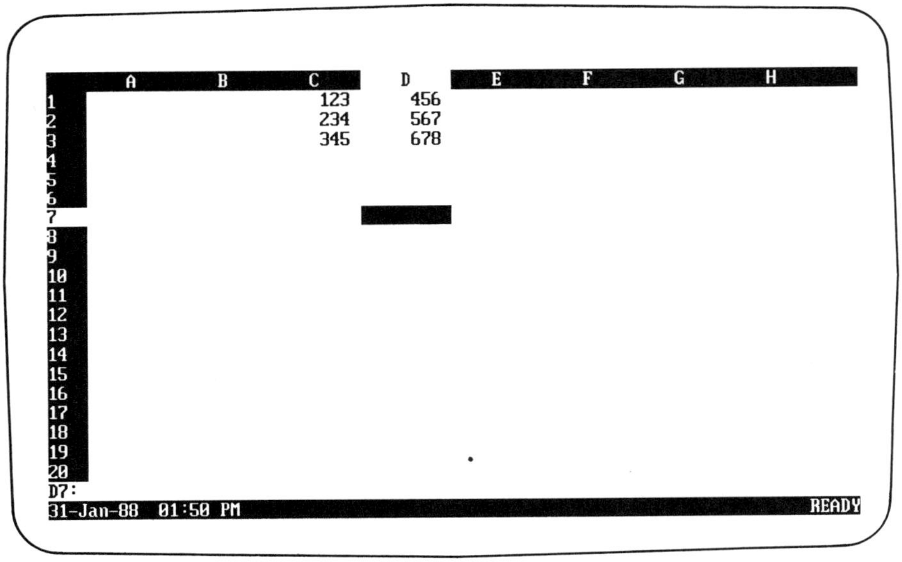

*Fig. 4.32. The worksheet before using the /**B**lock **M**ove command.*

To enter the appropriate block, start typing. The `D7..D7` disappears immediately. As you type, the characters appear where the D7..D7 was. To designate the proper source block for the example, enter *C1..D3* (you don't have to type two dots—just one). Then press Enter.

Quattro then asks you to `Enter the Destination for cells:`. Again, a default block already is specified for you. The block is just a one-cell block this time, but, as before, the cell address is the address of the cell at which the selector was located when you initiated the command. To enter your own block, start typing again. For the destination block, you can specify just the single cell E1. Quattro is smart enough to know that E1..F3 is implied and uses that block. As soon as you finish designating the destination block and pressing Enter, the selector returns immediately to where it was when you initiated the command. Figure 4.33 shows the results of the /**B**lock **M**ove operation.

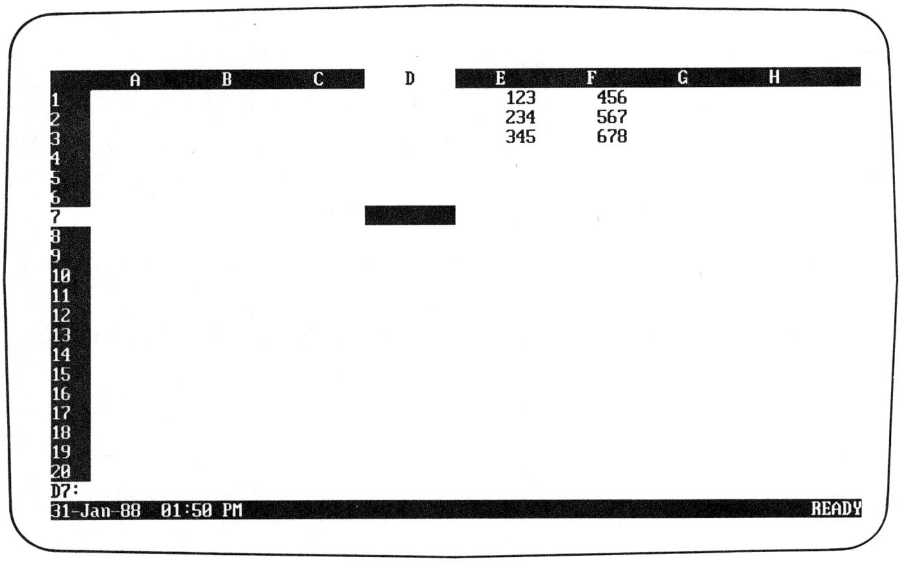

Fig. 4.33. The result of the /Block Move operation.

One point of this example is that the cell selector does not have to be positioned at the beginning of the destination or source blocks when you initiate a command. You can designate either block while the cell selector is positioned anywhere on the worksheet.

All the formulas involved in a /**B**lock **M**ove operation are updated automatically. For example, suppose that you have a simple three-cell worksheet that contains the following data:

A1 = +D1*100
C1 = 15
D1 = +C1

Now, suppose that you /**B**lock **M**ove the contents of cell D1 to cell E1. The formula in cell A1 would be altered to the following:

A1 = +E1*100
C1 = 15
E1 = +C1

You must be careful about the finality of the /**B**lock **M**ove command. When you move a block of cells, the destination block is overwritten completely by the source block, and the previous contents of those cells are lost forever unless you are using the Transcript add-in or quit Quattro without saving. If other cells exist whose formulas depend on the cell addresses of the lost cells, the other cells are given the value ERR instead of the cell address. For example, suppose that you add one more cell to the preceding example:

E2 = +E1

Then you repeat the move operation (/**B**lock **M**ove D1 E1). The value of cell E2 will change from 0 to ERR, and the contents of that cell will become +ERR. The cell to which E2 once referred, E1, has been overwritten as a result of the /**B**lock **M**ove operation.

Using the Expanding Cell Selector for Pointing to Blocks

As previously mentioned, Quattro's pointing capabilities can be used to specify a block of cells. This method is somewhat similar to menu pointing, but you will find that pointing to specify a block has a character all its own.

Suppose that you want to shift the contents of the block C1..D3 to E1..F3, but you don't want to enter the specific cell addresses from the keyboard. Assume that the cell selector was at cell D7 before you initiated the command. When Quattro asks for the source block, press Esc.

Esc is pressed to choose a cell address other that that of the default cell address (where the cell selector was located when the command was issued). Quattro automatically had designated D7 as one corner of the source block. If you do not press Esc but move the cell selector, you will see the reverse-video field begin to expand starting at cell D7. You can anchor cells yourself (that is, designate a cell as one corner of the source block) by entering a period (.) between addresses of the block's two outer corners when you enter a block. And you can tell whether a cell has been anchored by how it is designated in the descriptor line; for example, `D7..D7` indicates that the cell is anchored, and `D7` shows that the cell is not.

Because you want C1 to be one corner of the source block, move the cell selector up to this cell. You will see the address designation in the input line change as you move the cell selector upward from cell to cell. When you arrive at cell C1, press the period (.) to anchor the cell.

From this point on, cell C1 is referred to as the anchor cell, and the cell diagonally opposite the anchored cell is the free cell. A blinking underscore character is in the middle of the free cell. The blinking underscore helps you to visualize this process. Think of the highlighted area as a stretched rubber band, where one end has been anchored with a nail. As you pull the free end, the band (highlight) stretches in the direction of the pull (pointing).

At this point, cell C1 is both the anchor cell and the free cell. As you move the cell selector to the right and down to cell D3 to point to the other corner of the block, however, you will see the reverse-video field expand as you shift the free cell. You also will see the second part of the block designation change as you move from cell to cell. For example, `C1..D1` appears when you move the cell selector to cell D1.

When you reach cell D1, start moving down to cell D3. Now you will see the reverse-video field expand in a columnar fashion. When you reach cell D3, confirm the block specified in the input line by pressing Enter. The designation of the source block appears, as though you had entered the block from the keyboard (see fig. 4.34).

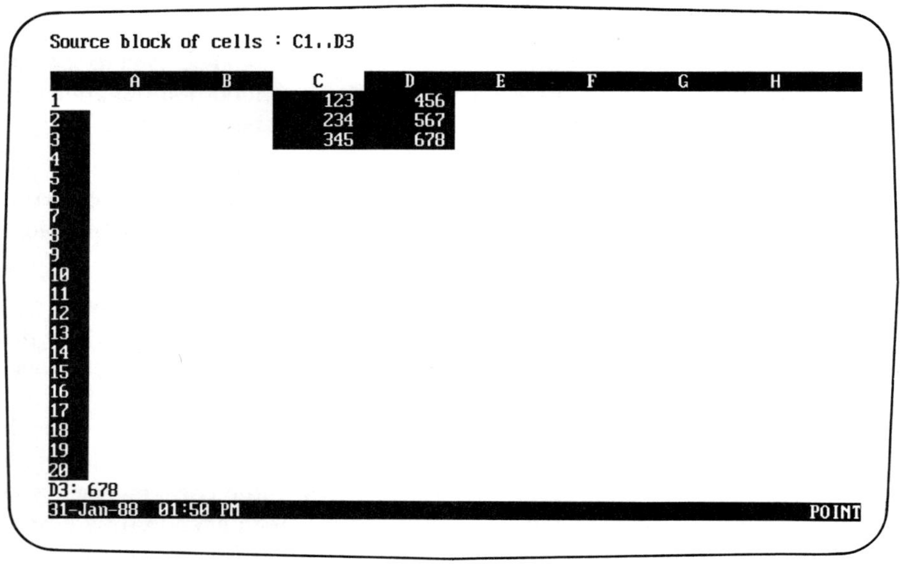

Fig. 4.34. Using the expanding cell selector to point to a block.

The process is similar for designating the destination block. After you specify the source block, the cell selector returns automatically to cell D7. You then move the cell selector over to E1 and press Enter. You can designate the destination block by pointing to the entire block, but remember that Quattro knows what you are implying when you enter just E1.

The Esc key can be used also when you are using a command but no cell has been anchored. Pressing Esc returns you to the previous command step. If you are in the middle of a formula, pressing the Esc key erases the cell address from the end of the formula and returns the cell selector to the current cell. In other words, with numbers already in cells A1..A3, if you type *@SUM(* in cell A4 and then point with the cell selector to cell A1, your formula so far will be @SUM(A1. If you press Esc, the formula again becomes @SUM(and the cell selector goes to cell A4.

The Backspace key also can be used for pointing to blocks. Pressing Backspace cancels the block specification, whether or not a cell has been anchored, and returns the cell selector to the location at which you began the command or formula.

Using the End Key for Pointing to Blocks

Quattro's use of the End key makes pointing to large blocks easy. The End key is used in combination with an arrow key to move the cursor to a logical boundary or edge of either a block or the spreadsheet borders. For example, if your cursor is on the label *January* in a row of month names, pressing the End key and then the right arrow key causes the cursor to jump to the cell just before the first empty cell to the right. This usually will be a *Total* column header.

For example, suppose that you want to move the contents of the block A1..C5 to the block that begins at cell A7. By now, you should be familiar with the /**B**lock **M**ove command. But you may not be familiar with using the End key to point to a block. When the block prompt `A1..A1` appears, press the End key and then the down-arrow key. The cell selector jumps to cell A5 (just before the empty cell), and the prompt reads `A1..A5`. Now move the cell selector by pressing the End key and then the right-arrow key. The prompt now reads `A1..C5`.

The End key can accelerate the process of pointing to blocks. Using the End key, you were able to define the block in the example with only four keystrokes. The process would have taken seven keystrokes if you used only the two arrow keys. The difference is dramatic when you work with larger blocks.

You can use the End key even in situations in which the key seems initially to be of little value. For example, figure 4.35 shows a worksheet consisting of two rows of information. One row is continuous; the other is broken. Suppose that you want to erase the contents of the broken row. To erase the contents, issue the /**B**lock **E**rase command. Quattro then prompts you for a block to delete. You can enter the block either by typing the coordinates or by pointing with the cell selector. If you point, you may want to try using the End key; however, because the block is not continuous, the End key will not move the selector easily from one end of the broken block to the other.

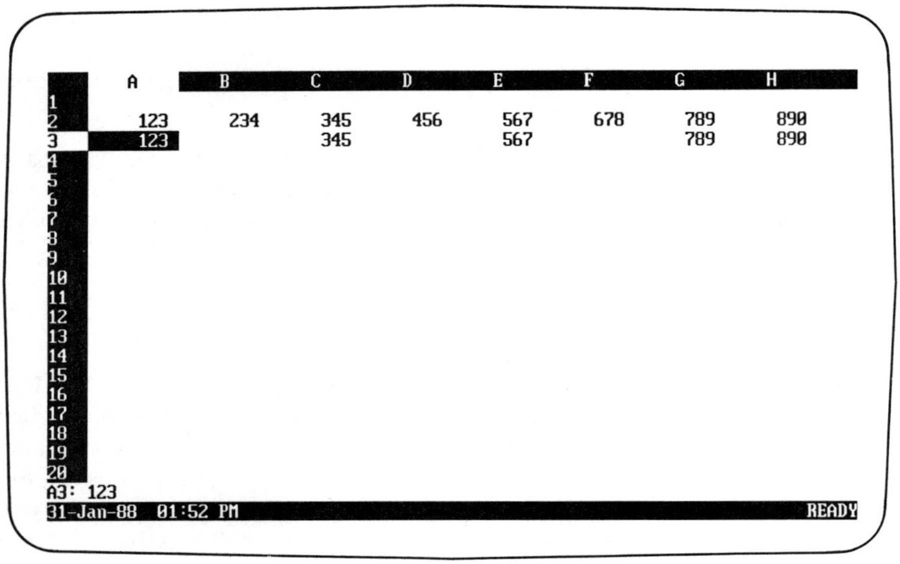

Fig. 4.35. A broken row next to a complete row.

Try this trick: When you specify the block, first move the cell selector *up* one row to cell A2; use the End key and the right-arrow key to move the cell selector to the end of the block; then move the cell selector down one row. Presto! The correct block has been specified. Figures 4.36, 4.37, and 4.38 illustrate this process. Use this technique as often as possible when you designate blocks—this technique is more convenient than simply using the right-arrow key to point.

Filling Blocks with Numbers

The command for filling blocks is /**B**lock **F**ill. /**B**lock **F**ill is useful for quickly creating a series of ascending or descending numbers such as record numbers for a database or month numbers for a worksheet.

/**B**lock **F**ill fills a block of cells with series of numbers that increase or decrease by a specified increment or decrement. For an example of the use of /**B**lock **F**ill, look at the year numbers used as titles in the sales forecast shown in figure 4.39.

When you issue the /**B**lock **F**ill command, Quattro first prompts you for the starting number of the series. The program then asks for the step (or incremental) value to be added to the previous value. Finally, Quattro prompts you for the ending value.

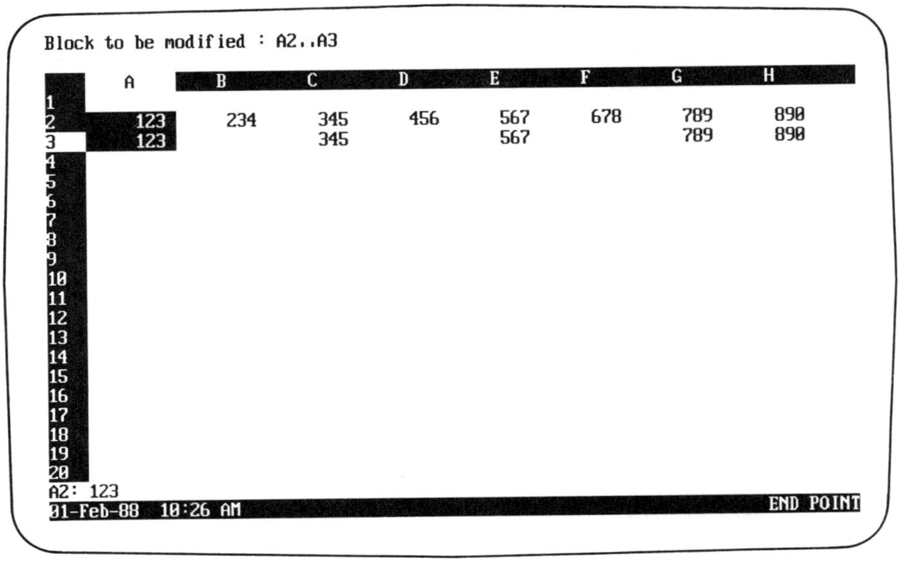

Fig. 4.36. The first step in using the End key on a broken row.

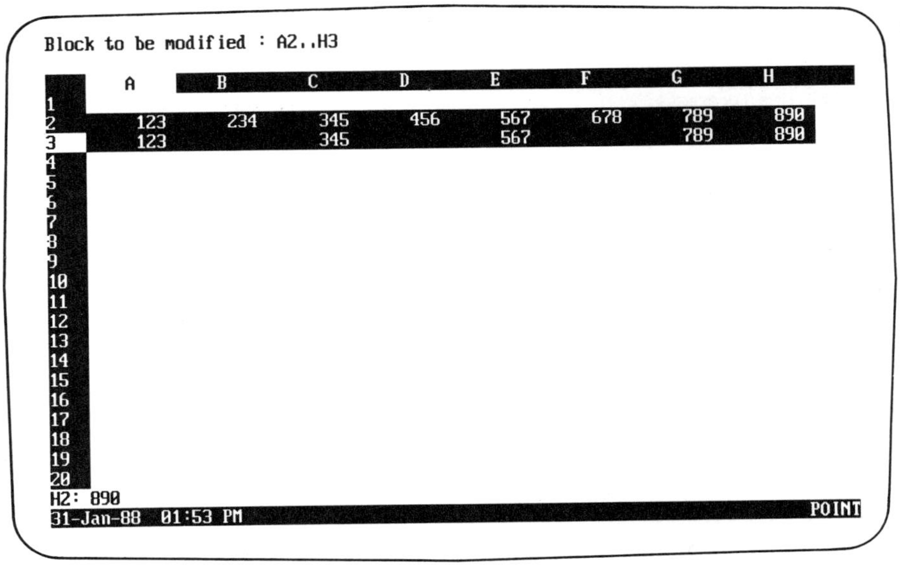

Fig. 4.37. The second step in using the End key on a broken row.

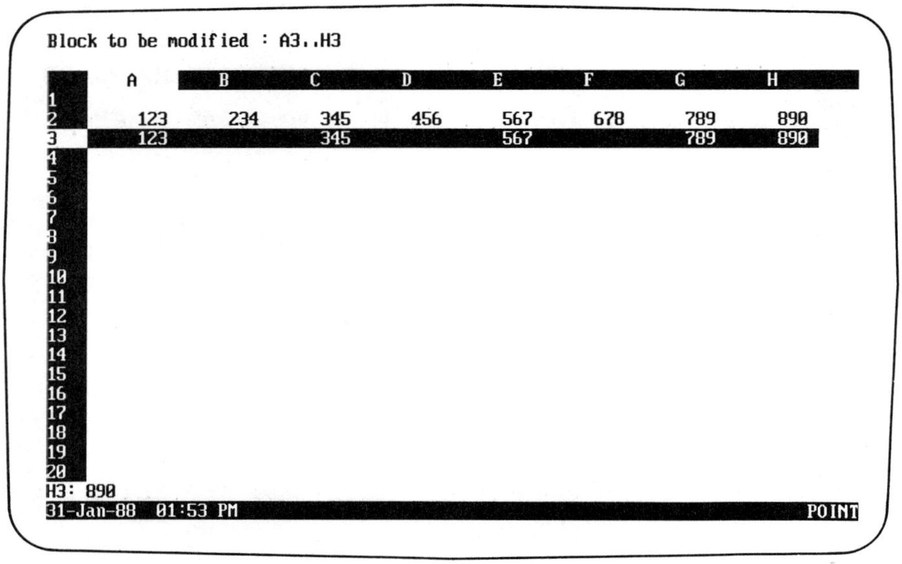

Fig. 4.38. The final step in using the End key on a broken row.

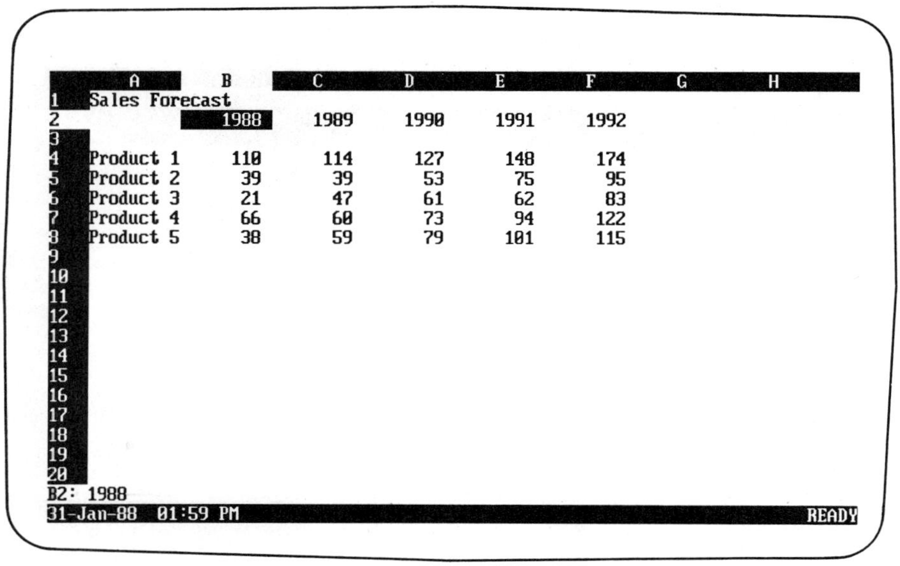

*Fig. 4.39. Entering year numbers with /**B**lock **F**ill.*

To enter a sequence of year numbers for a five-year forecast beginning in 1988, you need to start by specifying the block of cells to be filled. For this example, B2..F2 was chosen and then the beginning value, 1988, was entered. The incremental or step value in this example is one. The ending value is 1992 for a five-year forecast.

A disadvantage of the /**B**lock **F**ill command for year numbers is that you cannot center or left-justify the numbers after you create them. As numbers, they always will be right-justified. If you like your year numbers centered or left-justified, type them in as labels instead.

The /**B**lock **F**ill command also can work with the /**A**dvanced **W**hat-If command to build a list of interest rates, as shown in figure 4.40. In the figure, the column of interest rate values was entered with the /**B**lock **F**ill command. B7..B18 was specified for the block of cells to be filled, .05 for the starting value, and .01 for the step value. For the ending value, Quattro was allowed to default to 8,192, which is far beyond the ending value actually needed. The /**B**lock **F**ill command, however, fills only the specified block and doesn't fill cells beyond the end of the block.

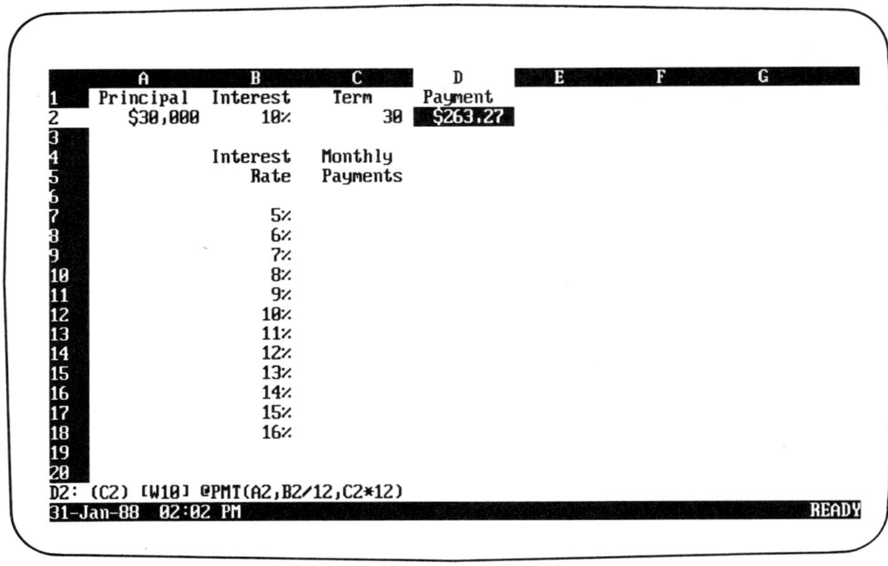

Fig. 4.40. Worksheet for monthly payment analysis.

You also can use cell references, formulas, and functions as arguments for the /**B**lock **F**ill command. If you want to fill a block of cells with incrementing dates, set the block and then use the @DATE function to set the start value—@DATE(88,12,1), for example. You also can use a cell formula, such as +E4, for the incremental value. In this case, E4 may contain the increment 7 so that you can have increments of one week at a time. You can enter the stop value @DATE(89,12,1), for example; or, if the stop date is in a cell, you can give that cell address as the stop value. Quattro allows many different combinations of commands.

Protecting Cell Contents and Areas of the Worksheet

Quattro has special features that protect areas of a worksheet from accidental destruction. With a series of commands, you can set up blocks of cells that cannot be changed without special effort. In fact, rows and columns containing protected cells cannot be deleted from the worksheet. These commands are particularly beneficial when you are setting up worksheets in which data will be entered by people who are not familiar with Quattro.

Cell protection primarily is set or unset by the /**D**efault **P**rotection command. The default setting for **P**rotection is **D**isable, or unset. This term means that each cell has the potential of being protected but is not protected at the moment. Setting and resetting the protection of specific cells and blocks are accomplished by the /**B**lock **A**dvanced **U**nprotect and **P**rotect commands.

You can think of the protection system as a series of electric fences that are set up around all the cells in the worksheet. The "juice" to these fences is turned off when a new worksheet is first loaded. All the cells in the worksheet can be modified, which is appropriate because you will want to have access to everything in the worksheet at this time. After you finish making all your entries in the worksheet, however, you may not want some areas modified, or you may want to set up special form-entry areas and not allow the cell selector to move anywhere else.

To accomplish either of these tasks, you must first activate protection, which is accomplished with the /**D**efault **P**rotection **E**nable command. After this command is issued, all the cells in the worksheet are protected. To continue the analogy, this command is like the switch that activates all the electric fences in the worksheet.

Now you can unprotect selectively certain blocks with the /**B**lock **A**dvanced **U**nprotect command. To use the analogy once again, you tear down the fences that surround these cells. You can, of course, reprotect these cells at any time by issuing the /**B**lock **A**dvanced **P**rotect command.

Suppose that you create a worksheet that includes a number of long and important formulas. You may want to protect these formulas against accidental modification or deletion by using Quattro's protection capability. But what if you need to make changes in several of these formulas? You could move around the worksheet, unprotecting cells, changing the formulas, and then protecting the cells again. Or you could use the /**D**efault **P**rotection **D**isable command to lower the fences around all the cells. After making the necessary changes, you could restore protection to all the cells by using the /**D**efault **P**rotection **E**nable command. When you enable protection again, any cells that were unprotected will remain accessible to you.

Managing Columns and Rows

The fundamental composition of the spreadsheet is a series of joined columns and rows. This section describes how to control column and row characteristics such as hiding columns, setting column widths, and inserting and deleting columns and rows.

Setting Column Widths

You can control the width of columns in the worksheet to accommodate data entries that are too wide for the default column width of nine characters. You also can reduce column widths, perhaps to give the worksheet a better-tailored appearance when a column contains narrow entries. In Quattro, you can set the width of all the columns in the worksheet at once or separately control the width of each column.

Suppose that you are setting up a projection of expenses for the next five years and want to display the full descriptions of the expense items (some of them 20 characters wide). You can set the first column of your projection of expenses to be 20 characters wide (to accommodate the descriptions) and then set the other columns to whatever width you want.

The command used to set individual column widths is /**C**olumn **W**idth. You can set one column width at a time either by entering a number or by using the left- and right-arrow keys followed by Enter. The advantage of the left- and right-arrow keys is that the column width expands and contracts each time you press a key. To get a good idea of what the width requirements are, experiment when you enter the command.

You need to remember two things about this command. First, you must position the selector in the proper column before you initiate the command. Otherwise, you will have to start over. Second, to reset the column width to the standard setting, you must use the /**C**olumn **R**eset command.

You also can control all the column widths in the worksheet at once. The command to use in Quattro is /Column **S**et_Global.

The /Column **W**idth command takes precedence over the /Column **S**et_Global command. That is, any column width previously set by the /Column **W**idth command will not be affected by a change in the global setting.

For example, if you set the width of column A to 12 by using the /Column **W**idth command and then change all the columns in the worksheet to a width of 5 by using the /Column **S**et_Global command, every column except column A will change to 5. Column A will remain at a width of 12 and will have to be reset to 5 with the /Column **R**eset command.

Hiding Columns

The /Column **H**ide command allows you to suppress the display of any columns in the worksheet. One important use for this command is to suppress display of unwanted columns when printing reports. When intervening columns are hidden, a report can display on a single page data from two or more separated columns.

Figures 4.41 and 4.42 show an example of the process of hiding columns. In the worksheet shown in figure 4.41, columns A through G are filled with numbers. Figure 4.42 shows the same worksheet after the /Column **H**ide command has been used to hide columns C, D, and E.

Numbers and formulas in hidden columns still are active, and cell references to cells in hidden columns continue to work properly. But the hidden columns do not appear on the display. You can tell which columns are missing only by noting the break in the column letters at the top of the display. The hidden columns are redisplayed temporarily, however, when you use certain commands, such as /**B**lock **C**opy or /**B**lock **M**ove; the hidden columns are marked with an asterisk (e.g., H*) during this temporary display.

When you select the /Column **H**ide command, Quattro prompts you for the block of columns to hide. You must invoke the command once for each block of adjacent columns that you hide.

To redisplay hidden columns, use /Column **E**xpose. When you select this command, all hidden columns are redisplayed with asterisks by the column letters at the top of the display. You are prompted for a block of columns to expose.

	A	B	C	D	E	F	G	H
1	111	222	333	444	555	666	777	
2	111	222	333	444	555	666	777	
3	111	222	333	444	555	666	777	
4	111	222	333	444	555	666	777	
5	111	222	333	444	555	666	777	
6	111	222	333	444	555	666	777	
7	111	222	333	444	555	666	777	
8	111	222	333	444	555	666	777	
9	111	222	333	444	555	666	777	
10	111	222	333	444	555	666	777	
11	111	222	333	444	555	666	777	
12	111	222	333	444	555	666	777	
13	111	222	333	444	555	666	777	
14	111	222	333	444	555	666	777	
15	111	222	333	444	555	666	777	
16	111	222	333	444	555	666	777	
17	111	222	333	444	555	666	777	
18	111	222	333	444	555	666	777	
19	111	222	333	444	555	666	777	
20	111	222	333	444	555	666	777	

H1:

31-Jan-88 02:02 PM READY

Fig. 4.41. The worksheet with numbers in columns A through G.

	A	B	F	G	H	I	J	K
1	111	222	666	777				
2	111	222	666	777				
3	111	222	666	777				
4	111	222	666	777				
5	111	222	666	777				
6	111	222	666	777				
7	111	222	666	777				
8	111	222	666	777				
9	111	222	666	777				
10	111	222	666	777				
11	111	222	666	777				
12	111	222	666	777				
13	111	222	666	777				
14	111	222	666	777				
15	111	222	666	777				
16	111	222	666	777				
17	111	222	666	777				
18	111	222	666	777				
19	111	222	666	777				
20	111	222	666	777				

H1:

31-Jan-88 02:04 PM READY

Fig. 4.42. The same worksheet with columns C, D, and E hidden.

If the screen has been split, certain Quattro commands affect only the current window. For example, the /**C**olumn **H**ide command can be used to hide a column in the current window without affecting the display in the other window.

Inserting Rows and Columns

Suppose that you have finished building a model in a worksheet but want to dress up its general appearance before you show the model to anyone. One technique for improving a worksheet's appearance is to insert blank rows and columns in strategic places to draw attention to headings and other important items.

The commands for inserting rows and columns in Quattro are /**C**olumn and /**R**ow **I**nsert. You can insert multiple rows and columns each time you invoke either of these commands. After you select /**C**olumn or /**R**ow **I**nsert, you are asked for an insert block. Depending on how you set up this block, one or more columns or rows are inserted.

Inserted columns appear to the left of the specified block, and inserted rows appear above the specified block. For example, suppose that you created the worksheet shown in figure 4.43. If you issue the /**C**olumn **I**nsert command and specify an insert block of A10..A10, a single blank column is inserted at column A, as shown in figure 4.44. Quattro automatically shifts all the values over one column and modifies all the cell formulas for the change. If you then specify /**R**ow **I**nsert and a block of A10..A10, Quattro inserts one blank row at row 10; the values that were contained in row 10 move down to row 11. Figure 4.45 illustrates the results of that operation.

Quattro does not have the capability to insert or delete partial rows and columns. But you can erase any areas that you want to delete and then move the resulting data, if desired.

Deleting Rows and Columns

Deleting rows and columns is the opposite of inserting them. Quattro allows you to delete multiple rows or columns with the /**C**olumn and /**R**ow **D**elete commands. After you choose either of these commands, Quattro asks you to specify a block of cells to be deleted. Just as for the Insert commands, the block you specify must include one cell from the row or column to be deleted.

For example, to delete rows 2 and 3 in the worksheet in figure 4.46, you should specify A2..A3. Other acceptable block designations are B2..B3, C2..C3, C2..G3, etc. The results of the deletion are shown in figure 4.47.

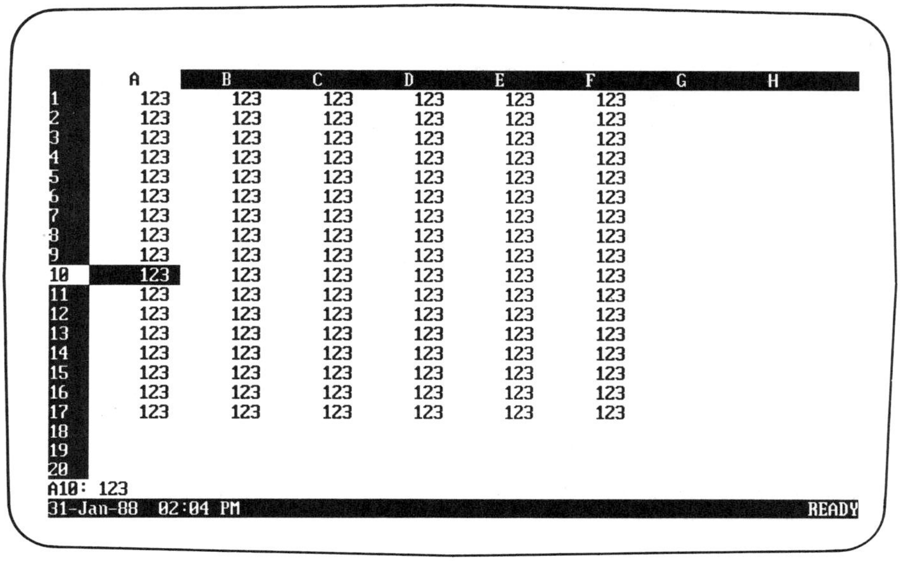

Fig. 4.43. The worksheet before using Insert commands.

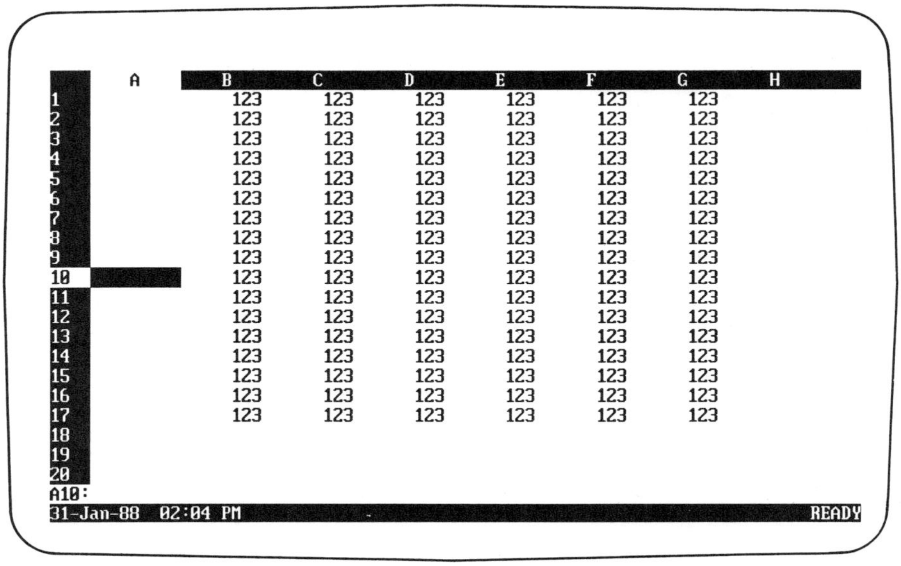

Fig. 4.44. The worksheet after inserting a column.

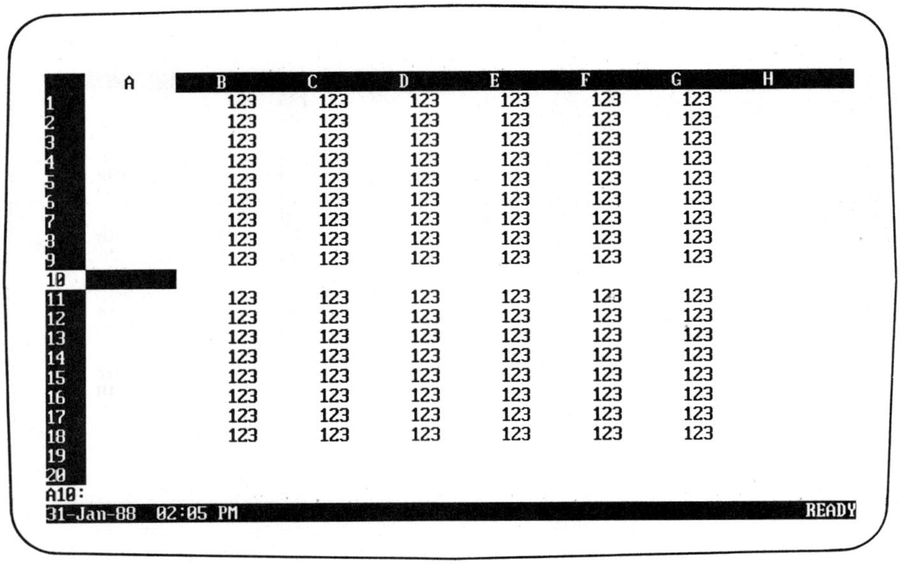

Fig. 4.45. The worksheet after inserting a row.

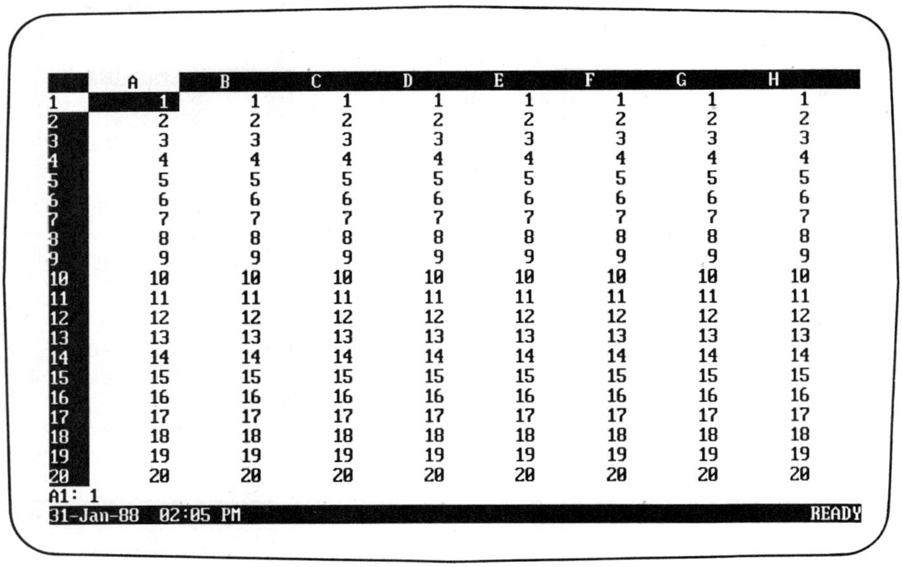

Fig. 4.46. The worksheet before deleting rows.

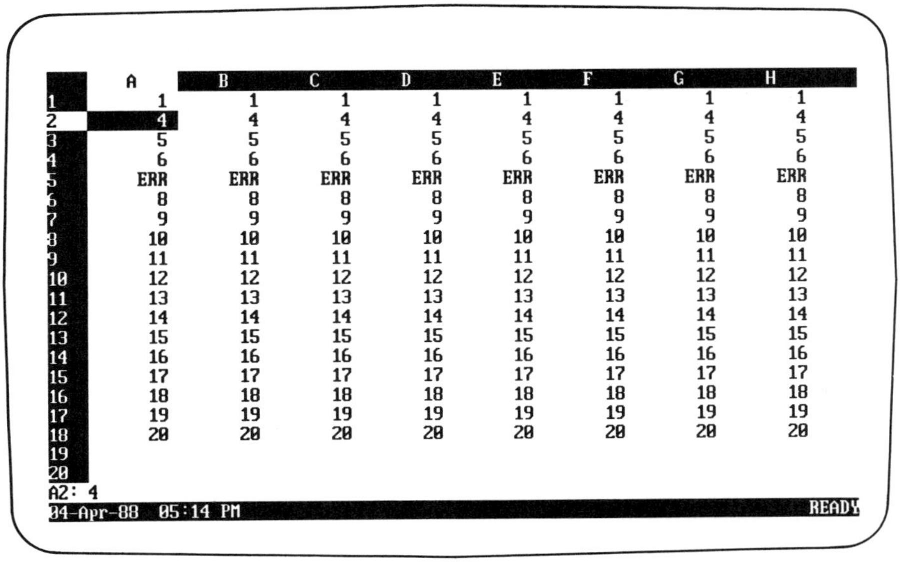

	A	B	C	D	E	F	G	H
1	1	1	1	1	1	1	1	1
2	4	4	4	4	4	4	4	4
3	5	5	5	5	5	5	5	5
4	6	6	6	6	6	6	6	6
5	ERR	ERR	ERR	ERR	ERR	ERR	ERR	ERR
6	8	8	8	8	8	8	8	8
7	9	9	9	9	9	9	9	9
8	10	10	10	10	10	10	10	10
9	11	11	11	11	11	11	11	11
10	12	12	12	12	12	12	12	12
11	13	13	13	13	13	13	13	13
12	14	14	14	14	14	14	14	14
13	15	15	15	15	15	15	15	15
14	16	16	16	16	16	16	16	16
15	17	17	17	17	17	17	17	17
16	18	18	18	18	18	18	18	18
17	19	19	19	19	19	19	19	19
18	20	20	20	20	20	20	20	20
19								
20								

A2: 4

04-Apr-88 05:14 PM READY

Fig. 4.47. The worksheet after deleting rows.

The easiest way to designate the block to be deleted is to point to cells in the appropriate row or column. You also can enter the cell addresses from the keyboard. Pointing to cells, however, helps you to avoid inadvertently choosing the wrong block.

Remember that when you use the Delete commands, the contents of the entire rows or columns you delete are gone forever—including all the cells in the rows or columns, not just the individual block of cells you specify. You may be able to get the values back if you previously saved a copy of the model on disk or if the Transcript add-in is active. But if you don't have a copy of the model, the rows' and columns' contents are lost. You would be wise to save prior to making deletions.

Notice that the worksheet in figure 4.47 is readjusted automatically so that all the contents below row 3 are shifted up. And all the formulas, command blocks, and named blocks are adjusted for the deletion. Formulas that contain references to the deleted cells are given the value ERR.

Deleting columns is similar to deleting rows. After you select the /Column Delete command, specify a block that includes at least one cell in each column to be deleted. For example, suppose that you wanted to delete column B in figure 4.48. A suitable block to designate for the /Column Delete command is B1..B1. Again, pointing is the best way to designate the block so that you avoid selecting the wrong column. Figure 4.49 shows the worksheet after column B is deleted.

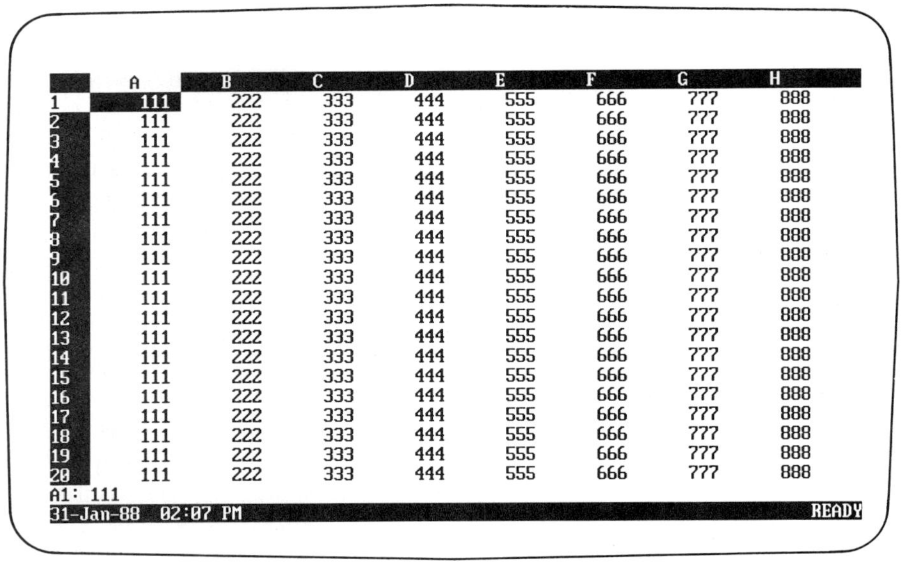

	A	B	C	D	E	F	G	H
1	111	222	333	444	555	666	777	888
2	111	222	333	444	555	666	777	888
3	111	222	333	444	555	666	777	888
4	111	222	333	444	555	666	777	888
5	111	222	333	444	555	666	777	888
6	111	222	333	444	555	666	777	888
7	111	222	333	444	555	666	777	888
8	111	222	333	444	555	666	777	888
9	111	222	333	444	555	666	777	888
10	111	222	333	444	555	666	777	888
11	111	222	333	444	555	666	777	888
12	111	222	333	444	555	666	777	888
13	111	222	333	444	555	666	777	888
14	111	222	333	444	555	666	777	888
15	111	222	333	444	555	666	777	888
16	111	222	333	444	555	666	777	888
17	111	222	333	444	555	666	777	888
18	111	222	333	444	555	666	777	888
19	111	222	333	444	555	666	777	888
20	111	222	333	444	555	666	777	888

A1: 111
31-Jan-88 02:07 PM READY

Fig. 4.48. The worksheet before deleting columns.

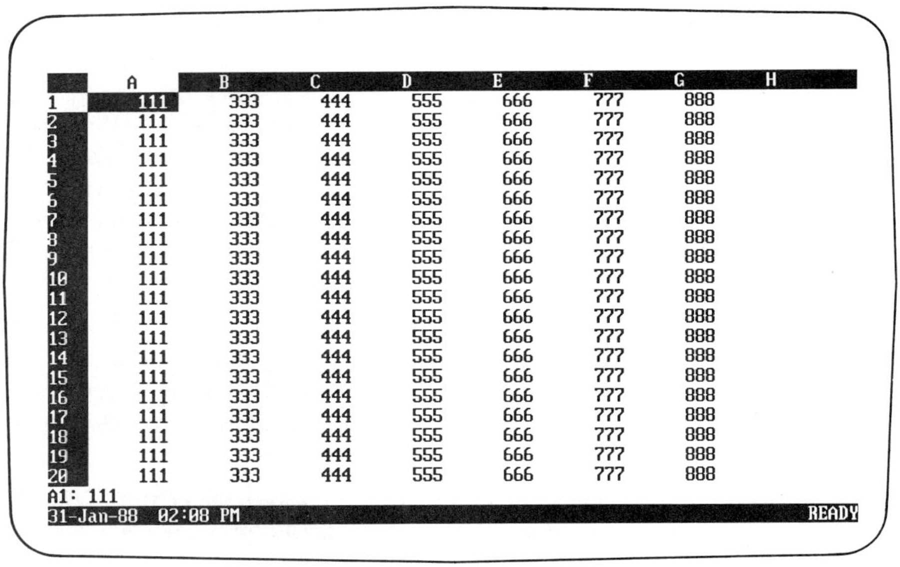

	A	B	C	D	E	F	G	H
1	111	333	444	555	666	777	888	
2	111	333	444	555	666	777	888	
3	111	333	444	555	666	777	888	
4	111	333	444	555	666	777	888	
5	111	333	444	555	666	777	888	
6	111	333	444	555	666	777	888	
7	111	333	444	555	666	777	888	
8	111	333	444	555	666	777	888	
9	111	333	444	555	666	777	888	
10	111	333	444	555	666	777	888	
11	111	333	444	555	666	777	888	
12	111	333	444	555	666	777	888	
13	111	333	444	555	666	777	888	
14	111	333	444	555	666	777	888	
15	111	333	444	555	666	777	888	
16	111	333	444	555	666	777	888	
17	111	333	444	555	666	777	888	
18	111	333	444	555	666	777	888	
19	111	333	444	555	666	777	888	
20	111	333	444	555	666	777	888	

A1: 111
31-Jan-88 02:08 PM READY

Fig. 4.49. The worksheet after deleting columns.

Erasing the Worksheet from Memory

The /Column Delete and /Row Delete commands are different from the /Block Erase command. The difference is best explained by using the analogy of a paper spreadsheet. The manual equivalent of the /Column Delete and /Row Delete commands is to cut apart the columnar sheet (using a pair of scissors), remove the unwanted columns and/or rows, and then paste the pieces of the sheet back together. When you delete a row or column, all data and formulas are deleted, and the display cell formats, the column widths, and the /Block Advanced Unprotect settings all are lost. The /Block Erase command, on the other hand, is like using an eraser to erase blocks of cells from the sheet. Do not forget the difference between these powerful commands.

In native Quattro terms, two differences exist between deleting cells by using the /Column Delete and /Row Delete commands and erasing cells by using /Block Erase. First, the /Column Delete and /Row Delete commands delete entire columns and rows within a worksheet, whereas /Block Erase erases particular blocks of cells, which may be as small or as large as you want. Second, the worksheet is readjusted automatically to fill in the gaps created by the deleted columns or rows when you use the /Column Delete and /Row Delete commands. With the /Block Erase command, the cells in the block that was erased are merely blanked.

Erasing the Worksheet

The /Erase command clears the entire spreadsheet from memory. This command not only erases all the contents of the worksheet but also restores all settings to their default condition, destroys any block names or graph names in the worksheet, and clears any title lock or window split in the worksheet.

Be sure that you understand the difference between the /Erase command and the /Block Erase A1..IV8192 command. The /Block Erase command removes the contents of every cell in the worksheet, except those that are protected. It does not, however, alter any of the Default settings, including column widths or print settings. /Erase, however, literally restores the Quattro worksheet to its default configuration. After the /Erase command is issued, the worksheet is exactly as it was when loaded.

Obviously, the /Erase command is a powerful and potentially destructive command. For this reason, Quattro prompts `Lose your changes?` and forces you to type a *y* for **Yes** or to point to `Yes` and press Enter, if the spreadsheet has been changed since it was last saved to a file. Otherwise, the sheet is erased instantly.

Once a worksheet is erased in this way, it cannot be recovered by normal means unless, again, you are using the Transcript add-in. Always save your worksheets before you erase them. To learn how to save your worksheet, see Chapter 8.

Laying Out the Spreadsheet

Quattro provides three methods for laying out the general appearance of the spreadsheet. The first, /**L**ayout **T**itles, allows you to freeze on-screen the columns and rows used as titles. The second option, **W**indows, gives you two independent display areas so that you can see two parts of the spreadsheet at once. The third option gives you control over where on the display the descriptor line will be placed.

Freezing Titles on the Screen

The /**L**ayout **T**itles command is similar to the /**L**ayout **W**indows command. Both commands allow you to see one area of a worksheet while you work on another. The unique function of the /**L**ayout **T**itles command, however, is that it freezes all the cells to the left or above (or both to the left and above) the cell selector's current position so that those cells cannot move off the screen.

A classic example of the advantage of this command occurs when you enter the items on a pro forma Balance Sheet and Income Statement. Suppose that you are trying to set up a budget to project the level of the financial statement items month by month for the next year. Because the normal screen, without any special column widths, shows 20 rows by 7 columns, you undoubtedly will have to shift the screen so that cell A1 is no longer in the upper left corner. In fact, if you enter the month headings across row 1 and the Balance Sheet and Income Statement headings down column A, as shown in figure 4.50, you must scroll the screen several different times in order to enter all the items.

To keep the headings in view on the screen, even when you scroll the screen, enter the /**L**ayout **T**itles command when the cell selector is highlighting cell B2. When you enter the command, the following Titles menu items appear:

Horizontal
Vertical
Both
Clear

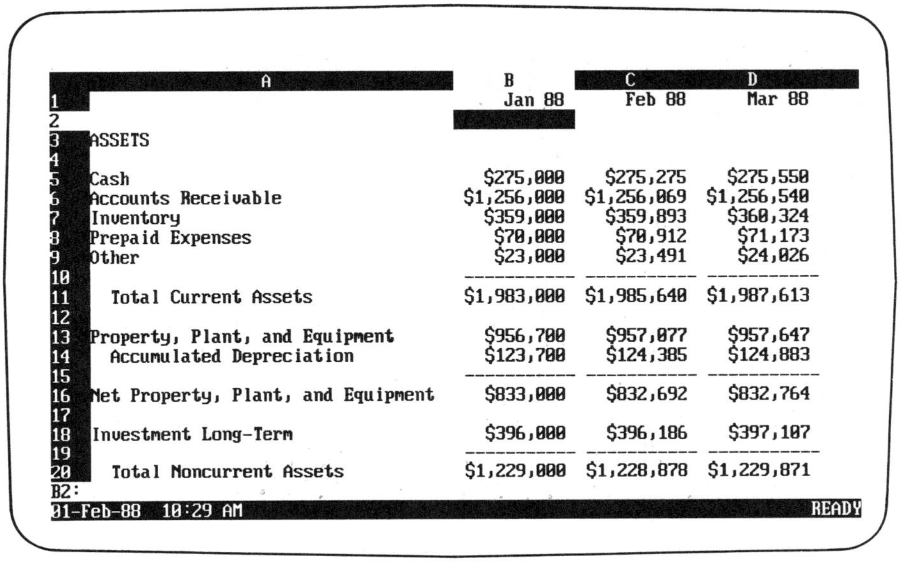

	A	B	C	D
1		Jan 88	Feb 88	Mar 88
2				
3	ASSETS			
4				
5	Cash	$275,000	$275,275	$275,550
6	Accounts Receivable	$1,256,000	$1,256,069	$1,256,540
7	Inventory	$359,000	$359,893	$360,324
8	Prepaid Expenses	$70,000	$70,912	$71,173
9	Other	$23,000	$23,491	$24,026
10		----------	----------	----------
11	Total Current Assets	$1,983,000	$1,985,640	$1,987,613
12				
13	Property, Plant, and Equipment	$956,700	$957,077	$957,647
14	Accumulated Depreciation	$123,700	$124,385	$124,883
15		----------	----------	----------
16	Net Property, Plant, and Equipment	$833,000	$832,692	$832,764
17				
18	Investment Long-Term	$396,000	$396,186	$397,107
19		----------	----------	----------
20	Total Noncurrent Assets	$1,229,000	$1,228,878	$1,229,871

B2:
01-Feb-88 10:29 AM READY

Fig. 4.50. A balance-sheet worksheet.

If you select **H**orizontal, all rows on the screen above the cell selector become frozen. That is, they don't move off the screen when you scroll up and down. If you select **V**ertical, all columns to the left of the cell selector are frozen and move only when you scroll up and down (but not when you move left and right). The **B**oth option freezes all rows above and all columns to the left of the cell selector. Remember to move the cell selector to the desired location before executing the /**L**ayout **T**itles command. **C**lear defrosts the worksheet titles.

In the pro forma example, the **B**oth option was selected. In this case, when you scroll right and left as well as up and down, the headings always remain in view. Figures 4.51 and 4.52 show two examples of how this process works. In figure 4.51, we scrolled across the spreadsheet to display columns F, G, and H, while keeping the headings in Column A on the screen. In figure 4.52, we scrolled down the spreadsheet to display rows 21 through 39, while keeping the headings in row 1 on the screen.

When you freeze rows or columns, you cannot move the cell selector into the frozen area. In the example, if you try to move the cell selector into cell A2 from cell B2, Quattro beeps and does not allow the cell selector to move into the protected area. Similarly, using the Home key moves the cell selector only to the upper left cell in the unfrozen area. In the example, this is cell B2. Normally, the Home function moves the cell selector to cell A1.

	A	F	G	H
1		May 88	Jun 88	Jul 88
2				
3	ASSETS			
4				
5	Cash	$276,900	$286,491	$297,654
6	Accounts Receivable	$1,345,521	$1,387,255	$1,258,731
7	Inventory	$345,654	$356,124	$321,564
8	Prepaid Expenses	$70,456	$71,546	$74,511
9	Other	$23,451	$19,456	$27,564
10		-----------	-----------	-----------
11	Total Current Assets	$2,061,982	$2,120,872	$1,980,024
12				
13	Property, Plant, and Equipment	$956,456	$1,025,654	$946,787
14	Accumulated Depreciation	$159,448	$168,999	$169,878
15		-----------	-----------	-----------
16	Net Property, Plant, and Equipment	$797,008	$856,655	$776,909
17				
18	Investment Long-Term	$409,222	$419,546	$412,548
19		-----------	-----------	-----------
20	Total Noncurrent Assets	$1,206,230	$1,276,201	$1,189,457

H2:

01-Feb-88 10:40 AM READY

Fig. 4.51. Moving to the right in the worksheet after setting titles.

	A	B	C	D
1		Jan 88	Feb 88	Mar 88
21		-----------	-----------	-----------
22	Total Assets	$3,212,000	$3,214,518	$3,217,484
23		==========	==========	==========
24				
25	LIABILITIES			
26				
27	Notes Payable	$276,000	$276,694	$277,036
28	Accounts Payable	$378,000	$378,616	$378,973
29	Accrued Expenses	$98,000	$98,822	$98,862
30	Other Liabilities	$25,000	$25,914	$26,119
31		-----------	-----------	-----------
32	Total Current Liabilities	$777,000	$780,046	$780,990
33				
34	Long Term Debt	$333,000	$333,009	$333,660
35		-----------	-----------	-----------
36	Total Liabilities	$1,110,000	$1,113,055	$1,114,650
37				
38				
39	STOCKHOLDER'S EQUITY			

B21: (C0) ' -----------

01-Feb-88 10:43 AM READY

Fig. 4.52. Moving down in the worksheet after setting titles.

One exception to this restriction occurs when you use the F5 (GoTo) key. If you use the GoTo function to jump to cell A1, you will see two copies of the title rows and/or columns. Figure 4.53 shows the example when you use the F5 key to go to cell A1. The dual set of titles can be confusing.

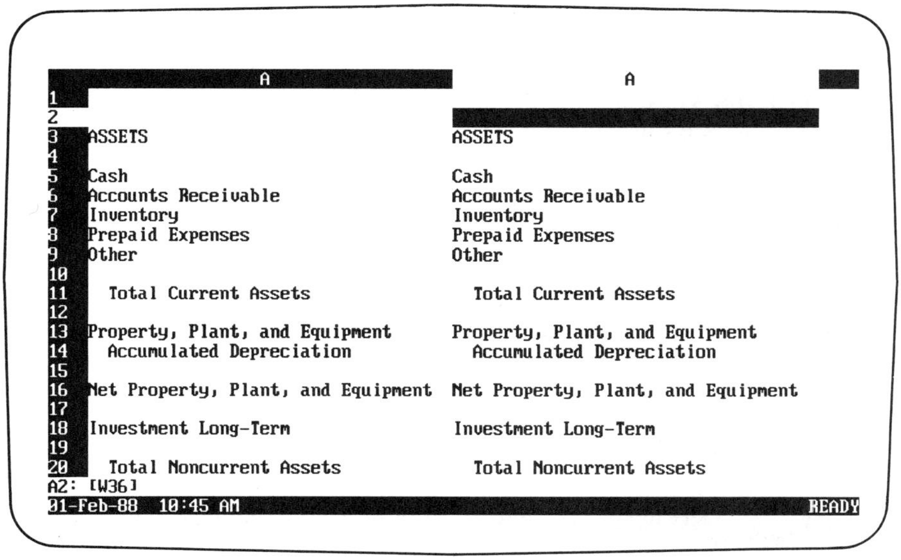

Fig. 4.53. The display after using the F5 (GoTo) key to move to cell A1.

The frozen areas also are accessible in other situations when you're in POINT mode. In the example, suppose that you wanted to define cell B6 as equal to A1. You would move the cell selector to cell B6, type + to begin the formula, and then use the cursor-movement keys to point to cell A1. In this case, the cell selector is allowed to move into the protected area, and Quattro does not beep.

Splitting the Screen

You can split the Quattro screen display into two parts, either horizontally or vertically. This feature helps you to overcome some of the inconvenience of not being able to see an entire spreadsheet at one time.

Suppose, for example, that you are working on a large model that spans several columns and that you are having trouble keeping track of how the changes made in one area of the worksheet are affecting another area. By splitting the screen, you can make the changes in one area and immediately see their effect in the other.

The command for splitting the screen is /**L**ayout **W**indows. When you enter this command, the following menu choices appear:

Horizontal
Vertical
Sync
Unsync
Clear

Horizontal and **V**ertical split the screen in the manner indicated by their names. The screen splits at the address at which the cell selector is positioned when you enter **H**orizontal or **V**ertical. In other words, you don't have to split the screen exactly in half. Remember that the dividing line requires no less than one row or one column on one side, depending on how you split the screen.

After you split the screen by using **H**orizontal, the cell selector appears in the top window. When you create a **V**ertical division, the cell selector appears in the left window (see fig. 4.54). To jump the division between the windows, use the F6 (Window) key.

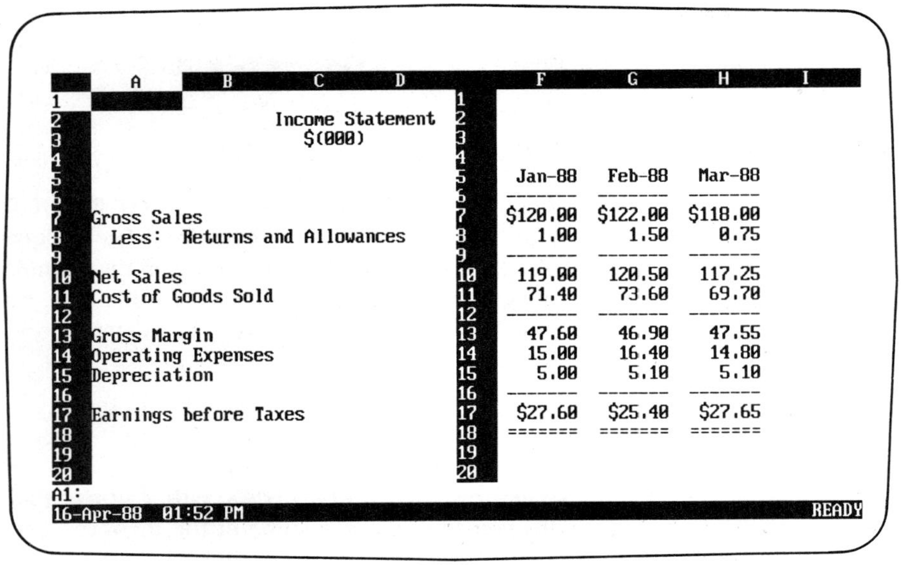

Fig. 4.54. A vertically split screen.

The **S**ync and **U**nsync options work as a pair. In **S**ync screen mode, when you scroll one screen, the other screen automatically scrolls with it. Horizontally split screens always keep the same columns in view, and vertically split screens always keep the same rows. **S**ync is the standard default for Quattro.

Unsync screens allow you to control one screen independently of the other in all directions. In fact, you even can show the same cells in the two different windows.

The **C**lear option removes the split-window option and reverts the screen to a single window display. When you use this option, the single window takes on the settings of the top or left-hand window, depending on how the screen was split.

Saving Your File before You /Quit

When you use the /**Q**uit command, you exit Quattro entirely, and all unsaved information is lost. To keep from losing the information, you need to save your file before you use /**Q**uit. File operations are explained in detail in Chapter 8, but you should learn as early as possible the basic operation of saving a file. And you should develop the habit of saving your file frequently.

The /**F**ile **S**ave command allows you to save or update an entire worksheet to a file on disk. This command makes an exact copy of the current worksheet, including all the display formats, block names, and settings you have specified.

To save your current worksheet, use the /**F**ile **S**ave command and then respond to the `Enter file name:` prompt by typing the name you have chosen for your file. Then press Enter. Your file is saved to disk. If you again invoke the /**F**ile **S**ave command after the current worksheet has been saved, Quattro uses the name you assigned to the file as the default file name.

Don't use a name that you used before unless you want your current worksheet to replace the one with the same name on disk. If you do type in a name that is already in use, Quattro asks whether you really do want to replace the existing file or back it up. Select **R**eplace if you do want to replace the existing file; if you're not sure, choose backup. Otherwise, to respecify, press Esc and type a new name. To cancel, select **C**ancel.

Whenever you have to choose a file name for a file command, Quattro helps you by displaying a list of the Quattro files on the current drive and directory. If the file name you want is in the list, you can select it by pointing and pressing Enter. If you want to replace an existing file, you can point to one of the entries on the list and then press Enter. Otherwise, you can type in the file name you want. Some characters are not allowed in file names; if the program does not accept the name you enter, check Chapter 8 for the rules for file names. Whatever name you use, Quattro automatically supplies a .WKQ extension.

To call a file back into main memory from disk, use the /**F**ile **R**etrieve command. Again, Quattro displays a list of all the file names currently on disk in the current directory and drive.

For information on using other than the current drive and directory to store your files, see Chapter 8.

Chapter Summary

This chapter laid the foundation for you to master Quattro. You learned about several of Quattro's most important, basic commands, including the commands that affect the entire worksheet and those that affect only certain designated blocks of cells. A wide variety of other fundamentals were covered: setting column widths, inserting rows and columns, hiding columns, protecting cells, erasing the worksheet, splitting the screen display, and freezing titles on the screen.

You learned also how to move and copy data from one part of the worksheet to another, and you learned how to make formulas that are copied or moved end up the way you want them, by using relative and absolute addressing. Finally, you learned how to save your file before quitting Quattro.

Now that you know the fundamentals of building a spreadsheet and manipulating the data on that spreadsheet, you're ready to dress up your work—to make it look the way you want it to look. The next chapter shows you how to use Quattro's **D**isplay_Format commands to control the appearance of your worksheet.

CHAPTER

5

Formatting Cell Contents

You may have discovered already that Quattro expects you to enter data in a certain form. If, for example, you try to enter *1,234*, the program beeps, switches to EDIT mode, and waits for you to remove the comma. You get the same response if you try to enter *10:08 AM*; the colon and the *AM* are the offenders. If you try to enter *$9.23*, the program accepts the entry but omits the $. If you could not change the way data is displayed, Quattro would have limited usefulness.

But you can control data display—not only for commas, currency, and time but also for a variety of other purposes. Formats control how cell contents are displayed. You change formats with one of the /**B**lock **D**isplay_Format or the /**D**efault **F**ormats **D**isplay commands. Quattro offers 10 format options:

Fixed
Scientific
Currency
, (comma)
General
+/- (horizontal-bar graph)

Percent
Date (includes **T**ime format)
Text
Hidden

These formats affect primarily the way numeric values are displayed in a worksheet. **T**ext format, for instance, causes a formula to appear in a cell as a formula rather than as a value. **H**idden format affects the display of every kind of entry.

Table 5.1 gives all the formats available in Quattro.

This chapter shows you how to use all 10 formats and how to control International formats. You learn to use the /**B**lock **R**eformat command for text formatting. Finally, the chapter deals with some format problems and offers possible solutions.

Setting Block and Default Formats

The commands for controlling formats are /**D**efault **F**ormats **D**isplay and /**B**lock **D**isplay_Format. The former controls the formatting of all the cells in the worksheet, and the latter controls specific blocks within the worksheet.

Generally, you use the /**D**efault **F**ormats **D**isplay command before you start to enter data in a worksheet. You should choose a format that applies to the majority of cells. This choice helps reduce the number of cells that need to be formatted individually after the spreadsheet is created. Once you have set all the cells to a default format, you can use the /**B**lock **D**isplay_Format command to override the **D**efault format setting for specific cell blocks.

The /**B**lock **D**isplay_Format command takes precedence over the /**D**efault **F**ormats **D**isplay command. As a result, whenever you change the default format, all the numbers and formulas affected change automatically unless they have been previously formatted with the /**B**lock **D**isplay_Format command. In turn, when you format a block, the format for that block overrides any formats already set by /**D**efault **F**ormats **D**isplay. If you want to save a default format permanently, use the /**D**efault **U**pdate command to update Quattro's definition file, which defines Quattro's start-up default settings (see Chapter 13 for more information).

Table 5.1
Quattro Format Options

Format	*Key*	*Explanation*
Fixed	F	Fixes the number of decimal places displayed
Scientific	S	Displays numbers in scientific notation
Currency	C	Displays currency symbols (such as $) and commas marking thousands
,	,	Inserts commas to mark thousands and multiples of thousands
General	G	Displays values with up to 10 decimals or in scientific notation
+/-	+	Creates horizontal-bar graphs or time-duration graphs on computers that do not have graphics capability. Each symbol equals an integer number. Positive numbers display as pluses; negative numbers as minuses.
Percent	P	Displays a decimal number as a whole percentage number with a percent sign (%)
Date	D	Displays a number as a date. The number must be in the form of a Julian date, such as 31040, or 31,040 days from January 1, 1900 (day 1). Time formats are found under the Date format command.
Text	T	Continues to evaluate formulas as numbers
Hidden	H	Hides contents from display and printing but still evaluates contents
Reset	R	Resets the cell format to the default format and shows any previously hidden cell contents

When you invoke either format command, the menu that appears contains the following entries:

Fixed
Scientific
Currency
, [Financial]
General
+/-
Percent
Date
Text [Show Formulas]
Hidden
Reset

Each format has special characteristics and specific uses. These characteristics and uses are discussed in the following pages.

General Format

Although not the first item on the menu, **G**eneral format is discussed first because it is the default format for all new worksheets unless you have used the /**D**efault **U**pdate command to modify the formats.

When numbers are displayed in **G**eneral format, trailing zeros to the right of the decimal point are not displayed. If numbers are too large or too small to be displayed normally, scientific notation is used.

Some examples of numbers displayed in **G**eneral format are

123.456
5.63E+14
-22.1
1.9E-09

General format does not control how labels are displayed. Labels are displayed as left-justified, right-justified, or centered, depending on the setting you make with the /**D**efault **F**ormats **A**lign or the /**B**lock **L**abel_Align command. Left-justification is the default.

General is the default setting for the /**D**efault **F**ormats **D**isplay. You can see the default setting by entering /**D**efault **F**ormats and then expanding the menu by pressing the plus (+) key located next to the numeric keypad. To close the view of these default settings, press the minus (-) key on the numeric keypad. Figure 5.1 shows the default format settings.

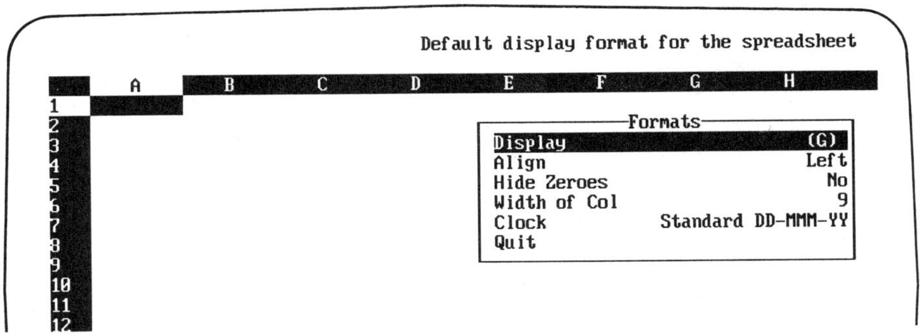

Fig. 5.1. Quattro's default display format.

All formats specified with /**B**lock **D**isplay_Format show format indicators on the descriptor line at the lower left of the spreadsheet. These indicators describe the cell on which the pointer rests. You do not have to enter these indicators; Quattro automatically provides them when you assign a block display format. When you use /**B**lock **D**isplay_Format and specify **G**eneral format for a block, the number on the descriptor line is preceded by the indicator (G) whenever the cell pointer is in the formatted block.

Fixed Format

Quattro's **F**ixed format is similar to **G**eneral format in that **F**ixed format does not display commas or dollar signs. The difference is that **F**ixed format lets you control the number of places displayed to the right of the decimal point. When you select **F**ixed format, Quattro prompts you for the number of decimal places you want displayed. When you enter a whole number into a formatted cell, Quattro enters a decimal point and the specified number of zeros to the right of the decimal. Sometimes, the number of decimal places you selected is fewer than the number of decimal places in the numbers you enter. Quattro rounds these numbers as displayed in the worksheet to the selected number of decimal places.

Notice that only the numbers as displayed are rounded; the numbers Quattro actually stores in the cells are not. For example, suppose that cell F33 contains the value 1.26, and the cell is formatted **F**ixed with 1 decimal place. You see 1.3 on-screen. But cell F33 still contains the value 1.26. If you are looking at the result of a formula in a cell formatted as **F**ixed, or as another Block format, you can use the F2 (Edit) key to bring the formula to the input line, and then press the F9 key to calculate the formula. This test immediately shows you the effect that display rounding has on that formula. Press the Esc key to remove the calculated number, or it will replace the original formula in the cell.

The following are examples of numbers in **Fixed** format:

In the Descriptor Line	*In the Cell*	*Displayed in the Worksheet*
(F0)15.5	15.5	16
(F2)1000.2145	1000.2415	1000.21
(F3)-21.405	-21.405	-21.405
(F4)93.1	93.1	93.1000

You do not have to enter the format indicator (for example, FØ) in the descriptor line. Quattro enters the indicator automatically. The indicator for the default format, however, does not appear in the descriptor line. For example, if you have not used the /**D**efault **F**ormats **D**isplay command to change the default from F2, (F2) does not appear in the descriptor line.

You can enter decimal numbers in two ways: with the decimal point (.12) or with the percent sign (12%). In F2 format (Fixed with two decimal places), for example, if you enter either .12 or 12%, the worksheet contains 0.12.

Fixed format can be useful when you want to control the number of places to the right of the decimal point without the automatic removal of insignificant digits, as occurs in **G**eneral format. **F**ixed format is particularly appealing when you want all the numbers in your columns to show the same number of decimal places.

Scientific Format

Scientific format causes Quattro to display numbers in exponential scientific notation. You will recall that this notation is used in **G**eneral format when numbers are too large or too small to be displayed any other way. By choosing **S**cientific format instead of **G**eneral format, however, you can control the number of decimal places and so determine the degree of precision with which numbers are displayed. Quattro's **G**eneral format controls the number of decimal places by default. Numbers that are rounded for display in the worksheet keep their values in the cell to the same precision as they were entered. Some examples follow:

In the Descriptor Line	*In the Cell*	*Displayed in the Worksheet*
(S2)27.1	27.1	2.71E+101
(S4)453.235	453.235	4.5324E+102
(S1)-21	-21	-2.1E+101
(S0)-1	-1	-1E+100

Currency Format

Currency format displays numbers in cells with a currency indicator before each entry and with commas separating hundreds from thousands, hundreds of thousands from millions, and so on. Negative values appear in parentheses ( ). The dollar sign is the default for the currency indicator.

Currency format also gives you the option of controlling the number of places to the right of the decimal point. If you are having trouble displaying values that are too large for the column width, this control is helpful because you can override the default setting of two places to the right of the decimal point.

If the value you want to display in Currency format is too large for the column width, instead of the value a series of asterisks fills the cell. This substitution occurs for all formats. The problem of space is particularly acute with Currency format, however, because the dollar sign, commas, and parentheses take up space. The best way to handle this situation is to experiment with the formatting parameters and the column width until you get the appearance you want.

You may recall that column width is controlled through either the /**C**olumn **W**idth or /**D**efault **S**et **G**lobal **W**idth command. The former controls specific columns in the worksheet, and the latter controls at the same time all the columns that have not been set individually.

Numbers that appear in the descriptor line are preceded by the indicator (C) for **C**urrency. This format indicator is followed by an integer, also within the parentheses. This number indicates the number of decimal places you have chosen. The following examples show how numbers appear in the descriptor line, how they are stored in the cell, and how they are displayed in the worksheet with **C**urrency format. Notice that numbers rounded with the **F**ormat command are not stored in the cell as rounded numbers; the full value is still available for all calculation purposes.

In the Descriptor Line	*In the Cell*	*Displayed in the Worksheet*
(C2)45	45	$45.00
(C2)1612.3	1612.3	$1,612.30
(C3)22.805	22.805	$22.805
(C1)105.56	105.56	$105.6
(C2)-210.99	-210.99	($210.99)

Depending on how cell-specific you want the control, cell formats are controlled with the /**D**efault **F**ormats **D**isplay or the /**B**lock **D**isplay_Format command followed (in this case) by **C**urrency.

Financial (Comma) Format

The , (comma), or financial, format resembles **Currency** format, except that the numbers are displayed without dollar signs. Commas separate hundreds from thousands, hundreds of thousands from millions, and so on. Parentheses () identify negative numbers. After the , (comma) format has been chosen, you can specify the number of decimal places.

This format can be particularly useful in financial statements for displaying all the numbers, except those at the tops and bottoms of columns, with commas but without dollar signs. For example, a portion of a balance sheet follows:

Cash	$1,750
Receivables	3,735
Inventories	9,200
Current Assets	$14,685

The numbers corresponding to Receivables and Inventories are displayed with , (comma) format, and those corresponding to Cash and Current Assets are displayed with **Currency** format.

The +/- Format

The +/- format creates a horizontal-bar graph of plus or minus signs, depending on the value of the number you enter in the cell. Asterisks are displayed if the size of the bar graph exceeds the column width. If zero is entered in a cell, a period (.) is displayed on the graph and left-justified in the cell.

In the Descriptor Line	*In the Worksheet*
(+)6	++++++
(+)-4	----
(+)0	.

Some applications use this format to mark values in a long column of numbers. As you scan the column, the +'s and -'s stand out and are easy to locate (see fig. 5.2).

Percent Format

The **Percent** format is used to display percentages; after you select **Percent**, you select the number of decimal places. The values displayed in the worksheet are the entered values multiplied by 100 and followed by a percent sign. Notice that numbers rounded for display purposes are not altered in the cell.

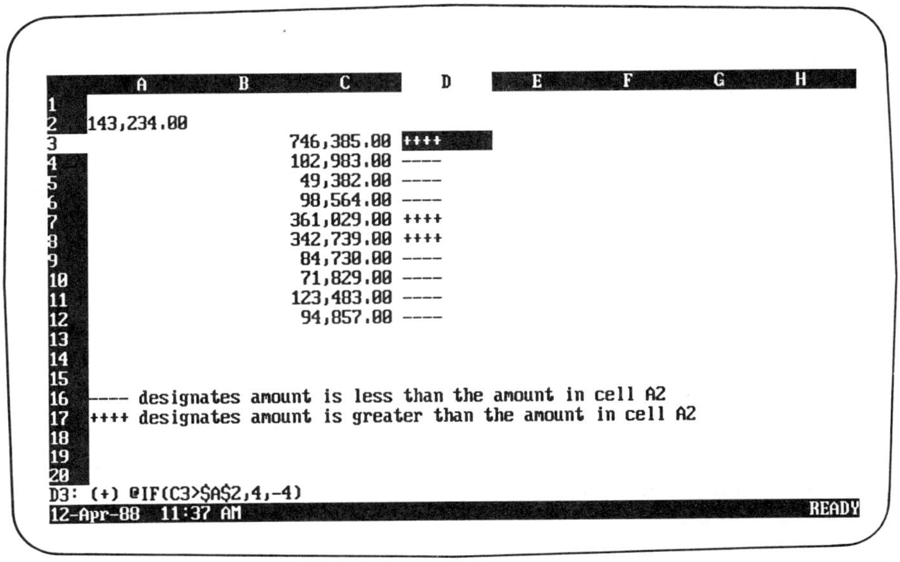

Fig. 5.2. Using the +/- format to identify values.

In the Descriptor Line	*In the Cell*	*Displayed in the Worksheet*
(P0).12	.12	12%
(P4)12.134	12.134	1213.4000%
(P2).5675	.5675	56.75%

One difficulty with this format is that your natural inclination is to enter integers instead of decimals (for example, 12 instead of .12 in the first example). But Quattro persists in its method of storing cell contents in only one way and allowing you to control only the display of the output. This problem can be alleviated by entering an integer and then entering a percent sign before you press the Enter key.

Date and Time Formats

Quattro internally represents any date as an integer equal to the number of days from January 1, 1900, to that date. For example, January 1, 1900, is represented by the number 1; December 31, 2099, is represented by 73050. To enter a date into the worksheet, you use one of the date functions: @DATE, @DATEVALUE, or @NOW. Quattro also allows you to press Ctrl-D to enter directly into a cell a label like 10-DEC-88. After you press Ctrl-D, Quattro automatically converts entered text to the correct serial-days number and formats the cell as a date.

Quattro calculates a period of hours as a decimal fraction of a day. The calculations are based on a 24-hour clock, military time. Therefore, the number 0.5 equals noon because 50 percent of the day has elapsed. To enter a time into the worksheet, use one of the time functions: @TIME, @TIMEVALUE, or @NOW.

To display a date or time in its proper format, use either the /**B**lock **D**isplay_Format **D**ate or /**D**efault **F**ormats **D**isplay **D**ate command; to format for time, use /**B**lock **D**isplay_Format **D**ate **T**ime or /**D**efault **F**ormats **D**isplay **D**ate **T**ime. When you use the /**B**lock **D**isplay_Format **D**ate command, any block you have set using the **D**ate format appears in one of five date and four time formats. When you use the /**D**efault **F**ormats **D**isplay **D**ate command, dates or times (as well as all other numbers entered in any cell in the worksheet) are displayed in the selected date and time format.

The five date and four time formats you can specify with the /**B**lock **D**isplay_Format **D**ate and /**D**efault **F**ormats **D**isplay **D**ate commands are shown in tables 5.2 and 5.3.

Table 5.2
Date Formats

Number	*Description*	*Example*
1	Day-Month-Year	
	DD-MMM-YY	19-Jul-88
2	Day-Month	
	DD-MMM	19-Jul
3	Month-Year	
	MMM-YY	Jul-88
4	Long International	
	MM/DD/YY	07/19/88
	or DD/MM/YY	19/07/88
	or DD.MM.YY	19.07.88
	or YY-MM-DD	88-07-19
5	Short International	
	MM/DD	07/19
	or DD/MM	19/07
	or DD.MM	19.07
	or MM-DD	07-19

Table 5.3
Time Formats

Number	*Description*	*Example*
1	Hour:Minute:Second	
	HH:MM:SS AM/PM	11:37:43 PM
2	Hour:Minute	
	HH:MM AM/PM	11:37 PM
3	Long International	
	HH:MM:SS	23:37:43
	or HH.MM.SS	23.37.43
	or HH,MM,SS	23,37,43
	or HHhMMmSSs	23h37m43s
4	Short International	
	HH:MM	23:37
	or HH.MM	23.37
	or HH,MM	23,37
	or HHhMMm	23h37m

For more information on date and time functions and formats, see Chapter 6.

Text Format

Text format displays formulas as they are entered in the input line, not the computed values, which Quattro normally displays. Numbers entered in this format are displayed in the same format as numbers in **G**eneral format.

Probably the most important application of this format is debugging. Because with **T**ext format you can display all the formulas, finding and correcting problems is a relatively easy task. If the characters in your formulas exceed the cell width, you see one character fewer than the column-width setting. Therefore, you may have to widen the cell width to see your complete formulas. **T**ext format also is useful to show database query criterion.

Some examples of **T**ext format follow:

In the Descriptor Line	*In the Worksheet*
(T)+C4/B12	+C4/B12
(T)(A21*B4)	(A21*B4)
(T)567.6	567.6

Hidden Format

Hidden format suppresses the display of cell contents for any block that you indicate after you invoke the /**B**lock **D**isplay_Format **H**idden command. If you want to hide all the cells in a column or block of columns, use the /**C**olumn **H**ide command (discussed in Chapter 4).

Although a cell with **H**idden format appears as a blank cell on the screen, the cell contents are displayed in the descriptor line when you place the cursor over that cell. Because the hidden cell is included in calculations, all formulas and values can be calculated and are readjusted when values are changed.

You may think that you can disguise entries in cells by allowing long labels of alphanumeric characters to overwrite hidden cells. For example, suppose that you put a value in cell F5, hide the value by using the /**B**lock **D**isplay_Format **H**idden command, and then put a long label in cell E5 in an attempt to overwrite the apparently blank cell F5. Quattro does not let cell F5 be overwritten; even if you use /**B**lock **D**isplay_Format **H**idden to hide a cell that contains data, the cell still blocks out long labels.

The Reset Format Command

The /**B**lock **D**isplay_Format **R**eset command resets the format of the indicated block to the default setting. When the format of a block is reset, the format indicator for any cell within the block disappears from the descriptor line.

When you issue the /**B**lock **D**isplay_Format **R**eset command, hidden columns are displayed with an asterisk temporarily next to the column letter (see fig. 5.3). After you reset the format for the block you select, the hidden columns again disappear.

International Formats

Quattro allows you to select the punctuation and currency signs displayed by comma and **C**urrency formats and to control the way the date and time are displayed when you use the special **I**nternational **D**ate and **T**ime formats. To control these settings globally for the worksheet, use the /**D**efault **I**nternational command.

The **P**unctuation option of the /**D**efault **I**nternational command gives you a choice of eight ways to punctuate numbers and to delimit function arguments. (See Chapter 6 for explanations of functions and arguments.) The default is the standard American convention of a period between an integer and its

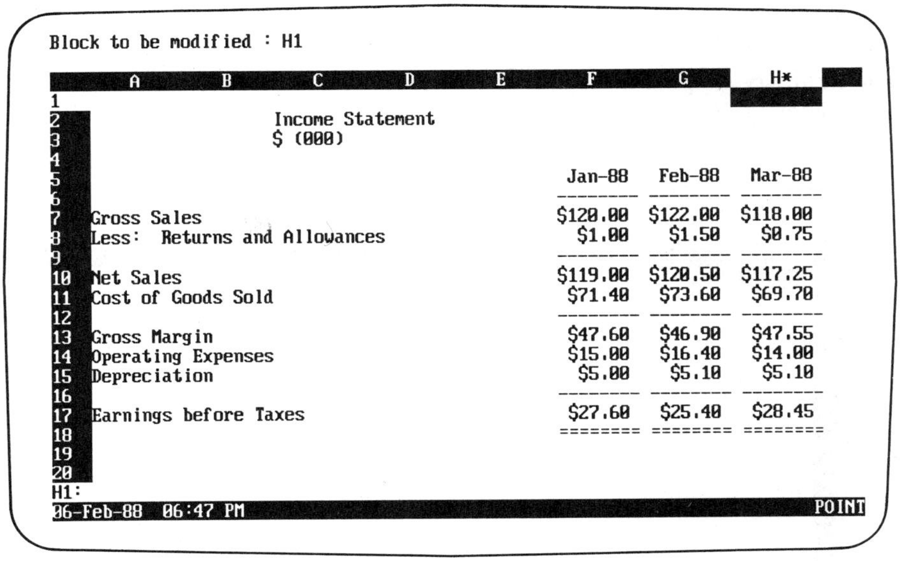

Fig. 5.3. Hidden column (H) marked with an asterisk.

fractional component, commas to mark thousands, and commas to delimit function arguments. You can change the default, however; seven other combinations are available for punctuating numbers.

The **C**urrency option allows you to change the currency symbol displayed by **C**urrency format and to specify whether that symbol is a prefix or a suffix.

The **D**ate and **T**ime options allow you to set the **I**nternational **D**ate and **T**ime formats. You have four choices each for date and time formats. The default format for dates is MM/DD/YY (01/16/88) and for times, HH:MM:SS in 24-hour time (19:25:33).

Using the /Block Reformat Command for Formatting Text

Quattro's /**B**lock **R**eformat command is something of an orphan. This command provides Quattro with the first hint of word-processing capabilities but is completely unsupported by other text-processing tools. For this reason, you can think of the /**B**lock **R**eformat command as an advanced formatting tool rather than as a simple word processor.

As you have seen, Quattro allows text entries wider than the width of the column in which they are entered. The labels overwrite adjoining cells unless a cell already contains text or numbers. After you have entered the text, use the /**B**lock **R**eformat command to block the text into the space you indicate. For example, suppose that you type the line of text shown on the Quattro worksheet in figure 5.4.

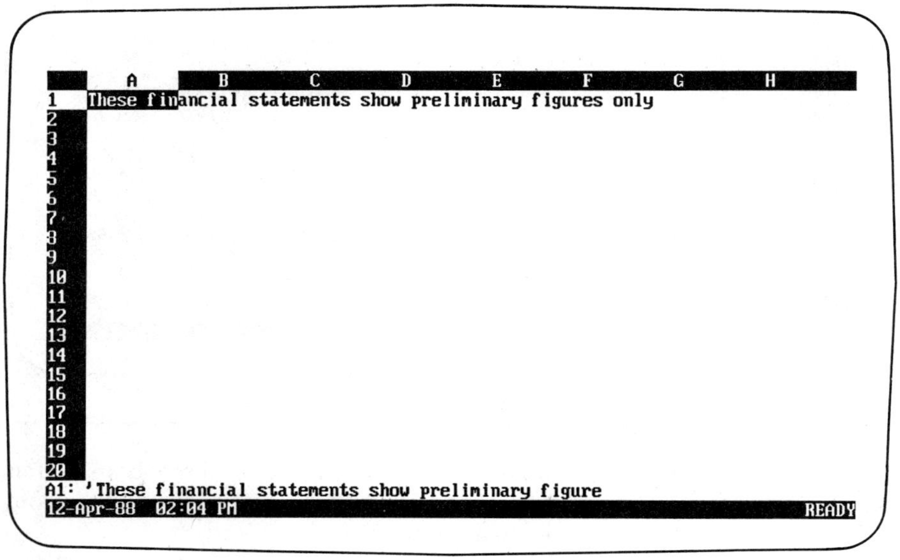

Fig. 5.4. Spreadsheet with long label in cells A1 through F1.

Notice that this label, which is entered in cell A1, extends across the cells from A1 through F1. Using the /**B**lock **R**eformat command, you can ask Quattro to justify this text into columns A and B; A, B, and C; or A, B, C, and D. By issuing the command /**B**lock **R**eformat **a1..c1**, you can specify that the text be blocked into three nine-character columns (A, B, and C). Figure 5.5 shows the results of this command.

This command can be used to fine-tune the captions and notes that are commonly attached to financial documents. But /**B**lock **R**eformat has some limitations. The worst of these limitations is that the command pushes down any entries in cells below the cell being justified. Normally, this effect is not a problem, but in some cases the rearrangement can mess up a carefully constructed worksheet.

For example, figure 5.6 shows a sample worksheet. Figure 5.7 shows the same sheet after the /**B**lock **R**eformat command has been used. The labels that were aligned in the first figure are no longer aligned in the second. Be careful when you use /**B**lock **R**eformat; its results are sometimes difficult to predict.

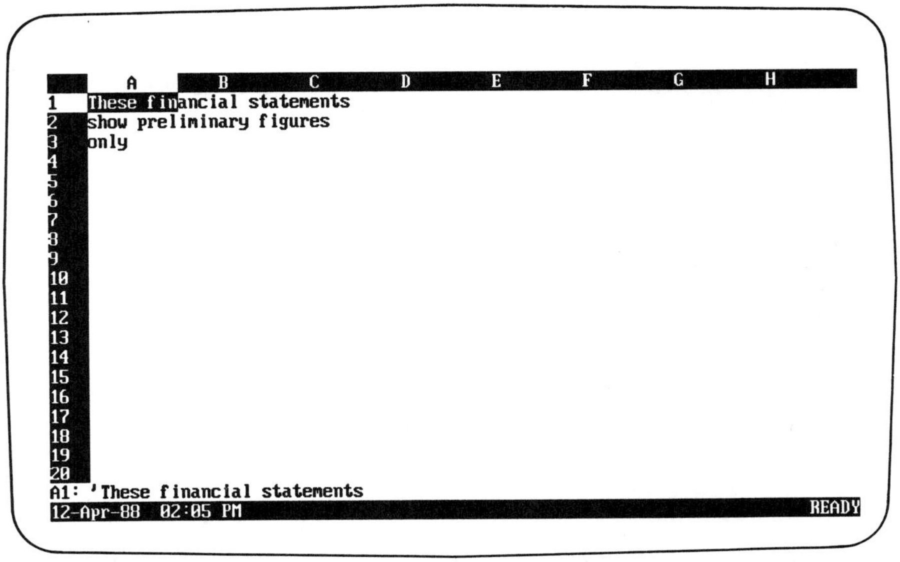

*Fig. 5.5. Results of the /**B**lock **R**eformat command.*

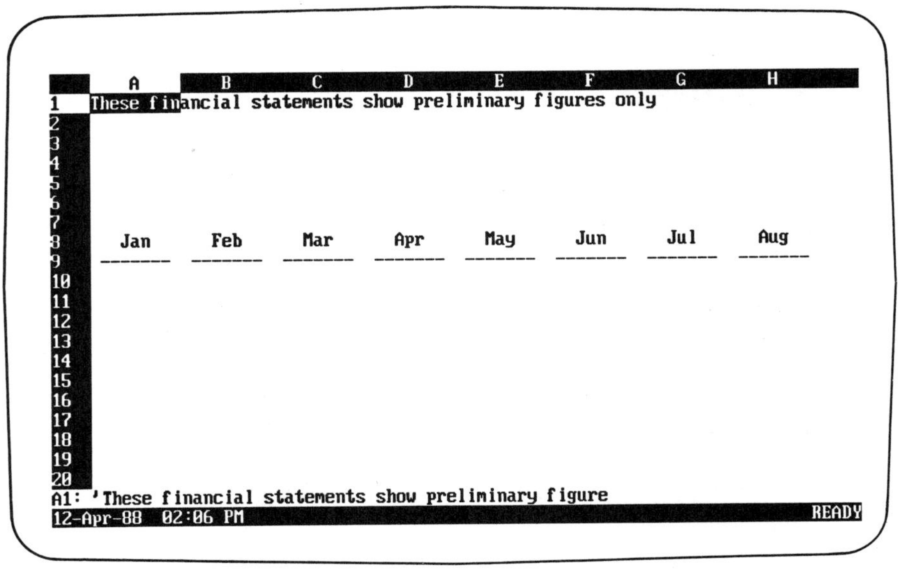

*Fig. 5.6. Spreadsheet before /**B**lock **R**eformat is used.*

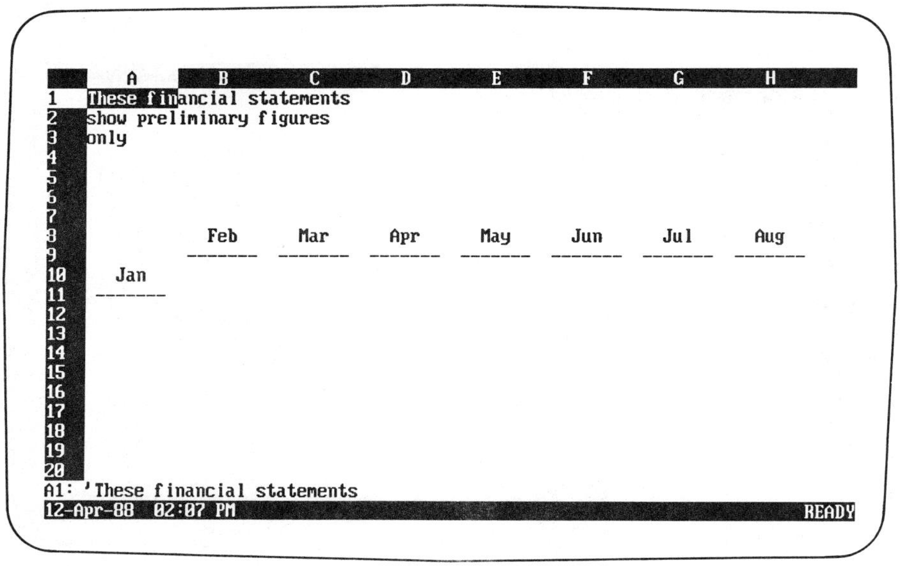

Fig. 5.7. Alignment problems after /Block Reformat is used.

You also can use /**B**lock **R**eformat to debug complex formulas. See Chapter 6 for a discussion of this technique.

Using Conditional Cell Colors

The main reason for using a spreadsheet is to help you make better decisions about business matters. Usually, Quattro does an exceptional job supporting decisions. However, sometimes a spreadsheet may get so large or complex that you cannot determine quickly which cells contain important or unusual data. Quattro has the capability to assign different colors to cells that need to be highlighted more than usual. This feature is called conditional coloring.

The conditional coloring feature is found on the /**D**efault **C**olors **C**onditional menu. From this menu, you can control the color of error cells and the display of exceptionally large or small numbers. Figure 5.8 shows an invoice aging database. It is used to evaluate the performance of the person charged with collecting on accounts. Because the database contains so many numbers, the model uses conditional colors to highlight unusually high or low records.

Figure 5.8 shows the application as you are entering a **S**mallest_Normal_Value of 22. Any number below 22 will appear in the cell color you assign through the **B**elow_Normal_Color menu. After setting a lower limit of 22, enter a

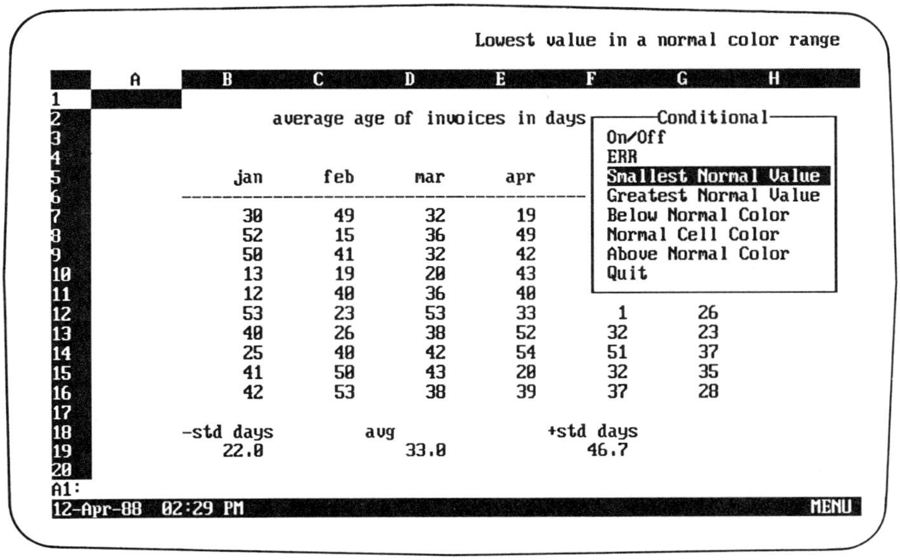

Fig. 5.8. The /Default Colors Conditional menu.

Greater Normal Value of 46.7. As soon as you have completed the settings, select the **O**n/off option to enable conditional coloring. Figure 5.9 shows how the change in colors makes seeing the unusual amounts easier.

Dealing with Formatting Problems

Despite the ease with which you ordinarily use Quattro's formats, you may encounter some problems while using them. For one thing, Quattro has no provision to left-justify or center numbers. Unlike labels, numbers can be right-justified only.

Having only right-justified numbers can create an unsightly appearance when you need to display different-size numbers in the same column (see fig. 5.10). Because of this problem, the /**B**lock **F**ill command for numbers used as column headers is less than convenient. (The /**B**lock **F**ill command is discussed in Chapter 4.) The only way around this particular problem is to make the *Quarter* numbers labels; then you can control the alignment.

Another problem with appearance occurs when, in the same column, you center labels that are an odd number of characters long and labels that are an even number of characters. The results may appear to be slightly out of kilter. If the column is an even number of characters wide, labels that are an

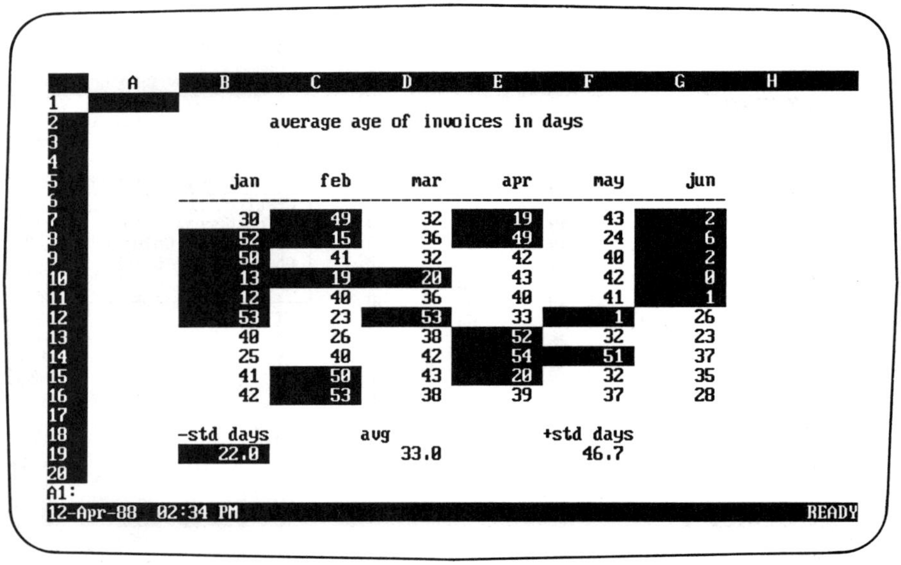

Fig. 5.9. A spreadsheet with conditional coloring.

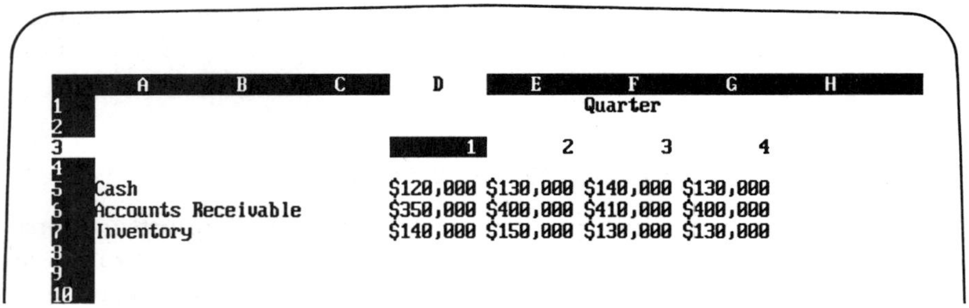

Fig. 5.10. Right-justified numeric labels above columns of numbers.

even number of characters center exactly, but labels that are an odd number of characters do not. If the column is an odd number of characters wide, the reverse is true. The following example illustrates this problem.

Column Even Number of Characters Wide	*Column Odd Number of Characters Wide*
1234567890	123456789
RALPHS	RALPHS
SOFT	SOFT
SHOES	SHOES

You really have no way around this problem except to try different alignments by inserting blanks or extra characters wherever possible. The problem of alignment is one that you will have to learn to live with and do your best to work around.

Because the /**B**lock **D**isplay_Format and /**D**efault **F**ormats **D**isplay commands punctuate numeric values, Quattro may display asterisks in the cell. As has been explained, this display occurs when the requested format exceeds the column width. The solution is to widen the column to accommodate the punctuation. Additional information on this procedure can be found in Chapter 4 of this book.

Chapter Summary

In this chapter, you have learned how to display your data as currency, dates, and times, and in financial, percent, and several other formats. You also learned how to hide a block of cells for purposes of appearance and security, and how to control international formats. You learned how to use the /**B**lock **R**eformat command to justify long labels. Finally, you saw how to make your exceptional data more visible by using conditional colors.

Now that you have learned formatting, you know most of the basics of building a spreadsheet, and you probably are already a competent user of Quattro. The next two chapters take you a long way toward becoming a master of the Quattro spreadsheet. Chapters 6 and 7 show you how Quattro's extensive library of preprogrammed functions makes the spreadsheet a powerful and easy-to-use tool for data analysis and manipulation.

CHAPTER

6

Using Basic Spreadsheet Functions: The Heart of Quattro

The most powerful tools within the Quattro spreadsheet are the spreadsheet's functions. Functions are built-in subroutines that save you time and effort and keep you from having to reinvent the wheel. Most functions provide you with shortcuts for, or features entirely unavailable with, standard spreadsheet operations.

To illustrate the use of functions as a class, let's take a quick look at the @SUM function, perhaps the most commonly used of all the functions. You can use @SUM in place of repetitive addition. For example, to add a list of hypothetical numbers in cells A1 through A5, you can simply enter the function @SUM(A1..A5) rather than +A1+A2+A3+A4+A5. Although adding a string of five numbers is not a big deal, imagine if you had to type in fifty-five numbers! You can see that a function like @SUM can be a tremendous time-saver.

Quattro has an especially rich set of functions. The general categories of functions include the following:

Statistical
Mathematical
Logical
Financial
Date and Time
Table and Array Handlers
Database Statistical
Text Handlers
Macro-Related Special
Engineering/Scientific
Programmer's

Quattro's functions are designed to maintain complete compatibility with Lotus 1-2-3. Additionally, Quattro has some advanced functions of its own—such as @CELLINDEX, @CURVALUE, @FILEEXISTS, @HEXTONUM, and @NUMTOHEX—which will be of interest to application developers.

This chapter and the following one explore all of Quattro's functions, with the emphasis on practical application examples to demonstrate how you can use the functions in your worksheets. This chapter covers the basic spreadsheet functions: statistical, mathematical, logical, financial, and date and time. The remaining functions are discussed in Chapter 7, "Using Advanced Spreadsheet Functions."

Function Syntax

All Quattro spreadsheet functions begin with the @ (at) symbol. This character informs the program that the information following the @ is a function name rather than a simple label.

Almost all functions include one or more "arguments," which are the data Quattro requires to perform the function. A function's arguments immediately follow the function name and are enclosed in parentheses, as in @ISSTRING(cell_reference). In the earlier @SUM example, the block *A1..A5* is the function's argument.

Some functions have multiple arguments, which must be differentiated or separated from one another. Quattro accepts commas as separator characters. For example, the function to figure mortgage payments, @PMT, must be told three things: a principal amount, an interest rate, and the term of the mortgage. Each of these pieces of information is an individual argument. Thus the syntax of the @PMT function is

@PMT(principal,rate,term)

Function arguments can be composed of a variety of types of data and references. For instance, the @SUM function can calculate:

Numbers	@SUM(5,4,3,2,1)
A series of cell references	@SUM(A1,G1,A21,G21)
A block-oriented reference	@SUM(B5..M20)
Spreadsheet functions and formulas	@SUM(@AVG(B5..B10),5+5)
Any combination of the above	@SUM(23.5,A1..B10,@MAX(A1..M99))

Many functions also take text, date, or keyword information as their arguments. These argument types are described with the appropriate functions throughout this chapter.

The use of arguments within functions is limited only by your needs and imagination. Remember, the real power of the spreadsheet lies in its functions.

Quattro checks each spreadsheet operator and function before it is calculated to make sure that the function has the correct syntax (everything is in the right order), sufficient arguments, and an equal number of opening and closing parentheses. If your computer beeps when you try to enter a function or formula, the syntax checker has probably detected an inconsistency. After the beep, the cursor will move to the first trouble spot in the formula and automatically put you in EDIT mode.

Tip When the syntax checker detects an error, the program does not allow the formula to be entered into the cell. The formula remains on the input line, vulnerable to unintentional keystrokes that can undo all the effort you have invested in the formula. I made a fatal slip on several occasions when trying to edit the formula, because the Esc key on my keyboard is just to the right of the Backspace key. (Pressing Esc erases the formula in the input line.) Beware!

Tip To prevent the accidental loss of an incomplete formula (perhaps caused by a syntax error), press the Home key, type a leading apostrophe (') in the formula, and press Enter. This action puts the formula's label equivalent in the cell. If you do accidentally press Esc, you only need to press the Edit key (F2) to restore the formula.

One of Quattro's nicer touches is the addition of the syntax checker to fix a problem without your intervention. For example, suppose that you want to enter a logical operator such as >= (greater than or equal to). In Lotus 1-2-3, Release 2.01, you must enter the operators in the correct order, or the syntax checker reports an error. In Quattro, however, if you enter the operator in the reversed form =>, Quattro automatically swaps the operators into the correct order.

Quick Function Entry Aid

Another convenient feature of Quattro is its quick @function entry lister. This feature, assigned to the Alt-F3 function key set, provides you with a quick reference list of all the functions available in Quattro. A portion of the list, which is arranged in alphabetical order, is shown in figure 6.1.

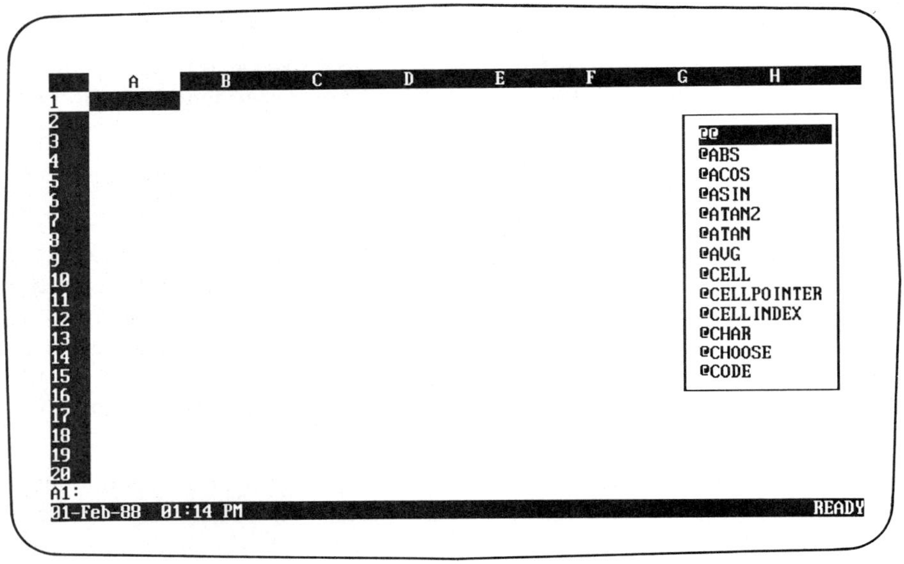

Fig. 6.1. The @function entry lister.

You can locate with the arrow keys the function you want to use. If you then press Enter, Quattro obliges by placing the @ sign and the function name on the input line. This method is usually quicker than typing and can help prevent typographical errors. Figure 6.2 shows the result of pressing the Enter key while the cursor is located on the @MEMEMSAVAIL function.

Tip To see the syntax required for certain functions while the function list is displaying, simply press the plus key (+) on the numeric keypad. The list window then expands to indicate the function's full syntax, including the arguments. For example, `@INDEX` changes to `@INDEX(block,col,row)`. You'll find this prompter handy if you have trouble remembering the syntax of hundreds of functions.

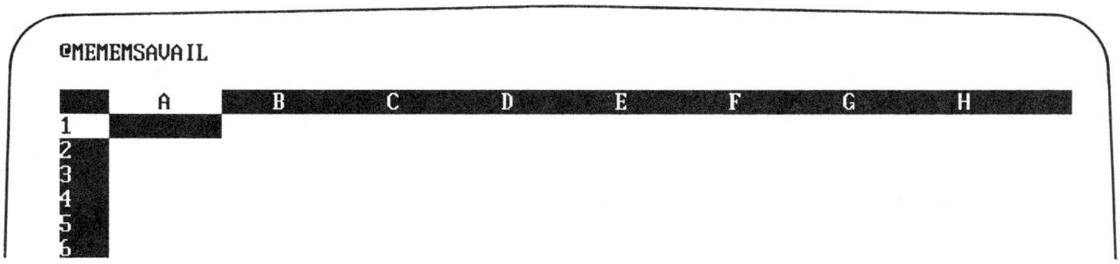

Fig. 6.2. The result of pressing Enter with the cursor on @MEMEMSAVAIL.

Math Operators

To manipulate numbers, you must indicate how you want a series of variables to be handled. Mathematical operators are the standard tools you use.

Just as you would expect, Quattro has an extensive list of operators to facilitate efficient handling of numbers and other types of data. The following table lists Quattro's available mathematical operators in their order of precedence, or normal order of calculation:

^	exponentiation
+	positive
-	negation
*, /	multiply, divide
+, -	add, subtract
&	text (string) addition

Comparison Operators

In addition to the mathematical operators, Quattro has a full complement of logical operators that makes the program more than adequate for making decisions in the spreadsheet. Here's a complete listing of Quattro's comparison operators:

<	less than
<=	less than or equal to
>=	greater than or equal to
>	greater than
=	equal
<>	not equal
#NOT#	logical NOT
#OR#	logical inclusive OR
#AND#	logical AND

Precedence

So that Quattro can provide consistent results when evaluating formulas or functions, the program evaluates formula operators in a consistent order—the order of precedence. As mentioned previously, the list of mathematical operators appears in order of precedence.

Normally, if all operators in a formula are of equal precedence (as addition and subtraction are), evaluation of the formula proceeds from left to right. If the operators are not equal in precedence, the operators with the highest precedence are evaluated from left to right, and then the other operators are evaluated in their turn, according to the normal order of precedence.

If you prefer, you can use parentheses to force the order in which Quattro will evaluate a formula. The formula

```
5-1*2^2
```

returns 1 as the answer (2 squared times 1, subtracted from 5). If you add parentheses in this way:

```
((5-1)*2)^2
```

the answer is 64 (the result of 5 minus 1 multiplied by 2, and then the whole thing squared). The rule of parentheses is that the material enclosed in the most deeply nested set of parentheses is always evaluated first, then calculation proceeds to the least-nested parentheses. After all parenthetical expressions have been evaluated, nonparenthesized expressions are evaluated normally from left to right.

Now that you know a little about Quattro's functions and formulas and how they are constructed, I'll introduce some handy techniques for editing and debugging.

Editing and Debugging Functions and Formulas

A few years ago, in the dark ages of spreadsheets (VisiCalc 1.0 on the Apple II), I needed to create an application that understood and could track time. Unfortunately, not until recently were spreadsheets given the capability to tell time. So in those days I had to create a complex network of highly integrated and extremely long formulas. As I proceeded with the development, I learned some unpleasant facts about working with formulas. These experiences led to the development of Gobel's laws:

1. You'll be 85 percent done with a formula but get distracted and completely forget what you were doing.
2. The difficulty of completing a formula is equal to the square of its length. Additionally, the difficulty factor is cubed by the number of functions in the formula.

Gobel's First Law

To illustrate what I mean by the first law, think about the most difficult formulas you ever tried to create. No doubt the most frustrating thing about the process was interruptions.

As you began building the formula in your mind, an intellectual glee overtook you because you thought of a brilliant approach to solving a stubborn problem. Surely, you thought, this idea would cause your name to be etched in the annals of algorithmic glory. Then, without warning, somebody taps lightly on your shoulder and asks that dreaded question: "Got a minute?" The formula in your mind comes crashing down as you are forced to turn your attention to the offending miscreant who saw you "doing nothing."

You can easily prevent such a turn of events from ever transpiring. The best advice is to get the formula down on paper first; that is, describe the formula logically. Before you begin to enter a formula, state its construction in logical English terms. That way you will be insulated from the complexities and frustration of trying to satisfy the spreadsheet's syntax requirements while you invent the formula. You will also avoid the need to track down multiple cell references.

For example, the basic formula for GROSS PROFIT is SALES minus COST OF GOODS SOLD. That equation is intuitive and easy to write. This technique also leads to the good habit of using block names for cells.

The Acid Test for Debugging Formulas

Now I'd like to show you the acid test that proves the technique. If you want to understand fully the formula that follows, consult the section dealing with the @IF function. For now, however, please follow along.

In one of my high-level seminars, we had some extra time at the end of the day, so I asked whether anyone had an application that they wanted to develop. To my surprise, the unanimous request of the class was to create a football pool application. Not being a gambler myself, the class had to instruct me on how to determine whether a bettor won or lost. The project turned out to be a difficult challenge.

Because I had learned my lesson about jumping into the spreadsheet with half-baked formulas, I resisted the temptation to start typing formulas. Instead, the class developed the formula in English. Here is the resulting algorithm. All it does is determine whether you won the bet.

> "Subtract the score of the underdog team from the team favored to win. If the result is less than the line (what odds makers expect), and you chose the underdog team, you win. Otherwise, you lose. Or, subtract the score of the underdog team from the team favored to win. If the favored team beat the line, and you chose the favored team, you win; otherwise, good-bye money."

With the formula succinctly stated in English, proceeding with the implementation of the formula was easy. Here it is, with block names rather than cell references:

```
@IF(FAV_SCR-OTHER_SCR<=LINE#AND#YRTEAM=0)#OR#
   (FAV_SCR-OTHER_SCR>LINE#AND#YRTEAM),BET,BET*-1.1)
```

Even though we were able to enter the formula, we still needed a method to verify that the formula was working as planned. We thus used a technique to decompile, or break apart, the formula into its basic components. This method employs the little-used /**B**lock **R**eformat command.

Using /Block Reformat To Compile and Decompile Formulas

The /**B**lock **R**eformat command was originally designed as a simple word-processing capability to allow you to create a consistent right margin based on the current column width. The command uses spaces in the text to determine where to break lines.

I'll use this command to demonstrate how to "untie" a formula after you enter it in a worksheet. Note the formula shown in the input line of figure 6.3. This worksheet holds all the data necessary for determining whether you won or lost a bet, based on the results of the game between teams A and Z. Right now, the formula indicates (in cell H4) that you lost 11 dollars. Is that conclusion correct? To find out, edit the formula. Type an apostrophe (') at the beginning of the formula, as shown in the input line, to convert the formula into plain text (a label).

```
@IF((D4-E4<=C4#AND#G4=0)#OR#(D4-E4>C4#AND#G4),F4,F4*-1.1)

        G         H         I    J    K    L    M    N
1    chosen
2      team    result
3   ------------------
4         0       -11
5         1       -22
6         0         5
7         0        33
8         0        32
9         0     -17.6
10        1         7
11        1     -20.9
12        0        10
13        1      -7.7
14        0         3
15        1     -17.6
16        0     -29.7
17        1     -15.4
18        1         1
19        0        17
20        1         8
H4: @IF((FSCR-OSC<=LINE#AND#YRTM=0)#OR#(FSCR-OSC>LINE#A
01-Feb-88  02:00 PM                                    EDIT
```

Fig. 6.3. A formula to determine whether you won or lost a bet.

Next, copy the label to an out-of-the-way cell. Then insert spaces into the formula at the boundaries of the conditional components of the formula, such as before opening and after closing parentheses, as shown in figure 6.4. Note that the column is being set at quite a narrow width (3). You can almost always use 3 as the new width. This step is important. The right edge of the highlighted block will be used as the right margin when the formula label is reformatted.

After adjusting the column width, invoke the /**B**lock **R**eformat command. After you press Enter to indicate the block, Quattro divides the formula label into separate cells at and below the original cell, based on the justification highlight and the strategically placed spaces in the label. Figure 6.5 illustrates the results.

The next step is to remove the leading apostrophes so that Quattro treats the components like formulas. Figure 6.6 shows the results: the individual formulas' calculations. Notice that block names are displayed now that the formula has been changed to text.

Now you can examine the larger formula's individual actors. By examining the results of the smaller formulas and their referenced values, you can much more easily verify whether the overall formula is logically correct.

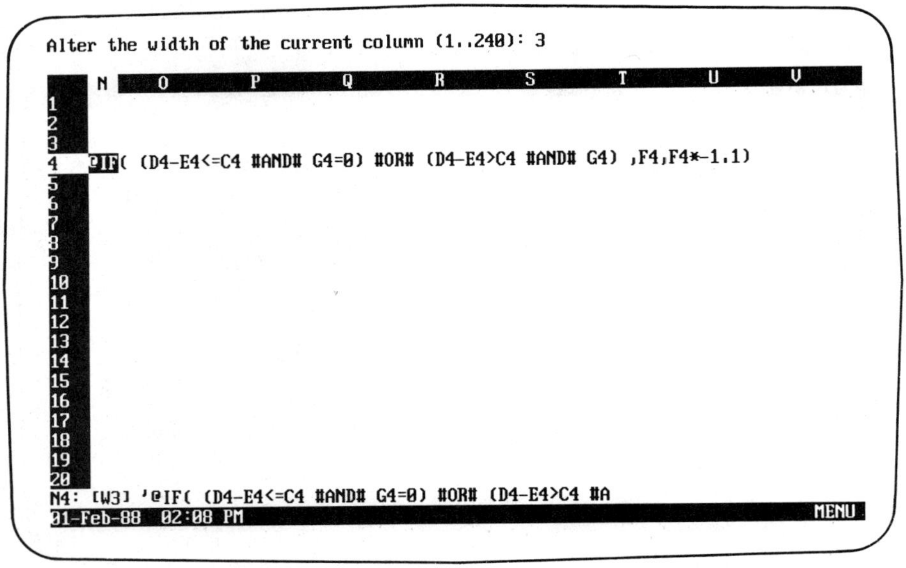

Fig. 6.4. Preparing to reformat the label.

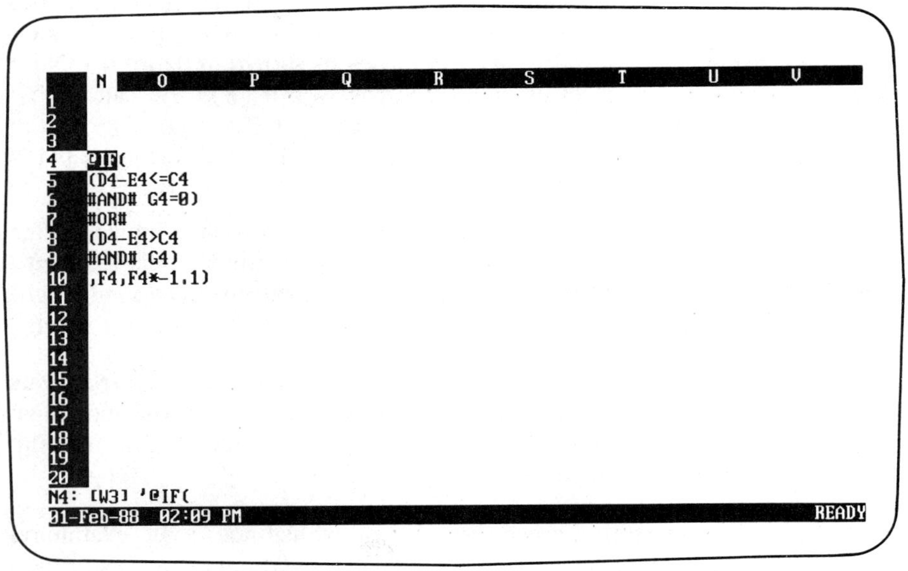

*Fig. 6.5. The result of selecting /**B**lock **R**eformat.*

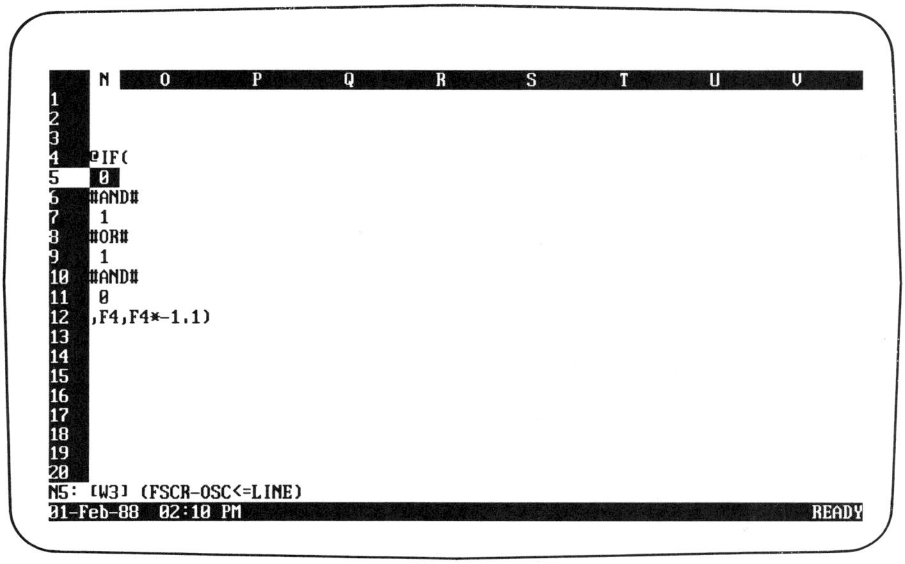

Fig. 6.6. Testing the individual formulas.

The next three figures illustrate one of the best features of this reformatting technique: the fact that you can return the excerpted components to their original positions in the overall formula. You must first reconvert the formulas to labels and then reinvoke the /**B**lock **R**eformat command. Note in figure 6.7 that this time the cursor highlight is pointing at a wide right margin. You must indicate a wide right margin so that the entire "paragraph" of formulas will be reformatted into the original top cell.

Note: If you are combining a large number of formulas into a single line, you can extend the reformatting pointer highlight beyond the 72 characters visible on the display. 240 is the maximum number of characters that can be reformatted into a single cell.

Figure 6.8 shows the formula label after it has been glued back together. You can now edit the label to remove the spaces and leading apostrophe.

Figure 6.9 shows the final product: a complex formula that has been designed, constructed, debugged, and tested in the most efficient, productive way possible.

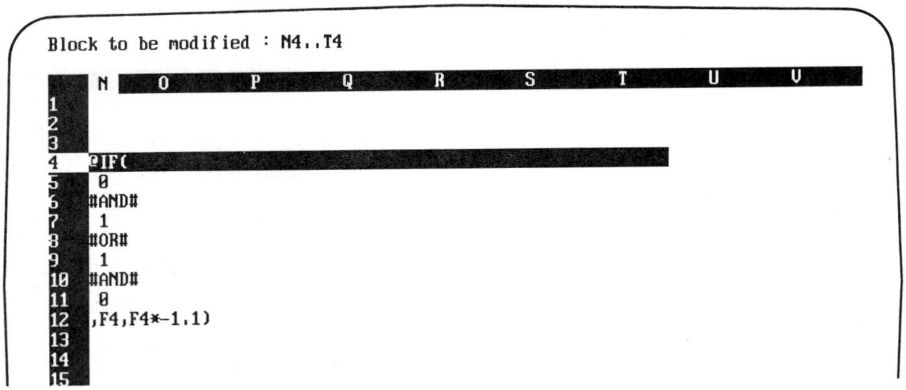

Fig. 6.7. Widening the column for the reformat procedure.

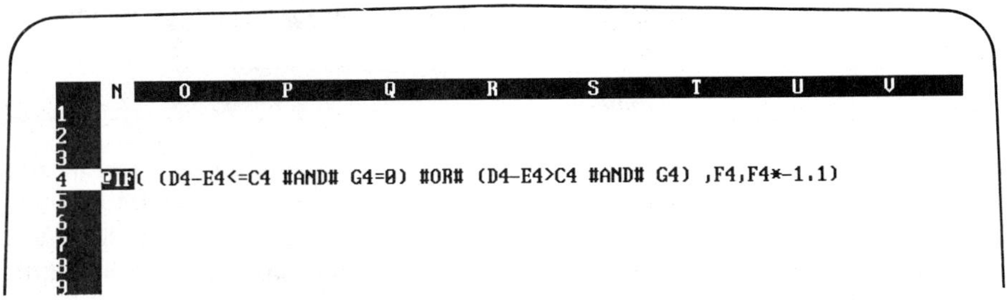

Fig. 6.8. After reformatting the label in one line.

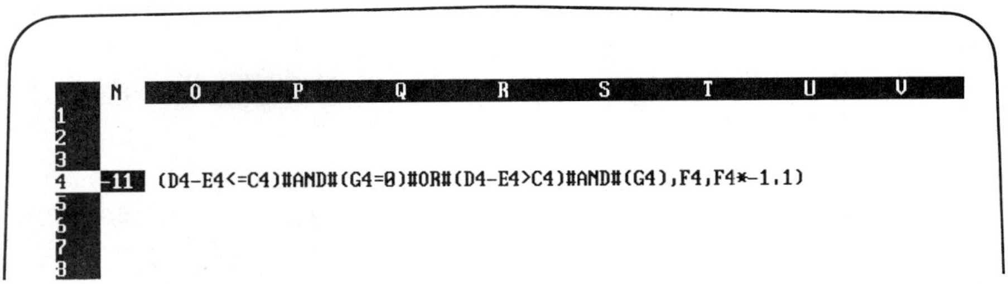

Fig. 6.9. The debugged and tested formula.

Gobel's Second Law

To illuminate the second law—the one that says the longer and more complex the formula, the greater the likelihood that it won't work—consider this series of @IF functions and the possible results. Notice how quickly the complexity of the formulas increases as the formula is developed.

Although the @IF function is discussed in detail later in the chapter, here's a brief explanation of the function's syntax. The @IF function is often called an IF-THEN-ELSE statement. The function evaluates a condition and returns one of two results: the THEN argument if the condition is true, and the ELSE argument if the condition is false.

Formula 1: @IF(A1,1,2)

This formula yields a simple condition (is A1 true?) and two possible results (1 if true, and 2 if false). These factors are not too tough to keep track of.

Formula 2: @IF(A1=B1,1,2)

This one still has only two possible results, but now the condition is more complex. Now consider the next function.

Formula 3: @IF(A1<=B1,@MAX(SALES,B1),@MIN(SALES,A1))

The THEN portion is @MAX(SALES,B1), and the ELSE portion is @MIN(SALES,A1)). The condition is considerably more complex, and the THEN and ELSE portions of the @IF function are much more sophisticated. Now you have to be sure not to misspell the functions or enter an incorrect order within the arguments of the functions. You have to be sure that the THEN and ELSE portions of the @IF function are in their proper places.

Formula 4: @IF(#NOT#A1#OR#NOT#B1=@SUM(BLOCK),
@RAND*@SUM(BLOCK),@DSUM(BLOCK,0,CRIT)

This formula contains so many possible combinations and permutations, you would have a difficult time formulating, constructing, debugging, and optimizing it. Using the /**B**lock **R**eformat technique can help you find any errors.

Some eagle eyes among you will immediately note the missing closing parenthesis needed by the overall @IF function. A missing parenthesis is a common problem during the construction of formulas. A second error in the formula is found between OR and NOT. Two pound (#) signs should be included at that point. The statement should read

@IF(#NOT#A1#OR##NOT#B1 . . .

After fixing these problems (if you succeed in finding them), you press the Enter key with a sense of impending victory. But no! How can the thing still be beeping at you? Easy.

Perhaps you didn't notice that you accidently pressed the space bar when the edit cursor was at the right end of the formula. You thus caused the dreaded "dangling space" problem. This insidious little bug is exceedingly difficult to track down because you can't see the space character. When you press Enter, the edit cursor jumps to the position the space occupies, thus guaranteeing that you won't see the problem. Figure 6.10 shows a formula that looks okay but has a dangling space.

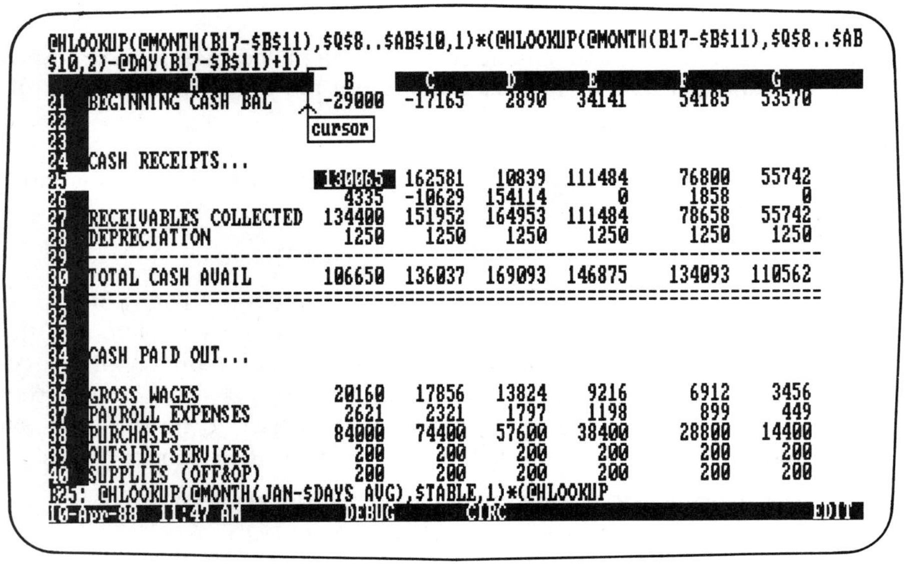

Fig. 6.10. An invisible dangling space.

My experience has been that you can spend hours trying to track down this problem. Why? Because you are looking for something logical, such as a missing comma or parenthesis. If you ever have an error crop up, and you can't discover the source, press the End key on the cursor keypad. If the edit cursor moves farther to the right than the formula, you've found the culprit. Figure 6.11 shows the edit cursor after the End key was pressed. Note that you can now see the space. Simply press Backspace to eliminate it.

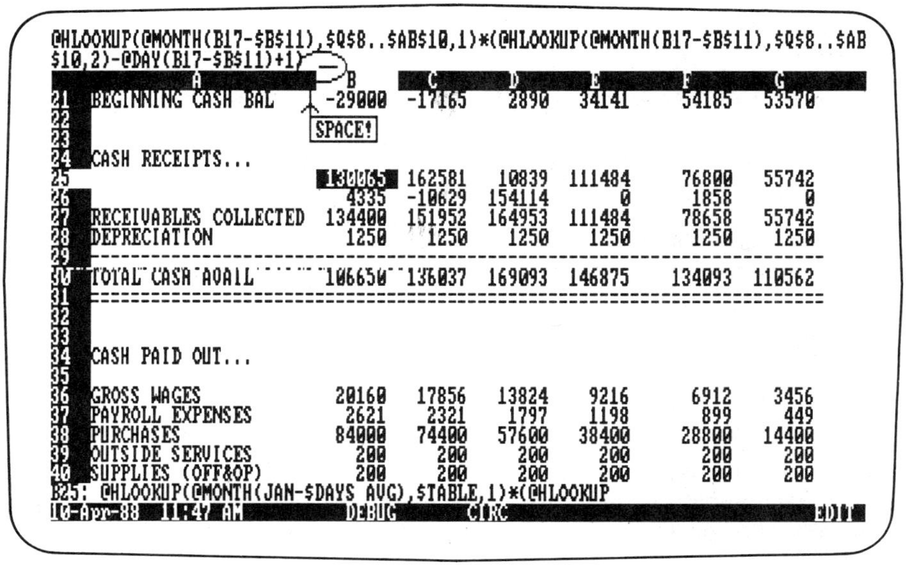

Fig. 6.11. After pressing the End key.

A Summary

By now, you might think that dealing with the problems that can (and will) arise from developing complex formulas is just not worth the time or frustration. But as you become more comfortable with spreadsheet formulas and the debugging functions, you will no doubt want to begin using some extremely sophisticated formulas. And the process will be much easier and more rewarding if you use the editing techniques I've described:

1. Use something you already know, English, to prototype complex formulas.

2. Use the /**B**lock **R**eformat method to create the individual pieces of the formula in separate cells and then knit them together after you have fully constructed, debugged, and optimized the pieces.

Now let's take a close look at Quattro's variety of @functions.

Statistical Functions

As you work in the Quattro spreadsheet, you will no doubt find that you will use statistical functions more often than any other. This fact may surprise you, when you consider how few people (maybe you included) enjoy the study of statistics in school.

Fortunately, most of Quattro's statistical functions are quite practical for day-to-day use. Among these, the @SUM or summation function is preeminent in frequency of use, followed perhaps by @AVG (the averaging function), @MIN, and @MAX. Less often used are @COUNT, @VAR, and @STD.

All the statistical functions accept an unlimited number of arguments (up to the character limit of each cell). Pay special note to this characteristic, because it leads to more efficient and powerful applications.

The syntax for the statistical functions is

@STATFUNC(1,2,3,4, . . . n)

where *STATFUNC* refers to the function's name, and the arguments can refer to a single cell, a block name, a number, a formula, a function, or any combination or number of combinations. Each entry in the list of arguments must be separated from the next entry by a comma.

Table 6.1 lists Quattro's statistical functions.

Table 6.1
Statistical Functions

Function	*Calculates*
@SUM(L1,L2,Ln)	Total of the values contained within the lists
@AVG(L1,L2,Ln)	Average of the values contained within the lists
@COUNT(L1,L2,Ln)	Number of elements in the lists; number of filled cells within a block
@MAX(L1,L2,Ln)	Largest value within the lists
@MIN(L1,L2,Ln)	Smallest value within the lists
@STD(L1,L2,Ln)	Standard deviation of the list values
@VAR(L1,L2,Ln)	Statistical variance of the values contained within the lists

Basic Statistical Functions

Quattro's simpler statistical functions are @SUM, @AVG, @COUNT, @MAX, and @MIN. The most basic of these, @SUM, has many uses outside as well as within a statistical context.

@SUM

@SUM computes the sum of a list or block of entries. The summation function is an alternative to the repetitive use of addition. For example, you can replace the formula +A1+A2+A3 with a block reference in the function @SUM(A1..A3). The longer the list of numbers to add, the more useful @SUM becomes.

@SUM accepts several different kinds of arguments, including numbers, a series of cell references, block-oriented references, spreadsheet functions and formulas, and any combination of these. For some specific examples, see the section entitled "Function Syntax."

The @SUM function ignores any references to empty cells or cells containing text. These cells are considered to be equal to 0 (zero).

@AVG

The @AVG function gives the average of a list of numbers. You can average any type of numeric data with this function. Figure 6.12 shows a simple example of how to use the @AVG function. This table averages several columns of data.

Tip You must be careful when defining blocks to average. Be sure that you *never* include any cells (such as column headings or the dotted line at the end of the column) that are not involved in the actual calculation.

The @AVG function includes as a part of the averaging calculation any cell that is nonblank. Figure 6.13 illustrates what happens when extraneous cells are referenced. The block reference has been extended to include row 14, the row containing the dashes.

Note that the answer in column C is now 292 and not 325 as it was in figure 6.12. The reason is that the sum of the numbers in the column is being divided by 10 rather than 9. In other words, the formula references 10 rows, but the column contains only 9 valid numbers.

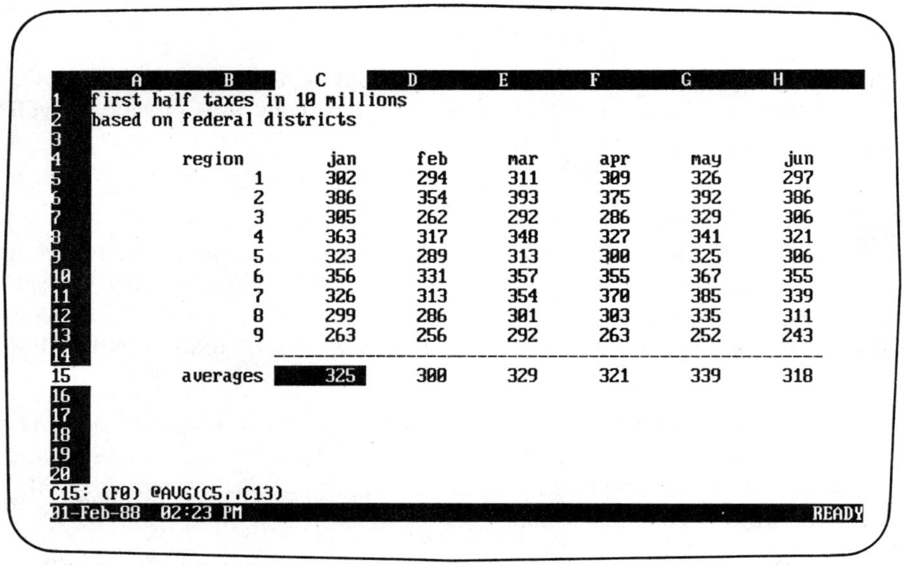

Fig. 6.12. An example of the @AVG function.

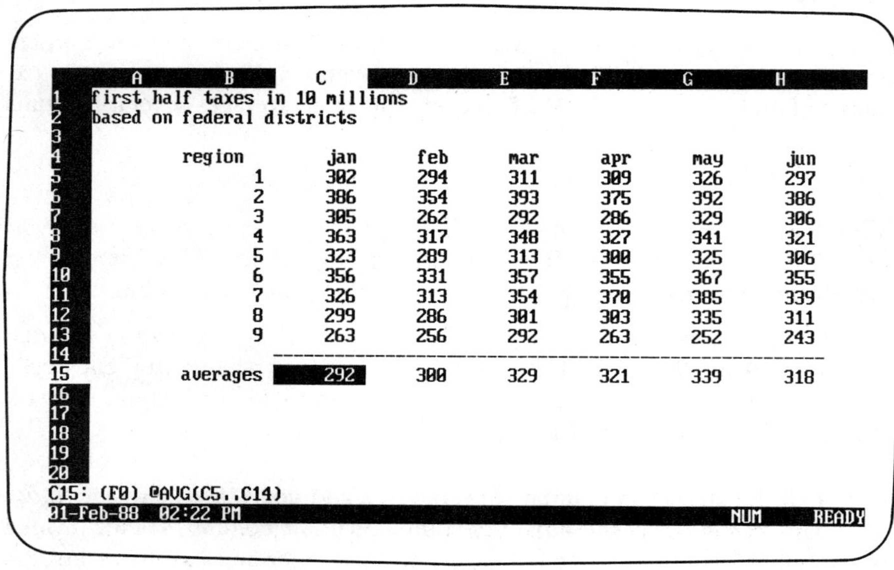

Fig. 6.13. Including a label in the @AVG calculation.

Including extra rows in statistical functions has become the habit of many users. This technique facilitates inserting rows at the end of a table without damaging formulas. Although valid when used with @SUM, this method shouldn't be used with @AVG.

How will @AVG react if one or more of the cells are simply empty? Figure 6.14 shows that the calculation proceeds correctly. The empty cell, C13, is ignored in the average.

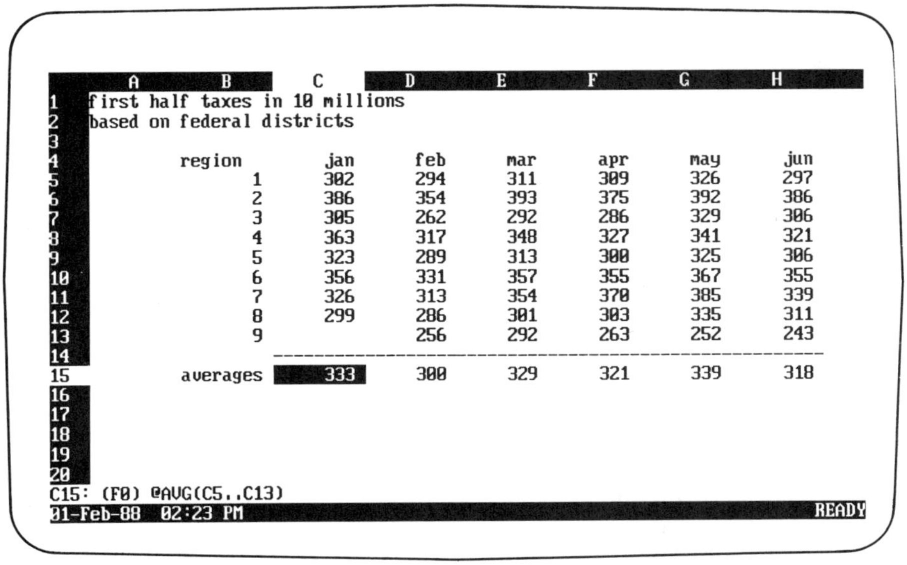

	A	B	C	D	E	F	G	H
1	first half taxes in 10 millions							
2	based on federal districts							
3								
4		region	jan	feb	mar	apr	may	jun
5		1	302	294	311	309	326	297
6		2	386	354	393	375	392	386
7		3	305	262	292	286	329	306
8		4	363	317	348	327	341	321
9		5	323	289	313	300	325	306
10		6	356	331	357	355	367	355
11		7	326	313	354	370	385	339
12		8	299	286	301	303	335	311
13		9		256	292	263	252	243
14			----------	----------	----------	----------	----------	----------
15		averages	333	300	329	321	339	318
16								
17								
18								
19								
20								

C15: (F0) @AVG(C5..C13)

01-Feb-88 02:23 PM READY

Fig. 6.14. Including a blank cell in the @AVG calculation.

@COUNT

The @COUNT function is designed to count the number of elements in a list. The elements counted can include numbers, text, dates, and times. Another way of thinking of @COUNT is that it indicates how many of the referenced cells contain data.

Tip Do not use a single cell reference within an @COUNT function, because the function will return an error if the cell is blank. Figure 6.15 shows an @COUNT function that is looking at a completely empty cell (A3). Yet the function returns an answer of 1. You are looking at a bona fide bug. Please don't blame Borland for the problem. Lotus 1-2-3 has had the problem for years, and no doubt Borland wants to be compatible right down to having the same bugs!

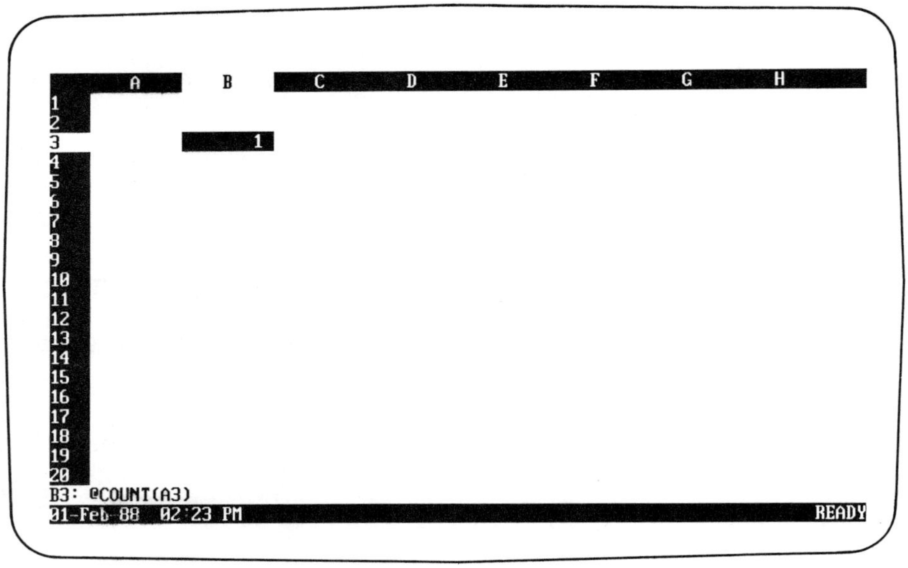

Fig. 6.15. The results of using a single cell reference with @COUNT.

Tip To prevent inaccurate single-cell counting, simply make the cell a block-oriented reference (A3..A3), as shown in figure 6.16.

All the caveats that apply to @AVG also apply to @COUNT. You must not include any extra cells. If you do, the count is likely to be wrong. Figure 6.17 shows what will happen if you include too many cells in your counting function. The @COUNT function counts everything, not just numbers. The column heading and dashed line labels are included in the count. For an accurate count, the function should be changed to @COUNT(C5..C13).

You might be surprised by the fact that the @COUNT function is also insensitive to the @ERR or @NA functions (discussed later in this chapter). The function counts cells displaying ERR and NA just as it would count any other cell entry.

@MAX

The @MAX and @MIN functions are frequently overlooked because their operations seem too obvious and not very useful. As you will see, however, these functions have some secrets to yield.

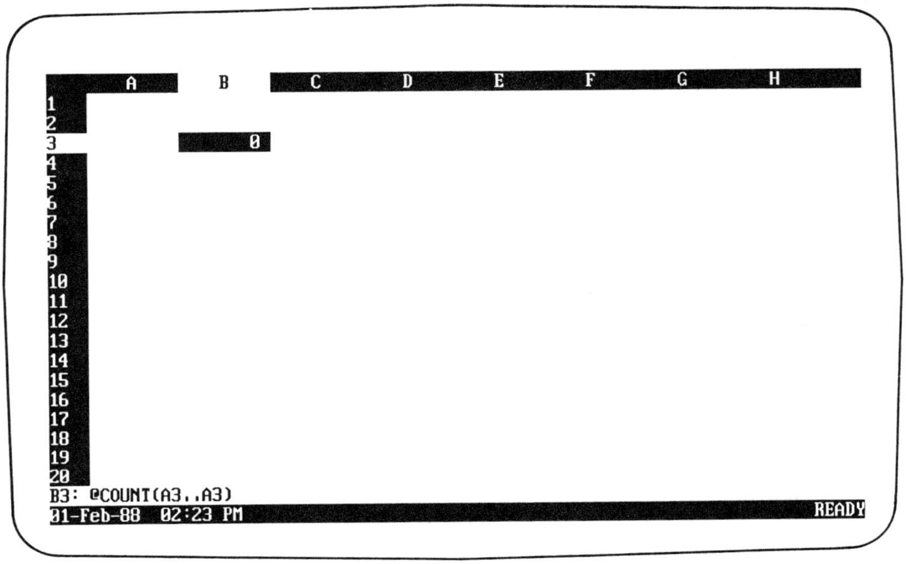

Fig. 6.16. After changing the cell reference to a block-oriented reference.

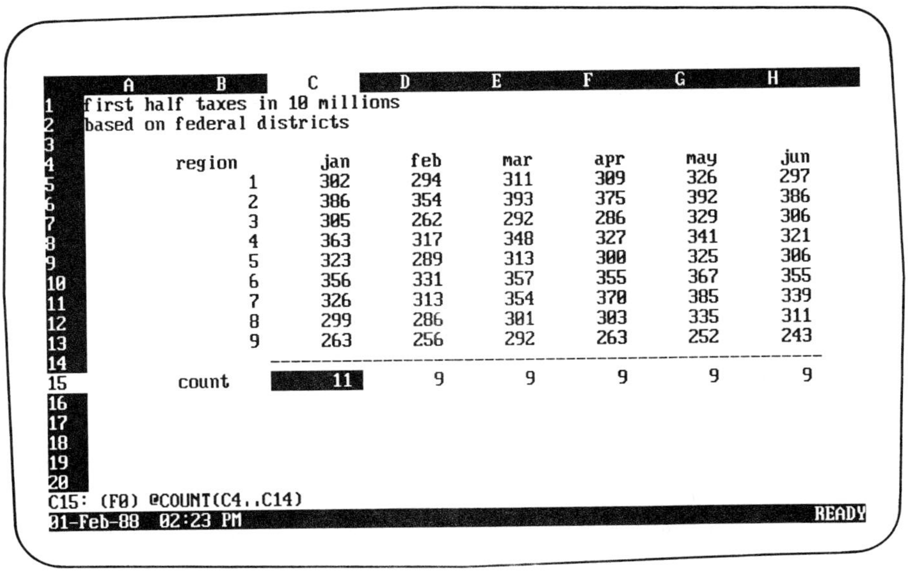

Fig. 6.17. Including extra cells in the @COUNT function.

@MAX displays the maximum or largest numerical value found in a given block of cells. The @MAX function, like the other statistical functions, requires a list-oriented argument. Unlike some of the other functions, however, @MAX is not designed to be used with cells containing text.

Figure 6.18 shows a simple use of the @MAX function. In this example, @MAX finds the region contributing the greatest number of tax dollars in any month.

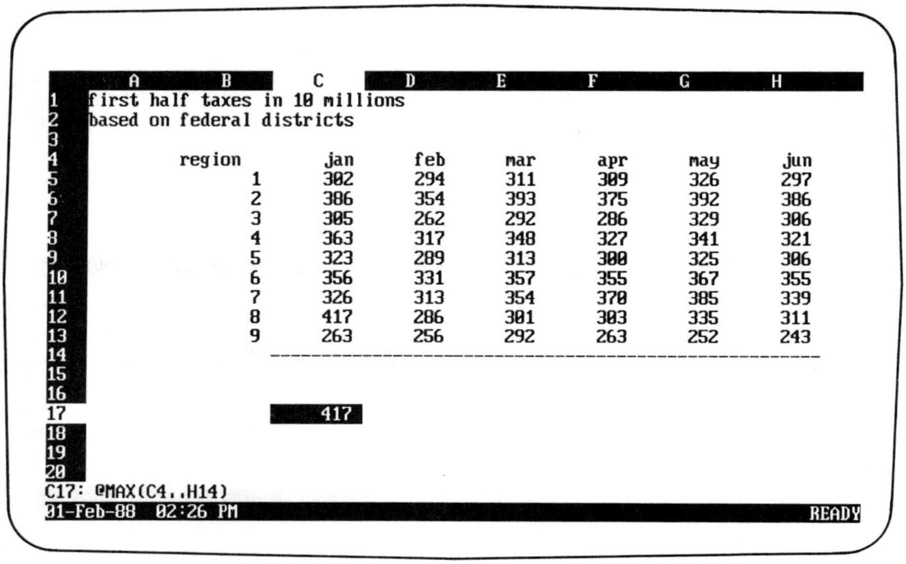

first half taxes in 10 millions
based on federal districts

region	jan	feb	mar	apr	may	jun
1	302	294	311	309	326	297
2	386	354	393	375	392	386
3	305	262	292	286	329	306
4	363	317	348	327	341	321
5	323	289	313	300	325	306
6	356	331	357	355	367	355
7	326	313	354	370	385	339
8	417	286	301	303	335	311
9	263	256	292	263	252	243

417

C17: @MAX(C4..H14)
01-Feb-88 02:26 PM READY

Fig. 6.18. A simple @MAX example.

Only the highest number in the table, 417, has been chosen. As you can see, this number is drawn from cell C12.

The @MAX function has no trouble with block references that include text or blank cells, because the function is looking for the largest number. Text cells and blank cells are valued at zero and are thus not a problem—unless you are looking for the largest negative number. If you are searching for the largest negative number and have included in the block accidental references to blank or text cells, your answer will always be 0 (zero) and incorrect.

If a cell referenced by @MAX has the value ERR or NA, @MAX displays ERR.

Let's look at another practical use of @MAX. A common problem with spreadsheet budgeting is that the formulas do not have realistic limits on them. To illustrate the problem and how @MAX can help, let's pretend that you are about to introduce a brand new consumer product, a disposable shaver that counts how many times you have used it and throws itself away before you destroy your skin.

The time has come for you to decide how much money to allocate to the advertising budget. Like nearly everyone before you, you decide to make advertising a percentage of sales. Why? Because. You set up the budget line item and discover a sad fact. Look at figure 6.19.

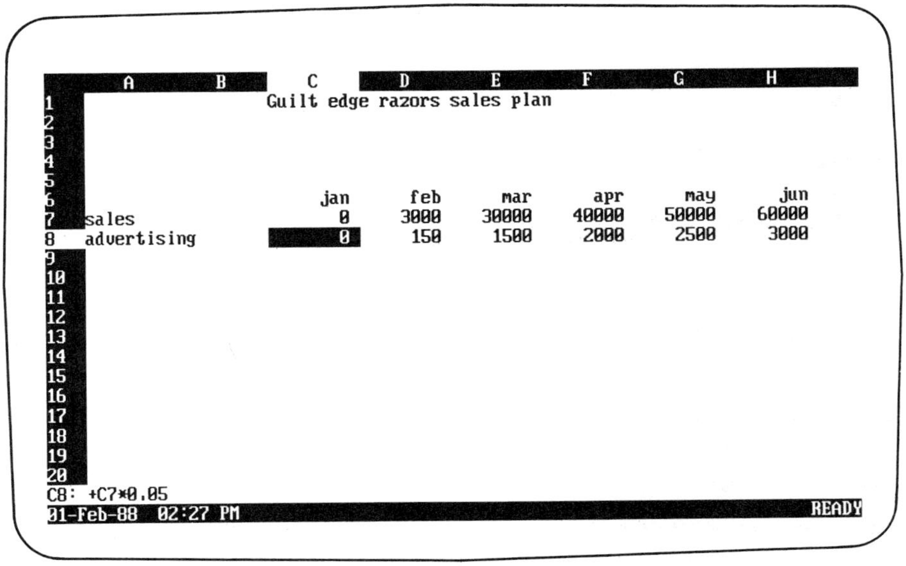

Fig. 6.19. A sales plan that sets advertising at a percentage of sales.

Yes, of course. If you are introducing a new product, you have had no sales yet. Thus you will have no money for advertising until something is sold. But nothing will be sold until you have advertised the product.

The @MAX function can neatly solve this and like problems. You can use @MAX to put a limit on how low a calculation will be allowed to go (put a floor under a calculation).

Figure 6.20 uses an @MAX function with two arguments. The first argument is an absolute reference to a floor, or limiting number, in cell D3. The second argument refers to the sales line item (C7), which in the first two months is quite low.

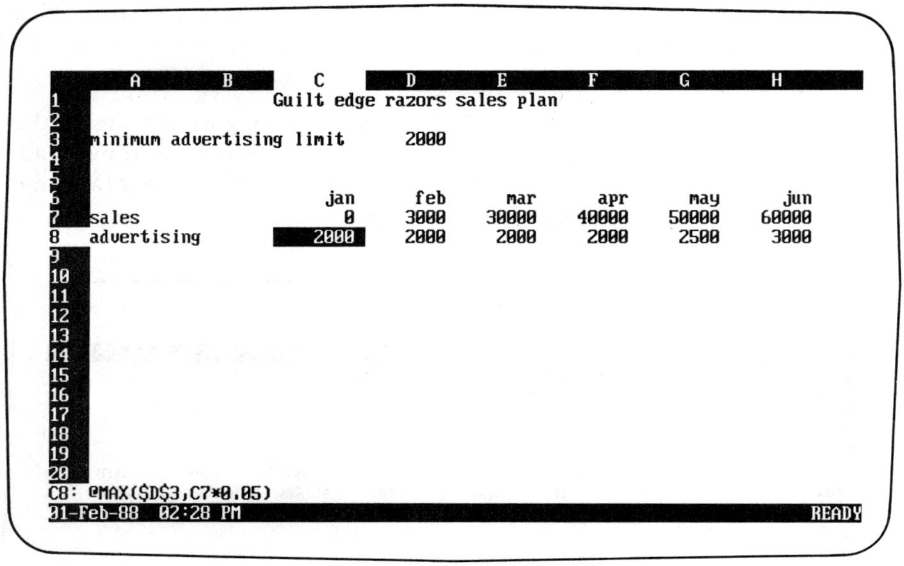

Fig. 6.20. Using @MAX to set a lower limit.

Now, advertising for the first months is guaranteed by the @MAX choice of the larger number. In the case of the first two months, @MAX chooses 2000 rather than 5 percent of sales, which is equal to 0. Once the 5 percent calculation exceeds the floor limit, @MAX begins to use this calculation.

The next section shows how to combine @MAX and @MIN to put upper and lower limits on line item calculations.

@MIN

The @MIN function is like @MAX except that @MIN selects the *lowest* value occurring in a given block of cells.

Tip Do not include in an @MIN function any cells that are blank or that contain text. @MIN considers blank cells and text cells to be equal to 0 (zero) and will probably incorrectly select such a cell, unless cells containing negative numbers are included in the argument.

In the example described with the @MAX function, a floor limit was placed on a line item. The @MIN function can perform the reciprocal service by placing an upper limit on growth.

Using the advertising budget as an example, imagine that you have just been made the managing director of Rolls Royce Motor Cars Ltd. One of your first tasks is to approve the next year's budget. Unfortunately, much unnecessary expenditure appears to be planned. If you spend advertising pounds beyond a certain limit, you will be throwing money away for two reasons:

1. You are production limited. Cloning cows to make sure that the leather in the front and back seats match takes a long time.

2. You are market limited. Only so many people in the world have the money to buy a car like your product. So if you advertise excessively, the "commoners" will just become mad at you because they can't afford your product.

Figure 6.21 shows a model that puts the cap on advertising with @MIN.

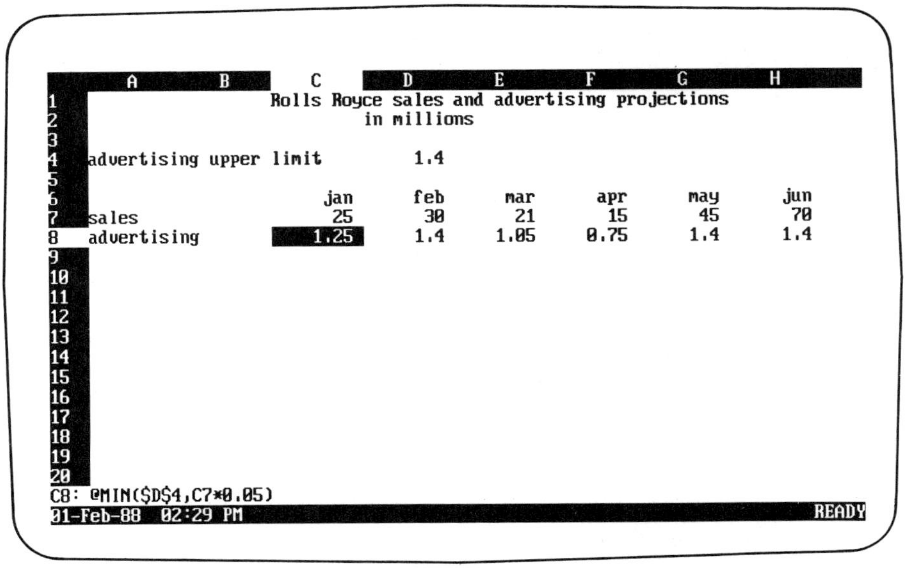

Fig. 6.21. Using @MIN to set an upper limit.

To complete the discussion of @MIN and @MAX, figure 6.22 demonstrates how to use both functions to put upper and lower limits on a budget line item.

Notice that the budget is limited on the low end for both January and February. The next three months use the normal sales-times-percent calculation. The last month in the model is limited on the upper end. Here's the formula that produces these results:

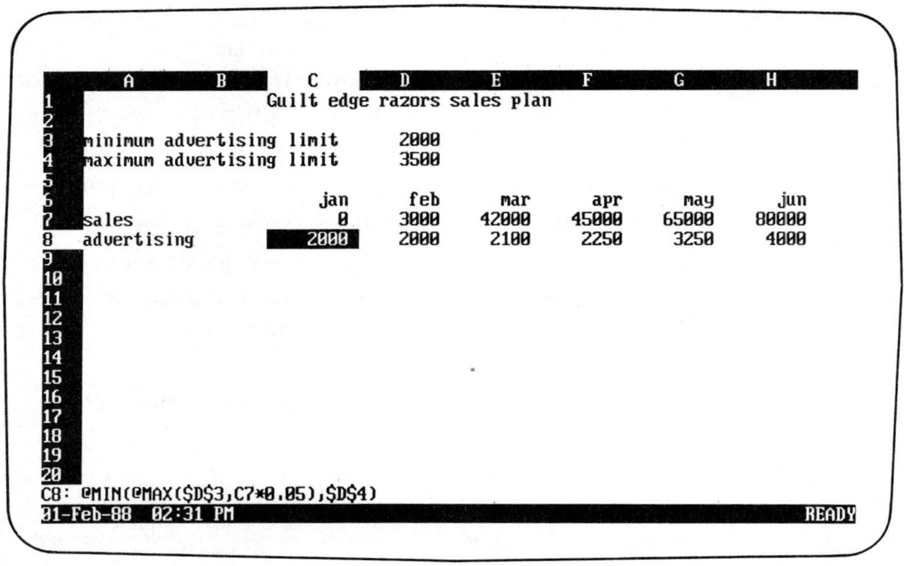

Fig. 6.22. Combining @MAX and @MIN to set lower and upper limits.

@MIN(@MAX(D3,C7*0.05),D4)

This formula is an example of using one function as the argument for another function. The @MIN function takes care of the upper limit by choosing either the last argument, D4, or the result of the @MAX function. This technique may seem confusing, but try it out. Once you've used it, you may find that you have much less need for the @IF function.

Advanced Statistical Functions

Quattro has two advanced statistical functions: @STD, which computes the *standard deviation* of a population; and @VAR, which computes the population *variance*. Variance and standard deviation are related dispersion statistics. The variance is the amount of deviation from the mean. The standard deviation, closely related to the variance, is the degree of deviation from the mean. The automatic calculations provided by @STD and @VAR can save you much time and effort in statistical analysis.

@STD

Standard deviation is the part of statistics that gives most statistics students a big headache. But in Quattro, working with standard deviation is not that difficult once you see how you can use the @STD function.

The syntax for @STD is

@STD(values_list)

where *values_list* can be a block of cells containing values, a list of numbers, or the result of formulas.

A more precise version of the averaging function, @STD gives you an indication of how well the average number (usually called the *mean*) describes the data being averaged. The lower the standard deviation number returned, the more accurately the mean describes the data. A standard deviation of 0 (zero) means that no data entries deviate from the mean. For example, the function @STD(5,5,5,5) returns 0. The mean, of course, is 5.

You can use @STD as an easy method for finding situations that are exceptional or out of the normal or acceptable range. The answer generated by the @STD function is a number that is a distance of one standard deviation from the mean. The formula @AVG(0,1,2,3,4) returns 2. The formula @STD(0,1,2,3,4) results in 1.4. (See row 2 of fig. 6.23.) But what do these results tell you?

As a general rule, 67 percent of the values in a population of values will fall one standard deviation from the mean. Thus, in this case, 67 percent of the values included in the functions' calculations are between .6 and 3.4. (Add and subtract the standard deviation of 1.4 from the mean of 2.) Obviously, this particular answer is not very helpful, because the quantity of elements in the values list is small. When you are dealing with a large group of elements, however, the @STD function can help you grasp the overall nature of your data.

Figure 6.23 illustrates a series of numbers with averaging functions in column A, and the @STD function applicable to the number series in column K. Note that in row 8, the numbers do not deviate from the average at all (@STD = 0.0), and in row 14, a significant deviation is evidenced (@STD = 3544.0).

The type of data that @STD best describes in general business applications is time-series data dealing with a single kind of data. Some examples include temperature over time, widths of gaps in car doors, time to process invoices, intelligence in the population, and many others.

Figure 6.24 shows a block of numbers that are a record of how many days passed before a customer paid a bill. For instance, the first entry under January indicates that, during the period being tracked, 30 days elapsed between an invoice and receipt of payment.

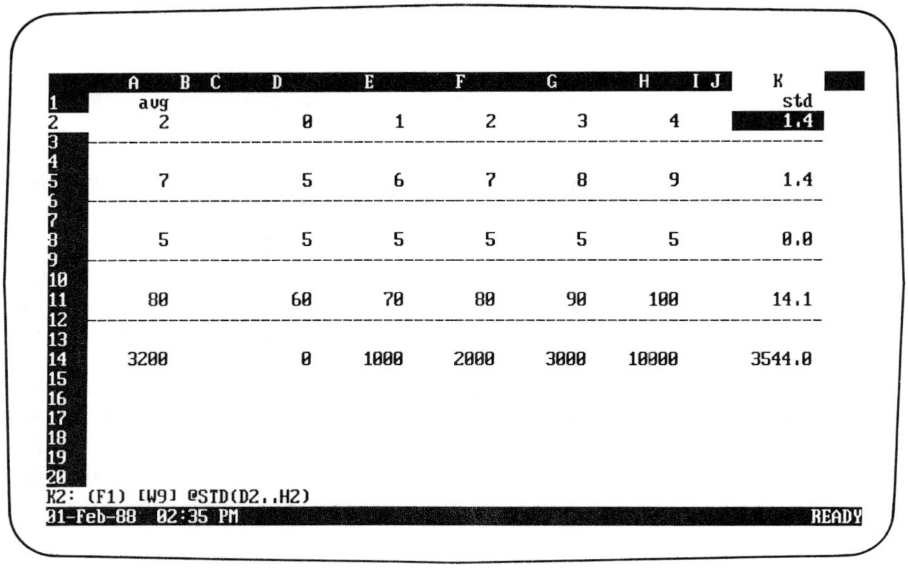

Fig. 6.23. Some sample averaging and standard deviation calculations.

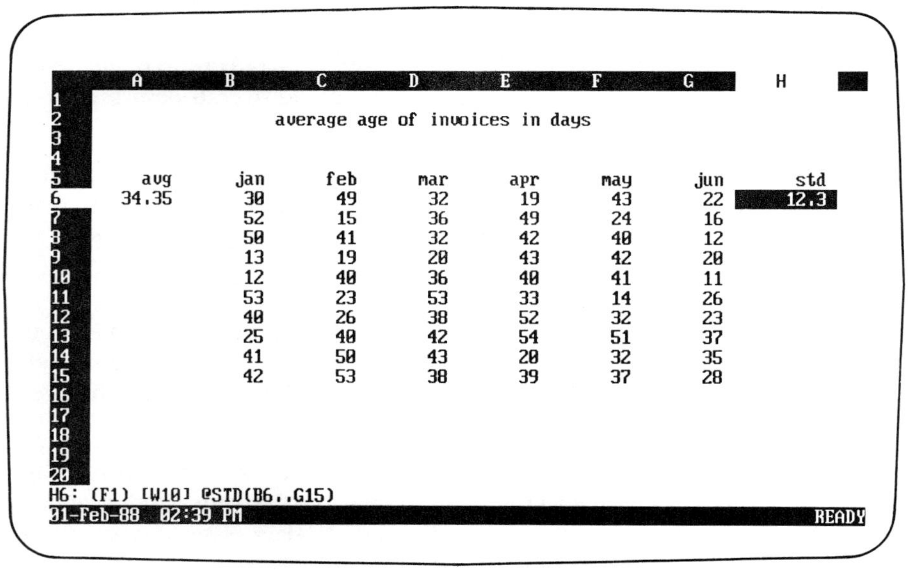

Fig. 6.24. An invoice-aging analysis.

In column A, the @AVG function shows that during the first six months of the year, payment was received, on average, 34.35 days after invoicing. Column K holds the standard deviation, 12.3, of the same block of numbers. What can you gather from these statistics? If you just look at the average number, you might conclude that everything is in pretty good shape. Yet the standard deviation number reveals that some figures significantly deviate from this average. In other words, things are NOT running smoothly in the collections department.

Figure 6.25 illustrates how to use both the average number and the standard deviation to get a better picture of the overall situation. At the bottom of the figure, the standard deviation has been subtracted from the average (column B) and added to the average (column F). These simple formulas tell the controller that 67 percent of all the numbers in the block referenced are between 22.0 and 46.7 (days). From a management perspective, the controller should determine what led to the early payments so that this customer behavior can be encouraged, and examine and discourage the late payments.

	A	B	C	D	E	F	G	H
1								
2			average age of invoices in days					
3								
4								
5	avg	jan	feb	mar	apr	may	jun	std
6	----------	----------	----------	----------	----------	----------	----------	----------
7	34.35	30	49	32	19	43	22	12.3
8		52	15	36	49	24	16	
9		50	41	32	42	40	12	
10		13	19	20	43	42	20	
11		12	40	36	40	41	11	
12		53	23	53	33	14	26	
13		40	26	30	52	32	23	
14		25	40	42	54	51	37	
15		41	50	43	20	32	35	
16		42	53	38	39	37	28	
17								
18		-std days		avg		+std days		
19		22		34.4		46.7		
20		+D19-H7				+D19+H7		

D20:

01-Feb-88 02:42 PM READY

Fig. 6.25. Using @AVG and @STD to obtain a clearer analysis.

Tip Do not include external cell references that are blank or contain text, NA, or ERR. The @STD function considers blank cells to be active and equal to zero, and will dangerously skew the results. If referenced cells contain text, NA, or ERR, the @STD function returns ERR.

Technically, the Quattro standard deviation function gives you the standard deviation of a population, not a sample. To get a completely accurate answer, you thus need all the data involved rather than merely a random sample, such as 10 percent of the data.

@VAR

The @VAR function is a statistic that describes the variability of a list of numbers. The syntax of @VAR is

@VAR(values_list)

where *values_list* can be a list of numbers, the result of a series of formulas, a reference to external values, or a mix of all these components.

The @VAR function is infrequently used. The formula to determine the variance of a list of numbers is part of the formula that leads to the more useful standard deviation: the standard deviation of a population is the square root of the variance.

Mathematical Functions for General Use

Although many of the functions grouped under the category of math functions are not of primary interest to business-oriented spreadsheet users, several of these functions provide critical resources for intermediate to advanced spreadsheet users and developers.

This section explores math functions that can round numbers, remove decimal values from numbers, recognize overall patterns within values, generate random numbers, and convert negative values to positive values automatically. Table 6.2 summarizes these functions. See the section in Chapter 7 entitled "Engineering and Scientific Functions" for information on mathematical functions especially useful to the scientific and engineering fields.

@ROUND

In contrast to the formatting commands that round numbers only in terms of the display, the @ROUND function rounds numbers both in the display and also in memory. Use of this function can eliminate the accumulated error phenomenon, which occurs when @SUM formulas that add columns of numbers appear to give incorrect answers because of rounding in the display and not in memory. For example:

Table 6.2
General Mathematical Functions

Function	*Description*
@ROUND(number,places)	Rounds a number to a specified number of decimal places
@INT(number)	Computes the integer portion of a specified number
@MOD(number,divisor)	Computes the remainder (modulus) of a division operation
@RAND	Generates random numbers
@ABS(number)	Computes the absolute value of a number

```
  3.3
  3.3
 +3.3
 ----
 10.0
```

The syntax of the @ROUND function is

@ROUND(number,places)

where *number* is the number to be rounded and can be either a number, a cell reference, a formula, or a block name. The second argument, *places*, indicates the number of decimal places. For instance, @ROUND(123.45,1) results in the number 123.5.

You can use either a positive or negative number for the places argument. Using a negative number rounds a number to some whole number. For example, the function @ROUND(123.45,-1) rounds to 120.

@INT

The first "utility" function for users is the @INT function. The integer function truncates a number to the next lower whole number. Digits to the right of the decimal point are eliminated. Thus, the number 123.45 becomes 123 in both memory and the display when adjusted with @INT(123.45).

The syntax for the integer function is

@INT(number)

where *number* can be a number, a cell reference, a formula, or a block name.

Although @INT provides only the whole-number equivalent of a real number, you can combine this function with other spreadsheet operators and functions to yield great utility. For instance, you may want to isolate the decimal amount of a number. Consider the following formula:

4.56-@INT(4.56)

This formula efficiently removes the whole number from the number 4.56, which leaves the decimal part (0.56) as the remainder.

Because @INT not merely displays but also stores only the whole-number portion, you can combine @INT with @NOW to isolate the integer portion of the current date so that you can use it in calculations. For more information, refer to the discussion of @NOW in the "Date and Time Functions" section of this chapter.

@MOD

The @MOD function name is short for *modulus*, another name for the remainder of a division operation. For example, you can divide 5 into 7 only once, with a remainder of 2. The syntax of the @MOD function is

@MOD(number,divisor)

where *number* can be a number, a cell reference, a formula, or a block name. The function @MOD(7,5) gives you the number 2.

At first glance this information may appear to be just another little piece of spreadsheet trivia. The @MOD function can prove to be a powerful tool, however, in both spreadsheets and macro logic.

Suppose that you are given the task of determining on what day of the week any date occurred. If you were asked about Thanksgiving Day, you would have no problem. Almost everybody knows that Thanksgiving always falls on a Thursday. But what about your own birthday? On what day did that fall last year?

The following formula determines the day of the week of any date within the range of dates that Quattro can deal with (December 31, 1899, to December 31, 2178):

@MOD(@DATE(87,12,15),7)

The result of this particular formula is the number 3. The number being divided is the date December 15, 1987. The divisor is the number 7. Why 7? Because each week contains 7 days, and if you divide a serial date by 7, the remainder tells you on what day of the week that date occurred or will occur. (For more on the @DATE function, see this chapter's "Date and Time Functions" section.)

A result of 3 means that the date occurs on a Tuesday, the third day of the week. Following is a table that shows the days of the week and the corresponding day numbers:

0 = Saturday
1 = Sunday
2 = Monday
3 = Tuesday
4 = Wednesday
5 = Thursday
6 = Friday

Why would a 0 mean a date occurred on a Saturday? Because Saturday is the seventh day of the week. If you divide 7 into the seventh day of the week, you get no remainder. In other words, the remainder is 0.

The @MOD function can be invaluable in some database applications when you want to examine transactions or records based on the day of the week. A conditional formula such as @MOD(date,7)=3, where *date* is the block name for the first record under a Date field name, will select only those records that occurred on a Tuesday, no matter what month, day, or year they happen to be.

Another use of the @MOD function can tell you whether a number is odd or even. Figure 6.26 contains two functionally identical formulas. The formula @IF(@MOD(6,2),"ODD","EVEN") divides 6 by 2, which results in an answer of 0 (zero) because no remainder is left. Thus the @MOD function's answer of 0 is used by the @IF function to indicate a false condition (0). Because the condition is false, the @IF function chooses the second alternative on the right (EVEN). If a remainder did exist, it would be a 1, and the @IF function would return the answer ODD. (For more details on the syntax of the @IF function, refer to the "Logical Functions" section of this chapter.)

@RAND

The @RAND function is a random number generator. A random number generator can provide you with a statistically valid random list of numbers upon which to base a calculation. You may need a random number, for example, when you are conducting an audit of purchase orders.

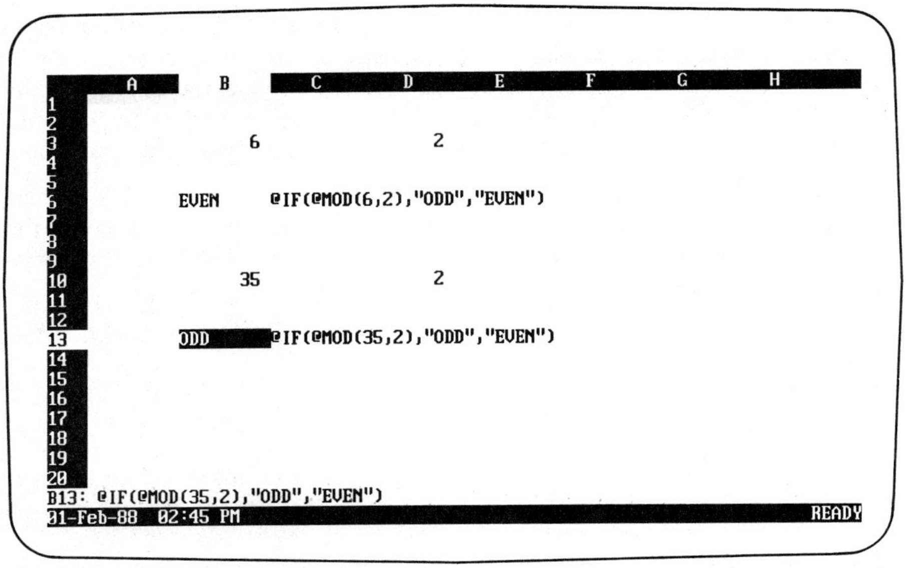

Fig. 6.26. Using @MOD to tell you whether a number is odd or even.

The syntax for this function is simply @RAND. No argument is required. The @RAND function generates a number greater than 0 and less than 1. Of course, this capability is not terribly useful by itself. To produce a range of numbers for the purchase-order audit, for example, you need to use other factors in concert with the @RAND function.

Suppose that you need to audit purchase-order numbers ranging from number 1500 to 2000. To produce the appropriate range of numbers, in this case 500 numbers (2000-1500), you might multiply the @RAND function by 500, as shown in the formula in cell B3 of figure 6.27.

The results of this formula change every time the spreadsheet is recalculated. The formula produces numbers such as those listed in figure 6.27. This list illustrates two problems. First, and most obvious, you don't need all the precision to the right of the decimal point (@RAND defaults to this number of decimal places). Second, the fact that the number 500 doesn't show up in the list is no accident. The reason is that the formula is multiplying by 500 a number which is less than 1.

The solution to the first problem is simply to nest the entire formula inside the @INT function. The solution to the second problem is to use the number 501 rather than 500. The new formula is

```
@INT(@RAND*501)
```

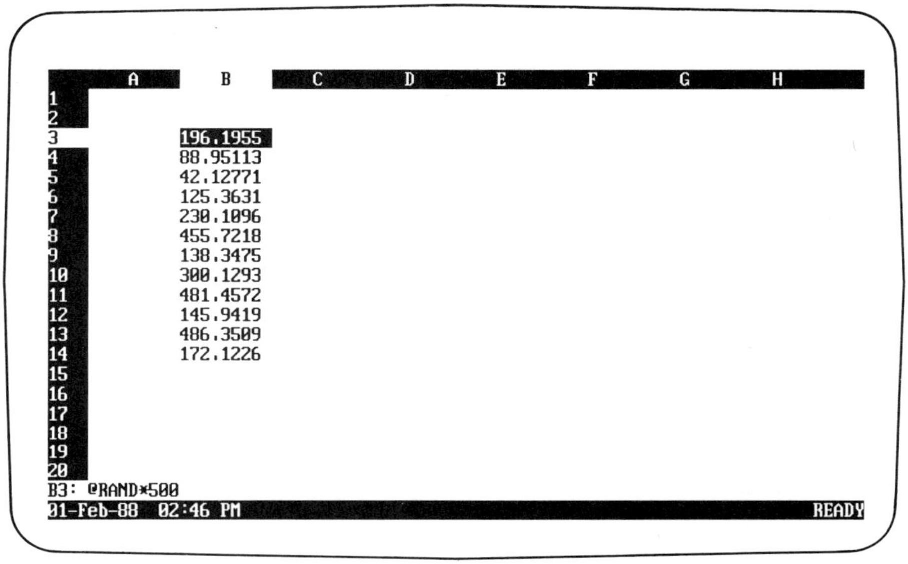

Fig. 6.27. A list of random numbers.

This new formula can create a list of numbers similar to the one in figure 6.28. As you can see, the list is now composed of whole numbers, including an instance of the number 500. (Keep in mind, however, that the number 500 will not appear every time you recalculate the worksheet.)

But this formula does not completely satisfy the purchase order example. The random numbers must be numbered between 1500 and 2000. To finish the task, you must modify the formula by adding the starting number, in this case 1500, to the formula:

@INT(@RAND*501)+1500

If you add a number to a randomly generated number, the number added becomes, in effect, a floor or starting number. Figure 6.29 shows a sample of the list produced with this formula.

Once you have completed the generation of the random list, it's a good idea to convert the numbers in the list to their equivalent values to prevent any change to the list by an accidental recalculation. You can convert the numbers with the /**B**lock **A**dvanced **V**alues command. This advanced command also generates a unique list that eliminates any duplications.

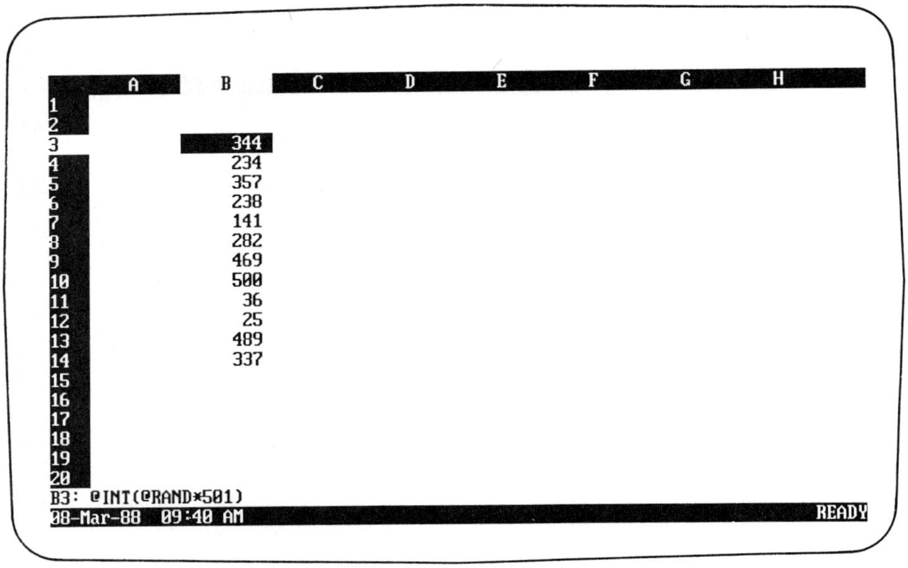

Fig. 6.28. Using @INT with @RAND to generate random whole numbers.

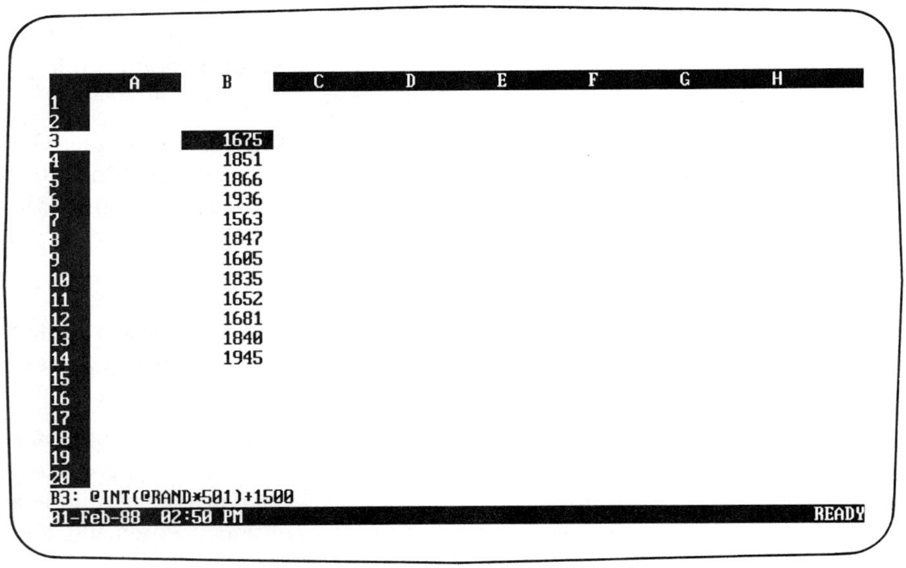

Fig. 6.29. After setting a starting number of 1500.

Tip Unlike other spreadsheets, the @RAND function in Quattro is not automatically reevaluated every time you press the Calc key. Quattro uses minimal recalculation to save time. With minimal recalculation, Quattro recalculates only the formulas that depend on data which has changed since the last recalculation.

Tip If you want to use @RAND for model simulations, ensure that all the factors which adjust the function are external cell references. Then you can force a recalculation just by entering a new variable in the referenced cell.

@ABS

The @ABS function computes the absolute value of a number. Use this function when you need to convert a value from negative to positive. The syntax for @ABS is

@ABS(number)

where *number* can be a number or a cell reference.

The @ABS function is particularly useful when a calculation in one area of your spreadsheet results in a negative value that you need to use as a positive value in another area of your spreadsheet. For example, you can reference a depreciation calculation for use in the expense portion of an income statement. Figure 6.30 shows how you can use the @ABS function for this purpose. Cell B8 contains the formula @ABS(B15); this formula returns to cell B8 the absolute value of the value contained in cell B15. Although B15 contains negative 33, the formula in B8 returns positive 33. The other cells in row 8 contain similar formulas.

Logical Functions

The quintessential reason for Quattro's existence is the program's capability to perform what-if analysis. One of the major factors contributing to this capability is Quattro's repertory of logical and related table-handling functions. This section explores these logical functions and discusses how you can use them most efficiently.

Table 6.3 lists the logical functions, with brief descriptions of their actions.

@IF

The most important and most useful of the logical functions is the @IF function, which allows the spreadsheet to perform decisions in an automated fashion. The syntax of the @IF function is

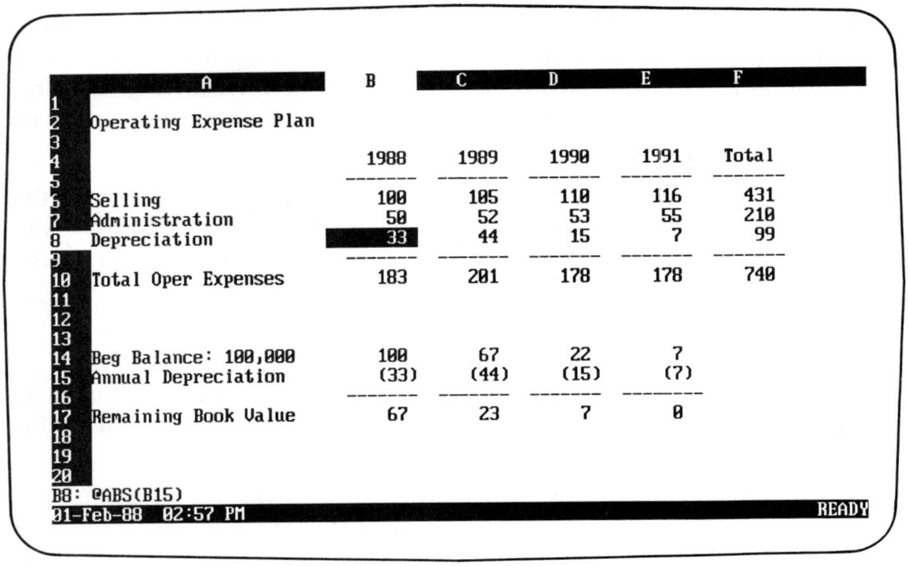

	A	B	C	D	E	F
1						
2	Operating Expense Plan					
3						
4		1988	1989	1990	1991	Total
5		-------	-------	-------	-------	-------
6	Selling	100	105	110	116	431
7	Administration	50	52	53	55	210
8	Depreciation	33	44	15	7	99
9		-------	-------	-------	-------	-------
10	Total Oper Expenses	183	201	178	178	740
11						
12						
13						
14	Beg Balance: 100,000	100	67	22	7	
15	Annual Depreciation	(33)	(44)	(15)	(7)	
16		-------	-------	-------	--------	
17	Remaining Book Value	67	23	7	0	
18						
19						
20						

B8: @ABS(B15)
01-Feb-88 02:57 PM READY

Fig. 6.30. Using @ABS in the worksheet.

Table 6.3
Logical Functions

Function	*Description*
@IF(condition,a,b)	Tests condition, and if condition is true, returns a; if condition is false, returns b
@ISSTRING(cell reference)	Results in 1 if cell is text, and 0 if cell is not
@ISNUMBER(cell reference)	Displays 1 if cell contains a value, and 0 if cell does not contain a value (is text)
@TRUE	Returns a value of 1
@FALSE	Returns a value of 0
@ISNA(cell reference)	Displays 1 if referenced cell is NA; otherwise, returns 0
@ISERR(cell reference)	Displays 1 if referenced cell is ERR; otherwise, returns 0

@IF(condition,true_result,false_result)

where *condition* can be any number, or any comparison statement that uses a logical operator such as equal (=) or greater than (>). The *true_result* and *false_result* arguments each can be any number, text, formula, function, or mix of the above, as long as data types within the calculations are in agreement. (For example, "5 + DAVE" makes no sense.)

The @IF function was briefly discussed at the beginning of this chapter. As you may recall, @IF evaluates the condition and returns true_result if the condition is true, and false_result if the condition is false. For example, the formula @IF(A1=5,500,A1*10) results in the number 500 if A1 is equal to 5, and returns a value that is 10 times whatever is in A1 if A1 is not equal to 5.

It is important to remember that you have complete flexibility as to what can be placed in the results arguments. The formula @IF(A1=5,500,"OOPS") displays the text OOPS in the cell if A1 is not equal to 5.

Multiple Conditional Tests

If you must test for more than two possible conditions, you might want to consider the use of the logical operators #NOT#, #AND#, and #OR#.

The colloquial expression "God willing and the creek don't rise" provides an example of several possible eventualities. You can use these variables:

God willing

creek don't rise

in this @IF function:

@IF(B2="god wills"#AND#B3="creek don't rise","ok","swim")

This function determines what will happen based on the contents of the variables.

Enter this formula, with appropriate cell references for the variables, into your spreadsheet. Then modify the variables to see how the logical operators affect the results. Figures 6.31 and 6.32 illustrate the example.

Nested @IF Functions

On those occasions when you need more than two selections from a logical test, you can nest @IF functions within @IF functions. An example of a situation in which this kind of formula might be appropriate is a program to categorize the aging of receivables. Typically, receivables are tracked or aged

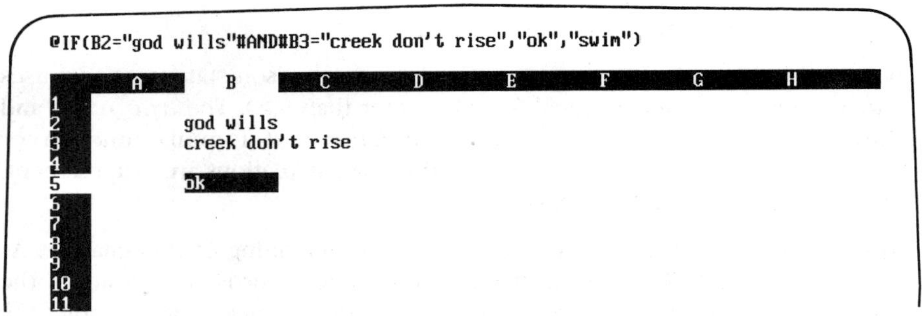

Fig. 6.31. An example of a multiple conditional test.

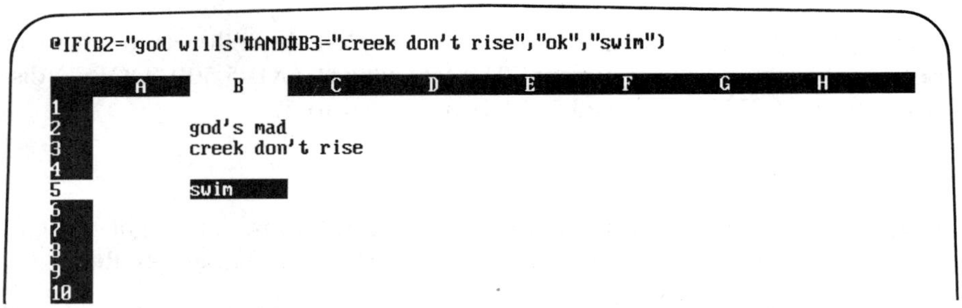

Fig. 6.32. The same example with a different result.

according to a standard time test. Specifically, the test tells management whether a receivable is less than 30 days old or equal to 30, 60, or 90 days so that appropriate action can be taken.

The following formula illustrates the use of a nested @IF function that notifies you of the status of each invoice:

@IF(A1<=30,"CURRENT",@IF(A1<60,"OVERDUE",@IF(A1<90,"PROBACCT","OYVEY")))

Note that the order of the conditional tests within the formula is important. Once a true expression is found, the rest of the formula is ignored. Thus, you should place the current condition test first in the formula. If the receivable is current, then no other tests on the other @IF functions will be performed. The final "OYVEY" in the formula is there to account for a receivable that doesn't satisfy any of the conditions (that is, one that is older than 90 days). This element serves as final "backstop" result.

Tip Always place the most likely situation in the first conditional test in a nested @IF statement. Your logical functions then calculate faster and, more importantly, lead to much shorter, more efficient solutions.

Tip To help you to avoid excessive or insufficient closing parentheses, remember that usually you will have as many closing parentheses at the end of a nested @IF function as you have @IFs within the formula.

Tip Nested @IFs are not the most intuitive or efficient logic structures. If you find that you need more than three levels of nesting, the @IF function is the wrong one to use. Look into using an @CHOOSE, @VLOOKUP, @HLOOKUP, or @INDEX function as a probable alternative.

Testing Transactions with @IF

If you are working with some kind of journal or transaction log, entering formulas into the spreadsheet in expectation of future entries may be convenient. An example is the classic checkbook register. Although in a manual checkbook register you would never think of entering balances into the future, in a spreadsheet you might enter the formula that returns current balances into cells where no transactions have occurred so that you save formula entry time later.

Unfortunately, taking this route results in a display of the current balance column similar to the example in figure 6.33. Note the balances carried beyond the actual transactions (G16..G20).

```
        A          B      C       D                 E              F        G       H I
1   ACCT MGR                  Beg Bal ==>               $2,099.27      22-Dec-88    X
2                                                                                   A T
3               Check         Payment/                             Clr              C Y
4      Date     Number Type    Credit   Description of Xaction      ?     Balance   T P
5   ================================================================================I E
6   23-Feb-89    4669   15     (657.00)     Liberia Mutual          N     1,442.27
7   23-Feb-89    4670   12     (235.17)    Alan Ross Agency         N     1,207.10
8   23-Feb-89    4671    8    1,250.00         Paycheck             Y     2,457.10
9   23-Feb-89    4672    3     (220.45)        Goodyarn             N     2,236.65
10  23-Feb-89    4673    7     (928.63)  Core St. Master Card       N     1,308.02
11  23-Feb-89    4674   21                       Void                     1,308.02
12  27-Feb-89    4675    1     (450.00)     Travel Advance          Y       858.02
13  04-Mar-89           19   (1,209.00)           IRS               N     (350.98)
14  04-Mar-89           20     (123.04)          Vepco              N     (474.02)
15  04-Mar-89            1      (35.00)          Lunch              Y     (509.02)
16                                                                        (509.02)
17                                                                        (509.02)
18                                                                        (509.02)
19                                                                        (509.02)
20                                                                        (509.02)
G16: (,2) [W10] +G15+D16
01-Feb-88  03:08 PM                                                  NUM      READY
```

Fig. 6.33. Entering formulas before transactions are input.

It would be useful if you could instruct Quattro to examine one of the cells to the left of the current-balance cell to determine whether a transaction has occurred. Figure 6.34 illustrates the use of a simple and efficient conditional testing technique that helps you test for the existence of a transaction.

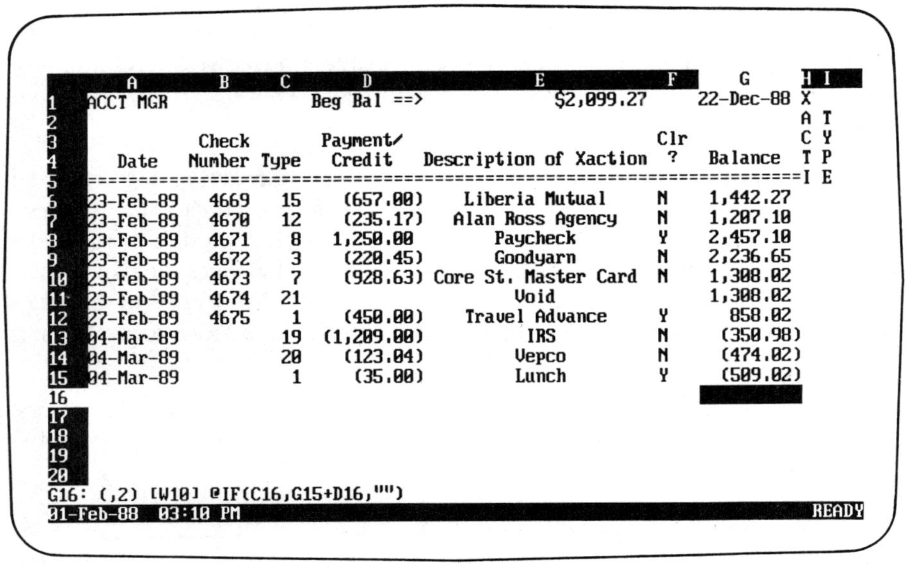

	A	B	C	D	E	F	G	H	I
1	ACCT MGR			Beg Bal ==>	$2,099.27		22-Dec-88	X	
2								A	T
3		Check		Payment/		Clr		C	Y
4	Date	Number	Type	Credit	Description of Xaction	?	Balance	T	P
5	==========	======	====	==========	======================	===	==========	I	E
6	23-Feb-89	4669	15	(657.00)	Liberia Mutual	N	1,442.27		
7	23-Feb-89	4670	12	(235.17)	Alan Ross Agency	N	1,207.10		
8	23-Feb-89	4671	8	1,250.00	Paycheck	Y	2,457.10		
9	23-Feb-89	4672	3	(220.45)	Goodyarn	N	2,236.65		
10	23-Feb-89	4673	7	(928.63)	Core St. Master Card	N	1,308.02		
11	23-Feb-89	4674	21		Void		1,308.02		
12	27-Feb-89	4675	1	(450.00)	Travel Advance	Y	858.02		
13	04-Mar-89		19	(1,209.00)	IRS	N	(350.98)		
14	04-Mar-89		20	(123.04)	Vepco	N	(474.02)		
15	04-Mar-89		1	(35.00)	Lunch	Y	(509.02)		
16									
17									
18									
19									
20									

G16: (,2) [W10] @IF(C16,G15+D16,"")

01-Feb-88 03:10 PM READY

Fig. 6.34. Using @IF to test for the existence of a transaction.

The conditional portion of the formula in cell G16 of figure 6.34 is simply a reference to the transaction Type column (column C). The condition is considered false if the cell either contains a zero or is blank. The @IF function considers all numbers not equal to zero to be true, even if they are negative.

By examining the Type column, the function can determine whether a transaction exists. If the condition is true, the result is the balance found; if the condition is false (transaction type not entered in column C), the formula returns the two double quotation marks found in the false_result portion of the formula. The two double quotation marks result in a null or blank display, as shown in cell G16 of figure 6.34.

Tip Use two double quotation marks with nothing between them (" ") to provide for a blank or null display as a result of a formula calculation.

Other Logical Functions

Although the @IF function is the most frequently used logical function, Quattro features some others that bear mentioning. These include @ISSTRING, @ISNUMBER, @TRUE, @FALSE, @ISNA, and @ISERR.

@ISSTRING

@ISSTRING is a function that returns a 1 if the cell being examined is a label (text), and a 0 if the cell is a value or formula. The syntax of the function is

@ISSTRING(cell_reference)

If the cell referenced is blank or contains NA or ERR, the result of @ISSTRING will be false, or 0.

This function is often used to determine the type of data that was entered in response to a macro that requested user input. For example, in the macro line

{IF @ISSTRING(DATA_ENTERED)}{DO_NEXT}

the IF keyword can use @ISSTRING to determine whether an error condition was caused by the user typing incorrect data. (Refer to Chapter 16, "Quattro Command Language Reference," for more information on the IF command.)

@ISNUMBER

The @ISNUMBER function is the exact opposite of @ISSTRING. If the cell referenced by @ISNUMBER is a value, formula, or contains NA or ERR, the function returns 1. Otherwise, the formula yields 0, a false result. For example, @ISNUMBER(A1) displays a 0 if A1 contains a label. Otherwise, the function returns a 1 for true if A1 is either blank or contains a value.

@TRUE

@TRUE takes no argument and is numerically equal to 1. You can use this function as an argument in an @IF function or a macro's condition.

To further the idea of a readable approach to writing functions and macros, you might combine an operator such as #NOT# with an @TRUE function. For example, the function:

@IF(PROFITABLE=#NOT#@TRUE,"YOU'RE_FIRED","WE_WANT_MORE!")

This function is highly readable, self-documenting, and quite distressing in its message.

@FALSE

Like @TRUE, the @FALSE function takes no arguments. You simply enter @FALSE.

@FALSE is numerically equivalent to 0. In fact, using this function instead of the number 0 offers no advantage, with the possible exception of use in a macro statement. In a macro, the code {IF MACRO_DONE=@FALSE} is more readable and self-documenting than the macro statement {IF MACRO_DONE=0}.

@ISNA

@ISNA tests a cell argument and returns 1 (true) only if the cell being examined is the function @NA or is a dependent cell of a cell containing an @NA function. (For more information on @NA, see Chapter 7's section entitled "Macro-Related Special Functions.") If the *label* NA is evaluated, however, @ISNA returns a 0 for false.

The syntax for the function is

@ISNA(cell_reference)

You can use @ISNA to signal that a condition or variable in the spreadsheet has not been supplied. For example, suppose that you suspect you have forgotten to enter quantities sold in an invoicing application. To trap this condition, you might have a formula such as:

@IF(QUAN_SOLD=0,@NA,QUAN_SOLD*UNIT_PRICE)

If the block named QUAN_SOLD equals 0, the function displays NA. Otherwise the function multiplies the quantity sold by the unit price. You can use the @ISNA function to signal a user that an NA "flag" has been raised somewhere in the spreadsheet.

@ISERR

@ISERR tests a cell argument and returns 1 (true) if the cell being examined is the function @ERR or is a dependent cell of a cell containing an @ERR function. (For more information on @ERR, refer to Chapter 7's section entitled "Macro-Related Special Functions.") If the evaluation of a spreadsheet cell results in the value ERR, the @ISERR function returns 1. If the *label* ERR is evaluated, however, @ISERR returns a 0 for false. The syntax for the function is

@ISERR(cell_reference)

where *cell_reference* can be a cell reference, formula, or function.

One handy use of the @ISERR function is trapping a situation that might lead to a spreadsheet error. One of the most frequent causes of ERR is when the program attempts to divide a number by 0. This error is appropriately known as a "divide-by-zero" error. If a number is divided by zero, Quattro doesn't know what the answer should be. So the program just gives up and displays ERR.

To prevent the propagation of ERR-valued cells in a spreadsheet, you can nest @ISERR as a condition within an @IF function, as the following example shows:

```
@IF(@ISERR(A1/B1),0,A1/B1)
```

In this example, if B1 contains a 0, the @ISERR formula becomes true. Thus 0 (the *true_result* argument) is displayed rather than the nagging ERR message. Otherwise, the @ISERR function is false, and the division operation proceeds normally.

Error Suppression

On many occasions in an application, ERRs can show up. The @IF/@ISERR method discussed in the previous section is a handy way to trap these potential errors. But another way to perform this operation is to use the #NOT# operator.

For example, look at this formula:

```
@IF(#NOT#B1,0,A1/B1)
```

The #NOT# operator turns to 0 (false) any number that is not equal to 0, and turns to 1 (true) any number that is equal to 0. Thus, in the example, the statement #NOT#B1 becomes true if B1 contains 0. This method of trapping the divide-by-zero error is less intuitive than the @ISERR example but is also shorter and uses less memory because the @ISERR function is not needed. As you can see, Quattro provides the flexibility to solve the same problem in different ways.

Financial Functions

The financial functions in Quattro are a convenience feature for those of you who must perform financial analyses on a frequent basis. The functions fall into three general categories: cash-flow analysis, debt/investment, and depreciation functions. Table 6.4 provides a look at the functions within these categories, along with a brief description of each function.

Table 6.4
Financial Functions

Cash-Flow Analysis Function	*Calculates*
@NPV(rate,cash_flows_block)	Net present value of uneven cash flows based on discount rate
@IRR(guess,cash_flows_block)	Internal rate of return of a series of cash flows
@PV(payment,interest,term)	Present value of investment based on equal payments per period
@FV(payment,interest,term)	Payout (future value) of investment based on equal payments per period

Debt/Investment Function	*Calculates*
@PMT(principal,interest,term)	Principal and interest payment per period
@RATE(fv,pv,term)	Interest rate required to achieve other arguments (future value, present value, and term)
@TERM(payment,interest,fv)	Number of periods needed to achieve other arguments (payment, interest, and future value)
@CTERM(interest,fv,pv)	Number of compounding periods needed to achieve interest, future value, and present value

Depreciation Function	*Calculates*
@SLN(cost,salvage,life)	Straight-line depreciation
@SYD(cost,salvage,life,period)	Sum-of-the-years'-digits depreciation
@DDB(cost,salvage,life,period)	Double-declining-balance depreciation

Generally speaking, all the financial functions use values rather than string data types as function arguments.

@NPV

The @NPV function returns the present value of an estimated series of unequal cash flows (or outflows) where payments are made at the end of the periods. The syntax of @NPV is

@NPV(discount_rate,cash_flows_block)

where *discount_rate* can be either a number in the cell or a reference to a cell containing a discount rate to be applied to the cash-flow values, and *cash_flows_block* must be a block reference to a series of cells containing estimated cash flows.

Figure 6.35 shows that the net present value of the cash flows in cells C5 through C10 is $91,889.78, based on an 8 percent discount rate, in contrast to the sum of the cash flows, $115,000, in cell C12.

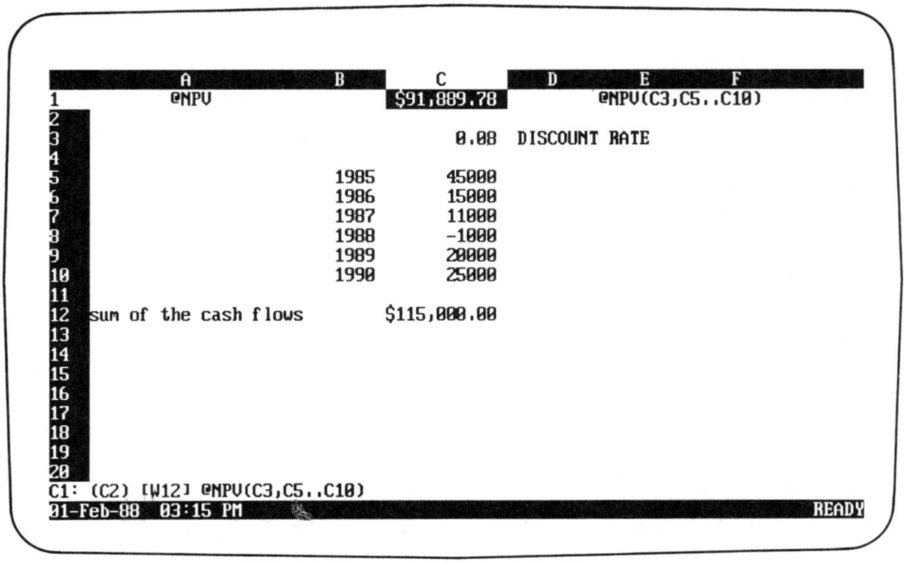

Fig. 6.35. The @NPV function.

To calculate net present value when the payment is made at the beginning of the period, use the formula

@NPV(discount_rate, cash_flows_block) + initial investment

A good use of the @NPV function is to find out whether a service contract is a good value. In the case of a vehicle service contract, how do you know whether the price is fair? First, you must estimate the repair expenses that you might incur during the period covered by the extended warranty. Then, use those figures as the cash flows argument in an @NPV function. You will then have a number that you can compare to the price of the service contract.

Here's another example. Suppose that you want to set aside an amount that, when invested at 8 percent, will cover the costs of running a vehicle. Figure 6.36 shows an example of how you can calculate the amount to save. The formula in cell C12 [@NPV(C10,C4..G6)] indicates that $5,296 is necessary to cover costs of $8,644 (C14) over the three years shown.

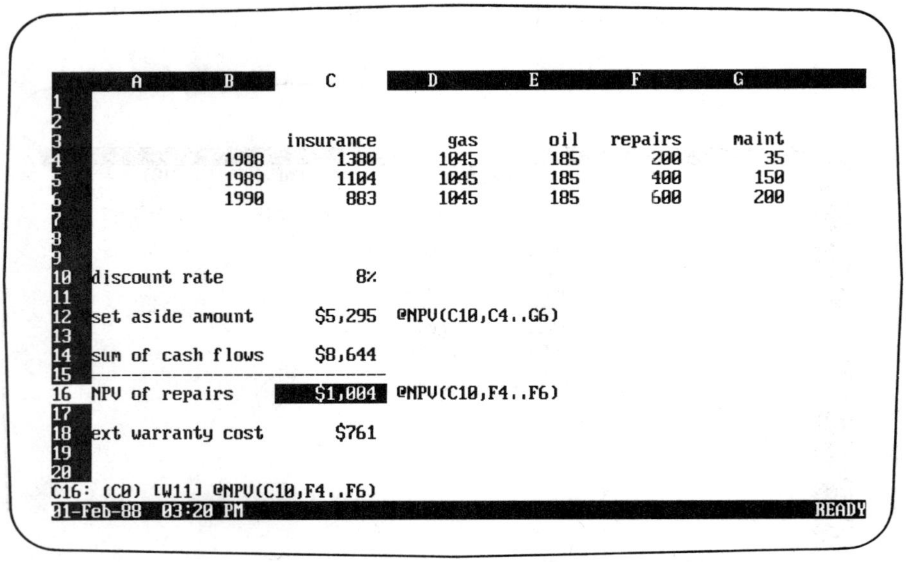

Fig. 6.36. A practical example of using @NPV.

In addition to determining the set-aside amount, the model also evaluates whether to buy a service warranty on the vehicle or take your chances on the car. The formula in cell C16 is the net present value of the costs of repairs over the three years. Cell C18 represents the price of the service contract.

The comparison shows that the service contract priced at $761 is the better way to go if your repair estimates are correct.

Models such as this one that make effective use of @NPV can help you to determine the true cost of an investment over its life.

@IRR

The @IRR, or internal rate of return, function is one of the most misunderstood of all financial analysis techniques. You should use @IRR to determine break-even points on an investment with variable cash flows. The function does not determine the profit on an investment but is best used for risk comparison purposes, such as comparing the rate of return on treasury bills (relatively riskless) with the return from drilling wells in an oil field.

The syntax for the @IRR function is

@IRR(guess_rate,cash_flows_block)

where *guess_rate* is a value or reference to a value that gives the @IRR function a place to start, and the *cash_flows_block* is the group of cells holding the periodic cash flows estimated for the investment.

The @IRR function is an internally iterative function, which means that it is a goal-seeking, or an approximation, function. Because the @IRR function has an infinity of possible rates from which to choose, the function uses the guess rate to get "in the neighborhood" of the eventual answer. This tactic is similar to aiming a cannon. A sighter gives the operator of the artillery piece the approximate coordinates of the target. Having this information, the gunner fires at the target. The sighter then feeds back the result to the gunner. This process continues until the target is hit. Once the aim is selected, the @IRR function internally calculates until it reaches an answer well above 99 percent accuracy.

The second @IRR argument is a multicell block that contains an initial outflow or negative number representing the initial investment. The succeeding cells hold your best estimates of projected cash flows.

The example in figure 6.37 illustrates how bad your initial aim can be for the guess number. In this case, the number chosen is 10000 percent. No matter what the guess number is, it will not have an effect on the outcome of the calculation. Only the cash flows will be considered once the calculation is initiated.

The internal rate of return of the sample investment is 12.37 percent (cell B1). This figure indicates that the net present value of all the cash flows is zero dollars if the discount rate is 12.37 percent. Stated another way, if the

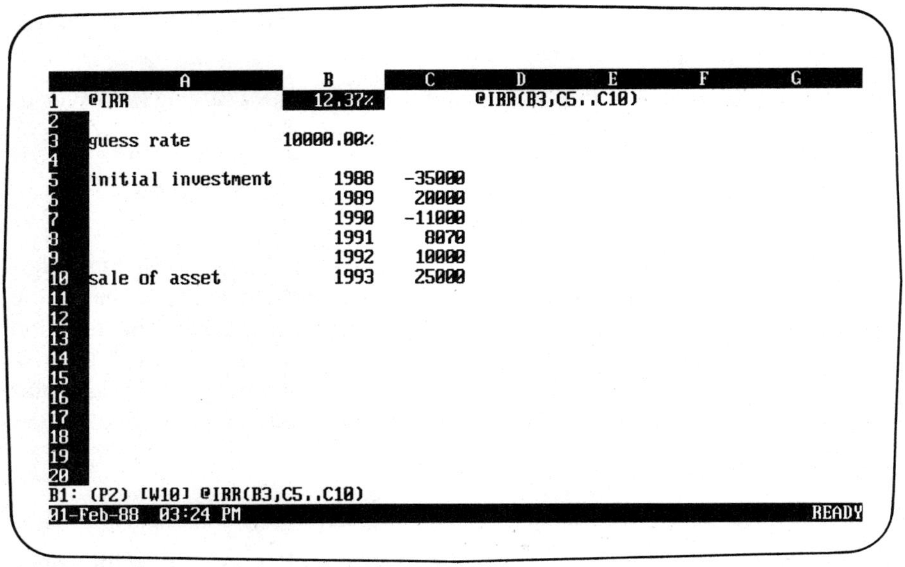

Fig. 6.37. Using a large guess rate.

inflation rate is 12.37 percent during the period of the cash flows, the investment is truly worthless. If the inflation rate is higher, then the investment will lose money. So, of course, the prudent investor will first determine the likelihood of that inflation rate and, second, evaluate the risk of the investment against the projected return. If a secure investment will provide the same return as a risky venture, common sense dictates taking the conservative course.

On a personal note, I suggest that you use the @IRR and @NPV functions with great care. They are completely dependent on the untenable premise that you can predict the future. You can't. @IRR and @NPV are useful as guidelines and for comparison only.

On a positive note, Quattro's implementation of the @IRR function is the fastest and least sensitive to the guess number of all the spreadsheets I have worked with.

Tip An implied but unstated presumption of the @IRR function is that you can and will be able to reinvest the cash flows at the rate that @IRR returns (in the example, 12.37 percent). This reinvestment may or may not be possible in reality.

@PV

The @PV, or present value, function is similar to the @NPV function in that they both present the true cost of a loan or value of an investment. In contrast to @NPV, which returns the present value of an estimated series of unequal cash flows, @PV shows the present value of a consistent payment. The syntax for @PV is

@PV(payment,interest,term)

where *payment* is the constant periodic payment, *interest* is the periodic interest rate, and *term* is the number of periods that the payment will be made.

The @PV function calculates the present value of an investment based on the "time value of money" principal. The time value of money is one of the first lessons that must be learned to manage money in business. This rule asserts that having the use of money is itself worth something. If this assumption is true, then a given amount of money available right now is worth more than that same amount of money in the future.

I learned the time value of money as a little boy. Every day about noon, the ice cream man, ringing his bells, would drive his truck into the neighborhood. I knew in my heart that the ice cream man gained secret satisfaction by leaving before I could get my money. So I would hurry to my mom and beg for the requisite nickel.

At this point, moms being what they are, she would say to me "I'll give you a nickel today, but if you wait until the end of the week, I'll give you a whole quarter." As I'm sure you guessed, I took the nickel. The opportunity to use that nickel in the present was much more attractive (and delicious) than the use of a quarter in the future.

The @PV function is helpful in determining which one of several financing options is least expensive from a consistent standpoint. The example in figure 6.38 shows how you can compare a variety of financing options to purchase a computer. Note that the formula @PV(C5,C7/12,C9) returns a present value of 6,405 in cell C3. Although the interest rate in C7 is higher than some other options, the present value is lowest for this scenario, which makes this option the least expensive of the financing plans.

Take note that in the formula the interest rate is divided by 12 to result in a monthly interest rate. Otherwise, the @PV function would assume that you wanted to know the present value of periodic payments made for 24 *years* rather than 24 months. The interval of the payments must agree with the period of the interest rate.

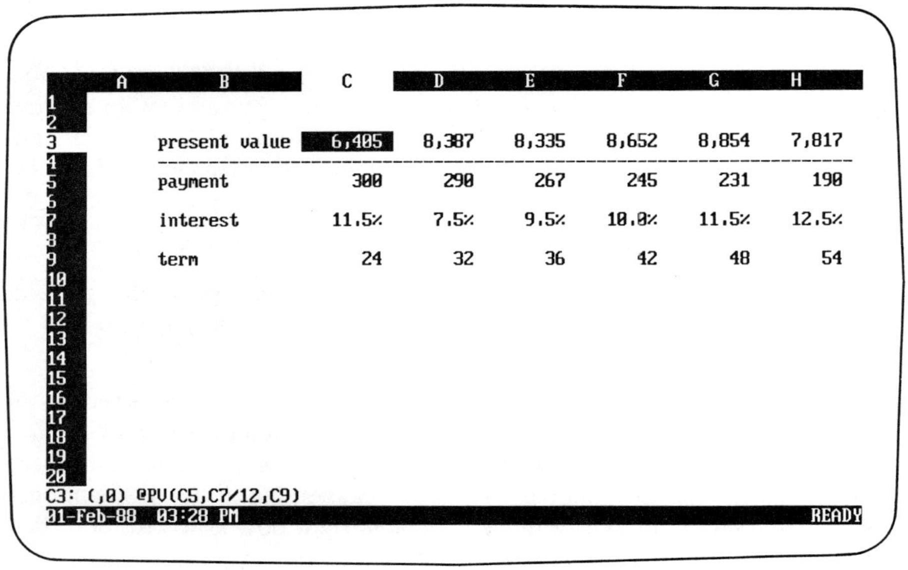

Fig. 6.38. Comparing various investment options with @PV.

@FV

The @FV, or future value, function indicates how much money will be earned by the end of an investment when the investment is made on a regular basis with a constant amount. The syntax for @FV is

@FV(payment,interest,term)

where *payment* is the constant periodic payment, *interest* is the periodic interest rate, and *term* is the number of periods that the payment will be made. @FV presumes that payments are made at the end of each period.

If you put $100 a month in an investment for 48 months at 12 percent annual interest, the future value function tells you that your payout, or future value, will be $6,122.26. The formula for this calculation is

@FV(100,0.12/12,48)

Figure 6.39 demonstrates an example of the @FV function. Note that you can use cell references or block names in place of the actual numbers.

To calculate the future value of an investment made at the beginning of the period, use the formula

@FV(payment,interest,term)*(1+interest)

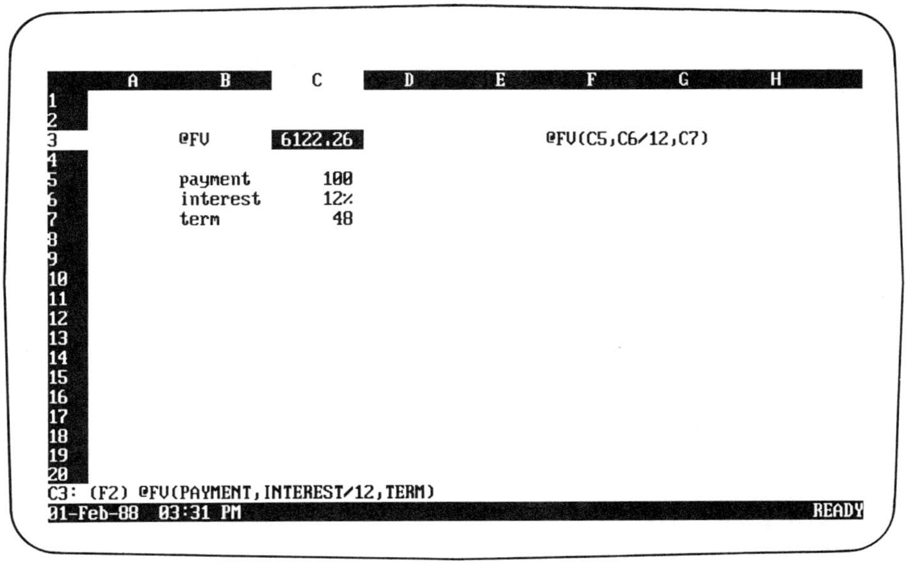

Fig. 6.39. The @FV function.

@PMT

Because of its general utility, @PMT is the financial function that you probably will use most often. The @PMT function returns the principal and interest payment per period (that is, the monthly payment) based on the principal borrowed (loaned), the periodic interest rate, and the number of periods (life) of the loan. The syntax for @PMT is

@PMT(principal,interest,term)

where *principal* is the amount borrowed or loaned, *interest* is the interest rate applied to the loan, and *term* is the life of the loan. For example, to find the monthly payment for a 5-year (60-month) loan at 9.5 percent annual interest for an $8,000 car, use the formula @PMT(8000,9.5%/12,60).

The @PMT function presumes that the payment occurs at the end of each period. To calculate a payment made at the beginning of the period, use the formula

@PMT(principal,interest,term)/(1+interest)

Tip As with the other cash-flow financial functions, in an @PMT formula, the periods for the interest and term arguments must agree. For instance, if the term of the loan is described as 360 months, then the interest rate must be specified as a monthly interest rate (unless you want the answer for a 360-*year* loan). Application of this rule usually results in the enhanced syntax of @PMT(principal,interest/frequency,term), where *frequency* is the type of period implied in the term argument.

Note the example in figure 6.40. The principal, interest, and term in the function are external references to cells C3, C4, and C5. Obviously the number 360 in the cell used for the term argument (C5) is the life of the loan in number of months. The formula is informed of that fact because the 9.5 percent interest rate is divided by 12 (months) in the formula. In this way, the interest and term arguments are made to agree.

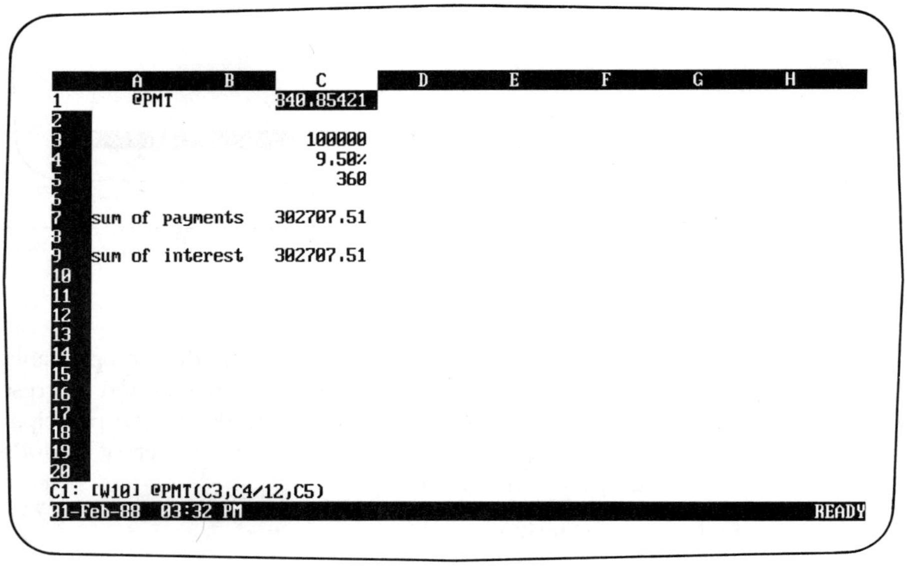

Fig. 6.40. Determining a periodic payment with @PMT.

The next figure shows an example of what happens if you don't match the interval between cash flows to the interest rate. Note in figure 6.41 that the @PMT function accepts the interest argument as an annual amount, which means that you will be paying $9,500 dollars a year for 360 years to amortize the mortgage. In other words, maybe a fraction of a cent is applied toward principal for the first 200 years!

For more information on the applications of @PMT, see the example in the section on /Advanced What-If in Chapter 12.

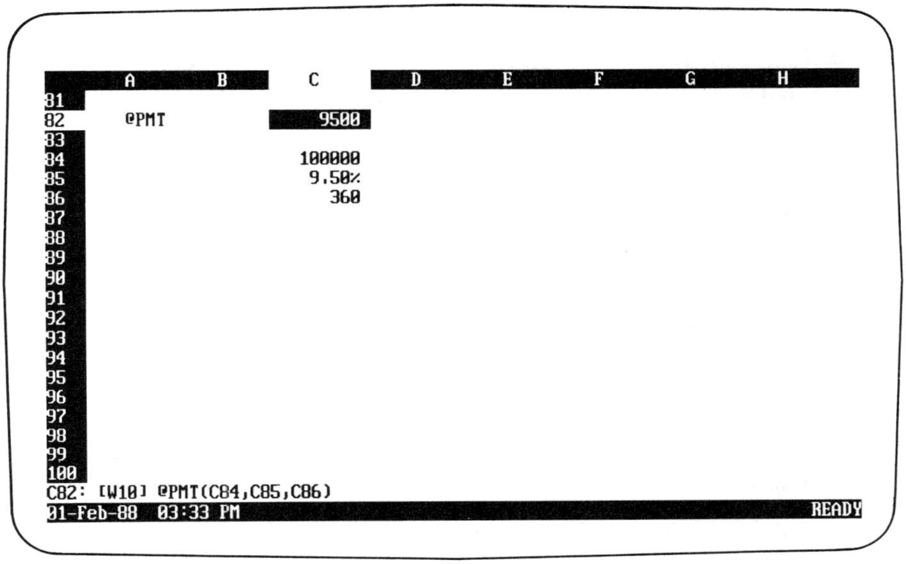

Fig. 6.41. The results of failing to match the term period with the interest rate.

@RATE

The @RATE function is used to determine the implied interest rate of an investment when only the payout value, present value, and term (compounding periods) of an investment are known. Determining what interest rate you will need in order to achieve optimal financial results is useful.

The syntax for @RATE is

@RATE(futurevalue,presentvalue,term)

Consider this simple example of @RATE. What interest rate is required for $10,000 to grow to $20,000 if the $10,000 is invested for 7 years? The formula @RATE(20000,10000,7) quickly shows that a 10.41 percent interest rate is needed.

As is true with several financial functions, you may need to factor the term argument to obtain the answer you need. For instance, if you want to find the monthly interest rate required for the problem posed in the previous paragraph, you need to multiply the term by 12 (months). The adjusted formula of @RATE(20000,10000,7*12) results in the monthly rate of .83 percent.

Tip If you specify a monthly compounding period rather than an annual period, @RATE will reach the future value with a lower interest rate. In the previous example, if you multiply .83 percent by 12, you will find that the answer is less than 10.41 percent, the yearly rate.

@TERM

The @TERM function answers the question, "How long must I wait for my investment to grow to a future value based on regular payments?" The @TERM function's syntax is

@TERM(payment,interest,futurevalue)

where *payment* is the amount invested per period, *interest* is the fixed rate applied to the payments, and *futurevalue* is the targeted value of the investment at maturity.

The formula @TERM(1000,0.1,10000) results in a term of 7.27 years, as shown in figure 6.42.

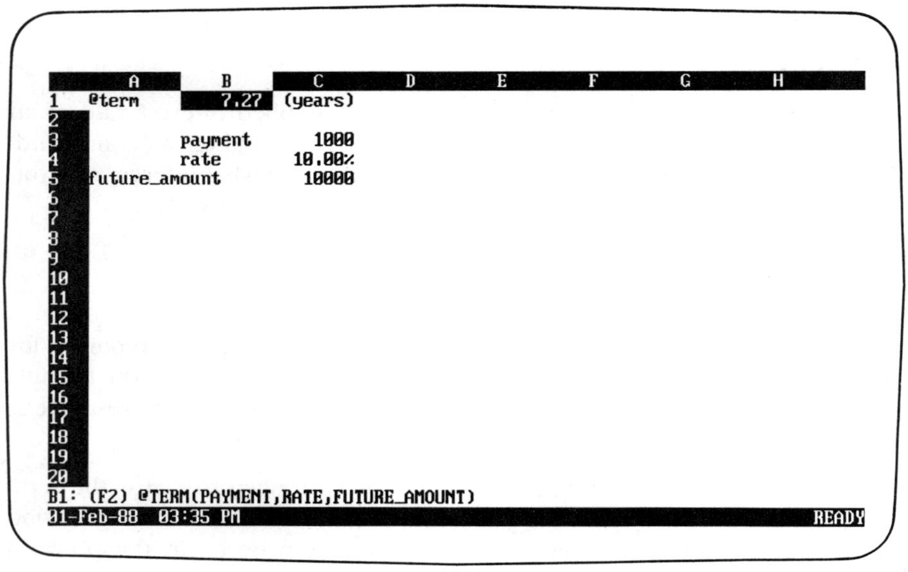

Fig. 6.42. The @TERM function.

The @TERM function presumes that the payment amount will be payed at the end of each period (that is, at the end of the year). If you want to determine the term when the payment is made at the beginning of the month, you can use the formula @TERM(payment,interest,futurevalue/(1+interest)). When payments on an annuity (an investment account where equal payments are made at regular periods) are made at the beginning of the period, the formula is known as annuity due. Figure 6.43 shows an annuity-due calculation using the same arguments as the standard annuity in figure 6.42. Note that the term of the annuity is shortened by half a year just by making payments at the beginning of the period.

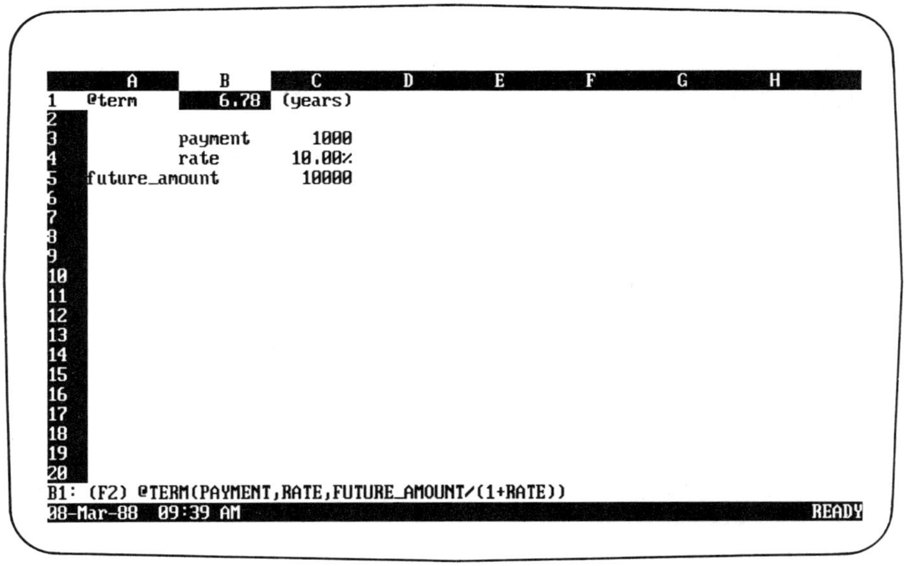

Fig. 6.43. The @TERM function adjusted for payments made at the beginning of a period.

@CTERM

The @CTERM function is a more advanced version of @TERM. @CTERM allows you to determine the term of an annuity based on the compounding rate of the investment. The syntax for @CTERM is

@CTERM(interest,futurevalue,presentvalue)

where *interest* is the interest rate per compounding period, *futurevalue* is the desired payout of the investment, and *presentvalue* is the lump sum amount originally invested.

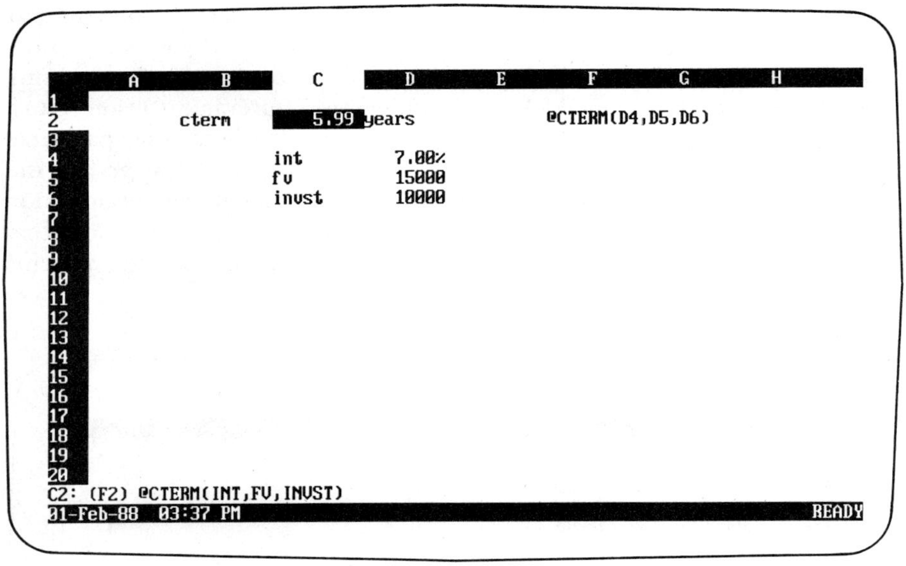

Fig. 6.44. The @CTERM function.

The formula @CTERM(0.7,15000,10000) results in the compound term of 5.99 years (see fig. 6.44) for $10,000 to grow to $15,000 dollars at 7 percent compounded annually.

The next figure illustrates how to use different compounding rates, such as daily or monthly compounding. In figure 6.45, notice that the interest argument (cell C3) must be divided by the compounding rate in order to introduce the effect of compounding, and that the entire formula is then also divided by the compounding rate to cause the formula to return an annual term.

As the figure illustrates, the term will be 5.81 years for monthly compounding: daily compounding results in a wait of 5.79 years.

Tip When figuring daily compounding, use 360 rather than 365 days. Banks and other financial institutions use a standard figure of 360. (Perhaps they still use a lunar calendar.)

@SLN

The @SLN function determines the annual depreciation allowable for tax purposes with the straight-line depreciation method. The syntax for @SLN is

@SLN(cost,salvage,life)

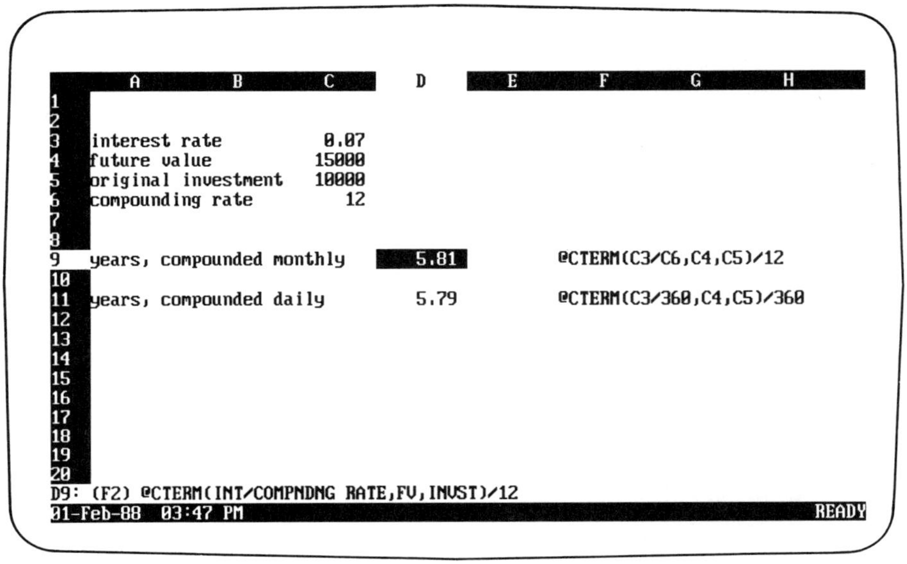

Fig. 6.45. Using monthly and daily compounding rates with @CTERM.

where *cost* is the total amount paid for the asset, *salvage* is the residual value that the asset is expected to retain, and *life* is the life of the asset in years. (The IRS determines many classes of asset life. Refer to IRS publications for current information.)

The formula @SLN(10000,0,5) results in the answer 2000. Thus, you can depreciate the asset $2,000 for each of the five years of its life. If the asset has a salvage value, it will be used to reduce the cost basis of the asset.

For another example of this depreciation function, refer to the discussion of the @CHOOSE function in Chapter 7's "Table and Array-Handling Functions" section.

@SYD

The @SYD function determines the annual depreciation allowable with the sum-of-the-years'-digits depreciation method. The syntax for @SYD is

@SYD(cost,salvage,life,yearnumber)

where *cost* is the total amount paid for the asset, *salvage* is the residual value that the asset is expected to retain, *life* is the life of the asset, and *yearnumber* is the year of the asset on which to base depreciation.

If you want to use @SYD to figure the second year's depreciation on a $10,000 truck with a five-year life, use the formula @SYD(10000,0,5,2). The result is 2666.67. If the truck has a salvage value, it will be used to reduce the cost basis of the asset. Each *yearnumber* used results in a different depreciation result.

Tip The @SYD function may leave a residual value in the asset after its useful life. You can depreciate this value using the straight-line method.

@DDB

The @DDB function determines the annual depreciation allowable with the double-declining-balance depreciation method. The syntax for @DDB is

@DDB(cost,salvage,life,yearnumber)

where *cost* is the total amount paid for the asset, *salvage* is the residual value that the asset is expected to retain, *life* is the life of the asset, and *yearnumber* is the year of the asset on which to base depreciation.

Double-declining-balance is the fastest depreciation method available in Quattro's suite of depreciation functions. The only quicker method is to "expense" an asset. (See section 179D of IRS regulations.)

If you want to use @DDB to figure the third year's depreciation on an $8,000 computer with a salvage value of $500 and a three-year life, use the formula @DDB(8000,500,3,3). The result is 388.89. Each *yearnumber* used results in a different depreciation result.

Tip The @DDB function may leave a residual value in the asset after its useful life. You can depreciate this value using the straight-line method.

Date and Time Functions

Quattro's date and time functions are useful for applications that need to use dates and times in calculations. Spreadsheets that implement project management, tickler files, and accounts payable/receivable can all benefit from these functions. The date and time functions allow dates and times to be treated as numeric data, which makes adding or subtracting one date from another easy.

One of the hidden features of Quattro is its capability to create date numbers without the assistance of the functions listed here. This feature is activated by the Ctrl-D keystroke combination. By pressing Ctrl-D before you enter a label, such as 3-SEP-88, you tell Quattro to convert that label into the date's numeric equivalent. You must press Ctrl-D before entering each date. As a bonus, the cell is instantly formatted in the default long international date format. (For more on formatting, see Chapter 4.)

Dates and times in Quattro are represented as numeric values. A date is an integer, where 1 is equal to January 1, 1900. Since that time, about 32000 days have elapsed. So if you enter a date with Ctrl-D or with one of the following functions, you will see a number of about this magnitude. Usually, you will want to format date numbers with a date format.

The earliest date that Quattro can handle is December 31, 1899, which the program represents as 0 (zero). The largest date available is December 31, 2178, which Quattro represents as the number 65380.

The time-handling capability is based on fractions of serial numbers. For example, 8:00 a.m. is represented by the decimal fraction 0.333333. You should note that any of the functions, such as @NOW, that depend on the computer's internal clock, or any time function that references an @NOW function, may not be accurate if the spreadsheet is not updated frequently.

Table 6.5 summarizes Quattro's date and time functions and includes a brief explanation of what they do.

Table 6.5
Date and Time Functions

Function	*Description*
@DATE(yy,mm,dd)	Determines the serial-number date based on the year, month, and day
@DATEVALUE(date_string)	Converts a date string to a serial number
@DAY(value)	Extracts the day of month number from a serial number
@MONTH(value)	Extracts the month number from a serial number
@YEAR(value)	Extracts the year number from a serial number
@TODAY	Returns current date value
@NOW	Returns current date and time value

Function	*Description*
@TIME(hh,mm,ss)	Determines the serial-number time based on the hours, minutes, and seconds
@TIMEVALUE(time_string)	Converts a time string to a fractional serial number
@SECOND(value)	Extracts the second number from a serial number
@MINUTE(value)	Extracts the minute number from a serial number
@HOUR(value)	Extracts the hour number from a serial number

@DATE

The @DATE function is used to enter the numeric form of a date so that Quattro can perform date calculations, such as determining the number of days between two dates. The syntax for @DATE is

@DATE(yy,mm,dd)

where *yy* is the last two or three digits of the year number, *mm* is a month number from 1 through 12, and *dd* is a day number from 1 through 31.

All the arguments for @DATE must be numeric rather than string-oriented data. The arguments can be numbers, references to external cells, or the results of other formulas.

To use the @DATE function on a date such as September 12, 1988, enter @DATE(88,9,12) into a cell. Quattro displays the number 32398. This figure represents the number of days that have elapsed since December 31, 1899. This form of notation is known as a Julian date.

As is true with most of the date functions, if you want the number that results from the @DATE function to look like a date, you must format the cell with the /**B**lock **D**isplay Format **D**ate command.

If you need to generate a date in the next century, such as January 1, 2001, enter the year number as a three-digit number, as in @DATE(101,1,1). The 101 argument means the year that is 101 years after 1900.

If you want to generate the day name for any date, use the following formula:

@MOD(@DATE(yy,mm,dd),7)

This formula will result in a number between 0 and 6. If you divide the number 7 into a date that falls on the seventh day of the week, the remainder will always be 0, which corresponds to Saturday. The function @MOD(@DATE(41,12,7),7), which refers to December 7, 1941, results in a 1 for Sunday. If you want the function to generate the actual day name rather than a number, you can use the @VLOOKUP function, as shown in figure 6.46.

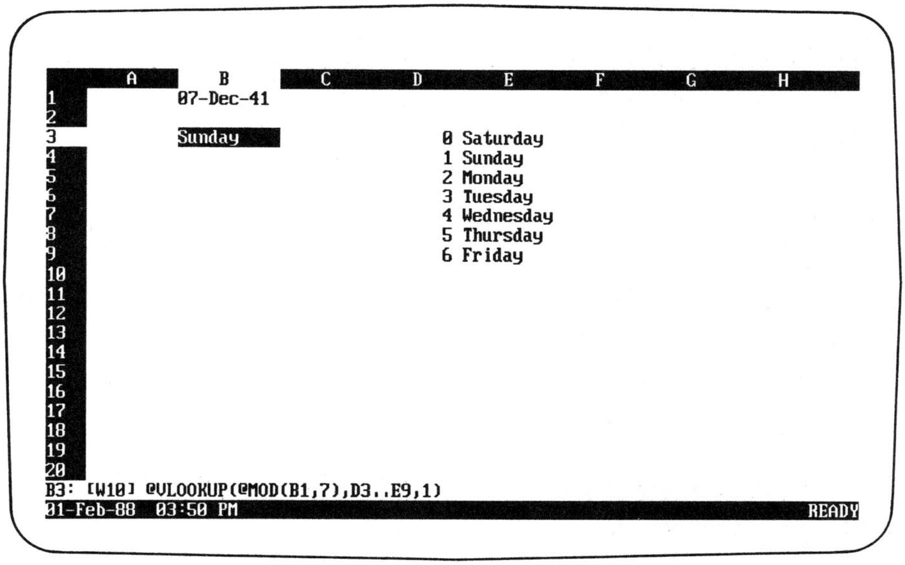

Fig. 6.46. Finding a date's particular day of the week.

For more information, see the section on @MOD in this chapter and the section on @VLOOKUP in Chapter 7.

@DATEVALUE

The @DATEVALUE function allows you to create a numeric date by using text. Thus you can enter the string "10-DEC-88" and have the @DATEVALUE function translate the string into the equivalent date number of 32487. The syntax for @DATEVALUE is

@DATEVALUE(date_string)

where *date_string* can be a quoted string or a reference to a cell containing a label or a string-oriented formula.

The @DATEVALUE function requires that the date string be written in one of the available date formats under the /**B**lock **D**isplay Format **D**ate menu. To illustrate this point, you may use within the @DATEVALUE function any of the date patterns shown in figure 6.47.

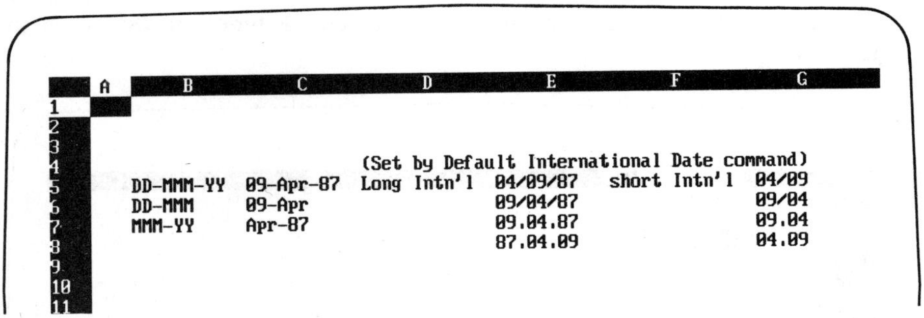

Fig. 6.47. Date formats available for use with @DATEVALUE.

Note that although the strings "09-apr-87", "09.04.87", and "04/09/87" return the identical answer, normally the "09-apr-87" format is simplest to enter.

Not all the entry formats are available at a given time. Some of the acceptable formats depend on which of the international date formats are selected as defaults.

@DAY

The @DAY function returns the day number for any valid date. The formula @DAY(@TODAY) gives the day's number for today. If today is March 5, the function returns the number 5. The syntax for @DAY is

@DAY(value)

where *value* is any number from 0 through 65380, Quattro's lowest and highest date numbers. Normally, the value argument will be either a formula or a reference to another date cell.

This function may seem rather redundant, because anyone with good eyesight can see the day of a date in the spreadsheet. The following example illustrates just why the @DAY function can prove useful in certain circumstances.

Figuring amortizations is a common use of the Quattro spreadsheet. In developing an amortization table, generating the date for the monthly payment may be desirable. At first this step seems simple. Why not just add 31 days to the previous payment date to come up with next month's date? This method will work for about 8 months. Then, the table will begin to skip months. Why? Because many months are not 31 days long. Some are 30 days, and February is usually but not always 28 days.

The example in figure 6.48 uses the @DAY function to produce an accurate next-month date that will not accumulate any date errors during the life of the mortgage. Notice in the figure that all the dates follow each other on exactly the same day of the month.

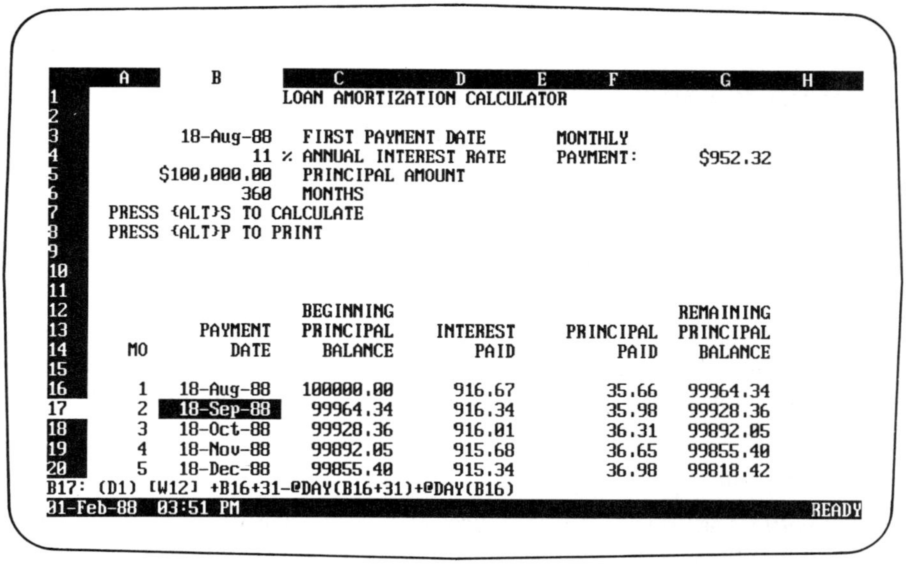

Fig. 6.48. Using @DAY to produce a series of monthly dates.

Figure 6.49 breaks this rather complex formula into its components, with an explanation of each part. The individual pieces of the formula are contained in column B, where the resulting numbers are displayed. The entire formula is repeated in cell C2. Column C describes the operation being performed by each formula segment, and column D illustrates these same steps as they appear formatted as dates.

@MONTH

The @MONTH function returns the month number, a number from 1 to 12, for any valid date. The formula @MONTH(@TODAY) gives the month number for today's date. If today is March 5, the function returns the number 3. The syntax for @MONTH is

	A	B	C	D
1		32183	i.e. February 10th to March 10th	10-Feb
2			+B1+31-@DAY(B1+31)+@DAY(B1)	
3				
4	step 1	32214	add 31 days to prev date	12-Mar
5	step 2	12	add 31 days to prev date and subtract from step 1	29-Jan
6	step 3	10	add day of prev date to step 2	10-Mar
7				
8				
9				
10				

Fig. 6.49. Studying the formula.

@MONTH(value)

where *value* is any number from 0 through 65380, Quattro's lowest and highest date numbers. Normally, the value argument will be either a formula or a reference to another date cell.

@YEAR

The @YEAR function returns the year number—a number from 0 (1900) to 178 (2178)—for any valid date. The formula @YEAR(@TODAY) gives the year number for today's date. If today is March 5, 1988, the function returns the number 88. The syntax for @YEAR is

@YEAR(value)

where *value* is any number from 0 through 65380, Quattro's lowest and highest date numbers. Normally, the value argument will be either a formula or a reference to another date cell.

@TODAY

The @TODAY function gives the date number based on the current date taken from the system clock. The date number is always presented as an integer number. The @TODAY function does not accept any arguments.

The result returned by @TODAY is not always current. To ensure that the answer is correct, press the Calc key (F9) or perform a menu operation, such as /**B**lock **C**opy, that will update the cell.

This function can be useful in some applications—in a tickler file, for example. You can use a formula such as

@IF(@TODAY>=DUE_DATE,"check the project","")

to indicate whether a project has passed its due date.

@NOW

The @NOW function gives a number representing both the date and time (for example, 32202.65) based on the current time taken from the system clock. The date portion of the number is an integer number, and the time portion is expressed as a decimal. In the number 32202.65, the date is represented by 32202, and the time is indicated by .65. The @NOW function does not accept any arguments.

The result returned by @NOW is not always current. To ensure that the answer is correct, press the Calc key (F9) or perform a menu operation, such as /**B**lock **C**opy, that will update the cell.

To generate just the day number of the current date, use the @TODAY function. To isolate just the time of day, use the formula @NOW-@TODAY.

You can also format a cell containing the @NOW function. Figure 6.50 shows first the serial number produced by the @NOW function (cell B4), then the number formatted as a date (cell B5), and, finally, the number formatted as time (cell B6).

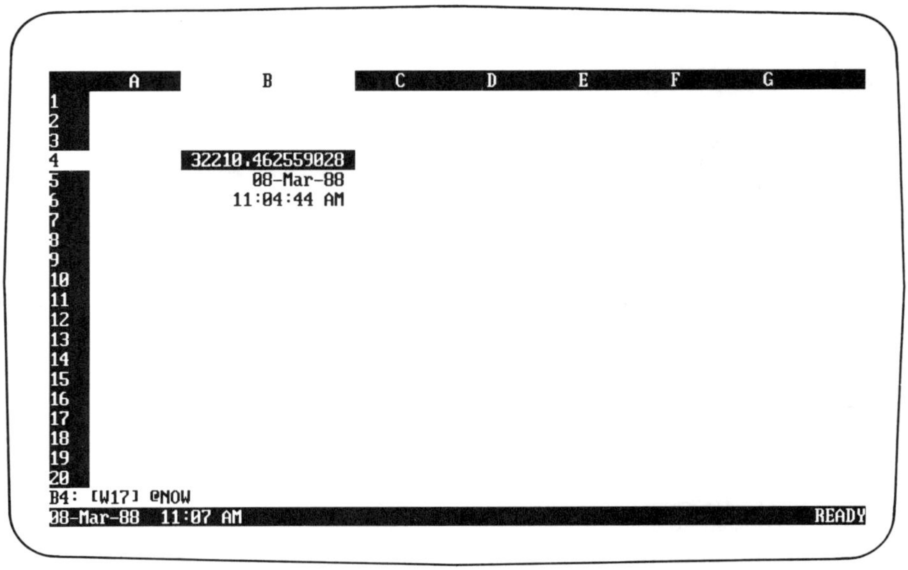

Fig. 6.50. @NOW formatted for date and time.

Notice that although the formatted cells show just the date or time, the number in memory still contains both a whole number (date) and the decimal number (time). Figure 6.51 shows a way to enter the formula if you want to isolate the current time. In the formula

@NOW-@INT(@NOW)

the @INT isolates the whole-number date portion, which is then subtracted from the entire serial number returned by @NOW.

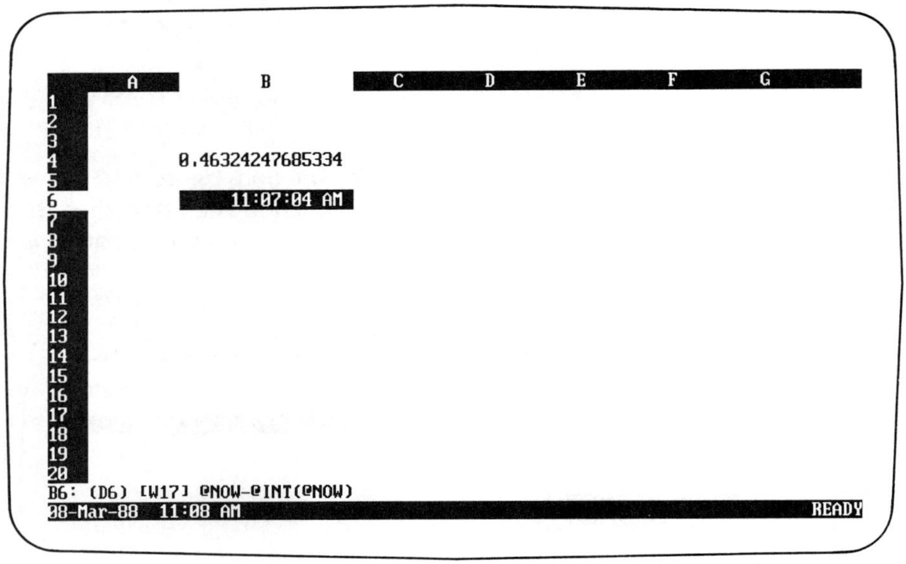

Fig. 6.51. Isolating the time portion of the current date with @NOW and @INT.

If you use an @NOW function for some decision-making purpose in an @IF statement or as the criterion in a database, you might experience some difficulties as a result. For instance, this condition:

@NOW=@DATE(87,12,15)

will always be false except for one brief moment: exactly at midnight on December 15, 1987.

The correct formula for date comparisons of this type is

@INT(@NOW)=@DATE(87,12,15)

This formula removes the time portion of the @NOW function, thus making it a "date to date" comparison.

@NOW can also be useful in macros that are time sensitive. For more information, see the section in Chapter 16 that describes the WAIT macro keyword.

@TIME

The @TIME function is used to enter a numeric form of time so that Quattro can perform calculations on the entry. For example, you may want the program to compute the number of seconds between two times. The syntax for @TIME is

@TIME(hh,mm,ss)

where *hh* is an hour numbered from 0 to 23, *mm* is a minute number from 0 to 59, and *ss* is the number of seconds from 0 to 59. All the arguments for @TIME must be numeric rather than string-oriented data. The arguments can be numbers, references to external cells, or the results of other formulas.

To use the @TIME function on a time such as 08:25:00, enter @TIME(08,25,00) in a cell. Quattro then displays the number `0.350694`. This number is a decimal portion of one day. A day is equal to 1. Any time is therefore a portion or fraction of a day. The decimal 0.5 is equal to noon, because half a day has elapsed. As is true with most of the time functions, if you want the number that results from the @TIME function to look like a time, you must format the number with the /**B**lock **D**isplay Format **D**ate **T**ime command.

Although you can use Ctrl-D to facilitate the entry of date information, no shortcut is available for time data. Therefore, to perform time calculations, you must be familiar with the time functions.

@TIMEVALUE

The @TIMEVALUE function allows you to create a numeric time from a string of text. Thus, you can enter the string "12:00:00" and have the @TIMEVALUE function translate the string into the equivalent time number (0.5 for 12:00 Meridian). The syntax for @TIMEVALUE is

@TIMEVALUE(time_string)

where *time_string* can be a quoted string or a reference to a cell containing a label or a string-oriented formula.

The @TIMEVALUE function requires that the time string be written in one of the available time formats under the /**B**lock **D**isplay Format **D**ate **T**ime menu. Specifically, the four valid formats are

HH:MM:SS	AM/PM
HH:MM	AM/PM
HH:MM:SS	(24-hour clock)
HH:MM	(24-hour clock)

For example, the function @TIMEVALUE("06:00:00 AM") returns the decimal fraction 0.25.

To determine the time that elapses between two particular times, simply subtract one time from another and then format the result in long international format, the third choice in the previous list.

@SECOND

The @SECOND, @MINUTE, and @HOUR functions are the reverse of the @TIME function. The @TIME function returns a decimal number representing a time; @SECOND, @MINUTE, and @HOUR extract from a decimal number specific units of time.

The @SECOND function returns a number between 0 and 59 that represents the seconds portion of a time. The syntax for the @SECOND function is

@SECOND(value)

where *value* is any number, usually a decimal number that represents a time.

For example, the formula

@SECOND(@TIMEVALUE("12:10:35"))

results in the number 35. The @TIMEVALUE function changes the string argument to a number, and the @SECOND function extracts the portion of the number that represents the seconds.

@MINUTE

The @MINUTE function returns a number between 0 and 59 that represents the minutes portion of a time. The syntax for the @MINUTE function is

@MINUTE(value)

where *value* is any number, usually a decimal number that represents a time.

Because a date is a whole number in Quattro, the @MINUTE function returns an answer of 0 to indicate midnight (zero hour). Notice the example in figure 6.52. @TODAY always represents the date number in integer form, so @MINUTE(@TODAY) returns 0 (see cell A1).

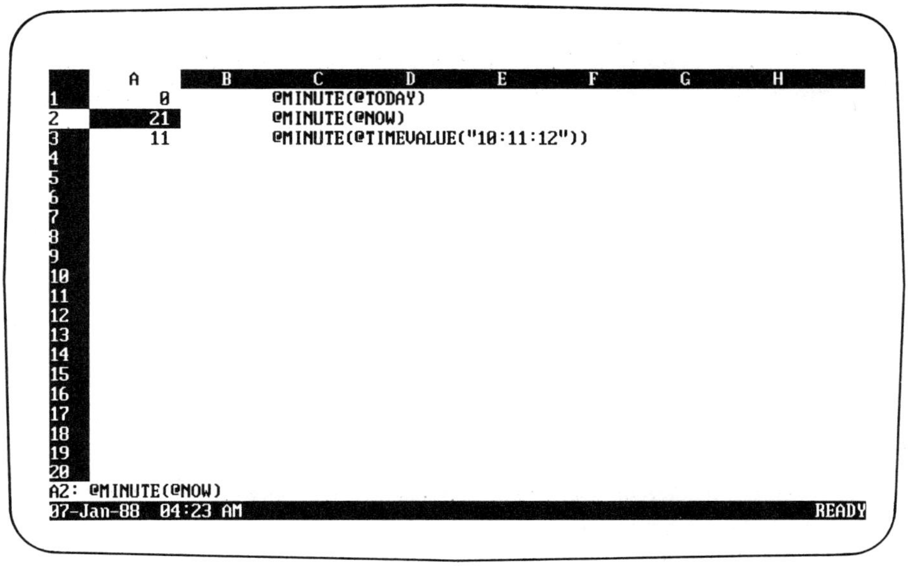

Fig. 6.52. Some examples of the @MINUTE function.

The formula in cell A2, @MINUTE(@NOW), extracts the minute number, 21, from the time. Note at the bottom of the figure the time that the figure was created: 04:23 a.m. Cell A2 was calculated two minutes before the figure was created.

@HOUR

The @HOUR function returns a number between 0 and 23 that represents the hours portion of a time. The syntax for the @HOUR function is

@HOUR(value)

where *value* is any number, usually a decimal number that represents a time.

Like the @MINUTE function, @HOUR returns an answer of 0 to indicate midnight (zero hour). Hour numbers are similar to military time (for example, 1500 hours). Figure 6.53 shows some @HOUR examples.

The formula in cell A2, @HOUR(@NOW), extracts the military time, 15 hours, which equals 3:00 p.m. Note that the figure was created at 3:41 p.m. The @HOUR function stripped off the minutes and seconds information.

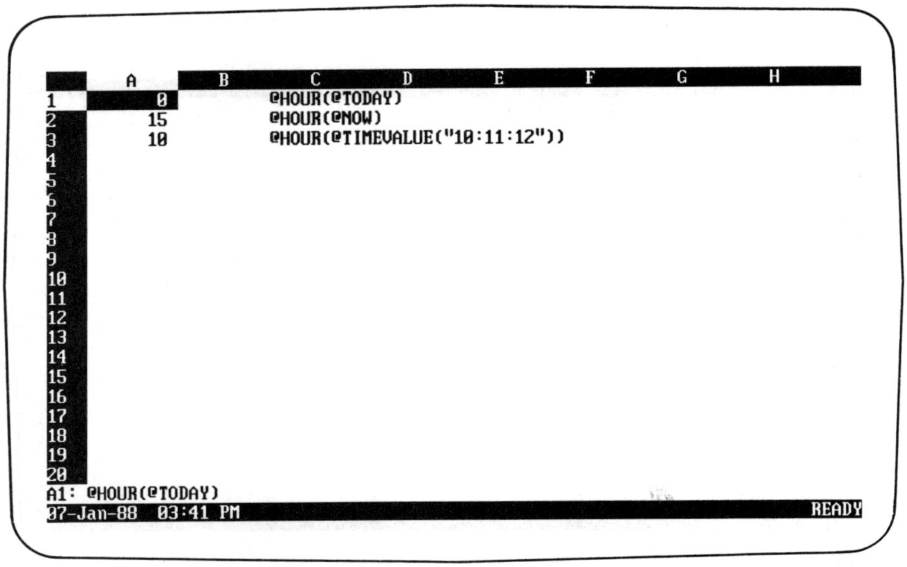

Fig. 6.53. Some examples of the @HOUR function.

Chapter Summary

This chapter introduced you to some powerful tools in Quattro's repertoire—the spreadsheet functions. The statistical, mathematical, logical, financial, and date/time functions can make your spreadsheet work a breeze. But this chapter is only the beginning. Chapter 7 covers advanced functions, such as table and array-handling, database statistical, text-handling, macro-related special, engineering/scientific, and programmers' functions.

CHAPTER

7

Using Advanced Spreadsheet Functions

Now that you have mastered Quattro's basic spreadsheet functions, you are probably ready to venture into some of the program's more sophisticated features—the advanced spreadsheet functions. This category includes functions to look up and index data, perform statistical analysis on selected records from a database, manipulate text strings, provide information about particular cells, and conduct trigonometric and logarithmic calculations.

First, let's look at a group of functions that can help you produce more efficient models.

Table and Array-Handling Functions

So many times in my travels, I have seen sophisticated spreadsheet applications that work but are overly large and unnecessarily complex. One of the functions most frequently abused in these spreadsheets is the @IF function.

@IF functions can be tortured creatures when pushed to four, five, and even more levels of nesting. Although I congratulate anyone with the patience and preciseness needed to accomplish this kind of juggling act, Quattro offers several alternatives that are superior to highly nested @IF statements.

This section explores several functions that significantly extend the decision-making and modeling power of Quattro. These functions, which include @CHOOSE, @VLOOKUP, @HLOOKUP, @INDEX, and @@, are listed in table 7.1.

Table 7.1
Table and Array-Handling Functions

Function	*Description*
@CHOOSE(key,argument, argument, . . .)	Selects an alternative result based on the key
@VLOOKUP(selector,table, offset_col)	Returns from a vertical table the data that corresponds to the selector value
@HLOOKUP(selector,table, offset_row)	Returns from a horizontal table the data that corresponds to the selector value
@INDEX(table,col_offset, row_offset)	Retrieves data from a table at the column and row offsets specified
@@(indirect cell reference)	Displays the contents of the cell specified as a label in the indirect cell reference

@CHOOSE

The @CHOOSE function uses a key value, which you provide, to select an entry from a list. The function has the following syntax:

@CHOOSE(key,argument,argument,...argument)

@CHOOSE displays the argument whose position in the list matches the key you indicated. (The first position corresponds to a key of 0, the second position corresponds to a key of 1, and so on. This system, which is used by many Quattro functions, is called an offset numbering system.) For example, the function

@CHOOSE(2,3,4,5)

returns the number 5 because 5 is in the third position in the list (offset position 2). If you change the key to 0, as in

@CHOOSE(0,3,4,5)

the function returns the number 3.

The first argument (the key) in the @CHOOSE function can be a number, a cell reference, a formula, or a function with numeric value. The remaining arguments can have either numeric or alphanumeric (string) values.

You can also use the @CHOOSE function to select formulas that will vary in different situations. For example, the percentage rate used to compute depreciation under the modified ACRS depreciation system varies with the useful life of the asset. Thus, an asset with a three-year life is depreciated in the first year of its life at a rate different from that of an asset with a five-year life. You could set up a depreciation table, as shown in figure 7.1, and use @CHOOSE to determine the correct depreciation calculation for a particular asset.

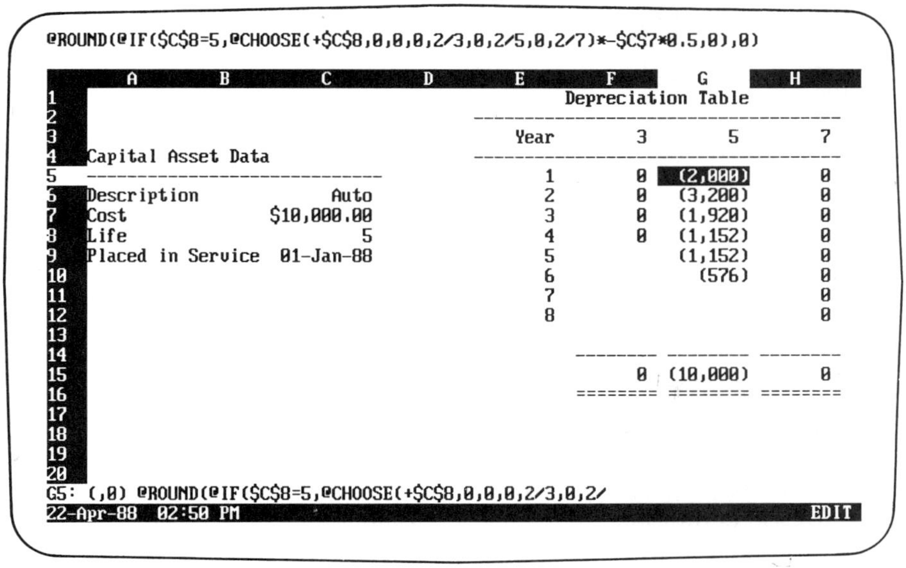

Fig. 7.1. Using the @CHOOSE function to determine the correct modified ACRS depreciation calculation.

You should consider the @CHOOSE function whenever you have a formula that may result in 3 to 10 alternatives. A nested @IF function should work well if you have 3 or less alternatives. But with more than 3, the length of the @IF formula becomes unwieldy and difficult to debug, edit, or update. If you have more than 10 alternatives, @VLOOKUP and @HLOOKUP may be more helpful than @CHOOSE.

@VLOOKUP

The vertical lookup function is best explained by looking at an example of a manual table that uses a similar process. The most familiar example is the dreaded IRS tax tables.

The tax tables are identical in structure to a vertical lookup table. Take a look at the sample table in figure 7.2 and consider how you find your hypothetical tax debt within the table.

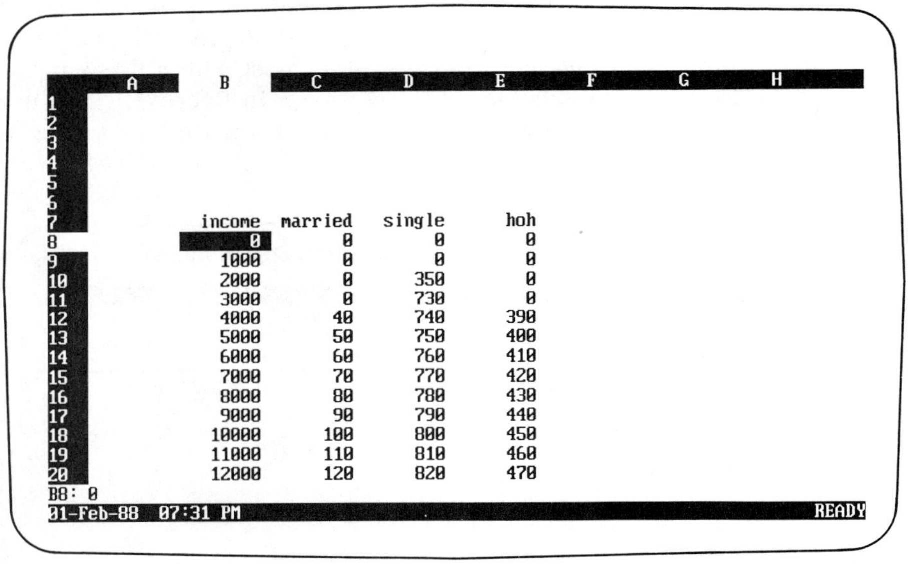

income	married	single	hoh
0	0	0	0
1000	0	0	0
2000	0	350	0
3000	0	730	0
4000	40	740	390
5000	50	750	400
6000	60	760	410
7000	70	770	420
8000	80	780	430
9000	90	790	440
10000	100	800	450
11000	110	810	460
12000	120	820	470

Fig. 7.2. An IRS tax table.

First, you look down the leftmost column to find the appropriate range of taxable income. Once you have found the correct row in the table, you look along the top of the table to find the applicable family status. Then you know which column to use. To find the tax amount, you "look up" the tax at the intersection of the row and column selected.

During the manual selection process, you perform an implied if-then process on the leftmost column to find the correct row. As your eye scans the income ranges starting at the top of the column, you no doubt silently use the rule "If my taxable income is greater than the row I am looking at, look at the next row down." So you go down the column until you find the first entry that is greater than your taxable income and then select the entry just before that one.

If you followed that explanation, then you know exactly how the @VLOOKUP function works. Instead of using your eye to scan a table, @VLOOKUP uses an internal if-then test on the leftmost column of a specified table. The syntax of the @VLOOKUP function is

@VLOOKUP(selector,table,offset_col)

Now let's use the tax table to explain @VLOOKUP's syntax. Figure 7.3 shows how to implement a table lookup function when emulating a previously existing manual system. To use this model, you enter adjusted gross income in cell B2. The @VLOOKUP function in cell B5 uses this income number as the *selector* argument. The function's second argument, the *table*, contains cell references that correspond to the top left cell (B8) and the bottom right cell (E42) of the table. You can also use a block name for this argument.

Perhaps the most difficult argument to visualize is the *offset_col*. This number is simply a number used by @VLOOKUP to determine at which column in the table to look to find the tax. In figure 7.3, the offset argument is found in cell B3. In this case, the offset number specifies an offset of 2, which means that @VLOOKUP will select the third column (remember, in an offset numbering system, the leftmost column is 0).

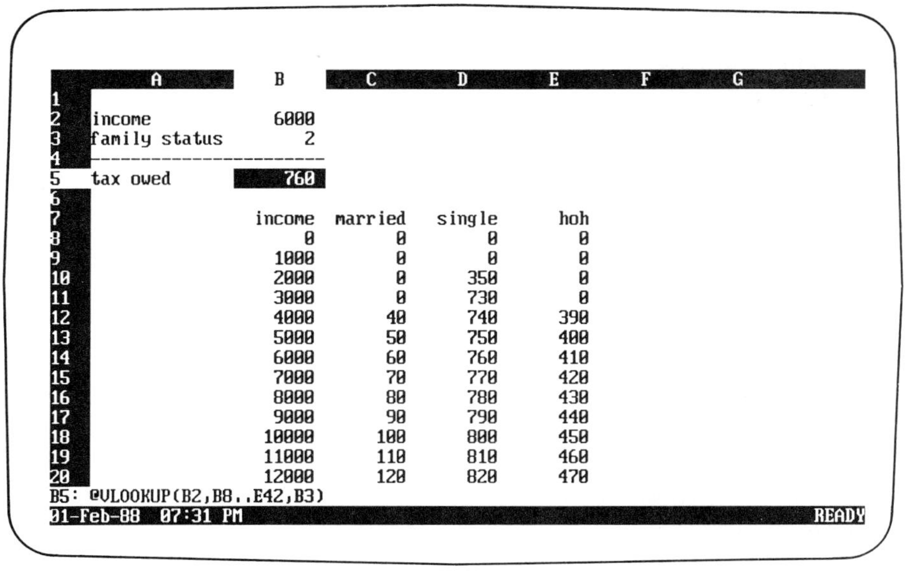

	A	B	C	D	E	F	G
1							
2	income	6000					
3	family status	2					
4	-----------------------						
5	tax owed	760					
6							
7		income	married	single	hoh		
8		0	0	0	0		
9		1000	0	0	0		
10		2000	0	350	0		
11		3000	0	730	0		
12		4000	40	740	390		
13		5000	50	750	400		
14		6000	60	760	410		
15		7000	70	770	420		
16		8000	80	780	430		
17		9000	90	790	440		
18		10000	100	800	450		
19		11000	110	810	460		
20		12000	120	820	470		

B5: @VLOOKUP(B2,B8..E42,B3)

01-Feb-88 07:31 PM READY

Fig. 7.3. Using @VLOOKUP to find the appropriate tax.

To see how the @VLOOKUP function found the answer, look down the column until you come to the row that is greater than or equal to 6000 (the selector argument). This row turns out to be row 14 in the sample spreadsheet. If you move across this row to the offset column (the third column), you will find the number 760.

The value of lookups is that you can include any number of variables in a table—up to the size of the spreadsheet. This function is especially valuable when you need to determine such things as unit pricing, discount levels, tax rates, salary rates, vacation accrual rates, and so on, where the possible alternatives in the table change regularly.

@HLOOKUP

The @HLOOKUP function has nearly the same arguments as @VLOOKUP. The syntax of the @HLOOKUP function is

@HLOOKUP(selector,table,offset_row)

Only the third argument, *offset_row*, differs from @VLOOKUP. This argument specifies the offset row, not the column, where the function is to look up the data. @HLOOKUP differs from @VLOOKUP in that the horizontal lookup table stretches across rather than down the spreadsheet. Thus the selector argument searches across the top row of the table from left to right rather than along the leftmost column from top to bottom as in @VLOOKUP.

Why would you want to use @HLOOKUP? It gives you the flexibility to lay out a table in exactly the way you want. If the table looks or fits better in the spreadsheet in a horizontal layout, you can use @HLOOKUP rather than @VLOOKUP.

Figure 7.4 shows an application that uses the @HLOOKUP function to determine how much vacation time has accrued for any employee, based on the number of years the employee has been with the company. This application could prove useful in budgeting for vacation times.

In figure 7.4, cell B1 contains the number of years an employee has worked for the company. This number serves as the selector argument in the @HLOOKUP function in cell B3. The table argument is a reference to the table that encompasses cells B8 through K9.

To find the correct vacation accrual for 6 years of employment, @HLOOKUP looks at the top left cell in the table. The selector number, 6, is greater than 1, the first number, so the lookup proceeds horizontally to the right until the function finds a number greater than or equal to 6. In this case, the column looked up is column G. The function then proceeds to offset row 1 to find the correct vacation amount (the number 3 in cell G9).

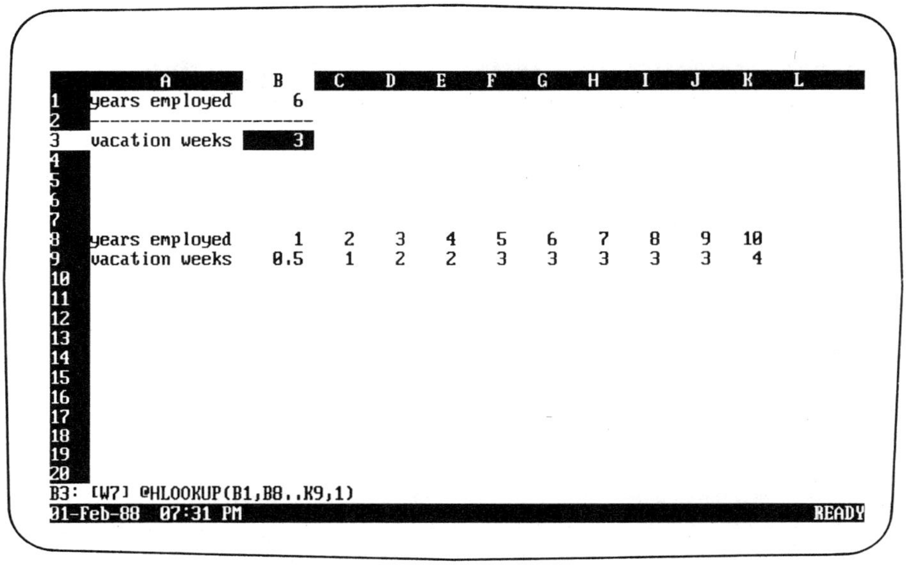

Fig. 7.4. A simple @HLOOKUP example to find the number of vacation weeks earned.

Figure 7.5 enhances the application so that it works with multiple employees. Note that references to the table argument have been made absolute (B12..K13) to allow for copying of the lookup function.

In this version of the vacation budgeting model, the vacation weeks due is found for individual employees in the database. Each employee has a horizontal lookup formula associated with the employee's database record. As you can see, the function in cell E5 looks to cell C5 for its selector argument, years employed.

Tip Always make absolute the references to a lookup function's table argument, whether they are cell references or a block name. Absolute references prevent dangerous errors if you need to copy the function later.

Tip If you copy any lookup function whose table reference is relative, the function will "walk off the table" as the formula is copied. At best, you will get an ERR or 0 display. At worst, you will get answers that may appear correct but are a result of the function looking in the wrong area of the spreadsheet for the table. Figure 7.6 illustrates what would have happened if the table reference in cell E5 of figure 7.5 had been copied down the column as a relative reference. Note that the table argument now refers to a nonexisting table in B13..K14.

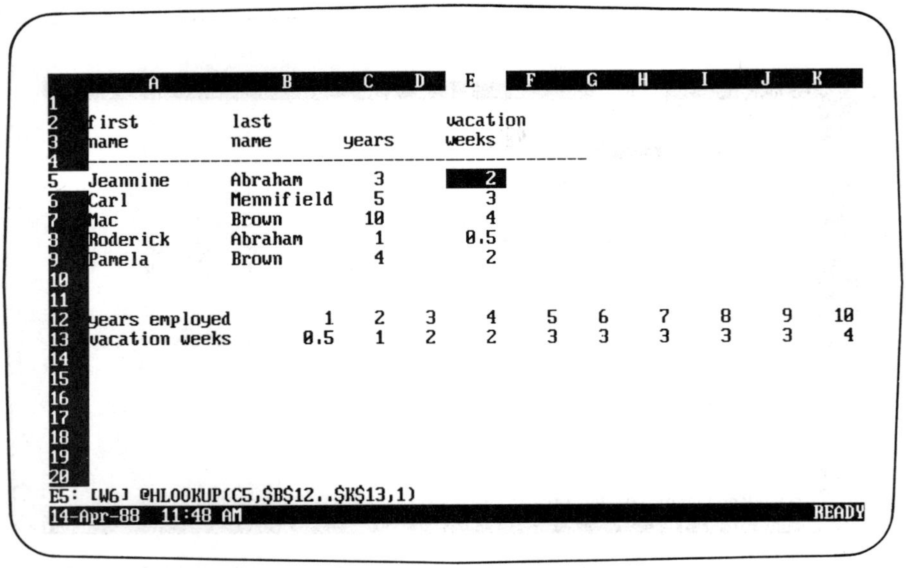

Fig. 7.5. The @HLOOKUP vacation model for multiple employees.

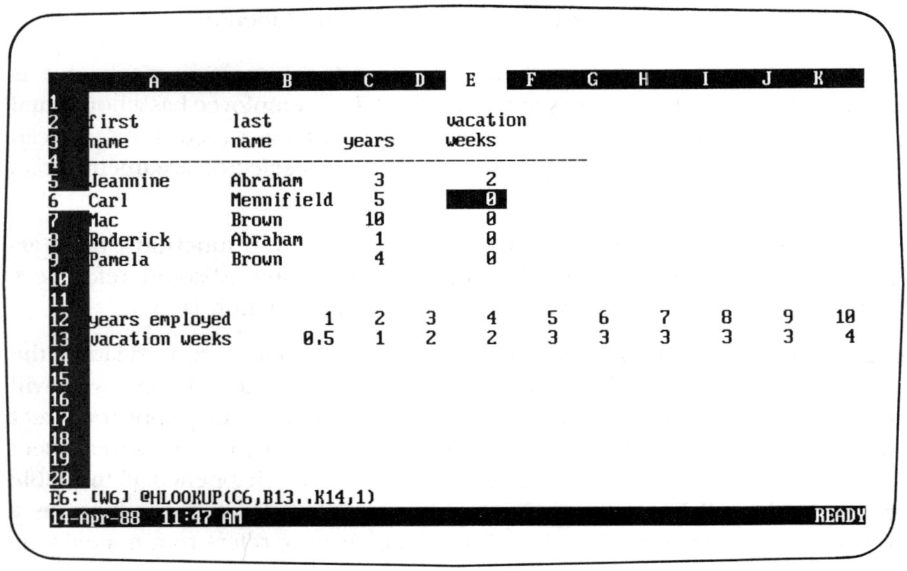

Fig. 7.6. The result of forgetting to make references absolute.

Tip Be sure to use ascending numbers in the index (zero offset) column or row of all tables. If you don't, the lookup function will stop searching at the first number that satisfies its selection criteria. For instance, if an @HLOOKUP table has the numbers 1, 2, 3, 4, 9, and 7—in that order—in the index (top) row, the function will never find the 7 because the lookup test (greater than or equal to the entry but less than the next entry) will be satisfied before the 7 is ever reached (for example, a selector number of 8 is greater than 4 and less than 9), so 4 will be chosen as the index point.

The next discussion of lookup tables shows how you can use text or labels to control a lookup function.

Text Lookups

Quattro has no limitation on what kind of data you can look up in a table. Figure 7.7 shows the vacation application as it indicates the amount of vacation a new employee should receive in the first year. As you can see, the @HLOOKUP function finds and returns the text `no vac`.

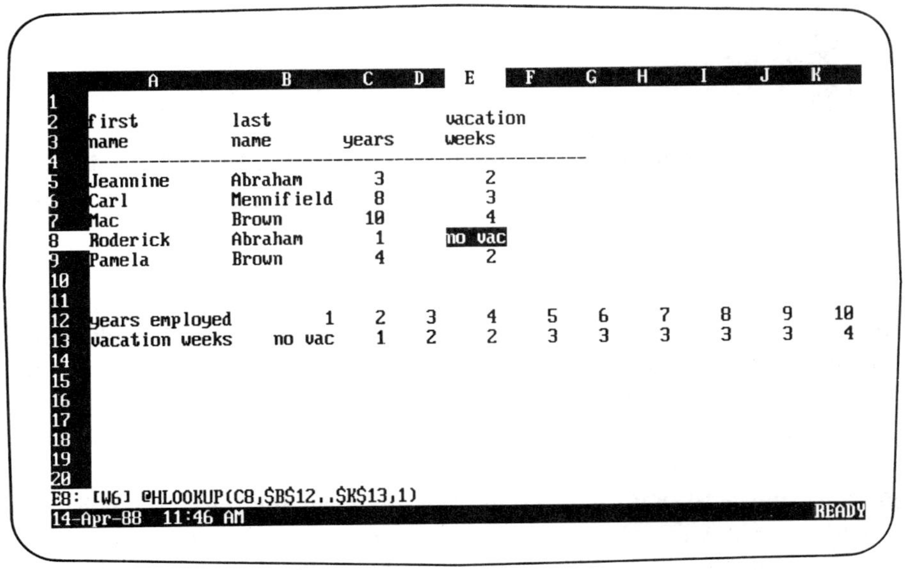

	A	B	C	D	E	F	G	H	I	J	K
2	first	last			vacation						
3	name	name	years		weeks						
5	Jeannine	Abraham	3		2						
6	Carl	Mennifield	8		3						
7	Mac	Brown	10		4						
8	Roderick	Abraham	1		no vac						
9	Pamela	Brown	4		2						
12	years employed	1	2	3	4	5	6	7	8	9	10
13	vacation weeks	no vac	1	2	2	3	3	3	3	3	4

E8: [W6] @HLOOKUP(C8,B12..K13,1)
14-Apr-88 11:46 AM READY

Fig. 7.7. Including text in a lookup table.

In addition to finding text within a table, both @VLOOKUP and @HLOOKUP can successfully use text as the selector argument for a table search. This feature may come in handy if you want to create an application that uses

English rather than some numbering system for lookups. Then, a casual employee could simply enter words to find the correct offset.

For example, you can use text selectors to embellish the vacation model from the preceding figures to apply the correct weeks of vacation based on both years employed and the category of employment, such as part-time, exempt, nonexempt, and executive (see fig. 7.8).

```
      A                B          C    D    E    F    G    H    I    J    K    L
1                  2
2
3  first name      last        years     emp status     vacation due
4  ------------------------------------------------------------------
5  Jeannine        Abraham       3       nonexempt           2
6  Carl            Mennifield    8       exempt              4
7  Mac             Brown        10       executive           5
8  Roderick        Abraham       5       nonexempt           3
9  Pamela          Brown         4       part-time           1
10
11
12 emp status
13 --------------                1    2    3    4    5    6    7    8    9   10
14 executive                     2    2    3    3    3    4    4    4    5    5
15 exempt                        1    2    2    3    3    3    3    4    4    4
16 nonexempt                     1    1    2    2    3    3    3    3    3    4
17 part-time                   0.5  0.5  0.5    1    1    2    2    2    2    3
18
19
20
A1: [W14] @VLOOKUP(E5,$A$14..$A$17,0)
14-Apr-88  11:20 AM                                                     READY
```

Fig. 7.8. Using text as the selector argument.

To find the vacation weeks for a particular employee status, the application performs a horizontal lookup, as in the previous examples, to determine the column in the table that corresponds to the years-employed selector argument.

A new column, "emp status," has been added to the database in figure 7.8. This column contains the data that will be used to determine the correct offset for the @HLOOKUP function. The argument for the offset must be numeric, so a way must be found to make an employee's status equivalent to some offset number. Cell A1 contains just such a function.

The @VLOOKUP function in A1 uses the text in E5 as the selector argument in the one-column table at A14..A17. The offset number in the lookup function is a 0 (zero). When looking in the index column for the answer, lookup functions return the offset position of the selected point in the table rather than the table entry itself.

The sample function in A1 tells you that the selector argument `nonexempt` holds the second offset position from the top of the table (counting from zero). You can use this number as the offset number argument within another lookup function if you add 1 to it. Figure 7.9 illustrates how.

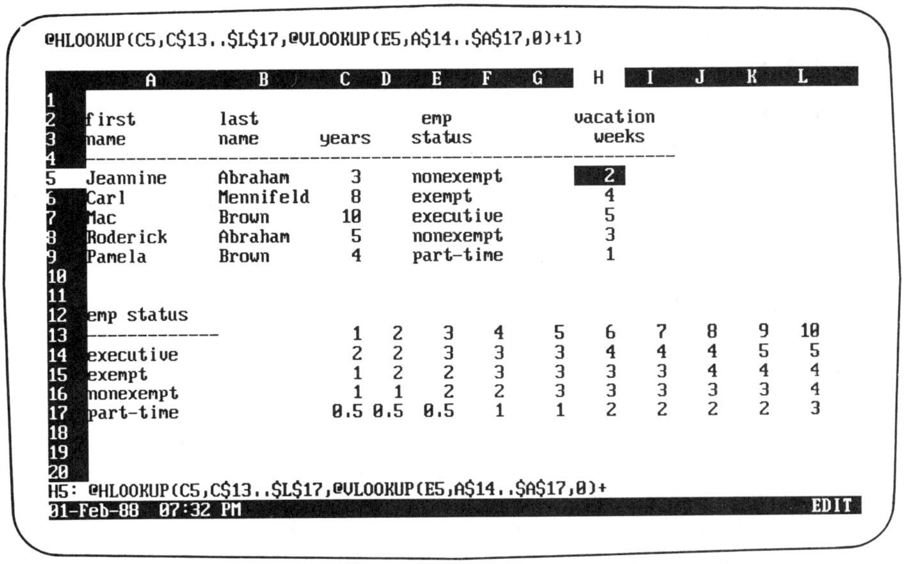

```
@HLOOKUP(C5,C$13..$L$17,@VLOOKUP(E5,A$14..$A$17,0)+1)

        A            B        C   D    E      F    G    H    I    J    K    L
1
2  first        last                emp               vacation
3  name         name       years    status              weeks
4  ---------------------------------------------------------------
5  Jeannine     Abraham      3      nonexempt             2
6  Carl         Mennifeld    8      exempt                4
7  Mac          Brown       10      executive             5
8  Roderick     Abraham      5      nonexempt             3
9  Pamela       Brown        4      part-time             1
10
11
12 emp status
13 -------------          1    2    3    4    5    6    7    8    9   10
14 executive              2    2    3    3    3    4    4    4    5    5
15 exempt                 1    2    2    3    3    3    3    4    4    4
16 nonexempt              1    1    2    2    3    3    3    3    3    4
17 part-time            0.5  0.5  0.5    1    1    2    2    2    2    3
18
19
20
H5: @HLOOKUP(C5,C$13..$L$17,@VLOOKUP(E5,A$14..$A$17,0)+
01-Feb-88  07:32 PM                                              EDIT
```

Fig. 7.9. The complete @HLOOKUP formula, which includes an @VLOOKUP as the offset argument.

Figure 7.9 is the final application. The @HLOOKUP function in cell H5 is similar to the simple examples shown previously, with the exception of the offset argument. This argument is supplied by the @VLOOKUP function that was illustrated in figure 7.8.

To understand this nested lookup function, here's a description in English: "Look at the number of years this employee has worked. Then find the corresponding column in the vacation table (C13..L17). Now look at the employee's status and find its position in the status table (A14..A17). Add 1 to the position number. Now use this number to determine how many rows deep to look into the vacation table."

The lookup function finds the answer, 2, at cell E16, the column for the third year of employment, and the row corresponding to a nonexempt employee.

You may be wondering why you should go to all this trouble. This kind of formula makes it much less likely that you will need macros in an application.

You want to avoid macros when you can, because macros are always going to be slower and harder to maintain than a well-implemented @function (yes, I know—never say always). (For more on macros, refer to Chapter 15.)

The next function is the little-known @INDEX function. If you need actuarial tables or similar constructs, @INDEX is the function for you.

@INDEX

The @INDEX function is much more specialized than @CHOOSE, @VLOOKUP, or @HLOOKUP. @INDEX can search a table without needing a formal selector or offset number as the lookup functions do. The syntax for the @INDEX function is

@INDEX(table,col_offset,row_offset)

The @INDEX function searches the specified *table* at the *col_offset* and *row_offset* supplied, and returns the value or text found at the resulting coordinate.

A good application of @INDEX is shown in figure 7.10. In this model, you need to enter only a starting and an ending month number to find the days between the months from one year to the next.

```
     A    B    C    D    E    F    G    H    I    J    K    L    M    N    O
1  Table showing the number of days from any date in one month to the same
2  date in any other month.  Enter starting and ending month as a number.
3
4                                from        to       days between months
5                                   7         9             303
6            from
7        to   jan  feb  mar  apr  may  jun  jul  aug  sep  oct  nov  dec
8       jan   365   31   59   90  120  151  181  212  243  273  304  334
9       feb   334  365   28   59   89  120  150  181  212  242  273  303
10      mar   306  337  365   31   61   92  122  153  184  214  245  275
11      apr   275  306  334  365   30   61   91  122  153  183  214  244
12      may   245  276  304  335  365   31   61   92  123  153  184  214
13      jun   214  245  274  304  334  365   30   61   92  122  153  183
14      jul   184  215  243  273  304  335  365   31   62   92  123  153
15      aug   153  184  212  243  273  304  334  365   31   31   92  122
16      sep   122  153  181  212  242  273  303  334  365   30   61   91
17      oct    92  123  151  182  212  243  273  304  335  365   31   61
18      nov    61   92  120  151  181  212  242  273  304  334  365   30
19      dec    31   62   90  121  151  182  212  243  274  304  335  365
20
K5: @INDEX(C8..N19,F5-1,H5-1)
01-Feb-88  07:32 PM                                                   READY
```

Fig. 7.10. Finding the number of days between two particular months with @INDEX.

The @INDEX function in cell K5 first identifies the block where the table is located. Notice that the table does not include the month names in row 7 or column B. The second argument, the column offset, uses the number 7 (the starting month number) in cell F5. Remember that an offset numbering system starts counting at 0, which means that unless you modify the offset number, the column identified will be the eighth column (August) rather than the seventh column (July). To make the month number entered correspond to the correct column offset, you must simply subtract 1 from the month number (F5-1). The same thing also applies to the row offset argument in cell H5 (the ending month number). For your reference, the number found by the @INDEX function is in cell I16.

Tip In an @INDEX function, be sure that the referenced column and row numbers are converted to offset arguments. You usually need to factor the numbers by subtracting 1 from each argument.

Figure 7.11 illustrates another example of the @INDEX function. This spreadsheet gives the annual cost of a homeowner's insurance policy based on two things: the value of the home to the nearest ten thousand and the area where the house is located.

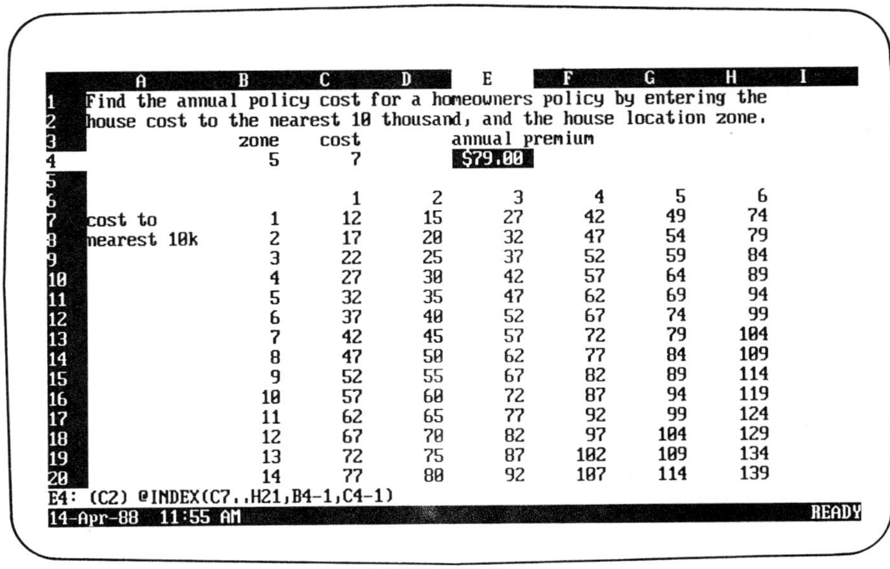

	A	B	C	D	E	F	G	H	I
1	Find the annual policy cost for a homeowners policy by entering the								
2	house cost to the nearest 10 thousand, and the house location zone.								
3		zone	cost		annual premium				
4		5	7		$79.00				
5									
6			1	2	3	4	5	6	
7	cost to	1	12	15	27	42	49	74	
8	nearest 10k	2	17	20	32	47	54	79	
9		3	22	25	37	52	59	84	
10		4	27	30	42	57	64	89	
11		5	32	35	47	62	69	94	
12		6	37	40	52	67	74	99	
13		7	42	45	57	72	79	104	
14		8	47	50	62	77	84	109	
15		9	52	55	67	82	89	114	
16		10	57	60	72	87	94	119	
17		11	62	65	77	92	99	124	
18		12	67	70	82	97	104	129	
19		13	72	75	87	102	109	134	
20		14	77	80	92	107	114	139	

E4: (C2) @INDEX(C7..H21,B4-1,C4-1)
14-Apr-88 11:55 AM READY

Fig. 7.11. Another @INDEX example.

The @INDEX function in cell E4 looks at the table found in cells C7 through H21. By using the number in the zone cell for the column offset and cost for the row offset, the system locates the annual cost in cell G13.

@@

The @@ (pronounced *at at*) function is one of the more arcane tools of Quattro. @@ allows you to address a cell, and therefore its contents, indirectly.

The @@ function is easy to understand if you think of it this way: High-rise apartment or condominium buildings usually have a phone system outside the door that enables you to call a resident. To ensure privacy, the phone systems don't show residents' names but instead list apartment numbers. If you know the apartment number, you are then cross-referenced to another number to dial on the phone. This indirect referencing, first to apartment, then to phone extension, is exactly what the @@ function does.

Of course, most people simply wait nonchalantly by the door until someone else goes in. Then they grab the door just before it closes.

Indirect addressing allows a spreadsheet developer to create an application that can deal with variables more flexibly. The syntax for @@ is

@@(indirect cell reference)

The @@ function expects that the cell referenced will contain a label. The label will be a text version of a cell address or block name. The text referenced by the @@ function contains a pointer to the cell holding the data needed by the @@ function. Figure 7.12 shows a simple example. The label `D4` is in cell A1. The @@ function in cell A4 is referencing the text in cell A1. By looking at cell A1, the function locates its ultimate reference, the contents of cell D4 (the label `indirect`).

The next example of @@ shows a flexible method of performing "what-if" analysis in the spreadsheet. You can use the model in figure 7.13 to find the annual payment for a house costing $100,000 with a term of 30 years. This model allows you simply to select (move the cell selector to) the interest rate you want to try and press Calc (F9).

In figure 7.13, the cell selector shows a cell containing the @PMT function. The first argument uses the principal amount in cell D3, and the last argument sets the term of the loan at 30 years. The interesting part of the formula is the @@ function that represents the interest rate argument. The @@ function's argument is A1, and in cell A1 is the indirect address to F3 where the rate of 8 percent is located. This interest rate is what the @PMT function uses.

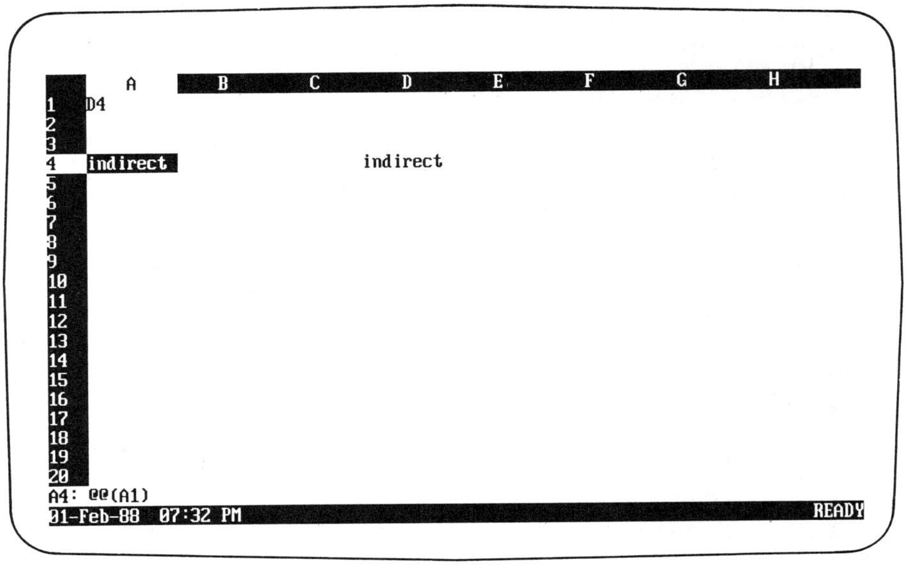

Fig. 7.12. The @@ function.

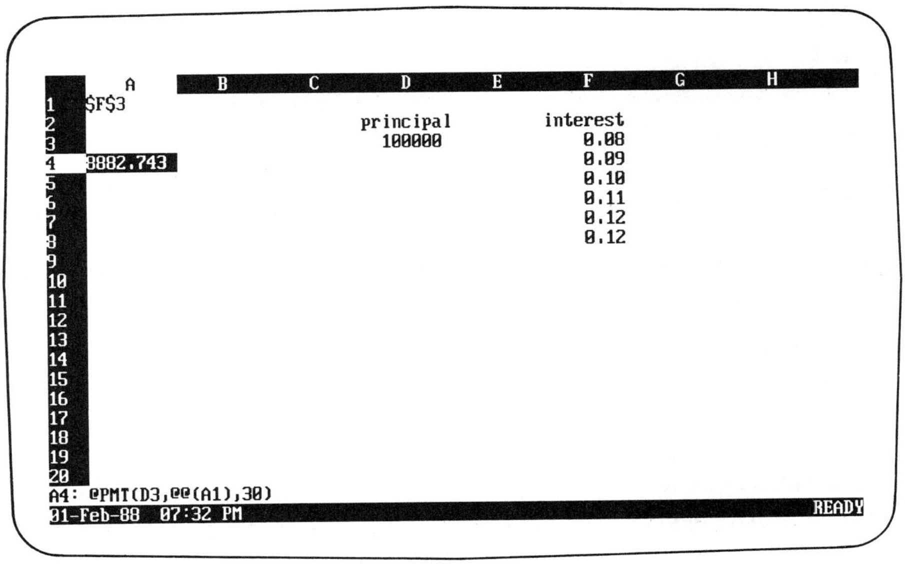

Fig. 7.13. Using @@ within an @PMT function.

Figures 7.14 and 7.15 point out the portion of the model that gives it flexibility from the user's standpoint. Cell A1 of figure 7.14 contains the formula

@CELLPOINTER("address")

which provides information about the cell selector's location just before the most recent recalculation. (For more information, refer to the discussion of @CELLPOINTER in this chapter's "Macro-Related Special Functions" section.) As you can see, the cell selector was at cell F3 when the spreadsheet was last calculated.

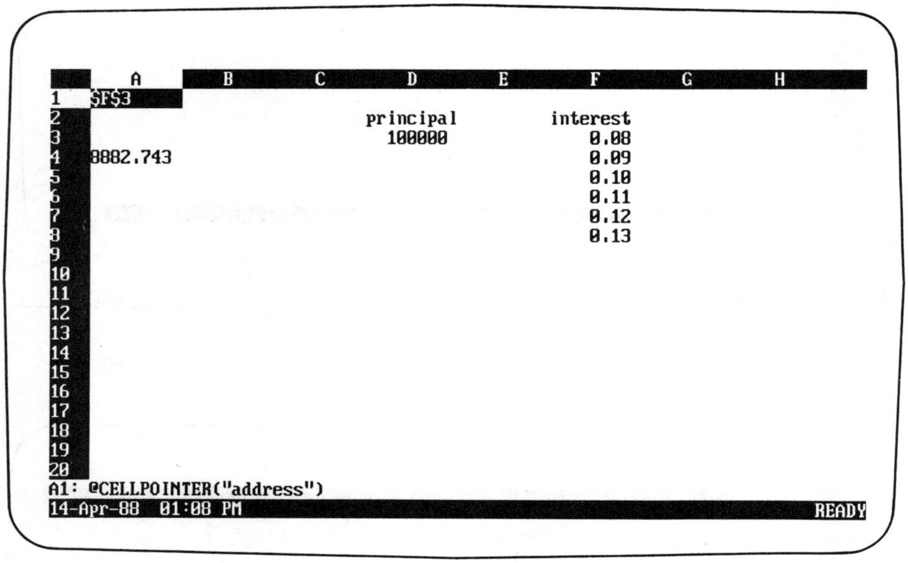

Fig. 7.14. The @@ refers to cell A1, which references cell F3 in the interest rate column.

Figure 7.15 shows what happened after the cell selector was moved to cell F8 and Calc was pressed.

In this instance, the @CELLPOINTER function returned the address F8, and the @@ function in cell A4 used this new reference to the interest rate list to fulfill the rate argument for the @PMT function.

The @@ function is similar in nature to the DISPATCH macro command. Look for this command in Chapter 16, "Quattro Command Language Reference," if you want to create a "point and shoot" macro menu in the spreadsheet.

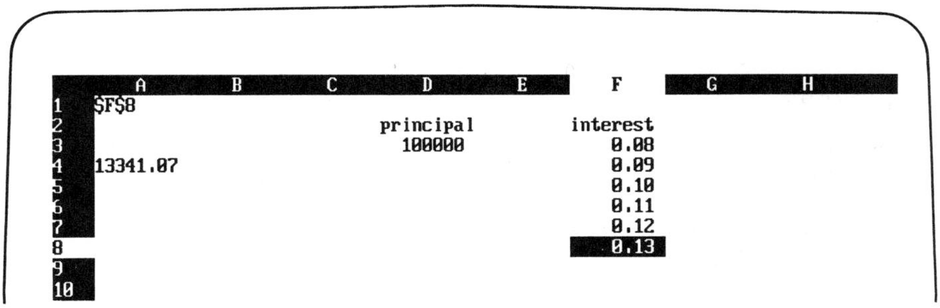

Fig. 7.15. After pressing Calc, which changes the reference in cell A1.

The table functions are some of the most powerful functions in Quattro. By becoming familiar with them, you will find that your applications will be more powerful and flexible and easier to maintain. If you are a macro lover and have not investigated the more advanced forms of these functions, you are really missing something.

Database Statistical Functions

The database statistical functions are nearly identical to the statistical functions described in Chapter 6. The difference is in the way that the database statistical functions determine which values to include in the manipulation.

For instance, the @SUM function totals all the values in its argument. Conversely, the @DSUM function allows you to specify which group or numeric range of values to sum. The database statistical functions provide a way to specify criteria for statistical evaluation. You can thus formulate functions that can answer requests such as "give me the average age for everyone between 21 and 70 years," "show me the sum of the sales for expenses greater than $500," or "give me a count of salespersons who exceeded quota."

The database statistical functions are usually associated with databases or data tables, but you are not limited to this type of application. You can use these functions to evaluate any column of values that has a unique column header.

Table 7.2 lists the database statistical functions and includes a brief description of each function.

The syntax for the database statistical functions is

```
@DFUNCTION(table_block,offset_col,criteria_block)
```

Table 7.2
Database Statistical Functions

Function	*Calculates*
@DSUM(table_block,col_offset, criteria_block)	The total of the values selected based on the criterion
@DAVG(table_block,col_offset, criteria_block)	The average of values selected from a table
@DCOUNT(table_block,col_offset, criteria_block)	The number of nonblank cells within a given block
@DMAX(table_block,col_offset, criteria_block)	The highest value based on the criterion
@DMIN(table_block,col_offset, criteria_block)	The lowest value based on the criterion
@DSTD(table_block,col_offset, criteria_block)	The standard deviation of the selected values
@DVAR(table_block,col_offset, criteria_block)	The variance of the selected values

where @DFUNCTION represents the name of the function. Following is a description of the arguments:

1. The *table_block* is a block encompassing the top left through the bottom right cells of the table to be analyzed. The *table_block* reference must include the row that contains column headers.

2. The *offset_col* argument allows you to specify which of many possible columns within the table to analyze.

3. The *criteria_block* is a reference to two or more vertical cells that contain the selection criteria for the statistical operation. The criteria_block consists first of a label in the top cell of the block that matches one of the column headers in the table. The second component of the criteria_block is a cell entry that provides an example of what elements of the target column should be included in the statistical operation. This cell must contain either a logical expression that evaluates to true (1) or false (0), or a string for statistics on text within a table. The entry must include a reference to the cell directly below the appropriate column header in the table.

If you plan to copy the database statistical formula to other locations in the spreadsheet, be sure that the table_block reference is absolute.

@DSUM

The @DSUM function returns the total of the values of entries selected from a table. The entries must meet specific criteria to be selected.

An example of the @DSUM function is shown in figure 7.16. This example shows how @DSUM can make selections based on more than one criterion. The checkbook application keeps track of which transactions have cleared the bank and which have not, and can exclude any deposit entries from the outstanding checks calculation.

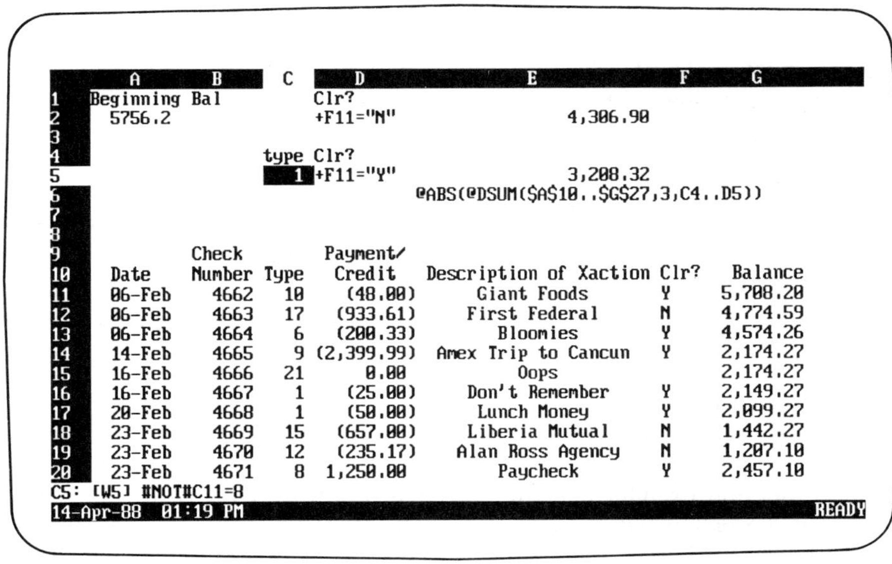

	A	B	C	D	E	F	G
1	Beginning Bal			Clr?			
2	5756.2			+F11="N"	4,306.90		
3							
4			type	Clr?			
5			1	+F11="Y"	3,208.32		
6					@ABS(@DSUM(A10..G27,3,C4..D5))		
7							
8							
9		Check		Payment/			
10	Date	Number	Type	Credit	Description of Xaction	Clr?	Balance
11	06-Feb	4662	10	(48.00)	Giant Foods	Y	5,708.20
12	06-Feb	4663	17	(933.61)	First Federal	N	4,774.59
13	06-Feb	4664	6	(200.33)	Bloomies	Y	4,574.26
14	14-Feb	4665	9	(2,399.99)	Amex Trip to Cancun	Y	2,174.27
15	16-Feb	4666	21	0.00	Oops		2,174.27
16	16-Feb	4667	1	(25.00)	Don't Remember	Y	2,149.27
17	20-Feb	4668	1	(50.00)	Lunch Money	Y	2,099.27
18	23-Feb	4669	15	(657.00)	Liberia Mutual	N	1,442.27
19	23-Feb	4670	12	(235.17)	Alan Ross Agency	N	1,207.10
20	23-Feb	4671	8	1,250.00	Paycheck	Y	2,457.10

C5: [W5] #NOT#C11=8

14-Apr-88 01:19 PM READY

Fig. 7.16. A model using @DSUM to total checks that have cleared the bank.

To obtain the sum of cleared transactions, the @DSUM formula in cell E5 sums only those records that have cleared (have a Y in column F). The criterion for this function is a reference to cells D4..D5. The criterion formula in D5 is +CLR?=Y. The @DSUM formula selects only cleared transactions and then sums the selected records from the third offset, column D.

The other database summation in cell E2 performs a similar totaling of the checks in the database that have not cleared (+CLR?=N).

If you include C4..C5 in the @DSUM function's criteria_block argument, you exclude any deposit entries, which are coded as 8 in the Type column (column C) of the table. The logical formula in C5 uses the complex operator #NOT# to exclude the transaction type of 8:

#NOT#C11=8

The limit for criteria is 32 fields.

@DAVG

The @DAVG function returns the average of numbers selected from a block. @DAVG uses the same formula, sum/count, as the @AVG function. The difference lies in the fact that @AVG averages all elements within a block, but @DAVG can examine the same block and return an average of selected elements meeting specific criteria.

In figure 7.17, notice the formulas in cells B9 and B14. The function in B9 is providing a simple @AVG of the numbers in B3..B7. The function in B14 is the function

@DAVG(B2..H7,0,B17..B18)

This formula can be interpreted as "use the table at B2..H7, and then average the numbers in the leftmost column (offset 0) that satisfy the criterion found in cells B17..B18." Only the numbers in the January column that satisfy the condition in cell B18, +B3>300, will be averaged. In other words, the function is averaging only the numbers in column B that are greater than 300.

The formula in cell B18 is formatted as text (with /**B**lock **D**isplay **F**ormat **T**ext) so that the underlying formula rather than the result is displayed. When a criteria is first entered in an unformatted cell, either 0 or 1 displays. The @DAVG function examines all the entries in the main table in the column starting at the cell specified in the criterion formula and includes all "true" entries (those that evaluate to 1).

Figure 7.18 helps to illustrate this concept by extending the model. More @DAVG functions have been created to average the rest of the model based on criteria in rows 14 and 15. The criteria in cell B15 is still formatted as text, but the rest of the criteria are in the general format.

Tip You should always format criterion formulas as text so that you can see the underlying formula.

	A	B	C	D	E	F	G	H
1								
2		jan	feb	mar	apr	may	jun	jul
3		327	294	311	309	326	297	317
4		417	354	393	375	392	386	411
5		333	262	292	286	329	306	314
6		335	286	301	303	335	311	320
7		264	256	292	263	252	243	252
8		----------	----------	----------	----------	----------	----------	----------
9	total @AV	335	290	318	307	327	309	323
10								
11								
12								
13	@DAVG of entries							
14	>300	353						
15								
16								
17	criteria	jan						
18		+B3>300						
19								
20								

B14: (F0) @DAVG(B2..H7,0,B17..B18)

01-Feb-88 07:32 PM READY

Fig. 7.17. An @DAVG example.

	A	B	C	D	E	F	G	H
1								
2		jan	feb	mar	apr	may	jun	jul
3		327	294	311	309	326	297	317
4		417	354	393	375	392	386	411
5		333	262	292	286	329	306	314
6		335	286	301	303	335	311	320
7		264	256	292	263	252	243	252
8		----------	----------	----------	----------	----------	----------	----------
9	total @AV	335	290	318	307	327	309	323
10								
11								
12								
13	@DAVG of entries							
14	>300	353	354	335	329	346	334	341
15								
16								
17	criteria	jan	feb	mar	apr	may	jun	jul
18		+B3>300	0	1	1	1	0	1
19								
20								

C14: (F0) @DAVG(C2..I7,0,C17..C18)

01-Feb-88 07:32 PM READY

Fig. 7.18. Expanding the @DAVG model.

@DCOUNT

The @DCOUNT, or database count, function returns the number of nonblank cells selected from a table. In the example in figure 7.19, note the text in cell B20, which shows you what is contained in the formula in B19. This formula is the criterion that instructs the @DCOUNT function to count only those elements in column 0 (jan) that are greater than 300 and less than 400. This logical formula is the method that allows you to specify a range of values for a database formula.

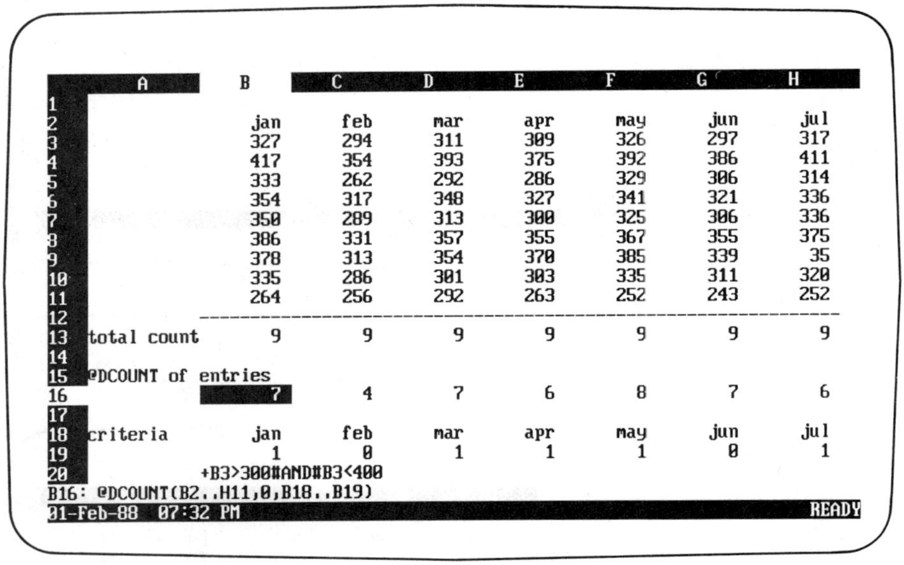

	A	B	C	D	E	F	G	H
1								
2		jan	feb	mar	apr	may	jun	jul
3		327	294	311	309	326	297	317
4		417	354	393	375	392	386	411
5		333	262	292	286	329	306	314
6		354	317	348	327	341	321	336
7		350	289	313	300	325	306	336
8		386	331	357	355	367	355	375
9		370	313	354	370	385	339	35
10		335	286	301	303	335	311	320
11		264	256	292	263	252	243	252
12		----------	----------	----------	----------	----------	----------	----------
13	total count	9	9	9	9	9	9	9
14								
15	@DCOUNT of entries							
16		7	4	7	6	8	7	6
17								
18	criteria	jan	feb	mar	apr	may	jun	jul
19		1	0	1	1	1	0	1
20		+B3>300#AND#B3<400						

B16: @DCOUNT(B2..H11,0,B18..B19)

01-Feb-88 07:32 PM READY

Fig. 7.19. Counting only specified entries with @DCOUNT.

@DMAX

The @DMAX function returns the highest value from entries that are selected from a table.

Figure 7.20 illustrates an application of the @DMAX function. The function is using a criterion that focuses on the region column header. The criterion formula +B3>=5 means that the @DMAX formulas in row 17 will find the maximum value from regions 5 through 9. The @DMAX formula in cell D17 uses an offset of 2, which causes the @DMAX function to find the highest value in the third column from the left (column D).

	A	B	C	D	E	F	G	H
1								
2		region	jan	feb	mar	apr	may	jun
3		1	327	294	311	309	326	297
4		2	417	354	393	375	392	386
5		3	333	262	292	286	329	306
6		4	354	317	348	327	341	321
7		5	350	289	313	300	325	306
8		6	386	331	357	355	367	355
9		7	378	313	354	370	385	339
10		8	335	286	301	303	335	311
11		9	264	256	292	263	252	243
12			----------	----------	----------	----------	----------	----------
13	@MAX all regions		417	354	393	375	392	386
14								
15	@DMAX regions 5-9							
16								
17	region		386	331	357	370	385	355
18	+B3>5							
19								
20								

D17: @DMAX(B2..I11,2,A17..A18)

01-Feb-88 07:32 PM READY

Fig. 7.20. Finding the maximum value with @DMAX.

@DMIN

The @DMIN function returns the lowest value from entries that are selected from a table.

In figure 7.21, the @DMIN function, like @DMAX in the previous figure, uses a criterion that focuses on the region column header. The criterion formula +B3<5 means that the @DMIN formulas in row 17 will find the minimum value from regions 1 through 4.

@DSTD

The @DSTD function returns the standard deviation of the values that are selected from a table. The @DSTD function is the square root of the @DVAR function. (For more information on standard deviation and variance, refer to the section in Chapter 6 entitled "Advanced Statistical Functions.")

The sample database in figure 7.22 illustrates the use of @DSTD in a classic IQ scenario. Note: The IQ numbers in the database were generated randomly.

The criteria in cells F1 and F2 limit the data used by the @DSTD function in cell F4 to only those subjects in the database that are older than 15 years

	A	B	C	D	E	F	G	H
1								
2		region	jan	feb	mar	apr	may	jun
3		1	327	294	311	309	326	297
4		2	417	354	393	375	392	386
5		3	333	262	292	286	329	306
6		4	354	317	348	327	341	321
7		5	350	289	313	300	325	306
8		6	386	331	357	355	367	355
9		7	378	313	354	370	385	339
10		8	335	286	301	303	335	311
11		9	264	256	292	263	252	243
12			-------	-------	-------	-------	-------	-------
13	@MIN all regions		264	256	292	263	252	243
14								
15	@DMIN regions 1-4							
16								
17	region		327	262	292	286	326	297
18	+B3<5							
19								
20								

D17: @DMIN(B2..I11,2,A17..A18)
01-Feb-88 07:32 PM READY

Fig. 7.21. Finding the minimum value with @DMIN.

of age. The formula in cell F5 is an @DAVG function. The numbers in cells F7 and G7 show the result of adding and subtracting the standard deviation from the average. In a larger population, these numbers would indicate that 67 percent of the entries in the database would fall between these numbers.

The second set of statistics on the right-hand side of figure 7.22 shows the standard deviation and average for males in the database.

@DVAR

The @DVAR function returns the variance of the values that are selected from a table. The @DVAR function returns a number equal to the square of the standard deviation.

Text Functions

Quattro's text functions—or string functions, as they are otherwise known—give you comprehensive control over the manipulation, conversion, and display of text in the spreadsheet. Some of the functions, such as @LEFT, @MID, and @RIGHT, perform text "cut-and-paste" operations. @VALUE, @STRING, @N, and @S allow you to convert text to numbers and numbers

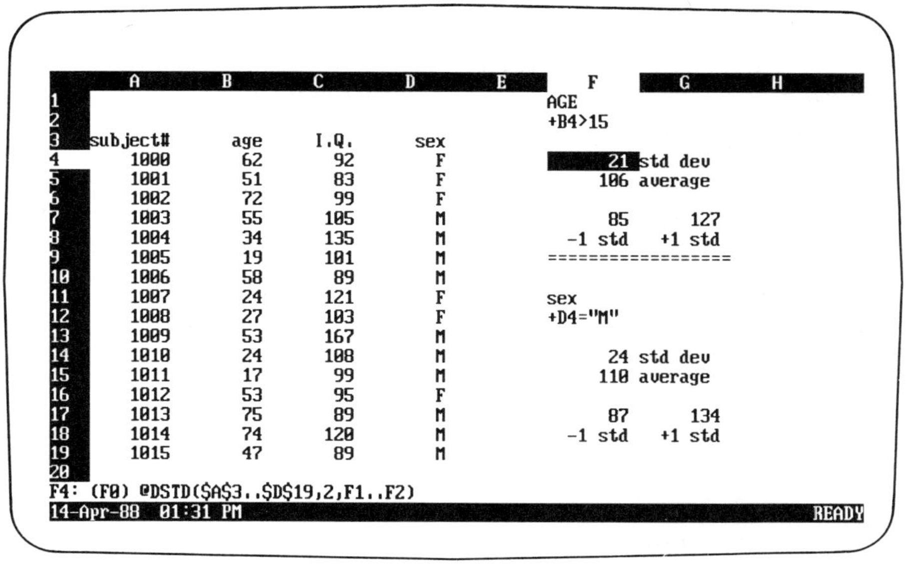

Fig. 7.22. Using @DSTD to compute the standard deviation in a group of IQ scores.

to text. @CHAR, @CODE, @FIND, @REPLACE, and @TRIM provide a number of features that facilitate the integration of text from external sources, such as a word processor. And @UPPER, @LOWER, and @PROPER let you control a string's case.

Table 7.3 summarizes the string functions. Note that you must always enclose string arguments in double quotation marks. Or you can use cell addresses rather than the string text.

@FIND

As its name implies, the @FIND function is used to find where text occurs within another string. The result of @FIND is a number equal to the starting position of the found text. (The numbering of characters starts at 0, so @FIND returns an offset number.) The syntax for @FIND is

@FIND(search_string,source_string,start_number)

The first argument, *search_string*, is the text you want to find. It can be either a quoted string (a string enclosed in double quotation marks) or a reference to a cell that contains a string.

The second argument, *source_string*, is the string that you are searching. It can be a quoted label or a cell reference.

Table 7.3
Text Functions

Function	*Description*
@FIND(search_string,source_string, start_number)	Returns starting number of found text
@MID(string,start_number,length)	Extracts the characters from the middle of a string from start number through length
@LEFT(string,length)	Extracts a specified number of characters from the left of the string
@RIGHT(string,length)	Extracts a specified number of characters from the right of the string
@EXACT(string1,string2)	Returns 1 (true) if string1 and string2 are exact matches; otherwise, returns 0 (false)
@REPLACE(string,start_number, length,replacement)	Replaces string with replacement at start number for specified length
@LENGTH(string)	Displays number of characters in string
@LOWER(string)	Displays lowercase version of string
@UPPER(string)	Displays uppercase version of string
@PROPER(string)	Displays proper case version of string (initial letter in each word uppercase, remaining letters lowercase)
@REPEAT(string,number)	Repeats a text string a specified number of times
@N(single cell reference)	Returns contents of cell reference as numeric data type (text=0)

Function	*Description*
@S(block reference)	Returns contents of cell in upper left corner of block as string data type (values=" ")
@STRING(value,decimal_places)	Converts value to string showing specified number of decimal places
@VALUE(string)	Converts string to value equivalent
@TRIM(string)	Removes redundant spaces from string
@CLEAN(string)	Removes all nondisplayable ASCII characters from string
@CHAR(ASCII number)	Returns the character that corresponds to the specified ASCII number
@CODE(string)	Gives the ASCII number for the first character in string

The last argument, *start_number*, is a number that tells the @FIND function where to begin its search. If the start number is less than the position number of the found text, the start number will have no effect on the result of @FIND. For example, if the position number is 15, you could choose 0, 9, or 12 as the start number and obtain the same result. If the search string occurs only once in the subject text (the source string), the start number *must* be lower than the start position of the search string.

For example, the formula

@FIND("the","now is the time",0)

results in an answer of 7, which is where the first character of the found string occurs in the larger string. But the function

@FIND("q","que",2)

results in an error because the @FIND function starts looking at the second offset position, which falls after the occurrence of the letter *q*.

Why then do you even need to specify a start number? In some cases, you may want to find the position of the second or third occurrence of a substring within a string. The start number provides a way for you to begin the search after the first instance of the text.

@FIND's capability to skip text is illustrated in detail in the following section on the @MID function. For now, let's take a brief look at two @FIND formulas that are identical except for the start-number argument.

In the formula

@FIND("honest","an honest man...honest",0)

the answer given is the number 3, because the first *honest* in the source string begins at the third offset position.

In the formula

@FIND("honest","an honest man...honest",5)

the answer given is the number 16, because the start number, 5, tells the @FIND function to begin searching after the first *honest* in the source string.

Figure 7.23 illustrates a practical use of @FIND. Note that the figure includes examples of @MID and @LEFT, which are discussed in the following sections. This figure contains a list of names that need to be rearranged so that each first name comes first, followed by the middle initial and the last name. You can use @FIND to help isolate the last names from the list of full names in column A, based on the location of the space character that consistently follows each last name.

The formula in cell E5, which is written in text format in F5 for illustration, uses the @FIND function to return a number that describes the offset position of the first space character. The numeric position of the space always corresponds with the number of characters that you need to extract from the left. The section entitled "@LEFT and @RIGHT" shows you how to use this number to extract the last names.

@MID, @LEFT, and @RIGHT are a class of functions that extract portions of text from strings of text. These functions are called "substring" functions. Another way of describing them is that they do the cutting in "cut-and-paste" operations. The next function, @MID, can extract the first names from the middle of the strings in column A.

@MID

The @MID, or "middle," function allows you to extract text from the middle of a specified string. The syntax for @MID is

@MID(string,start_number,length)

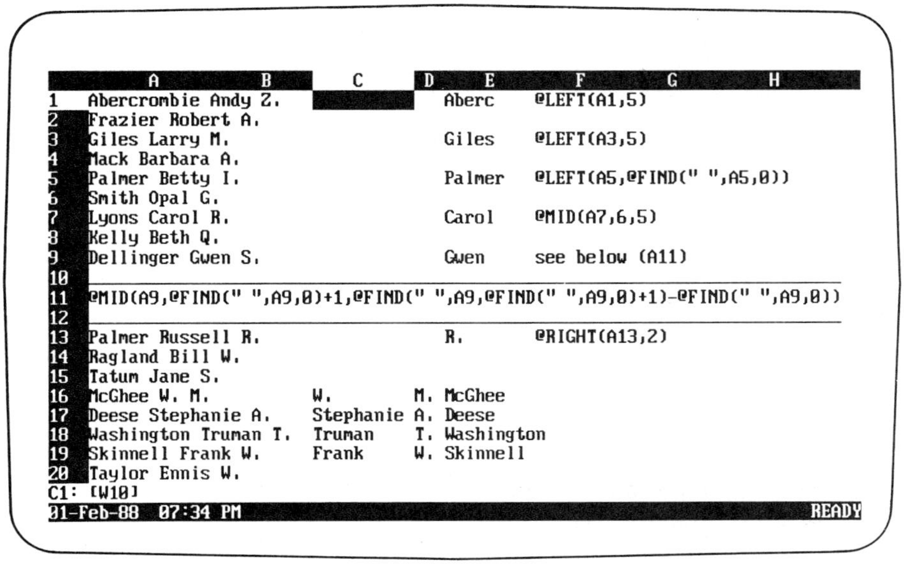

```
          A           B         C       D    E          F             G           H
1   Abercrombie Andy Z.                      Aberc      @LEFT(A1,5)
2   Frazier Robert A.
3   Giles Larry M.                           Giles      @LEFT(A3,5)
4   Mack Barbara A.
5   Palmer Betty I.                          Palmer     @LEFT(A5,@FIND(" ",A5,0))
6   Smith Opal G.
7   Lyons Carol R.                           Carol      @MID(A7,6,5)
8   Kelly Beth Q.
9   Dellinger Gwen S.                        Gwen       see below (A11)
10
11  @MID(A9,@FIND(" ",A9,0)+1,@FIND(" ",A9,@FIND(" ",A9,0)+1)-@FIND(" ",A9,0))
12
13  Palmer Russell R.                        R.         @RIGHT(A13,2)
14  Ragland Bill W.
15  Tatum Jane S.
16  McGhee W. M.          W.          M. McGhee
17  Deese Stephanie A.    Stephanie A. Deese
18  Washington Truman T.  Truman      T. Washington
19  Skinnell Frank W.     Frank       W. Skinnell
20  Taylor Ennis W.
C1: [W10]
01-Feb-88  07:34 PM                                                        READY
```

Fig. 7.23. Using @FIND, @MID, @LEFT, and @RIGHT to rearrange a list of names.

The *string* argument can be a quoted label or a reference to a cell that contains text. The *start_number* is an offset number that tells the @MID function where to start "cutting" the string. If you specify a start number of 0 (zero), the @MID function becomes equivalent to @LEFT. The *length* argument tells the @MID function how many characters it should return, beginning with the starting position.

An example of @MID is

@MID("back in the USSR",5,6)

The result of this formula is the substring *in the*. The *i* in the word *in* is the fifth offset character, and counting six positions to the right results in *in the*.

Normally, the @MID function's string argument is a reference to another cell. The start-number and length arguments can be either a constant, as in the previous example, or a formula that makes the decision based on the string being evaluated. An example of the latter method is using the @FIND function as the second and third arguments in the @MID function. For example, look at the formula in cell E9 of figure 7.23. (The formula is written in text format in cell A11.) This formula makes use of the @FIND function's capability to detect spaces in a string of multiple words.

If you simply need to know where to begin cutting, you can use the @FIND technique in a formula such as

@MID("ab cd",@FIND(" ","ab cd",0),99)

In this sample, the @FIND function returns the offset number of the first space, 2. The @MID function then returns all the remaining characters because the length argument (99) is greater than the length of the string.

Tip Use a large number, such as 99, as the length argument in an @MID function if you want to extract all text to the right of the starting number.

Before constructing the formula, it's always a good idea to write in English the operations that must be performed on a representative string. This step makes creating the formula easier.

For example, the @MID formula in figure 7.23 is designed to pull the first names from the middle of the strings. Look at the name in cell A9 (`Dellinger Gwen S.`). You want the formula to determine where to start and where to stop extracting so that the name `Gwen` is pulled from the string. The English logic for the operation is as follows:

- Find the starting point of the string.
- Determine the ending point of the string.
- Subtract the starting point from the ending point to get the length.
- Add 1 to the starting point and ending point to convert from offsets.

The formula to implement this logic appears convoluted at first glance, yet when you break down the formula it is quite simple. The first portion of the formula:

@MID(A9,@FIND(" ",A9,0)+1,

determines the source string (A9) and the starting number for the @MID function.

The next portion of the formula finds the correct number of characters to cut from the middle. The first part:

@FIND(" ",A9,@FIND(" ",A9,0)+1)

finds the position number of the second space. You can translate this statement to mean: "Find the first space and add 1 to it. Now use that number as the starting point for the other @FIND function." Because you will always begin looking one character after the first space, this part of the formula always finds the position of the second space.

The last part of the formula:

-@FIND(" ",A9,0))

subtracts the starting number from the ending number. This operation gives the original @MID function the answer it needs to complete the length argument.

I admit that the formula is a little complex. When you consider that you need to create the formula only once and can copy it anywhere on a spreadsheet with little modification, however, you can see how worthwhile the formula can prove to be. Another benefit of this kind of string math function is that it demonstrates the power of Quattro's functions when you use them in concert.

@LEFT and @RIGHT

The @LEFT function returns portions of text beginning from the left of the referenced string. The syntax for the @LEFT function is

@LEFT(string,length)

The *string* argument is the string from which you want to extract a portion. This argument can be a quoted label, a formula that results in a string, or an external reference to a cell containing text. (If a referenced cell contains values, the result of the @LEFT function is ERR.) The *length* argument indicates the number of character positions in a string to be extracted.

The function

@LEFT("we the people",6)

returns the text *we the*. Although only five characters are visible in this string, the @LEFT function counts the space between *we* and *the*.

Figure 7.23 shows an example of how you can use @LEFT. The formula in cell E1 refers to the name in cell A1. (Look at cell F1 to see the formula written in text format.) The length argument in that function is 5. As a result, the string `Aberc` is returned from the left of the name.

As you can see from cells E1 and E3, the @LEFT function's length argument needs to be more dynamic when determining how many characters to use from the left so that the last names are consistently extracted from the full names in column A. Fortunately, the @FIND function can step in, as shown in the formula in cell E5. For more on @FIND, refer to this chapter's discussion of that function.

The @RIGHT function is the last of the cut-and-paste functions. As you no doubt anticipated, the @RIGHT function extracts a string from the right side of a larger string. The syntax for @RIGHT is

@RIGHT(string,length)

The *string* argument can be a quoted label or a reference to another cell that contains text. The *length* argument can be either a constant number, a reference to a cell value, or the result of a formula.

For example, the function

@RIGHT("face",3)

results in the display of `ace`.

In figure 7.23, the @RIGHT function completes the application that rearranges names by extracting the middle initial. This function is quite simple to construct because the middle initial is represented by a consistent number of characters (2). The formula in E13 is displaying `R.`, the result of cutting the last two characters from the right of the string in cell A13. (The formula is displayed in text format in cell F13.)

@EXACT

The @EXACT function can determine whether two sets of text are exactly alike in spelling and case. The syntax for @EXACT is

@EXACT(string1,string2)

where *string1* and *string2* are either quoted strings or references to cells that contain strings.

The @EXACT function is more rigorous than the @IF function when comparing text. The @IF function returns a 1 (for true) for two strings that are spelled the same, even if one is in uppercase, and the other in lowercase. In the case of @EXACT, however, if the strings are not identically spelled *and* cased, the function returns the number 0 (zero) for false.

One use for @EXACT is in a password macro that scrupulously checks the exactness of the password entry. Such a macro might look like this:

```
{GETLABEL "Enter your password...",PASSENTRY}
{IF @EXACT(PASSENTRY,PASSWORD)}{LET_EM_IN}
{KICK_EM_OUT}
```

The @EXACT function compares the password entry, PASSENTRY, with the true password that is stored in PASSWORD. If the function evaluates as true (the password and entry are identical), the program proceeds to LET_EM_IN. If not, operation jumps to KICK_EM_OUT.

@REPLACE

You can use the @REPLACE function to modify small portions of text in a cell without manually editing the cell. The syntax for @REPLACE is

@REPLACE(string,start_number,length,replacement)

The *string* argument can be a quoted string, a string formula, or a cell reference that holds text. The *start_number* tells the function where to begin the replacement. The *length* tells the function how many characters to replace, starting from the start number. As it implies, the *replacement* argument is the text that will replace the cut text. This argument can also be a quoted string, a string formula, or a reference to a string-valued cell.

The formula

@REPLACE("in the end",7,3,"beginning")

results in the new string *in the beginning*. The 7 is used to start the replacement at the seventh offset position. The 3, or length, tells @REPLACE to cut the *end* from the original string.

Figure 7.24 demonstrates @REPLACE by altering the sexist nature of the phrase "Now is the time for all good men to come to the aid of their country." The formula in cell A5

@REPLACE(A3,@FIND("men",A3,0),3,"people")

uses the @FIND function to locate the starting position of "men". Then @REPLACE extracts "men" and inserts "people".

The @REPLACE function is in Quattro mainly for the sake of compatibility with 1-2-3.

Tip Use the /**B**lock **S**earch/Replace menu commands to perform replacements, because this process is easier and more efficient than the @REPLACE function.

@LENGTH

The @LENGTH function returns the number of characters contained in any text string. The syntax for @LENGTH is

@LENGTH(string)

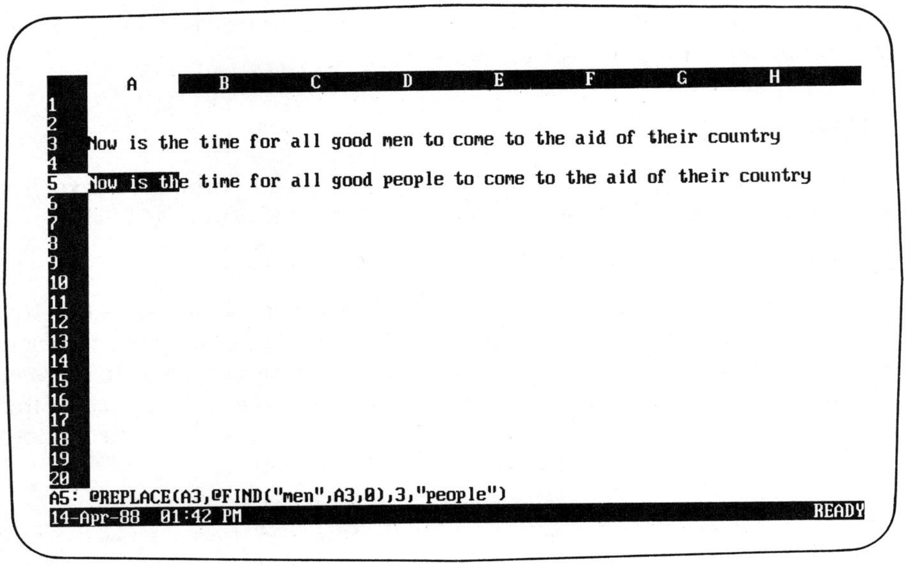

Fig. 7.24. Changing a string with @REPLACE.

The *string* argument can be a quoted string or an external reference to a cell that contains a string.

The result of the function

@LENGTH("we are not amused")

is the number 17, the number of characters (including spaces) in the argument.

The @LENGTH function is usually used to facilitate the manipulation of text in some fashion, either in a macro or in a formula used to generate a more structured screen display.

An example of such an application is a macro that automatically centers text in the middle of the screen (or page). The following macro determines how many space characters to "pad" in front of a string to force it to the center of the display:

```
{CALC}{EDIT}{HOME}{RIGHT}
@REPEAT(" ",@INT((72-@LENGTH(@CELLPOINTER("contents")))/2))~
```

Before showing the macro's effect, let's investigate the variety of functions nested together to perform the centering function.

In the most nested function, @CELLPOINTER, the "contents" argument returns the contents of the current cell. The cell selector should be on the first title to center. The next function, @LENGTH, determines the length of this text. Then the length of the title is subtracted from the width of the display (72 characters). The resultant number at this point is the number of character positions on the screen line not occupied by the title.

The formula then divides this result by 2 and converts the number to an integer with @INT. The macro uses this number when editing the title and padding the line with the correctly repeated number of spaces.

Figure 7.25 shows the condition of the spreadsheet before the macro is activated.

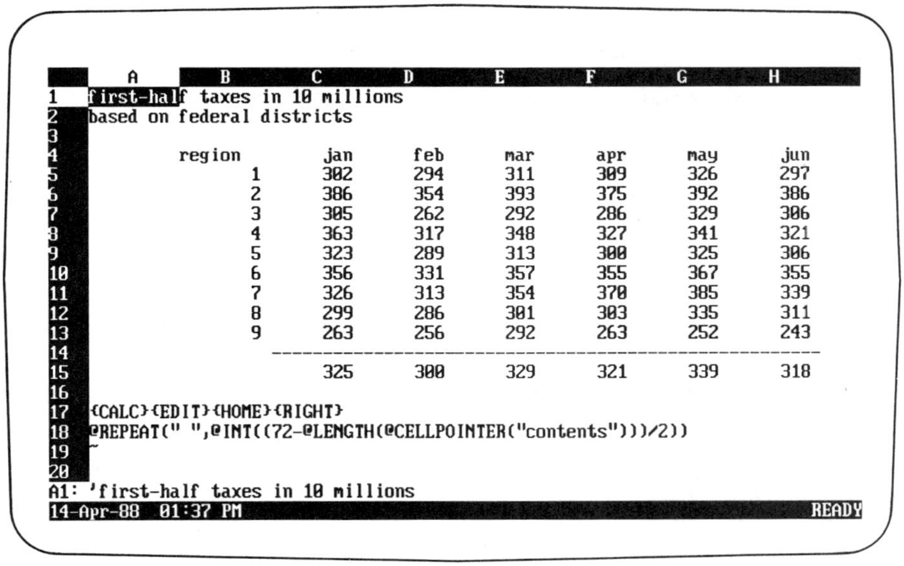

```
        A          B         C         D         E         F         G         H
1   first-half taxes in 10 millions
2   based on federal districts
3
4              region       jan       feb       mar       apr       may       jun
5                   1       302       294       311       309       326       297
6                   2       386       354       393       375       392       386
7                   3       305       262       292       286       329       306
8                   4       363       317       348       327       341       321
9                   5       323       289       313       300       325       306
10                  6       356       331       357       355       367       355
11                  7       326       313       354       370       385       339
12                  8       299       286       301       303       335       311
13                  9       263       256       292       263       252       243
14                    ------------------------------------------------------------
15                          325       300       329       321       339       318
16
17  {CALC}{EDIT}{HOME}{RIGHT}
18  @REPEAT(" ",@INT((72-@LENGTH(@CELLPOINTER("contents")))/2))
19  ~
20
A1: 'first-half taxes in 10 millions
14-Apr-88  01:37 PM                                                          READY
```

Fig. 7.25. A macro that uses @LENGTH to center titles.

Figure 7.26 shows the result of executing the macro by using the /**M**acro **E**xecute command with the cell selector in cell A1. The Edit key (F2) has been pressed so that you can see in the input line the spaces preceding the title.

Figure 7.27 shows the result of executing the macro with the cell selector in cell A2. This example demonstrates the flexibility of the @LENGTH function and its accomplices, because the macro placed the second title in the correct location relative to the title's own length. As you can see, you can use this centering macro on a line of *any* length.

```
          A     B        C         D         E         F         G         H
 1                  first-half taxes in 10 millions
 2 based on federal districts
 3
 4       region         jan       feb       mar       apr       may       jun
 5                1     302       294       311       309       326       297
 6                2     386       354       393       375       392       386
 7                3     305       262       292       286       329       306
 8                4     363       317       348       327       341       321
 9                5     323       289       313       300       325       306
10                6     356       331       357       355       367       355
11                7     326       313       354       370       385       339
12                8     299       286       301       303       335       311
13                9     263       256       292       263       252       243
14             ------------------------------------------------------------
15                      325       300       329       321       339       318
16
17 {CALC}{EDIT}{HOME}{RIGHT}
18 @REPEAT(" ",@INT((72-@LENGTH(@CELLPOINTER("contents")))/2))
19 ~
20
A1: '                first-half taxes in 10 million
14-Apr-88  01:44 PM                                                    READY
```

Fig. 7.26. Centering the first title.

```
          A     B        C         D         E         F         G         H
 1                  first-half taxes in 10 millions
 2                     based on federal districts
 3
 4       region         jan       feb       mar       apr       may       jun
 5                1     302       294       311       309       326       297
 6                2     386       354       393       375       392       386
 7                3     305       262       292       286       329       306
 8                4     363       317       348       327       341       321
 9                5     323       289       313       300       325       306
10                6     356       331       357       355       367       355
11                7     326       313       354       370       385       339
12                8     299       286       301       303       335       311
13                9     263       256       292       263       252       243
14             ------------------------------------------------------------
15                      325       300       329       321       339       318
16
17 {CALC}{EDIT}{HOME}{RIGHT}
18 @REPEAT(" ",@INT((72-@LENGTH(@CELLPOINTER("contents")))/2))
19 ~
20
A2: '                  based on federal districts
14-Apr-88  01:45 PM                                                    READY
```

Fig. 7.27. Centering the second title with the same flexible macro.

This application is an excellent example of the power that you can have when you combine @functions with macros. If you prefer, you can use the macro to center titles on printed output simply by replacing the 72 in the formula with 80, 132, or 240, depending on your printer width and setup. For more information, see this chapter's sections on the @REPEAT and @CELLPOINTER functions, and the discussion of macros in Chapter 15.

@LOWER, @UPPER, and @PROPER

@LOWER, @UPPER, and @PROPER offer three ways to convert the case of a string value. The @LOWER function takes any text argument and forces all the characters into lowercase. The @UPPER function takes any text argument and forces all the characters into uppercase. The @PROPER function capitalizes the first letter of each word and lowercases the remaining letters in each word. For example, @PROPER("sample text") returns `Sample Text`. The syntax for these three functions is

@FUNCTION(string)

The *string* can be any text argument enclosed in double quotation marks, any single cell reference containing text, or any formula that results in a string. References to values, @NA, or @ERR result in ERR. Figure 7.28 shows the effects of @LOWER and @UPPER.

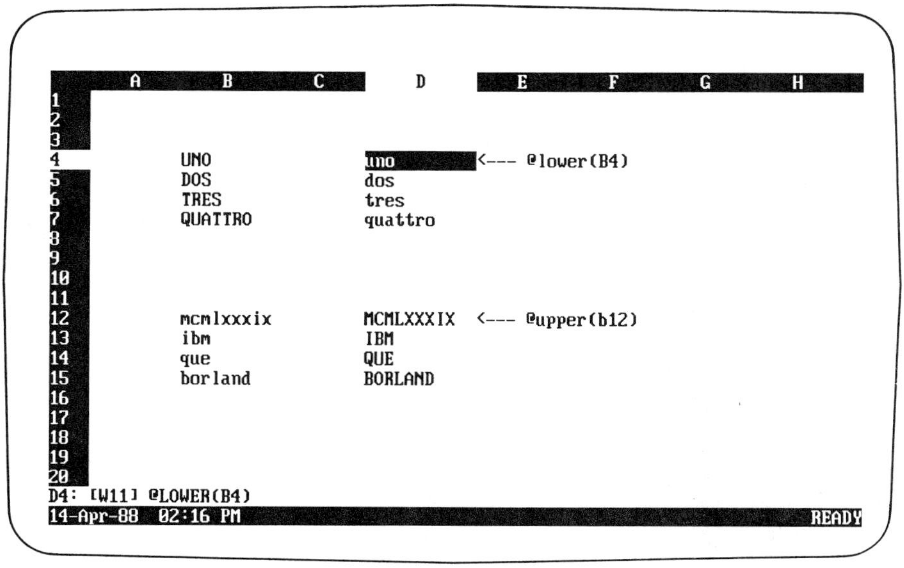

Fig. 7.28. Examples of the @LOWER and @UPPER functions.

Figure 7.29 shows the results in column D of using @PROPER on the list of words in column B.

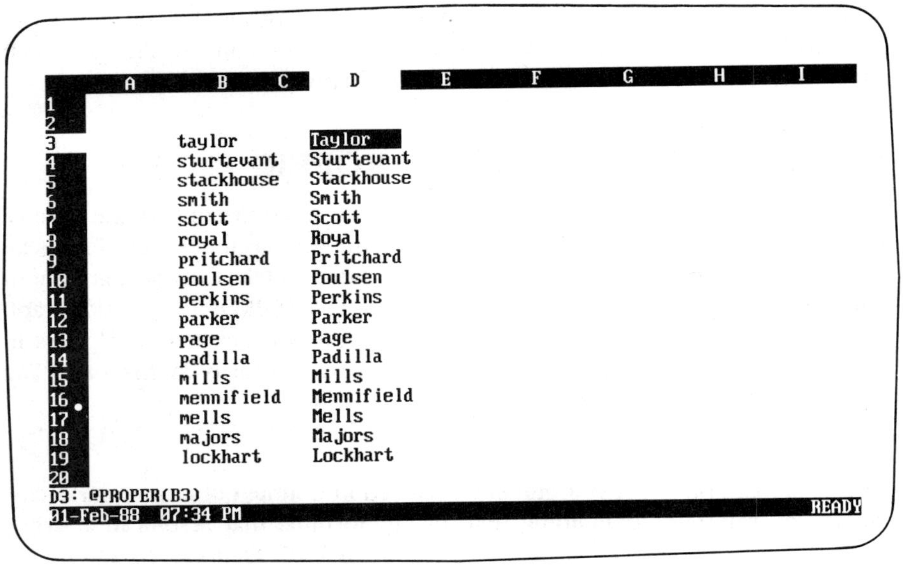

Fig. 7.29. The results of using @PROPER on column B.

@REPEAT

The @REPEAT function repeats one or more characters in a cell a specified number of times. The syntax for @REPEAT is

@REPEAT(string,number)

where *string* is any quoted string or any cell reference to a label in the spreadsheet. The *number* is a number, or reference to a cell containing a number, that indicates how many times the string should be repeated.

Figure 7.30 illustrates an example of the use of @REPEAT. In this illustration, the string "*=" is repeated 10 times in cell B3.

Tip You can easily change the appearance of dividing lines in the spreadsheet by using external absolute references to the string and number arguments in an @REPEAT function, as shown in figure 7.31.

By changing the cells referenced, you automatically change all your spreadsheet dividing lines, as shown in figure 7.32, where the string "*=" has been replaced with "[]" and the repeat factor has been raised to 30.

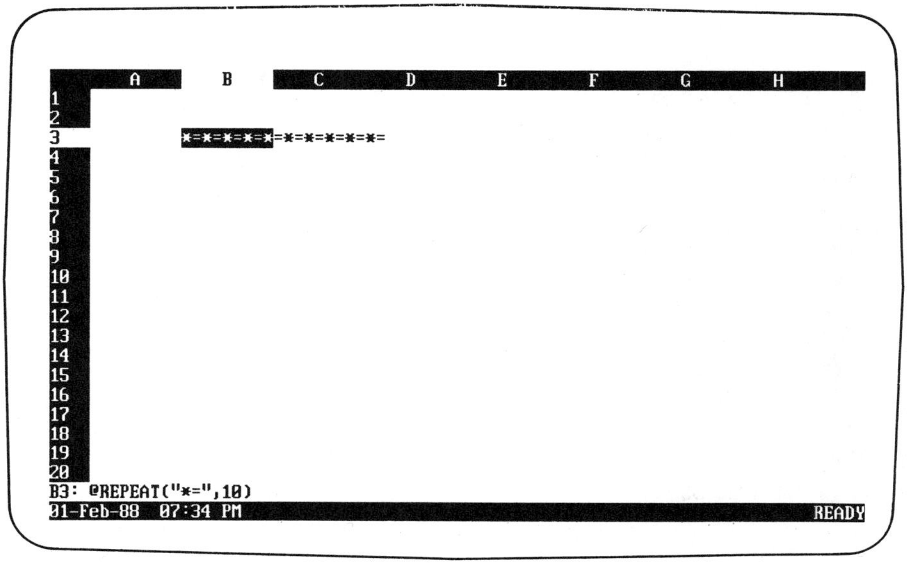

Fig. 7.30. Repeating characters with @REPEAT.

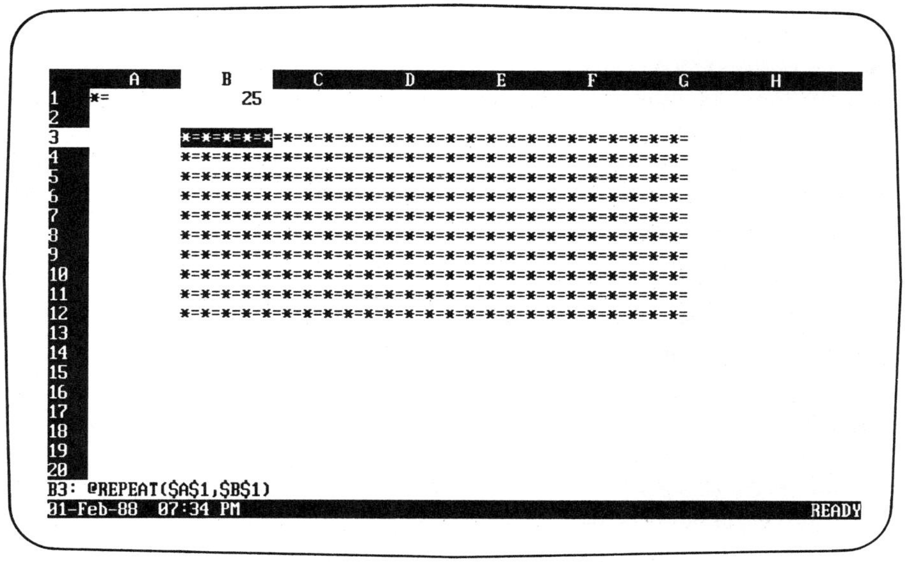

Fig. 7.31. Absolute cell references as @REPEAT arguments.

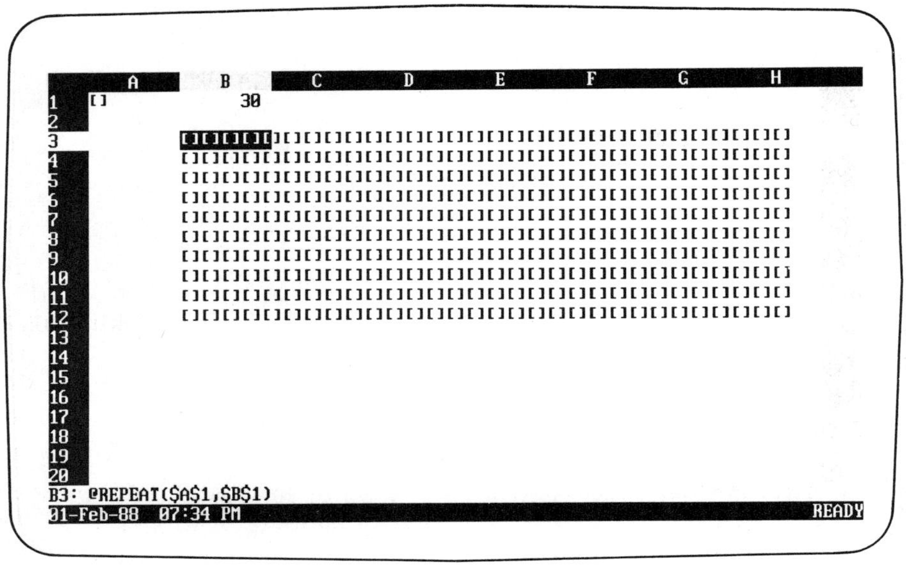

Fig. 7.32. After modifying the referenced cells.

The most practical use of @REPEAT occurs when you use it in combination with the @LENGTH function. You can then repeat characters based on the length of another text string.

You can use @LENGTH and @REPEAT to maintain an even right margin. One situation in which you might want an even right margin is in check writing. Writing out a check amount would be more convenient if you didn't have to fill in the trailing spaces manually to complete the amount line. The next example shows you how @LENGTH and @REPEAT can work together to produce a handy result.

This formula in cell A5 of figure 7.33:

+A3&@REPEAT("-",40-@LENGTH(A3))

first references the text in cell A3. Then the concatenation operator (&) adds to cell A3 the result of the string formula at the operator's right. This formula repeats the dash (-) character to a consistent ending point. The function finds the regular ending point (40) by first determining how long the text in cell A3 is and then subtracting this length from 40. The result becomes the repeat factor for the @REPEAT function.

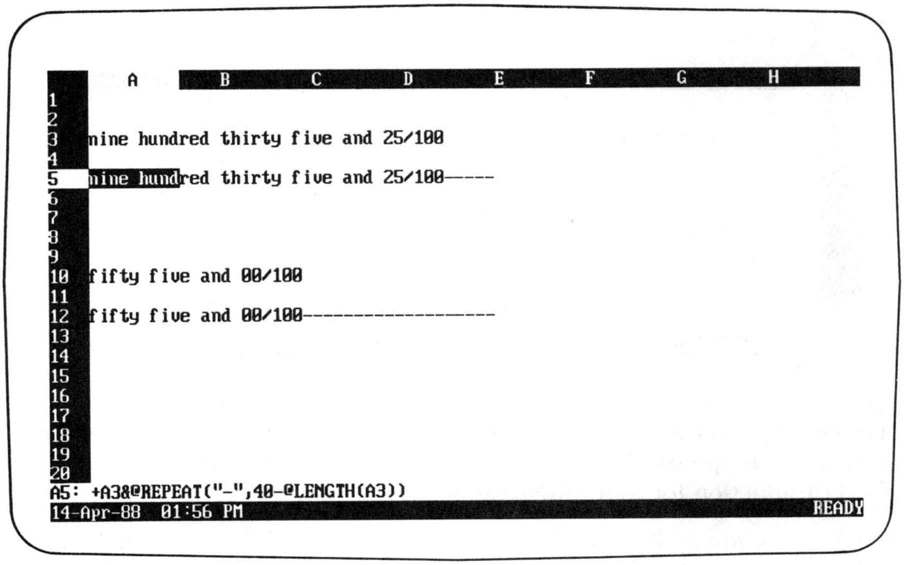

Fig. 7.33. Using @REPEAT and @LENGTH to create an even right margin.

Cell A12 in figure 7.33 demonstrates the formula's effectiveness. This cell contains the same formula found in cell A5 but uses a different check amount. The same stopping point for the dashes is maintained.

For another example of dynamic string sizing, see the discussion of the @LENGTH function in this chapter.

@N and @S

The @N and @S functions give you a way to test for the presence of strings or values. The @N function treats all cells as if they are numeric. If a cell contains a number, @N returns that number. If the referenced cell contains text, @N returns the number 0 (zero). The syntax for @N is

@N(block reference)

Although you can use numbers or text as the function's argument, that method serves no purpose, because @N is useful only when viewing an external cell. Figure 7.34 illustrates the effect that @N has when referencing a variety of cells.

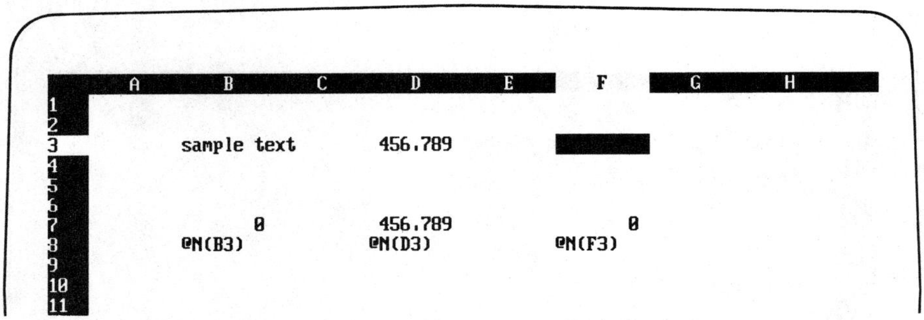

Fig. 7.34. An example of @N.

The @N function exists so that you can force a reference to a cell to be a numeric data type no matter what kind of data is in the cell. See the similar @VALUE function for more information.

The @S function is the opposite of the @N function. @S treats a referenced cell as a string. Although similar to the @STRING function, the @S function is not quite the same as @STRING. The @STRING function converts a number into that number's string equivalent. The @S function treats a referenced cell's contents as either the text within it or as a null string if the cell contains a value. The syntax for @S is

@S(block reference)

The @S function's argument must be a block reference to a single cell, such as @S(A1..A1), rather than a single cell reference, such as @S(A1). Without the @S function, a formula that refers to an empty cell results in 0 (zero). In many cases, you might prefer that a cell containing a formula not result in a display if the referenced cell is empty.

The next figure shows an application that allows you to enter new names to a list of city names. In figure 7.35, the formulas in column A that look at these city names use the @S function, which suppresses the zeros. The formulas in column C reference the same cells but do not use the @S function. The zeros in column C are not appropriate.

As you can see, the top of the application has room for you to enter more city names. As new city names are typed in, the @S formulas in column A will recognize and display these cities. If the @S function were not there, the formula to reference a new city entry would display a 0 at the current cell-selector location. This technique can be useful to a company experiencing a regional expansion. By referencing a list of current regions, with room for more regions as they become established, you can add a region to your bud-

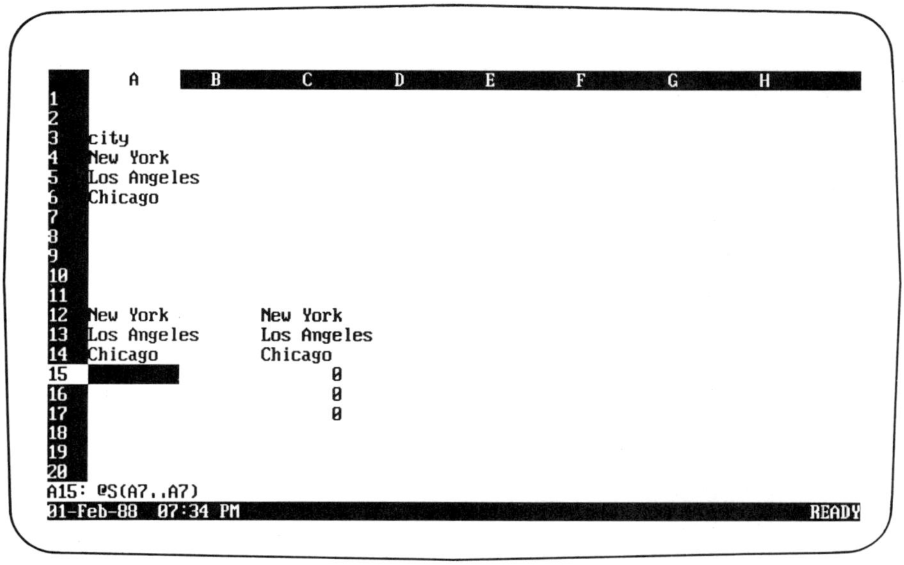

Fig. 7.35. Suppressing zero displays for empty cells by using the @S function.

geting model as easily as typing in the new city name. The model will recognize the new city and display it throughout the model in the appropriate cells.

This example also illustrates a major difference between @S and @N. @S does not display a cell's contents at all unless they are text. But @N displays all cells' contents as numbers. If a cell contains text, the result of @N is 0.

@STRING

The @STRING function converts a number to its string equivalent. That is, a value such as 6 is converted by the @STRING function to a label 6. The difference between a value and a label is highlighted in figure 7.36, which shows several examples of @STRING. Note that the number 6 in cell B3 is right-aligned, but its label equivalents in cells B5..B11 are left-aligned.

The syntax of @STRING is

@STRING(value,decimal_places)

The first argument, the *value* to convert, can be a number, a formula that results in a number, or a reference to a cell containing a number. The second argument, *decimal_places*, allows you to specify the number of decimal places you want displayed in the resultant string.

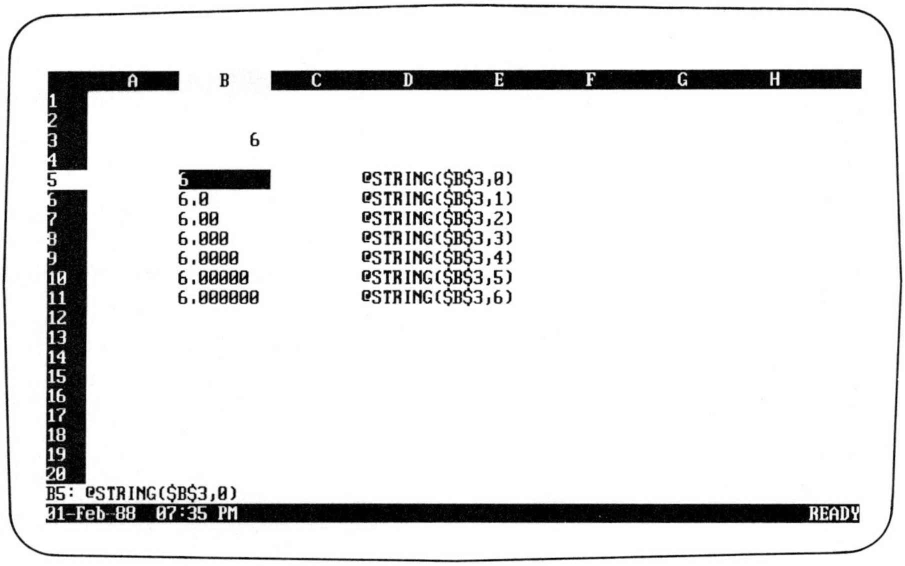

Fig. 7.36. Converting a value to a string with a specified number of decimal places.

Tip The decimal_places argument causes a number's string equivalent to appear rounded according to the same rules as the @ROUND function. For example, the function @STRING(456.75,0) results in the string 457 because of the rounding effect.

The @STRING function is most often used when a value needs to be combined (concatenated) with text. The Quattro syntax checker does not allow text and numbers to be combined directly. If you try to do so, the result will be ERR. The @STRING function provides a method to alleviate this problem.

@VALUE

The @VALUE function takes a text argument that looks like a number and converts the text to its numeric equivalent. Unlike its partner, @STRING, the @VALUE function does not have a rounding argument. The syntax for @VALUE is simply

@VALUE(string)

where *string* can be a quoted string, a cell reference, or a formula.

Like the @STRING, @S, and @N functions, @VALUE is used to help make data types conform to one another in a formula.

If the string has extra spaces, the @VALUE function automatically trims them when converting the string to a number. If you want to remove extra spaces but not change the string to a value, you need the @TRIM function.

@TRIM

The @TRIM function removes any extra spaces from a string. Whenever more than one space falls between two characters, @TRIM removes those extra spaces. The @TRIM function leaves one space in instances where trimming occurs. The syntax of the @TRIM function is

@TRIM(string)

Figure 7.37 illustrates the operation of the @TRIM function. Line 6 contains a string with extra spaces, and line 7 shows that same line after @TRIM has been used.

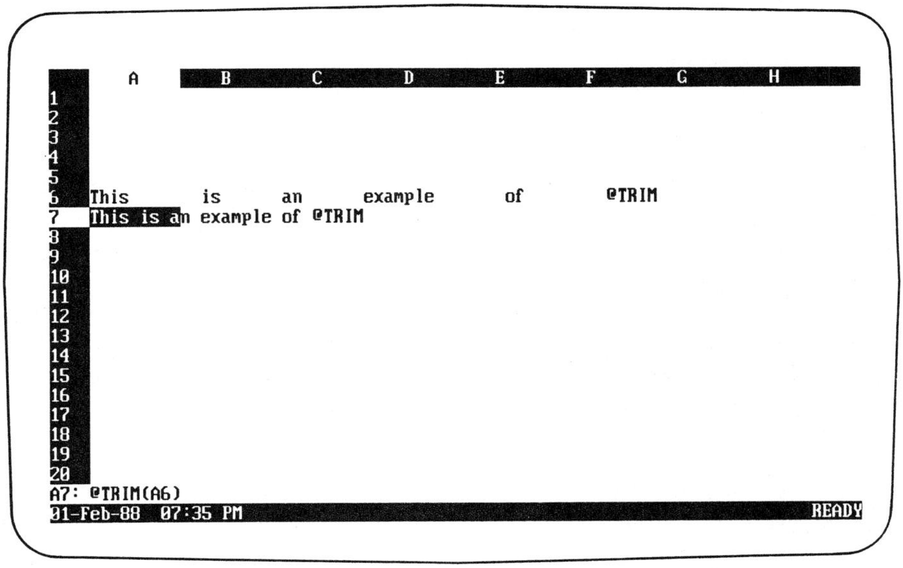

Fig. 7.37. Trimming extra spaces with @TRIM.

You can use the @TRIM function to validate data-entry routines so that extra spaces are not accidentally entered. Here is an example of a small macro that performs this validation service (for information on macro fundamentals, refer to Chapter 15):

{GETLABEL "Please enter your full name:",ENTRY}
{LET ENTRY,@TRIM(ENTRY)}

The first statement puts the user's name in the cell with the block name ENTRY. The second statement @TRIMS any extra spaces from the name in the ENTRY cell.

Another use of the @TRIM function is to remove extra spaces in imported ASCII text files (files imported with the /**F**ile **I**mport command). Frequently, these files will have spaces that unnecessarily preserve left and right margins.

@CLEAN

As its name implies, the @CLEAN function performs a cleanup operation on text. The function's usefulness, however, is limited to those situations involving the importation of data from other programs that Quattro can't translate directly or from files created during a communications session. The syntax for @CLEAN is

@CLEAN(string)

The *string* argument will usually be a reference to a cell containing a line of text rather than a single character or word.

Tip When used in Quattro, the @CLEAN function doesn't do anything. It is simply included to ensure complete compatibility with 1-2-3, which is not to imply that Quattro is therefore less powerful. On the contrary, although 1-2-3 can't display many of the ASCII characters, Quattro does so quite nicely. The @CLEAN function exists in 1-2-3 because odd characters within a 1-2-3 spreadsheet may not be readily seen. Such would not be the case in Quattro. Smiling faces, hearts, spades, and so on are immediately apparent in Quattro. See the following section on @CHAR for more information on extended ASCII characters.

@CHAR

The @CHAR function gives you access to many characters not available from the keyboard, as well as normal keyboard characters. The syntax for @CHAR is

@CHAR(ASCII number)

For instance, if you need to display the fraction *1/2*, you can use the @CHAR function with an argument of 171, as figure 7.38 proves.

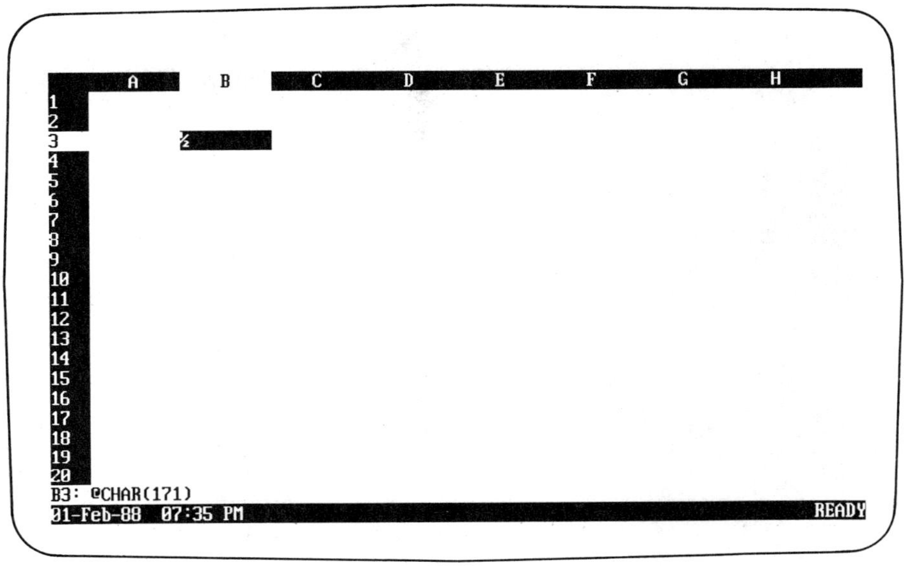

Fig. 7.38. Displaying an ASCII character.

If the @CHAR function references a fractional number, then the number is rounded to either the next higher or lower number before a character is returned. If you prefer that the number not be rounded, use the formula

@CHAR(@INT(ASCII number))

Figure 7.39 provides a complete listing of the nonstandard or extended ASCII characters available in Quattro.

Tip In 1-2-3, you can generate non-keyboard characters with the Compose key (Alt-F1). Because this function key was used so infrequently, the designers at Borland did not include the Compose key with the Quattro program. You can obtain the effect of 1-2-3's Compose key by using the @CHAR function and then using the menu system to perform a /**B**lock **A**dvanced **V**alues operation, which removes the @CHAR function and leaves the character. You can then work with the character just as you can any other character in the worksheet.

The @CODE function is the reverse of @CHAR.

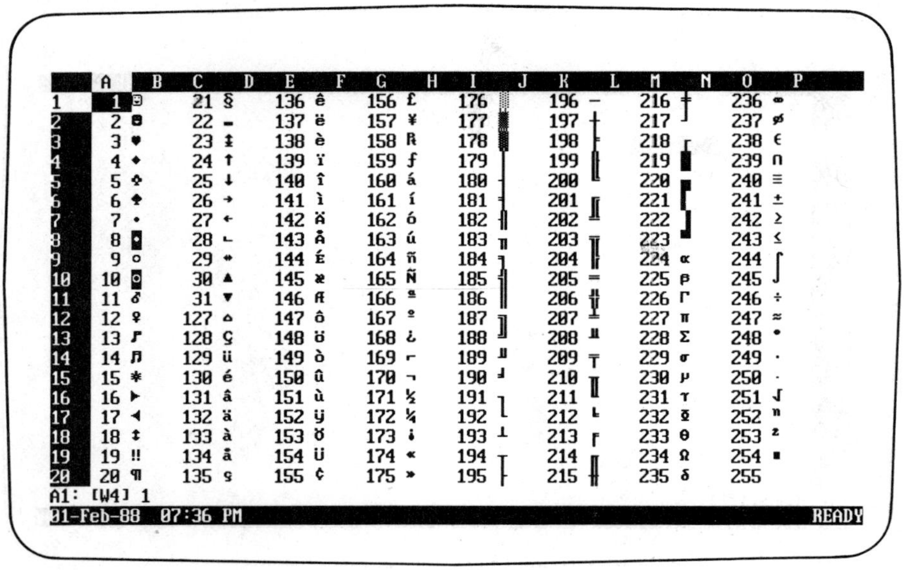

Fig. 7.39. The extended ASCII characters.

@CODE

The @CODE function takes a string or text argument and returns the ASCII code for that specified string. The syntax for @CODE is

@CODE(string)

The *string* argument can be a character or group of characters enclosed by quotation marks, or any reference to a cell that contains text. Note, however, that if a referenced string is longer than one character, the @CODE function returns the ASCII number for only the first character in the string.

The function @CODE("A") returns the number 65. The formula @CODE("NOW IS THE TIME") results in the number 78, the ASCII code for the N in NOW.

Macro-Related Special Functions

The functions in this section are most valuable when used in concert with macro keyword commands (see Chapter 16). But the special functions can also be useful in the spreadsheet. Functions such as @ERR and @NA, for example, can be quite helpful for trapping spreadsheet errors.

Unfortunately, however, these functions are underutilized. The software manuals contain few clues to tell you that these functions are designed mainly to enhance the power and intelligence of the Quattro macro commands.

Note: This section contains many macro examples to illustrate the utility of this special group of functions. For information on macro fundamentals, read Chapter 15.

Table 7.4 is a list of the special functions, with brief descriptions of their actions.

Table 7.4
Macro-Related Special Functions

Function	*Description*
@CELL("attribute",block)	Returns specified attribute of upper left cell of block
@CELLPOINTER("attribute")	Returns specified attribute of current cell
@CELLINDEX("attribute",block, offset_col,offset_row)	Returns specified attribute of cell at column and row offsets of block
@NA	Sets current cell to NA
@ERR	Sets current cell to ERR
@ROWS(block)	Calculates number of rows in block
@COLS(block)	Calculates number of columns in block
@CURVALUE(initial_menu_name, specific_menu_action)	Returns current value of a menu setting
@FILEEXISTS(FILENAME.EXT)	Returns 1 if file name exists; otherwise, returns 0 (argument can include drive and path name)
@MEMAVAIL	Shows available DOS memory
@MEMEMSAVAIL	Shows available expanded memory

@CELL and @CELLPOINTER

The @CELL and @CELLPOINTER functions return information about the setting of a specified cell. The syntax for @CELL is

@CELL("attribute",block)

where *"attribute"* is either a quoted string or a reference to a cell containing one of the available attribute arguments, which are listed in table 7.5. (Note that you also use these attributes for the @CELLPOINTER and @CELLINDEX functions.) The *block* argument specifies the block that the @CELL argument should examine. @CELL returns the requested attribute for the top left cell of the block.

Table 7.5
Cell Attributes for @CELL, @CELLPOINTER, and @CELLINDEX

Attribute	*Function Returns*
"address"	Cell address of specified cell as an absolute reference
"col"	Column 1 to 265 of specified cell
"contents"	Exact contents of specified cell
"format"	Format number of cell
"prefix"	Either ', ", or ^ for left, right, or centered label
"protect"	1 if specified cell is protected; 0 if not protected
"row"	Row 1 to 8192 of specified cell
"type"	Data type of cell contents: *v* for value, *l* for label, *b* for blank
"width"	Column width of cell (1 to 240)

The format option returns the format of the specified cell, using a predefined code from the following list:

Code	*Format*
Fn	Fixed, to *n* places
En	Scientific, to *n* places
Cn	Currency, to *n* places
Pn	Percent, to *n* places

,n	Punctuated, to *n* places
G	General
+	+/-
D1-D5	Date formats
D6-D9	Time formats
T	Text contents of source cell
H	Hidden

An example of @CELL is

@CELL("address",DATA_BASE)

This formula returns the address of the top left cell of a block named DATE_BASE, no matter where it is located. The result of the *"address"* argument is an absolute address (for example, A1).

A major reason to use @CELL is to keep track of the address of the top left cell of a block. When a macro is moving around a block of cells, the @CELL function can tell the macro where this block has been moved.

The syntax for @CELLPOINTER is

@CELLPOINTER("attribute")

where *"attribute"* is either a quoted string or a reference to a cell containing one of the reserved strings listed in table 7.5. Note that @CELLPOINTER does not include a ***block*** argument. @CELLPOINTER returns the requested attribute for the current cell—the cell where the cell selector was positioned at the time of the most recent spreadsheet update (recalculation).

The @CELLPOINTER function is the most versatile of the "CELL" functions. Generally speaking, @CELLPOINTER provides macros with a method to determine the status of the current cell. For example, if a macro needs to know whether the cell selector is currently positioned on an empty cell, the formula @CELLPOINTER("type") returns the necessary information. The "type" argument returns a string of either *v* (for value), *l* (for label), or ***b*** (for blank). A sample macro statement is

{IF @CELLPOINTER("type")="b"}{QUIT}

Figure 7.40 contains another example of a macro that includes @CELLPOINTER. This macro uses the @CELLPOINTER("row") and @CELLPOINTER("col") functions to keep a user within an area of the spreadsheet bounded by row 100 and column Z (column 26). The IF keyword statements provide the "Big Brother" control of the cell selector. The rest of the macro simply allows the user to type at the keyboard without interference from the macro (unless the user ventures out of bounds). Appropriately, this macro is named FENCE.

For more information on the GET and BRANCH keywords, see Chapter 16.

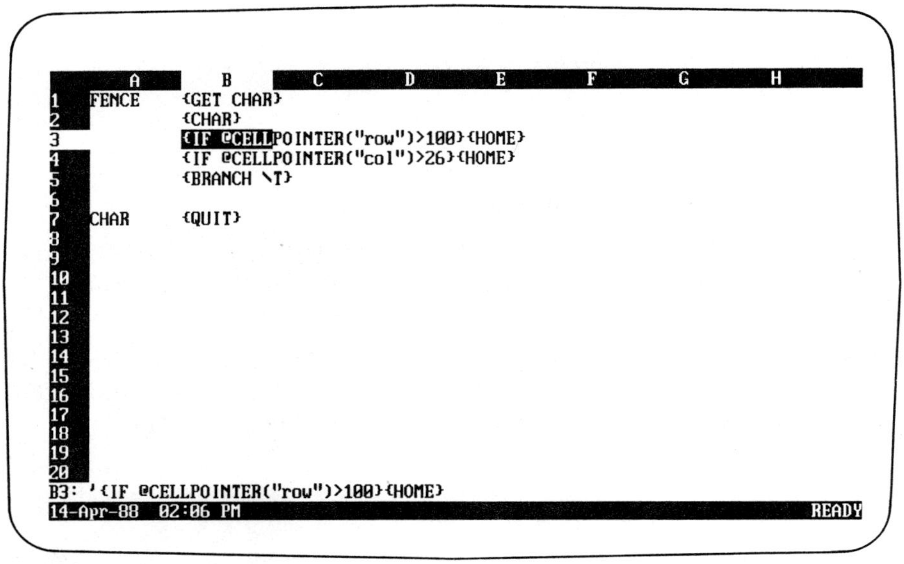

Fig. 7.40. Using @CELLPOINTER in a macro to keep the user in a limited area of the spreadsheet.

The macro in figure 7.41 deletes blank rows until the cell selector "lands" on the cell containing the word STOP. The macro command that performs the test is

{IF @S(@CELLPOINTER("contents"))="STOP"}{QUIT}

@CELLINDEX

Like @CELL and @CELLPOINTER, the @CELLINDEX function returns information about the setting of a specified cell. The syntax for @CELLINDEX is

@CELLINDEX("attribute",block,offset_col,offset_row)

where *"attribute"* is either a quoted string or a reference to a cell containing one of the reserved strings listed in table 7.5. The *block* argument specifies the block that the @CELLINDEX argument should examine. The *offset_col* is the column offset number within the block, and the *offset_row* is the offset

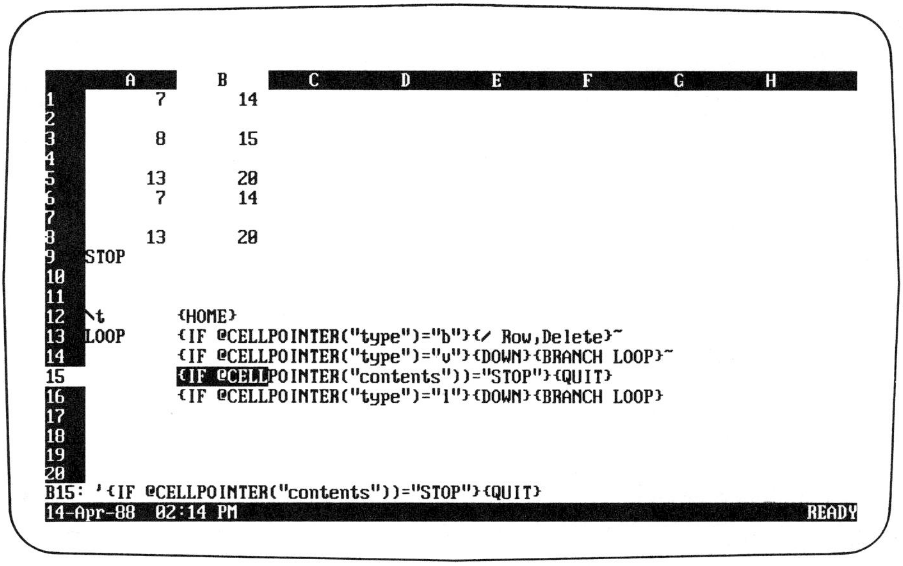

Fig. 7.41. Using @CELLPOINTER to tell a macro when to quit.

number indicating how many rows deep to look in the block. @CELLINDEX returns the requested attribute for the intersection of the column and row offset within the block.

@NA and @ERR

The @NA function sets the value of the cell to NA (not available). The syntax for @NA is simply @NA.

The best use of @NA is in formulas, such as @IF and @CHOOSE formulas. As an example, consider a formula that has the job of determining, based on a purchase quantity, whether a customer gets a discount. The function

@CHOOSE(QUANTITY,@NA,0.03,0.05,0.08)

would display NA if the threshold for discounts was not achieved; in other words, if the block named QUANTITY contains the number 0 (key = 0). Any cell that references a cell with the value of @NA will also be NA, or may even have the value ERR.

The @ERR function sets the value of the cell to ERR. The syntax for @ERR is simply @ERR.

The best use of @ERR is in formulas in which you need to flag an application error, such as in situations where the spreadsheet is not aware of what constitutes an error. To illustrate the point, assume that you have an application which requires the entry of a person's age into a database. What if the user enters an age of 703 rather than 73? This error will badly skew any statistics performed on the data. So, a formula such as

@IF(@MAX(AGE_COLUMN)>100,@ERR,@STATISTICALFUNCTION())

will notice any age greater than 100 and display ERR; otherwise, the statistical function will be performed.

Any cell that references a cell with the value of @ERR will also be ERR.

@ROWS and @COLS

The @ROWS function returns the number of rows contained within the specified block. The @COLS function returns the number of columns contained within the specified block. The syntax for these functions is

@ROWS(block)
@COLS(block)

where *block* can be a block cell reference or a named block reference. For example, @ROWS(A10..G15) returns the number 6 because the defined block contains 6 rows. If the block named AREA encompasses cells A1..G5, then @COLS(AREA) returns the number 7 because the defined block includes 7 columns.

The @ROWS and @COLS functions are useful in macros when you want to control the distance that the cell selector moves. For example, the macro

{UP @ROWS(DATABASE)-1}

always moves the cell selector to the first or top row of a database if the cell selector begins in the last row of the database. And the macro

{LEFT @COLS(DATABASE)-1}

always moves the cell selector to the first or key column of a database if the cell selector begins in the last column of the database.

@ROWS and @COLS may also be useful in PUT, @CELLINDEX, and @INDEX formulas or in any function that specifies a column offset as one of its arguments.

@CURVALUE

The @CURVALUE function is used to determine the current settings, such as column widths and printer settings, for selected menu choices. The syntax for @CURVALUE is

@CURVALUE("initial_menu_name","specific_menu_action")

where *initial_menu_name* is the menu choice from the menu that first appears when you press the slash key (/), and *specific_menu_action* is the menu choice that holds the setting you want. Both arguments must be quoted strings.

To illustrate, the formula

@CURVALUE("print","block")

returns the block that Quattro last printed (current /**P**rint **B**lock setting). If the block last printed was located in cells B3 through D16, the result of the example formula is B3..D16.

Figure 7.42 shows a macro program that tests the current value of the resource directory. If the directory is not C:\SS\Q, the fix routine is called. The fix routine (starting at cell B9) first brings up the default resource directory menu choice. Then the resource directory is reset to the specified directory. Finally, the macro returns to cell B3 to retrieve the file.

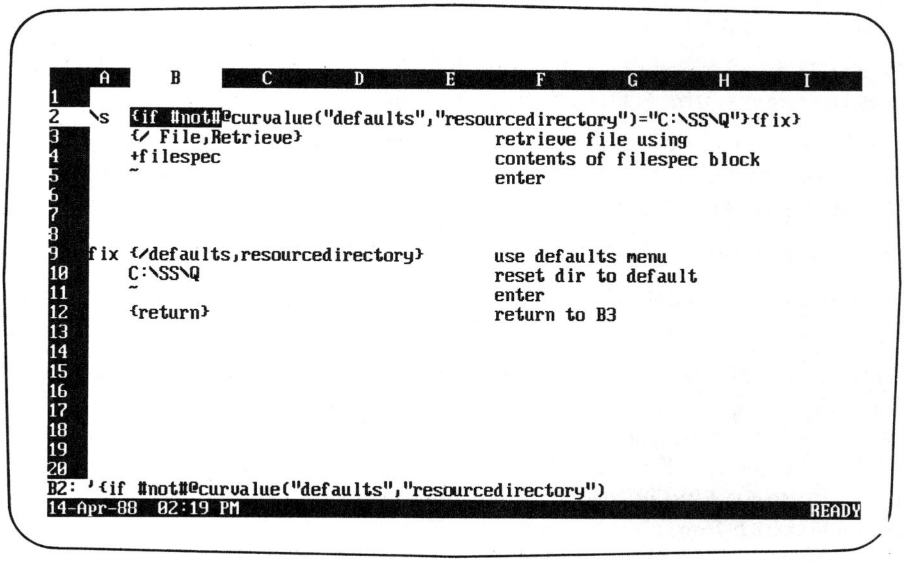

Fig. 7.42. A macro example that uses the @CURVALUE function.

@FILEEXISTS

The @FILEEXISTS function is a logical or Boolean function that returns a true or false result after testing the file-name argument of the function. The syntax for @FILEEXISTS is

@FILEEXISTS([d][path]FILENAME.EXT)

where *[d]* is an optional drive letter, such as B:, *[path]* is an optional path specification to the file, such as \SS\SSFILE\, and *FILENAME.EXT* is the name and extension of the file being tested. You can also use as the argument a cell reference to a file name. If a value, unquoted string, or blank cell is used as the argument, an ERR results.

For example, the formula @FILEEXISTS("BUDGET.WKQ") examines the current default data directory to determine whether the BUDGET file exists. If the file is found, the function returns a 1 (one); if the file is not found, a 0 (zero) results.

Figure 7.43 shows how you can increase the @FILEEXISTS function's flexibility by making the file-name argument an external reference. The second row of the spreadsheet has been set up to accept the various components of a file name. Cell B4 uses a string concatenation formula (+A2&B2&C2&D2) to put together all the pieces of the name. (The formula is shown in text form at cell D4.) Using the resulting file name from cell B4, the @FILEEXISTS function returns a result of 0, which means that the file does not exist in the given drive and directory.

Figure 7.44 shows a successful search for a file on a hard disk directory. Note that the value of the @FILEEXISTS function is a 1.

@FILEEXISTS can be extremely useful when you are doing macro-driven file consolidations with the /**F**ile **C**ombine **C**opy, **A**dd, and **S**ubtract menu commands. For instance, the macro command

{IF#NOT#@FILEEXISTS(FILESPEC)}{BRANCH OOPS}

branches to the OOPS macro if the file name in the FILESPEC block does not exist.

Tip For the @FILEEXISTS function to do its job, it must physically check for the file's existence every time the sheet is recalculated. On a slow computer, this process can degrade performance. Worse, if the drive being searched does not contain a disk, a hard error (the kind that kills macros) occurs. You can use the ONERROR macro command to trap the `Drive open` error if you use @FILEEXISTS in a macro. See the discussion of ONERROR in Chapter 16.

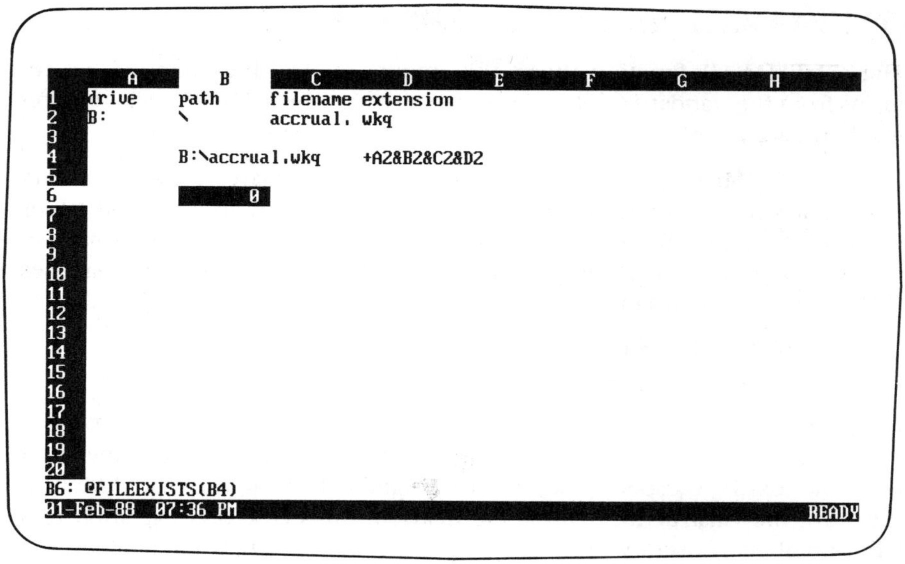

Fig. 7.43. Checking for the existence of a file.

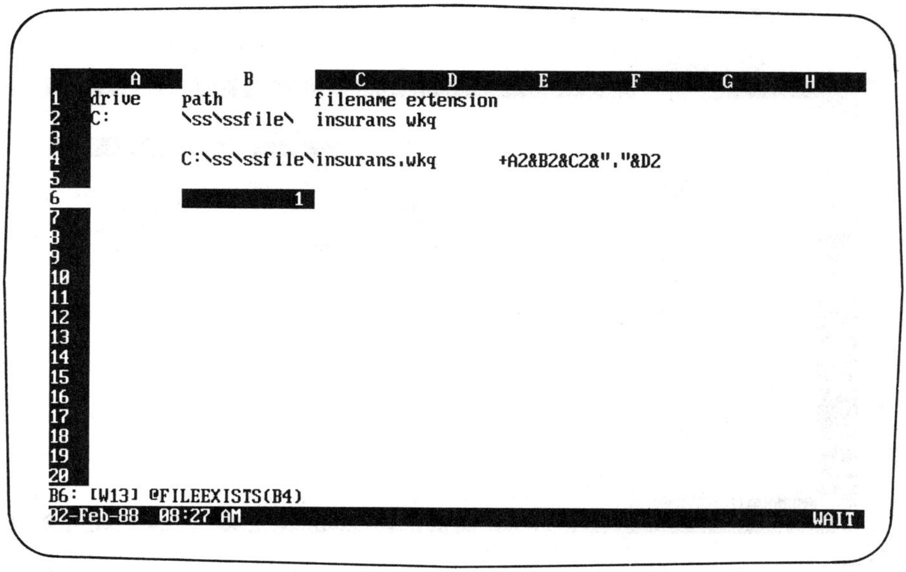

Fig. 7.44. A successful @FILEEXISTS test.

@MEMAVAIL and @MEMEMSAVAIL

The @MEMAVAIL function shows the amount of available memory that remains from the standard 640K DOS memory space. The @MEMAVAIL function needs no argument, so the syntax is simply @MEMAVAIL.

One use of @MEMAVAIL is in an application that adds large amounts of data or formulas to a spreadsheet. An application that creates amortization tables is a good example. The macro statement to prevent the excessive growth of the table beyond the current memory limit could be an IF statement that uses @MEMAVAIL. For instance, the statement

```
{IF @MEMAVAIL<20000}No memory: Press Enter and save file
  {GET CHAR}{ESC}{QUIT}
```

tests available memory. If less than 20K remain, the message `Press Enter and save file` appears on the input line. After the user presses Enter (or any other key), the text is "escaped," and the macro quits. Then the user should follow the "save file" instruction. You could distribute this type of application to a large number of users without worrying about how much memory the individual users' machines might have.

Figure 7.45 shows the @MEMAVAIL function along with a display of the hardware status menu screen for comparison.

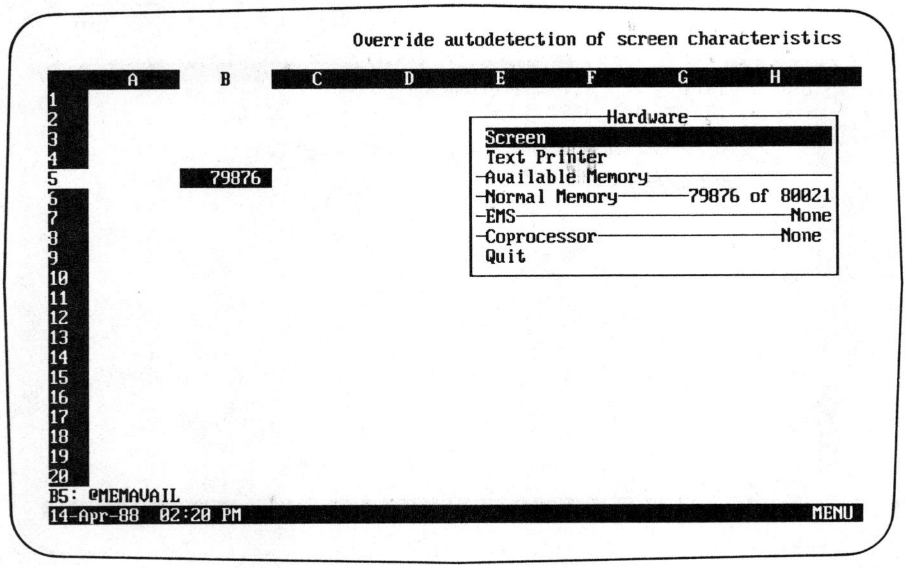

Fig. 7.45. The @MEMAVAIL function.

The @MEMEMSAVAIL function shows the amount of memory that remains from expanded memory (memory that extends beyond the standard 640K DOS memory space). The @MEMEMSAVAIL function requires no argument.

EMS stands for expanded memory standard, a memory-management method that tricks DOS into thinking that more than 640K of memory is available. You must have an expanded memory manager (software and hardware) to use EMS.

As is true of @MEMAVAIL, the @MEMEMSAVAIL function can warn a running macro of the fact that memory is running out. See the discussion of @MEMAVAIL for details.

Tip You can use the memory functions to get a feel for which kinds of formulas and functions use the most memory, because you can see the available memory decrement instantaneously as data is entered.

Engineering and Trigonometric Functions

Quattro's engineering and trigonometric functions will be most useful to those of you in the scientific and engineering fields. Table 7.6 summarizes these functions.

@SQRT

The @SQRT, or square root, function returns a number that when multiplied by itself (squared) equals the argument of the function. @SQRT's operation is the opposite of squaring. The syntax for @SQRT is

```
@SQRT(value)
```

where *value* is any positive number. If you use a negative number as the argument, the function returns ERR. You can use the formula @SQRT(@ABS(value)) to get the square root of any number, whether negative or positive.

You can also use @SQRT to modify the @STD (standard deviation) function so that @STD returns a sample standard deviation rather than the standard deviation of the population. The formula to find the @STD for the sample is

```
@SQRT(@[D]COUNT(ARG)/
@[D]COUNT(ARG)-1)*@[D]STD(ARG)
```

where *[D]* means that you can use either statistical or database statistical functions, and *ARG* represents any legal argument.

Table 7.6
Engineering and Trigonometric Functions

Trigonometric Function	*Description*
@SQRT(value)	Returns square root of value
@PI	Returns the value of the constant *pi* (circumference/diameter)
@SIN(x)	Returns sine of angle x
@COS(x)	Returns cosine of an acute angle x
@TAN(x)	Returns tangent of angle x
@ASIN(x)	Returns arcsine
@ACOS(x)	Returns arccosine
@ATAN(x)	Returns arctangent
@ATAN2(x/y)	Returns inverse tangent of the angle x/y
@DEGREES(radians_value)	Converts radians to degrees
@RADIANS(degrees)	Converts degrees to radians
Logarithmic Function	*Description*
@EXP(power_value)	Raises *e* to a specified power
@LN(value)	Calculates natural logarithm of value
@LOG(value)	Calculates base 10 logarithm of value

The example in figure 7.46 shows the relative effects on the validity of the standard deviation statistic based on the population standard deviation and the sample standard deviation. The formula for sample standard deviation, which uses @SQRT, is in cell F8.

To find a root greater than the square root, you can nest the @SQRT function for the root you need. Thus, to get the fourth root of 81, the formula is @SQRT(@SQRT(81)).

```
         A          B          C          D          E          F          G          H
1                                                          age
2                                                          +B4>15
3   subject#       age        I.Q.        sex
4        1000       62          92          F              20.76119 std dev population
5        1001       51          83          F                   106 average
6        1002       72          99          F                    16 count
7        1003       55         105          M
8        1004       34         135          M              21.44206 std dev sample
9        1005       19         101          M
10       1006       58          89          M
11       1007       24         121          F                    85       127
12       1008       27         103          F                -1 std    +1 std
13       1009       53         167          M              ==================
14       1010       24         108          M
15       1011       17          99          M
16       1012       53          95          F
17       1013       75          89          M
18       1014       74         120          M
19       1015       47          89          M
20
F8: [W9] @SQRT(F6/(F6-1))*F4
02-Feb-88  08:31 AM                                                               READY
```

Fig. 7.46. Using @SQRT to find the sample standard deviation.

@PI

The @PI function returns the transcendental constant *pi*, which is approximately 3.1415. Pi is the ratio of a circle's circumference to its diameter. The syntax for this function is simply @PI.

Following are some examples of how you can use @PI in calculations:

- @PI * radius^ = the area of a circle
- @PI * diameter = the circumference of the circle
- Degrees * @PI/180 converts to radians (See this section's discussion of @RADIANS.)

@SIN, @COS, and @TAN

The @SIN, @COS, and @TAN functions return the sine, cosine, and tangent, respectively, of an angle (x) in radians. The syntax for these three functions is

@SIN(x)
@COS(x)
@TAN(x)

where *x* is an angle in radians or an external cell reference to an angle. As mentioned previously, you can compute the radians by using this formula:

Radians = Degrees * @PI/180

The argument for the @SIN function must be between -90 (-pi/2) degrees and +90 (+pi/2) degrees. For example, the function @SIN(@RADIANS(90)) equals 1. Alternatively, @SIN(@RADIANS(-90)) equals -1.

The answer supplied by the @COS function is the cosine of the angle. For example, the formula @COS(@RADIANS(45)) returns the cosine of a 45-degree angle, 0.707.

The result of the @TAN function has no upper or lower limit. The formula @TAN(@RADIANS(90)) equals 1.63E+16, @TAN(@RADIANS(45)) results in 1, and @TAN(@RADIANS(-45)) equals -1.

@ASIN, @ACOS, @ATAN, and @ATAN2

The @ASIN, @ACOS, @ATAN, and @ATAN2 functions compute the arcsine, arccosine, arctangent, and four-quadrant arctangent, respectively, of the specified angle in radians.

The syntax for @ASIN and @ACOS is

@ASIN(x)
@ACOS(x)

where *x* is a value or external reference to a value between -1 and 1. If the number exceeds these boundaries, the function returns ERR.

The formula @ASIN(1) equals 1.571. If you nest the formula within the @DEGREES function, as in

@DEGREES(@ASIN(1))

the radians result of this @ASIN function is converted to 90 degrees.

The @ACOS function returns the arccosine, which is the reciprocal of the @COS function. The function @ACOS(-1) returns an answer of 3.141593 (pi).

The syntax for @ATAN is

@ATAN(x)

where *x* is the angle in radians whose tangent is *x*. The @ATAN function returns a value greater than -90 (-pi/2) degrees and less than +90 (+pi/2) degrees. For example, @ATAN(1) equals .7854. By nesting the function within the @DEGREES function, as in

@DEGREES(@ATAN(1))

you obtain the result of 45.

@ATAN2 returns the arctangent, or inverse tangent, of the angle x/y. The result returned is the angle in radians, y/x. The syntax for this function is

@ATAN2(x,y)

for the angle whose tangent equals x/y.

Here are some sample @ATAN2 functions:

- @ATAN2(-1,0) = 3.1416 or pi radians
- @ATAN2(1,1) = .7854 radians
- @DEGREES(@ATAN2(1,1)) = 45 degrees

The acceptable range of arguments for @ATAN2 is from -3.14159 (-pi) to 3.14159 (+pi). Any argument exceeding these bounds causes a result of ERR.

@DEGREES

The @DEGREES function converts a number of radians to the equivalent degrees. The syntax is

@DEGREES(radians_value)

The following formulas both return an answer of 180 degrees:

@DEGREES(@COS(-1))

@DEGREES(@PI)

@RADIANS

The @RADIANS function converts degrees to radians. The syntax for @RADIANS is

@RADIANS(degrees)

One degree is equal to .017453 radians. Thus the formula @RADIANS(1) returns .017453. The formula for @RADIANS is @PI/180.

@EXP

The @EXP, or exponentiation, function raises the constant *e* (approximately 2.71828) to a specified power. The syntax for @EXP is

@EXP(power_value)

where *power_value* is a number that will be used as the exponent for *e*. The lowest and highest allowable arguments for @EXP are -708 and +709.

The formula @EXP(1) is *e* to the first power. You can use @EXP to generate the constant when you need it in other calculations.

The @EXP function is inversely related to the next function, @LN. The function @EXP(@LN(4)) equals 4, and @LN(@EXP(4)) also equals 4.

@LN

The @LN function calculates the natural logarithm of a positive number where *e* (2.71828) is the base number. The syntax for @LN is

@LN(value)

where *value* is any positive number. A negative number results in ERR.

For example, the function @LN(2.71812818) returns approximately 1 as the result; @LN(8)/@LN(2) equals 3.

@LOG

The @LOG function returns the base 10 logarithm of a number. The syntax for @LOG is

@LOG(value)

where *value* can be any positive or negative number. @LOG determines the order of magnitude of a number. For example, the formula @LOG(100) equals 2; @LOG(1000000) equals 6.

Tip You can use @LOG as an approximation for the number of whole-number places of a value. For example, are you talking hundreds or millions?

The function

@INT(@LOG(@ABS(valued cell reference)))+1

returns the number of whole-number places for any value. If the valued cell reference is 100, the answer will be 3 (places). If the value referenced is -198012, the answer will be 6.

@LOG(x) and the exponentiation operation 10^@LOG(x) have an inverse relationship.

Programmers' Functions

The majority of spreadsheet users have little use for the programmers' functions. The primary value of these functions, which include @HEXTONUM and @NUMTOHEX, is for programmers who need to do conversions between decimal numbers (base 10) and hexadecimal numbers (base 16).

@HEXTONUM

The @HEXTONUM function converts hexadecimal numbers to decimal numbers. The syntax for @HEXTONUM is

@HEXTONUM("hexvalue")

where *hexvalue* is a string representing a value based on the hexadecimal system. The primary numbers for hexadecimal are 0, 1, 2, 3, 4, 5, 6, 7, 8, 9, A, B, C, D, E, and F. Hexadecimal F is equal to decimal 15; thus the function @HEXTONUM("F") returns the value 15.

Figure 7.47 shows hexadecimal numbers AAAA through FFFFFFFF in column E, and their decimal equivalents in column G. Note that the hexadecimal numbers FFFF, FFFFF, FFFFFF, and FFFFFFFF are equal to some of the common microprocessor memory limits (8080, 8088/6, 80286, 80386).

@NUMTOHEX

The @NUMTOHEX function converts decimal numbers to hexadecimal numbers. The syntax for @NUMTOHEX is

@NUMTOHEX(decimal_value)

where *decimal_value* is a number based on the decimal system (base 10). The primary numbers for hexadecimal are 0, 1, 2, 3, 4, 5, 6, 7, 8, 9, A, B, C, D, E, and F. Hexadecimal "F" is equal to decimal 15; thus the function @NUMTOHEX(15) returns the value F.

Figure 7.48 shows decimal numbers 0 through 15 in column A, and their hexadecimal equivalents in column B.

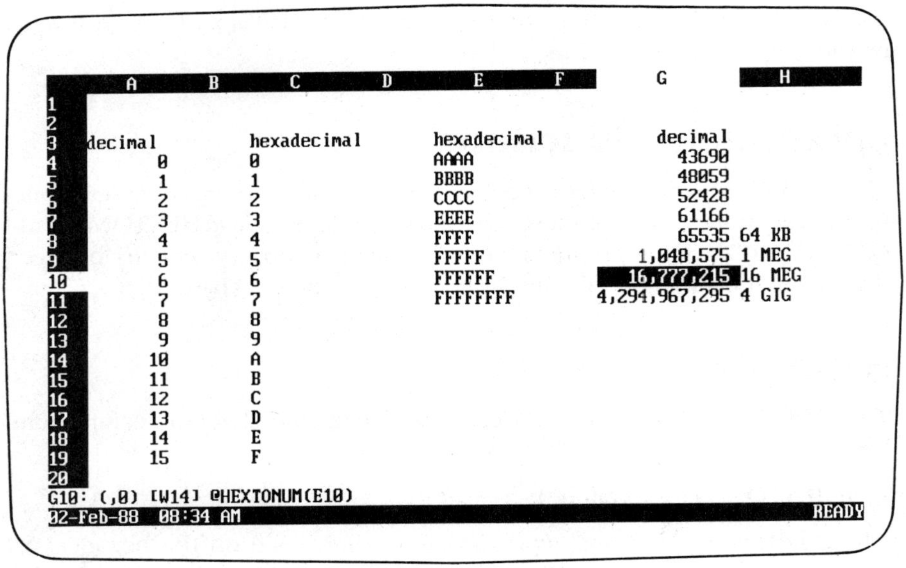

Fig. 7.47. Converting hexadecimal numbers to their decimal counterparts.

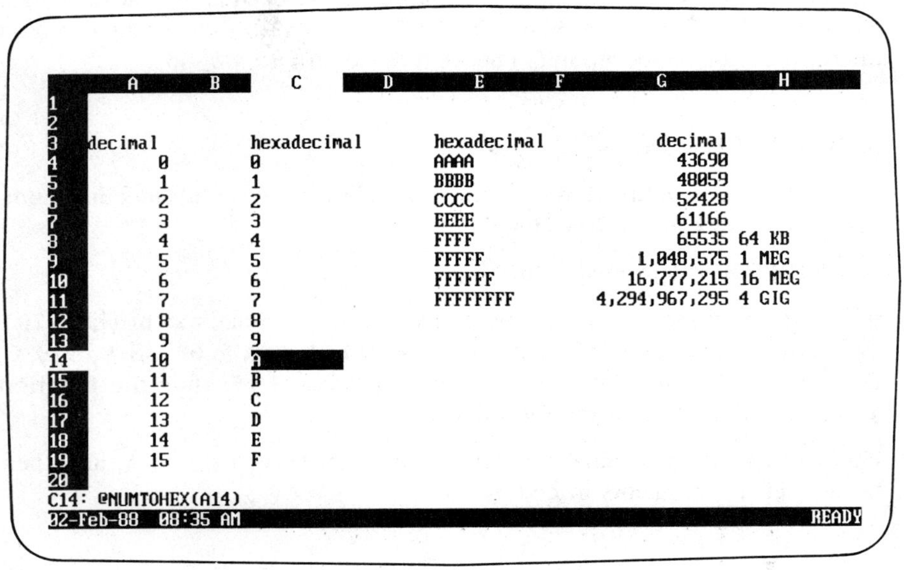

Fig. 7.48. Using @NUMTOHEX to convert decimal numbers to hexadecimal.

Chapter Summary

Now, please indulge me as I pass along some homilies that may help to make your life with spreadsheet functions easier. I hope these tips will serve you as well as they have me.

I'm often told by new users that some function I'm demonstrating is "interesting," but that they will never need it. Yet six months later they have found the function to be indispensable. So you should always presume that a function will come in handy at some time in the future, even if the function doesn't seem useful at the moment.

Think of the plethora of functions in Quattro as a well-stocked toolbox. Although you may not need those special wrenches often, when you do need them, nothing else will work.

If you need some special functionality, always assume that Quattro already has the function. For instance, when I needed a function that could tell when a cell was blank, I used Quattro's help system to track down the @CELLPOINTER function with the "type" argument.

Develop a library file of your most useful, well developed functions. You will then find that you have more time to build bulletproof, efficient functions that are reusable. Thus your formula technique will improve at the same time as your productivity. Don't reinvent the wheel.

Be sure to use block names such as SALES rather than cell-oriented references (A3..N3) as much as possible. By using block names, your functions will be much more readable and therefore self-documenting.

Get in the habit of formulating problems in English before typing in the spreadsheet. This preliminary step will not only make developing complex functions easier, but will also lead you to new methods of solving problems that might not otherwise have occurred to you.

When developing a decision-making formula, such as a nested @IF function, always put the most likely alternative first in the results argument of the function. This tactic leads to much shorter, simpler, less-nested functions.

Furthermore, be sure to examine your conditional logic in @IF functions to see whether you can state a condition in a simpler way. Literally several hundred ways to state a condition may be available, but usually only two or three of them are efficient.

Do your best to avoid putting variables within functions. Instead, as much as possible, structure your functions so that variables are in other cells and are referred to. Any spreadsheet will then be easier to use because you won't need to change any formulas in order to perform "what-if" analysis.

If you are having trouble coming up with a solution to a tough problem, don't spend hours banging away at the keyboard. Get out of the chair (which may be hard to do) and take a brisk walk. Try not even to think about the problem for 15 or 20 minutes. If you're at all like me, a good answer will pop into your head before you know it.

If you've used a spreadsheet for more than a week or two, you may have already experienced this next dilemma, but I'll say it anyway. NEVER show a spreadsheet to your boss until you have worked with it for at least a couple of weeks. Spreadsheets can sense when your boss is looking, and they love to throw eggs.

Finally, don't show an amazing formula of which you are especially proud to someone who doesn't use spreadsheets. They will either say, "Yeah, that's nice . . .," or will be convinced that you are absolutely nuts to go to so much trouble just to balance a couple of numbers!

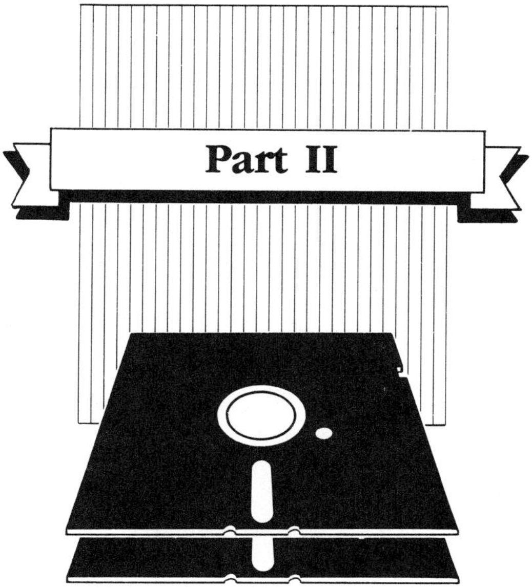

Managing Quattro Files, Reports, and Graphs

Includes

Managing Files in Quattro

Printing Professional Reports

Graphing with Quattro

CHAPTER

8

Managing Files in Quattro

Storing, retrieving, and deleting files to and from disks are capabilities common to all spreadsheet programs. What makes Quattro unique is the scale with which it performs these functions, thanks to its additional translation and file compression features.

Quattro was written for users who intend to mix and match many large files and move them in and out of storage frequently. In fact, with its file translation capabilities, Quattro can serve as a translation device between otherwise incompatible programs such as dBASE® and Paradox. A complete listing of all file operation commands can be found in Appendix A, "Command Reference Tables."

This chapter will show you how to

- Save, edit and name files
- Retrieve files
- Use passwords to protect files
- Translate files

- Retrieve portions of files
- Combine separate files
- Delete files
- List different types of files
- Import files, using the /File Import command

A General Description of Quattro Files

Quattro file names, like all DOS file names, can be up to eight characters long, not including a three-character extension. The three basic rules for file names are as follows:

1. File names may include the characters A through Z, 0 through 9, and the underscore (_). Depending on your system, you may be able to use other special characters, but Quattro does not accept the characters <, >, and *. Although Quattro uses a period to separate the file name from the extension, the program does not accept the period (.) within the file name. For example, Quattro does not accept the file name SALES1.1.TXT.

2. File names may not contain blank spaces. Many people use the underscore (_) to represent a blank space.

3. Lowercase letters are converted automatically to uppercase in file names.

Although you determine the eight-character name, Quattro creates the extension automatically according to the type of file you are handling. The possible file extensions are

.WKQ For worksheet files
.PRN For print and graph files
.EPS For files with Postscript graphics compatibility
.PIC For files with 1-2-3 graphics compatibility

Experienced 1-2-3 users should note that the program uses .WKQ as a file extension for worksheets rather than .WK1. This difference allows Quattro to distinguish between Quattro worksheets and worksheets from 1-2-3 and Symphony. Happily, Quattro can load any file from any release of 1-2-3 or Symphony. See the "Translating Files" section in this chapter for more information.

If you want, Quattro lets you supply your own file extension. To create a file name with your own extension, enter the file name according to the listed rules, type a period, and add an extension of one to three characters. Notice that any file name with your own extension is not displayed in the lists of .WKQ, .PIC, .EPS, or .PRN files. The /File Retrieve command, for example, retrieves all .WKQ files without your needing to specify an extension. You must specify special file extensions manually. To retrieve your specially named file, type the file name and extension after the `Enter name of file to retrieve:` prompt.

To see a list of files with your own extension (along with all other files), remove the default file name from the input line and replace the default file name with the wild-card pattern *.*. This displays all files in the directory (you then can choose a file to load). Although not fail-safe, creating file names with your own extensions can provide a level of security for those files for which you want to limit user access. Additional ways of limiting access to files are provided by Quattro's password system, described in this chapter.

Keep in mind that only one worksheet exists in a file, and that you can work on a worksheet only when it is in main memory.

Saving Files

The basic file function of storing files is easy to perform in Quattro. The /**F**ile **S**ave command allows you to save an entire worksheet as a file on disk. The /**F**ile **S**ave command makes an exact copy of the current worksheet, including all the formats, block names, and settings you have specified.

When you enter this command, Quattro tries to assist you by supplying a list of the current worksheet files on the disk. You can either point to one of the entries or enter a new file name. To enter a new file name, you must use the rules for correct file names. Quattro automatically supplies a .WKQ extension, as shown in figure 8.1.

Naming a New File

Remember to be expressive when naming a new file. True, you have only eight characters with which to name the file; but make those characters specific. In other words, choose a file name that relates something about the contents or purpose of the file. The following list provides some good examples of file names:

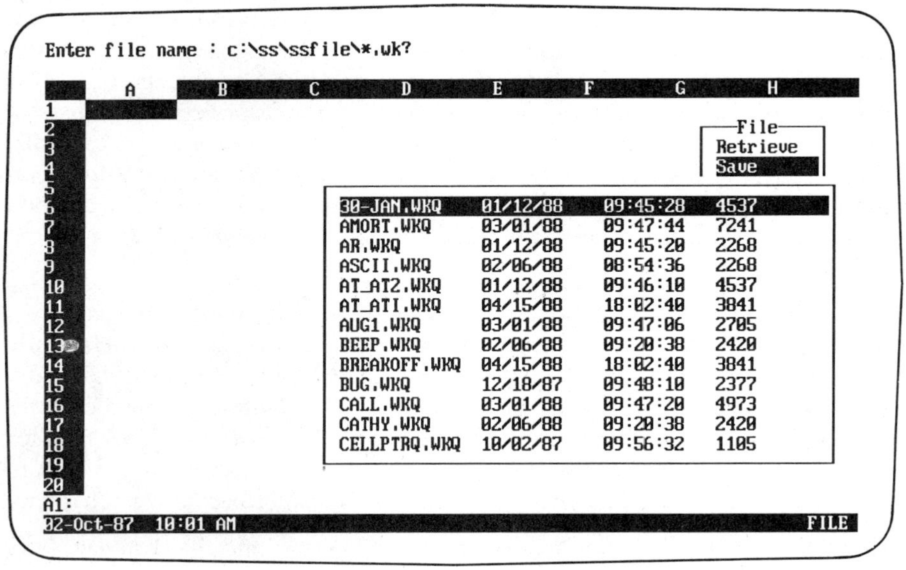

Fig. 8.1. File name list during /File Save.

File name	*Description*
INVWS-06	Inventory worksheet for June
PRO_RRNT	Pro forma worksheet for the planned restaurant
EMPLSTDP	Employee list for the Data Processing Department

If you work with many different worksheets that contain basically the same information, you need to make the names similar without, of course, using the same name. In the previous examples, the name INVWS-06 was given to an inventory worksheet for the month of June. Following this naming scheme, you would name the inventory worksheets for July and August INVWS-07 and INVWS-08, respectively. This naming technique will help you recall file names later.

After you've chosen the file name, type the name and press Enter. Quattro saves the file to that name and assigns .WKQ as a default extension.

Normally, the fact that Quattro assigns this extension poses no problem, because when Quattro displays a list of files, only the files beginning with the extension letters .WK are shown (for example, .WKQ or .WK1). At times, however, you may want to supply your own extension. For example, suppose that the pro forma worksheet file, PRO_RRNT, contains confidential information. When you type the file name, you can use an extension of .CFL to indicate that the file is confidential. In this case, type the name as PRO_RRNT.CFL.

Saving Later Versions

Sometimes when you are creating a Quattro model, you may want to save more than one version of the model on disk. If you do, you need to save the worksheet under two different file names, because each time you save a file under an existing name, the new file replaces the old one.

Suppose that you have been working on a cash management worksheet and have already saved it under the name CASHMGT. When you save the worksheet again, the name CASHMGT appears as the default name. Quattro displays the last file name as the default, to save you typing time and trouble.

If you want to create a new file name at this point, you have two options. You could simply type the new name (such as CASHMGT2) and press Enter. The easier method, however, is to modify the default name displayed by Quattro. Because changing the name to CASHMGT2 requires only adding one character to the default name, simply press the space bar once; then press the Backspace key to remove the blank space, type *2*, and press Enter.

In EDIT mode, you can make any changes as though you were editing a label in a worksheet cell. Normally, Quattro assumes that if you are not going to use the current file name, you will type a completely new file name. By pressing the space bar, however, you can make minor changes to the worksheet's path specification or the file name.

If you use a hard disk system, you may want to save your worksheets on floppy disks as insurance as well as on the hard disk. To do this, after you've saved the worksheet on the hard disk, issue /**F**ile **S**ave again. When you see the file name you have just saved (as the file on the hard disk), press the Esc key until the prompt `Enter file name:` is the only thing remaining. Then type the drive designation for the floppy disk and the new file name. Before pressing Enter, make sure that you have placed the correct floppy disk in the specified drive.

If you try to save a file that already has been saved to disk, Quattro responds with the message `File already exists` and the menu shown in figure 8.2.

If you choose **C**ancel, Quattro returns you to READY mode. The **R**eplace option writes the current spreadsheet over the previously saved file. **B**ackup makes the previously saved file a backup copy, giving it the file extension

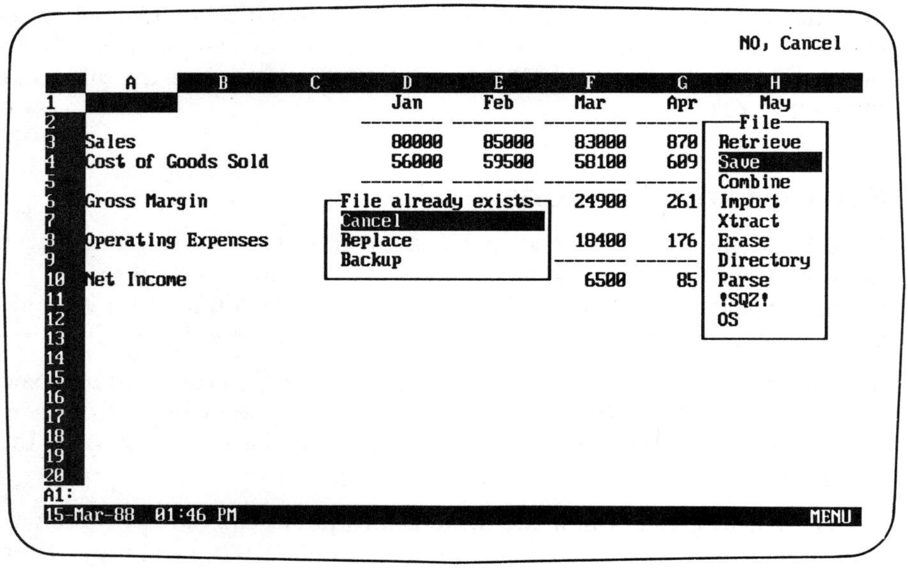

Fig. 8.2. Saving a previously saved file.

.BAQ. Remember: you can make only one backup per file name, no matter which file extension you use.

Retrieving Files

To call a file back into memory from disk, use the /**F**ile **R**etrieve command. Again, Quattro displays a list of all files on disk with extensions that match the pattern .WK?, such as .WKQ, .WK1, and .WK!.

Whenever you need to choose a file name, Quattro helps you by displaying a list of the files on the current drive and directory. If the file name you want is in the list, you can select it by moving the highlight bar to that name and pressing Enter. Otherwise, you can type the file name you want.

Quattro displays the list of file names in a box. Figure 8.3 shows the normal file display. If you press the plus sign (+) on the numeric keypad while the file catalog box is on-screen, you get an expanded description of each file, including the date and time of the file's creation or last modification, and the file's size. Figure 8.4 shows the expanded file display. Press the minus sign (-) on the numeric keypad to return to the normal file display.

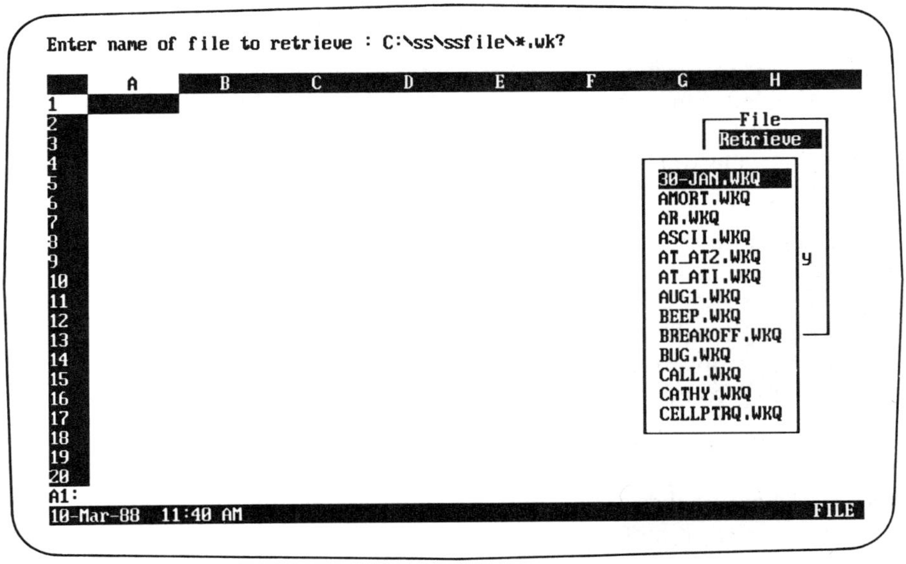

Fig. 8.3. The normal file display.

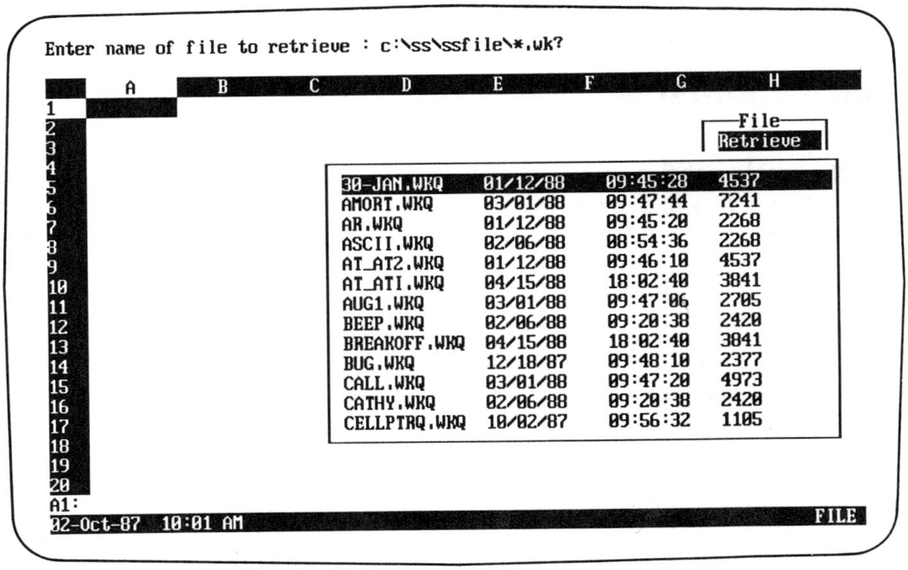

Fig. 8.4. The expanded file display.

Using Wild Cards for File Retrieval

When you are retrieving files, Quattro allows the use of *wild cards*. The asterisk (*) and the question mark (?) wild cards are helpful when you need to limit the number of files displayed on-screen or when you are unsure of the exact spelling of a file you want to retrieve.

The asterisk (*) wild card can be used in place of any combination of characters; the question mark (?) wild card stands for any one character. The asterisk can be used only when it follows other characters or is used by itself. Thus, to find INVWS-06.WKQ, the name INVWS-*.WKQ is acceptable but *WS-06.WKQ is not. The question mark, on the other hand, can be used in any character position. Therefore, instead of the incorrect retrieval name *WS-06.WKQ, you could enter ???WS-06.WKQ.

Suppose you want a listing of your inventory worksheets: INVWS-06.WKQ, INVWS-07.WKQ, and INVWS-08.WKQ. If you want to use a wild card to retrieve a listing of these files, you can enter one of the following names in response to the prompt `Enter name of file to retrieve:C\*.WK?`

INVWS-*.WKQ
INVWS-??.WKQ

Either of these names retrieves the files you want. Similarly, to list all files that have the extension .CFL (for confidential), you can type *.CFL. All files with the .CFL extension will be listed.

Retrieving Files from Subdirectories

Quattro keeps track of subdirectory names as well as file names. These names are displayed in the current directory, with the subdirectories indicated by the backslash (\) that appears after the subdirectory name. To suppress the display of worksheet files in the file catalog box so that only the directory names appear, use this wild-card pattern:

*.

This pattern shows only disk entries within the current directory that have no extension (see fig. 8.5). To list all subdirectories within the root directory for the C: drive, press Esc and type

C:*.

If you point to a subdirectory name and press Enter to select it, Quattro switches to that subdirectory and displays a list of its files. The list includes any subdirectories of this subdirectory. You then can specify a file name in that subdirectory.

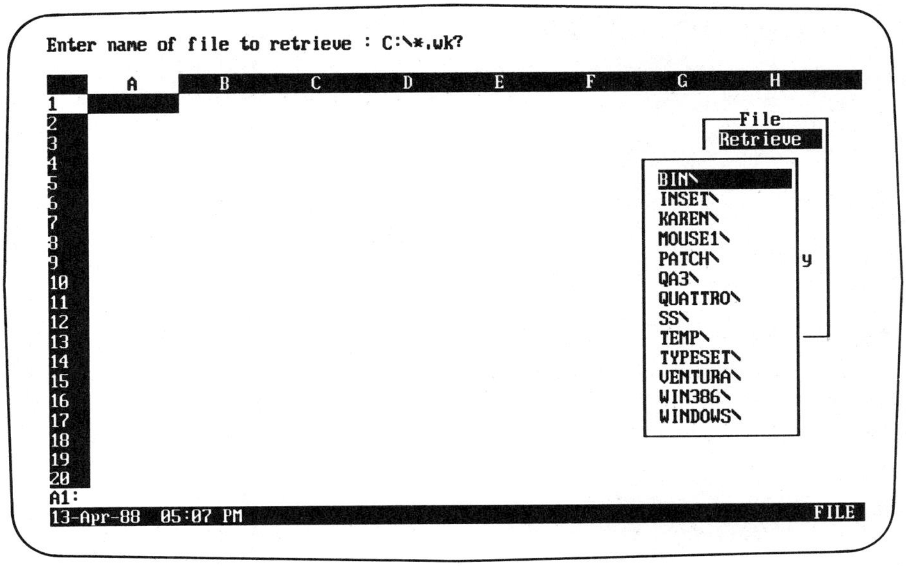

Fig. 8.5. Displaying subdirectories.

If you want to access a file on a different drive or in a directory that is not a subdirectory of the current directory, use the Esc key or the Backspace key. Pressing the Esc key once while the default path name is displayed changes Quattro from FILE mode to EDIT mode; you can then edit the file specification just as you would any cell entry. Pressing the Esc key a second time erases the current drive and subdirectory specification; you can then specify the drive and directory you want. (The /**D**efault **D**irectories command is an exception: for this command, the default path name appears in the input line in EDIT mode; pressing the Esc key once erases the path name.)

You can use the Backspace key to erase the path name, one directory at a time. To reverse the process, select a subdirectory name from the list of files and then press Enter.

Some valid file names, and drive and directory specifications are

B:\SAMPLE1.WKQ	Worksheet file on drive B:
C:\QUATTRO\SAMPLE1.WKQ	Worksheet file in subdirectory QUATTRO on drive C:

C:\QUATTRO\DATA*.WKQ	List of all .WKQ files in subdirectory DATA of subdirectory QUATTRO on drive C:. Quattro displays the list and waits for you to select a specific file name.
A:*.*	List of all files on drive A:. Quattro displays all file names and waits for you to select a specific file name.

If you want to find out more about DOS path names and subdirectories, you can consult *Using PC DOS*, 2nd Edition, and *MS-DOS User's Guide*, 2nd Edition, both by Chris DeVoney; and *Managing Your Hard Disk*, by Don Berliner; all published by Que Corporation.

Translating Files

You no doubt have been frustrated at times because you could not easily access data you created with another software program. For instance, perhaps you have a large amount of information stored in a database file to which you want direct access. Or perhaps you want to do some calculations with your Quattro spreadsheet but save the results to a dBASE or 1-2-3 file.

Quattro has a wonderful capability to eliminate this "Tower of Babel" file confusion. Quattro can retrieve files without any intervention from the user if the files are in any of the following file formats: dBASE II® or dBASE III Plus, Paradox, 1-2-3 Release 1A and 2.x, Symphony, or Reflex. Quattro also can translate files into dBASE and 1-2-3 formats.

Quattro *translator files* (which have the extension .TRN) retrieve foreign file formats. Quattro uses these translator files whenever you specify to retrieve a file that has another program's special file extension, such as dBASE's .DBF extension. These extensions signal Quattro to use the translator files (which must be present in the same directory as the main Quattro program).

To illustrate file translation, suppose you want to translate a database created in Quattro to a dBASE III Plus file. In figure 8.6 the /**F**ile **S**ave command has been invoked. Rather than the default .WKQ extension, however, the file name has a .DBF extension.

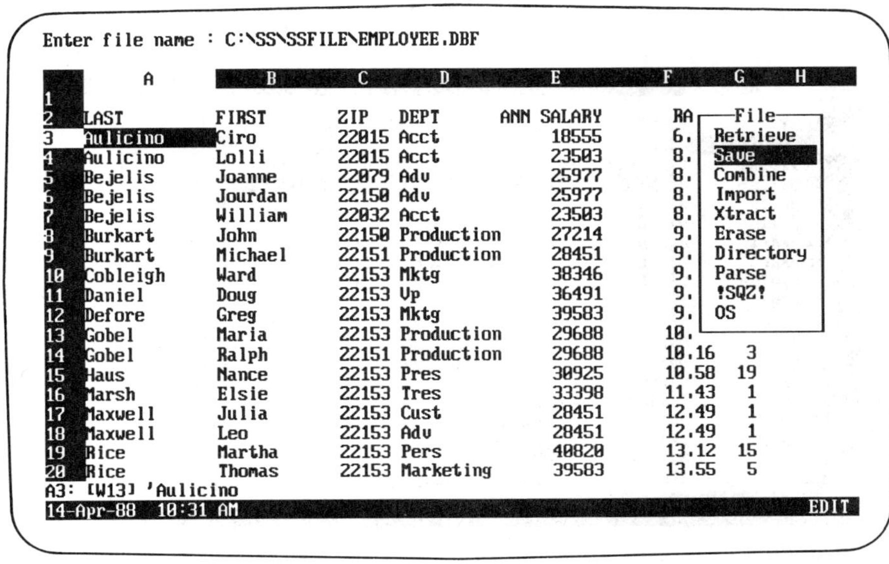

Fig. 8.6. Saving a database in Quattro.

When you press Enter, a box opens that provides you with options related to saving a dBASE file:

View Structure
Write dBASE File
Quit

If you are certain that Quattro will save the database file properly, you can go ahead and save the file. In most cases, however, choosing **V**iew Structure is a good idea, because you then can see how Quattro intends to structure the database when saving it. Figure 8.7 illustrates the result of choosing the **V**iew Structure command.

Notice in figure 8.7 that Quattro has mistakenly presumed that the database begins on row 1 of the spreadsheet. Because no column names were in the first row, Quattro assigned generic field names of A, B, C, and so on. To prevent this error, either ensure that the database in the spreadsheet is in the first row, or (more conveniently) use the /**F**ile **X**tract command so that you can specify the starting row for the database. Figure 8.8 shows the structure when the database is moved to A1..G19.

As you can see, the column headings have been included as part of the structure, and the data types now include numbers (as they should) rather than only character data types. Notice that the ANN SALARY column heading has

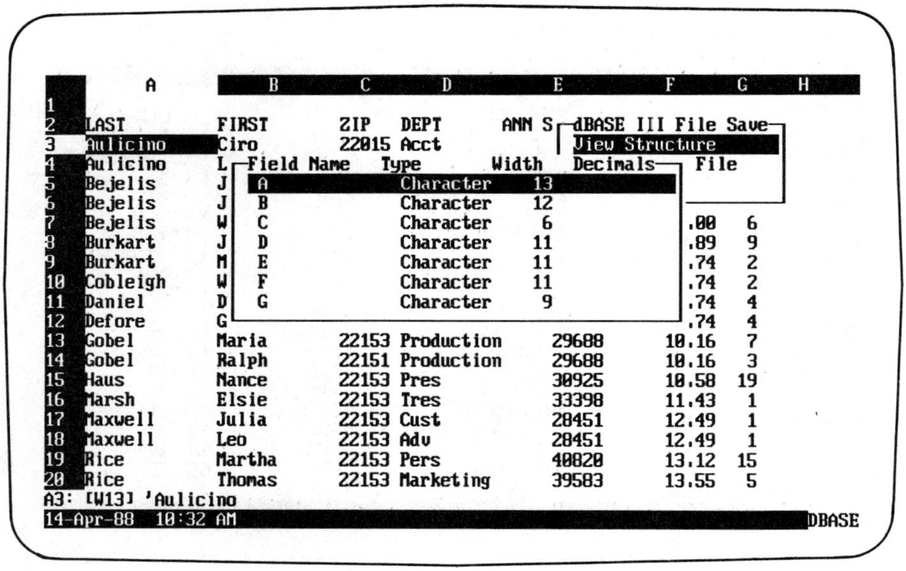

Fig. 8.7. The presumed database structure.

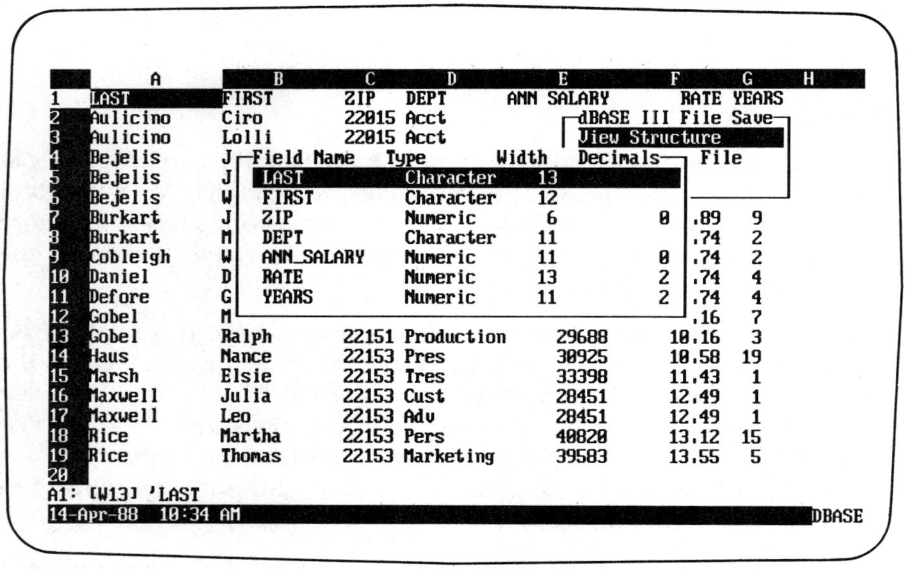

Fig. 8.8. The actual database structure.

been modified to include an underscore to connect the two words. dBASE does not accept a field name that contains a blank space. This space detection and correction feature prevents the problem that would otherwise have occurred when dBASE tried to use the file.

When the database area of the spreadsheet has been selected correctly, you can proceed to fine-tune the specific elements in the structure box before performing the translation. For instance, to modify the ANN_SALARY field, move the highlight bar in the structure box to the ANN_SALARY row and press the menu key (/). The resulting menu is shown in figure 8.9.

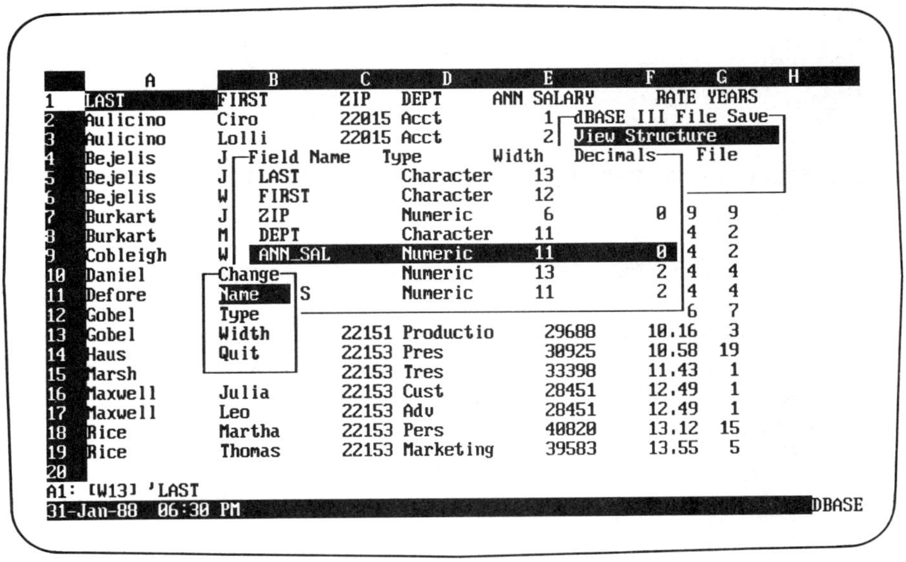

Fig. 8.9. Modifying the ANN_SALARY field.

Figure 8.9 shows the database structure after the field name has been modified, and as the column width and decimal specification are being changed. The field change menu allows you to modify the field name, data type, width, and decimals carried. The data types allowed are character, numeric, date, and logical. In this example, you do not need to change the data type from numeric. Figure 8.10 shows the structure after the changes have been made.

When you are satisfied with the structure, press the Esc key to move back up to the dBASE III File Save box, and choose **Write dBASE File** from the menu to save the file.

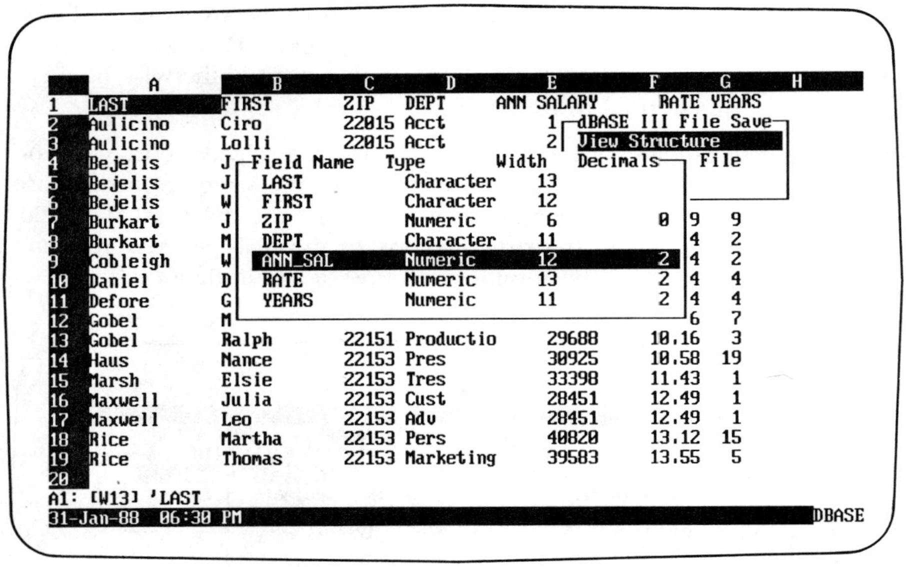

Fig. 8.10. The revised database structure.

The process for saving Quattro files to Paradox and Reflex database files is quite similar. Translations to 1-2-3, for example, do not require any special structuring steps. Simply type the /**F**ile **S**ave command, use a .WK1 extension, and press Enter.

To retrieve a file from any of these programs, simply use the appropriate extension. Quattro takes care of all the details automatically.

Using Password Protection

You can protect your files by using Quattro's password protection system. You can create a password with the /**F**ile **S**ave command so that your file can be retrieved only with the exact password.

To create a password, begin by selecting the /**F**ile **S**ave command. At the `Enter file name: *.wk?` prompt, type the file name, leave a space, and then type *p*, as shown in figure 8.11. After you press Enter, you will see a password prompt; type your password and press Enter again. Quattro then asks you to `Verify:`. Type the password once more (see fig. 8.12). Any difference between the first and second passwords results in nonacceptance.

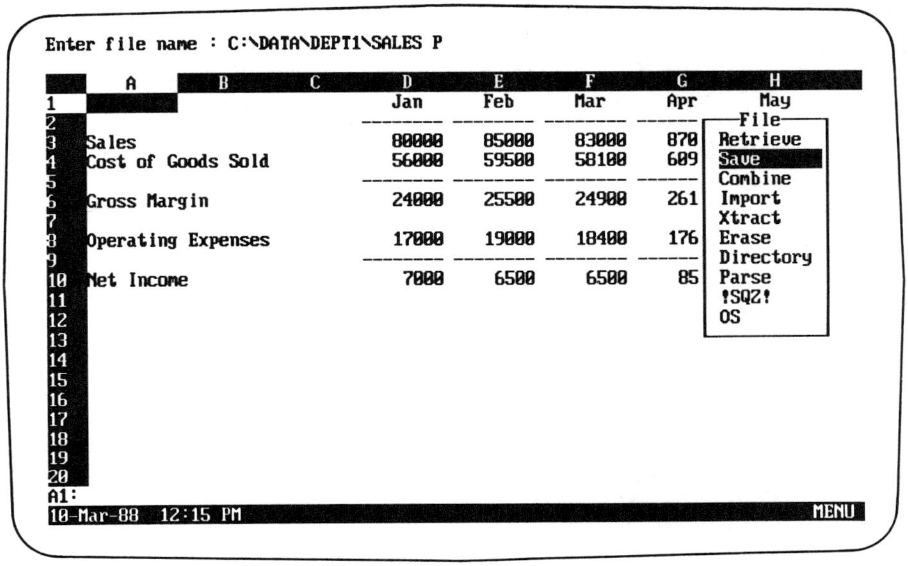

Fig. 8.11. Indicating that a password will be entered.

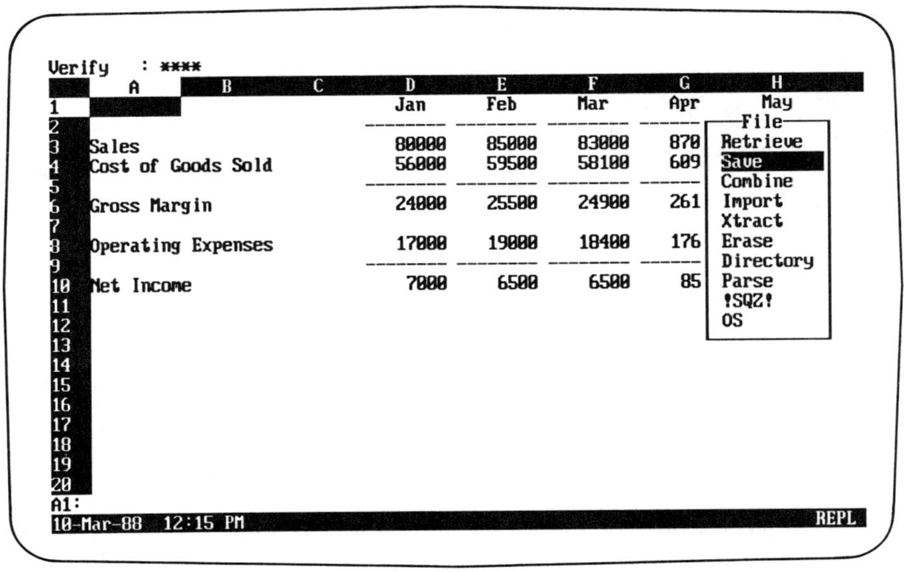

Fig. 8.12. Verifying the specified password.

After you issue /File **R**etrieve and enter your password correctly, the worksheet appears. But if you enter the password incorrectly, you get an error message indicating that an incorrect password was supplied, and the mode indicator flashes ERROR. Press Esc to return to a blank worksheet.

Quattro accepts any character in a password, which can be up to 16 characters long. Be sensitive to case, however: Quattro accepts the password only in the exact uppercase or lowercase letters you entered. For example, if you entered *pdfund* as your password, Quattro would not retrieve the file if you typed *PDFUND* or *PDfund* or any other combination of uppercase and lowercase letters. Be sure to remember your password.

To delete a password, retrieve the file that has the password you want to delete. Then, when you are ready to save the file, select the /File **S**ave command. When the prompt appears, press Esc to erase the [P] message that appears (see fig. 8.13). Proceed with the /File **S**ave operation, and Quattro will save the file without the password.

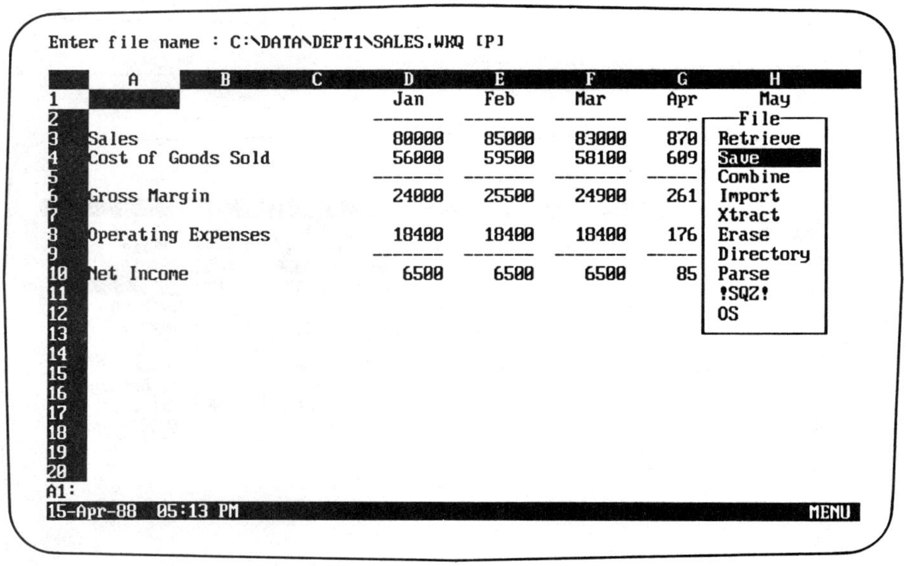

Fig. 8.13. Removing password protection.

To change a password, complete the first three steps for deleting the password name. After you have deleted [P], the prompt appears with the file name listed. Press the space bar, type *p*, and press Enter. Quattro then prompts you for a new password and asks you to verify it. Once you have completed these steps and saved the file, the new password is stored.

Deleting Files

When you save files to disk, you may eventually find that your disk is full. To alert you, Quattro flashes the message `Disk is full.` You can then either swap disks or delete one or more of the files occupying space on the disk.

There are two ways to delete stored files in Quattro. The first way is to use the /**F**ile **E**rase command. When you issue /FE, a menu box appears for you to indicate the type of file to erase: a **W**orksheet, **P**rinting, **G**raph, or **O**ther file. According to your choice (**W**, **P**, or **G**), Quattro shows you only .WKQ and .WK1 files, .PIC files, or .PRN files, respectively. If you choose **O**ther, Quattro lists all files. You then can point to the file you want to erase (or type its name) and press Enter.

You can use the wild-card characters mentioned earlier to display all the files of a certain type that are to be deleted. These are the same wild-card characters used for DOS and other commands throughout Quattro. You can use wild-card characters in several ways:

- * Matches the remaining characters of a file name. B* matches BOB, BARNEY, BOQUIST, and so on.
- ? Matches all characters in a single position in a file name. B?RD matches BARD, BIRD, and BYRD, but not BURT.

Be careful when you use the /**F**ile **E**rase command. Once a file has been deleted, that file cannot be recovered by conventional means. Always check and double-check that you really want to delete a file before you do so.

Another way to delete files is to use the /**F**ile **O**S command and the DOS DEL command. This method makes available the full power of DOS but requires more time to suspend Quattro execution, perform the DOS command, and return to Quattro.

Specifying Drives and Directories

You use the /**D**efault **D**irectories command to change the default drive and directory for files. Hard disk users can use the default directory setting to their advantage. For example, directories may be set up as shown in the diagram in figure 8.14. The default directory could then be set to C:\DATA. When a file is to be retrieved, the subdirectories DATA\DEPT1, DATA\DEPT2, and DATA\COMPANY are displayed. After you've chosen the proper directory, the files stored in that directory are displayed again so that you can make a choice. Setting the default directory this way saves time if you use worksheets in different subdirectories.

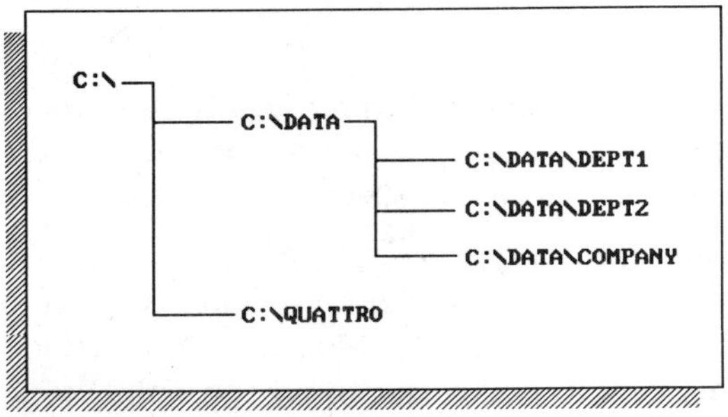

Fig. 8.14. Possible hard disk directories.

Two types of file directories can be specified: data and resource. The *data directory* contains your worksheet files. The *resource directory* holds three types of files. First, it holds the files that provide the help system (F1). Second, it holds a variety of files that provide information to Quattro, letting Quattro use your computer hardware efficiently. Third, the resource directory holds the QUATTRO.DEF file, which defines the default settings for Quattro. This is the file that is changed each time you use the /**D**efault **U**pdate command.

Sometimes, however, you will want to override the default directory setting temporarily. You may, for example, be doing a considerable amount of extracting, combining, and retrieving in one particular subdirectory on the hard disk. The /**F**ile **D**irectory command lets you specify another drive and directory for the duration of the current session.

Using Advanced File Handling Commands

The filing commands described in the preceding sections should serve most of your basic storage needs. This section illustrates the powerful advanced filing commands that Quattro offers. With these commands, you can "cut and paste" files. You also can temporarily access the operating system, shrink file sizes, and import and structure foreign data files.

Combining Files

Sometimes you will want to copy certain blocks of cells from other worksheets into strategic spots in the current worksheet. For example, if you work for a large firm, you may want to combine several divisions' balance sheets and income statements into one consolidated worksheet.

A simple technique for accomplishing this kind of consolidation is to develop and keep a copy of a *spreadsheet template*, or an "empty master" (a worksheet file with no data and usually only labels). You will always have an empty master ready when the time comes to perform a consolidation. When you start with an empty master, you can copy the first divisional worksheet into the master, leaving the original divisional worksheet file untouched.

Copying a block of cells can also be helpful when you want to combine quarterly data into a yearly statement. Again, the data and spreadsheet layout must be compatible, and you will benefit if you keep an empty master.

The command used to combine data in the preceding examples is /**F**ile **C**ombine. This command gives you the following menu options:

Copy	Pulls in an entire worksheet or a named block and causes the new contents to write over the corresponding cells in the existing worksheet. Cells in the worksheet that correspond to empty cells in the file or block being combined are not affected. (There is an important distinction here between empty cells and cells containing a blank in the combine file.)
Add	Pulls in the values from an entire worksheet or a named block and adds these values to the corresponding cells in the current worksheet. The **A**dd command affects only cells in the worksheet that are blank or contain numeric values. Cells containing formulas or labels are unchanged. Cells in the file being combined that contain labels or string formulas are not added.
Subtract	Pulls in an entire worksheet or a named block and subtracts the values from the corresponding cells in the current worksheet. When an existing cell is empty, the incoming value is subtracted from zero. Like **A**dd, **S**ubtract affects only cells in the worksheet that are blank or contain numeric values. Cells containing formulas or labels in the current worksheet are unaffected, and cells from the worksheet being combined that contain labels or string formulas are not subtracted.

The specified worksheet or named block is combined into the current worksheet, with the current position of the cell selector as the upper left corner of the block that is combined. For example, if the cell selector is at cell A1, the specified worksheet or named block is combined into the current worksheet starting at cell A1. If the cell selector is at cell AA100, the worksheet or block is combined into the current worksheet starting at cell AA100. Before you combine a block from another worksheet, be sure that your cell selector is in the proper cell. Whatever is being copied, added, or subtracted overwrites data that is currently in your worksheet relative to the starting selector location.

Only the /File Combine Copy command overwrites formulas. Adding or subtracting files adds or subtracts values contained in cells that do *not* already contain formulas. All formulas referencing the affected cells in the destination worksheet (in memory) then use the added or subtracted values.

When you use the /File Combine Copy command with worksheets or named blocks containing formulas, the cell references in those formulas are adjusted relative to the cell selector location where the worksheet or block is combined, including absolute cell references. After the combining process has been completed, the absolute cell references in cells that were combined into the current worksheet behave normally when you copy or move those cells.

Figures 8.15, 8.16, 8.17, and 8.18 show examples of the **C**opy and **A**dd options. Figure 8.15 shows a worksheet that I created and stored on disk. Figure 8.16 shows a similar worksheet that is stored in Quattro's memory. Figure 8.17 shows the results of combining these two worksheets, using the **C**opy option when the cell selector was in A1. Notice that the copied block completely replaced the previous worksheet. Figure 8.18 shows the results of combining these two worksheets with the **A**dd option, with the cell selector in A1. The **S**ubtract option is so much like the **A**dd option that I did not include it here.

	A B C	D	E	F	G	H
1		Jan	Feb	Mar	Apr	May
2		--------	--------	--------	--------	--------
3	Sales	$80,000	$85,000	$83,000	$87,000	$90,000
4	Cost of Goods Sold	$56,000	$59,500	$58,100	$60,900	$63,000
5		--------	--------	--------	--------	--------
6	Gross Margin	$24,000	$25,500	$24,900	$26,100	$27,000
7						
8	Operating Expenses	$17,000	$19,000	$18,400	$17,600	$20,000
9		--------	--------	--------	--------	--------
10	Net Income	$7,000	$6,500	$6,500	$8,500	$7,000
11						
12						

Fig. 8.15. Worksheet for /File Combine.

	Jan	Feb	Mar	Apr	May
Sales	$100,000	$120,000	$130,000	$150,000	$160,000
Cost of Goods Sold	$78,000	$96,000	$112,000	$120,000	$123,000
Gross Margin	$22,000	$24,000	$18,000	$30,000	$37,000
Operating Expenses	$15,000	$16,000	$17,500	$18,000	$21,000
Net Income	$7,000	$8,000	$500	$12,000	$16,000

Fig. 8.16. Another worksheet for /File Combine.

	Jan	Feb	Mar	Apr	May
Sales	$80,000	$85,000	$83,000	$87,000	$90,000
Cost of Goods Sold	$56,000	$59,500	$58,100	$60,900	$63,000
Gross Margin	$24,000	$25,500	$24,900	$26,100	$27,000
Operating Expenses	$17,000	$19,000	$18,400	$17,600	$20,000
Net Income	$7,000	$6,500	$6,500	$8,500	$7,000

Fig. 8.17. Worksheet after /File Combine Copy.

	Jan	Feb	Mar	Apr	May
Sales	$180,000	$205,000	$213,000	$237,000	$250,000
Cost of Goods Sold	$134,000	$155,500	$170,100	$180,900	$186,000
Gross Margin	$46,000	$49,500	$42,900	$56,100	$64,000
Operating Expenses	$32,000	$35,000	$35,900	$35,600	$41,000
Net Income	$14,000	$14,500	$7,000	$20,500	$23,000

Fig. 8.18. Worksheet after /File Combine Add.

Tip One excellent use of the /**F**ile **C**ombine **S**ubtract command is to "zero out" a spreadsheet simply by subtracting a file from itself. If you subtract a file from itself, all data (or "assumption") cells become equal to zero, and all cells referring to assumption cells also return to zero. This command can save much tedium when you want to reuse a spreadsheet that has accumulated a great deal of old data—for example, when the time comes to redo budgets for a new year.

All three options (**A**dd, **S**ubtract, and **C**opy) are useful in combining worksheets. The /**F**ile **C**ombine **A**dd command, which can be used to consolidate one worksheet with another, is especially helpful. For example, /FCA could be used by a business with several divisions to consolidate the income statements for each division into a company-wide statement.

Extracting Files

With the /**F**ile **X**tract command, you can save part of the worksheet file—either the formulas existing in a block of cells or the current values of the formulas in the block, depending on the option you select (**F**ormulas or **V**alues). Both options create a worksheet file that you can reload into Quattro with the /**F**ile **R**etrieve command. If you decide to extract only the current values, however, the resulting worksheet file contains numbers but no formulas. Selecting the **F**ormulas option creates a file with all the formulas, values, and other settings (graph names, block names, and column and window settings) intact.

The /**F**ile **X**tract command also requires that you specify the portion of the worksheet you want to save. The block to be saved can be as small as a cell or as large as the entire worksheet. For example, consider the amortization table shown in figure 8.19. Suppose that you want to make a graphic comparison of one year's interest and principal payments for three different loans. Your **X**tract block would be A28..G39.

When you use the **V**alues option with the /**F**ile **X**tract command, you can "lock" the current values in a worksheet. To lock the values, issue the command and select the **V**alues option. Then specify the portion of the worksheet you need as the block to extract. If necessary, you can select the entire worksheet as your block, saving the current values stored in the worksheet. You can think of this technique as taking a snapshot of the current worksheet.

The new, values-only file can be reloaded into the worksheet and printed or graphed, as previously mentioned. Figure 8.20 shows what the extracted portion of the worksheet looks like after it has been retrieved. If you compare the entry in the input line with the same entry in figure 8.19, you can see that the calculated value has replaced the formula.

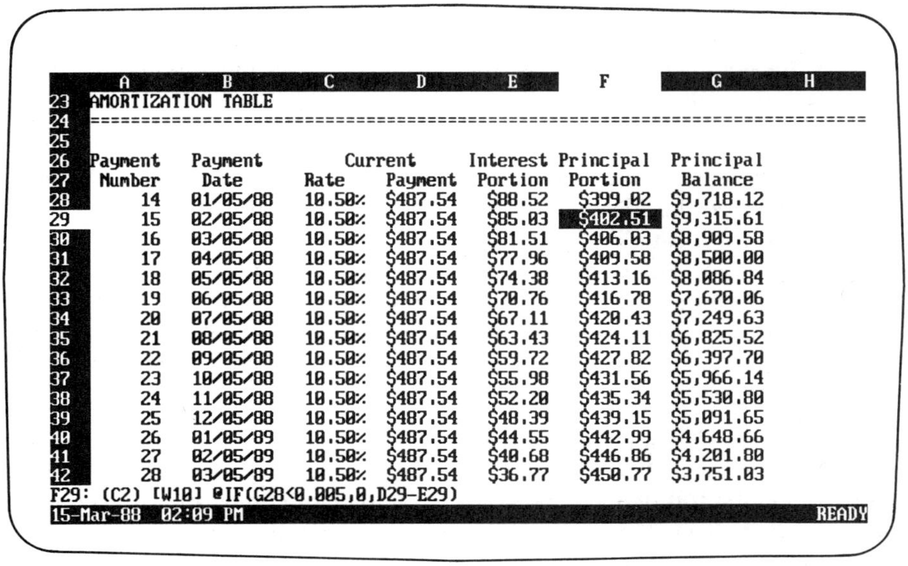

	A	B	C	D	E	F	G	H
23	AMORTIZATION TABLE							
24	==							
25								
26	Payment	Payment	Current		Interest	Principal	Principal	
27	Number	Date	Rate	Payment	Portion	Portion	Balance	
28	14	01/05/88	10.50%	$487.54	$88.52	$399.02	$9,718.12	
29	15	02/05/88	10.50%	$487.54	$85.03	$402.51	$9,315.61	
30	16	03/05/88	10.50%	$487.54	$81.51	$406.03	$8,909.58	
31	17	04/05/88	10.50%	$487.54	$77.96	$409.58	$8,500.00	
32	18	05/05/88	10.50%	$487.54	$74.38	$413.16	$8,086.84	
33	19	06/05/88	10.50%	$487.54	$70.76	$416.78	$7,670.06	
34	20	07/05/88	10.50%	$487.54	$67.11	$420.43	$7,249.63	
35	21	08/05/88	10.50%	$487.54	$63.43	$424.11	$6,825.52	
36	22	09/05/88	10.50%	$487.54	$59.72	$427.82	$6,397.70	
37	23	10/05/88	10.50%	$487.54	$55.98	$431.56	$5,966.14	
38	24	11/05/88	10.50%	$487.54	$52.20	$435.34	$5,530.80	
39	25	12/05/88	10.50%	$487.54	$48.39	$439.15	$5,091.65	
40	26	01/05/89	10.50%	$487.54	$44.55	$442.99	$4,648.66	
41	27	02/05/89	10.50%	$487.54	$40.68	$446.86	$4,201.80	
42	28	03/05/89	10.50%	$487.54	$36.77	$450.77	$3,751.03	

F29: (C2) [W10] @IF(G28<0.005,0,D29-E29)

15-Mar-88 02:09 PM READY

Fig. 8.19. Using /File Xtract on an amortization table.

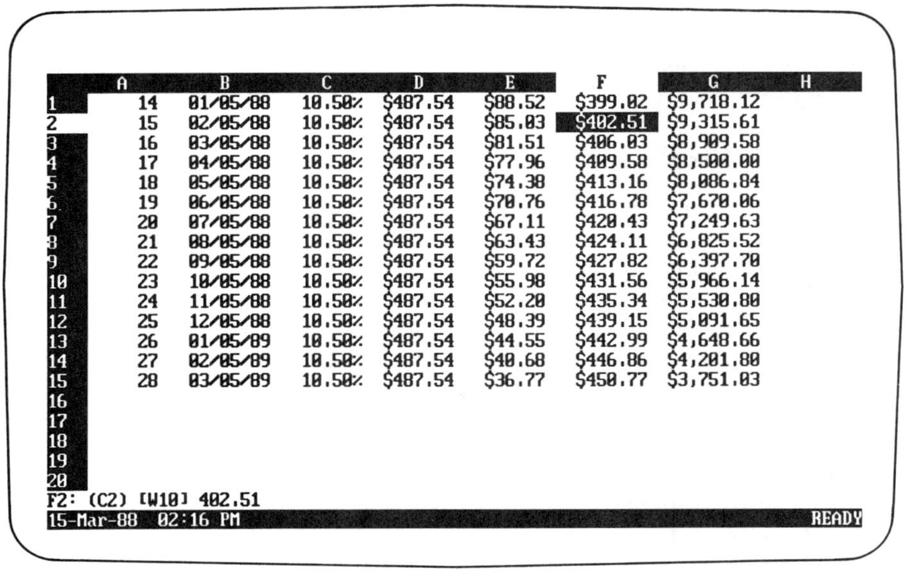

	A	B	C	D	E	F	G	H
1	14	01/05/88	10.50%	$487.54	$88.52	$399.02	$9,718.12	
2	15	02/05/88	10.50%	$487.54	$85.03	$402.51	$9,315.61	
3	16	03/05/88	10.50%	$487.54	$81.51	$406.03	$8,909.58	
4	17	04/05/88	10.50%	$487.54	$77.96	$409.58	$8,500.00	
5	18	05/05/88	10.50%	$487.54	$74.38	$413.16	$8,086.84	
6	19	06/05/88	10.50%	$487.54	$70.76	$416.78	$7,670.06	
7	20	07/05/88	10.50%	$487.54	$67.11	$420.43	$7,249.63	
8	21	08/05/88	10.50%	$487.54	$63.43	$424.11	$6,825.52	
9	22	09/05/88	10.50%	$487.54	$59.72	$427.82	$6,397.70	
10	23	10/05/88	10.50%	$487.54	$55.98	$431.56	$5,966.14	
11	24	11/05/88	10.50%	$487.54	$52.20	$435.34	$5,530.80	
12	25	12/05/88	10.50%	$487.54	$48.39	$439.15	$5,091.65	
13	26	01/05/89	10.50%	$487.54	$44.55	$442.99	$4,648.66	
14	27	02/05/89	10.50%	$487.54	$40.68	$446.86	$4,201.80	
15	28	03/05/89	10.50%	$487.54	$36.77	$450.77	$3,751.03	
16								
17								
18								
19								
20								

F2: (C2) [W10] 402.51

15-Mar-88 02:16 PM READY

Fig. 8.20. The extracted portion of the amortization table.

/**F**ile **X**tract **F**ormulas preserves any formulas that are in the extract block. This option can be particularly useful if your worksheet is too large to fit on one disk, because you can split the file across two disks and still preserve the formulas you need.

/**F**ile **X**tract **F**ormulas works like the /**B**lock **M**ove command; formulas reference cells relative to their position. If you have specified absolute addresses in the worksheet, the formulas are adjusted based on their new locations in the new file. For example, if you extract the block E5..E10, the new file contains this block in A1..A6; any formulas in E5..E10 will appear in the extracted file with cell references relative to their new location at A1..A6, even if you specified absolute addresses. The absolute addressing specifications are extracted to the new file, however, and the cell references will be treated as absolute addresses in their new context.

When extracting file formulas, remember that any formulas to be extracted must be accompanied by the cells they draw data from. For instance, if a formula in cell A100 depends on cell A1, the block defining the extract area must include cell A1. Otherwise, the resulting extract file is useless. Thus you usually will identify formula extracts that begin at the top left of a block to ensure that all necessary cells will be included in the extract.

Tip Beware of using the first-character method of menu selection for the /**F**ile **X**tract command. If you are not careful, you might inadvertently type /fe instead of /fx, because the word *extract* starts with an *e*. However, typing /fe selects the /**F**ile **E**rase command!

Accessing DOS from Quattro

As you use Quattro, you'll notice that before long you'll have several worksheet files that take up significant disk space. Hard disk users have less to worry about than floppy disk users in this respect. No matter what type of system you are using, however, you need to keep track of the amount of disk space used by your files. Few things are worse than getting a `Disk is full` error message after working on an important worksheet and trying to save it.

You can get around this problem by using Quattro's /**F**ile **O**S command. When you type /fo from READY mode, Quattro "steps aside" and displays the DOS prompt. (Even though the DOS prompt is displayed, Quattro and your worksheet are still in memory.) At the DOS prompt, you can enter the DOS CHKDSK command to see how much space is available on your disk. You also can use the FORMAT command to format a new disk, if you need to.

Hard disk users also can use /**F**ile **O**S to exit to DOS for checking and formatting disks. If your hard disk is almost full, you may want to erase old files—after ensuring that you have made backups.

When you are finished with the DOS operations, type *exit* to return to the Quattro worksheet. Now you can save the model you were working on.

Tip When you use /**F**ile **OS** to exit to DOS, *do not* start any program from DOS that alters memory, such as a memory-resident program. If you do, you won't be able to return to the Quattro worksheet. In effect, the memory-resident program "knocks the knees" out from under Quattro, and you will lose any work that you did not save.

Using !SQZ! To Compress Files

Just as a trash compactor squeezes all the air out of a trash bag, you can squeeze all the excess "air" out of a spreadsheet file. Repetitive, redundant, and unnecessary data can be removed or compressed so that the file you save to disk is significantly smaller than it otherwise would be. Quattro has such a file compressor: !SQZ!. The command /**F**ile **!**SQZ! shows you the current settings of the file squeezer.

If you want to squeeze a file when you save it, you simply type a *z* as the last character of the file name extension—for example, AMORT.WKZ. Quattro uses the current squeeze settings and saves the file in as little as 5% of the space needed to save the unsqueezed file. To retrieve a squeezed file, simply use the normal /**F**ile **R**etrieve command; Quattro unsqueezes the file automatically.

The command includes three options that deal with file compacting: whether to save blank cells, how to save values, and which version of the compression utility to use. Even if you leave all the defaults at their original settings, you will benefit from a significant compression of files. The options simply allow you to optimize the compression factor according to your needs. Type /f! to display the !SQZ! menu with the default settings (see fig. 8.21).

With the first option, **R**emove blanks, you can further compress a file by not saving blank cells. A formatted blank cell is a formatted cell that contains no data, labels, or formulas. Although you can save a significant amount of disk space with the **R**emove blanks option, you should avoid using this option if your spreadsheet contains a data-entry area or macro that depends on formatted blank cells.

The second option, "**S**torage of Values," allows you to instruct !SQZ! how to save displayed values that are based on formulas within the worksheet. Normally, Quattro saves both the formulas and the calculated values on the spreadsheet. The "**S**torage of Values" option can save you even more disk space by omitting the values, or by saving a slightly less-precise version of those numbers to disk.

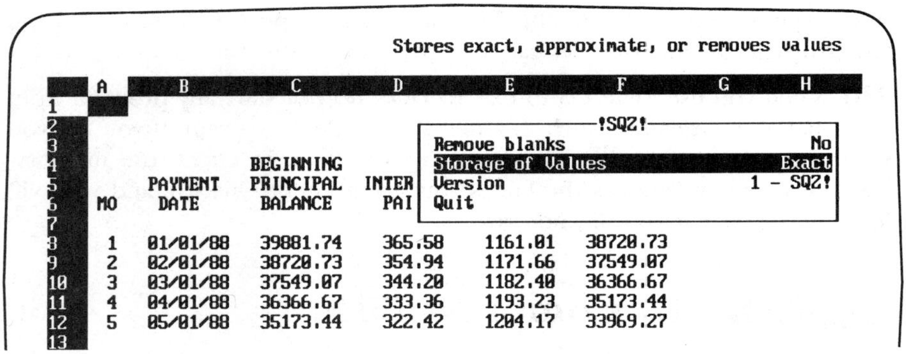

Fig. 8.21. The !SQZ! menu with default settings.

The choices available for "**S**torage of Values" let you determine how precisely and therefore how much space to devote to formula-based values in the file. The default is **E**xact, which saves numbers to the right of the decimal point to 15 places. The second option, **A**pproximate, saves 7 significant digits. For most applications, the **A**pproximate option supplies sufficient accuracy. The last "**S**torage of Values" option, **R**emove, simply eliminates the storage of displayed values based on formulas. **R**emove does not remove all numbers—just those driven by formulas. If you remove values in a file, you need to remember to press F9 (Calc) to regenerate the values after you retrieve the file.

The third !SQZ! option, **V**ersion, allows you to choose between the two versions of the !SQZ! utility. If you want to maintain compatibility with 1-2-3 files that were compressed with Turner Hall Publishing's SQZ!™ utility, use the first version of !SQZ!. If not, use the second version, which is more efficient. The second version is the equivalent of Turner Hall's new SQZ! Plus, for 1-2-3. Figure 8.22 shows the !SQZ! menu with alternate settings.

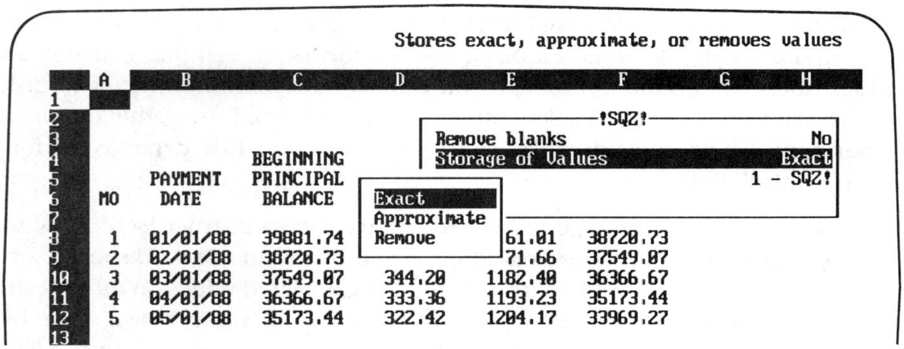

Fig. 8.22. Alternate settings for the !SQZ! menu.

Using !SQZ! on files is a cost-free alternative to purchasing greater disk capacity. To show you how "compressed" a squeezed file is, the file named AMORT in figure 8.23 was originally 40,849 bytes. After squeezing, the file uses a mere 5,804 bytes of file space: a compression factor of over 80%. Figure 8.23 shows an expanded listing of the AMORT file. Notice the difference in the sizes of the unsqueezed and squeezed files.

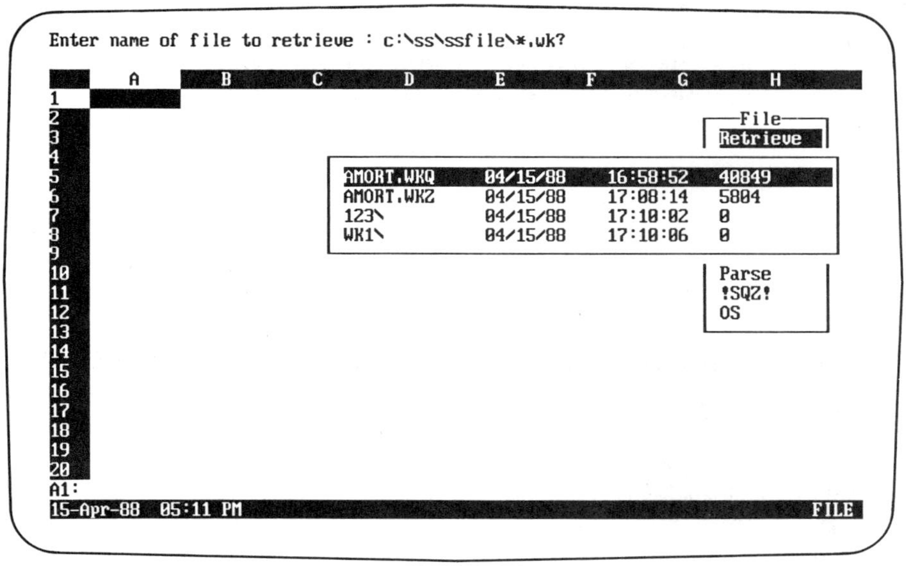

Fig. 8.23. Squeezed and unsqueezed sizes of the AMORT file.

Importing Files

The /**F**ile **I**mport command is used to copy standard ASCII (text) files from disk to specific locations in the current worksheet. Print (.PRN) files are an example of standard ASCII files. (.PRN files and their uses are covered in Chapter 9.) Other standard ASCII files include those produced by different word-processing and BASIC programs.

Figure 8.24 shows an example of an ASCII file. Notice that text is enclosed in quotation marks but values are not. Notice also that each "field" is separated, or *delimited*, by commas.

To import the file in figure 8.24 into the current worksheet, you start by placing the cell selector in the upper left corner of the block into which the data is to be imported and specifying /**F**ile **I**mport. You then specify **A**SCII

Text File and type the name of the file to import. Your worksheet should look like the one shown in figure 8.25. Notice that each line is imported as a long label and that the quotation marks and commas are imported as well.

```
"Part Name","Part Number","Qty","Cost","Retail"
"Hammer","H0101",12,1.95,3.99
"Wrench","W0998",15,3.25,5.99
"Standard Screw Driver","S0099",30,1.07,1.99
"Phillips Screw Driver","S0101",25,1.27,2.09
"Hack Saw","00201",5,4.22,6.99
"Jig Saw","10020",5,22.94,29.99
```

Fig. 8.24. An example of a delimited ASCII file.

```
      A        B        C        D        E        F        G        H
1  "Part Name","Part Number","Qty","Cost","Retail"
2  "Hammer","H0101",12,1.95,3.99
3  "Wrench","W0998",15,3.25,5.99
4  "Standard Screw Driver","S0099",30,1.07,1.99
5  "Phillips Screw Driver","S0101",25,1.27,2.09
6  "Hack Saw","00201",5,4.22,6.99
7  "Jig Saw","10020",5,22.94,29.99
8
9
10
11
12
13
14
15
16
17
18
19
20
A1: '"Part Name","Part Number","Qty","Cost","Retail"
10-Mar-88  03:28 PM                                              READY
```

Fig. 8.25. ASCII file imported into the worksheet.

If you import the file as Comma & "" Delimited File, it looks like the file shown in figure 8.26. Notice that no quotation marks or commas are imported and that each field is now contained in its own cell.

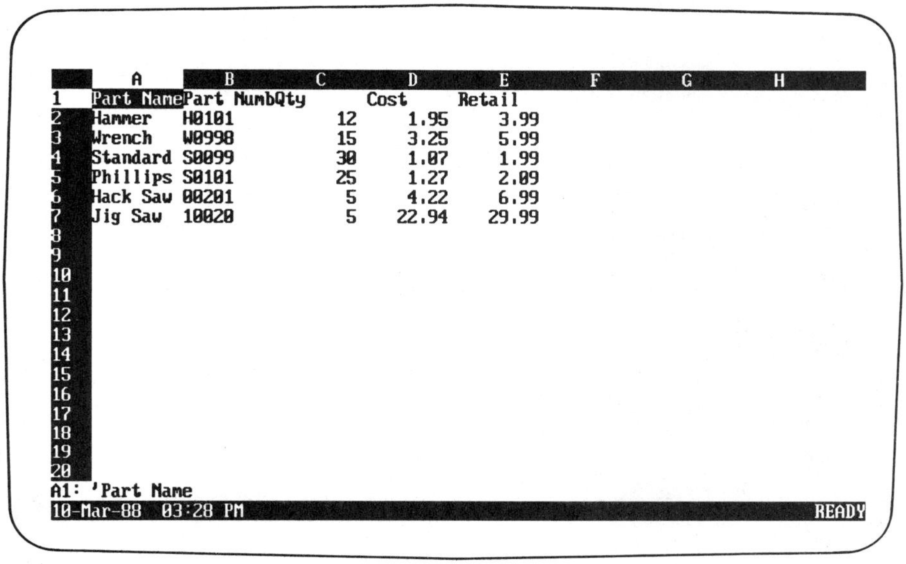

Fig. 8.26. The ASCII file imported as Comma & "" Delimited File.

Generally, use the **A**SCII Text File option to import an ASCII file that was created with a word processor and that you want to use as documentation to create a report. Use the **C**omma & "" Delimited File option when you import a delimited file. Remember that if you import a file with **C**omma & "" Delimited File, any column headings not enclosed in quotation marks are not imported. Headings that are enclosed in quotation marks are imported as labels.

Parsing To Make Import Files Usable

The /**F**ile **P**arse command is a flexible and easy method of extracting numeric, string, and date data from long labels and placing the data in separate columns. For example, suppose that you typed inventory data in a report composed with the WordStar word-processing program and you want to load the print-image file in Quattro. After you load the file by using the /**F**ile **I**mport command, you must reformat the data by using the /**F**ile **P**arse command.

The /File Parse Command

The /**F**ile **I**mport command loads the inventory data into the block A1..A16 (see fig. 8.27). Visually, the data is formatted in a typical spreadsheet block

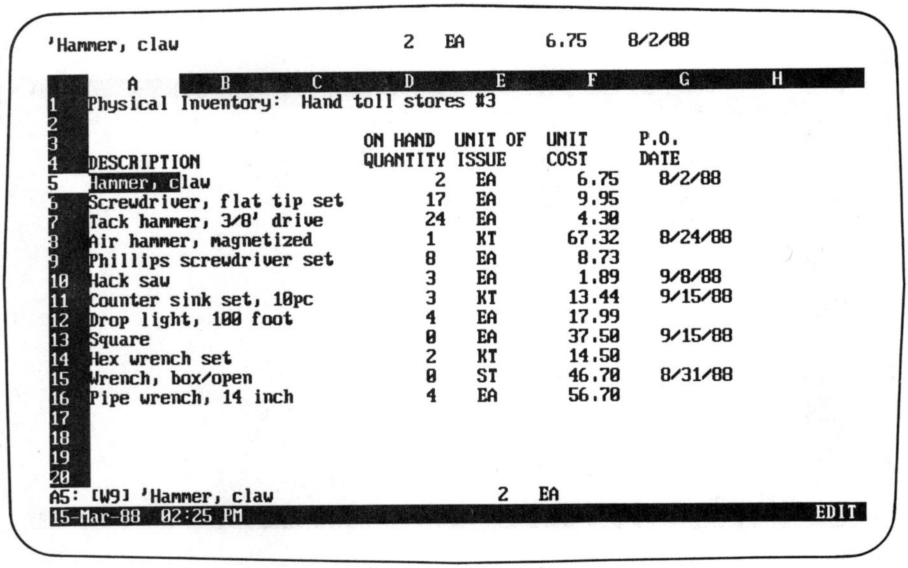

Fig. 8.27. Results of a /File Import command.

such as A1..G16, but the display is misleading. The current cell-selector location is A5; the entire contents of the row exist only in that cell as a long label, as the input line shows.

To break down the long label to columns, move the cell selector to the first cell to be parsed and select /**F**ile **P**arse. The following menu then appears:

Create
Edit
Input
Output
Go
Reset
Quit

Use **C**reate to create a newly inserted line in the data to be parsed. This option specifies the pattern or patterns for splitting the long labels into numbers, labels, and dates. The **E**dit option is used to modify the format line that is created. The format line is Quattro's "best guess" as to the structure of the data. The **E**dit option gives you an opportunity to refine Quattro's selections.

Use **I**nput to specify the block of cells to be parsed. The **O**utput option denotes the upper left corner of the block of cells that will hold the result of the parsing operation. **G**o performs the parse, based on the other settings. **R**eset clears the previously set input and output blocks.

To parse the data in figure 8.27, follow these steps:

1. Move the selector to A3, which is the first cell that has the data you want to break into columns. (You do not need to parse the title in cell A1.)

2. Parse the column headings in cells A3..A4 by creating one format line; then parse the data in A5..A16 by creating another format line.

Different format lines are necessary because the data is a mixture of label, numeric, and date data, and because all the headings are labels. Select **C**reate. A suggested format line is inserted in the data at A3, in a step that moves the remaining worksheet content down a line.

After creating a format line, you can edit it by selecting **E**dit. Use the format line to mark the column positions and the type of data in those positions. /**F**ile **P**arse uses the format line as a guideline to break down the data and move the data to its respective columns in the output block.

Format lines are made of combinations of certain letters and special characters. The letters denote the beginning position and the type of data; special symbols define the length and spacing of a field.

Symbol	*Purpose*
D	Marks the beginning of a **D**ate field
L	Marks the beginning of a **L**abel field
S	Marks the beginning of a **S**kip position
T	Marks the beginning of a **T**ime field
V	Marks the beginning of a **V**alue field
>	Defines the continuation of a field. Use one > for each position in the field (excluding the first position).
*	Defines blank spaces (in the data below the format line) that may be part of the block of data in the following cell

Create as many format lines as you need in your data. In the inventory example, you need to enter another format line at cell A6 and specify the format criteria for the data records that follow. Suggested format lines are shown in figure 8.28. To restore the **P**arse menu, press Enter after you finish editing.

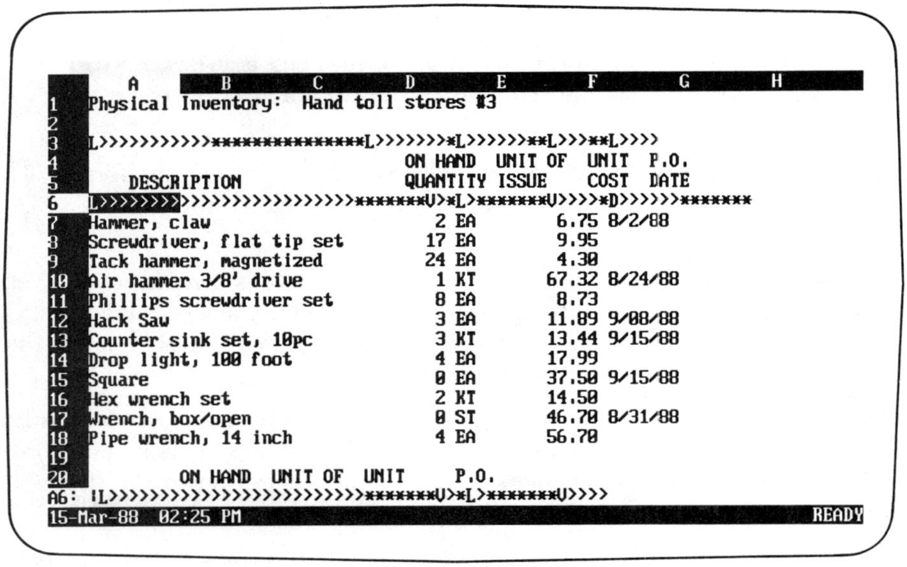

Fig. 8.28. Editing a format line in a /File Parse operation.

After setting up two format lines in the Physical Inventory example (see fig. 8.28), select **I**nput from the **P**arse menu. Point to or type the block A3..A18, which includes format lines, column headings, and data; then press Enter. Continue by selecting **O**utput from the **P**arse menu and by entering A20 as the upper left corner of a blank block to accept the parsed data. Complete the operation by selecting the **G**o option (see fig. 8.29).

The data displayed in individual cells may not be exactly what you want. You can make a few changes in the format and column width, and you also can add or delete information to make the newly parsed data more usable. These enhancements are not part of the /**F**ile **P**arse command. but they usually are necessary after importing and parsing data.

To produce the final inventory database shown in figure 8.30, follow these steps (if needed, see Chapters 4 and 5 for details on performing these steps):

1. Delete rows A3..A19 to remove the unparsed data and to move the parsed data up under the title.
2. Expand column A to make it 25 characters wide, and contract column C to make it 8 characters wide.
3. Reformat the P.O. DATE block in column E to the Date 4 format.
4. Insert at column E a column for the inventory value.

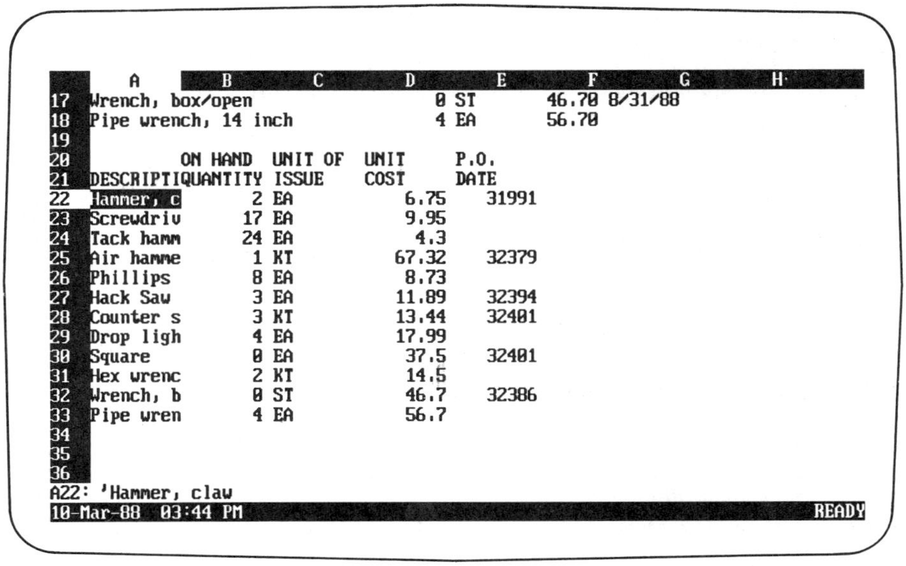

Fig. 8.29. Unsatisfactory results from a /File Parse operation.

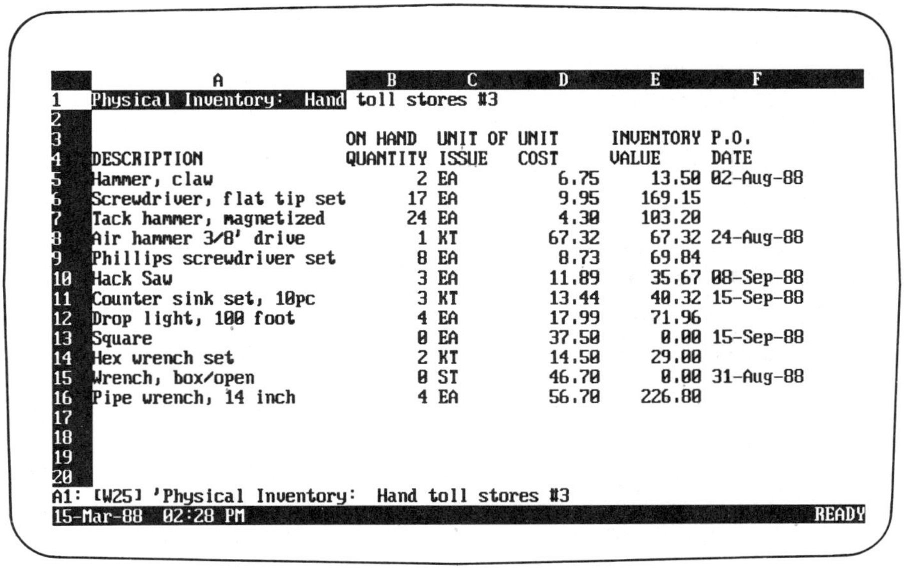

Fig. 8.30. Improving the appearance of parsed data.

5. Widen the new column E to 10 characters (the P.O. DATE should be column F).
6. Add the INVENTORY and VALUE headings in cells E3 and E4, respectively.
7. Enter in cell E5 the formula to compute the inventory value (+B5*D5).
8. /**B**lock **C**opy the formula in cell E5 to cells E6..E16.
9. /**B**lock **D**isplay_Format D5..E16 to the ", (financial)" format, and press Enter to accept the default of 2 decimal places.

Cautions about Using /File Parse

If you are parsing a value that continues past the end of the field, the data is parsed until a blank is encountered or until the value runs into the next field in the format line. This means that if you parse labels, you need to make sure that the field widths in the format line are wide enough so that you can avoid losing data because of blanks. If you parse values, the field widths are less critical.

Experiment on small amounts of data until you are comfortable using the /**F**ile **P**arse command. After you understand how this important command works, you will find many more applications for it—such as parsing data downloaded from a mainframe computer or automatically converting a long list of text dates to serial number dates. Every time you develop a new application, you should consider whether existing data created on another software program can be imported and then changed to Quattro's column and row format with /**F**ile **P**arse.

Chapter Summary

Quattro's file commands allow you to perform the basic operations of saving, retrieving, and deleting entire files. Although all spreadsheet programs perform these operations, Quattro has much more to offer. You can store and retrieve parts of files, and translate files from other programs such as 1-2-3, Symphony, and dBASE. With !SQZ!, you can conserve your precious disk space without buying an extra disk or utility. And parsing files provides a powerful tool for downloading and converting large chunks of data from other systems for use with the Quattro spreadsheet. All these file operations are efficient and easy to use.

Chapter 9 shows how you can produce effective reports based on your spreadsheet models, and how you can select from a wide variety of Quattro printing options.

CHAPTER

9

Printing Professional Reports

Quattro is a powerful tool for developing information presented in column-and-row format. You can enter and edit your spreadsheet and database files on-screen, as well as store the input on disk. But to make good use of your data, you often need the data in printed form: as a target production schedule, a summary report to your supervisor, or a detailed reorder list to central stores, for example.

By using Quattro's /**P**rint command, you can access many sublevels of print options to meet your printing needs. You can elect to output directly from Quattro to the printer or use the alternate /**P**rint **D**estination **F**ile sequence to create a print (.PRN) file; later, you can produce a printout of the file from within Quattro or from DOS, or you can incorporate the file into a word-processing file. What happens to the .PRN file if the original file is updated? Nothing. The .PRN file remains as a permanent record of how that original file appeared at one point in time.

This chapter shows you how to do the following:

- Choose between /**P**rint **D**estination **F**ile and /**P**rint **D**estination **P**rinter

- Print using default settings
- Print single or multiple pages
- Exclude segments within a designated print block
- Control paper movement
- Change the default settings
- Test the print format of large print blocks
- Print spreadsheet content cell by cell
- Prepare output for acceptance by other programs

Notice that printing graphs is not covered in this chapter. Printing graphs is covered in the next chapter.

Setting Up Your Reports

A frustrating situation sometimes occurs when you're setting up a spreadsheet for reports: the layout for attractive screen appearance may not work conveniently when the time comes to print out a report. For example, you may have widened several columns to add display formats to cells. Widening those columns causes no problem until you print the report and find that the report lines are too long. Although ways are available to adjust for this problem, a good idea is to prevent some of the more obvious problems before printing.

First, try to keep your columns as narrow as possible. Also, use a wide carriage printer if you have the option. Using a wide carriage printer gives you as much room as possible for characters printed across a page. Typically, you will want to print 14 columns to a report—12 columns (one for each month), a totals column, and a column of labels describing the line items. If each column is nine characters wide, then the report will be 131 characters—just enough to squeeze into the normal 132 characters that are available on a wide printer. Later in the chapter, you will learn how to use optional fonts that are available in most printers to "compress" the reports to approximately 240 characters (132 for a narrow printer) per line.

Second, always enter the entire line-item descriptors in column A. Following this procedure avoids the problem that can occur when the pieces of a line-item label are entered into separate columns. If you put the labels in columns A and B, for example, as soon as you need to adjust the width of either column A or B, many of the line items appear wrong.

Another good idea is to always highlight all the information you intend to print when using the **/Print Block** command. Often, text entries in cells "spill over" into adjacent cells to the right. If you don't identify those spillover cells, the text appearing there is omitted on the printout.

Often, a budget model has a large quantity of zeroes that can clutter up a report. Use the /**D**efault **F**ormats **H**ide_Zeroes command to suppress the display and, therefore, the printing of excessive zeroes.

As a final general tip, keep in mind that a short report almost always is preferred to a long report. Most long reports never are used—except to hold down a trash can.

Printing Basic Draft-Quality Reports

Quattro's Print menu is designed to handle both simple and complex worksheet printing needs. You need to know only about the main Print menu if you want to print quickly a report that doesn't require changing default print settings (such as those settings for paper size) or that doesn't require special enhancements (such as headers, footers, or different size and style of type). However, if you want to dress up your report or have special requirements for paper size, margins, or page length, you need to know about many commands available on menus that follow the main Print and Default Hardware Text_Printer menus.

This section shows you how to print draft-quality reports quickly and easily using a minimum of commands from the main Print menu. You learn how to print short reports of one page or less by using only two commands from the main Print menu. Then you learn how to print a report that spills onto more than one page. Later in the chapter, you learn how to use those commands that enhance reports, change type size and style, and automatically repeat border titles. You also learn how to produce printouts of complete formulas rather than their resulting values.

Using the Sample Cash-Flow Projector Spreadsheet

The large model in figure 9.1 occupies the block A1..W130; you are referred to this model throughout the chapter. This chapter focuses on the printing options (and problems) associated with such a large spreadsheet.

	A–D	E	F	G	H	I	J	K	L	M	N	O	P	Q	R	S	T
3	CASH FLOW PROJECTOR	Copyright (C) 1987 Que Corporation															
6	BALANCES IN WORKING CAPITAL ACCOUNTS			Dec	Jan	Feb	Mar	Apr	May	Jun	Jul	Aug	Sep	Oct	Nov	Dec	
8	Assets																
9	Cash			$17,355	$31,643	$34,333	$36,657	$35,614	$29,146	$20,000	$20,000	$20,000	$76,623	$198,464	$403,773	$788,353	
10	Accounts Receivable			493,151	510,780	533,597	551,287	577,314	614,997	641,802	750,544	879,271	989,501	1,097,616	1,170,646	1,218,036	
11	Inventory			163,833	169,209	176,671	189,246	206,788	228,828	269,990	296,527	324,230	345,629	311,575	194,481	(65,890)	
13	Liabilities																
14	Accounts Payable			125,000	130,754	139,851	150,186	163,731	180,350	203,669	225,085	243,320	258,740	238,844	174,080	55,781	
15	Line of Credit			0	0	0	0	0	0	1,834	8,327	2,035	0	0	0	0	
17	Net Working Capital			$549,339	$580,878	$604,750	$627,003	$655,984	$692,620	$726,289	$833,659	$978,146	$1,153,013	$1,368,812	$1,594,820	$1,884,718	
22	SALES	Oct	Nov	Dec	Jan	Feb	Mar	Apr	May	Jun	Jul	Aug	Sep	Oct	Nov	Dec	Total
24	Profit Center 1	$27,832	$23,864	$26,125	$31,336	$37,954	$43,879	$51,471	$56,953	$53,145	$54,140	$53,614	$52,015	$48,902	$44,091	$42,536	$570,036
25	Profit Center 2	13,489	21,444	20,140	22,572	24,888	25,167	32,588	40,140	37,970	34,587	33,463	28,939	24,153	27,060	26,701	358,228
26	Profit Center 3	126,811	124,382	123,618	131,685	129,044	131,723	139,221	141,879	149,803	147,108	147,032	153,440	149,990	145,198	150,510	1,716,633
27	Profit Center 4	94,285	92,447	89,010	95,473	98,008	96,986	95,318	103,538	108,146	108,642	106,065	110,401	112,018	111,956	107,522	1,254,073
28	Profit Center 5										115,000	175,000	225,000	300,000	325,000	350,000	1,490,000
30	Total Sales	$262,417	$262,137	$258,893	$281,066	$289,894	$297,755	$318,598	$342,510	$349,064	$459,477	$515,174	$569,795	$635,063	$653,305	$677,269	$5,388,970
33	Cash	10%	10%	10%	10%	10%	10%	10%	10%	10%	10%	10%	10%	10%	10%	10%	
34	Percent of 30 Days	20%	20%	20%	20%	20%	20%	20%	20%	20%	20%	20%	20%	20%	20%	20%	
35	Collections 60 Days	50%	50%	50%	50%	50%	50%	50%	50%	50%	50%	50%	50%	50%	50%	50%	
36	90 Days	20%	20%	20%	20%	20%	20%	20%	20%	20%	20%	20%	20%	20%	20%	20%	
38	Cash Collections				$263,437	$267,077	$280,066	$292,571	$304,827	$322,258	$350,735	$386,447	$459,566	$526,948	$580,275	$629,878	$4,664,085
43	PURCHASES	Oct	Nov	Dec	Jan	Feb	Mar	Apr	May	Jun	Jul	Aug	Sep	Oct	Nov	Dec	Total
45	Cost of Goods Sold																
46	Profit Center 1	33%	33%	33%	33%	33%	33%	33%	33%	33%	33%	33%	33%	33%	33%	33%	
47		$9,185	$7,875	$8,621	$10,341	$12,525	$14,480	$16,985	$18,794	$17,538	$17,866	$17,693	$17,165	$16,138	$14,550	$14,037	$188,112
48	Profit Center 2	29%	29%	29%	29%	29%	29%	29%	29%	29%	29%	29%	29%	29%	29%	29%	
49		$3,912	$6,219	$5,841	$6,546	$7,218	$7,298	$9,451	$11,641	$11,011	$10,030	$9,704	$8,392	$7,004	$7,847	$7,743	$103,886
50	Profit Center 3	50%	50%	50%	50%	50%	50%	50%	50%	50%	50%	50%	50%	50%	50%	50%	
51		$63,406	$62,191	$61,809	$65,843	$64,522	$65,862	$69,611	$70,940	$74,902	$73,554	$73,516	$76,720	$74,995	$72,599	$75,255	$858,317
52	Profit Center 4	67%	67%	67%	67%	67%	67%	67%	67%	67%	67%	67%	67%	67%	67%	67%	
53		$63,171	$61,939	$59,637	$63,967	$65,665	$64,981	$63,863	$69,370	$72,458	$72,790	$71,064	$73,969	$75,052	$75,011	$72,040	$840,229
54	Profit Center 5	30%	30%	30%	30%	30%	30%	30%	30%	30%	30%	30%	30%	30%	30%	30%	
55		$0	$0	$0	$0	$0	$0	$0	$0	$0	$34,500	$52,500	$67,500	$90,000	$97,500	$105,000	$447,000
57	Total Cost of Goods Sold	$139,673	$138,224	$135,908	$146,696	$149,930	$152,621	$159,910	$170,745	$175,908	$208,741	$224,476	$243,746	$263,189	$267,507	$274,075	$2,437,543
60	Inventory 0 Days in Advance	5%	5%	5%	5%	5%	5%	5%	5%	5%	5%	5%	5%	5%	5%	5%	
61	Purchasing 30 Days in Advance	50%	50%	50%	50%	50%	50%	50%	50%	50%	50%	50%	50%	50%	50%	50%	
62	Schedule 60 Days in Advance	30%	30%	30%	30%	30%	30%	30%	30%	30%	30%	30%	30%	30%	30%	30%	
63	90 Days in Advance	15%	15%	15%	15%	15%	15%	15%	15%	15%	15%	15%	15%	15%	15%	15%	
65	Inventory Purchases	$138,873	$141,363	$148,015	$152,072	$157,391	$165,196	$177,452	$192,785	$217,071	$235,277	$252,180	$265,145	$229,135	$150,413	$13,704	$2,207,821
67	Payment Cash	30%	30%	30%	30%	30%	30%	30%	30%	30%	30%	30%	30%	30%	30%	30%	
68	Schedule 30 Days	40%	40%	40%	40%	40%	40%	40%	40%	40%	40%	40%	40%	40%	40%	40%	
69	60 Days	30%	30%	30%	30%	30%	30%	30%	30%	30%	30%	30%	30%	30%	30%	30%	
71	Payment for Purchases			$142,612	$147,237	$152,451	$158,137	$166,531	$178,375	$195,471	$215,247	$234,886	$250,999	$250,453	$216,322	$133,017	$2,299,124

Row		Oct	Nov	Dec	Jan	Feb	Mar	Apr	May	Jun	Jul	Aug	Sep	Oct	Nov	Dec	Total
74																	
75	OPERATING EXPENSES	Oct	Nov	Dec	Jan	Feb	Mar	Apr	May	Jun	Jul	Aug	Sep	Oct	Nov	Dec	Total
76																	
77	Profit Center 1	$20,458	$20,760	$20,963	$21,529	$22,329	$22,802	$23,108	$24,099	$24,422	$24,431	$25,060	$25,646	$26,515	$26,639	$26,881	$293,461
78	Profit Center 2	14,377	15,002	15,587	15,946	16,790	17,355	17,739	18,195	18,610	19,412	19,546	20,348	20,860	21,729	21,785	228,315
79	Profit Center 3	25,921	26,393	27,339	27,554	28,286	28,464	29,275	29,292	29,578	30,246	30,358	31,041	31,680	32,048	32,525	360,347
80	Profit Center 4	13,922	14,885	15,801	16,130	16,800	17,651	18,039	18,789	19,704	20,400	20,939	21,589	21,833	22,024	22,154	236,052
81	Profit Center 5					10,000	14,000	18,000	20,000	22,000	22,470	22,837	22,995	23,364	24,023	24,806	224,495
82																	
83	Corporate Overhead	14,944	15,262	15,801	16,332	16,474	16,933	17,616	18,575	18,640	19,278	19,544	20,225	21,142	21,565	22,378	228,702
84																	
85	Total Expenses	$89,622	$92,302	$95,491	$97,491	$110,679	$117,205	$123,777	$128,950	$132,954	$136,237	$138,284	$141,844	$145,394	$148,028	$150,529	$1,571,372
86																	
87	Payment Cash	70%	70%	70%	70%	70%	70%	70%	70%	70%	70%	70%	70%	70%	70%	70%	
88	Schedule 30 Days	20%	20%	20%	20%	20%	20%	20%	20%	20%	20%	20%	20%	20%	20%	20%	
89	60 Days	10%	10%	10%	10%	10%	10%	10%	10%	10%	10%	10%	10%	10%	10%	10%	
90																	
91	Total Payment for Expenses			$94,266	$96,572	$106,523	$113,928	$121,153	$126,741	$131,236	$134,852	$137,342	$140,571	$143,973	$146,883	$149,515	$1,549,288
92																	
93																	

Row		Dec	Jan	Feb	Mar	Apr	May	Jun	Jul	Aug	Sep	Oct	Nov	Dec	Total
94															
95	CASH FLOW SUMMARY		Jan	Feb	Mar	Apr	May	Jun	Jul	Aug	Sep	Oct	Nov	Dec	Total
96															
97	Collection of Receivables		$263,437	$267,077	$280,066	$292,571	$304,827	$322,258	$350,735	$386,447	$459,566	$526,948	$580,275	$629,878	$4,664,085
98	Other Cash Receipts		0	0	0	0	0	0	0	0	0	0	0	50,000	50,000
99															
100	Cash Disbursements														
101	Payment for Purchases on Credit		147,237	152,451	158,137	166,531	178,375	195,471	215,247	234,886	250,999	250,453	216,322	133,017	2,299,124
102	Operating Expenses		96,572	106,523	113,928	121,153	126,741	131,236	134,852	137,342	140,571	143,973	146,883	149,515	1,549,288
103	Long-Term Debt Service		0	0	0	0	0	0	0	0	0	0	0	0	0
104	Interest Payment on Line of Credit														
105	Interest Rate	13.50%	13.50%	13.50%	13.50%	13.50%	13.50%	13.50%	13.50%	13.50%	13.50%	13.50%	13.50%	13.50%	
106	Payment		0	0	0	0	0	0	21	94	23	0	0	0	137
107	Income Tax Payments		5,340	5,413	5,677	5,930	6,179	6,532	7,109	7,833	9,315	10,681	11,762	12,767	94,538
108	Other		0	0	0	0	0	0	0	0	0	0	0	0	0
109															
110	Total Cash Disbursements		249,149	264,387	277,742	293,614	311,295	333,238	357,228	380,154	400,908	405,107	374,966	295,299	3,943,087
111															
112	Net Cash Generated This Period		$14,288	$2,690	$2,324	($1,043)	($6,468)	($10,980)	($6,493)	$6,293	$58,658	$121,841	$205,309	$384,579	$770,998
113															
114															

Row		Dec	Jan	Feb	Mar	Apr	May	Jun	Jul	Aug	Sep	Oct	Nov	Dec
115														
116	ANALYSIS OF CASH REQUIREMENTS	Dec	Jan	Feb	Mar	Apr	May	Jun	Jul	Aug	Sep	Oct	Nov	Dec
117														
118	Beginning Cash Balance		$17,355	$31,643	$34,333	$36,657	$35,614	$29,146	$20,000	$20,000	$20,000	$76,623	$198,464	$403,773
119	Net Cash Generated This Period		14,288	2,690	2,324	(1,043)	(6,468)	(10,980)	(6,493)	6,293	58,658	121,841	205,309	384,579
120														
121	Cash Balance before Borrowings		31,643	34,333	36,657	35,614	29,146	18,166	13,507	26,293	78,658	198,464	403,773	788,353
122	Minimum Acceptable Cash Balance		20,000	20,000	20,000	20,000	20,000	20,000	20,000	20,000	20,000	20,000	20,000	20,000
123														
124	Amount above/(below) Minimum Acceptable Balance		11,643	14,333	16,657	15,614	9,146	(1,834)	(6,493)	6,293	58,658	178,464	383,773	768,353
125														
126	Current Short-Term Borrowings		0	0	0	0	0	1,834	6,493	(6,293)	(2,035)	0	0	0
127	Total Short-Term Borrowings	0	0	0	0	0	0	1,834	8,327	2,035	0	0	0	0
128														
129	Ending Cash Balance		$31,643	$34,333	$36,657	$35,614	$29,146	$20,000	$20,000	$20,000	$76,623	$198,464	$403,773	$788,353
130														

Fig. 9.1. The Cash Flow Projector spreadsheet model.

Quickly Printing One Screenful of Data (PrtSc)

Perhaps the most overlooked way of printing is generating a "snapshot" of the information on-screen at any particular moment.

Before you print any portion of a Quattro spreadsheet, decide whether the output must be of "report" quality (suitable for official distribution or filing) or whether the output can be a "screen dump" (hard copy of the screen's contents).

Figure 9.2, for example, was produced by retrieving a Cash Flow Projector file and then pressing Shift-PrtSc. If you have an enhanced keyboard, simply press PrtSc.

```
        A        B        C        D         E         F         G
1    ====================================================================
2
3    CASH FLOW PROJECTOR                 Copyright (C) 1987 Que Corporatio
4
5    ====================================================================
6    BALANCES IN WORKING CAPITAL ACCOUNTS                          Dec
7    ==================================================== =========
8    Assets
9     Cash                                                      $17,355
10    Accounts Receivable                                       493,151
11    Inventory                                                 163,833
12
13   Liabilities
14    Accounts Payable                                          125,000
15    Line of Credit                                                  0
16                                                             --------
17   Net Working Capital                                       $549,339
18                                                             ========
19
20
A1: [W9] \=
07-Feb-88  03:01 PM                                                      READY
```

Fig. 9.2. The result of using the DOS Shift-PrtSc key.

The resultant screen dump captures everything on the screen, including such unwanted items as the descriptor line and status line. Such "quick and dirty" printouts may be adequate for interoffice memos and, because they capture the date-time display, for documenting model construction.

Printing Draft-Quality Reports on One Page or Less

To generate a default printout, you only need to specify on the Print menu a **B**lock to print, activate **G**o, and then select **Q**uit to return to the worksheet. All other selections are optional.

If you don't change any of the default print settings, and no other print settings were entered during the current worksheet session, then printing a page or less involves only a couple steps. As mentioned in the preceding paragraph, these steps include the following:

1. Highlight on the worksheet the block that you want printed.
2. Choose **G**o to begin printing.

Two other steps may be necessary if another person works on the same machine with the same program and possibly changed either the default settings or entered new settings in the Print menu during the current worksheet session. First, you can check the default hardware settings by selecting /**D**efault **H**ardware **T**ext_Printer. Second, the default page-layout settings can be seen by selecting the /**P**rint **P**age_Layout command. A quick review of these screens indicates whether the printer settings are the ones you indicated previously. You can clear any special settings that may have been entered for Print commands by another user; select the /**P**rint **R**eset **A**ll command to remove any settings for a particular worksheet.

If you are certain that all default settings are correct and no other settings were entered, you easily can print a report by completing the following sequence of operations. First, check that your printer is on-line and that your paper is positioned where you want the data to begin printing. Next choose /**P**rint. The main Print menu appears (see fig. 9.3) with the following options:

Block
Left_Heading
Top_Heading
Destination
Page_Layout
Format
Adjust_Printer
Reset
Go
Quit

Indicate the part of the worksheet that you want to print by selecting **B**lock and highlighting the area. Suppose that you want to print the December data

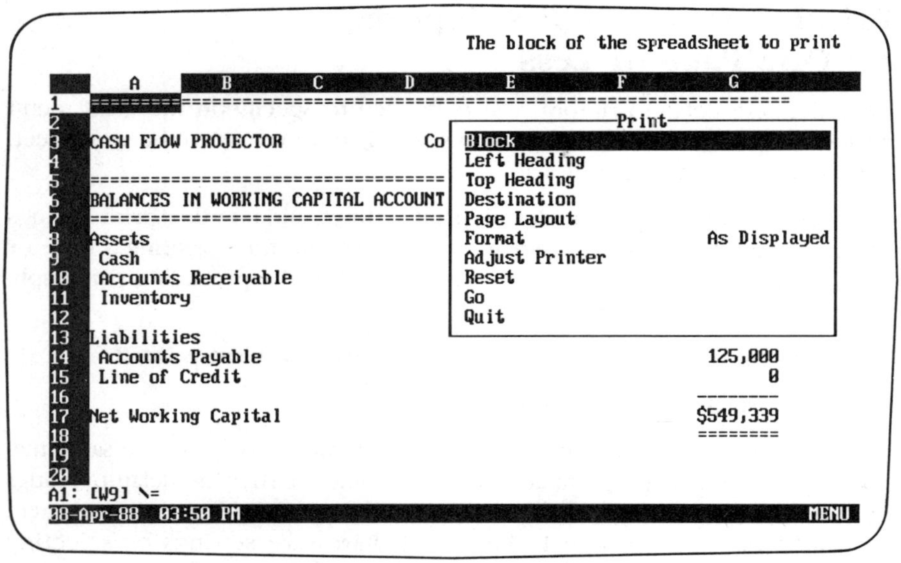

Fig. 9.3. The main Print menu.

for the *Balances in Working Capital Accounts* part of the Cash Flow Projector shown in figure 9.1. To print this small area, specify the block A1..G17.

You can use the PgUp, PgDn, Home, and End keys to designate blocks when you print. If you want to designate a block that includes the entire active area of the spreadsheet, anchor the top left corner of the print block, press the End key, and then press the Home key. Then press Enter.

After you enter the exact block that you want to print, select **G**o. Selecting **G**o after entering the block A1..G17 for the Cash Flow Projector produces the printout shown in figure 9.4. If you accidentally press Enter after you already used the Go option, the file prints a second time, which can be particularly disconcerting. You can stop printing by pressing Ctrl-Break twice.

Printing Reports Longer than One Page

If the area of your worksheet has more rows and columns than can be printed on one page, you can use the basic steps discussed in the preceding section for printing reports on one page or less. Setting the print block, however, so that a new page begins exactly where you want it to begin can be a bit tricky sometimes. Also, if you want to print a section of a large worksheet like the Cash Flow Projector in figure 9.1, you may need to use the /**P**rint **T**op_Heading command so that labels are repeated across the top of each page.

```
==============================================================================
CASH FLOW PROJECTOR                       Copyright (C) 1987 Que Corporatio
==============================================================================
BALANCES IN WORKING CAPITAL ACCOUNTS                                    Dec
============================================================= =========
Assets
 Cash                                                               $17,355
 Accounts Receivable                                                493,151
 Inventory                                                          163,833

Liabilities
 Accounts Payable                                                   125,000
 Line of Credit                                                           0
                                                                   --------
Net Working Capital                                                $549,339
```

Fig. 9.4. The result of printing one page with default settings.

To assure that information is printed on the pages as you want, remember that Quattro treats numeric and text data differently when splitting data from one page to the next. Numbers are printed complete, because they can span only one cell. Text, however, such as long labels that lie across several cells, may be split in awkward places from one page to the next.

Suppose, for example, that you want to print six months of data from the *Balances in Working Capital Accounts* section on the Cash Flow Projector worksheet in figure 9.1. Suppose, also, that you want to print your report on 8 1/2-by-11-inch paper, the default paper size. To print the report on this size paper with the default margin settings and a pitch of 10 characters per inch, you need two pages to print the entire report.

To print six columns of data from the *Balances in Working Capital Accounts* spreadsheet, complete these steps. After first checking that your printer is on-line and that your paper is positioned where you want the printing to begin, choose the /**P**rint command. The main Print menu appears:

Block
Left_Heading
Top_Heading
Destination
Page_Layout
Format
Adjust_Printer
Reset
Go
Quit

Because you want the labels in A6 through A17 in figure 9.1 to print on both pages, you must use the /**P**rint **T**op_Heading or **L**eft_Heading command. When you select /**P**rint **T**op_Heading or **L**eft_Heading, Quattro asks whether the labels that you want repeated are located down a column or across a row. For our sample report, choose **L**eft_Heading. (To print a report on two or more pages and repeat labels that are displayed across a row, select **T**op_Heading after choosing /**P**rint.)

After you choose **L**eft_Heading, the prompt `Row headings to print on left of each page:` appears. If your cell selector is located in the column where the labels appear, press Enter. If not, move your cell selector to the column and press Enter. Once you indicate which column or row of labels that you want repeated on each page, you do not need to include those labels in your actual print block. Quattro automatically places those labels in the first column or row on every page.

When you set the print block for reports that will print on more than one page, highlight all columns or rows except those columns or rows that you entered using the /**P**rint **T**op_Heading or **L**eft_Heading command. To print the January through June data for the *Balances in Working Capital Accounts* spreadsheet, you must highlight block H6..M18 (see fig. 9.1). Notice that this block does not include A6..D18, which is the block that contains the labels.

The last three steps involve aligning or setting up the page registration, selecting **G**o, and finally choosing **Q**uit after the printing is completed. Choosing /**P**rint **A**djust_Printer **A**lign helps to assure that printing begins at the top of all succeeding pages after the first.

This command actually informs Quattro that the paper has been adjusted physically to the desired starting point in the printer. In particular, make sure that you position your printer paper and use the /**P**rint **A**djust_Printer **A**lign command whenever you manually have rolled the paper in or out of the printer or aborted a print job.

The resulting printed pages of the *Balances in Working Capital Accounts* spreadsheet are shown in figures 9.5a and 9.5b.

BALANCES IN WORKING CAPITAL ACCOUNTS	Jan	Feb	Mar
Assets			
Cash	$31,643	$34,333	$36,657
Accounts Receivable	510,780	533,597	551,287
Inventory	169,209	176,671	189,246
Liabilities			
Accounts Payable	130,754	139,851	150,186
Line of Credit	0	0	0
Net Working Capital	$580,878	$604,750	$627,003

Fig. 9.5a. First page of a report printed on two pages.

BALANCES IN WORKING CAPITAL ACCOUNTS	Apr	May	Jun
Assets			
Cash	$35,614	$29,146	$20,000
Accounts Receivable	577,314	614,997	641,802
Inventory	206,788	228,828	269,990
Liabilities			
Accounts Payable	163,731	180,350	203,669
Line of Credit	0	0	1,834
Net Working Capital	$655,984	$692,620	$726,289

Fig. 9.5b. Second page of a report printed on two pages.

Hiding Segments within the Designated Print Block

Because the /Print commands require the specification of a block to print, you can print only rectangular blocks from the spreadsheet. Nevertheless, you can suppress the display of cell contents within the block. You can eliminate one or more rows, hide one or more columns, or remove from view a segment that spans only part of a row or a column. The results of each of the following illustrations print on one page, using default settings.

Excluding Rows

To exclude rows from printing, you must mark the rows for omission. Do this procedure by typing a double vertical bar (||) in the blank leftmost cell of the print block of each row that you want to omit. Only one of these vertical bars appears on-screen, and neither vertical bar appears on the printout. A row marked in this way does not print, but the suppressed data remains in the spreadsheet and is used in any applicable calculations.

Suppose, for example, that you want to print the *Cash Flow Summary* line descriptions from the Cash Flow Projector model. When the /Print command prompts you for a block to print, specify A94..D112. The printout of the contents of rows 94 through 112 is shown in figure 9.6a.

```
======================================
CASH FLOW SUMMARY
======================================
Collection of Receivables
Other Cash Receipts

Cash Disbursements
 Payment for Purchases on Credit
 Operating Expenses
 Long-Term Debt Service
 Interest Payment on Line of Credit
  Interest Rate
  Payment
 Income Tax Payments
 Other

Total Cash Disbursements

Net Cash Generated This Period
```

Fig. 9.6a. Printout of individual cash-disbursements rows.

Now suppose that you don't want the printout to show the cash-disbursements detail (rows 100 through 109). Do not use a worksheet command to delete the rows! Instead, prevent the row from printing by typing a double vertical bar in the leftmost cell of each row to be omitted. Because the leftmost cell is not blank, however, you need to make an adjustment. The simplest method is to insert a new column A and narrow it to a one-character width. Then type || in cell A100 and copy that entry to cells A101..A109.

When you execute the **P**rint command, be sure to specify the expanded block A94..E112 (not A94..D112 or B94..E112). Figure 9.6b shows the resulting printout.

```
======================================
CASH FLOW SUMMARY
======================================
Collection of Receivables
Other Cash Receipts

Total Cash Disbursements

Net Cash Generated This Period
```

Fig. 9.6b. Individual cash-disbursements rows omitted.

To restore the spreadsheet after you finish printing, delete column A with the /**C**olumn **D**elete command.

Excluding Columns

As you learned from Chapter 4, you can use Quattro's /**C**olumn **H**ide command to specify columns that you don't want to display on-screen. If these marked columns are contained in a print block, the columns do not appear on the printout.

Suppose, for example, that you are working with the Cash Flow Projector model and that you want to print only the descriptions and the January-through-March Sales/Cash Collections information contained in block A21..J40. Issue the /**C**olumn **H**ide command and specify columns E1..G1 to suppress the October-through-December data. The resulting printout is shown in figure 9.7.

SALES		Jan	Feb	Mar
Profit Center 1		$31,336	$37,954	$43,879
Profit Center 2		22,572	24,888	25,167
Profit Center 3		131,685	129,044	131,723
Profit Center 4		95,473	98,008	96,986
Profit Center 5				
		--------	--------	--------
Total Sales		$281,066	$289,894	$297,755
		========	========	========
	Cash	10%	10%	10%
Percent of	30 Days	20%	20%	20%
Collections	60 Days	50%	50%	50%
	90 Days	20%	20%	20%
		--------	--------	--------
Cash Collections		$263,437	$267,077	$280,066
		========	========	========

Fig. 9.7. The printout after hiding columns E, F, and G.

To restore the columns, select /**C**olumn **E**xpose. When the hidden columns (marked with an asterisk) reappear on-screen, you can specify which column or columns to display.

Excluding Blocks

If you want to hide only a partial row, a partial column, or an area that partially spans one or more rows and columns, use the /**B**lock **D**isplay_Format **H**idden command to mark the blocks.

Perhaps your spreadsheet includes documentation that you want to save on disk but omit from the printout. For example, you may want to omit the copyright message in the third row of the Cash Flow Projector model. To omit the message, issue the /**B**lock **D**isplay_Format **H**idden command and specify cell E3. (Although the message spans several cells, the message is entered in E3.) Then print the block A1..G7 (see fig. 9.8).

After you finish printing, select /**B**lock **D**isplay_Format **R**eset (or any other desired display format) and then specify the block E3..E3 to restore the copyright message. After hiding and resetting, you lose any other display formats that you indicated previously. Remember to reformat (Currency, for example) if necessary.

```
=====================================================================
CASH FLOW PROJECTOR
=====================================================================
BALANCES IN WORKING CAPITAL ACCOUNTS                              Dec
=============================================================  =======
```

Fig. 9.8. The printout after hiding block E3.

If you find yourself repeating print operations (hiding the same columns, suppressing and then restoring the same documentation messages, etc.), remember that you can save time and minimize frustration by developing and using print macros (see Chapter 15).

Controlling Paper Movement

Unless you stipulate otherwise, the top of a page is marked initially by the print head's position when you turn on the printer and load Quattro. If you print a block containing fewer lines than the default page length, the paper does not advance to the top of the next page; the next print operation begins wherever the preceding operation ended. If you print a block containing more lines than the default page length, Quattro automatically inserts page breaks in the document between pages, but the paper does not advance automatically to the top of the next page after the last page prints unless you specify such a procedure.

If you don't want to accept Quattro's automatic paper-movement controls, you can change the controls from the keyboard. You can specify the "top" of a page in any paper position, advance the paper by line or by page, and insert page breaks exactly where you want them.

Using the Print Menu's Line, Page, and Align Options

If you are using continuous-feed paper, position the paper so that the print head is at the top of the page and then turn on the printer. Do not advance the paper manually. Because Quattro coordinates a line counter with the current page-length setting, any lines you advance manually are not counted, and page breaks crop up in strange places.

If you want to advance the paper one line at a time (to separate several small printed blocks that fit on one page, for example), issue the /**P**rint **A**djust_Printer **S**kip_Line command. This command sequence causes the printer to skip a line.

If you want to advance to a new page after printing less than a full page, select the /**P**rint **A**djust_Printer **F**orm_Feed sequence. Whenever you issue this command, the printer skips to a new page. (The following section shows how you can embed a page-break symbol in the print block to instruct Quattro to advance automatically.)

In many cases, a faster way to advance the paper is to take the printer off-line, adjust the paper manually, put the printer on-line, and then issue the /**P**rint **A**djust_Printer **A**lign command. In fact, whether you adjust the paper off-line in this manner or on-line with the paper-control commands, you should issue **A**lign. /**P**rint **A**djust_Printer **A**lign, however, also resets the page counter, which you may not want done if you are numbering pages in a header or footer (see the section on "Headers and Footers").

Whenever you begin a print job at the top of a page, select **A**lign before selecting **G**o.

To print an existing footer option on the last page, use the /**P**rint **A**djust_Printer **F**orm_Feed command at the end of the printing session. If you select the **Q**uit command from the Print menu without issuing the /**P**rint **A**djust_Printer **F**orm_Feed command, this final footer does not print; although you can reissue the /**P**rint **A**djust_Printer commands, select **F**orm_Feed and the footer still prints.

Setting Page Breaks within the Spreadsheet

Look again at figure 9.1, which shows the entire Cash Flow Projector model.

Suppose that you want to print three months of data (October through December) for the *Sales* and the *Purchases* sections of the worksheet. To make sure that the *Purchases* section begins printing on a new page, you can insert a page break into the worksheet by using a command sequence or by typing a special symbol.

To enter a page break by using Quattro's commands, first move the cell selector to column A and then to one row above the row at which you want the page break to occur. Then select the /**P**rint **P**age_Layout **C**reate_Break command, which automatically inserts a new blank row containing a page-break symbol (|::). What you will see on-screen is ::, but the cell contents on the descriptor line will be |:: (shift-backslash).

For example, to insert a page break just above the first separating line in the Cash Flow Projector model's *Purchases* section, position the cell selector on A42 and then execute the command. Figure 9.9 shows the double-colon page-break symbol. To remove the inserted row and the page-break symbol after you finish printing, use the /**R**ow **D**elete command.

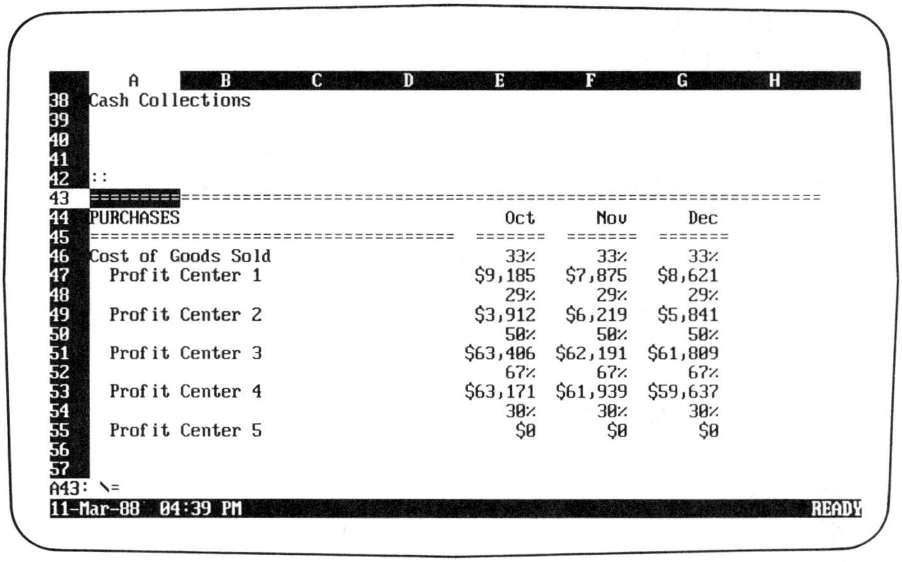

Fig. 9.9. Inserting a page-break symbol into the worksheet.

As an alternative, insert a blank row into your worksheet where you want a page break and then type a page-break symbol (|::) into a blank cell in the leftmost column of the print block in that row. The contents of cells in any row marked by the page-break symbol do not print.

Be careful when you alter a spreadsheet. You may alter formula results by inserting rows, or you may delete accidentally the wrong row after you finish printing. You may be able to avoid these problems by typing the page-break symbol into the leftmost column in the print block of a row that already is blank in your worksheet. First check to be sure that the row is blank; use the End key and the right-arrow key to scan across the row.

Changing the Print Options

You can use the /**D**efault **H**ardware **T**ext_Printer commands to change the default print settings. The new default settings remain in effect for all print operations performed in the current work session. If you want the new settings to be in effect whenever you load Quattro, return to the Default level of the command sequence and select the **U**pdate option.

You also can change print settings by using the selections on the Print Page_Layout menu shown in figure 9.10. The **M**argins_&_Length option and the **S**etup_String option override the **D**efault settings for margins, setup strings, and page length. These settings are provided to help you improve the readability of your reports.

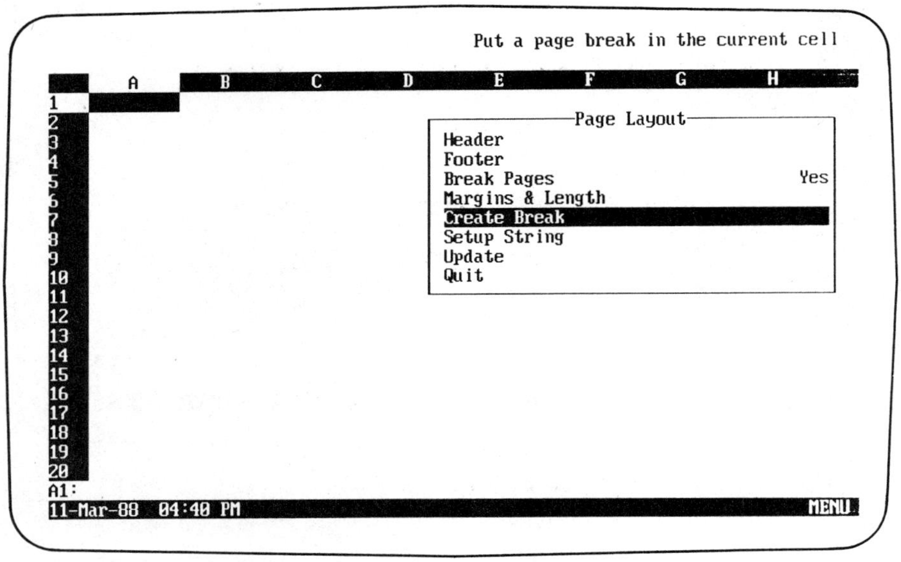

Fig. 9.10. The Print Page_Layout submenu.

Whatever print settings you use for your worksheet are saved with the file when you execute /**F**ile **S**ave. When you retrieve the file, the settings saved with that particular file are still in effect.

Headers and Footers

Quattro reserves three lines in a document for a header and an additional three lines for a footer. You can retain the six lines (regardless of whether you use them) or eliminate all six lines by selecting /**P**rint **P**age_Layout **B**reak_Pages **N**o (illustrated later in this chapter).

Technically, either the **H**eader or **F**ooter option lets you specify up to 240 characters of text within one line in each of three positions: left, right, and center. But from a practical standpoint, the overall header or footer line cannot exceed the number of characters printed per inch *multiplied by* the width of the paper in inches *minus* the right and left margins.

The header text, which is printed on the first line after any blank top-margin lines, is followed by two blank header lines (for spacing). The footer text line is printed above the specified bottom-margin blank lines and below two blank footer lines (for spacing).

Although all features of the text can be entered manually, Quattro provides special characters for controlling page numbers, the current date, and the positioning of text within a header or footer. These special characters follow:

Character	*Function*
#	Automatically prints page numbers, starting with 1
@	Automatically includes (in the form dd-mm-yy) the date that you entered when you loaded DOS
|	Automatically separates text Absence of a | mark left-justifies all text. The first | mark centers text that follows. The second | mark right-justifies remaining text.

For an illustration, you will reprint the Cash Flow Projector block A1..G17 after adding a header that includes all the preceding special characters.

To add the header, select /**P**rint, specify Block A1..G17, and then select **P**age_Layout **H**eader. At the prompt `A line of text to be printed at the top of each page:` type the following:

@|YOUR FIRM NAME|#

Then select **Q**uit from the Print Page_Layout menu; signal the top of the page to the printer, if necessary, by selecting **A**djust_Printer **A**lign; press Escape and then select **G**o. If you compare the printed header line shown in figure 9.11 with figures 9.5a and 9.5b, you can see how the temporary changes improve the report's appearance.

Whenever the print block exceeds a single-page output, the header is reproduced on each succeeding page and the page number increases by one. If you used the special page-number character (#) and want to print your report a second time before you leave the Print menu, you can reset the page counter

```
04-Apr-88                        YOUR FIRM NAME                        1

======================================================================

CASH FLOW PROJECTOR

======================================================================
BALANCES IN WORKING CAPITAL ACCOUNTS                              Dec
=============================================================  =========
Assets
 Cash                                                            $17,355
 Accounts Receivable                                             493,151
 Inventory                                                       163,833

Liabilities
 Accounts Payable                                                125,000
 Line of Credit                                                        0
                                                                --------
Net Working Capital                                             $549,339
                                                                ========
```

Fig. 9.11. The result of specifying a header.

and set the top of the form by choosing **A**lign from the Adjust_Printer menu before selecting **G**o.

If you specified a header line, but the centered or right-justified text doesn't print, make sure that the right-margin setting is appropriate for the current pitch (characters per inch) and paper width. To change the header, simply repeat the sequence to establish the text, press Esc to remove the display of the existing header from the input line, and press Enter. (You can delete a header or footer without removing other specified options.)

Left Headings and Top Headings

A printed report with lines of figures can be difficult—if not impossible—to interpret if you don't know what those figures represent. You can make your report easy to understand by using a special Quattro feature that lets you print specified columns and rows repeatedly on a multipage printout.

If you use the default Print settings to print the Cash Flow Projector model shown in figure 9.1, the report contains all necessary information. But without descriptions of what each line of figures represents, some pages may be difficult to interpret.

To improve a report, you may need to add certain column or row headings. Selecting **L**eft_Heading produces a column that appears as a border to a set of rows; selecting **T**op_Heading produces a row that appears as a border to a set of columns. Setting headings in a printout is analogous to freezing titles in the spreadsheet: **L**eft_Heading produces a border like a frozen vertical title display, and **T**op_Heading produces a column like a frozen horizontal title display.

To illustrate the process of creating headings, you will modify only a small portion of the report—the working-capital balances information in the block A1..S18 (refer to fig. 9.1). You will omit the blank columns (E and F) as well as the initial December column (G) and will use the **L**eft_Heading command to repeat the account names in columns A through D.

Select /**P**rint, specify **B**lock A1..S18, and then select **L**eft_Heading. When the message `Row headings to print on the left of each page:` appears in the input line, specify A1..D1. As you can see from figures 9.12a through 9.12d, the account names are repeated to coincide with the January-through-December dollar amounts.

If the designated border includes part of the print block, or the print block includes part of the border, you get the same information printed twice, which probably is not the result you want or expect.

If you want to print information with a horizontal border on every page, select the **T**op_Heading option. For example, you could use this option if you wanted to print out only the Liabilities information in rows 13 to 15.

Select the /**P**rint **L**eft_Heading or **T**op_Heading command sequence only when you want borders to be printed. If you select the sequence accidentally, the cell highlighted by the cell pointer is entered as either the **C**olumns or **R**ows you inadvertently selected. Should this occur, remove the selection by using the /**P**rint **R**eset **B**orders command sequence.

```
=====================================================================
CASH FLOW PROJECTOR

=====================================================================
BALANCES IN WORKING CAPITAL ACCOUNTS       Jan         Feb         Mar
==================================== =========   =========    ========
Assets
 Cash                                  $31,643     $34,333     $36,657
 Accounts Receivable                   510,780     533,597     551,287
 Inventory                             169,209     176,671     189,246

Liabilities
 Accounts Payable                      130,754     139,851     150,186
 Line of Credit                              0           0           0
                                      --------    --------     -------
Net Working Capital                   $580,878    $604,750    $627,003
                                      ========    ========     =======
```

Fig. 9.12a. Page 1 of a printed column border.

CASH FLOW PROJECTOR

BALANCES IN WORKING CAPITAL ACCOUNTS	Apr	May	Jun
Assets			
Cash	$35,614	$29,146	$20,000
Accounts Receivable	577,314	614,997	641,802
Inventory	206,788	228,828	269,990
Liabilities			
Accounts Payable	163,731	180,350	203,669
Line of Credit	0	0	1,834
Net Working Capital	$655,984	$692,620	$726,289

Fig. 9.12b. Page 2 of the printed column border.

CASH FLOW PROJECTOR

BALANCES IN WORKING CAPITAL ACCOUNTS	Jul	Aug	Sep
Assets			
Cash	$20,000	$20,000	$76,623
Accounts Receivable	750,544	879,271	989,501
Inventory	296,527	324,230	345,629
Liabilities			
Accounts Payable	225,085	243,320	258,740
Line of Credit	8,327	2,035	0
Net Working Capital	$833,659	$978,146	$1,153,013

Fig. 9.12c. Page 3 of the printed column border.

```
=====================================================================

CASH FLOW PROJECTOR

=====================================================================
BALANCES IN WORKING CAPITAL ACCOUNTS     Oct         Nov         Dec
==================================== =========   =========   =========
Assets
 Cash                                 $186,131    $337,995    $582,796
 Accounts Receivable                 1,097,616   1,170,646   1,218,036
 Inventory                             352,687     358,926     358,926

Liabilities
 Accounts Payable                      267,621     272,747     275,041
 Line of Credit                              0           0           0
                                      --------    --------    --------
Net Working Capital                 $1,368,812  $1,594,820  $1,884,718
                                      ========    ========    ========
```

Fig. 9.12d. Page 4 of the printed column border.

Be sure that any embedded page breaks and setup strings (see the next section) are not in the border. Embedded codes should be in the left column of the print block if the codes are to work properly.

Setup Strings

Setup strings are optional printer codes that you can use to change the size or style of type. To pass setup strings temporarily to the printer, use one of two methods: either select the **Setup** option from the Page_Layout menu and specify the appropriate ASCII code or embed the code in the spreadsheet. (Remember that you can establish a "permanent" or default setup string that will be used automatically whenever Quattro is loaded. To do so, access the Print Page_Layout menu shown in fig. 9.10 and then select **Update**.)

You will see both temporary methods by printing portions of the Working Capital Accounts information in the Cash Flow Projector report. The examples assume that an EPSON printer is being used. (The Quattro *Reference Manual* contains a "Printer Control Codes" section in Appendix C.)

To use the first method, first send a setup string (the decimal code for ASCII must not exceed 39 characters) by executing a Quattro command sequence. Assume that the print block is H1..S18 and that columns A1..D1 are established as a border at the left side of every printed page.

Access the Print Page_Layout menu, select **S**etup_String, type *\015* to indicate compressed print on an EPSON printer, and then press Enter. At this point, if you were to press Escape or **Q**uit from the menu and issue a **G**o command, the first printed page would contain only January-through-March amounts in compressed print.

Because you want the January-through-August amounts to fit on the page, you must establish margins that coincide with print pitch. Select **P**age_Layout **M**argins **R**ight from the Page_Layout menu. Then specify *136* (8 1/2 inches multiplied by 16 characters per inch in compressed mode). The resulting printout is shown in figures 9.13a and 9.13b.

CASH FLOW PROJECTOR

BALANCES IN WORKING CAPITAL ACCOUNTS	Jan	Feb	Mar	Apr	May	Jun	Jul	Aug
Assets								
Cash	$31,643	$34,333	$36,657	$35,614	$29,146	$20,000	$20,000	$20,000
Accounts Receivable	510,780	533,597	551,287	577,314	614,997	641,802	750,544	879,271
Inventory	169,209	176,671	189,246	206,788	228,828	269,990	296,527	324,230
Liabilities								
Accounts Payable	130,754	139,851	150,186	163,731	180,350	203,669	225,085	243,320
Line of Credit	0	0	0	0	0	1,834	8,327	2,035
	--------	--------	--------	--------	--------	--------	--------	--------
Net Working Capital	$580,878	$604,750	$627,003	$655,984	$692,620	$726,289	$833,659	$978,146
	========	========	========	========	========	========	========	========

Fig. 9.13a. Page 1 printed in compressed mode.

CASH FLOW PROJECTOR

BALANCES IN WORKING CAPITAL ACCOUNTS	Sep	Oct	Nov	Dec
Assets				
Cash	$76,623	$186,131	$337,995	$582,796
Accounts Receivable	989,501	1,097,616	1,170,646	1,218,036
Inventory	345,629	352,687	358,926	358,926
Liabilities				
Accounts Payable	258,740	267,621	272,747	275,041
Line of Credit	0	0	0	0
	--------	--------	--------	--------
Net Working Capital	$1,153,013	$1,368,812	$1,594,820	$1,884,718
	========	========	========	========

Fig. 9.13b. Page 2 printed in compressed mode.

To remove the temporary setup string, select **S**etup_String from the Print Page_Layout menu, press Esc, and then press Enter. Exit the Print Page_Layout menu by selecting **Q**uit or pressing Esc.

You use this method when you want all output from the current print operation to reflect the code condition. In the preceding illustration, for example, the contents in the entire print block, as well as the column borders, were printed in compressed mode.

If you want only a portion within a print block to reflect a special printing characteristic, you can embed a setup string in the spreadsheet instead of issuing several separate print commands. In blank rows preceding and following the area that requires special treatment, type a double vertical bar (||) and the appropriate ASCII code (or codes) separated by backslashes. (Insert a blank row, if necessary, making sure that the blank row does not disturb any formulas in your worksheet.) The first vertical bar does not appear in the worksheet, and neither the bars nor the print codes are printed. If you must embed a code in a row containing data, that data does not print.

If you want to print the first few rows of the Cash Flow Projector report in normal pitch, except for an enlarged title in row 3, you must first select /**P**rint **R**eset **A**ll to restore all print settings to default values. Then enter the following in the first cell of the first blank row (A2) to activate expanded print on an EPSON printer:

||\027\087\049

In the first cell of the next blank row (A4), shut off expanded print by entering the following:

||\027\087\048

If you specify A1..F8 as the print block, the printed output is similar to that shown in figure 9.14.

You can combine more than one print characteristic in a setup string if the combined setup code does not exceed the 39-character limit and your printer supports the combination. Check your printer manual for information about the compatibility of codes.

```
================================================================
CASH FLOW PROJECTOR
================================================================
BALANCES IN WORKING CAPITAL ACCOUNTS
================================================================
Assets
```

Fig. 9.14. The results of embedding a setup string in the worksheet.

A setup string contains the print-enhancement codes found in the printer manual. Each code consists of a backslash and three digits. If the manual says, for example, to use ESC E to turn on emphasized mode, look up the decimal equivalent for ESC (27) and for uppercase E (69). Because each code must contain three digits and begin with a backslash, you use \027\069 as the setup string to turn on emphasized mode. (Note: do not include spaces in a setup string.)

Page-Break Characters

The /**P**rint **P**age_Layout **C**reate_Break command inserts a page-break character in the cell at which the cursor is positioned. If data is in the cell, you must insert a blank row (using /**R**ow **I**nsert) first before issuing the /**P**rint **P**age_Layout **C**reate_Break command.

The page-break character is used when printing a block from the worksheet. You should realize that the best time to insert page-break characters is while you are building the worksheet. As you become more experienced in building worksheets and printing reports based on those worksheets, you will learn to think in terms of printed pages as you build. Thinking ahead saves time and minimizes confusion when you're ready to print.

The page break is effective only when positioned at the left edge of the block being printed. When the page break is in effect, the contents of the other cells in that page-break row within the print block are not printed.

Page Layout: Margins and Page Length

To change page layout temporarily, use the Print Page_Layout menu. If you want to change the margins or page length, select the **M**argins_&_Length option and then select **P**age_Length, **L**eft, **T**op, **R**ight, or **B**ottom from the submenu. The numbers at the right end of each line in the menu box denote the current setting, which you can change.

Be sure that you set left and right margins that are consistent with the width of your paper and the established pitch (characters per inch). The right margin must be greater than the left margin. And make sure that settings for the top and bottom margins are consistent with the paper's length and the established number of lines per inch.

The specified page length must not be less than the top margin *plus* the header lines *plus* one line of data *plus* the footer lines *plus* the bottom margin, unless you use the /**P**rint **P**age_Layout **B**reak_Pages **N**o command to suppress headers, footers, margins, and page breaks. To maximize the output on every printed page of a large spreadsheet, you can combine this option with setup strings that condense print and increase the number of lines per inch.

Printing a Listing of Cell Contents

You can spend hours developing and debugging a model spreadsheet and much additional time entering and verifying data. You should safeguard your work not only by making backup copies of your important files but also by printing the cell contents of important spreadsheets. Be aware, however, that this print job can eat up large chunks of time if you have a large worksheet.

You can print cell contents by selecting /**P**rint **F**ormat **C**ell-Formulas from the menu.

Choosing **C**ell-Formulas produces a listing that shows the width of the cell (if different from the default), the cell format, the cell-protection status, and the contents of cells in the print block, with one cell per line. By subsequently selecting **A**s_Displayed, the other **F**ormat option, you restore the default instructions to print the block as it appears on-screen.

You can produce a cell-by-cell listing of only the first seven columns and the first 18 rows of the Cash Flow Projector worksheet, for example, by selecting /**P**rint, specifying the block A1..G18, and then selecting **F**ormat **C**ell-Formulas. Return to the main Print menu by pressing Escape from the Format menu. Choose **A**djust_Printer **A**lign and then **G**o. The resulting one-cell-per-line listing is shown in figure 9.15.

Notice that within the specified print block, the contents of each cell in the first row are listed before the next row is presented. Information enclosed by parentheses indicates a block format established independently of the global format in effect. For example, the (C0) in cell G17 indicates that the cell was formatted (with a /**B**lock **F**ormat command) as **C**urrency, with zero decimal places.

Information enclosed by square brackets indicates a column width set independently of the global column width in effect. For example, the [W11] in cell G17 indicates that column G was set specifically to be 11 characters wide. Cell content is printed after the column-width and format information. The formula in G17 results in the $549,339 shown in the printed spreadsheet in figure 9.1.

```
A1: [W9] \=
B1: [W9] \=
C1: [W10] \=
D1: [W10] \=
E1: [W10] \=
F1: [W11] \=
G1: [W11] \=
A3: [W9] 'CASH FLOW PROJECTOR
D3: [W10] 'Copyright (C) 1987 Que Corporation
A5: [W9] \=
B5: [W9] \=
C5: [W10] \=
D5: [W10] \=
E5: [W10] \=
F5: [W11] \=
G5: [W11] \=
A6: [W9] 'BALANCES IN WORKING CAPITAL ACCOUNTS
G6: [W11] ^Dec
A7: [W9] \=
B7: [W9] \=
C7: [W10] \=
D7: [W10] \=
E7: [W10] \=
F7: [W11] \=
G7: [W11] ' =========
A8: [W9] 'Assets
A9: [W9] ' Cash
G9: (C0) [W11] 17355
A10: [W9] ' Accounts Receivable
G10: (,0) [W11] 493151
A11: [W9] ' Inventory
G11: (,0) [W11] 163833
A13: [W9] 'Liabilities
A14: [W9] ' Accounts Payable
G14: (,0) [W11] 125000
A15: [W9] ' Line of Credit
G15: (,0) [W11] 0
G16: [W11] '  --------
A17: [W9] 'Net Working Capital
G17: (C0) [W11] 549339
G18: [W11] '  ========
```

Fig. 9.15. A listing produced by using the Cell-Formulas option.

Resetting the Print Options

Selecting **/Print Reset** lets you eliminate all or a portion of the **Print** options that you chose earlier. Here are the **Reset** options:

All
Print_Block
Borders
Layout

You can clear every **Print** option, including the print block, by selecting **All**, or you can be more specific by using the other choices:

Menu	*Keystroke*	*Description Selection*
Print_Block	**P**	Removes the previous block specification
Borders	**B**	Cancels **C**olumns and **R**ows specified as borders
Layout	**L**	Eliminates local settings and returns to the default page-layout settings

Remember that you can automate many routine print operations by setting up print macros, which are discussed in Chapter 15. /**P**rint **R**eset **A**ll is usually the first instruction in this type of macro.

Preparing Output for Acceptance by Other Programs

Many word-processing and other software packages accept ASCII text files. You can maximize your chances of successfully exporting Quattro files to other programs if you select several **P**rint command sequences that eliminate unwanted specifications for page layout and page breaks.

Begin by selecting /**P**rint **D**estination **F**ile. Direct output to a .PRN file instead of to a printer by specifying a FILE NAME. After specifying the **B**lock to print, choose **P**age_Layout **B**reak_Pages **N**o. When you tell Quattro that you don't want page breaks, Quattro presumes that you also want to suppress all headers and footers from a print operation.

Then choose **Q**uit from the Page_Layout menu and create the .PRN file on disk by selecting **G**o. When you select **G**o, Quattro gives you the option of replacing, backing up, or appending (adding to) a file if the file name you specified already exists. After you choose the desired file-handling alternative, choose **Q**uit from the Print Destination File menu. Follow the instructions in your word-processing or other software package to import the specially prepared Quattro disk files.

Note of caution: If you don't use the **Q**uit command after choosing **G**o, the print file is not created properly. The act of choosing **Q**uit from the menu causes Quattro to place an EOF (end-of-file) marker at the end of the print file. If you find that the print files you create have a file size of 0 (zero) bytes, you omitted the **Q**uit command.

To restore the default printing of headers, footers, and page breaks, issue the /**P**rint **P**age_Layout **B**reak_Pages **Y**es command. You ordinarily choose

Break_Pages Yes when printing to the printer and **Break_Pages No** when printing to a file.

Managing Printer Settings

To minimize the keystrokes necessary for a print operation, Quattro makes certain assumptions about how you want your copy printed. The usual print operation produces 72 characters per line and 56 lines per page on 8 1/2-by-11-inch continuous-feed paper and uses the first parallel printer installed. You must know the current settings for your Quattro program, however.

Current Printer Hardware Settings

You should check the default settings before you print. To check the settings, issue the **/Default Hardware Text_Printer** command, which produces the menu shown in figure 9.16.

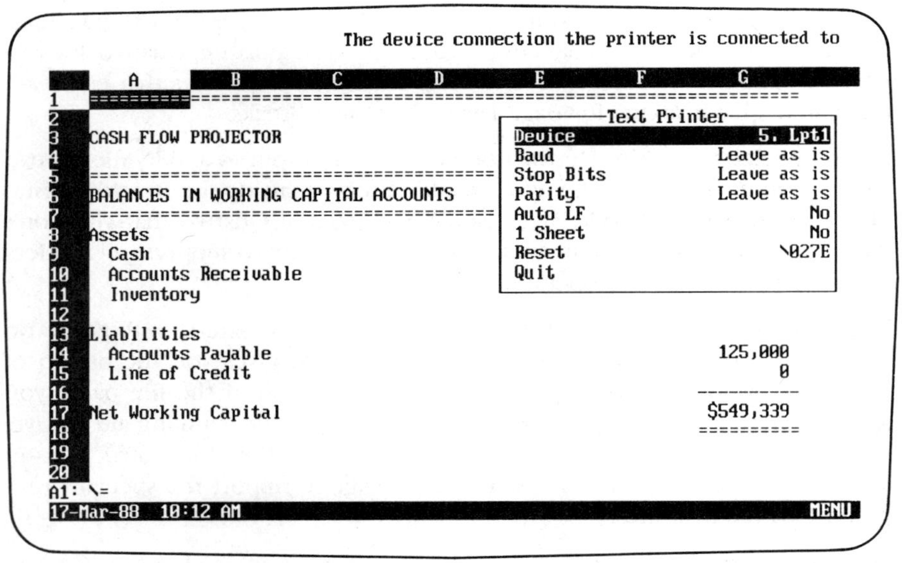

Fig. 9.16. The Default Hardware Text_Printer menu.

You use the Text_Printer menu to initiate changing a setting for the current work session and choose **Update** on the Default menu to make the change remain in effect every time you reload Quattro. You can view the current settings while in the Text_Printer menu; the current printer settings are displayed in a form similar to that shown in figure 9.17.

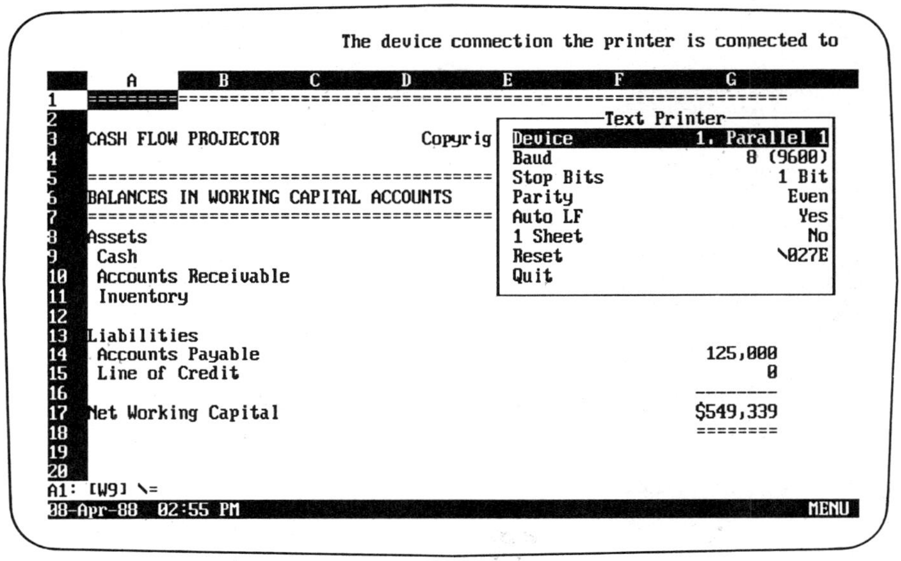

Fig. 9.17. A sample Default Hardware Text_Printer settings box.

Default Hardware Text_Printer Options

The Default Hardware Text_Printer options let you specify how to communicate with your printer and how to advance the page in the printer at the end of each line and each page.

If you want to change any of the print settings shown in the default settings box report, issue the /**D**efault **T**ext_Printer command. The first option in the submenu shown in figure 9.18, **D**evice, lets you determine which output port or device will be used to route information to the printer.

Use the **D**evice option to specify one of nine possible connections between your computer and your printer:

1 First parallel port (the default)
2 First serial port
3 Second parallel port
4 Second serial port
5 DOS Device LPT1
6 DOS Device LPT2

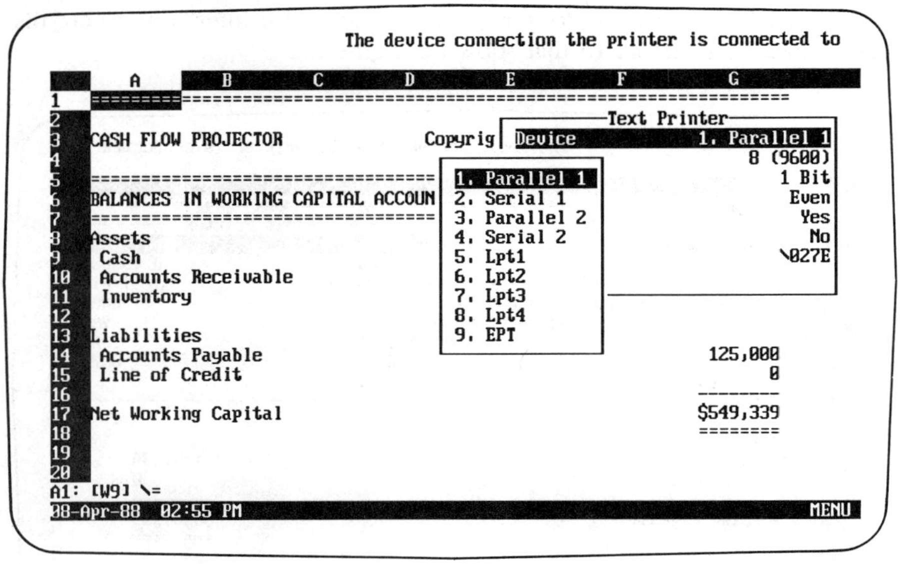

Fig. 9.18. The Default Hardware Text_Printer submenu.

7 DOS Device LPT3
8 DOS Device LPT4
9 DOS Device EPT

Choices 5 through 8 are usually applicable if your workstation is part of a local area network. If you select either serial port option (2 or 4), the default DOS serial port settings are used. If you want to modify these settings, you can use the Baud menu choice to specify the following baud rates (data transmission speed—for example, a 1200 baud rate roughly equals 120 characters per second):

1 110 baud
2 150 baud
3 300 baud
4 600 baud
5 1200 baud
6 2400 baud
7 4800 baud
8 9600 baud
9 19200 baud

Selection 9 (EPT) was added to the Device menu late in Quattro's development and, as a result, is not documented in the manuals. The EPT device is used with the IBM Page Printer laser printers. The EPT device port allows much higher transmission rates from the computer to the printer and, thus, superior laser printer throughput.

Use the **S**top **B**its and **P**arity options to modify the "envelope" that transports the data packets to the printer. This envelope only applies to printers that attach to a serial or RS-232 port on your computer, such as laser printers and daisy wheel printers. If you have a parallel printer, these settings are irrelevant. See your printer manual and the DOS manual or *Using PC DOS*, 2nd Edition, from Que Corporation for more information.

The **A**uto_LF setting specifies the printer's end-of-line procedure; **Y**es signals the printer to advance automatically a line when it receives a carriage return; **N**o means that the printer will not advance automatically a line when it receives a carriage return. With most printers, leave **A**uto_LF in its **N**o default setting. If you want your reports to be double-spaced, select **Y**es. Selecting **Y**es tricks Quattro into sending a second line-feed command to the printer.

The **1**_Sheet option controls page advancing. If you are using continuous-feed paper, do not change the **1**_Sheet option's default setting of **N**o. If you are using single sheets of paper, select **Y**es to change the default setting; printing then pauses at the end of each page so that you can insert a new sheet of paper. After you insert the page, press Enter to continue printing.

Page-Layout Options

For page layout, you must consider the length and width of the printer, paper, the number of lines that will print on one page (lines per inch), and the pitch (characters per inch). Because Quattro initially assumes 8 1/2-inch-by-11-inch paper and a printer output of six lines per inch, the default page length is 66 lines (11 inches times six lines per inch). Because of Quattro's default settings (two-line margins at the top and bottom), all 66 lines are not used if you keep the default top and bottom margins on each page. Every line ordinarily contains 10 or 12 characters per inch. You can vary the pitch by using setup strings, which were discussed earlier in this chapter.

Look again at figure 9.10. Five options determine default page-layout Margins_&_Length characteristics:

Page_Length
Left
Top
Right
Bottom

The Margins_&_Length menu box shows the current numbers for these page-layout settings.

To calculate the print width that will result on your report, subtract the current left-margin setting (default 4) from the current right-margin setting (default 76). Your report will be with the remaining characters (default 72) per line.

To calculate how many lines of your worksheet actually will be printed, you need to subtract not only the lines for top and bottom margins but also the lines that Quattro automatically reserves for a header and a footer. If you are using all default settings, for example, the actual number of lines (or rows) from your worksheet that will be printed is 56. Quattro assigns two lines each for the top and bottom margins and reserves three lines each for a header and a footer. These six lines are reserved even if you do not enter a header or footer. Because the default page length is 66, you subtract four lines for top and bottom margins and six lines reserved for a header and footer to get 56 lines printed. (To learn how to enter headers and footers on the printout, see the "Headers and Footers" section of this chapter.)

Page-Layout Setup Strings

The default setting for **S**etup_String is no setup string. No special printer-control codes, such as condensed print, eight lines per inch instead of six, or boldface type, are in effect. (For examples of setup strings, see the section "Changing the Print Options" in this chapter.)

Remember that if you use the /**D**efault **H**ardware **T**ext_Printer command to change print settings, the new settings remain in effect for the current work session. For the settings to remain the default whenever you start up Quattro, use the /**D**efault **U**pdate command after you have made the changes you want.

Chapter Summary

This chapter showed you how to create printed reports from your Quattro worksheets. You learned how to print quickly and easily by using the default settings and how to change the defaults. To customize your reports and make them more readable and understandable, you learned how to break the worksheet into pages; change the margins and page length; and provide headers, footers, and borders on the printout. You also discovered how to take full advantage of your printer's capabilities by passing setup strings to the printer.

Successfully printing large spreadsheets with a variety of options generally takes practice and some study of your printer manual. Use this chapter as a reference as you continue to experiment.

The next two chapters show you how to add visual effects to your reports. Chapter 10 shows you how to create graphs, view graphs on-screen, and print graphs on your printer or plotter.

CHAPTER

10

Graphing with Quattro

Even if Quattro provided only spreadsheet capabilities, the program would be extremely powerful. More information can be assembled quickly and tabulated electronically than could possibly be developed manually. But despite the importance of keeping detailed worksheets that show real or projected data, that data can be worthless if it cannot be readily understood.

To help decision makers who are pressed for time or unable to draw conclusions from countless rows of numeric data, and who may benefit from seeing key figures displayed graphically, Borland offers sophisticated graphics in Quattro. The program offers 10 types of business graphs as well as options for enhancing the graphs' appearance.

Quattro adds many welcome additions to the usual set of integrated spreadsheet graphics. For example, Quattro has the capability to mix different graph types in a single graph. This capability allows you to combine charting methods such as line and bar graphing.

This chapter shows you how to do the following:

- Meet minimum requirements for constructing graphs
- Enhance the appearance of a graph
- Preserve the graph on disk

- Edit the current contents of a graph
- Reset some or all graph settings
- Select an appropriate graph type
- Develop all graph types
- Print out the graph to a graphics printer or plotter

Reducing Data "Noise" with Graphs

The very power of a spreadsheet sometimes can be its downfall. For example, Quattro's workspace is the size of a football field, and you easily can get lost in the data.

Initially, users of spreadsheets were driven by the desire to do "what-if" analyses—to see many scenarios without having to commit to one prematurely. These what-if models were supposed to help managers better understand how future events might affect their business. But like many good ideas, this one got offtrack. The temptation to fill the sheet with multiple integrated models and huge amounts of data actually can cloud the decision-making process.

A way is needed to see the relationships of various parts of a model without being faced with printouts several inches thick.

The integrated graphics that Quattro helps to automate perform data reduction; instead of working through reams of paper, you can construct a pictorial version of the key data elements or reduce the data to its essentials. The graph then can show you any patterns and oddities that no amount of manual analysis would reveal.

The graph provides an added benefit. The graph can be used as a jumping off point for more sophisticated presentation graphics and desktop-publishing applications, because Quattro can produce Lotus- and PostScript-compatible graph files.

Basic Requirements for Creating a Graph

The number and variety of options used to generate a graph can be overwhelming to the new Quattro user; thus, the process of creating a first graph may seem overly difficult. But creating and displaying a simple graph actually is quite easy.

In this section, you learn how to apply all the options to a line graph. Then you learn how to construct all the other types of Quattro graphs.

But before creating your first graph, you must determine whether your hardware supports viewing and printing graphs and whether the spreadsheet on-screen contains data that you want to graph. You also should understand which type of graph is best suited for presenting specific numeric data in picture form.

Hardware and Software Setup

Quattro's graphics feature will be used to create and view a graph, store the graph's specifications for later use, and print the graph. Creating and storing a graph requires only that you have the Borland Quattro software installed on your equipment and that you correctly select options from the Graph menu.

To view a graph on-screen, you need a graphics monitor or a monitor with a graphics-display adapter. (Without such a monitor, you can construct and save a Quattro graph, but you must print the graph to view it.)

To print a graph, you use the **/Graph Print** command along with a graphics printer or other graphic output device supported by Quattro.

To create a graph, first load Quattro and retrieve a worksheet file containing the data that you want to graph. Suppose, for example, that you want to graph data from the 1988 CASH FLOW DATA spreadsheet, part of which is displayed in figures 10.1a and 10.1b.

	A B C	D	E	F	G	H	I
1	1988 CASH FLOW DATA						
2							
3	=========================	=========	=========	=========	=========	=========	=========
4	WORKING CAPITAL ACCOUNTS	Jan	Feb	Mar	Apr	May	Jun
5	=========================	=========	=========	=========	=========	=========	=========
6	Current Assets:						
7	Cash	$31,643	$34,333	$36,657	$35,614	$29,146	$20,000
8	Accounts Receivable	510,780	533,597	551,287	577,314	614,997	641,802
9	Inventory	169,209	176,671	189,246	206,788	228,828	269,990
10		---------	---------	---------	---------	---------	---------
11	Total Current Assets	711,632	744,601	777,189	819,715	872,970	931,792
12							
13	Current Liabilities:						
14	Accounts Payable	130,754	139,851	150,186	163,731	180,350	203,669
15	Other Short-term Debt	0	0	0	0	0	1,834
16		---------	---------	---------	---------	---------	---------
17	Total Current Liabilities	130,754	139,851	150,186	163,731	180,350	205,503
18							
19	Net Working Capital	$580,878	$604,750	$627,003	$655,984	$692,620	$726,289
20		=========	=========	=========	=========	=========	=========

Fig. 10.1a. The sample WORKING CAPITAL ACCOUNTS worksheet: January through June.

	A B C	J	K	L	M	N	O
1	1988 CASH FLOW DATA						
2							
3	=========================	=========	=========	=========	=========	=========	=========
4	WORKING CAPITAL ACCOUNTS	Jul	Aug	Sep	Oct	Nov	Dec
5	=========================	=========	=========	=========	=========	=========	=========
6	Current Assets:						
7	Cash	$20,000	$20,000	$76,623	$186,131	$337,995	$582,796
8	Accounts Receivable	750,544	879,271	989,501	1,097,616	1,170,646	1,218,036
9	Inventory	296,527	324,230	345,629	352,687	358,926	358,926
10		---------	---------	---------	---------	---------	---------
11	Total Current Assets	1,067,071	1,223,501	1,411,753	1,636,434	1,867,567	2,159,759
12							
13	Current Liabilities:						
14	Accounts Payable	225,085	243,320	258,740	267,621	272,747	275,041
15	Other Short-term Debt	8,327	2,035	0	0	0	0
16		---------	---------	---------	---------	---------	---------
17	Total Current Liabilities	233,412	245,355	258,740	267,621	272,747	275,041
18							
19	Net Working Capital	$833,659	$978,146	$1,153,013	$1,368,812	$1,594,820	$1,884,718
20		=========	=========	=========	=========	=========	=========

Fig. 10.1b. The sample WORKING CAPITAL ACCOUNTS worksheet: July through December.

To graph information from this spreadsheet's WORKING CAPITAL ACCOUNTS section, you need to know which numeric data you can plot and which data (numeric or label) you may be able to use to enhance the graph.

Account names are displayed across columns A, B, and C. Monthly headings and amounts appear in columns D through O. The numeric entries in rows 7, 8, 9, 14, and 15, as well as the formula results in rows 11, 17, and 19, are suitable for graphing as data points.

To develop graphs to view on-screen, select /**G**raph from the main Quattro menu to display the Graph menu. You usually will use two options from the main Graph menu. You may indicate which type of graph you want with the /**G**raph **G**raph_Type command. If you don't select a graph type, Quattro displays a stacked-bar graph, the initial default, which can be changed.

You must define at least one data series, which is a block of cells that contain values; you define this series with the /**G**raph **S**eries_Values command. When you select **S**eries_Values, you will choose among one of six data-series options. You should use the /**G**raph **X**-Axis_Values option as a data block only when you create an XY graph, which is explained later in this chapter. To display the graph, assuming that you have a graphics-equipped monitor, you then select **V**iew.

Selecting a Graph Type

Selecting one of the 10 available graph types is easy. When you select **Graph_Type** from the Graph menu, the options are displayed, as shown in figure 10.2.

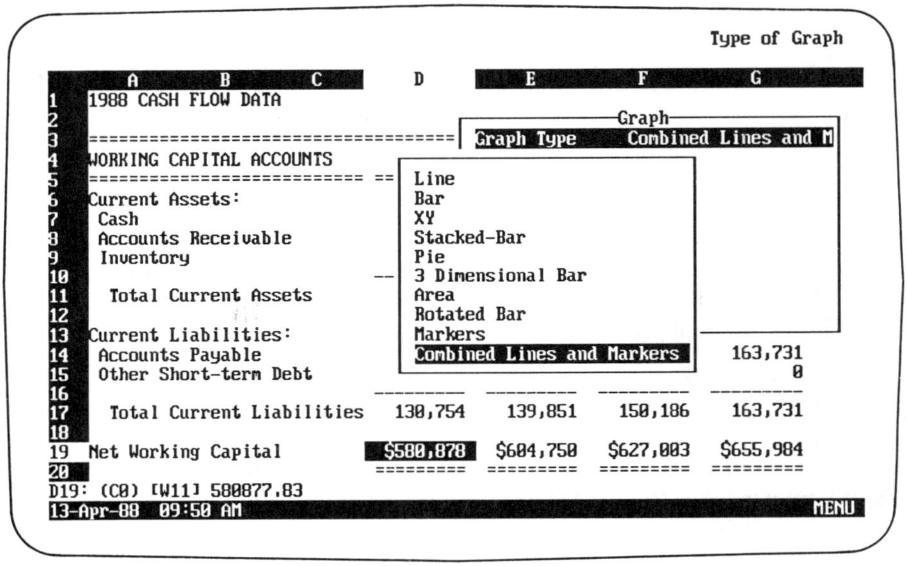

Fig. 10.2. The Graph_Type menu.

By selecting one of these options, you set that graph type and automatically restore the Graph menu.

To understand which graph type will best convey the meaning of specific numeric data, you must know something about plotting points on a graph. Review the two basic terms (*x-axis* and *y-axis*) illustrated in figure 10.3.

All graphs (except pie graphs) have two axes: the y-axis (the vertical left edge) and the x-axis (the horizontal bottom edge). Quattro automatically provides tick marks for both axes. The program also scales the adjacent numbers on the y-axis, based on the minimum and maximum figures included in the plotted data block(s). Generally, the y-axis corresponds to values/magnitudes, and the x-axis corresponds to time/trend data.

Every point plotted on a graph has a unique location (x,y): *x* represents the time period or the amount measured along the horizontal axis; *y* measures the corresponding values along the vertical axis. The intersection of the y-axis and the x-axis is called the *origin*. Notice that the origin of the graph

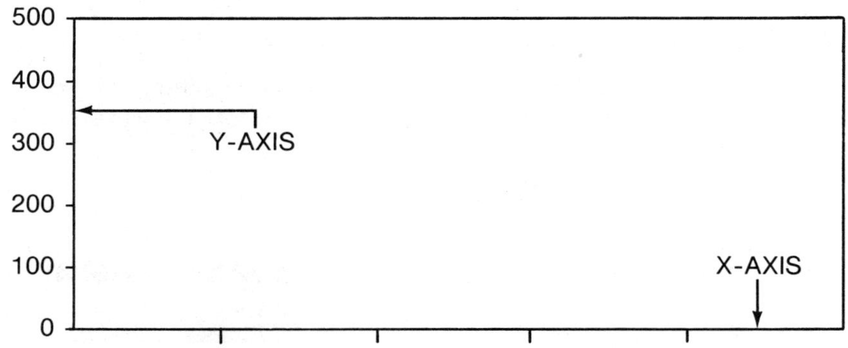

Fig. 10.3. The graph's x and y axes.

in figure 10.3 is 0 (zero). To minimize misinterpretation of graph results and to make graphs easier to compare, use 0 (zero) as the origin in your graphs. Later in this chapter, you will learn how to manually change the upper or lower limits of Quattro's scale.

Of the 10 Quattro graph types, all but the pie graph display both x- and y-axes. Line, bar, stacked-bar, rotated-bar, and markers graphs display values (centered on the tick marks) along the y-axis only. The XY graph displays figures on both axes. (A general statement about the use of each Quattro graph type precedes the explanation of how to construct that type of graph.)

Specifying a Worksheet Data Block

Quattro does not permit you to type in data to be plotted on a graph. Do not confuse the process of plotting data points with that of typing descriptions, such as titles, which is illustrated later in this chapter.

To create a graph, you must specify a location where the data can be found in the currently displayed spreadsheet; you specify the location as a data series in block form. To enter a data series from the Graph Series_Values menu, choose one of the following options:

1st_Series
2nd_Series
3rd_Series
4th_Series
5th_Series
6th_Series

Before you start building a graph, read the following general statements about the choice(s) required for each graph type:

Graph type	*Option(s)*
Line	Select as many as six data series after you have accessed separately the Graph Series_Values menu choices. You do not have to start with **1**st_Series.
Bar	Select as many as six data series after you have accessed separately the Graph Series_Values menu choices. You do not have to start with **1**st_Series. The data points in every data series are marked by a unique symbol. Multiple data series appear on the graph from left to right in numeric order. Every data series displayed in black and white has unique shading. Every data series displayed in color is assigned one of the colors supported by your particular graphics display card.
XY	To enter the data series being plotted as the independent variable, select **X**-Axis_Values from the main Graph menu. Plot at least one dependent variable (you usually would select **1**st_Series).
Stacked Bar	Follow the Bar graph instructions. In a stacked-bar graph, multiple data series appear from bottom to top in series-number order.
Pie	Enter only one data series by selecting **1**st_Series from the Graph Series_Values menu.
3-D Bar	Select as many as six data series after you have accessed separately the Graph Series_Values menu choices. You do not have to start with **1**st_Series. The data points in every data series are marked by a unique symbol. Multiple data series appear on the graph from left to right in numeric order. Every data series displayed in black and white has unique shading. Every data series displayed in

Graph type	*Option(s)*
	color is assigned one of the colors supported by your particular graphics display card.
Area	Follow the instructions for a line graph. An area graph charts the proportion of each series line to the overall total of all the lines. An area graph is similar to the stacked-bar graph type.
Rotated Bar	A rotated-bar graph is the same as a bar graph. The rotated-bar graph is simply a horizontal version of the bar graph.
Markers	Enter as many as six data series. You do not have to start with **1**st_Series. The data points in every data series are marked by a unique marking symbol.
Lines & Markers	Enter as many as six data series after you have accessed separately the Graph Series_Values menu choices. You do not have to start with **1**st_Series. The lines in every data series are marked by a unique marking symbol.

As you build your own graphs, refer to the preceding comments (organized by graph type).

Constructing a Combined Lines and Markers Graph

After you select the appropriate graph type for the data you will plot, producing a graph is easy. Using the Net Working Capital amounts in row 19 of figure 10.1a, you can create a combined-lines-and-markers graph of the January-through-June amounts or the January-through-December amounts. From Quattro's main menu, select /**G**raph to access the Graph menu.

The next step is to select Graph_**T**ype. Choose **C**ombined_Lines_&_Markers from the menu. If you don't make a choice from the Graph_Type menu, you are presented with a stacked-bar graph, Quattro's default type.

To enter the first-series value, choose **1st_Series** from the Series_Values menu and then respond to the input-line prompt `Values for this series:` by entering *D19..I19*.

By specifying the type of graph and the spreadsheet location of data to plot, you have completed the minimum requirements for creating a graph. If you press **View**, you see a graph similar to that shown in figure 10.4.

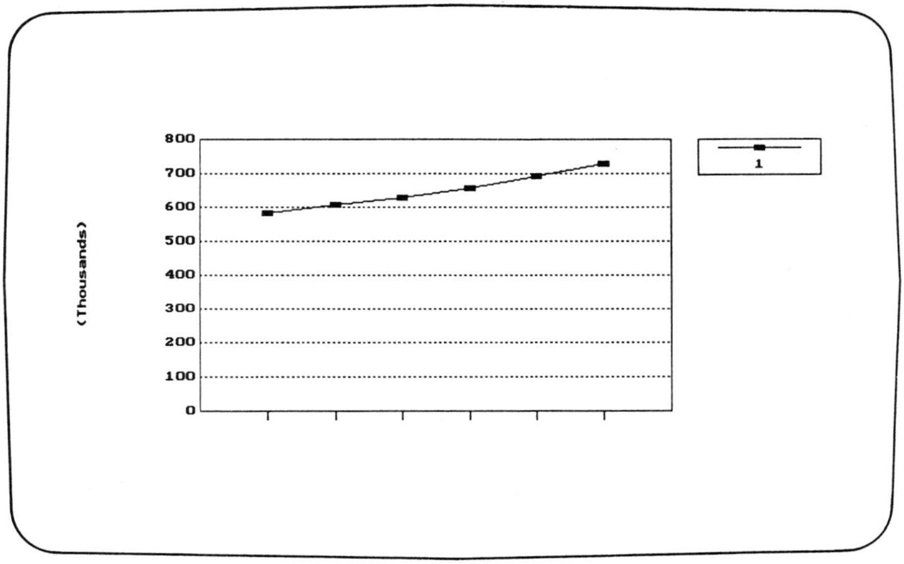

Fig. 10.4. A default line graph.

You know what this graph represents, but it may not mean much to anyone else. Although the six data points corresponding to the January-through-June figures have been plotted, none of the points has been labeled to indicate what the point represents. Notice, however, that Quattro automatically displays the `(Thousands)` indicator along the y-axis.

Before delving into the specific characteristics of each graph type, you should be aware of some available methods for improving the appearance of your graphs. These methods apply to all graph types, unless stated otherwise.

Enhancing the Appearance of a Basic Graph

As you know, you can create an on-screen graph by selecting from the main Graph menu a **Graph_Type**, the appropriate series values, and **View**. If you want to improve the appearance of your graph, select **Titles** or **Customize**.

As you add enhancements to your graphs, check the results frequently. Almost all the menus that allow you to customize graphs also provide a View option. Select **View** to check the most recent version of the graph. Press any key to exit the graph display and restore the current menu to the screen.

You also may notice that many of the graph menus have duplicate commands in addition to **View**. This characteristic may seem confusing at first, but you will find that being able to modify the same graph settings from several menus is a great convenience. For example, you can create a title for the bottom of a graph (x-axis) either by selecting /**Graph Titles X** or /**Graph Customize X**-Axis **Title**. Thus, Quattro lets you modify a graph setting wherever convenient. Discussions of the operation of duplicate menu commands are not repeated in the following sections.

To view the current graph from the worksheet's READY mode, press the F10 (Graph) key, which instantly redraws the graph with any updated information. Whenever you are not in MENU mode, you can use the F10 (Graph) key to view the graph. Press any key except F10 to return to the worksheet.

Adding Descriptive Labels and Numbers

To add descriptive information to a graph, use the /**Graph Titles** command. To label series values, use the /**Graph Customize Series Legends** and **Inter**ior_Labels options. The x-axis can be changed from the /**Graph X**-Axis_Values command. Figure 10.5 shows where these additional items will appear on your graph.

As you can see, interior labels appear within the graph. Descriptions entered with the **X**-Axis_Values option appear immediately below the x-axis. You can enter as many as four titles within one graph: two at the top and one to describe each axis. Legends describing the shading, color, or symbols assigned to data series in line or bar graphs appear at the top right corner of each graph. Legends are assigned automatically by Quattro, which means that the line color, symbol, or cross-hatching pattern for each series value is isolated in the legends box. Use the /**Graph Customize Series Legends** command to add descriptive information about each of the data series.

Using the Titles Option

If you select /**Graph Titles**, the following options are displayed in the menu box:

1st_Line
2nd_Line
X

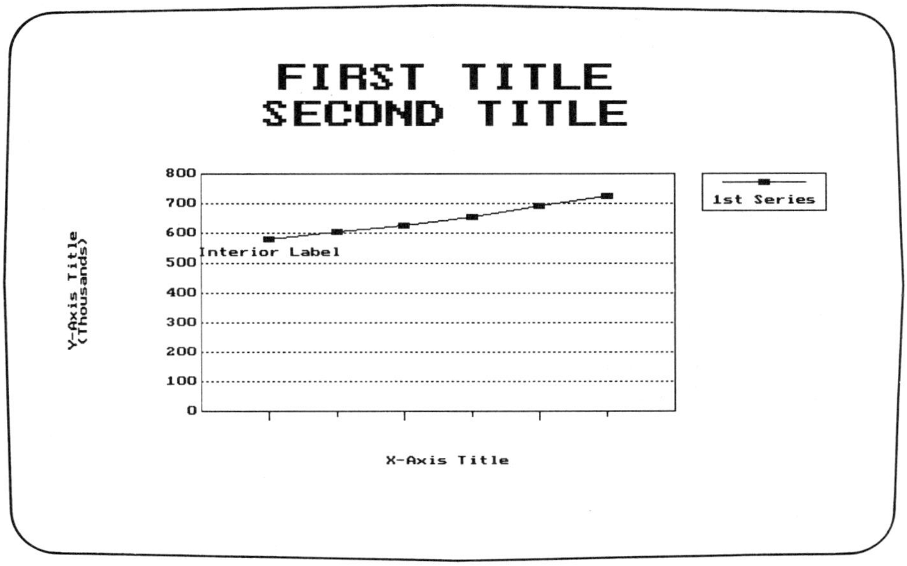

Fig. 10.5. Graph location of descriptive information.

Y
Size
Font
View
Quit

You can enter one or two centered titles at the top of your graph. When you enter two titles, the sizes of the two titles initially are the same. You will learn shortly how this default can be changed. You can enter titles by typing a new description, by specifying a block name, or by referencing the cell location of a label or a number already in the worksheet.

With the /**G**raph **T**itles **S**ize and /**G**raph **T**itles **F**ont commands, you have control of both the size and typestyle of titles. The **S**ize command lets you set the size of titles independently so that the second title can be made smaller than the first. The menu options for size are **A**utosize, **S**mall, **M**edium, and **L**arge.

The /**G**raph **T**itles **F**ont command gives you many optional typestyles for the titles in a graph. Eleven fonts are available. Having control of type fonts is nice but don't go overboard with them. The key is for a graph to convey a message; and the simpler it is, the better. Put another way, the graph's style should not overwhelm the graph's substance.

Both the **Titles** and the **Titles Size** command menus have their own View options. By using **View**, you can see immediately the results of your artistic modifications.

Suppose that you want to enhance the basic combined-lines-and-markers graph of the Net Working Capital amounts (refer to fig. 10.5). (Figures 10.1a and 10.1b contain the worksheet data for this graph.) You will enter four titles, using cell references for two of the titles and typing new descriptions for the others.

Select /**Graph Titles 1st_Line**; then, when Quattro prompts you for a title, type *ABC Company*. Press Enter.

Select **2nd_Line** and enter *\A19* to make `Net Working Capital` (the contents of cell A19) the second top-centered title. Press Enter. Then, to reproduce `1988 CASH FLOW DATA` beneath the x-axis, select **X** and enter *\A1*. To enter the fourth title, select **Y** and then enter *Actual Dollars*. Now check the graph by selecting **View**. Your graph should look like the enhanced graph in figure 10.6.

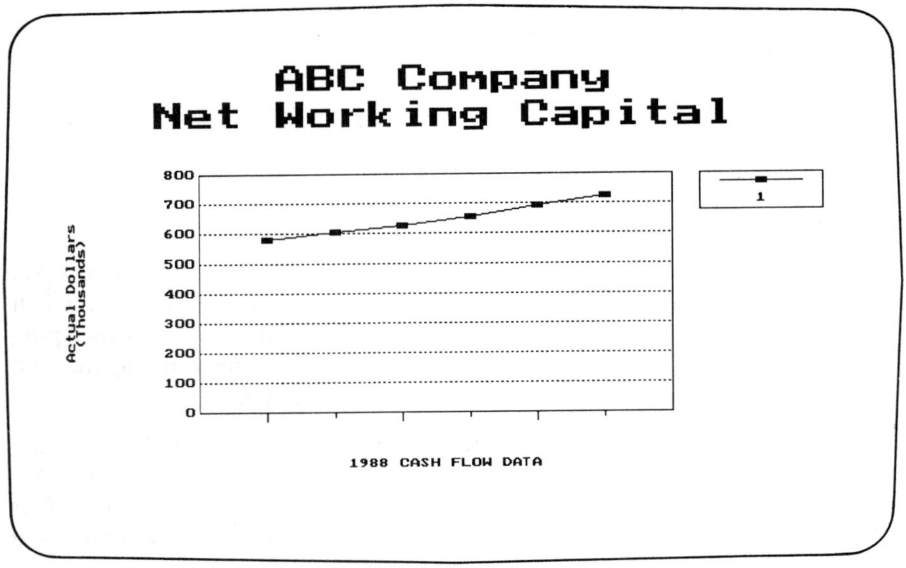

Fig. 10.6. Titles added to a line graph.

When you print the graph, the fonts that you selected for the titles are printed as nearly as possible to the screen display. The most accurate reproductions of graphs are accomplished with laser printers that support the PostScript page-description language.

To edit a title, use the command sequence that you used for creating the title. The existing text, cell reference, or block name appears in the input line, ready for editing. If you want to eliminate a title, press Esc and then press Enter.

The X-Axis and Y-Axis titles have no significance when you construct a pie graph.

Entering Labels within a Graph

After a series has been graphed, you can enter values or labels to explain each point plotted on the graph. You do so by first selecting **C**ustomize **S**eries **I**nterior_Labels from the main Graph menu and then specifying the data series (**1**st through **6**th) to which the interior labels apply. Instead of typing the labels (as you typed the titles), you must specify each interior-label block by pointing to an existing block in the worksheet, providing cell coordinates, or specifying a previously determined block name.

Continue to enhance your sample combined-lines-and-markers graph by entering the January-through-June headings from row 4 of the worksheet (refer to fig. 10.1a). First, select /**G**raph **C**ustomize **S**eries **I**nterior_Labels. The following submenu choices appear on-screen:

1st_Series
2nd_Series
3rd_Series
4th_Series
5th_Series
6th_Series
View
Quit

Associated with this submenu is a line at the top right of the screen explaining that the highlighted **1**st menu choice is used for specifying interior labels for the first series. The only series value currently defined in the Working Capital combined-lines-and-markers graph is the first series, which is defined as D19..I19.

To enter the six abbreviated monthly headings from row 4 in the worksheet, select **1**st_Series and then enter *D4..I4*. The following submenu appears:

Center
Left
Above
Right
Below
None (to reset)

From this submenu, select only one option for each interior-label block you are identifying. In other words, you cannot position one cell within an interior-label block *above* its associated data point and another cell within that same interior-label block *below* its associated data point.

To continue enhancing your graph, select **A**bove. As soon as you make your selection, the menu automatically returns to the Graph Customize Series Interior_Labels submenu. To examine the graph, select **V**iew. Your graph should resemble that in figure 10.7.

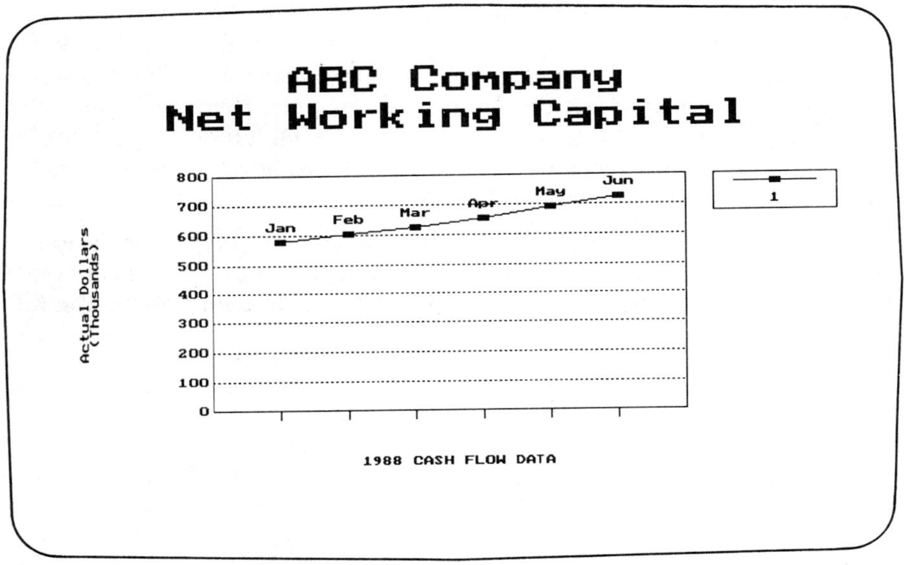

Fig. 10.7. Data-labels added within a line graph.

If you graph more than one data series, attach the interior labels to the data series with the largest figures. Then select **A**bove to position the interior labels above the data points plotted. To enter text or numbers as the plotted points, use the **C**enter option with line graphs that display **N**either lines nor symbols.

To edit either the block or position of the interior label, use the same command sequence that you used to create the interior label. Edit the current block or specify a different position.

To eliminate an interior label, follow the original setup sequence, overriding the existing interior-label block by substituting the address of any single blank cell in the worksheet.

To remove the January-through-June interior labels from within the sample Working Capital graph, select the following sequence:

/Graph **C**ustomize **S**eries **I**nterior_Labels **1**st_Series **D1** **A**bove

Note that you enter D1 to blank out the existing block.

Select **V**iew to check the graph. The graph should again resemble that shown in figure 10.6.

Note: You cannot use **I**nterior_Labels for a pie graph.

Entering Labels below the X-Axis

Instead of placing descriptive information within a graph, you may prefer to enter label information along the x-axis. The main Graph menu's **X**-Axis_Values option has two distinct functions. Use the option to position labels below the x-axis in trend graphs such as line, bar, and stacked-bar graphs. Or use the option to enter a data series in an XY graph. (XY graphs are discussed later in this chapter). You can use the **X**-Axis_Values option also to label slices of a pie chart.

Suppose, for example, that you want to enter the actual January-through-June Net Working Capital figures as labels below your sample graph's x-axis. Select **X**-Axis_Values from the main Graph menu and enter the block *D19..I19*. To keep the titles from overlapping, reduce the size of the graph by using **G**raph **T**itles **S**ize **X**_and_Y **M**edium. Select **V**iew. Your graph should look like that in figure 10.8.

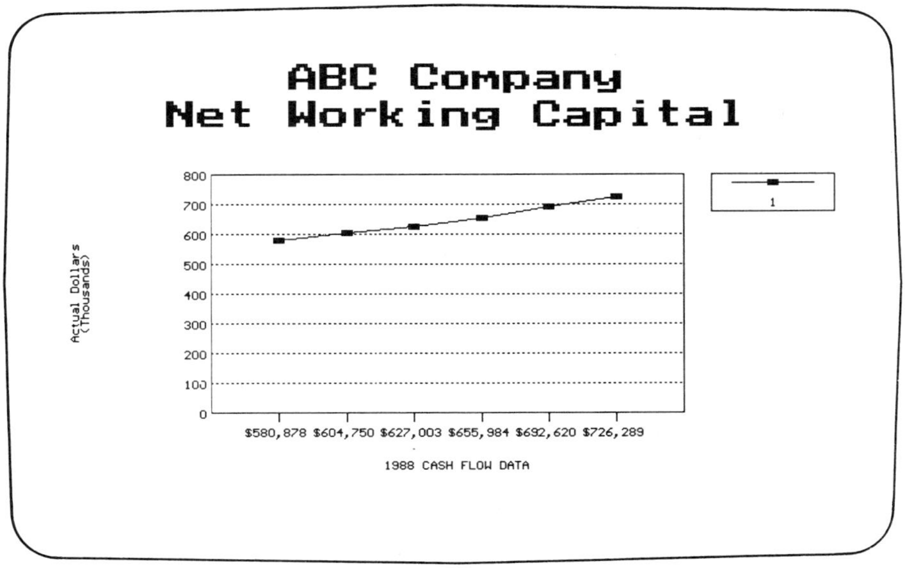

Fig. 10.8. Displaying values below the x-axis.

Notice that in this graph, the values used as descriptive labels below the x-axis display the same format shown in the worksheet.

You may remember that entries within the block you specify for descriptions can be either values or labels. To practice entering labels, you will change the Net Working Capital descriptive amounts to January-through-June headings. To do so, select **X**-Axis_Values from the main Graph menu and then type *D4..I4*. When you choose **V**iew to check the graph, your graph should resemble that shown in figure 10.9.

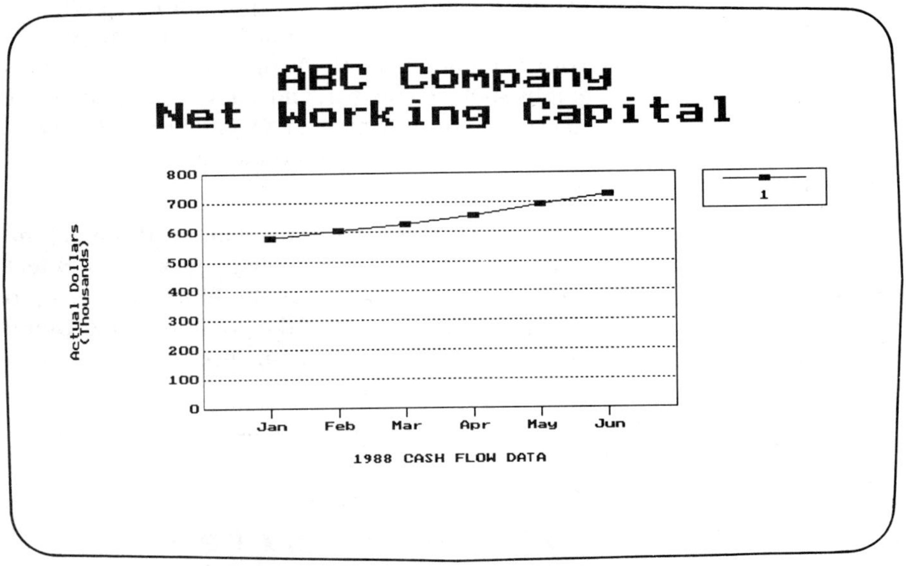

Fig. 10.9. Displaying labels below the x-axis.

If the x-axis labels or numbers are longer than 9 or 10 characters, parts of the extreme right or left descriptions may not be displayed. To edit the x-axis labels, select **X**-Axis_Values from the main Graph menu and then override the current block by typing or pointing to a different block. To eliminate the x-axis labels, select **/Graph Reset X**-Axis.

You cannot use **X**-Axis_Values to enter labels below the x-axis when you construct an XY or pie graph. (The x-axis can be used to place labels next to each pie slice in a pie graph, however.)

Using the Legend Option

Whenever a graph contains more than one set of data, you need to be able to distinguish between those sets. Quattro automatically creates a legend box to the right of each graph. As a default, Quattro displays the color, marker, or crosshatch pattern for each series value and puts the number of the associated series below the pattern displayed. The /**G**raph **C**ustomize **S**eries **L**egend command lets you assign a more descriptive label to these numbered legends (refer to table 10.1 for a summary of the assignments specific to each series value).

Table 10.1
Graph Symbols and Shading

Data Range	*Line Graph Symbols*	*Bar Graph B&W Shading*	*On-Screen Color*
A	□		Red
B	+		Blue
C	◊		White
D	△		Red
E	X		Blue
F	▽		White

Quattro assigns each series a default color, marker, or crosshatch pattern. If you find that you don't like the default series identifier, you can alter it by using the /**G**raph **C**ustomize **S**eries **M**arkers, /**G**raph **C**ustomize **S**eries **P**atterns, or /**G**raph **C**ustomize **C**olors **S**eries commands to modify the mark or crosshatch pattern. When you choose one of these commands, you then have an opportunity to select which series (**1**st_ through **6**th_Series) to which to apply the change(s).

The most recent version of the sample Working Capital combined-lines-and-markers graph displays the square symbol assigned to the data points entered as the first data series (refer to fig. 10.9). Suppose that you want to change the data to reflect two items, Total Current Assets (CA) and Total Current Liabilities (CL), rather than the single item reflecting Net Working Capital.

First, change the second title line to reflect the changed data. Select /**G**raph **T**itles **2**nd_Line, press Esc to remove the current cell reference, and enter *Components of Working Capital* as the new second title. You will retain the first series, respecifying the series value as Total Current Assets, and add a second series for the Total Current Liabilities.

To enter the Total Current Assets figures for the first six months of the year, select **/Graph Series_Values 1st_Series** and then either type *D11..I11* or press Esc once and point to the block. If you remove the anchor from the data-series block by pressing Esc, you must reanchor it by pressing the period (.) key. When the main Graph menu reappears, select **3rd_Series** and enter *D17..I17*. Choose **/Graph Customize Series Legends 1st_Series** and type *TOTAL CA*. Then select **Legends 3rd_Series** and type *TOTAL CL* at the prompt. When you select **View**, Quattro displays the modified graph (see fig. 10.10).

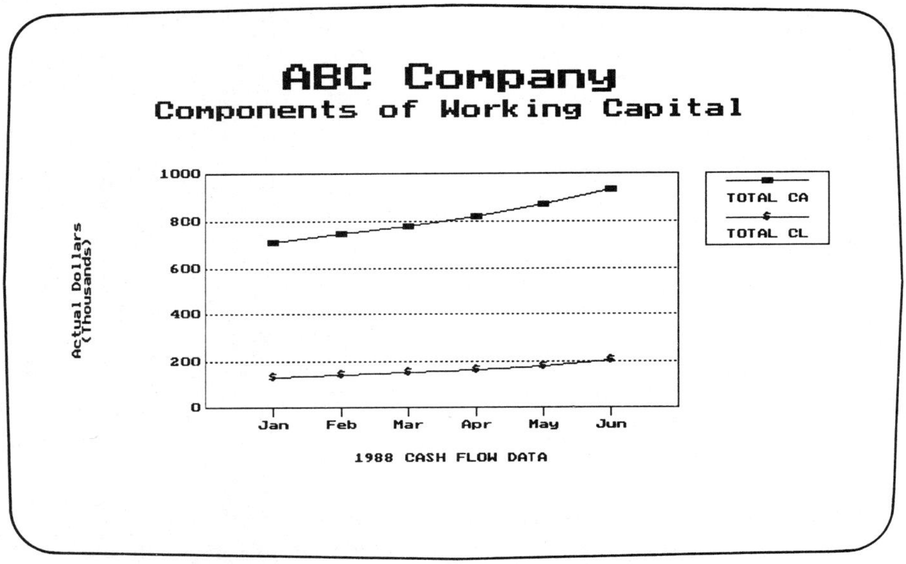

Fig. 10.10. Adding legends to the line graph.

If you want to edit a legend, use the same command sequence you used to create that legend. The existing text, cell reference, or block name appears in the input line, ready for you to edit. To eliminate a legend, press Esc and then press Enter.

Legends are appropriate only for graphs with two or more data series. You cannot use **Legends** for pie graphs, which can have only one data series.

Altering the Default Graph Display

All the previously described enhancements involve adding label or number descriptions to the basic minimal graph. Quattro supplies the additional default display items shown in figures 10.9 and 10.10.

For example, in both of these graphs, the figures (scale) along the vertical y-axis were set automatically, taking into account the minimum and maximum values in the series values plotted. The amounts are displayed in **G**eneral format. Within the graphs, Quattro automatically centers the symbols on data points plotted; black lines are used to connect the symbols, leaving the background clear. All labels that were included in the x-axis block are displayed below the graphs.

You can change any of these additional default graph display items. To continue enhancing the appearance of a basic graph, you will change the defaults in the simple combined-lines-and-markers graph. (Additional illustrations are included in this chapter's explanations of how to develop most graph types.)

Setting a Background Grid

Ordinarily, you will use the default (horizontal line grid) background for your graphs. But times may occur when you will want to impose a grid on a graph so that the data-point amounts are easier to read.

Selecting /**G**raph **C**ustomize **G**rids produces the following menu:

Color
Line_Type
Frame_Graph
View
Quit

The first option lets you override the default grid color (white) by presenting you with a menu of available grid colors from which to choose. The **L**ine_Type option lets you create one of several grid patterns that are listed next (choice 1 is the default):

Menu choice	*Effect*
1	Dotted grid (allows clear view of lines as they pass through the grids)
2 ________	Solid grid lines
3 - - - -	Dashed grid lines
4 — - —	Alternating dashed grid
5 +	Combined horizontal and vertical grid lines
6 |	Solid vertical grid only

Full_Frame	Puts a frame around graph by connecting the top and right borders of graph with a line
None	Clears grids from the graph

Figure 10.11 shows a graph with the + (horizontal and vertical) grid patterns.

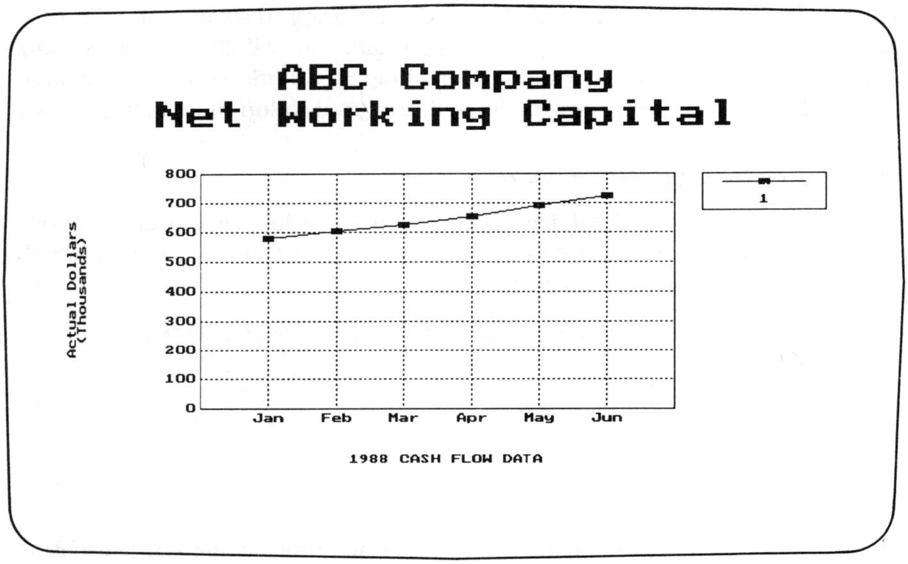

Fig. 10.11. A graph with horizontal and vertical grid patterns.

Experiment with different grids, repeating the command sequence and specifying other options. Whenever you want to eliminate a grid display, select /Graph Grids Line_Type None.

Note: You cannot use Grids for a pie graph.

Changing the X- and Y-Axis Scale Settings

When a graph such as the line, XY, bar, or stacked-bar graph is created, Quattro automatically sets scale values displayed on the y-axis, taking into account the smallest and largest numbers in the series values plotted. (For XY graphs only, Quattro also establishes x-axis scale values.)

If you need to force a numeric upper limit or origin other than the one chosen automatically by Quattro, use the /Graph Customize Y-Axis Scale command to change scaling to Manual. Once you set scaling to manual mode, you can enter the numeric upper and lower limits from the Y-Axis menu. Be sure that your menus are in expanded mode so you can see the current defaults for the upper and lower limits for the y-axis. If your menus are not in expanded mode, press + on the numeric keypad while in MENU mode.

You can use negative figures for scale values in line, XY, and bar graphs but not in stacked-bar or pie graphs. Also, the y-axis upper limit must be larger than the lower limit.

In addition to changing the upper and lower scale values, Quattro lets you determine the size of the increment between the maximum and minimum values (this increment is indicated by tick marks). For example, by using the /**G**raph **C**ustomize **Y**-Axis **I**ncrement command, you can change the scale along the y-axis of the graph shown in figure 10.11 from the default increment of 100,000 to an increment of 20,000 on each tick mark (580, 600, 620, 640, 660, 680, 700, 720, and 740).

You also can enter a skip factor to prevent the tick marks from appearing too crowded by using the **N**o._of_Minor_Ticks command (**N**o. represents Number).

Quattro automatically sets the display format of the scale values to **G**eneral—the same default global numeric display that you see when you access a blank worksheet. Notice that dollar signs, commas, and decimal points are not displayed along the y-axis in figure 10.11. You can change the format to any of the styles available from the Default Formats Display menu by using the /**G**raph **C**ustomize **Y**-Axis **F**ormat_of_Ticks command. Do not confuse the capability of altering the default format of the scale values with that of bringing in previously formatted worksheet numbers as interior labels.

Another y-axis scale display is the indicator that appears along the y-axis when a line, XY, bar, or stacked-bar graph is created. (On an XY graph, an indicator appears also along the x-axis.) This indicator appears as `(Thousands)` along the y-axis of the graph in figure 10.11.

Although you cannot change the indicator, you can suppress its display. To understand why you might want to suppress display of the indicator, imagine a worksheet that contains data with truncated trailing zeros (for example, a sales budget figure of 5,000,000 that has been entered in the worksheet as 5,000). Graphing the truncated figures produces the y-axis indicator `(Thousands)`, but you need `(Millions)`. You can suppress display of the indicator and type an appropriate indicator as part of the y-axis title. Select /**G**raph **C**ustomize **Y**-Axis **D**isplay_Scaling **N**o to eliminate the scale's magnitude indicator `(Thousands)`.

Using the sample graph shown in figure 10.11, practice changing y-axis scaling values by setting a minimum value of 580,000 and a maximum value of 740,000. Select /**Graph** **C**ustomize **Y**-Axis **S**cale **M**anual and enter a **L**ow limit of *580000* (without dollar signs or commas); then select **H**igh and enter *740000* (without dollar signs or commas) as the upper limit. Now select **V**iew. The graph should resemble that in figure 10.12.

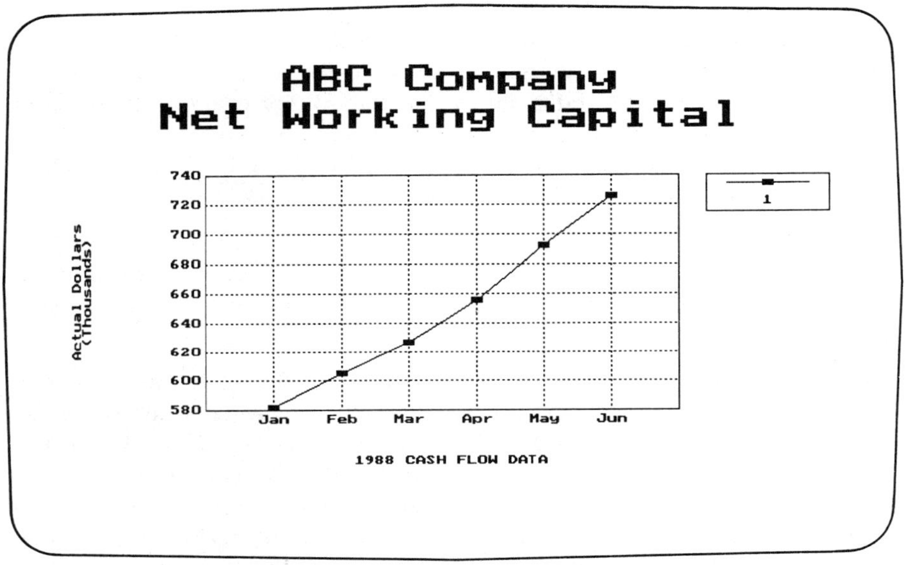

Fig. 10.12. Changed y-axis upper and lower limits.

If you compare figures 10.11 and 10.12, you can see that changing the origin gives you a different perspective on the magnitude of the increase in working capital. Notice also that Quattro has changed the increment between tick marks from $100,000, in figure 10.11, to $20,000, in figure 10.12.

You can change scale display format and suppress the scale indicator by using a few keystrokes. Suppose that you want to alter the y-axis title in the graph shown in figure 10.12 to indicate that the y-axis values are in thousands. Suppose also that you want to change the default **G**eneral format to **C**urrency format with zero decimal places and to suppress the automatic scale indicator.

Select /**Graph** **C**ustomize **Y**-Axis **T**itle and type *(in thousands)* to add this information to the existing `Actual Dollars` title. Change the display format by selecting **F**ormat_of_Ticks **C**urrency and specifying zero decimal places. To suppress automatic display of the indicator, immediately select **D**isplay_Scaling and then **N**o. Now choose **V**iew to see the graph (see fig. 10.13).

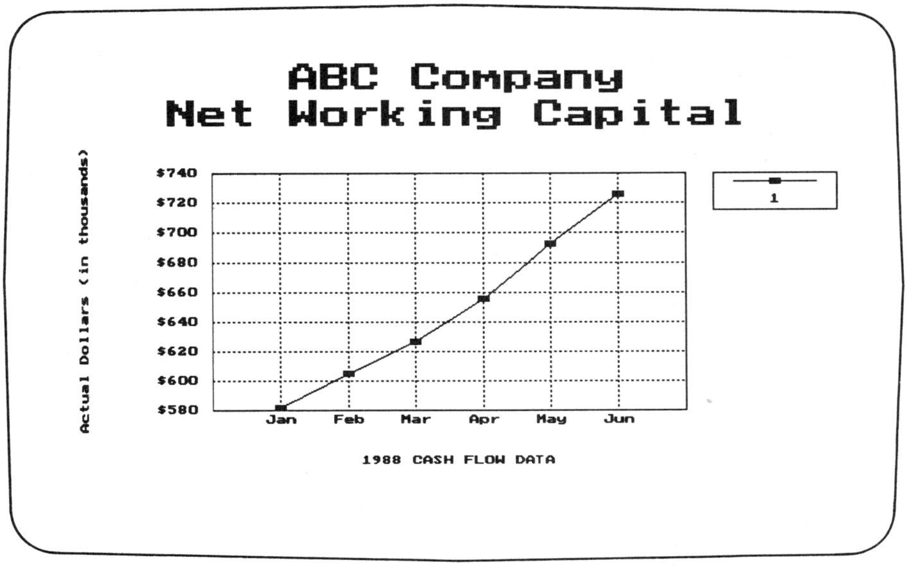

Fig. 10.13. Changed scale format and suppressed indicator.

To see the changes, compare the graphs in figures 10.12 and 10.13.

Now restore the indicator display by selecting /**G**raph **C**ustomize **Y**-Axis **D**isplay_Scaling **Y**es. Change the format and manual limits by repeating the command sequences used to establish the first changes, this time selecting alternative formats or entering alternative minimum or maximum values. Restore the automatic scale limits by choosing **S**cale **A**utomatic.

Almost all the options on the Graph Customize X-Axis menu are identical to the Y-Axis menu. Choose /**G**raph **C**ustomize **X**-Axis to adjust scaling on an XY graph.

Spacing Display of X-Axis Labels

If the labels on the x-axis are so long that they crowd together or overlap, you can use the /**G**raph **C**ustomize **X**-Axis **N**o._of_Minor_Ticks command to skip some x-axis labels. Use this option to improve the display. You seldom will need to set the factor higher than 4. If you would like to retain as many labels on the x-axis as possible, Quattro gives you the /**G**raph **C**ustomize **X**-Axis **A**lternate_Ticks command. This command staggers the labels so that they alternate on two different lines below the graph. Usually, this procedure prevents the labels from overwriting one another.

As an alternative, you can remove some of the x-axis labels. Suppose, for example, that the monthly headings below the x-axis in figure 10.13 were spelled out, which would crowd the display. To improve the display, select /Graph Customize **X**-Axis No._of_Minor_Ticks, enter *1*, and select View. The changed spacing is shown in figure 10.14.

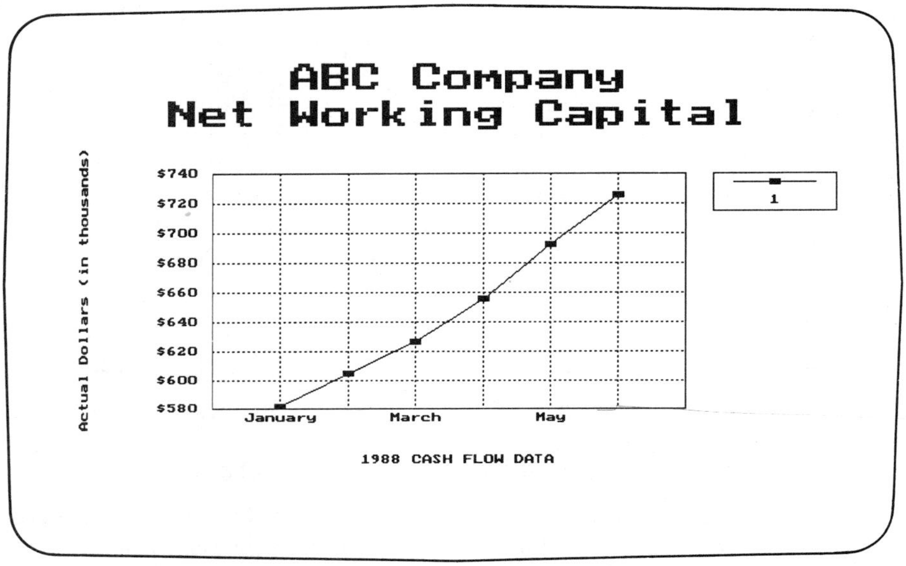

Fig. 10.14. Skipped labels on the x-axis.

As you can see, only the January, March, and May x-axis labels are displayed. To retain the x-axis labels but restore the default setting of using every label in the block, repeat the command sequence, specifying *0*.

The No._of_Minor_Ticks command does not apply to pie graphs.

Overriding Graph Types

One of Quattro's unique features is its capacity to mix graph types within the same graph. The /Graph Customize Series Override_Type command lets you specify the type of graphing for any series values in a graph. For example, you can use this command to set one of four data series to be a line graph while leaving the other three data series in bar-graph format. Thus, you can highlight more important data series while retaining the other series values in a graph. The graph types that can be intermixed follow:

Line
Markers
Combined_Lines_&_Markers
Bar
None (shows interior labels only)

Working with Multiple Graphs

You sometimes may need several graphs that each display different data. With Quattro, you can have multiple graphs in a spreadsheet file. Quattro can store multiple graphs in an area of the file known as the *graph stack*.

Multiple graphs in Quattro work like tray dispensers in cafeterias. Have you ever noticed how tray dispensers work? If you look downward at the top of the stack, you can see only one tray—the top one. If you remove the tray, the tray below it moves to the top of the stack and becomes visible. This same procedure applies to multiple graphs. You can see only one graph at a time, the one at the top of the stack. To see another graph, you must bring it to the top of the stack. The graph at the top of the stack is described as the *current graph*.

Graph names are part of a spreadsheet file just as formulas and labels are part of a spreadsheet file. If you want to be able to display and edit named graph settings in future spreadsheet sessions, the graph settings must be saved with the /**F**ile **S**ave command.

Creating Graph Specifications for Reuse

If you want to be able to view on-screen a graph that you created in an earlier graphing session, the graph must have been given a name when the graph was originally constructed (and the worksheet must have been saved, unless the same worksheet is still active). To name a graph, issue the /**G**raph **N**ame command to access the following menu:

Display
Store
Erase
Reset

Only one graph at a time can be the current graph. If you want to save a graph that you just completed (for subsequent recall to the screen) as well as build a new graph, you must first issue a /**G**raph **N**ame **S**tore command. The only way to store a graph for later screen display is to issue this command, which instructs Quattro to remember the specifications used to define the current graph. You cannot have multiple graphs if you don't name each of the graphs individually.

When Quattro prompts you for a graph name, provide a name that is up to 15 characters long.

You can use data from a single worksheet to create and name several different graphs. Just be sure to save the worksheet before you retrieve a different worksheet file or before you /**Q**uit Quattro. Graph specifications are stored with the worksheet file when you issue the /**F**ile **S**ave command.

To recall any named graphs from within the active spreadsheet, select /**G**raph **N**ame **D**isplay. When this command is issued, Quattro displays a list of all the graph names stored in the current worksheet. When the names are displayed, you can select the graph you want to redraw by either typing the appropriate name or pointing to the name on the list. By invoking **N**ame **D**isplay commands in rapid sequence, you create a "slide show" of Quattro graphics.

To delete a single named graph, issue the /**G**raph **N**ame **E**rase command. Again, Quattro lists all the graph names stored in the current worksheet. You can select the graph you want to delete by either typing the appropriate name or pointing to the name on the list.

If you want to delete all the graph names, issue the /**G**raph **N**ame **R**eset command. Using this command to delete the names of all graphs also deletes the parameters for all the graphs within that particular worksheet.

Resetting the Current Graph

You may have noticed that, throughout this chapter, instructions for editing or removing options have been given at the end of each new topic. These instructions are important because Quattro continues to use an enhancement in the next version of the same graph, or in a new graph, unless you take specific actions to remove that enhancement. For example, you can build a series of six different bar graphs by specifying the graph **T**ype for only the first one. You will recall that you did not have to respecify the titles you entered for the graph in figure 10.6 as you constructed the graphs in figures 10.7 through 10.9. Although you changed the second title to better explain the new data blocks in figure 10.10, that title was the only one of four that had to be changed.

If you want to make changes to only a few items in graph contents that involve enhancements, you can respecify or eliminate these items from the Customize menu. However, if the next graph you will construct is substantially different from the current one, you may want to use the /Graph **R**eset command. Selecting /Graph **R**eset produces this submenu:

Graph
1st_Series
2nd_Series
3rd_Series
4th_Series
5th_Series
6th_Series
X-Axis

Select **G**raph from this submenu only if you do not want to use any of the existing specifications in your new graph. This command, which ensures that no unwanted settings or enhancements from a previous graph carry over into the current one, usually precedes any graph construction automated by macros. (Creating and using macros is discussed in Chapter 15.)

As an alternative to a total graph reset, you can specify removal of an individual series value. All interior labels assigned to the reset series value also will be eliminated. By choosing **R**eset **X**-Axis, for example, you remove labels displayed below the x-axis, pie-slice labels, and x-axis information for an XY graph.

The following sections of this chapter discuss how to construct each type of graph.

Choosing the Right Graph

You have learned that you can use Quattro to build 10 types of graphs. Because more than one type can accomplish the desired presentation, choosing the best graph type sometimes can be strictly a matter of personal preference.

For example, selecting **L**ine, **B**ar, **3**-Dimensional_Bar, **R**otated_Bar, or **P**ie is appropriate if you plan to graph only a single series of values. At other times, however, only one form will do the job. Before you read the rest of this chapter, take a moment to learn—or review—the primary uses of each graph type.

Selecting an Appropriate Graph Type

You may want to review table 10.1 to refresh your memory about which series values are appropriate for each graph type. A brief summary of the use of each graph type follows:

Graph Type	*Purpose*
Line	This graph type shows the trend of numeric data across time. It is used, for example, to display monthly working-capital amounts during 1988. The line graph type does not display individual data points.
Bar	Similar to a line graph, a bar graph displays the trend of numeric data across time, but with vertical bars. It is used, for example, to display total current assets compared to total liabilities for each month during 1988.
XY	This graph type is used to compare one numeric data series to another numeric data series, to determine if one set of values appears to depend on the other. It is used, for example, to plot monthly Sales and Advertising Expenses to assess whether a direct relationship exists between the amount of sales and the dollars spent for advertising (regression analysis).
Stacked Bar	This graph type is used to graph two or more data series that total 100 percent of a specific numeric category. It is used, for example, to graph three monthly data series—Cash, Accounts Receivable, and Inventory (displayed one above the other)—to depict the proportions each comprises of total current assets throughout the year. (Do not use this type of graph if your data contains negative numbers.)
Pie	This graph type is used to graph only one data series, the components of which total 100 percent of a specific numeric category. It is used, for example, to graph the January Cash, Accounts Receivable, and Inventory amounts to depict the proportion each comprises of the January current assets. (Do not use this type of graph if your data contains negative numbers.)

3-Dimensional Bar	This graph type is similar to a bar graph except that bars are shaded to appear three-dimensional. It works best with few data items.
Area	This graph type is similar to a combination of line and stacked-bar graphs except that data is *cumulative* values. It is used, for example, to graph the January through December sales for Profit Centers 1-4, on a cumulative basis. (Do not use this type of graph if your data contains negative numbers.)
Rotated Bar	This graph type is the same as a bar graph. The rotated-bar graph is simply a horizontal version of the bar graph.
Markers	This graph type is similar to a line graph, but only data points are displayed.
Combined Lines & Markers	This graph type is a combination of line and marker graph types. It was the graph type used in the beginning of this chapter to build your Quattro graphing skills.

Building Graph Types

Although combined-lines-and-markers graphs were used to illustrate Quattro's general graph-enhancement options, most of the options can be used for all graph types. (As you know, certain options don't apply to specific types of graphs.)

The following discussion focuses on several graph types and explains which enhancements are particularly useful for specific graph types. The data in the SALES (by Profit Center) report shown in figures 10.15a and 10.15b is used to create the graphs. Line, bar, and stacked-bar graphs all are appropriate for graphing this monthly sales-by-profit-center information.

Combined-Lines-and-Markers Graphs

First, you use the worksheet data to create a combined-lines-and-markers graph. This graph type is an enhanced version of the basic line graph. The combined-lines-and-markers graph puts special marks, or symbols, where the line intersects the points on the x-axis. This feature helps you separate multiple lines in a graph. Most of the construction methods presented here also apply to the plain line and markers graphs.

	A	B	C	D	E	F	G	H
1	========	========	========	========	========	========	========	========
2	SALES		Jan	Feb	Mar	Apr	May	Jun
3	========	========	========	========	========	========	========	========
4	PC 1		$31,336	$37,954	$43,879	$51,471	$56,953	$53,145
5	PC 2		22,572	24,888	25,167	32,588	40,140	37,970
6	PC 3		131,685	129,044	131,723	139,221	141,879	149,803
7	PC 4		95,473	98,008	96,986	95,318	103,538	108,146
8			--------	--------	--------	--------	--------	--------
9	Total Sales		$281,066	$289,894	$297,755	$318,598	$342,510	$349,064
10			========	========	========	========	========	========

Fig. 10.15a. Sample sales data by profit center (January through June).

	A	B	I	J	K	L	M	N	O
1	========	========	========	========	========	========	========	========	==========
2	SALES		Jul	Aug	Sep	Oct	Nov	Dec	Total
3	========	========	========	========	========	========	========	========	==========
4	PC 1		$54,140	$53,614	$52,015	$48,902	$44,091	$42,536	$570,036
5	PC 2		34,587	33,463	28,939	24,153	27,060	26,701	358,228
6	PC 3		147,108	147,032	153,440	149,990	145,198	150,510	1,716,633
7	PC 4		108,642	106,065	110,401	112,018	111,956	107,522	1,254,073
8			--------	--------	--------	--------	--------	--------	----------
9	Total Sales		$344,477	$340,174	$344,795	$335,063	$328,305	$327,269	$3,898,970
10			========	========	========	========	========	========	==========

Fig. 10.15b. Sample sales data by profit center (July through December).

Because you are constructing a new graph, you need to reset the graph settings to remove any unwanted options that may have been carried over from your last graph operations.

You must enter the four data series as blocks: C4..N4, C5..N5, C6..N6, and C7..N7. You can choose any four of the menu's six **Series_Values** options (**1st** through **6th**). If you plan also to specify a corresponding legend, the best policy is to enter the data series in order (C4..N4 Profit Center 1 figures as the first series, C5..N5 Profit Center 2 figures as the second series, and so on). To produce a graph similar to that shown in figure 10.16, use the following command sequences:

/**Graph**	**Reset Graph**		
	Graph Type		Combined Lines & Markers
	Series Values		1st Series **C4..N4**
			2nd Series **C5..N5**
			3rd Series **C6..N6**
			4th Series **C7..N7**
	Titles	**1st Line**	**1988 SALES**
		2nd Line	**SAMPLE COMPANY**
		X	**SALES BY PROFIT CENTER**

Customize Series Legends 1st Series \A4
2nd Series \A5
3rd Series \A6
4th Series \A7
View
Quit

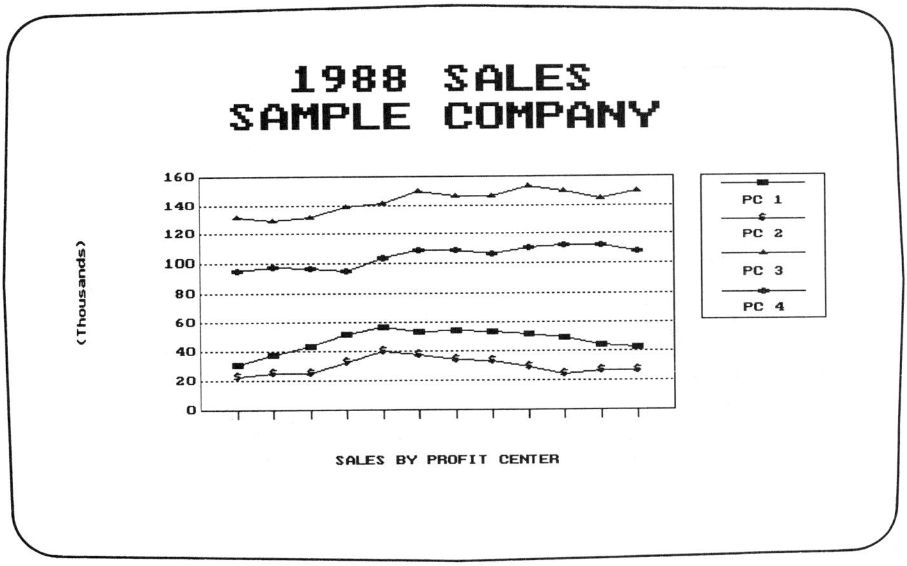

Fig. 10.16. A combined-lines-and-markers graph of profits by center.

Notice that the upper limit of the y-axis is set automatically at $160,000, which is slightly higher than the highest monthly sales amount in all the series values ($153,440 for September sales for Profit Center 3).

Notice that each of the four legends to the right of the graph displays the symbol used on a line in the graph. Always use legends for multiple-line graphs. Without legends, you will not know which data series each line represents. If you prefer certain symbols, you can pick the symbol to associate with each series by choosing /**G**raph **C**ustomize **S**eries **M**arkers.

Stacked-Bar Graphs

You may want to experiment with different graph types when you plot multiple time-series data. *Time-series* data is a sequential series of data that usually occurs over equal intervals of time. In business, this interval is frequently monthly or yearly. If the total of the series values produces a meaningful figure (for example, the combined January sales of each profit center equal total January sales), try using a stacked-bar graph. The series values in a stacked-bar graph are displayed as bars; these bars are plotted in order—1st_ through 6th_Series with the 1st_Series closest to the x-axis. After entering the command sequences to create figure 10.16, for example, you can create the stacked-bar graph shown in figure 10.17 by selecting **Graph_Type Stacked_Bar** from the main Graph menu and then selecting **View**.

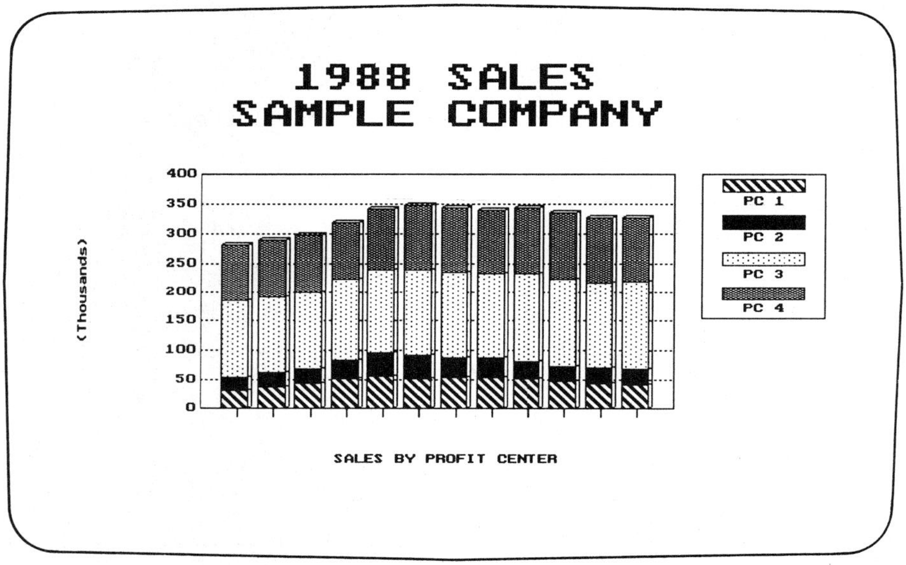

Fig. 10.17. Stacked-bar graph of sales by profit center.

All the options you set to produce the combined-lines-and-markers graph in figure 10.16 are carried over to the new stacked-bar graph. The legends (which show symbol assignments for the combined-lines-and-markers graph) change automatically to display the crosshatches of a black-and-white bar graph. Quattro also adjusts automatically the upper and lower limits of the y-axis. The new $400,000 upper limit in the stacked-bar graph exceeds the highest total sales month ($349,064 in June). In a stacked-bar graph, the lower limit always must be zero.

In a Quattro stacked-bar graph, you can customize the crosshatches or, where applicable, the bar's colors. Do this customizing through the **/Graph Customize Colors** and **/Graph Series Patterns** commands. Assuming that the current graph is shown in figure 10.17, use the following command sequences to produce the graph shown in figure 10.18.

/Graph	**Reset 2nd Series**
	Reset 3rd Series
	Reset 4th Series
	Series Values 3rd Series C5..N5
	5th Series C6..N6
	6th Series C7..N7
	Customize Series Legends 3rd Series \A5
	5th Series \A6
	6th Series \A7
	View

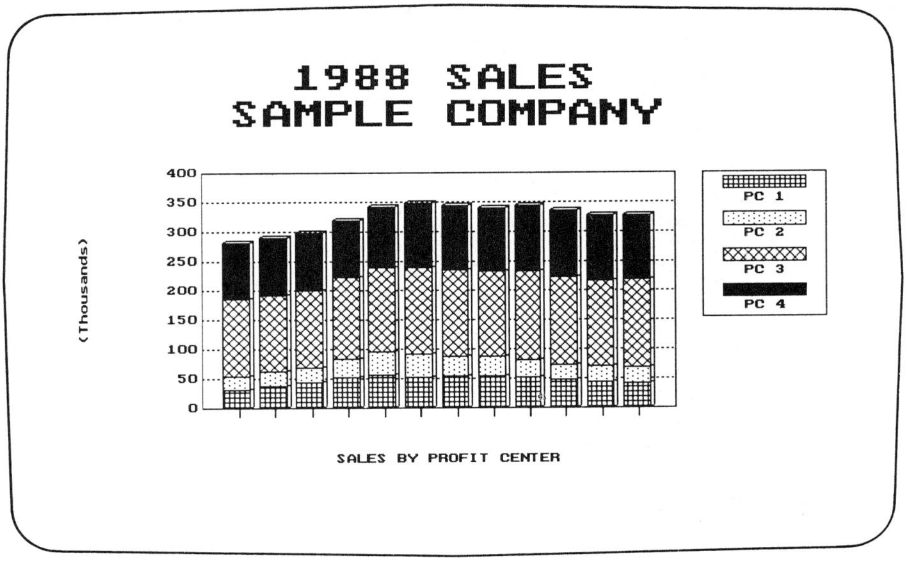

Fig. 10.18. Stacked-bar graph with customized crosshatches.

If you compare figures 10.17 and 10.18, you can see that changing the patterns of crosshatches makes the information easier to read. If you intend to view the stacked-bar graph in color, be sure to assign different colors to adjoining sections of the bars; otherwise, you may not be able to differentiate between two data items.

Area Graphs

Area graphs are similar to stacked-bar graphs in that the series values are stacked one on top of the other. The area graph, however, more clearly preserves the trend information in the graph. The area graph is similar in concept to a geological cross-section: You can see the "surface" of the data in the top line, which represents the total of the values of all the lines below. Thus, you can see how the individual lines contribute to the overall trend. Figure 10.19 shows the stacked-bar graph as an area graph.

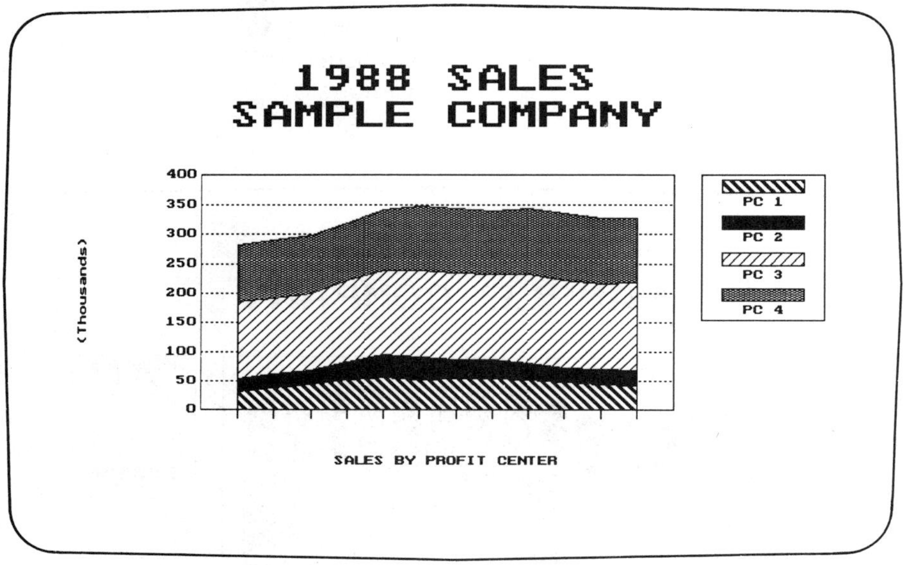

Fig. 10.19. An area graph.

Bar, 3-Dimensional-Bar, and Rotated-Bar Graphs

A bar graph also is appropriate for displaying the worksheet's sales-by-profit-center information (refer to figs. 10.15a and 10.15b). By plotting more than one value series, you can produce a comparative bar graph. In this kind of graph, the bars are displayed in the order the data series are entered, with the 1st_Series bar in the leftmost position.

Assuming that the stacked-bar graph shown in figure 10.18 is the current graph, experiment with the bar graph type by entering the following command sequences:

/Graph **G**raph **T**ype **B**ar
X-Axis **C2..N2**
View

Your graph should be similar to that shown in figure 10.20.

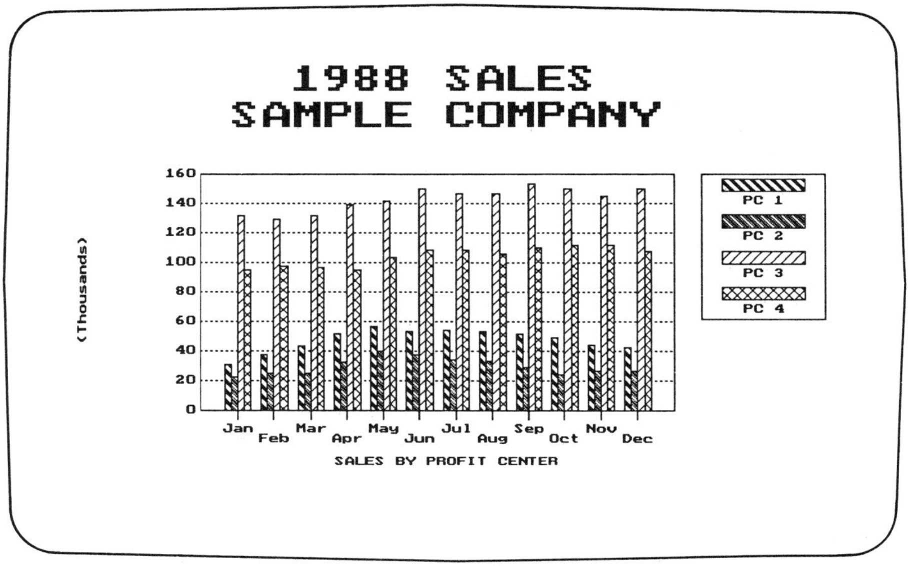

Fig. 10.20. A comparative bar graph.

In this graph, each of the four bars clustered around a tick mark on the x-axis represents the sales of one profit center. In every set of bars, the leftmost bar represents the 1st_Series value; the next bar represents the 2nd_Series; and so on. Monthly headings are centered under the x-axis tick marks. Quattro automatically has revised (to $160,000) the upper scale of the y-axis.

When you work with four data blocks, each of which contains 12 numbers, the display is crowded. You may prefer to create additional graphs, each comparing fewer data series or containing only one series value. For example, to compare only the two top profit centers, use the following command sequences:

/Graph **R**eset **1**st Series
Reset **3**rd Series
View

Compare your results to figure 10.21.

Notice that the legends for the deleted series values are not displayed. The legends have been deleted with the series values.

Ordinarily, you will want to graph comparative information (that is, use more than one data series) when the numbers to be plotted are classified in some way: by region, division, product line, and so on. By resetting series values in

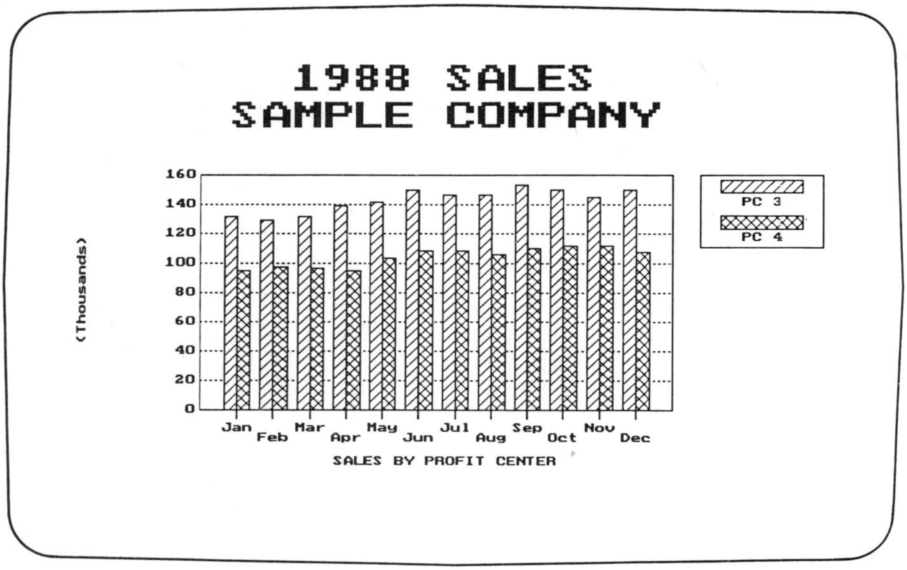

Fig. 10.21. Comparative bar graph showing only two series.

the current example, for example, you can produce a simple bar graph showing total annual sales of each profit center. Use the following command sequence to produce the graph in figure 10.22:

/Graph **R**eset **X**-Axis
Reset **5**th Series
Reset **6**th Series
X-Axis Values **A4..A7**
Series Values **1**st Series **O4..O7**
View

When you graph summary information, especially when the figures are large, you may want to display specific amounts as interior label descriptions within the graph or as x-axis labels below the graph. For example, the graph in figure 10.22 would be easier to understand if each profit center's specific contribution to total annual sales were shown above that profit center's bar.

You can use the **I**nterior_Labels command to enter numbers as well as labels. Access the main Graph menu and apply the following command sequences to the previous settings to produce the improved graph shown in figure 10.23:

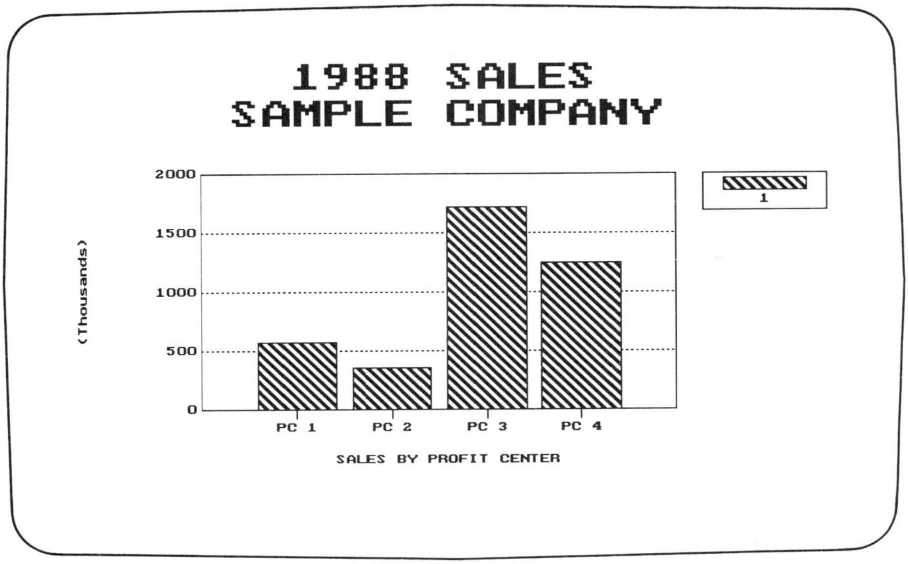

Fig. 10.22. Bar graph showing total annual sales for each profit center.

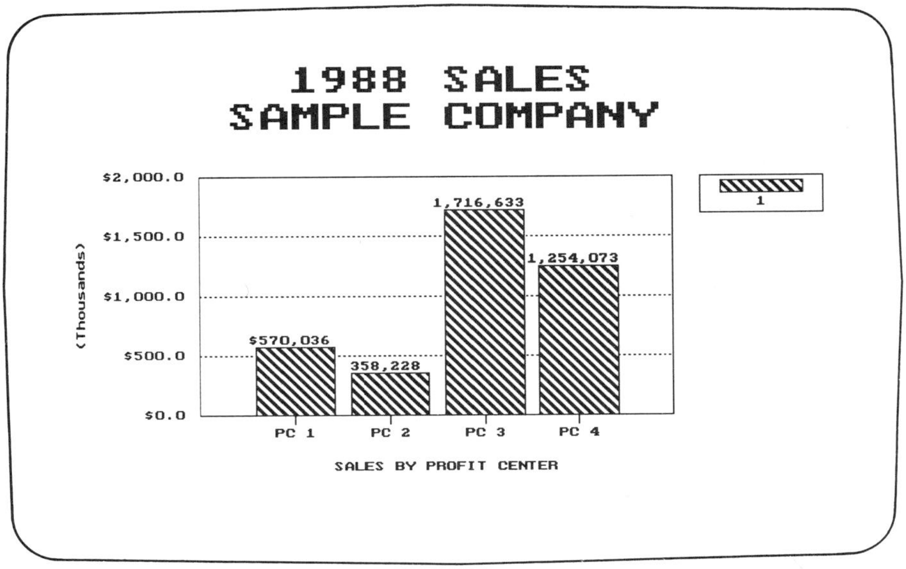

Fig. 10.23. Bar graph with interior labels.

/Graph Customize	Series	Interior_Labels 1st_Series O4..O7 Above
	X-Axis	Title **SALES BY PROFIT CENTER**
	Y-Axis	Format of Ticks Currency **1**
		View

The rotated-bar and 3-dimensional-bar graphs are variants of the standard bar graph. The rotated-bar graph displays the x-axis of the graph vertically, where the y-axis normally is, and the y-axis is placed at the bottom of the display. This rotation results in a bar graph in which the bars extend across the screen from left to right.

The 3-dimensional-bar graph is more visually appealing than a plain bar graph because the 3-dimensional-bar graph gives the effect of being three dimensional. This effect can be useful when you are using Quattro for a business presentation and want to vary graphing styles. To convert the current bar graph to a 3-dimensional-bar graph, first eliminate the interior labels and then choose **3**_Dimensional_**B**ar as the **G**raph_**T**ype (see fig. 10.24).

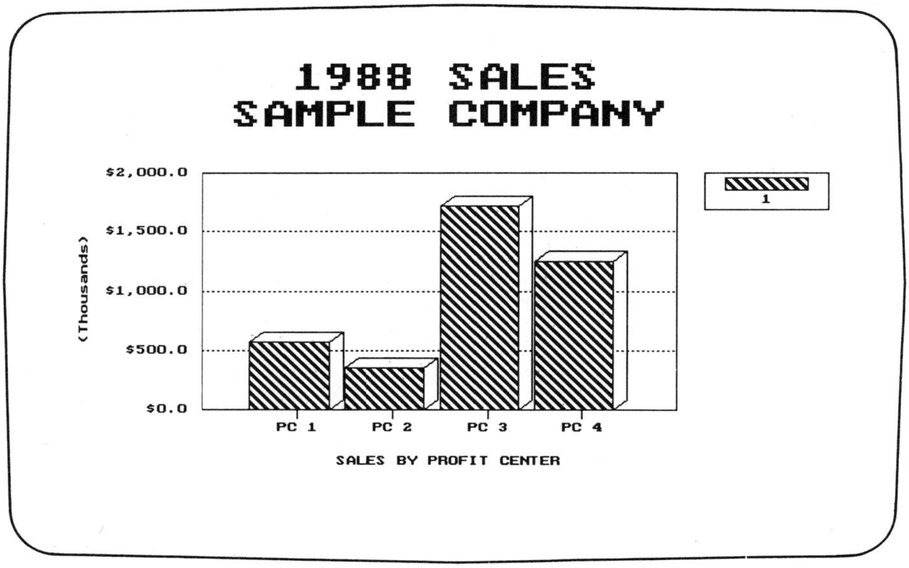

Fig. 10.24. A 3-dimensional-bar graph.

Be careful not to plot too many data series with 3-dimensional-bar graphs. If you do, the positive effect is lost, and the 3-dimensional effect actually becomes a distraction.

Pie Graphs

You can use a pie graph only for plotting a single data series in which all numbers are positive. The main Graph menu's **X**-Axis_Values and the **C**ustomize **P**ies commands are the only menu options that apply to a pie graph.

You create a pie graph by plotting each profit center's contribution to total sales. If you select /**G**raph **G**raph_Type **P**ie **V**iew, using the latest bar-graph settings, the graph in figure 10.25 is displayed.

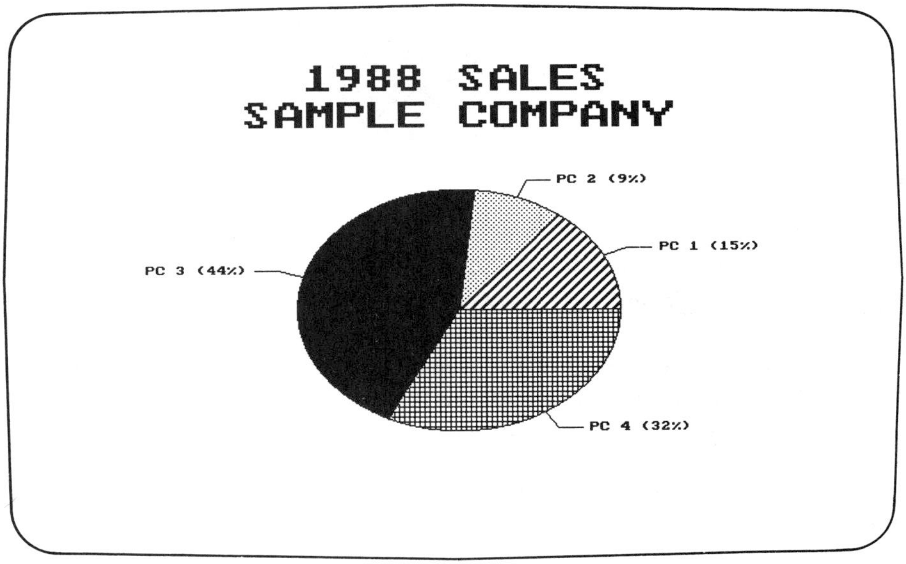

Fig. 10.25. A pie graph.

Quattro automatically calculates and displays in parentheses the percentage of the whole represented by each pie wedge. To suppress these percentages, use the /**G**raph **C**ustomize **P**ies **L**abel_Format **N**one command. Notice that the profit center labels, which you enter by using the main Graph menu's **X**-Axis_Values option, are the same as those on the bar graph.

You can change the shading or color with the **P**attern or **C**olor command from the menu displayed by the /**G**raph **C**ustomize **P**ies command. Quattro provides 12 different shading patterns for monochrome display and 128 different colors. You can display as many as 16 colors if you have an EGA or VGA color display and four colors on CGA color displays. Figure 10.26 shows some of the pie-graph shading patterns.

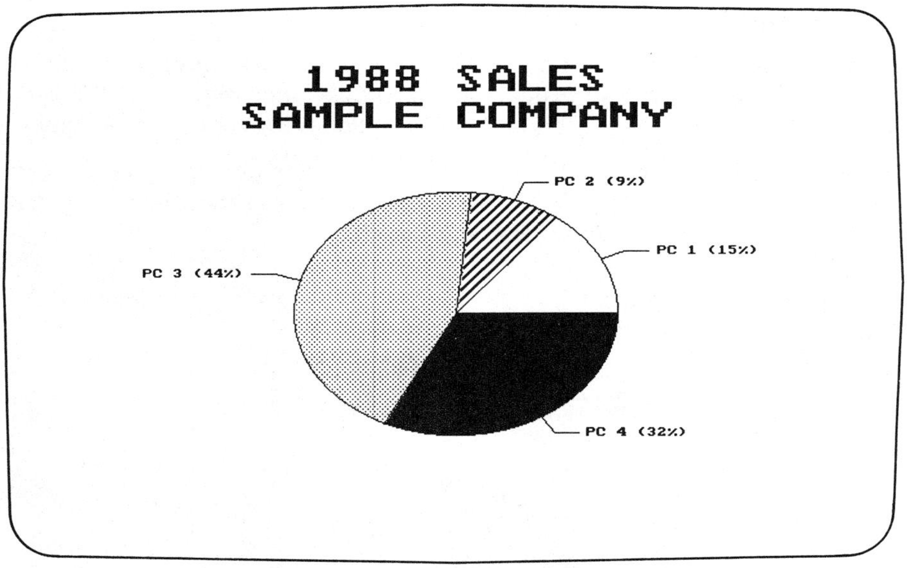

Fig. 10.26. Pie graph with customized shading patterns.

You can "explode" any or all of the wedges by using the /**G**raph **C**ustomize **P**ies **E**xplode command. To illustrate this feature, suppose that you emphasize Profit Center 3's top performance by exploding the 3rd_Series slice. Then select **V**iew to view the graph. As you can see from figure 10.27, the Profit Center 3 portion of the pie is now set apart (exploded) from the rest of the graph.

Marking each segment of the pie with an appropriate label is essential. In this case, you must label each profit center.

XY Graphs

The XY graph, also called a scatter plot, is a variation of a line graph. In this type of Quattro graph, two or more different data items from the same series values have the same x-axis value. Instead of showing time-series data, XY graphs illustrate the relationships of different attributes of data items: age and income, for example, or educational achievements and salary.

Think of one data item as the independent variable and consider the other item to be dependent on the first. Use the Graph menu's **X**-Axis_Values command to enter the independent variable and use one of the **1**st_ through **6**th_Series values options to enter the other item.

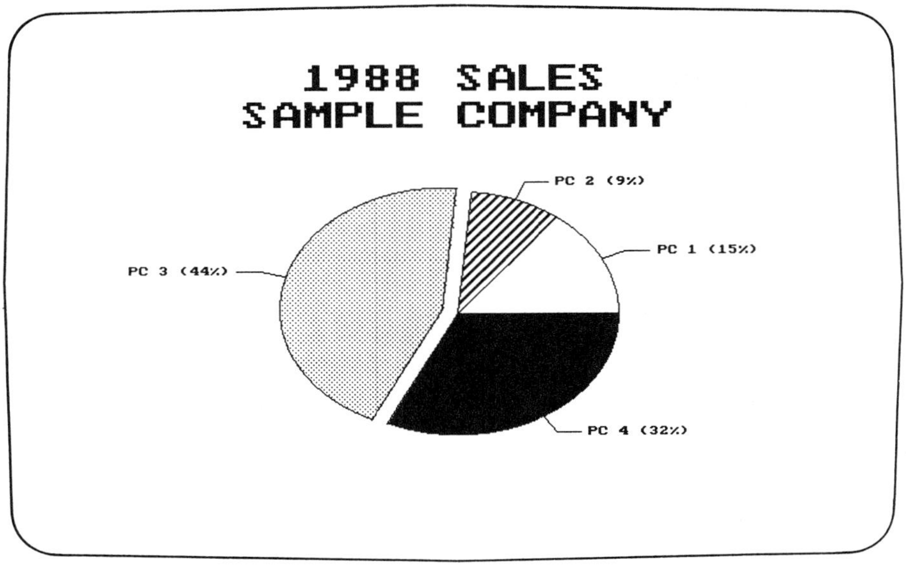

Fig. 10.27. An exploded pie graph.

Suppose that you want to create a graph that shows the correlation between the amount a profit center spends on advertising and the sales generated by that profit center. Somewhere in the spreadsheet, information is being tabulated to record each profit center's share of advertising dollars spent. To create an XY graph for Profit Center 1, use the sample % of Advertising Budget data for Profit Center 1 (see fig. 10.28) and the monthly sales data for Profit Center 1 from the worksheet in figure 10.15a and 10.15b.

Using the number of advertising dollars expended as the independent variable and sales as the dependent variable, you can construct an XY graph that includes titles and labels. To create the graph, issue the following command sequences:

/Graph	**R**eset **G**raph		
	Graph **T**ype **XY**		
	X-Axis Values **B17..B28**		
	Series Values **1**st Series **C4..N4**		
	Titles	**1**st-line	**SALES vs SHARE OF ADVERTISING**
		2nd-line	**PROFIT CENTER 1**
		X	**% of Advertising Budget**
	Customize **G**rids	**L**ine Type **N**one	
		View	

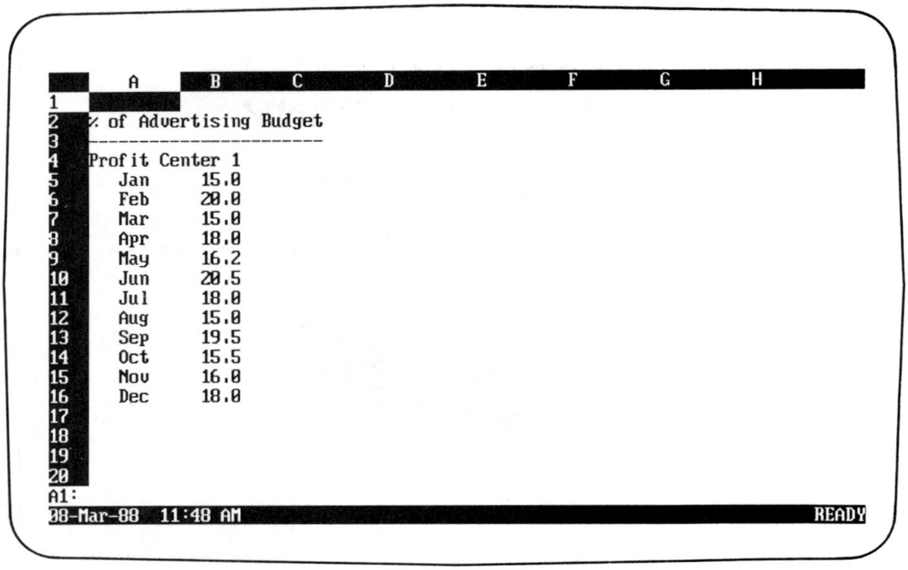

Fig. 10.28. Advertising data for comparison with sales data.

The initial XY graph should look like the one shown in figure 10.29.

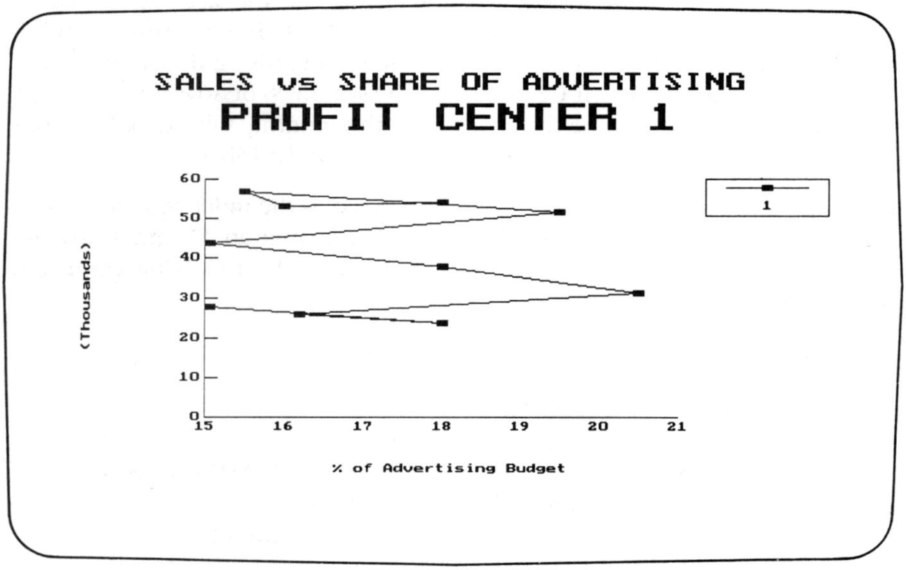

Fig. 10.29. XY graph showing advertising and sales data.

Because this graph displays the default lines typical of line graphs, using the graph to determine whether a relationship exists between the two data series plotted is difficult at best. But by overriding the XY graph with a markers graph, you can suppress display of the lines and make the graph easier to read. Assuming that the preceding XY graph with connecting lines is the current graph, issue the following command sequences:

/**G**raph **C**ustomize **S**eries **1**st Series
Override Type
Markers
View

The revised graph should resemble that shown in figure 10.30.

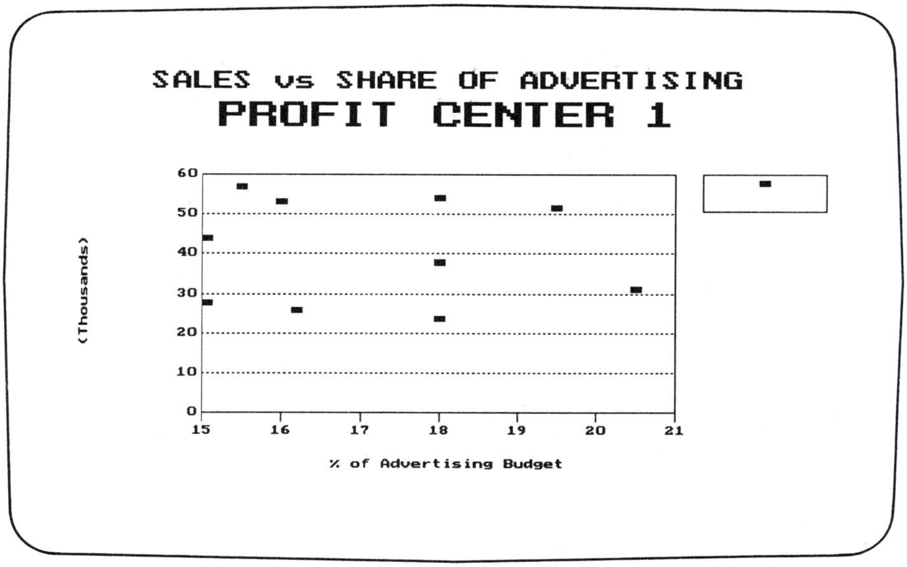

Fig. 10.30. The XY graph without lines (a scatter plot).

This XY graph without lines connecting the data points is called a scatter plot. If the symbols in a scatter plot seem to cluster along a single imaginary straight line among the data points, a strong relationship exists.

At first glance, the widely scattered data points in figure 10.30 seem to indicate no strong dependency of sales dollars on advertising dollars spent. Before you draw conclusions, however, manually set the lower scale limits of both axes to zero in order to avoid distortion in the graph due to scale differences. Use the following command sequences:

Customize	**X-Axis**	**Low 0**
		High .22
	Y-Axis	**Low 0**
		High 60000
		View

Then compare the results to figure 10.31.

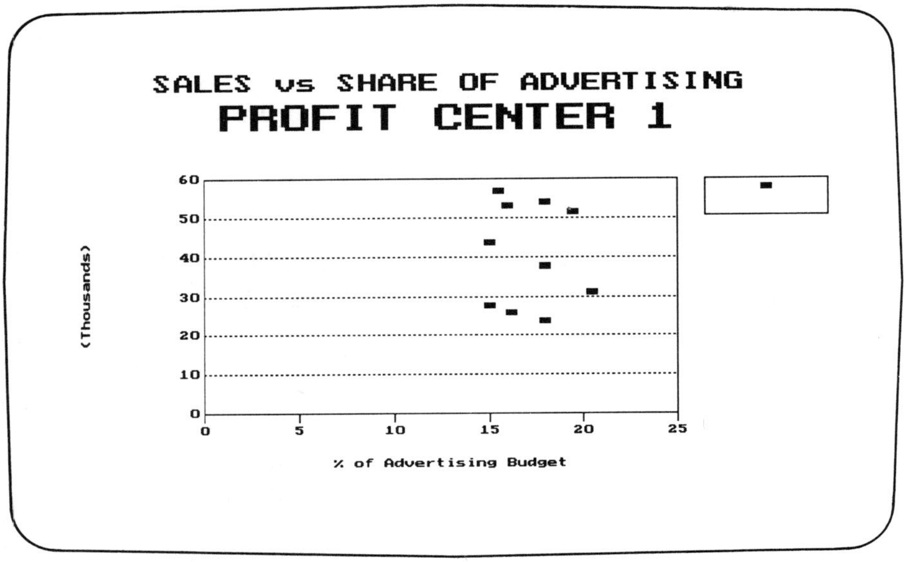

Fig. 10.31. The XY graph scaled proportionately.

Aren't you glad that you didn't jump to conclusions? As you can see, the revised graph seems to show a significant correlation between the sales generated and the advertising dollars expended for Profit Center 1 during 1987. (If you want to calculate data for a regression line to plot through the scattered symbols, use the /**A**dvance **R**egression command discussed in Chapter 15.)

Quattro's Graph Output

Unlike earlier generations of spreadsheets, Quattro has the capability to send graphs directly to a plotter or a printer. This capability is a great convenience over programs that require you to use an external graph-printing program. In addition to being more convenient, Quattro's graph printing commands are simpler to use because most of the information you see in the display of a Quattro graph can be sent directly to the output device. This feature simplifies immensely the task of printing graphs. Printing graphs is simpler because you do not have to exit Quattro and use a separate program to print graphs, which also had to be saved first.

To print a graph, you first must make it the current graph. The current graph is the graph displayed when you press F10 or choose one of the View commands.

You use the /Graph Print command to access the options on the main Graph Print menu. The options on this menu follow:

Option	*Effect*
Printers	Lets you select the graphics printer driver that best supports graphic output on your graphics output device
Destination	Gives you the option of sending the output to one of two printing devices or to a disk file
Layout	Defines the layout of the graph on a page
Colors	Allows you to modify the graph's output colors
Go	Prints the graph
Write EPS/PIC	Immediately creates a disk file you name in either PostScript or Lotus PIC file format, based on the current graph
Name	Names graph to print
Reset	Restores Graph Print settings to defaults
Update	Makes modifications to Graph Print definitions, just like Update on all menus

Before you print your first graph, you need to understand these options so that you can create the best Quattro setup for your graphics printer or plotter.

Selecting and Setting Up Printers

The command to set up graphics printers is /Graph Print Printers. Through the Printers command, you tell Quattro the kind of printer the program will be talking to and the way to treat this printer. You also use this option to select the resolution, which directly affects the speed and clarity of the graphics output.

Quattro accepts two graphics printing devices. If your graphics printing device is a plotter, you select **Plotter_Speed** from the menu. The prompt for this option instructs you to select a number from 0 to 9. The default is 0, which causes Quattro to send data to the hardware at the highest speed the hardware accepts. If you need to slow the device for special tasks, such as printing transparencies, use a low number, such as 2 or 3. The higher the number you select for **Plotter_Speed**, the faster the graphics output is.

The 1st_ and 2nd_Printer menus give you the options of setting up the communications parameters for a serial printer or plotter. You use the **Baud_Rate**, **Parity**, and **Stop_Bits** options. If you don't alter the default settings, Quattro uses the serial port settings initiated by the disk operating system. If the graphics printer is a parallel device, the serial settings are ignored.

Figure 10.32 shows some of the many printers supported by Quattro. One benefit of using Quattro is its support of PostScript laser printers, such as the Apple LaserWriter®.

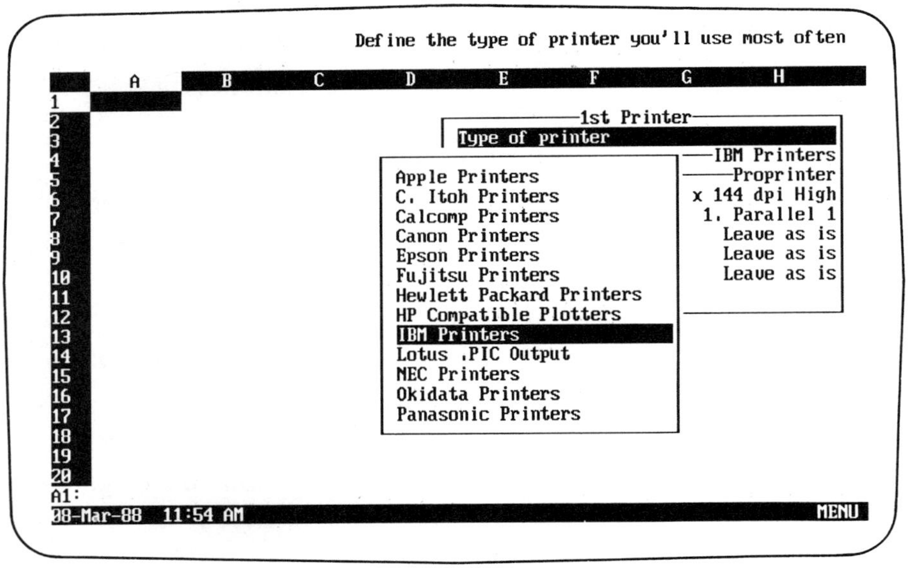

Fig. 10.32. Some of the printers supported by Quattro.

If your printer has more than one resolution option, you are prompted for the resolution. Figure 10.33 shows the resolution options for an IBM ProPrinter™.

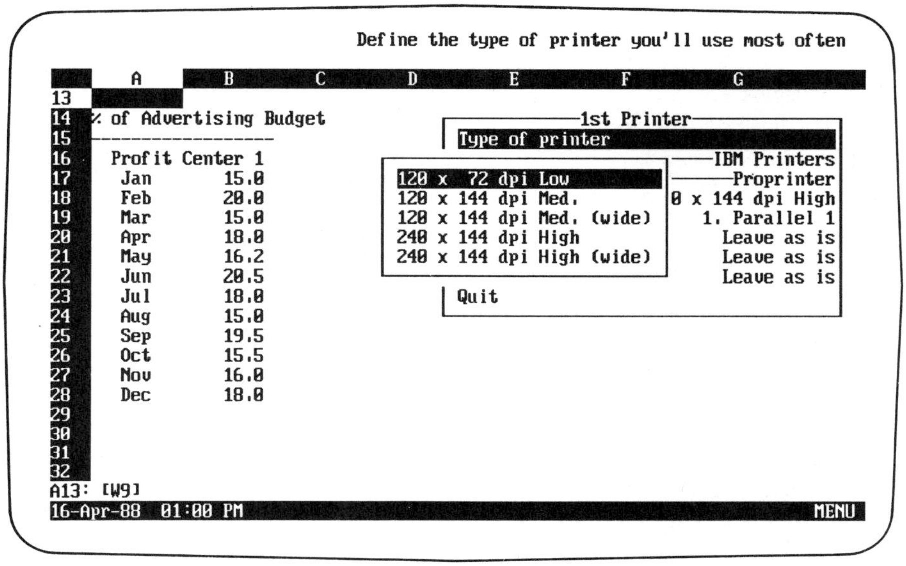

Fig. 10.33. Resolution options for the IBM ProPrinter.

Adjusting Graph Layout

Once you have told Quattro how to talk to your graphics printer, you may want to alter the way the graph is printed on the page. The **/Graph Print Layout** commands give you this capability.

When you first see the default settings, you may be a bit disconcerted to see that Quattro has set the **L**eft_Edge (margin), **T**op_Edge, **H**eight, and **W**idth all to 0. You may think that this setting produces a graph of no size at all. What actually results from the 0 settings is that Quattro makes the graph as large as possible, with no margins and no size restrictions.

To specify something other than the largest possible graph on a page, select the appropriate options and enter numbers in either inches or centimeters. The measurement system you use depends on the current setting of the **M**easurement command on the Layout menu. The default choice is inches. Figure 10.34 shows the Layout menu after the **L**eft_Edge and **T**op_Edge options have been modified to provide 1-inch and 1.5-inch margins, respectively.

Note also the **O**rientation option. This choice determines whether the graph is printed horizontally across the page in Landscape fashion or vertically on the page in Portrait fashion. The last option on the Layout menu is **B**reak_Page,

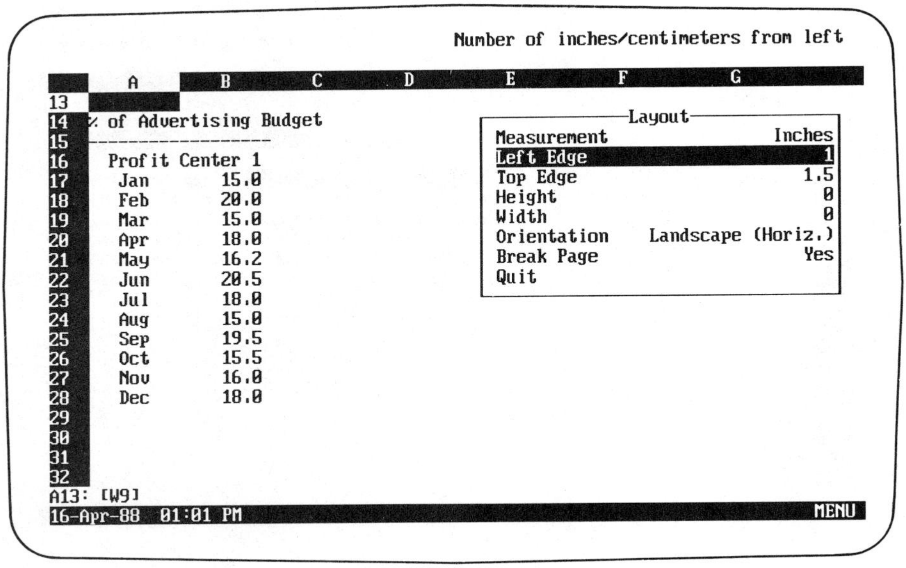

Fig. 10.34. Quattro's Layout menu.

which determines whether the page is advanced automatically after each graph is printed. Set this option to **N**o if you want to print more than one graph on a page.

You already may have been impressed by Quattro's effective use of colors in a graph. The graph printing commands continue this effectiveness by giving you control over the final color of the printed graph. The /**G**raph **P**rint **C**olors command lets you modify the colors of **P**ie and **S**eries graphs and the **T**itles, **F**rame, **G**rid, and **B**ackground colors (see fig. 10.35). If you modify the graph with the Colors menu commands, you can make these colors the default graph output colors by using the **U**pdate command on the Colors menu. If you want to override the default output colors with the screen colors, use the /**G**raph **P**rint **C**olors **C**opy_the_Screen's (colors) command.

Setting the Current Graph for Printing

Once the hardware, layout, and colors have been chosen, the next step is to make sure that the graph you want to print is the current graph. One way to make the graph current is to view the graph from one of the many graph menus that have a **V**iew option. Perhaps a surer method, however, is to use the /**G**raph **P**rint **N**ame command. This command lets you use a named graph setting as the current graph while you are in the graph-printing menu system. Figure 10.36 shows one of three named graphs being selected as the graph to print.

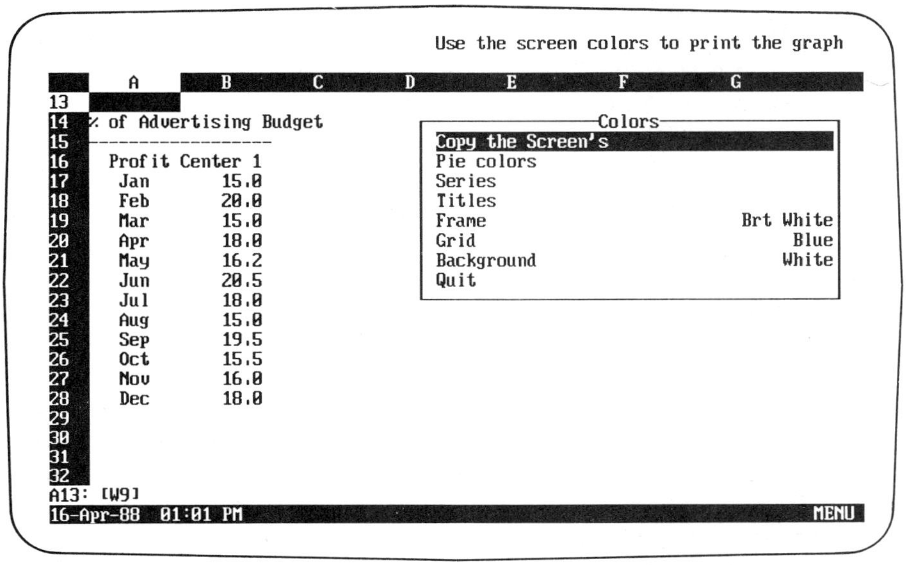

Fig. 10.35. The Colors menu.

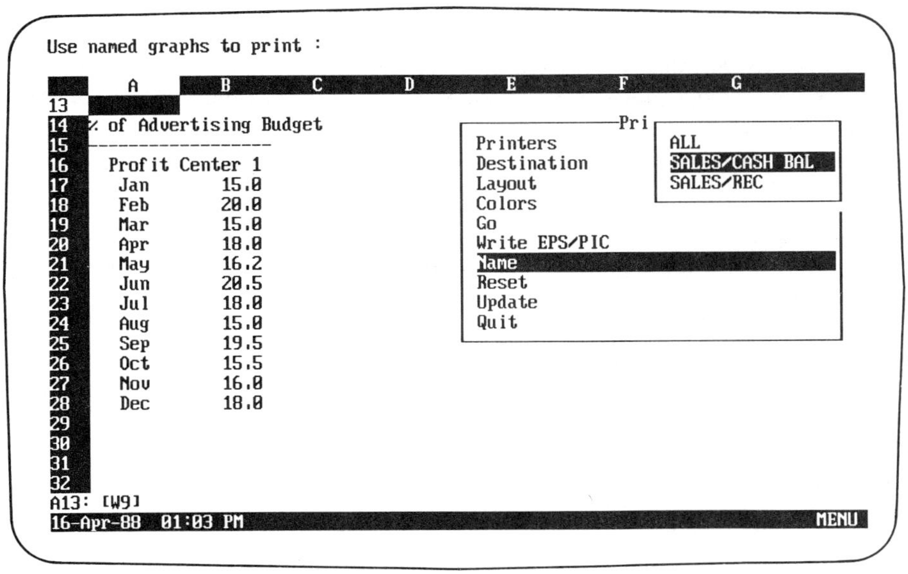

Fig. 10.36. Selecting a graph to print.

Now you're ready to print the graph. Printing can be done quite simply by selecting the **G**o command from the Graph Print menu. Quattro has several output options for your convenience. The **/G**raph **P**rint **D**estination command lets you specify which of two possible graphics devices you send the graph to. You also can tell Quattro that you want to save the graph in a file for later printing.

The **/G**raph **P**rint **D**estination **N**ame command lets you enter a file name for the graph. The default extension of the file name is .PRN. Also on the Destination menu is the **T**ype command. The **T**ype command controls the format used to store the graphic information in the file you name. This command gives you the option of sending a graph to a file at home, for instance, and printing the graph later on an expensive, high-quality laser printer.

The last output option on the Graph Print menu is the **W**rite_EPS/PIC command. You use this command to create a graph output file in PostScript (EPS) or Lotus format (PIC). When you select the **W**rite_EPS/PIC command, a submenu appears giving you the choice of the two file types. When you make a selection, you are prompted for a file name. Once you enter the file name, Quattro creates the file.

Chapter Summary

In this chapter, you saw how flexible and sophisticated Quattro graphics can be. You were introduced to the many options for setting up Quattro's graph environment with your screen hardware. You saw examples of the various graph types and learned when to use and how to set up each type. Significantly, you saw the relative simplicity of Quattro's integrated graph printing capability.

Now that you have completed this chapter, you probably have worked with both the spreadsheet and, of course, graphs. The next section in this book moves to more advanced aspects of Quattro: the database management commands. Specifically, the following chapter introduces the concept of a database and demonstrates how Quattro adds power to spreadsheets by providing sorting and database querying capabilities.

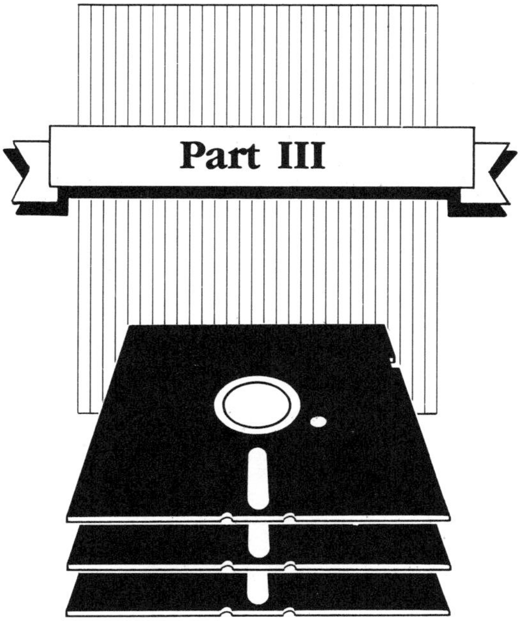

Part III

Managing Data with Quattro

Includes

Data Management

Quattro's Advanced Data Analysis Commands

CHAPTER

11

Data Management

In addition to the electronic spreadsheet and graphics, Quattro has a third capability: data management. Because the entire Quattro database resides in the spreadsheet within main memory (RAM), Quattro's database feature is fast, easy to access, and easy to use.

The increased speed is a result of the reduction in the time required to transfer data to and from disks. By doing all the work inside the spreadsheet, Quattro saves the time required for constant input and output to disk.

The Quattro database is easily accessed because Borland has made the entire database visible within the spreadsheet. You can view the contents of the whole database by using worksheet windows and cursor-movement keys to scroll through the database.

The ease of use is a result of integrating data management with the program's spreadsheet and graphics functions. The commands for adding, modifying, and deleting items in a database are the same ones you use for manipulating cells or groups of cells within a worksheet. And creating graphs from blocks in a database is as easy as creating them in a spreadsheet.

This chapter and the next deal with Quatro's data management capabilities. In particular, this chapter shows you how to

- Create a Quattro database
- Enter, modify, and maintain data records
- Carry out sort and query operations

What Is a Database?

A database is a collection of data organized so that you can list, sort, or search its contents. The database may contain any kind of information, from addresses to tax-deductible expenditures.

The smallest unit in a database is a *field*, or a single data item. For example, suppose that you want to develop an information base of present or potential corporate contributors for a not-for-profit organization. Your database might include the following fields of information:

Company Name

Company Address

ZIP Code

Contact Person

Phone Number

Last Contact Date

Contact Representative

Last Contribution Date

A database *record* is a collection of associated fields. In the preceding example, the accumulation of all data about one contributor forms one record.

In Quattro, a record is a row of cells within a database; a field is a single cell; and a database is a block of cells that spans at least one column and two rows. Although this definition does not distinguish between a database and any other block of cells, remembering that in Quattro a database is similar to any other group of cells will help you as you learn about the different /**A**dvanced **D**atabase commands covered in this chapter and the next. In many instances, you can use these database commands in what you may consider "nondatabase" applications, for example, as a checkbook register.

Because a database is actually a list, its manner of organization sets the database apart from ordinary blocks of cells. Just as a list must be organized to be useful, a database must be organized to permit access to the information it contains. Retrieval of information usually involves *key fields*. A database key field is any field on which you base a list, sort, or search operation. For example, you can use ZIP Code as a key field to sort the data in the contributor database and assign contact representatives to specific geographic areas. And you can prepare a follow-up contact list by searching the database for the key field Last Contact Date in which the date is less than one year ago.

What Can You Do with a Quattro Database?

The Quattro database has the spreadsheet's row-and-column format. Figure 11.1 shows the general organization of a Quattro database.

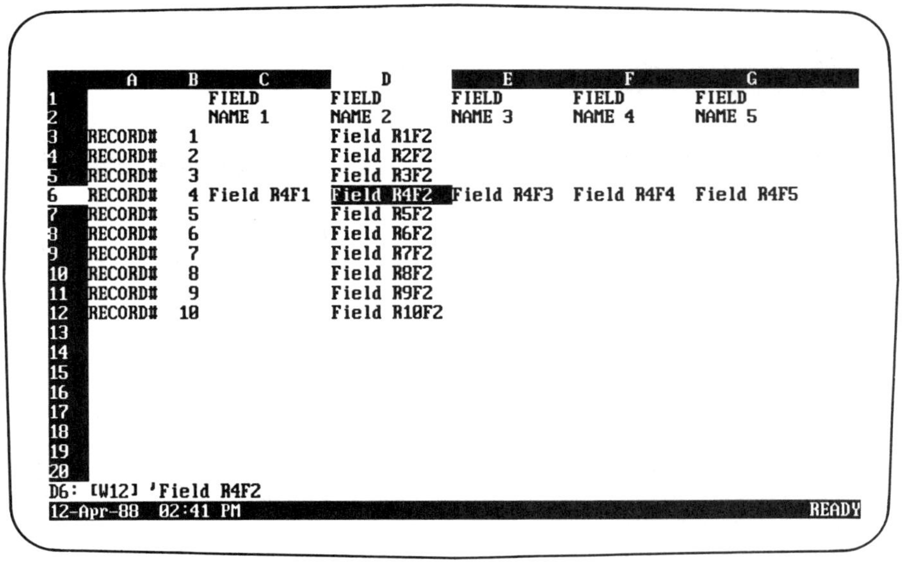

Fig. 11.1. Organization of the Quattro database.

Labels (field names) describing the data items appear as column headings. Information about each specific data item (field) is entered in a cell in the appropriate column. In figure 11.1, the highlighted cell (D6) represents data for the second field name in the database's fourth record.

In the Marketing Research database shown in figure 11.2, the highlighted row (row 5) contains the fields of information in the first record.

The major disadvantage of Borland's approach is the limitation imposed on the size of the database. With some popular database programs, you can get by with loading only portions of your database at once; with Quattro, the

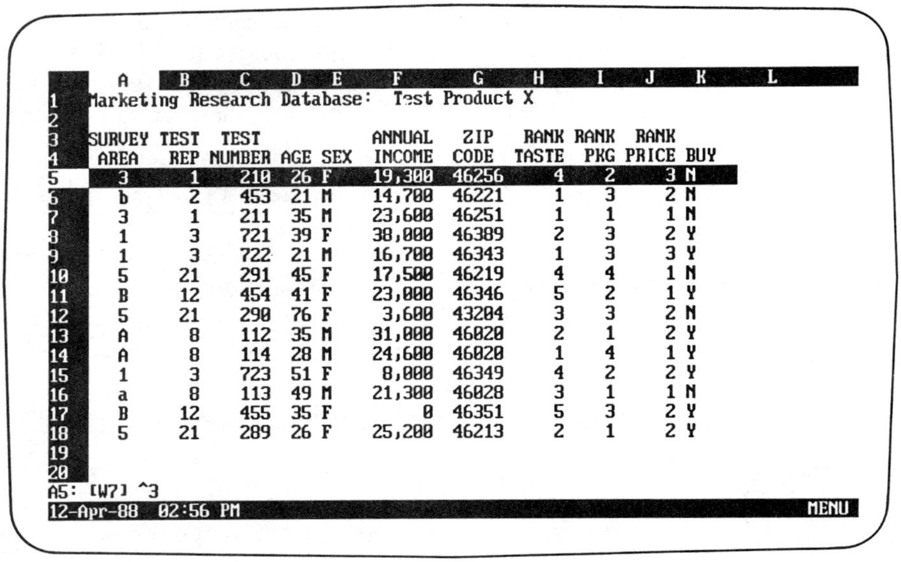

	A	B	C	D	E	F	G	H	I	J	K	L
1	Marketing Research Database: Test Product X											
2												
3	SURVEY	TEST	TEST			ANNUAL	ZIP	RANK	RANK	RANK		
4	AREA	REP	NUMBER	AGE	SEX	INCOME	CODE	TASTE	PKG	PRICE	BUY	
5	3	1	210	26	F	19,300	46256	4	2	3	N	
6	b	2	453	21	M	14,700	46221	1	3	2	N	
7	3	1	211	35	M	23,600	46251	1	1	1	N	
8	1	3	721	39	F	38,000	46389	2	3	2	Y	
9	1	3	722	21	M	16,700	46343	1	3	3	Y	
10	5	21	291	45	F	17,500	46219	4	4	1	N	
11	B	12	454	41	F	23,000	46346	5	2	1	Y	
12	5	21	290	76	F	3,600	43204	3	3	2	N	
13	A	8	112	35	M	31,000	46020	2	1	2	Y	
14	A	8	114	28	M	24,600	46020	1	4	1	Y	
15	1	3	723	51	F	8,000	46349	4	2	2	Y	
16	a	8	113	49	M	21,300	46028	3	1	1	N	
17	B	12	455	35	F	0	46351	5	3	2	Y	
18	5	21	289	26	F	25,200	46213	2	1	2	Y	
19												
20												

A5: [W7] ^3

12-Apr-88 02:56 PM MENU

Fig. 11.2. The first record in a database.

entire database must be loaded into memory before you can perform any data management operations.

Theoretically, the maximum number of records you can have in a Quattro database corresponds to the maximum number of rows in the spreadsheet (8,192 rows minus 1 row for the field names). Realistically, however, the number of records in a specific database is limited by the amount of available memory: internal memory (RAM), disk storage, and space allocated within the database to hold data extracted by Query commands.

If your computer has 640K of internal memory, you can store in a single database only about 800 400-byte (character) records or 6,000 50-byte records. Disk operating system commands and the Quattro program instructions occupy the remaining memory. (To provide a frame of reference, each record in the Marketing Research database shown in fig. 11.2 contains 67 characters.) For large databases, you need to extend the internal memory capacity beyond 640K by adding an expanded memory board, such as Intel's Above Board.

If you use floppy disks for storage of database files, you are limited to files that total less than 360,000 characters (1.2 million characters on a high-density 5 1/4-inch disk or 1.44 million on a high-density/high-capacity 3 1/2-inch disk). On a hard disk, a database of 4,000 500-byte records occupies two million characters, or two megabytes.

When you estimate the maximum database size you can use on your computer equipment, be sure to include enough blank rows to accommodate the maximum output you expect from activities such as the extract operations.

You access the menu of /Advanced Database commands from the main Quattro menu. If the database commands don't do everything you need, all the options on the main menu can be used as well on databases as on spreadsheets; thus, all the power of Quattro is at your fingertips.

If you prefer to use a specialized program—such as dBASE®, Paradox, or Reflex™—for your database, use Quattro's file-translation capabilities (see Chapter 8) to import files so that you can take advantage of Quattro's data and graphing commands.

If you can deal with Quattro's memory constraints and the somewhat time-consuming method of using menu options to manipulate data, you'll have a powerful data management tool.

When you select /Advanced from the Quattro menu, the following options are displayed in the Advanced menu box:

Database
What-If
Regression
Frequency
Matrix
Quit

The true data management operations, Sort and Query (search) options, are found under Database. Both Sort and Query are described in detail in this chapter. The other Advanced options (What-If, Regression, Frequency, and Matrix) are considered, more appropriately, data creation or analysis operations. They are described in the next chapter.

Creating a Database

You can create a database as a new file or as part of an existing spreadsheet. If you decide to build a database as part of an existing worksheet, choose a worksheet area that will not be needed for anything else. This area should be large enough to accommodate the number of records you plan to enter during the current session and in the future. If you add the database to the side of the spreadsheet, be careful about inserting or deleting spreadsheet rows that may also affect the database. If you add a database below an existing spreadsheet, be careful not to disturb predetermined column widths in the spreadsheet portion when you adjust column widths to the widths of database fields.

Setting Up a Database

After you have decided which area of a worksheet to use or decided to create a new file, you create a database by entering field names (column headers) across a row and entering data in cells as you would for any other Quattro application. The mechanics of entering database contents are simple; the most critical step in creating a useful database is planning your field names carefully.

Quattro's data retrieval techniques rely on locating data by field names. A common error in setting up a database is choosing a field name (and entering data) without thinking about the output you want from that field. For example, suppose that you establish GIFTDATE as a field name to describe the last date a contribution was made. Then you enter dates as labels, in the general form 'XX/XX/XX. Although you can search for a GIFTDATE that matches a specific date, you won't be able to perform a math-based search for all GIFTDATE entries within a specified period of time or before a certain date. To get maximum flexibility from Quattro's database commands, enter dates in your databases in the following form (see Chapter 6 for more information):

@DATE(year_number,month_number,day_number)

Before you begin listing the kinds of data items you think you may need, write down the output you expect from the database. For example, you might use the following information from the sample database:

Company Name

Company Address

Contact Person

Phone Number

Last Contact Date

Contact Representative

Last Contribution Date

You also need to consider any source documents that might provide input to the file. If you enter database content from a standard source document, such as a marketing research survey form, you can increase the speed of data entry by setting up the field names in the same order as the corresponding data items on the form.

When you are ready to set up your database, you must specify for each item a field name, the column width, and the type of entry.

Tip You also can use Ctrl-D for direct entry of dates. Press Ctrl-D; then type the date as a label (but without the apostrophe). As the entry format use 01-

Jan-88, 01-Jan, Jan-88, 01/01/88, or 01/01. Quattro automatically creates the numeric date equivalent and formats the display of the cell as a date.

You then need to determine how specific the information in each column will be, adjust the column width (if desired), and determine whether you will enter data as numbers or as labels. For example, if you want to sort by area code all records containing telephone numbers, you should enter telephone numbers as two separate fields (columns): area code (XXX) and the phone number XXX-XXXX. Entering the numbers as two separate fields allows for two different types of searches in the future. Because you will not need to perform math functions on telephone numbers, enter them as labels. Otherwise, Quattro will interpret the hyphen (-) as a minus sign.

Finally, be sure that the kind of data in each column of the database is consistent. That is, if you start a column with numeric data, all entries in that column must be numeric. This practice is called *data typing*. The data type is the kind of data a cell contains. Quattro supports three data types: numeric, string, and date. Unless a column's data type remains consistent, you cannot get accurate results from sorting and querying operations.

Entering Field Names and Formatting a Database

After you have planned your database, you can build it. To help you understand how the process works, consider a Marketing Research database created as a new database on a blank worksheet. Before you start to create a database, make sure that you are working in READY mode. After you select the appropriate area of the worksheet for the database, enter the field names across the top two rows (see fig. 11.3).

In the figure, the highlight bar rests on row 4, the field name row. The field names must be labels, even if they are the numeric labels '1, '2, etc. Although you can have more than one row for the field names, Quattro uses only the names that appear in the row directly above the first record in the database. For example, the first field name in the Marketing Research database (rows 3 and 4 of column A) is SURVEY AREA. Only AREA (the portion in row 4) will be referenced as a field name in sort and query operations.

Keep in mind that all field names should be unique; any duplication of names confuses Quattro when you search the database. The field names in figure 11.3 are acceptable because, although some words in row 3 are repeated (TEST and RANK), each field name in row 4 is unique.

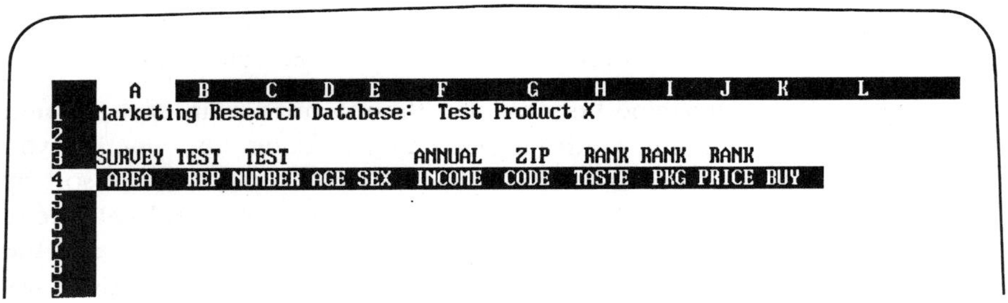

Fig. 11.3. Field names entered into a new database.

To control the manner in which cells are displayed, use Quattro's /**B**lock **D**isplay_Format and **C**olumn **W**idth options. (See Chapter 4 for a detailed discussion of these commands.) In figure 11.2, notice that the format in column F is comma (financial) with no decimal places and that column widths on the worksheet vary from 4 to 7 characters.

Note also that whenever a right-aligned column of numeric data is adjacent to a left-aligned column of label information (AGE and SEX or INCOME and CODE, for example), the data looks crowded. You can insert blank columns to change the spacing between fields; but if you plan to sort the database, do not leave any blank rows. Blank rows are sorted to the top of the database. If you have a large number of blank rows, you may think that you have lost the database because empty rows are at the top and valid data is pushed below the current display.

Entering Data

After you have set display formats, altered the column widths, entered field names, and added columns for spacing, you can enter records in the database. To enter the first record, move the cursor to the row directly below the field-name row; then enter the data across the row as you do any place in the spreadsheet.

In the sample Marketing Research database, the contents of the AREA, REP, NUMBER, SEX, CODE, and BUY fields are entered as labels; the contents of the AGE, INCOME, TASTE, PKG, and PRICE fields are entered as numbers. As a rule of thumb, you use numeric entries if you need to perform calculations on the data. Otherwise, enter data as labels. For example, you do not use area code data in formulas, so you can enter area codes as labels with no bad consequences. Figure 11.4 shows the initial data and the column spacing for this database.

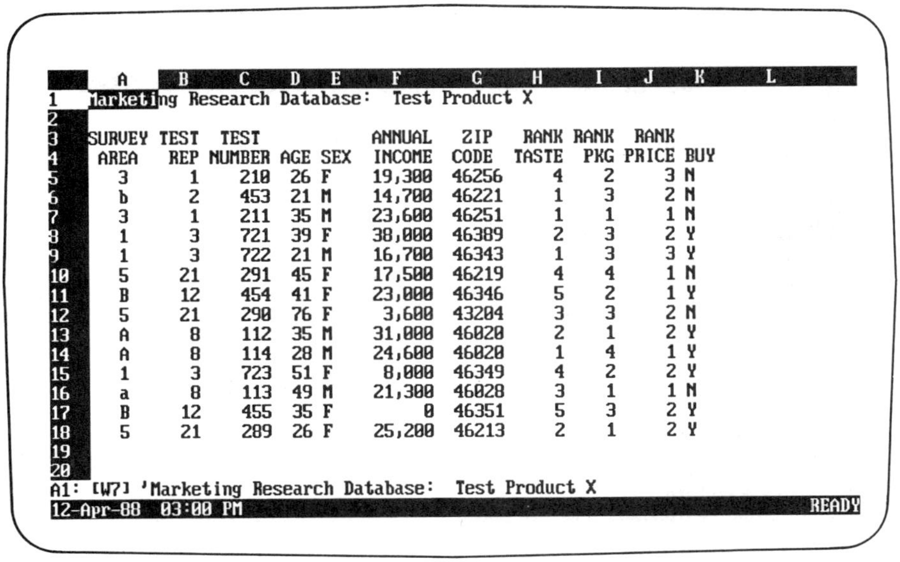

	A	B	C	D	E	F	G	H	I	J	K	L
1	Marketing Research Database: Test Product X											
2												
3	SURVEY	TEST	TEST			ANNUAL	ZIP	RANK	RANK	RANK		
4	AREA	REP	NUMBER	AGE	SEX	INCOME	CODE	TASTE	PKG	PRICE	BUY	
5	3	1	210	26	F	19,300	46256	4	2	3	N	
6	b	2	453	21	M	14,700	46221	1	3	2	N	
7	3	1	211	35	M	23,600	46251	1	1	1	N	
8	1	3	721	39	F	38,000	46389	2	3	2	Y	
9	1	3	722	21	M	16,700	46343	1	3	3	Y	
10	5	21	291	45	F	17,500	46219	4	4	1	N	
11	B	12	454	41	F	23,000	46346	5	2	1	Y	
12	5	21	290	76	F	3,600	43204	3	3	2	N	
13	A	8	112	35	M	31,000	46020	2	1	2	Y	
14	A	8	114	28	M	24,600	46020	1	4	1	Y	
15	1	3	723	51	F	8,000	46349	4	2	2	Y	
16	a	8	113	49	M	21,300	46028	3	1	1	N	
17	B	12	455	35	F	0	46351	5	3	2	Y	
18	5	21	289	26	F	25,200	46213	2	1	2	Y	
19												
20												

A1: [W7] 'Marketing Research Database: Test Product X

12-Apr-88 03:00 PM READY

Fig. 11.4. The new Marketing Research database.

This Marketing Research database is used periodically throughout the chapter to illustrate the results of using **D**ata commands. The fields are limited to a single screen display; but in real-life applications, you track many more data items. You can maintain as many as 256 fields (the number of columns available) in a Quattro database. You can use all 8,192 rows in the spreadsheet if you have enough memory.

Using the Form Input Command

You can help inexperienced users who may need to enter data into your Quattro database by using the /**A**dvanced **D**atabase **F**orm_Input command. With /**A**dvanced **D**atabase **F**orm_Input, you can limit the movement of the cell pointer to only the cells that you want available for editing and data entry. This limited area becomes a form-input area.

The **F**orm_Input command allows movement only to cells that have protection removed by the /**B**lock **A**dvanced **U**nprotect command. You must use the /**B**lock **A**dvanced **U**nprotect command when you set up the special form-entry areas mentioned previously. For example, suppose that you want to restrict the access to only the main database area of the employee database shown in figure 11.5. As part of the setup for form input, the database's cells have been unprotected.

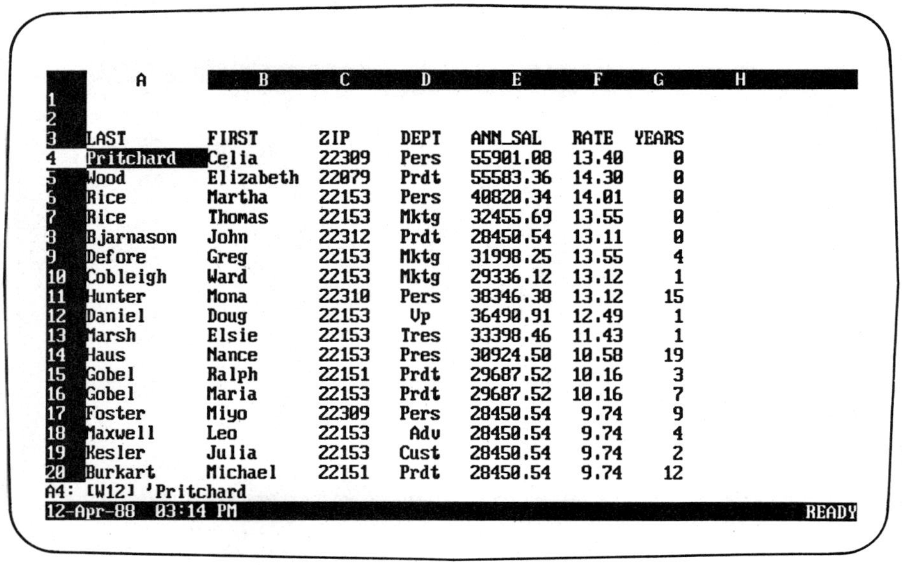

	A	B	C	D	E	F	G	H
1								
2								
3	LAST	FIRST	ZIP	DEPT	ANN_SAL	RATE	YEARS	
4	Pritchard	Celia	22309	Pers	55901.00	13.40	0	
5	Wood	Elizabeth	22079	Prdt	55583.36	14.30	0	
6	Rice	Martha	22153	Pers	40820.34	14.01	0	
7	Rice	Thomas	22153	Mktg	32455.69	13.55	0	
8	Bjarnason	John	22312	Prdt	28450.54	13.11	0	
9	Defore	Greg	22153	Mktg	31998.25	13.55	4	
10	Cobleigh	Ward	22153	Mktg	29336.12	13.12	1	
11	Hunter	Mona	22310	Pers	38346.38	13.12	15	
12	Daniel	Doug	22153	Vp	36490.91	12.49	1	
13	Marsh	Elsie	22153	Tres	33398.46	11.43	1	
14	Haus	Nance	22153	Pres	30924.50	10.58	19	
15	Gobel	Ralph	22151	Prdt	29687.52	10.16	3	
16	Gobel	Maria	22153	Prdt	29687.52	10.16	7	
17	Foster	Miyo	22309	Pers	28450.54	9.74	9	
18	Maxwell	Leo	22153	Adv	28450.54	9.74	4	
19	Kesler	Julia	22153	Cust	28450.54	9.74	2	
20	Burkart	Michael	22151	Prdt	28450.54	9.74	12	

A4: [W12] 'Pritchard

12-Apr-88 03:14 PM READY

Fig. 11.5. The employee database.

When you invoke the **Form_Input** command, Quattro prompts you to designate a data input block. In the example in figure 11.5, this block could be the block A1..G20 or the block A3..Z99. The exact size of the block doesn't matter, as long as the block includes all the unprotected cells. Figure 11.6 shows the input block as it is being defined by entering the cell references at the prompt.

After the block has been designated, the cell selector jumps immediately to cell A4 and waits for you to enter a number or label. The upper left corner of the input block is positioned at the upper left corner of the screen. In the example, the field names are not unprotected; yet, in order for the user to keep track of the columns, the field names are included in the overall form input block so that they will remain on-screen.

Don't press Enter to process the input; use one of the arrow keys. In the example, you might use the right arrow to move the cursor to G4. Notice that pressing the right arrow again causes the cell selector to jump to cell A5, automatically wrapping the cursor around to the next unprotected cell.

Once again, you will want to make a cell entry and use an arrow key to move on. The /**A**dvanced **D**atabase **F**orm_Input command remains in effect until you press the Enter key or the Esc key. When you press either key, the cell selector returns to the upper left corner of the input block, and the worksheet

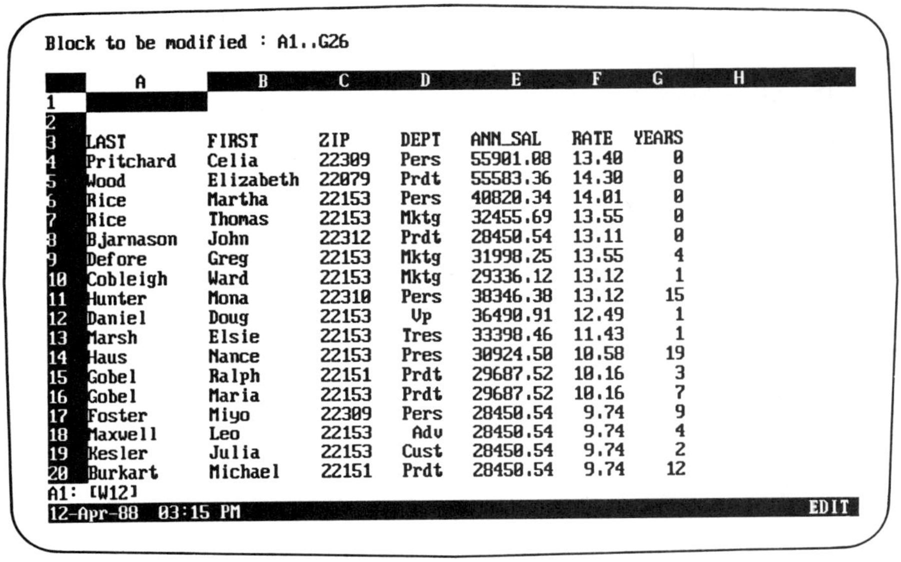

Block to be modified : A1..G26

	A	B	C	D	E	F	G	H
1								
2								
3	LAST	FIRST	ZIP	DEPT	ANN_SAL	RATE	YEARS	
4	Pritchard	Celia	22309	Pers	55901.08	13.40	0	
5	Wood	Elizabeth	22079	Prdt	55583.36	14.30	0	
6	Rice	Martha	22153	Pers	40820.34	14.01	0	
7	Rice	Thomas	22153	Mktg	32455.69	13.55	0	
8	Bjarnason	John	22312	Prdt	28450.54	13.11	0	
9	Defore	Greg	22153	Mktg	31998.25	13.55	4	
10	Cobleigh	Ward	22153	Mktg	29336.12	13.12	1	
11	Hunter	Mona	22310	Pers	38346.38	13.12	15	
12	Daniel	Doug	22153	Vp	36490.91	12.49	1	
13	Marsh	Elsie	22153	Tres	33398.46	11.43	1	
14	Haus	Nance	22153	Pres	30924.50	10.58	19	
15	Gobel	Ralph	22151	Prdt	29687.52	10.16	3	
16	Gobel	Maria	22153	Prdt	29687.52	10.16	7	
17	Foster	Miyo	22309	Pers	28450.54	9.74	9	
18	Maxwell	Leo	22153	Adv	28450.54	9.74	4	
19	Kesler	Julia	22153	Cust	28450.54	9.74	2	
20	Burkart	Michael	22151	Prdt	28450.54	9.74	12	

A1: [W12]
12-Apr-88 03:15 PM EDIT

Fig. 11.6. Defining the data input block.

returns to the same position on the screen as before the /**A**dvanced **D**atabase **F**orm_Input command was issued.

To automate the process of entering data in the database, include the /**A**dvanced **D**atabase **F**orm_Input command in a keyboard macro that executes automatically when a database is loaded. With this macro, a Quattro novice can enter information into the database with no risk of erasing or overwriting important information. (See Chapters 15 and 16 to learn how to create macros.)

Modifying a Database

Thanks to Quattro, maintaining the accuracy of the database content is as easy as creating the database.

To add and delete records in a database, you use the same commands for inserting and deleting rows that you use for any other application in Quattro. Because records correspond to rows, you begin inserting a record with the /**R**ow **I**nsert command. You then fill in the various fields in the rows with the appropriate data. Figure 11.7 shows an example of inserting a record in the middle of the Marketing Research database.

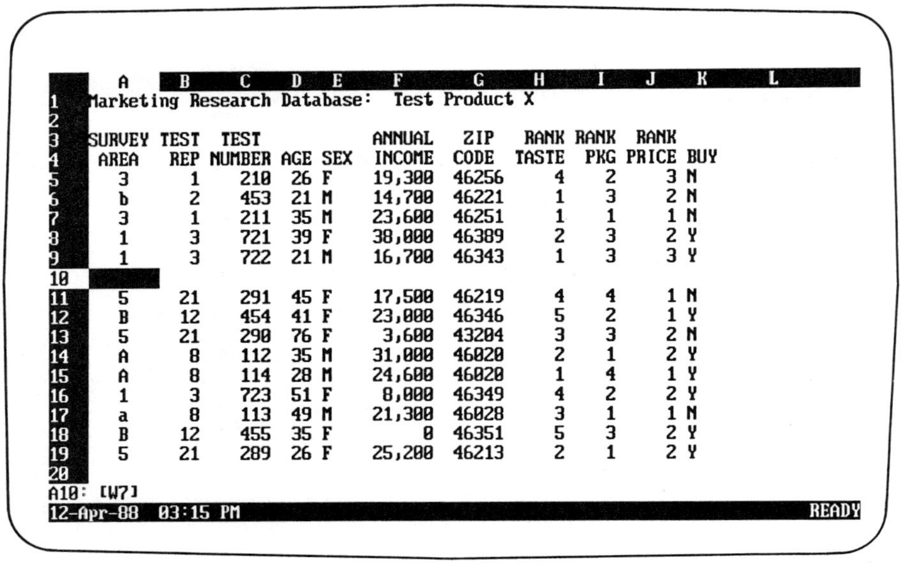

	A	B	C	D	E	F	G	H	I	J	K
1	Marketing Research Database: Test Product X										
2											
3	SURVEY	TEST	TEST			ANNUAL	ZIP	RANK	RANK	RANK	
4	AREA	REP	NUMBER	AGE	SEX	INCOME	CODE	TASTE	PKG	PRICE	BUY
5	3	1	210	26	F	19,300	46256	4	2	3	N
6	b	2	453	21	M	14,700	46221	1	3	2	N
7	3	1	211	35	M	23,600	46251	1	1	1	N
8	1	3	721	39	F	38,000	46389	2	3	2	Y
9	1	3	722	21	M	16,700	46343	1	3	3	Y
10											
11	5	21	291	45	F	17,500	46219	4	4	1	N
12	B	12	454	41	F	23,000	46346	5	2	1	Y
13	5	21	290	76	F	3,600	43204	3	3	2	N
14	A	8	112	35	M	31,000	46020	2	1	2	Y
15	A	8	114	28	M	24,600	46020	1	4	1	Y
16	1	3	723	51	F	8,000	46349	4	2	2	Y
17	a	8	113	49	M	21,300	46028	3	1	1	N
18	B	12	455	35	F	0	46351	5	3	2	Y
19	5	21	289	26	F	25,200	46213	2	1	2	Y
20											

A10: [W7]

12-Apr-88 03:15 PM READY

Fig. 11.7. Inserting a record into a database.

To delete records, move your cell selector to the row or rows you want to delete and use the /**R**ow **D**elete command. Because you do not have an opportunity to verify the block before you issue the command, be extremely careful when you specify the records to be deleted. If you want to remove only inactive records, consider first using the **E**xtract command from the Query menu in order to store the extracted inactive records in a separate file before you delete the records (see "Searching for Records" in this chapter).

To add a new field to a database, position the cell selector anywhere in the column that will be to the right of the inserted column. Issue /**C**olumn **I**nsert command, and then fill the field with values for each record. For example, to insert a DATE field between the NUMBER and AGE fields in the Marketing Research database, position the cell selector on any cell in the AGE column, issue the /**C**olumn **I**nsert command, and then type the new field name in D3 and D4 (see fig. 11.8).

Because maintaining data is costly in time and computer memory, you may not feel justified keeping certain seldom-used data fields in the database. To delete the TEST DATE field, for instance, position the cell selector anywhere in that column and then use the /**C**olumn **D**elete command.

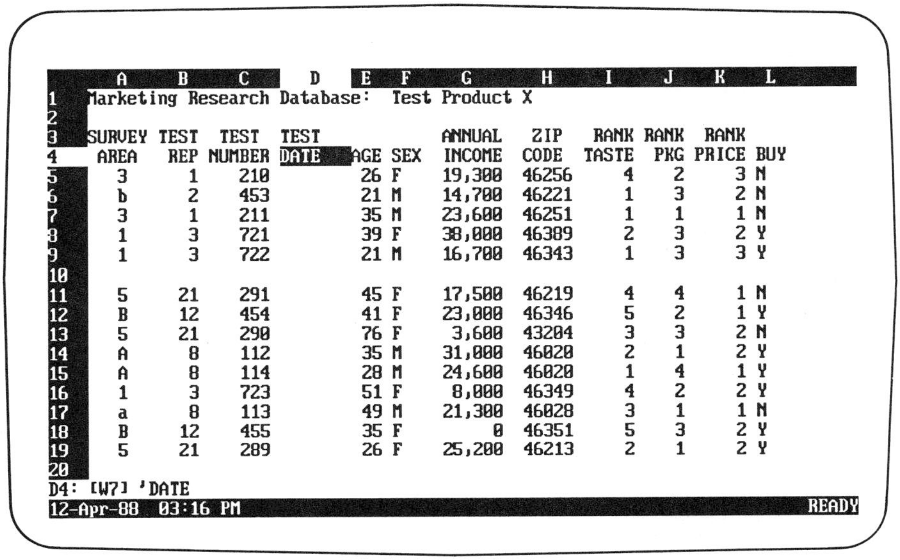

	A	B	C	D	E	F	G	H	I	J	K	L
1	Marketing Research Database: Test Product X											
2												
3	SURVEY	TEST	TEST	TEST			ANNUAL	ZIP	RANK	RANK	RANK	
4	AREA	REP	NUMBER	DATE	AGE	SEX	INCOME	CODE	TASTE	PKG	PRICE	BUY
5	3	1	210		26	F	19,300	46256	4	2	3	N
6	b	2	453		21	M	14,700	46221	1	3	2	N
7	3	1	211		35	M	23,600	46251	1	1	1	N
8	1	3	721		39	F	38,000	46389	2	3	2	Y
9	1	3	722		21	M	16,700	46343	1	3	3	Y
10												
11	5	21	291		45	F	17,500	46219	4	4	1	N
12	B	12	454		41	F	23,000	46346	5	2	1	Y
13	5	21	290		76	F	3,600	43204	3	3	2	N
14	A	8	112		35	M	31,000	46020	2	1	2	Y
15	A	8	114		28	M	24,600	46020	1	4	1	Y
16	1	3	723		51	F	8,000	46349	4	2	2	Y
17	a	8	113		49	M	21,300	46028	3	1	1	N
18	B	12	455		35	F	0	46351	5	3	2	Y
19	5	21	289		26	F	25,200	46213	2	1	2	Y
20												

D4: [W7] 'DATE
12-Apr-88 03:16 PM READY

Fig. 11.8. Inserting a field into a database.

The process of modifying the contents of database fields is the same as that for modifying the contents of cells in any other Quattro application. As you learned in Chapter 3, you change the cell contents either by retyping the cell entry or by using the F2 (Edit) key and editing the entry.

All other commands, such as those for moving cells, formatting cells, displaying the contents of worksheets, and so on, are the same for the database and other spreadsheet applications.

Sorting Database Records

Quattro's data management capability lets you change the order of records by sorting them according to the contents of the fields. Selecting /**A**dvanced **D**atabase **S**ort produces the following command menu:

Block
1st_Key
2nd_Key
3rd_Key
4th_Key
5th_Key
Go

Reset
Sort_Order
Quit

To sort the database, start by designating a sort block. This block must be long enough to include all the records to be sorted and wide enough to include all the fields in each record. If you sort only some of the columns of a database, you destroy the relationships within the records. Remember not to include the field-name row in this block; otherwise, the field-name row will be sorted with the other records in the database. (If you are unfamiliar with how to designate or name blocks, see Chapter 4.)

The block does not have to include all the rows in the database. If part of the database already has the organization you want, or if you don't want to sort all the records, you can sort only a portion of the database.

Tip Remember: When you sort, do not include the field names in your block.

After specifying the sort block, you must specify the keys for the sort. *Keys* are the fields to which you attach the highest priority when the database is sorted. The field with the highest priority is the 1st Key, and the field with the next highest priority is the 2nd Key. For example, to sort by last name and then by department, indicate last name as the 1st key and department as 2nd key. You must set a 1st Key, but other sort keys are optional. After selecting the key fields, you must choose between ascending and descending order.

Tip Sorting database records is equivalent to moving the rows. As a precaution (to allow you to restore the data to its original order), save the database with /**F**ile **S**ave before you issue a **S**ort command.

Adjusting the Sort Order

Quattro's **S**ort_Order command gives you the capability to change the program's basic sorting rules. For instance, by default Quattro puts numbers before labels when sorting in ascending order. No law of the universe says that you must adhere to this order; and for your purposes sorting labels with a higher priority than numbers may be more convenient. To modify the basic order, choose **S**ort_Order and then **N**umbers_before_Labels from the Sort Order menu. Then, you can choose Yes or No to suit your needs.

In addition to giving priority to numbers or labels, you also can select a true alphabetic sort or a sort based on the ASCII numbers of the characters. Most of the time, alphabetic sort is preferred. Figure 11.9 shows the Sort Order menu and its options.

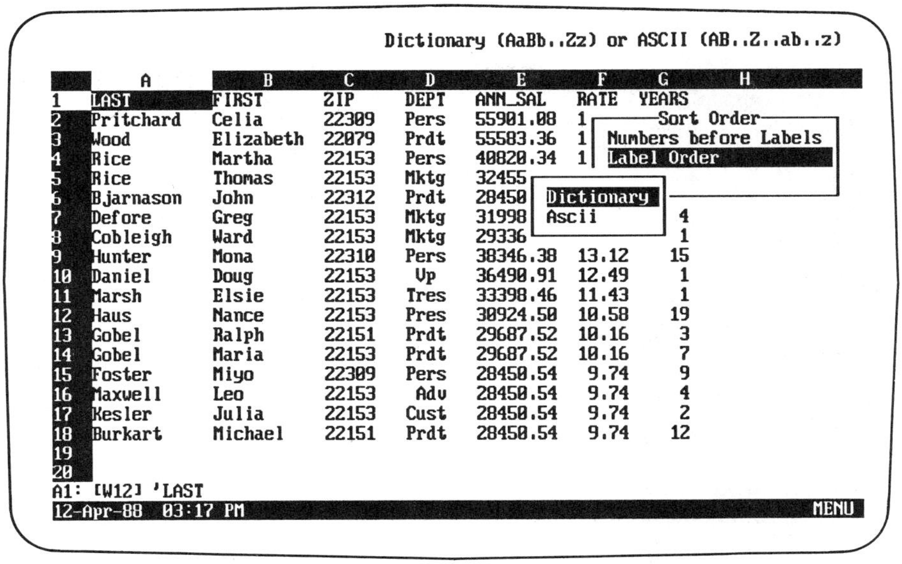

Fig. 11.9. The Sort Order menu.

ASCII sorting is case-sensitive sorting: uppercase letters are all sorted before lowercase letters in an ascending sort. **D**ictionary sorting ignores case. The **D**ictionary and **N**umbers_before_Labels options both sort in the following order:

Blank spaces

Special characters (!, #, $, etc.)

Numeric Characters (1, 2, 3, 4, etc.)

Alpha Characters (A, b, etc.)

Using a One-Key Sort

A simple example of a database sorted according to a primary key (often called a single-key database) is a dictionary. All the entries in the dictionary are sorted in ascending alphabetical order using the defined word as the primary key. Ascending order means that data is sorted from the lowest to the highest value (1, 2, 3, etc.) or label (A, B, C, etc.). Descending order moves from the highest to the lowest (10, 9, 8, etc., and Z, Y, X, etc.)

An ascending alphabetical sort can be used to reorder the records in the address database shown in figure 11.10.

	A	B	C	D	E	F
1	LAST	FIRST	STREET ADDRESS	CITY	STATE	ZIP
2	Harrington	James	12344 Arlington Lane	Covington	KY	41011
3	Thomas	Brian	18499 Central Park Ave.	New York	NY	12945
4	Leugers	Karen	21 Hill St. Apt. 34	San Fancisco	CA	34892
5	Englert	Michael	234 Orange St.	Buffalo	NY	13427
6	Smith	Margaret	2341 Kyles Lane	Hoboken	NJ	00125
7	Pryor	Aaron	2341 Milford St.	Cincinnati	OH	45209
8	Cleary	Esther	238 Higgins St. Apt 14	Spokane	WA	89042
9	Wolf	Barbara	3098 Arnold Ave.	Dallas	TX	57820
10	Wright	Ned	31238 Carolina St.	Kettering	OH	43289
11	Saunders	Ronald	3214 Keystone Ave.	Indianapolis	IN	46250
12	McGruder	Mary	331 Park Lane Apt. 32	Raleigh	NC	23459
13	Simpson	Jeremy	3509 Ludlow Ave.	Newport	KY	43892
14	Rooney	Kevin	391 Atwater Ave. Apt. 3	Providence	RI	02912
15	Franks	Mike	4284 Knight Circle	Rochester	NY	09025
16	Sorrenson	Sarah	432 Keys Crescent	Bloomington	IN	47401
17	Holland	Earl	4983 Drake Rd.	Cincinnati	OH	45243
18	Tuke	Samuel	9038 Greenup St.	Seekonk	RI	02915
19	Malvern	Thomas	939 Dime Circle	Nashville	TN	47341
20						

A1: [W12] 'LAST

14-Apr-88 10:56 AM READY

Fig. 11.10. The address database.

You can use Quattro's sorting capability to reorder records alphabetically on the LAST name field. Select /**A**dvanced **D**atabase **S**ort **B**lock. At the prompt for a block to sort, respond with A2..F19.

After you specify the sort block, the Advanced Database Sort menu returns to the screen. This menu is one of Quattro's "sticky" menus. (The Print menu is another.) Sticky menus remain displayed and active until you choose **Q**uit or press Esc. This sticky menu is helpful because you don't have to choose /**A**dvanced **D**atabase **S**ort at the beginning of each command.

After specifying the sort block, select **1**st_Key and then enter or point to the address of any entry in the column containing the **1**st_Key field. Remember that in this case you can point to blank or field-name cells. For example, you can enter A1 as the **1**st_Key in the address database. Quattro then asks you to enter a sort order (**A**scending or **D**escending). For this example, choose **A**scending order and press Enter. Finally, you choose **G**o from the menu to execute the sort. Figure 11.11 shows the address database sorted in ascending alphabetical order by last name.

You can add a record to an alphabetized name-and-address database without having to insert a row in order to place the new record in the proper position. Simply add the new record to the bottom of the current database, expand the sort block, and then sort the database again by last name.

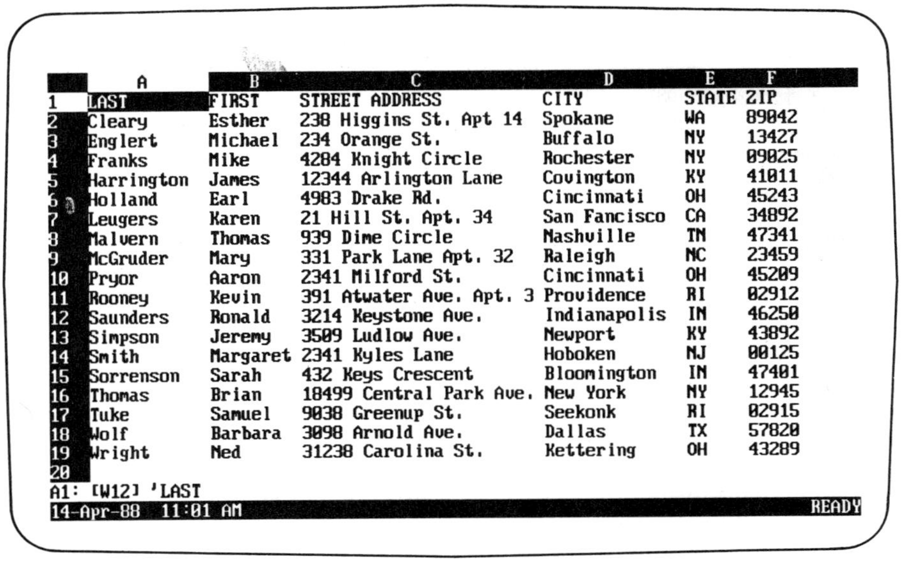

	A	B	C	D	E	F
1	LAST	FIRST	STREET ADDRESS	CITY	STATE	ZIP
2	Cleary	Esther	238 Higgins St. Apt 14	Spokane	WA	89842
3	Englert	Michael	234 Orange St.	Buffalo	NY	13427
4	Franks	Mike	4284 Knight Circle	Rochester	NY	09825
5	Harrington	James	12344 Arlington Lane	Covington	KY	41011
6	Holland	Earl	4983 Drake Rd.	Cincinnati	OH	45243
7	Leugers	Karen	21 Hill St. Apt. 34	San Fancisco	CA	34892
8	Malvern	Thomas	939 Dime Circle	Nashville	TN	47341
9	McGruder	Mary	331 Park Lane Apt. 32	Raleigh	NC	23459
10	Pryor	Aaron	2341 Milford St.	Cincinnati	OH	45209
11	Rooney	Kevin	391 Atwater Ave. Apt. 3	Providence	RI	02912
12	Saunders	Ronald	3214 Keystone Ave.	Indianapolis	IN	46250
13	Simpson	Jeremy	3509 Ludlow Ave.	Newport	KY	43892
14	Smith	Margaret	2341 Kyles Lane	Hoboken	NJ	00125
15	Sorrenson	Sarah	432 Keys Crescent	Bloomington	IN	47401
16	Thomas	Brian	18499 Central Park Ave.	New York	NY	12945
17	Tuke	Samuel	9038 Greenup St.	Seekonk	RI	02915
18	Wolf	Barbara	3098 Arnold Ave.	Dallas	TX	57820
19	Wright	Ned	31238 Carolina St.	Kettering	OH	43289
20						

A1: [W12] 'LAST

14-Apr-88 11:01 AM READY

Fig. 11.11. The sorted address database.

Sorting on Two or More Keys

Quattro can handle as many as five-key sorts. The key with highest priority is called the primary key; others are secondary keys. Your telephone book's Yellow Pages provide an example of sorting on more than one key. Records are sorted first according to business type (the primary key), then by business name (secondary key), and third by address (secondary key).

For practice with a two-key sort (first by one key and then by another key within the first sort order), refer again to the address database. This database can be reordered so that records are sorted first by state and then by city within state.

You designate the block A2..F19 as the sort block. Select **1st_Key** from the Sort menu and enter E1 as the field location of the initial sort key. (Remember that you can specify any cell in column E.) Choose **A**scending order for the sort by STATE. Select **2nd_Key**, enter D1, and choose **A**scending sort order by CITY. Figure 11.12 shows the results of issuing the **G**o command after you have specified the two-key sort.

As you can see, records are now grouped first by state in alphabetical order (California, Indiana, Kentucky, and so on) and then by city within state (Bloomington, Indiana, before Indianapolis, Indiana). When you determine

	A	B	C	D	E	F
1	LAST	FIRST	STREET ADDRESS	CITY	STATE	ZIP
2	Leugers	Karen	21 Hill St. Apt. 34	San Fancisco	CA	34892
3	Sorrenson	Sarah	432 Keys Crescent	Bloomington	IN	47401
4	Saunders	Ronald	3214 Keystone Ave.	Indianapolis	IN	46250
5	Simpson	Jeremy	3509 Ludlow Ave.	Newport	KY	43892
6	Harrington	James	12344 Arlington Lane	Covington	KY	41011
7	McGruder	Mary	331 Park Lane Apt. 32	Raleigh	NC	23459
8	Smith	Margaret	2341 Kyles Lane	Hoboken	NJ	00125
9	Thomas	Brian	10499 Central Park Ave.	New York	NY	12945
10	Englert	Michael	234 Orange St.	Buffalo	NY	13427
11	Franks	Mike	4204 Knight Circle	Rochester	NY	09025
12	Holland	Earl	4903 Drake Rd.	Cincinnati	OH	45243
13	Pryor	Aaron	2341 Milford St.	Cincinnati	OH	45209
14	Wright	Ned	31230 Carolina St.	Kettering	OH	43289
15	Tuke	Samuel	9038 Greenup St.	Seekonk	RI	02915
16	Rooney	Kevin	391 Atwater Ave. Apt. 3	Providence	RI	02912
17	Malvern	Thomas	939 Dime Circle	Nashville	TN	47341
18	Wolf	Barbara	3098 Arnold Ave.	Dallas	TX	57820
19	Cleary	Esther	238 Higgins St. Apt 14	Spokane	WA	89042
20						

A1: [W12] 'LAST

31-Jan-88 04:37 PM READY

Fig. 11.12. The address database after a two-key sort.

whether to use 1st, 2nd, or higher sort keys, be sure to request a reasonable sort. For example, do not try to sort first on city and then on state within city. Also, whenever possible, you may want to have the key fields as the leftmost fields in your database. By having the key fields as the first one or two fields in the database, you won't have to hunt for the results of the sort. As in the example, however, you'll find that this visual advantage isn't always feasible.

The capability to sort on more than two keys can be useful when you have several columns in which you may have sorting "ties." For example, suppose that you want to reorder the four fields of student information in the college database shown (in part) in figure 11.13.

You can reorder the records to sort first on MAJOR field of study (1st Key), then on SEX within each field of study (2nd Key), and then on AGE within each group of male or female students (3rd Key). Although subdividing each age group into the STATUS of full- or part-time student is not particularly significant in this small sample database, you can add additional sorts within sorts when appropriate.

To generate four-key sorts, you simply identify the key columns to sort in their order of precedence and specify ascending or descending order, just as you do for a one- or two-key sort.

Column to be used as first sort key : B1

	A	B	C	D	E	F	G	H
1	STATUS	MAJOR	SEX	AGE				
2	Full	Accounting	M	22				
3	Part	Finance	F	19				
4	Full	Accounting	F	27				
5	Full	Marketing	F	33				
6	Full	Administration	M	20				
7	Part	Finance	M	19				
8	Part	Accounting	F	26				
9	Full	Accounting	F	35				
10	Full	Marketing	F	19				
11	Full	Accounting	F	20				
12	Full	Finance	M	19				
13	Full	Finance	M	31				
14	Full	Finance	M	26				
15	Part	Accounting	F	29				
16	Full	Accounting	F	42				
17	Part	Accounting	M	27				
18	Part	Finance	F	48				
19	Part	Marketing	F	33				
20	Part	Administration	M	19				

B1: [W16] 'MAJOR

12-Apr-88 03:29 PM CAPS NUM POINT

Fig. 11.13. The college database before sorting.

In the sorted database (fig. 11.14), notice that major fields of study are grouped alphabetically, that study fields are subdivided into female and male categories, and that each subgroup is further sorted by age. For example, the six female accounting majors rank in age from 20 to 42 years. Splitting a duplicate age (Finance M 19 or Marketing F 33, for example) into a fourth subdivision (by status) does not produce meaningful data.

Restoring the Presort Order

Look at the Marketing Research database shown in figure 11.15. If you sort the original contents of the database on any field, such as the REP field, you cannot restore the records to their original order. If you add a record-number column to the database before any sort, however, you can sort the records on any field and then restore the original order by resorting on the record number field.

Figure 11.16 shows the record-number field NUM, which has been added in column A. After you have sorted the database on another column, you can sort again on the NUM field to restore the records to their original order. Another way to restore sort order is to use Transcript, the add-in program supplied with Quattro. Transcript can add an UNDO capability to Quattro (see Chapter 14 for more information).

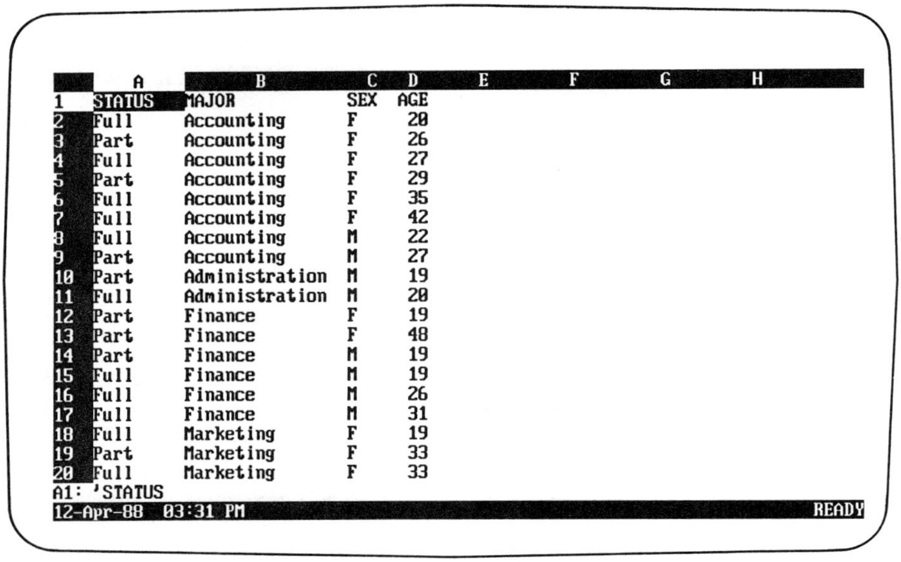

	A	B	C	D
1	STATUS	MAJOR	SEX	AGE
2	Full	Accounting	F	20
3	Part	Accounting	F	26
4	Full	Accounting	F	27
5	Part	Accounting	F	29
6	Full	Accounting	F	35
7	Full	Accounting	F	42
8	Full	Accounting	M	22
9	Part	Accounting	M	27
10	Part	Administration	M	19
11	Full	Administration	M	20
12	Part	Finance	F	19
13	Part	Finance	F	40
14	Part	Finance	M	19
15	Full	Finance	M	19
16	Full	Finance	M	26
17	Full	Finance	M	31
18	Full	Marketing	F	19
19	Part	Marketing	F	33
20	Full	Marketing	F	33

A1: 'STATUS
12-Apr-88 03:31 PM READY

Fig. 11.14. The sorted college database.

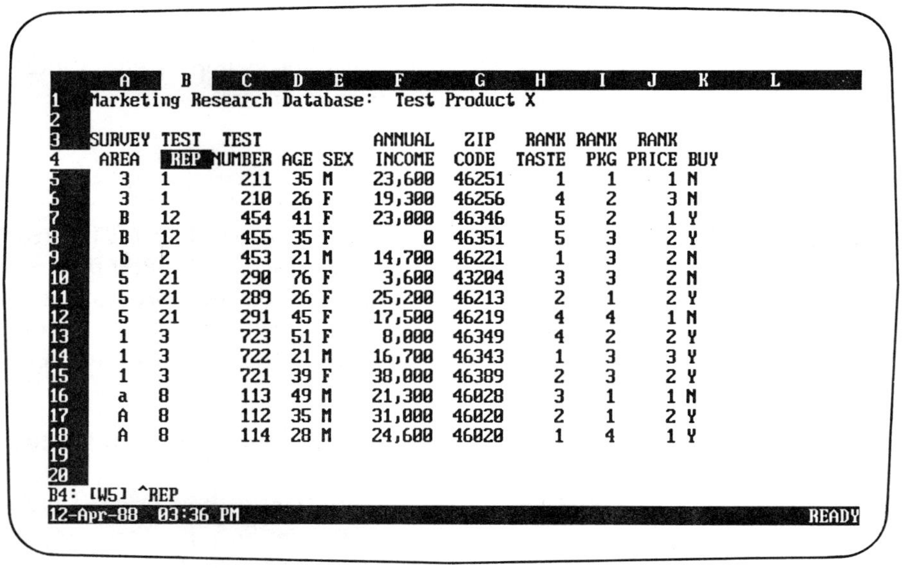

	A	B	C	D	E	F	G	H	I	J	K
1	Marketing Research Database: Test Product X										
2											
3	SURVEY	TEST	TEST			ANNUAL	ZIP	RANK	RANK	RANK	
4	AREA	REP	NUMBER	AGE	SEX	INCOME	CODE	TASTE	PKG	PRICE	BUY
5	3	1	211	35	M	23,600	46251	1	1	1	N
6	3	1	210	26	F	19,300	46256	4	2	3	N
7	B	12	454	41	F	23,000	46346	5	2	1	Y
8	B	12	455	35	F	0	46351	5	3	2	Y
9	b	2	453	21	M	14,700	46221	1	3	2	N
10	5	21	290	76	F	3,600	43204	3	3	2	N
11	5	21	289	26	F	25,200	46213	2	1	2	Y
12	5	21	291	45	F	17,500	46219	4	4	1	N
13	1	3	723	51	F	8,000	46349	4	2	2	Y
14	1	3	722	21	M	16,700	46343	1	3	3	Y
15	1	3	721	39	F	30,000	46389	2	3	2	Y
16	a	8	113	49	M	21,300	46028	3	1	1	N
17	A	8	112	35	M	31,000	46020	2	1	2	Y
18	A	8	114	28	M	24,600	46020	1	4	1	Y
19											
20											

B4: [W5] ^REP
12-Apr-88 03:36 PM READY

Fig. 11.15. The sorted Marketing Research database.

	A	B	C	D	E	F	G	H	I	J	K	L
1		Marketing Research Database:					Test Product X					
2												
3	REC	SURVEY	TEST	TEST			ANNUAL	ZIP	RANK	RANK	RANK	
4	NUM	AREA	REP	NUMBER	AGE	SEX	INCOME	CODE	TASTE	PKG	PRICE	BUY
5	1	3	1	210	26	F	19,300	46256	4	2	3	N
6	2	b	2	453	21	M	14,700	46221	1	3	2	N
7	3	3	1	211	35	M	23,600	46251	1	1	1	N
8	4	1	3	721	39	F	38,000	46389	2	3	2	Y
9	5	1	3	722	21	M	16,700	46343	1	3	3	Y
10	6	5	21	291	45	F	17,500	46219	4	4	1	N
11	7	B	12	454	41	F	23,000	46346	5	2	1	Y
12	8	5	21	290	76	F	3,600	43204	3	3	2	N
13	9	A	8	112	35	M	31,000	46020	2	1	2	Y
14	10	A	8	114	28	M	24,600	46020	1	4	1	Y
15	11	1	3	723	51	F	8,000	46349	4	2	2	Y
16	12	a	8	113	49	M	21,300	46028	3	1	1	N
17	13	B	12	455	35	F	0	46351	5	3	2	Y
18	14	5	21	289	26	F	25,200	46213	2	1	2	Y
19												
20												

A4: [W4] 'NUM

12-Apr-88 03:37 PM READY

Fig. 11.16. The Marketing Research database restored to original order.

Searching for Records

You have learned how to use the **Sort** option to reorganize information from the database by sorting records according to key fields. In this section, you learn how to use **Query**, the data retrieval command, to locate, edit, extract, or delete the records you find.

The Physical Inventory database shown in figure 11.17 is used to illustrate the basic concepts of Quattro's search (also called query) operations.

Looking for records that meet certain conditions is the simplest form of searching a Quattro database. To determine when to restock items, for example, you can use a search operation to find any records with an on-hand quantity of fewer than four units.

Once you have located the information you want, you can extract (copy) the selected records from the database and put them in another section of the worksheet. For example, you can extract all records with a purchase order (P.O.) date, and print the extracted area as a record of pending purchases.

With Quattro's search operations, you can perform a variety of other activities. You have the option of looking for only the first occurrence of a specified field value in order to develop a list of unique field entries. For instance, you

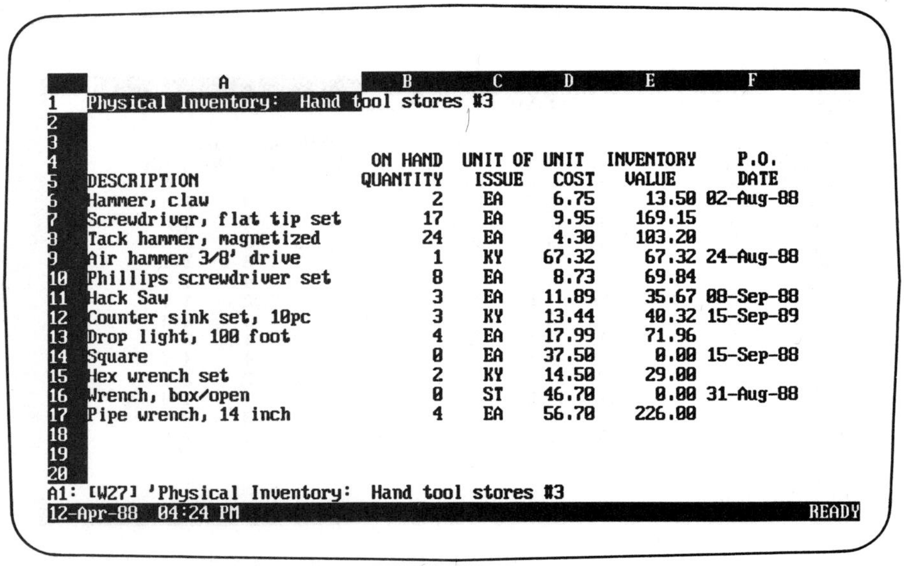

	A	B	C	D	E	F
1	Physical Inventory: Hand tool stores #3					
2						
3						
4		ON HAND	UNIT OF	UNIT	INVENTORY	P.O.
5	DESCRIPTION	QUANTITY	ISSUE	COST	VALUE	DATE
6	Hammer, claw	2	EA	6.75	13.50	02-Aug-88
7	Screwdriver, flat tip set	17	EA	9.95	169.15	
8	Tack hammer, magnetized	24	EA	4.30	103.20	
9	Air hammer 3/8' drive	1	KY	67.32	67.32	24-Aug-88
10	Phillips screwdriver set	8	EA	8.73	69.84	
11	Hack Saw	3	EA	11.89	35.67	08-Sep-88
12	Counter sink set, 10pc	3	KY	13.44	40.32	15-Sep-89
13	Drop light, 100 foot	4	EA	17.99	71.96	
14	Square	0	EA	37.50	0.00	15-Sep-88
15	Hex wrench set	2	KY	14.50	29.00	
16	Wrench, box/open	0	ST	46.70	0.00	31-Aug-88
17	Pipe wrench, 14 inch	4	EA	56.70	226.80	
18						
19						
20						

A1: [W27] 'Physical Inventory: Hand tool stores #3

12-Apr-88 04:24 PM READY

Fig. 11.17. The Physical Inventory database.

can search the ISSUE field to extract a list of the different units of measure. You also can delete selected inventory records, for example, records for which quantity on-hand equals zero (if you don't want to reorder these items).

Setting Minimum Search Requirements

To initiate any search operation, you issue the /**A**dvanced **D**atabase **Q**uery command. Then, you need to select the operation from the Advanced Database Query menu:

Block
Assign_Names
Formula_Criterion
Criteria_Table
Locate
Extract
Unique
Output_Block
Delete
Reset
Quit

You use the **B**lock, **C**riteria_Table, and **O**utput_Block options to specify blocks for the search operations. **B**lock and **C**riteria_Table, respectively, define the area to be searched and the area that will contain the search conditions. These areas must be specified in all **Q**uery operations. If the search condition is simple, however, you can use a simple **F**ormula_Criterion rather than a criteria table (more on this subject later). An output block must be established if you want to copy records or parts of records to an area outside the database.

The **A**ssign_Names command is used to create block names in the first record of the database. These block names correspond to the field names (column headers). This command makes phrasing your criteria more logical and convenient. The last two menu options signal the end of the current search operation. **R**eset removes all previous **Q**uery selections so that you can specify a different search area and different conditions. **Q**uit takes you back to MENU mode.

The **L**ocate, **E**xtract, **U**nique, and **D**elete options on the Query menu are summarized in table 11.1. They are discussed in more detail in the rest of this chapter.

Table 11.1
Search Options

Option	*Keystroke*	*Description*
Locate	L	Moves down through the search block and positions the cursor on records that match given criteria. You can enter or change data in the records as you move the cursor through them.
Extract	E	Creates copies, in a specified area of the worksheet, of all or some fields in records that match given criteria
Unique	U	Similar to Extract, but recognizes that some fields in the search block may contain duplicate entries. Duplicates are not copied to output block.
Delete	D	Deletes all records that match given criteria and shifts the remaining records to fill in the gaps that remain

To perform a **Query** operation, you must specify a search block and either a criteria table or a formula criterion and select one of the four search options. Before issuing a **Unique** or **Extract** command, you also must specify an output block.

Defining the Search Block

The *search block* for the /**A**dvanced **D**atabase **Q**uery command is the block of records you want to search. The specified area does not have to include the entire database. In the Physical Inventory database shown in figure 11.17, specifying a search block of A4..F16 defines the area of search as the entire database. In the sorted college database (fig. 11.14), entering A1..D9 as the search block limits the search area to the records for the accounting majors.

Whether you search all or only a part of a database, you must include the field-name row in the search block. If field names occupy space on more than one row, specify only the row directly above the first record to start the search block. In the Physical Inventory database, for example, even though rows 3 and 4 both contain portions of the field names, you start the search block with row 4 (by entering A4..F16 instead of A3..F16).

Select /**A**dvanced **D**atabase **Q**uery **B**lock and specify the search block by typing or pointing to a block or by using an assigned block name (see Chapter 4). You do not have to specify the search block again unless you choose to search a different block of data.

Defining the Criteria Table

In previous instructions for using Quattro applications, you learned to communicate cell locations to Quattro. When you want Quattro to search for records that meet certain criteria, you must be able to talk to Quattro in terms the program understands. Quattro provides two methods for specifying search criteria. The first method discussed is the **C**riteria_Table command. The criteria table is a special block that you define. It is used to hold the conditions of the search and so serves as a filter when only certain records are extracted. The second, **F**ormula_Criterion, is explained in the section "Using the Formula Criterion Command" in this chapter.

Suppose that you want to identify in the address database all records that contain OH in the STATE field. When the database is on-screen and Quattro is in READY mode, type *STATE* in cell H2 and *OH* in cell H3 (see fig. 11.18). Type the name *Criteria Table* in cell H1 only if you want the name for documentation; cell H1 is not directly involved in the search procedure.

Select /**A**dvanced **D**atabase **Q**uery, and specify A1..F19 as the search block. The Query menu is displayed as soon as you enter the search block. Select

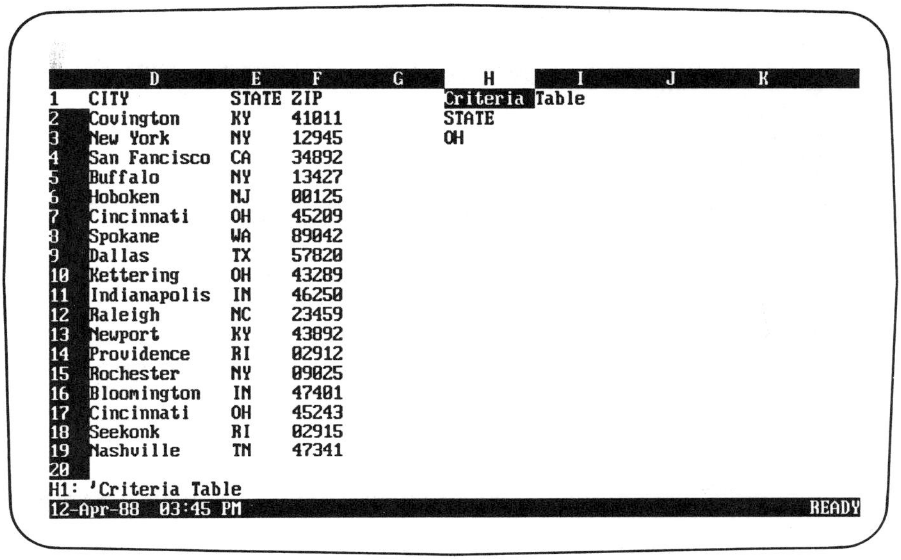

Fig. 11.18. A criteria table created in the address database.

Criteria_Table, and then type, point to, or name the block H2..H3 as the location of your search condition. The Query menu again returns to the screen.

You can use numbers, labels, or formulas as criteria. A criteria table can be up to 32 columns wide and two or more rows deep. The first row must contain the field names of the search criteria (STATE in row 2 of fig. 11.18). The rows below the unique field names contain the actual criteria, (OH in row 3). The field names in the search block and the criteria table must match exactly.

By designating the search block and criteria table, you have completed the minimum requirements for executing a **L**ocate or **D**elete command.

Tip Be sure to enter the specific field names above the conditions in the worksheet (in READY mode) before you use the /**A**dvanced **D**atabase **Q**uery **C**riteria_Table command sequence.

Issuing the Locate Command

When you select **L**ocate from the Query menu, a highlight bar moves through the search block to the first record that meets the condition specified in the criteria table. In the example, the highlight bar rests on the first record that includes OH in the STATE field (see fig. 11.19).

	A	B	C	D	E	F
1	LAST	FIRST	STREET ADDRESS	CITY	STATE	ZIP
2	Harrington	James	12344 Arlington Lane	Covington	KY	41011
3	Thomas	Brian	18499 Central Park Ave.	New York	NY	12945
4	Leugers	Karen	21 Hill St. Apt. 34	San Fancisco	CA	34892
5	Englert	Michael	234 Orange St.	Buffalo	NY	13427
6	Smith	Margaret	2341 Kyles Lane	Hoboken	NJ	00125
7	Pryor	Aaron	2341 Milford St.	Cincinnati	OH	45209
8	Cleary	Esther	238 Higgins St. Apt 14	Spokane	WA	89042
9	Wolf	Barbara	3098 Arnold Ave.	Dallas	TX	57820
10	Wright	Ned	31238 Carolina St.	Kettering	OH	43289
11	Saunders	Ronald	3214 Keystone Ave.	Indianapolis	IN	46250
12	McGruder	Mary	331 Park Lane Apt. 32	Raleigh	NC	23459
13	Simpson	Jeremy	3509 Ludlow Ave.	Newport	KY	43892
14	Rooney	Kevin	391 Atwater Ave. Apt. 3	Providence	RI	02912
15	Franks	Mike	4284 Knight Circle	Rochester	NY	09025
16	Sorrenson	Sarah	432 Keys Crescent	Bloomington	IN	47401
17	Holland	Earl	4983 Drake Rd.	Cincinnati	OH	45243
18	Tuke	Samuel	9038 Greenup St.	Seekonk	RI	02915
19	Malvern	Thomas	939 Dime Circle	Nashville	TN	47341
20						

A7: [W12] 'Pryor

14-Apr-88 11:00 AM MENU

Fig. 11.19. The first record that meets the criterion.

By pressing the down-arrow key, you can move the highlight bar to the next record that conforms to the criterion. You can continue pressing the down-arrow key until the last record that meets the search conditions has been highlighted (see fig. 11.20).

Pressing the up-arrow key moves the cursor to the preceding record that conforms to the search criteria. Pressing the Home and End keys positions the cursor, respectively, on the first and last records in the database, regardless of the established search criteria. You use the right-arrow and left-arrow keys to move the single-character blinking cursor to different fields in the highlighted record. Then, you can enter new values or use the Edit key to update the current values in the field.

One caution: If you change the record so that it no longer satisfies the **L**ocate criteria and then move away from that record, you cannot use the arrow keys to return to the record during the **L**ocate operation.

To end the **L**ocate operation and return to the Query menu, press Enter or Esc. To return directly to READY mode, press Ctrl-Break.

Using the Formula Criterion Command

Quattro provides another method for establishing a search criterion: the **F**ormula_Criterion command. With **F**ormula_Criterion, you use a single formula

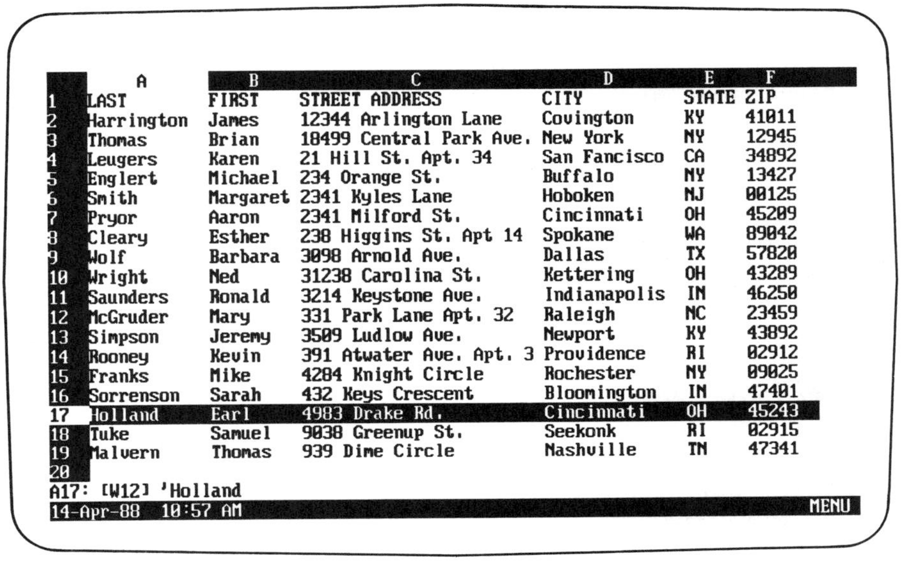

	A	B	C	D	E	F
1	LAST	FIRST	STREET ADDRESS	CITY	STATE	ZIP
2	Harrington	James	12344 Arlington Lane	Covington	KY	41011
3	Thomas	Brian	10499 Central Park Ave.	New York	NY	12945
4	Leugers	Karen	21 Hill St. Apt. 34	San Fancisco	CA	34892
5	Englert	Michael	234 Orange St.	Buffalo	NY	13427
6	Smith	Margaret	2341 Kyles Lane	Hoboken	NJ	00125
7	Pryor	Aaron	2341 Milford St.	Cincinnati	OH	45209
8	Cleary	Esther	238 Higgins St. Apt 14	Spokane	WA	89042
9	Wolf	Barbara	3098 Arnold Ave.	Dallas	TX	57820
10	Wright	Ned	31238 Carolina St.	Kettering	OH	43289
11	Saunders	Ronald	3214 Keystone Ave.	Indianapolis	IN	46250
12	McGruder	Mary	331 Park Lane Apt. 32	Raleigh	NC	23459
13	Simpson	Jeremy	3509 Ludlow Ave.	Newport	KY	43892
14	Rooney	Kevin	391 Atwater Ave. Apt. 3	Providence	RI	02912
15	Franks	Mike	4204 Knight Circle	Rochester	NY	09025
16	Sorrenson	Sarah	432 Keys Crescent	Bloomington	IN	47401
17	Holland	Earl	4983 Drake Rd.	Cincinnati	OH	45243
18	Tuke	Samuel	9038 Greenup St.	Seekonk	RI	02915
19	Malvern	Thomas	939 Dime Circle	Nashville	TN	47341
20						

A17: [W12] 'Holland
14-Apr-88 10:57 AM MENU

Fig. 11.20. The last record that meets the criterion.

as the criterion to search a database. This formula can set a single criterion or several at once.

Tip Using Formula_Criterion overrides any existing criteria tables.

You use Formula_Criterion to enter formula-based criteria. For an example, suppose that you want to use this method to search the address database for names of people who live in Ohio. You can create a formula that sets this condition.

Before defining the formula, use the **A**ssign_Names command to assign block names that are the same as the field names. The names are placed in the first row of the database and can be used to create formula criteria.

Choose /**A**dvanced **D**atabase **Q**uery; from the Query menu, select **F**ormula_Criterion. At the prompt for the Formula Criterion, enter the following logical formula:

STATE="OH"

Figure 11.21 shows the use of the **F**ormula_Criterion command with the formula entered. Figure 11.22 shows the result after the **L**ocate command has been issued. Use this command when you have a short criterion and don't need the flexibility of multifield criteria offered by the **C**riteria_Table command.

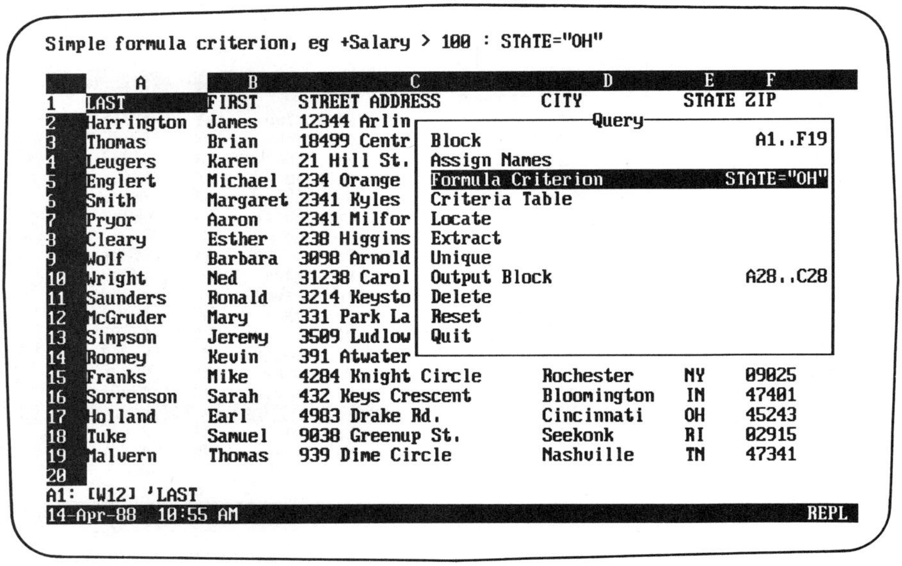

Fig. 11.21. Issuing the Formula Criterion command.

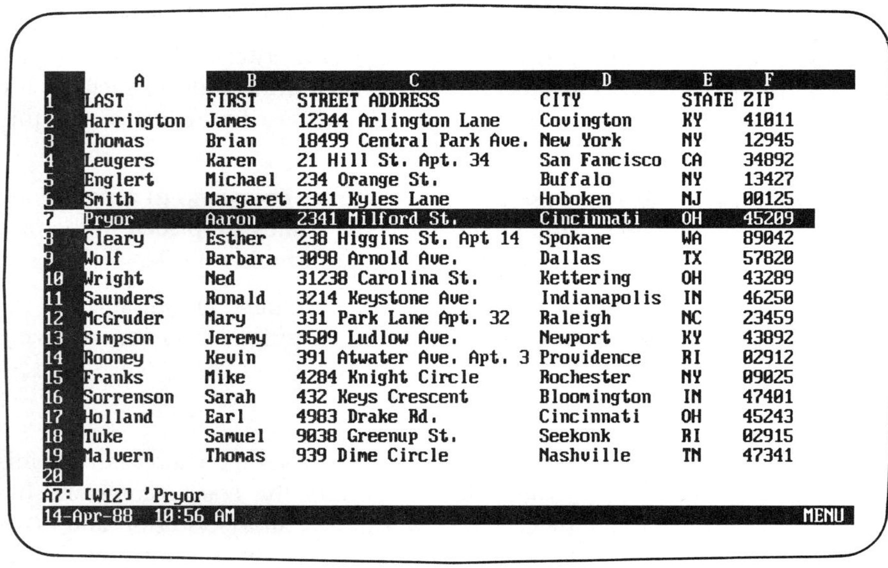

Fig. 11.22. The first record that meets the formula criterion.

Listing All Specified Records with the Extract Command

The **Locate** command has limited use, especially in a large database. Most of the time you need to generate a report based on categories in the database rather than simply locate data within the database.

As an alternative to the **Locate** command, you can use the **Extract** command. With **Extract**, you can copy to a blank area of the worksheet only the records that meet the conditions. You can view a list of all the extracted records, print the block of extracted records, or even use the /**F**ile **X**tract command to copy only the extracted record block to a new file on disk. (Be careful not to confuse /**F**ile **X**tract with /**A**dvanced **D**atabase **Q**uery **E**xtract.)

Defining the Output Block

Before you issue the /**A**dvanced **D**atabase **Q**uery **E**xtract command, you must define a criteria table and an output block. To define the output block, choose a blank area in the worksheet as the output block to receive records copied in an extract operation. Place the block to the right of or below the database. In figure 11.23, for example, both the criteria table and the output block have been placed below the records in the address database.

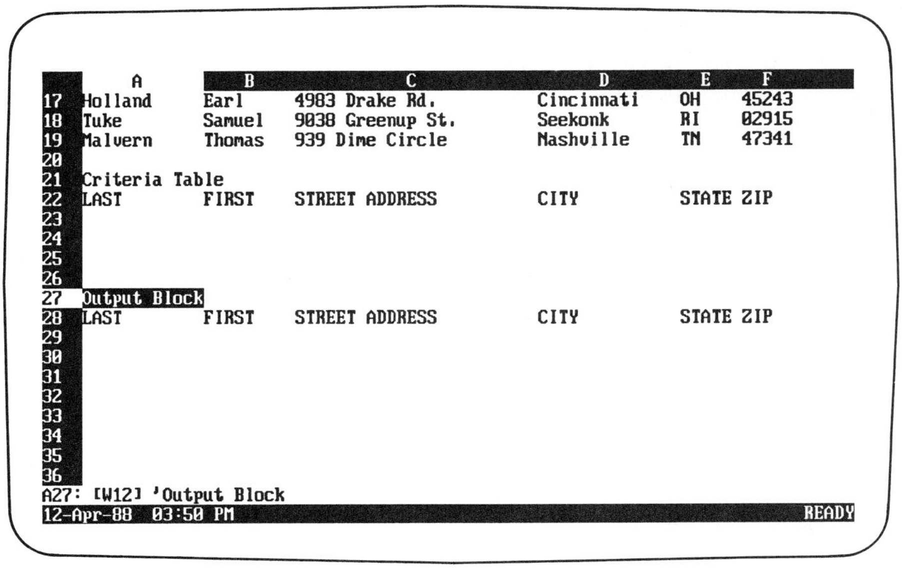

Fig. 11.23. The defined output block.

Tip Extract also outputs to areas that are not blank. You must be careful to specify a block of blank cells as the output block.

In the first row of the output block, copy the names of only the fields whose contents you want to extract. You do not have to copy these names in the same order as they appear in the database. (In fig. 11.23, the *Output Block* entry in cell A27 is for documentation purposes only, and all field names in row 28 have been reproduced in the order of the database.)

The field names in both the criteria table and output block must match exactly the corresponding field names in the search block. To avoid mismatch errors, use the /**B**lock **C**opy command to copy the database field names into the criteria table and output block.

Select /**A**dvanced **D**atabase **Q**uery **O**utput; then type, point to, or name the block location of the output area. You can create an open-ended extract area by entering only the output field-name row as the block, or you can set the exact size of the extract area. Use the latter method when you want to retain additional data that is located below the extract area. For example, as you can see in figure 11.23, naming A28..F36 as the output block limits incoming records to eight (one row for field names and one row for each record).

To limit the size of the extract area, enter the upper left and lower right cell coordinates of the entire output block. The first row in the specified block must contain the field names. You must have enough remaining rows to accommodate the maximum number of records you expect to receive from the extract operation. If you do not allow sufficient room in the fixed output area, the extract operation aborts after Quattro has filled the output block; and an error message states that you have too many selected records to fit into the output block.

To create an open-ended extract area, which does not limit the number of incoming records, specify as the output block only the row containing the output field names. For example, by naming A28..F28 as the output block in figure 11.23, you define the area to receive records from an extract operation without limiting the number of records.

An extract operation overwrites all existing data in the output block. If you use only the field-name row to specify the output area, all data below that row down to row 8192 may be destroyed to make room for the incoming extracted records.

Executing the Extract Command

You have two ways to execute an **E**xtract command. (1) You enter the search conditions in a criteria table in the worksheet. (2) You enter a formula criterion; type the output field names (or indicate the output block address); and set the search block, criteria table (optionally), and output block from the Database Query menu.

To accelerate what seems to be a time-consuming setup process, establish a standard search block, criteria table, and output block and then store the block names for these locations. Keeping in mind the limit of 32 criteria fields, you can establish a single criteria table that encompasses all the key fields on which you might search (the block A22..F23 in fig. 11.23). By establishing this block, you save the time needed to specify a criteria table for each different extract. If the criteria table contains many unused field names, however, you lose some speed of execution.

For an illustration of the extract process, turn again to the address database (fig. 11.20). Suppose that you want to create a list of all records with OH in the STATE field. Assume that rows 22 and 28 contain the field names, respectively, for the criteria table and the output block. Enter *OH* in cell E23. Select /**A**dvanced **D**atabase **Q**uery and specify the search block (A1..F19), criteria table (A22..F23), and output block (A28..F28). Then choose **E**xtract from the Query menu. The output block in figure 11.24 contains three extracted records, each of which meets the condition of STATE = OH.

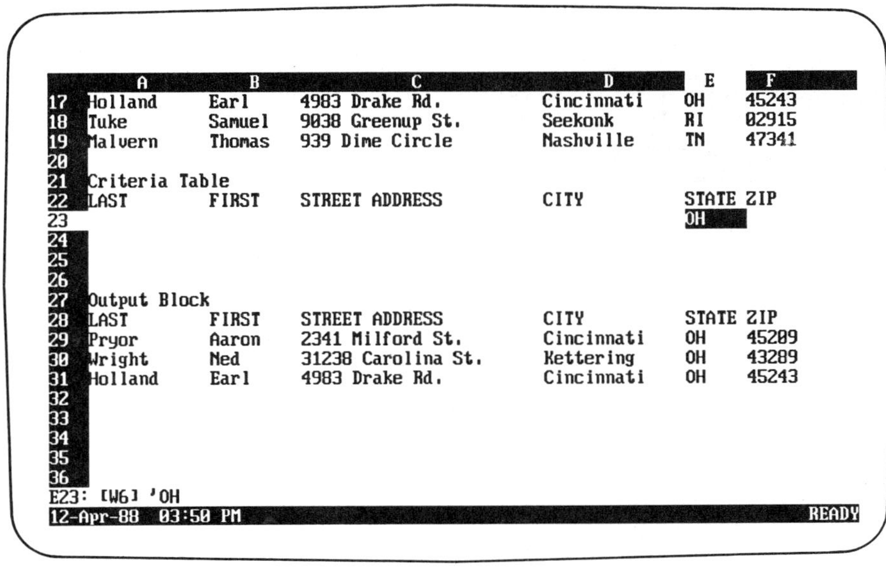

	A	B	C	D	E	F
17	Holland	Earl	4983 Drake Rd.	Cincinnati	OH	45243
18	Tuke	Samuel	9038 Greenup St.	Seekonk	RI	02915
19	Malvern	Thomas	939 Dime Circle	Nashville	TN	47341
20						
21	Criteria Table					
22	LAST	FIRST	STREET ADDRESS	CITY	STATE	ZIP
23					OH	
24						
25						
26						
27	Output Block					
28	LAST	FIRST	STREET ADDRESS	CITY	STATE	ZIP
29	Pryor	Aaron	2341 Milford St.	Cincinnati	OH	45209
30	Wright	Ned	31238 Carolina St.	Kettering	OH	43289
31	Holland	Earl	4983 Drake Rd.	Cincinnati	OH	45243
32						
33						
34						
35						
36						

E23: [W6] 'OH

12-Apr-88 03:50 PM READY

Fig. 11.24. Three records extracted from the address database.

You do not have to extract entire records or maintain the order of field names within the extracted records. For example, you can combine the first- and last-name fields into a new field, NAME, which you locate in column G. Then you extract only the NAME and CITY information from records that have OH in the STATE field. To do this, type *NAME* in cell G1 and then type the string formula *+B2&" "&A2* in cell G2. This formula causes the first and last names in cells A2 and B2 to be combined with a space between them (see Chapter 7 for more information about text-based formulas and functions). Copy the formula in cell G2 to the block G3..G19, issue the /**B**lock **A**dvanced **V**alue command to convert to values the formulas in G2..G19 (see fig. 11.25).

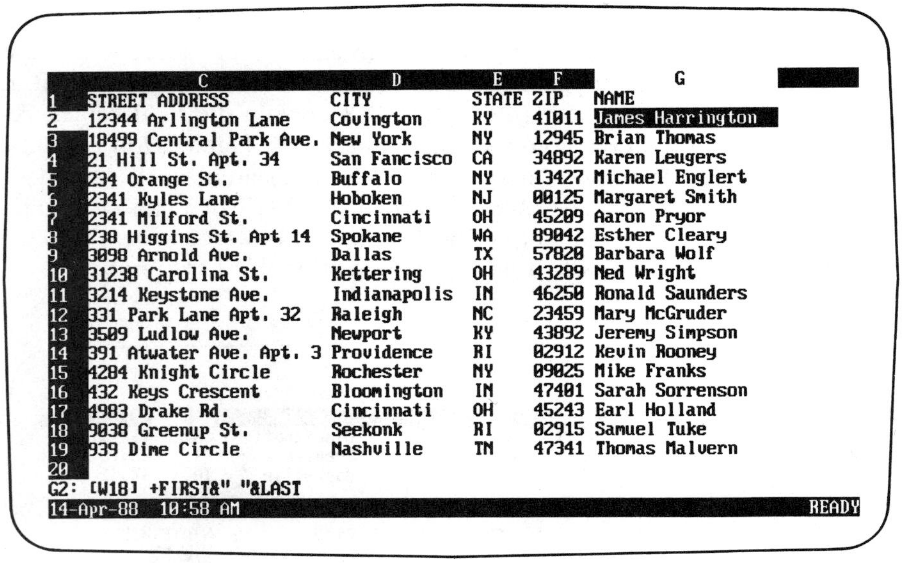

	C	D	E	F	G
1	STREET ADDRESS	CITY	STATE	ZIP	NAME
2	12344 Arlington Lane	Covington	KY	41011	James Harrington
3	10499 Central Park Ave.	New York	NY	12945	Brian Thomas
4	21 Hill St. Apt. 34	San Fancisco	CA	34892	Karen Leugers
5	234 Orange St.	Buffalo	NY	13427	Michael Englert
6	2341 Kyles Lane	Hoboken	NJ	00125	Margaret Smith
7	2341 Milford St.	Cincinnati	OH	45209	Aaron Pryor
8	238 Higgins St. Apt 14	Spokane	WA	89042	Esther Cleary
9	3098 Arnold Ave.	Dallas	TX	57820	Barbara Wolf
10	31238 Carolina St.	Kettering	OH	43289	Ned Wright
11	3214 Keystone Ave.	Indianapolis	IN	46250	Ronald Saunders
12	331 Park Lane Apt. 32	Raleigh	NC	23459	Mary McGruder
13	3509 Ludlow Ave.	Newport	KY	43892	Jeremy Simpson
14	391 Atwater Ave. Apt. 3	Providence	RI	02912	Kevin Rooney
15	4204 Knight Circle	Rochester	NY	09025	Mike Franks
16	432 Keys Crescent	Bloomington	IN	47401	Sarah Sorrenson
17	4983 Drake Rd.	Cincinnati	OH	45243	Earl Holland
18	9038 Greenup St.	Seekonk	RI	02915	Samuel Tuke
19	939 Dime Circle	Nashville	TN	47341	Thomas Malvern
20					

G2: [W18] +FIRST&" "&LAST

14-Apr-88 10:58 AM READY

Fig. 11.25. The address database after a new NAME field has been added.

Next, erase the field names in row 28 by using /**B**lock **E**rase. Type the new field name, NAME, in cell A28; skip column B (for spacing purposes); and enter the second output field, CITY, in cell C28. Then respecify the output block as A28..C28. Expand both the search block and criteria table to include the new column G. Then issue the /**A**dvanced **D**atabase **Q**uery **E**xtract command. This operation extracts the name and city information for all records of individuals living in Ohio (see fig. 11.26).

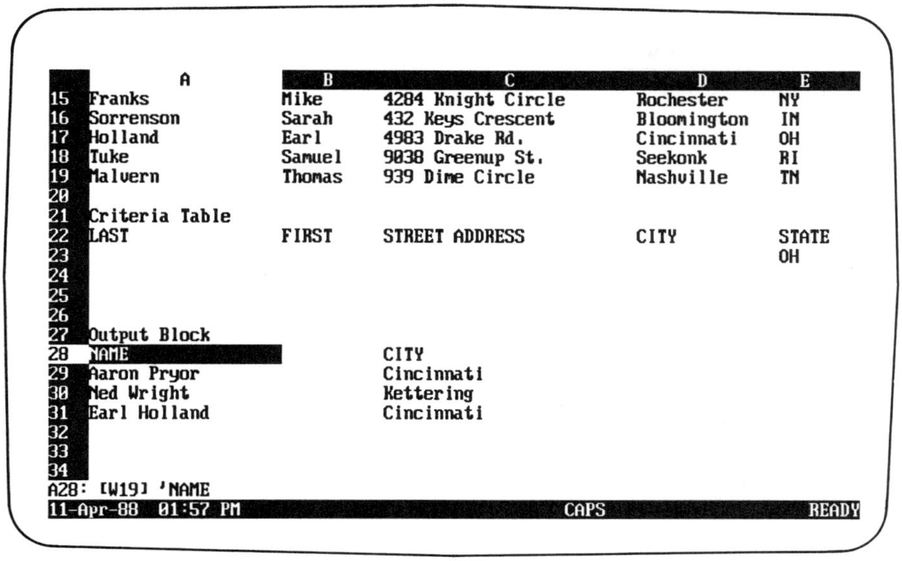

Fig. 11.26. The output block of the revised address database.

Using More Complicated Criteria

In addition to an exact-match search on a single label field, Quattro permits a wide variety of record searches: on exact matches to numeric fields, on partial matches of field contents, on fields that meet formula conditions, on fields that meet all of several conditions, and on fields that meet either one condition or another.

Look first at variations of queries on single fields.

Wild Cards in Criteria Tables

You can use Quattro's wild cards for matching labels in database operations. The characters ?, *, and ~ have special meaning when used in the criteria table. The question mark (?) instructs Quattro to accept any single character in that specific position and can be used only to locate fields of the same length. The asterisk (*), which tells Quattro to accept any and all characters that follow, can be used on field contents of unequal length. By placing a tilde (~) at the beginning of a label, you tell Quattro to accept all values except those that follow. Table 11.2 gives examples of how you can use wild cards in search operations.

Table 11.2
Using Wild Cards in Search Operations

Enter	*To locate*
N?	NC, NJ, NY, etc.
BO?L?	BOWLE but not BOWL
BO?L*	BOWLE, BOWL, BOLLESON, BOELING, etc.
SAN*	SANTA BARBARA, SAN FRANCISCO
SAN *	SAN FRANCISCO only
~N*	Strings in specified fields that do not begin with the letter N

Use the ? and * wild-card characters when you are unsure of the spelling used in field contents. Be sure that the results of any wild-card extract operation are what you need. And be extremely careful when you use wild cards in a **D**elete command. If you are not careful, you may remove more records than you intend.

Formulas for Searching Numeric Fields

To set up formulas that query numeric fields in the database, you can use the following relational operators:

>	Greater than
>=	Greater than or equal to
<	Less than
<=	Less than or equal to
=	Equal to
<>	Not equal to

If you create a formula that references the first field entry in the numeric column you want to search, Quattro moves down the column testing the formula on each cell until the program reaches the end of the specified search block. You can place the formula anywhere below the criteria table's field-name row (unlike text criteria, which must be directly below the associated field name). For example, you can use a formula based on information already in the Marketing Research database in figure 11.16 to extract the records of test participants who are at least 45 years old. First, type the formula *+D5>=45* in cell D22 (see fig. 11.27). Notice that +D5 is replaced by the block name +AGE. This replacement occurs because you used the /**A**dvanced **D**atabase **Q**uery **A**ssign_Names command to assign the field name AGE to D5 as a block name.

Notice that the formula is displayed in the descriptor line and that a zero (0) is displayed in cell D22. The formula checked whether the content of cell

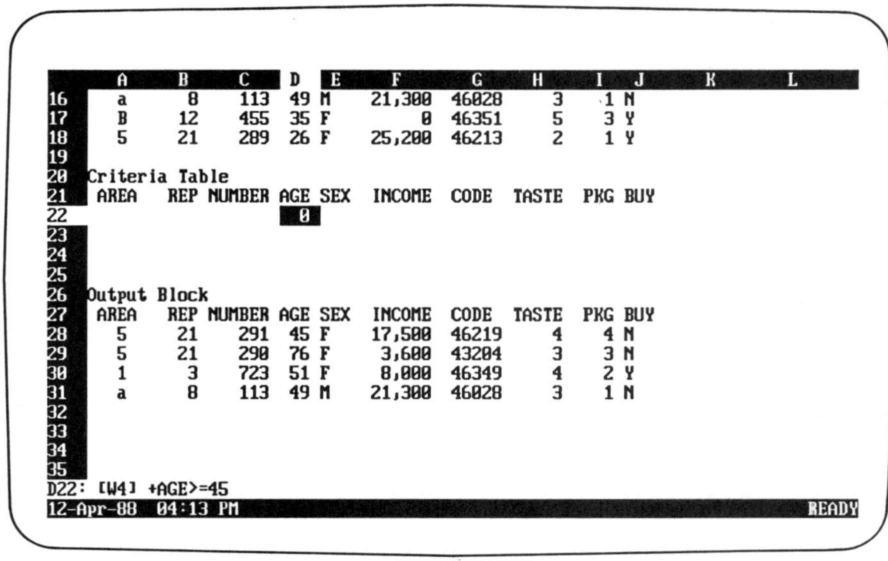

Fig. 11.27. Entering a formula into the criteria table.

D5 (AGE = 26) is greater than or equal to 45 and returned the zero (0) to indicate a false condition. (To better understand the search condition, you can use the /**B**lock **D**isplay_Format **T**ext command to change the display from 0 to the underlying formula.

After you have specified the search block, criteria table, and output block, executing an extract operation produces four records for which AGE equals or exceeds 45 years. A criterion of +D5>45 extracts only three records; the formula +D5=45 extracts only one record.

To reference cells outside the database, use formulas that include absolute cell addressing. (For addressing information, refer to Chapter 4.) For example, suppose that immediately after you issue the preceding command (to extract records based on AGE), you want to extract the records of Marketing Research database respondents whose income exceeds the average income of all respondents.

To extract these records, you must first return to READY mode. Then, you must calculate the average income by entering @AVG(G5..G18) in a blank cell (G24) away from all database blocks (see fig. 11.28).

Next, type the formula +G5>G24 as the criterion under INCOME in cell G22 (again see fig. 11.28). The +G5 tells Quattro to test (starting in cell G5) INCOME contents against the average income in cell G24 and to continue

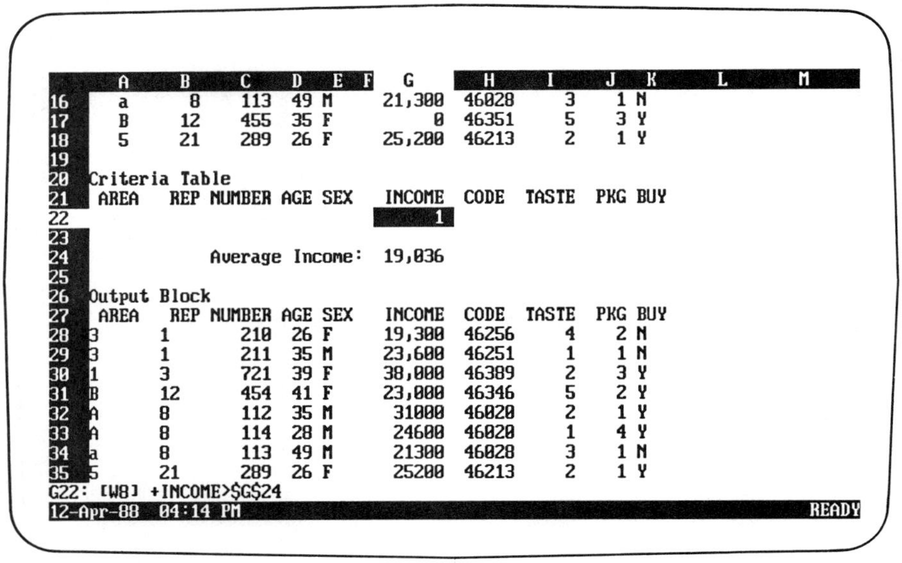

Fig. 11.28. Using a formula to reference a cell outside the database.

down column G to the end of the search block (row 18), comparing each subsequent income cell with the average income in cell G6. The use of the absolute cell reference (G24) ensures that all cells are compared to the same average figure.

With the program still in READY mode, press the F7 (Query) key to repeat the most recent query operation (Extract, in this example). The F7 shortcut eliminates the need to select /**A**dvanced **D**atabase **Q**uery **E**xtract. Use the shortcut method only when you do not want to change the locations of the search block, criteria table, and output block. As you can see from figure 11.28, the extracted records show that eight of the Marketing Research database participants have incomes greater than the average income of all respondents.

Compound Conditions in a Criteria Table

Now that you have seen how to perform a **L**ocate or **E**xtract operation with only one criterion, you are ready to learn how to use multiple criteria for your queries. You can set up multiple criteria as AND conditions (in which all the criteria must be met) or as OR conditions (in which any one criterion must be met). To draw an analogy, you can search a music department's library for sheet music requiring drums AND trumpets or for music for drums OR trumpets. The AND condition is likely to produce fewer selections than the OR condition.

You indicate two or more criteria, all of which must be met, by specifying all the conditions on the criterion row immediately below the field names. The multiple criteria in row 24 of the college database requests the records for which MAJOR equals Accounting and SEX equals Male (see fig. 11.29). When you issue the **Extract** command, Quattro extracts two records that meet both conditions. Quattro ignores uppercase and lowercase differences. You also can set multiple conditions in a formula by using special conditional operators (explained in the section "Special Operators.")

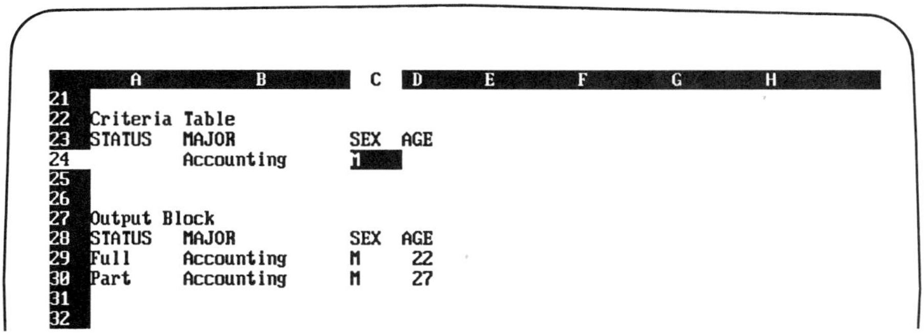

Fig. 11.29. Using two criteria in the criteria table.

If you maintain a criteria table that includes many fields, you can quickly extract records based on different conditions. For example, you can access READY mode, change M to F in cell C24 (under SEX), and press the F7 (Query) key. Quattro immediately copies the records of female accounting majors to the output block (see fig. 11.30).

You can continue to add conditions to the criteria table. Enter the additional criteria only in the row immediately below the field-name row. For example, the extracted records in figure 11.31 are limited to female accounting majors who are under 30 years old.

Criteria placed on the same row have the effect of a logical AND; they tell Quattro to locate or extract records that meet this field condition AND this field condition AND this field condition, and so on. Criteria placed on different rows have the effect of a logical OR; that is, they tell Quattro to locate or extract on this field condition OR that field condition, and so on. You can set up a logical OR search on one or more fields. (For more information about logical operators, see Chapter 6.)

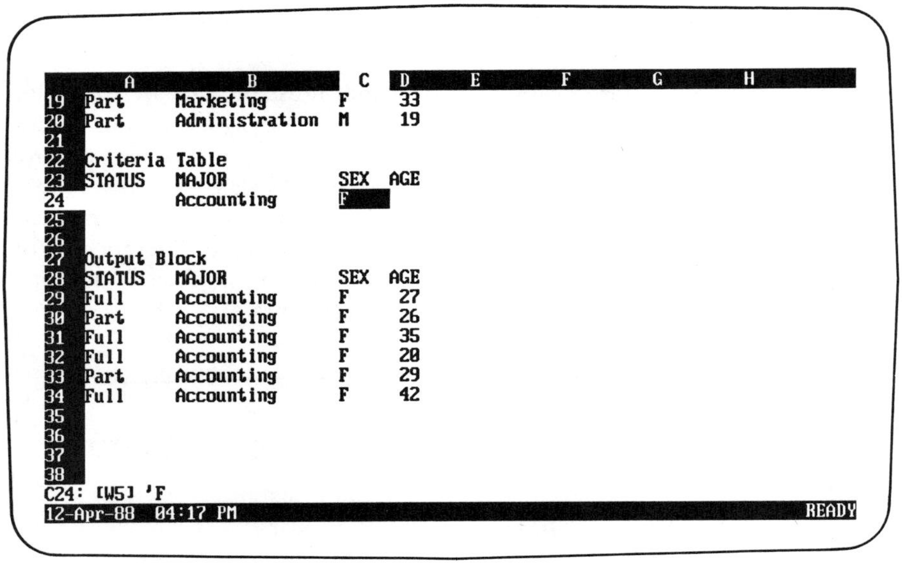

Fig. 11.30. Changing conditions in the criteria table.

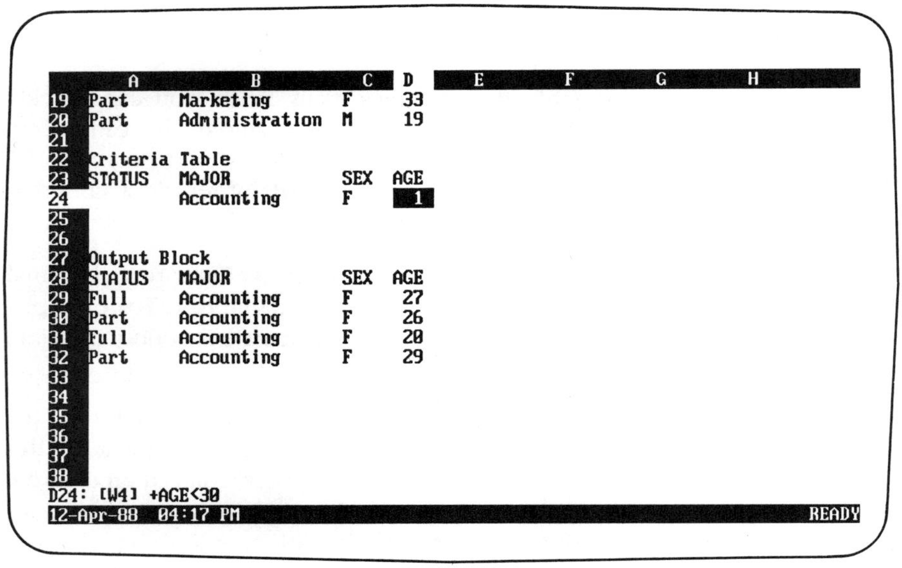

Fig. 11.31. Adding conditions to the criteria table.

Searching a single field for more than one condition is the simplest use of an OR condition. To illustrate the concept, you can extract from the Physical Inventory database (refer to fig. 11.17) the records whose unit of issue is either KT (kit) or ST (set).

Under the ISSUE criteria field, type one condition immediately below the other (see fig. 11.32). Be sure to expand the criteria table to include the additional row. As you can see from the output block in figure 11.32, four records in the Physical Inventory database have either KT or ST for a unit of issue.

```
         A                          B        C          D         E          F
12 Counter sink set, 10pc           3       KY        13.44     40.32   15-Sep-89
13 Drop light, 100 foot             4       EA        17.99     71.96
14 Square                           0       EA        37.50      0.00   15-Sep-88
15 Hex wrench set                   2       KY        14.50     29.00
16 Wrench, box/open                 0       ST        46.70      0.00   31-Aug-88
17 Pipe wrench, 14 inch             4       EA        56.70    226.00
18
19 Criteria Table
20 DESCRIPTION                 QUANTITY   ISSUE      COST      VALUE       DATE
21                                          KY
22                                          ST
23
24 Output Block
25 DESCRIPTION                 QUANTITY   ISSUE      COST      VALUE       DATE
26 Air hammer 3/8' drive            1       KY        67.32     67.32   24-Aug-88
27 Counter sink set, 10pc           3       KY        13.44     40.32   15-Sep-89
28 Hex wrench set                   2       KY        14.50     29.00
29 Wrench, box/open                 0       ST        46.70      0.00   31-Aug-88
30
31
C22: [W8] ^ST
12-Apr-88  04:26 PM                                                         READY
```

Fig. 11.32. Searching one field for two conditions.

You also can specify a logical OR condition on two or more different field conditions. For example, suppose that you want to search the Marketing Research database for records in which age is greater than 50 OR in which income exceeds $25,000. Figure 11.33 shows the setup of the criteria in rows 22 and 23. Note that the criteria are on two different rows in the criteria table.

To set up these criteria, you type *+D5>50* in cell D22. In the next row, enter *+G5>25000* in cell G23. (Remember that you can type formulas under any field name; you could have entered the two formulas in cells A22 and A23, for example.) Adjust the criteria table to include the OR condition by expanding the criteria table down a row.

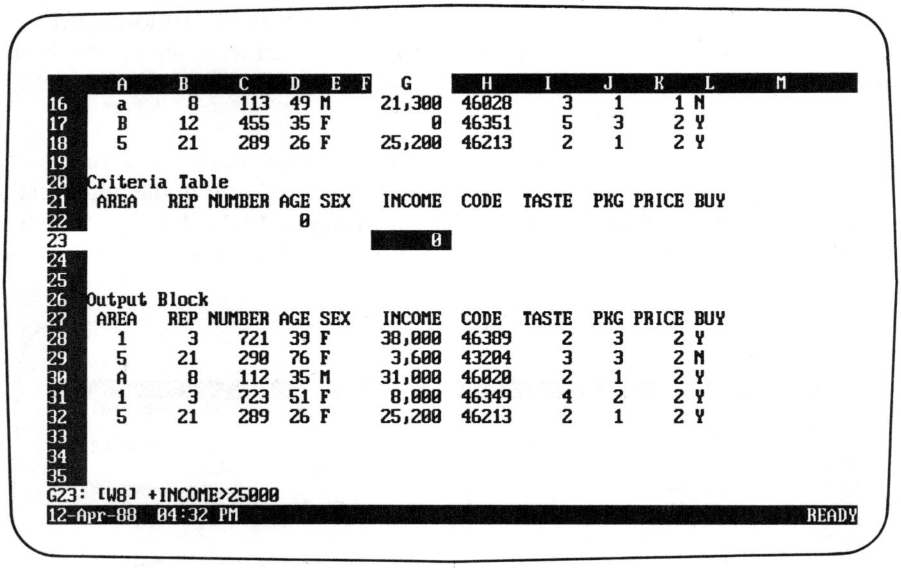

Fig. 11.33. Searching two fields for two conditions.

When you issue the **E**xtract command, five records are copied to the output block. Although rows 29 and 31 in figure 11.33 do not reflect INCOME contents exceeding $25,000, these rows do contain AGE contents above 50. Only one condition OR the other had to be met before the copy was made.

To add additional OR criteria, move to a new row, enter the new condition, and expand the criteria table to include the row containing the new condition. If you reduce the number of rows involved in an OR logical search, be sure to shrink the criteria table.

Although no technical reason prevents you from mixing AND and OR logical searches, the results of a mixed **Q**uery operation may not be of much use because they are so difficult to verify. Follow the format of placing each AND condition in the row immediately below the criterion field-name row, and each OR condition in a separate row below. For example, if you want to search the Marketing Research database (fig. 11.16) for records in which BUY equals Y (Yes) and INCOME is either less than $10,000 or greater than $30,000, erase the AGE search condition in cell D22 and then enter the AND and OR conditions in the following cells:

	G	H	I	J	K	L	M	N
22	+G5<10000							Y
23	+G5>30000							Y

By specifying these conditions, you tell Quattro to search for records in which INCOME is less than $10,000 AND the BUY response is Yes (row 22) OR for records in which INCOME is greater than $30,000 AND the BUY response is Yes (row 23). The criteria table (A21..N23) remains unchanged. Repeating the Y in cell N23 is critical (even though you have entered Y in cell N22) because if Quattro locates a blank cell within a criteria table, the program selects all records for the field name above that blank cell.

Test the logic of your search conditions on a small sample database in which you can verify search results easily by scrolling through all records and noting which should be extracted. For example, if the Marketing Research database contained hundreds of responses, you could test the preceding AND-OR search conditions on the small group of 14 records shown in figure 11.16. (Issuing an **E**xtract command should copy to the output area only the records in rows 8, 13, 15, and 17.)

String Searches

If you want to search on the partial contents of a field, you can use functions in a formula. For example, suppose that you can remember only the street name, Keystone, for a record you want to extract from the address database. If you can safely assume that all street addresses start with a number and have a space before the street name (XXX Streetname), you can use the formula shown in the input line of figure 11.34 as the search criterion in cell C23.

The double quotation marks (" ") in the formula instruct Quattro to start the search after a blank space is encountered (between the street number and street name). The 1,8 portion of the formula instructs the program to search on the first through the eighth character positions matching "keystone", thereby eliminating any need to know whether Street, Ave., Avenue, and so on, is part of the field. Issuing the **E**xtract command produces one record in the output block (row 29). You also can use compound criteria and search on both CITY and part of the STREET ADDRESS field. (See Chapter 7 for an in-depth description of the @MID and @FIND functions.)

Special Operators

To combine search conditions within a single field, use the special operators #AND# and #OR#. Use the special operator #NOT# to search for a negative search condition, that is, anything that is *not* the given condition.

Use #AND# or #OR# to search on two or more conditions within the same field. For example, suppose that you want to extract from the Physical Inventory database all records with an August, 1987, purchase-order date (DATE). Establish the criterion by requesting an extract of all dates later than

```
@MID(C2,@FIND(" ",C2,0)+1,8)="Keystone"

         A          B                C                    D            E      F
10 Saunders     Ronald   3214 Keystone Ave.       Indianapolis  IN     46250
11 McGruder     Mary     331 Park Lane Apt. 32    Raleigh       NC     23459
12 Simpson      Jeremy   3509 Ludlow Ave.         Newport       KY     43092
13 Wolf         Barbara  3098 Arnold Ave.         Dallas        TX     57820
14 Rooney       Kevin    391 Atwater Ave. Apt. 3  Providence    RI     02912
15 Franks       Mike     4284 Knight Circle       Rochester     NY     09025
16 Sorrenson    Sarah    432 Keys Crescent        Bloomington   IN     47401
17 Holland      Earl     4983 Drake Rd.           Cincinnati    OH     45243
18 Tuke         Samuel   9038 Greenup St.         Seekonk       RI     02915
19 Malvern      Thomas   939 Dime Circle          Nashville     TN     47341
20
21 Criteria Table
22 LAST         FIRST    STREET ADDRESS           CITY          STATE ZIP
23                                              0
24
25
26
27 Output Block
28 LAST         FIRST    STREET ADDRESS           CITY          STATE ZIP
29 Saunders     Ronald   3214 Keystone Ave.       Indianapolis  IN     46250
C23: [W24] @MID(STREET ADDRESS,@FIND(" ",STREET ADDRESS
15-Apr-88  08:28 AM                                                    EDIT
```

Fig. 11.34. Using a string search formula.

July 31, 1987, AND earlier than September 1, 1987. In figure 11.35, the formula condition has been entered in cell A21. (Keep in mind that you do not have to type a formula under the associated field name, DATE in this example.) The extracted records are displayed in rows 26 through 28.

You use the #AND#, #OR#, and #NOT# operators to enter (in one field) conditions that can be entered some other way (usually in at least two fields). For example, you can enter +C5="KT"#OR#C5="ST" in a single cell in row 21 (any cell in the criteria table A20..F21) as an alternative criterion entry for producing figure 11.32 (unit of issue as KT or ST in the Physical Inventory database).

Use #NOT# at the beginning of a condition to find anything that does *not* conform to that condition. For example, if the Physical Inventory database had only three units of issue—KT, ST, and EA (each)—you could produce the results shown in figure 11.32 by specifying the criterion #NOT#"EA" in cell C21 of the criteria table A20..F21.

You also can enter this kind of criterion into the /Advanced **D**atabase **Q**uery **F**ormula_Criterion menu. Use this command if you do not already have a criteria table set up.

```
        A                                  B      C        D          E         F
10 Phillips screwdriver set                8     EA     8.73      69.84
11 Hack Saw                                3     EA    11.89      35.67 08-Sep-88
12 Counter sink set, 10pc                  3     KY    13.44      40.32 15-Sep-89
13 Drop light, 100 foot                    4     EA    17.99      71.96
14 Square                                  0     EA    37.50       0.00 15-Sep-88
15 Hex wrench set                          2     KY    14.50      29.00
16 Wrench, box/open                        0     ST    46.70       0.00 31-Aug-88
17 Pipe wrench, 14 inch                    4     EA    56.70     226.00
18
19 Criteria Table
20 DESCRIPTION                     QUANTITY  ISSUE   COST     VALUE       DATE
21                                       1
22
23
24 Output Block
25 DESCRIPTION                     QUANTITY  ISSUE   COST     VALUE       DATE
26 Hammer, claw                            2     EA     6.75      13.50 02-Aug-88
27 Air hammer 3/8' drive                   1     KY    67.32      67.32 24-Aug-88
28 Wrench, box/open                        0     ST    46.70       0.00 31-Aug-88
29
A21: [W27] +DATE>@DATE(88,7,31)#AND#DATE<@DATE(88,9,1)
12-Apr-88  04:44 PM                                                          READY
```

Fig. 11.35. Using the #AND# special operator.

Performing Other Types of Searches

In addition to the **Q**uery and **L**ocate commands, you can use the Query menu's **U**nique and **D**elete commands for searches. By issuing the **U**nique command, you can produce (in the output block) a copy of only the first occurrence of a record that meets a specified criterion. And you can update the contents of your Quattro search block by deleting all records that meet a specified criterion. After entering the conditions, you need to specify only the search block and criteria table before you issue the **D**elete command.

Searching for Unique Records

Ordinarily, the **U**nique command is used to copy into the output area only a small portion of each record that meets the criterion. For example, if you want a list of measurements used in the Physical Inventory database, set up an output block that includes only the unit of ISSUE (see fig. 11.36). To search all records, leave blank the row below the field-name row in the criteria table A19..F20. Then, with the search block defined as A4..F16 and the output block set at A24, select **U**nique to produce (in rows 25 through 27) a list of the three units of measure.

As another example, you can produce from the college database a list of the majors selected by current students. To do so, you specify in the output area

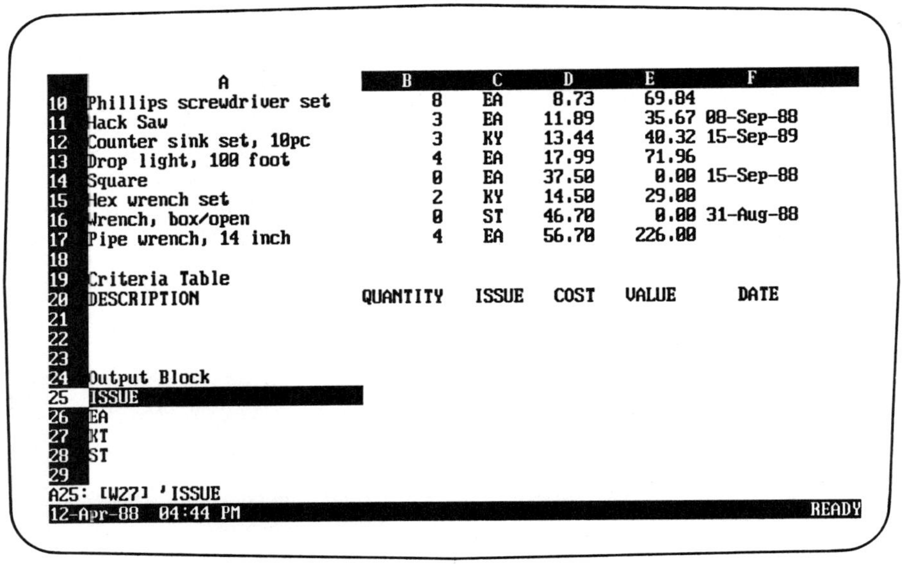

Fig. 11.36. Result of the Unique command.

only the field name MAJOR, leave blank the row under field names in the criteria table, and execute the Unique command.

Deleting Specified Records

As you know, you can use the /**R**ow **D**elete command sequence to remove records from a spreadsheet. If you want a fast alternative to this one-by-one approach, use the **D**elete command to remove unwanted records from your database files. Before you select **D**elete from the Query menu, simply specify the block of records to be searched (search block) and the conditions for the deletion (criteria).

For example, suppose that you want to remove from the address database all records with a STATE field beginning with the letter N. Specify a search block of A1..F19 and a criteria table of A22..F23, and use the criterion N* in cell E20. Then, issue the **D**elete command to remove all records for states that begin with N. As you can see from figure 11.37, the remaining records pack together in rows 2 through 14, and the search block automatically adjusts to A1..F14.

Be extremely careful when you issue the Delete command. To give you the opportunity to verify that you indeed want to select the **D**elete command,

	A	B	C	D	E	F
1	LAST	FIRST	STREET ADDRESS	CITY	STATE	ZIP
2	Harrington	James	12344 Arlington Lane	Covington	KY	41011
3	Leugers	Karen	21 Hill St. Apt. 34	San Fancisco	CA	34892
4	Pryor	Aaron	2341 Milford St.	Cincinnati	OH	45209
5	Cleary	Esther	238 Higgins St. Apt 14	Spokane	WA	89042
6	Wright	Ned	31238 Carolina St.	Kettering	OH	43289
7	Saunders	Ronald	3214 Keystone Ave.	Indianapolis	IN	46250
8	Simpson	Jeremy	3509 Ludlow Ave.	Newport	KY	43892
9	Wolf	Barbara	3098 Arnold Ave.	Dallas	TX	57820
10	Rooney	Kevin	391 Atwater Ave. Apt. 3	Providence	RI	02912
11	Sorrenson	Sarah	432 Keys Crescent	Bloomington	IN	47401
12	Holland	Earl	4983 Drake Rd.	Cincinnati	OH	45243
13	Tuke	Samuel	9038 Greenup St.	Seekonk	RI	02915
14	Malvern	Thomas	939 Dime Circle	Nashville	TN	47341
15						
16						
17						
18	Criteria Table					
19	LAST	FIRST	STREET ADDRESS	CITY	STATE	ZIP
20					N*	

E20: [W6] 'N*

12-Apr-88 04:47 PM READY

Fig. 11.37. Using the Delete command.

Quattro displays the following menu on which the least dangerous command (**C**ancel) is highlighted as the default:

Cancel
Delete

Choose **C**ancel to abort the delete command. Select **D**elete to verify that you want to execute the delete operation.

You can guard against deleting the wrong records by one of three precautionary measures. Before you issue a **Q**uery **D**elete command, you can

1. /**F**ile **S**ave the database, using a name such as TEMP, to create a copy of the original. Then, if the logic of the delete conditions proves faulty, you can retrieve this copy, which is the original file.
2. Perform an **E**xtract based on the delete conditions, view the records to verify that they are the ones to be removed, and then perform the **D**elete operation.
3. If you do lose data, you can use Quattro's Transcript add-in program to restore deleted records (see Chapter 14).

Chapter Summary

This chapter introduces and explains the basic database capabilities of Quattro. You learned how to create and modify a database. The /Advanced Database Sort and /Advanced Database Query commands, explained in this chapter, provide many options for working with the records in your database. You can rearrange the records in a database and find and extract records according to any criteria you want to use. Because the Quattro database is stored in the spreadsheet, all these activities can be accomplished quickly and easily.

Chapter 12 continues the discussion of databases by introducing and explaining more advanced database analysis activities.

CHAPTER

12

Quattro's Advanced Data Analysis Commands

Quattro's data analysis commands are the "number crunching" commands of the program. If you need to manipulate and analyze large tables of numbers, then the database statistical functions, what-if table, commands, and advanced frequency analysis commands may be just what you need.

The commands discussed in this chapter are, appropriately, under the Advanced menu. If your data management needs are usually met by the @SUM function, you may not need the features in this chapter. The /**A**dvanced **R**egression and /**A**dvanced **M**atrix commands will be of interest mainly to marketing researchers, demographers, and those interested in operations research.

Quattro's database statistical functions are similar to the spreadsheet statistical functions (described in Chapter 6). The database functions, which have been modified to manipulate database fields, are another powerful feature of Quattro.

Like the standard statistical functions, the database statistical functions perform complex calculations. (In Quattro, these functions are called aggregation and counting functions.) In one simple formula, a function performs a calculation that would otherwise require several formulas. This efficiency and ease of application make these functions excellent tools for data management and report generation.

The Quattro statistical functions include

@DCOUNT	Gives the number of items in a list
@DSUM	Sums the values of all the items in a list
@DMIN	Gives the minimum of all the items in a list
@DMAX	Gives the maximum of all the items in a list
@DSTD	Gives the standard deviation of all the items in a list
@DVAR	Gives the variance of all the items in a list
@DAVG	Gives the arithmetic mean of all the items in a list

The general form of these functions is

@Dfunction(input block, column, criteria table)

In order to work, a database function must have three elements, or arguments: an input (database) block, a column number, and a criteria table. The first element, the ***input block***, is a definition of the database block itself. The input block specified includes unique column headings in the top row, and each row below the headings contains related information (name, address, and so on) in the appropriate columns. (For more information on function arguments, see Chapter 6.)

The second argument, the column number, is a number that identifies the column of the input block on which the function will operate. The database functions begin counting columns starting from the left column of the data area (input block). The leftmost column of the table is numbered as column 0 (zero), not column 1.

Finally, the database function must have a criteria table, which is a spreadsheet block consisting of at least two rows. The first row duplicates at least one—and possibly many—of the column headings in the first row of the input block. The second row holds the labels or logical (true-false) formulas that make up the selection criteria. The criteria table limits or filters the information in statistical operations. One example of this filtering is a criterion that excludes part-time employees. This type of criterion can be entered manually into a cell below the first-row label that corresponds to the appropriate field name.

The input block and criteria table are the same as those used by the /**A**dvanced **D**atabase **Q**uery command (see Chapter 11).

The following example uses the database statistical functions. Suppose that you want to compute the mean, variance, and standard deviation of the average interest rates offered by money market funds for a given week. If you are unfamiliar with the concepts of mean, variance, and standard deviation, you can read more about them in Chapter 6. At this point, the assumption is that you know what these terms mean. The following explanation simply shows you how to use these functions with databases.

Figure 12.1 shows the Money Market database and the results of the database functions. Notice that the functions to find the maximum and minimum rates of return also are included.

	A	B	C	D	E
1	Money Market Database (7 day average yield)			Database	Statistics
2				-----------------	
3	NAME	WEEK 1		Count	17
4	Alliance Group Capital Reserves	7.7		Mean	7.7
5	Bull & Bear Dollar Reserves	7.7		Variance	0.057
6	Carnegie Cash Securities	7.4		Std Dev	0.238
7	Colonial Money Market	7.9		Maximum	8.2
8	Equitable Money Market Account	7.8		Minimum	7.3
9	Fidelity Group Cash Reserves	8.0			
10	Kemper Money Market	7.7			
11	Lexington Money Market	8.1			
12	Money Market Management	7.8			
13	Paine Webber Cash	7.9			
14	Prudential Bache	7.4		Criteria	Table
15	Saint Paul Money Market, Inc	7.6		WEEK 1	
16	Shearson T-Fund	8.2		1	
17	Short Term Income Fund	7.9			
18	Standby Reserves	7.6			
19	Summit Cash Reserves	7.3			
20	Value Line Cash Fund	7.7			

D16: +B4>7
21-Apr-88 10:10 AM READY

Fig. 12.1. Database functions used in Money Market database.

The functions are located in column E and labeled in column D. The functions and their arguments are

Count	@DCOUNT(A3..B20,1,D13..D14)
Mean	@DAVG(A3..B20,1,D13..D14)
Variance	@DVAR(A3..B20,1,D13..D14)
Std Dev	@DSTD(A3..B20,1,D13..D14)
Maximum	@DMAX(A3..B20,1,D13..D14)
Minimum	@DMIN(A3..B20,1,D13..D14)

Look at the @DCOUNT function in cell E3. The first argument shows that the function uses the block A3..B20 as its input block, or source data. The 1 (one) in the second argument of the formula tells the @DCOUNT function which column of the input block to operate (count) in. Remember that function arguments always begin counting with 0 (zero). In this case, column A is the leftmost column of the input block, so it is column 0. This @DCOUNT function is counting the entries in column B (offset of 1). The criteria table block is D13..D14. The formula in D14 (+B4>7) causes the @DCOUNT function to include in the count only the values in column B that are greater than 7. Cell references in a criteria formula are made to the first cell below the column names in the input block (B4). The answer in E3 indicates that column B contains 17 entries greater than 7.

Figure 12.1 shows that the week's mean return for 17 different money market funds works out to an annual percentage rate of 7.7 (cell E4) with a variance of 0.057 (cell E5). This result means that about 68 percent of the money market funds return between 7.46 and 7.94 percent annually. The following formulas show how you arrive at these figures:

One Std. Dev. below mean 7.7 - 0.238 = 7.46

One Std. Dev. above mean 7.7 + 0.238 = 7.94

The result of the @DMIN function (cell E8) shows that the lowest rate of return is 7.3 percent. Summit Cash Reserves returns at this rate. This value is almost two standard deviations below the mean. That figure—two standard deviations below the mean—is computed as follows:

Two Std. Devs. below mean 7.7 - (2 x 0.238) = 7.22

Because approximately 95 percent of the population falls within plus or minus two standard deviations of the mean, Summit Cash Reserves is close to being in the lowest 2.5 percent of the population of money market funds for that week; 5 percent is divided by 2 because the population is assumed to be normal. (See Chapter 6 for further discussion of how to interpret statistical functions.)

The Shearson T-Fund returns 8.2 percent, the highest rate. The @DMAX function in cell E7 has found the highest rate (cell B16) to be slightly more than two standard deviations (E6) above the mean (E4), which is the highest 2.5 percent in a normally distributed population.

By setting up the proper criteria, you can analyze any portion of the database you want. For example, you may want to know the effect of changing the input block.

How do the statistics change if funds returning less than 7.5 percent are excluded from the statistics? Figure 12.2 gives the answer. Note that the count, mean, variance, and standard deviation all change because of the new criterion in cell D14 (+B4>7.5).

	A	B	C	D	E
1	Money Market Database (7 day average yield)			Database	Statistics
2				----------	----------
3	NAME	WEEK 1		Count	14
4	Alliance Group Capital Reserves	7.7		Mean	7.8
5	Bull & Bear Dollar Reserves	7.7		Variance	0.031
6	Carnegie Cash Securities	7.4		Std Dev	0.175
7	Colonial Money Market	7.9		Maximum	8.2
8	Equitable Money Market Account	7.8		Minimum	7.6
9	Fidelity Group Cash Reserves	8.0			
10	Kemper Money Market	7.7			
11	Lexington Money Market	8.1			
12	Money Market Management	7.8			
13	Paine Webber Cash	7.9			
14	Prudential Bache	7.4		Criteria	Table
15	Saint Paul Money Market, Inc	7.6		WEEK 1	
16	Shearson T-Fund	8.2		1	
17	Short Term Income Fund	7.9			
18	Standby Reserves	7.6			
19	Summit Cash Reserves	7.3			
20	Value Line Cash Fund	7.7			

D16: +B4>7.5

21-Apr-88 10:11 AM READY

Fig. 12.2. Using database statistical functions to analyze changes in the Money Market database.

Obviously, the database statistical functions can tell you a great deal about the database as a whole and about how to interpret the values it contains. Suppose that you add several more weeks' data to the database, as shown in figure 12.3. The database statistical functions can be used to analyze all or part of the larger database.

The use of block names in the @DCOUNT function helps you understand what the formula is doing. The input block (DB) starts at A3 and extends through G20. The offset of 3 means that the statistics shown reflect values

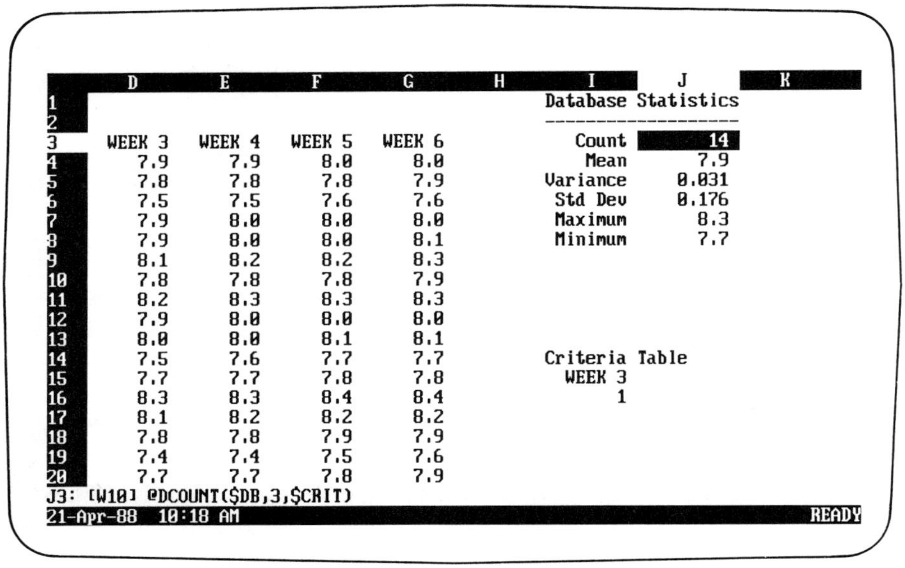

Fig. 12.3. A portion of the Money Market database with several weeks' data added.

selected from column D. The criterion has not changed from figure 12.2 except that the user has changed the label in I13 to match the column header in column D (WEEK 3).

You can use all the methods you have seen so far to interpret the statistics in figure 12.3. The input block, column, and criteria table used for the data from the third week of our example are as follows:

Input block	A3..G20
Column	3 (for the fourth column)
Criteria table	I13..I14

From this information, you can determine how the formulas have been set up for each week. The criteria table displayed in figure 12.3 (I13..I14) shows the criterion used to select the values for the third week.

Table Building

Table building is an extension of the what-if process, in which the spreadsheet instantly shows the effects of changing variables, such as discount rates, inflation rates, salary levels, and so on. In fact, you can duplicate the functions performed by the table-building feature by performing a series of what-if analyses. This method takes a prohibitive amount of time, however. Table building automates the what-if process so that you can make a thorough analysis with a minimal amount of effort.

Table building automates the what-if process through iteration: Quattro takes sets of values and substitutes them one at a time for existing values in the worksheet. You provide the values for substitution and tell Quattro where to substitute them. The program automatically records the results.

This procedure may sound mysterious, but it is actually simple; Quattro does most of the work internally. All you have to know is how to set up the appropriate blocks; Quattro takes care of the rest.

The /**A**dvanced **W**hat-If command, which performs the table building, makes Quattro a superlative program for performing what-if analysis. Although the /**A**dvanced **W**hat-If command may take some time to learn, you will find it one of the most powerful in Quattro. In fact, the strength of this command rivals that of similar commands in more sophisticated mainframe decision-support systems. When you consider the command's strength and its ease of implementation, you will find that the /**A**dvanced **W**hat-If command is an excellent feature.

The purpose of the /**A**dvanced **W**hat-If command is to structure the what-if analysis. The command lets you build a table of input values, which the program substitutes one at a time into your model. Quattro then records the results in the table next to the input values. The /**A**dvanced **W**hat-If **1**_Variable command builds a table of results based on one variable referenced by one or more formulas. The /**A**dvanced **W**hat-If **2**_Variables command builds a table of results based on two variables but only one formula.

As a demonstration, look at a simple example that builds a table of interest rates and shows their effects on the monthly payments of a 30-year mortgage, as shown in figure 12.4.

By using the /**A**dvanced **W**hat-If **1**_Variable command, you can have Quattro substitute in the input cell the interest rates you have entered in column B. After calculating the results, Quattro lists the monthly payments in column C next to the corresponding interest rates.

Before entering the /**A**dvanced **W**hat-If **1**_Variable command, you enter the interest rate values in a column. (To enter those values, you can use the /**B**lock **F**ill command, which was covered in Chapter 4.) Cells B7..B18 hold the interest rates.

For the next step, you need to enter either the appropriate formula for calculating the results or the cell address from which to draw those results. This entry goes to the right of the column of interest rates and one row above

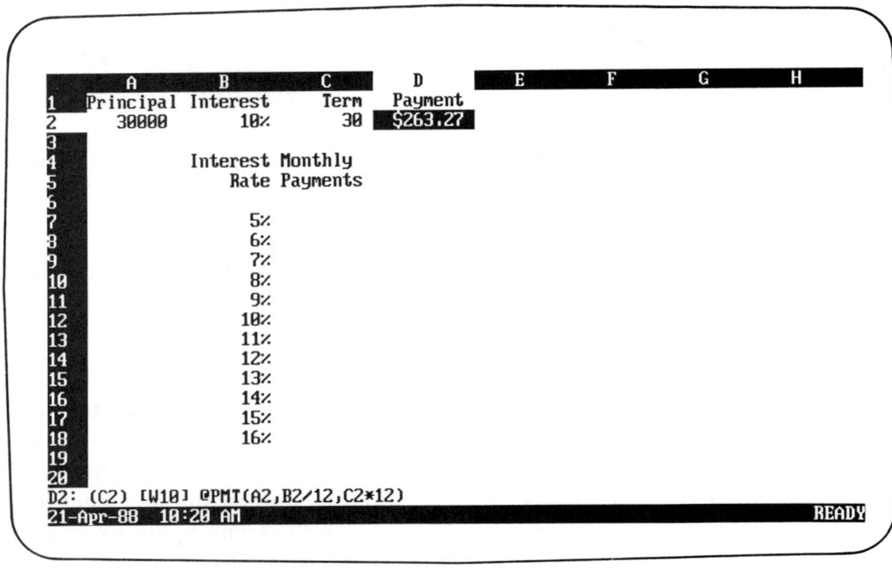

Fig. 12.4. Building a table of interest rates for a 30-year mortgage.

the first entry. The entry is located in this position because the top left cell is the input cell, where Quattro substitutes the various interest rates in order to calculate and complete the data table.

The value +D2 is entered in cell C6, as shown in figure 12.5, but you could enter in C6 the formula for computing the value. The formula in cell D2 is

@PMT(A2,B2/12,C2*12)

In the formula A2 is the principal amount; B2 is the annual interest rate, which is divided by 12 to yield a monthly rate; and C2 is the term in years, which is multiplied by 12 to give the number of months in the life of the loan. The +D2 appears because the /**B**lock **D**isplay-**F**ormat **T**ext command was issued for cell C6, causing the formula rather than the value to be displayed.

At this point, you issue the /**A**dvanced **W**hat-If **1**_Variable command. Quattro then prompts you to specify a *table block*, a block of cells that includes the column of interest rates and the column where the results are to appear. In this example, you enter B6..C18 in response to the prompt. Notice that this block specification includes the formula row.

Then the program prompts you to enter an *input cell*. This cell is the cell to which the @PMT function refers for its interest rate argument. That is, the

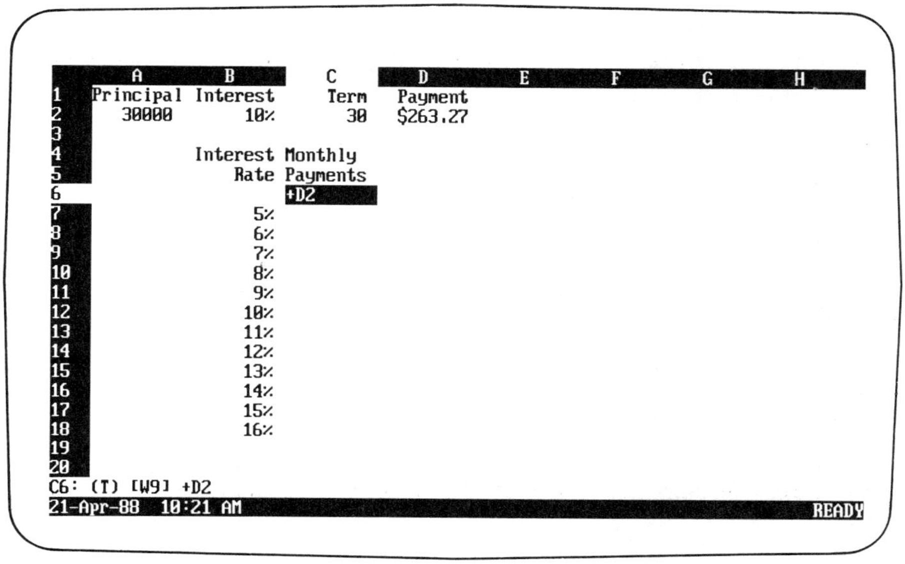

Fig. 12.5. Entering the formula for computing payments at different interest rates.

input cell is the cell to which all the values in the column of interest rates relate. In a manner of speaking, Quattro plugs into cell B2, one after the other, the values of the interest-rate column. The @PMT function uses each new variable as its interest argument. The function places to the right of the appropriate interest rate variable each answer generated.

While Quattro calculates the results, the WAIT mode indicator flashes in the lower right corner of the screen. When the calculation is finished, the mode changes to READY. Now the table contains all the payment values (see fig. 12.6).

If you want to try some other input values, you can change the values and then press the Alt-F7 (Table) key to recalculate the table automatically. When the table is recalculated, Quattro uses the command parameters you specified in the previous /**A**dvanced **W**hat-If command.

A more complicated example, shown in figure 12.7, uses the /**A**dvanced **W**hat-If **2**_Variable command, which requires two input variables instead of one. Using more variables increases the breadth of the sensitivity analyses you can perform. This example is designed to show the effects on total cost of changes

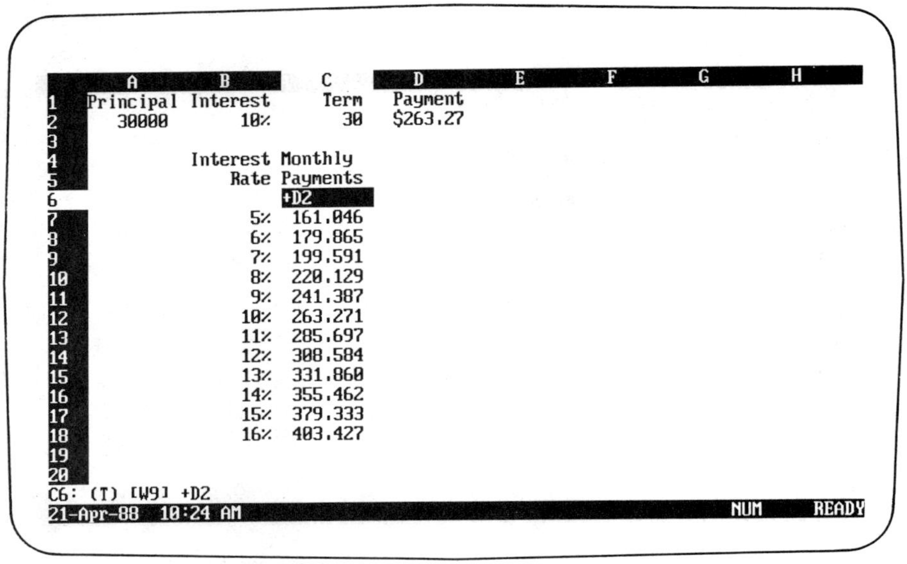

Fig. 12.6. The finished table of interest rates.

in order quantity and order point. You are looking for the combination of order point and order quantity that minimizes Cumulative Costs to Date at the end of a 12-month period.

The lower left portion of figure 12.7 shows the result of using the /**A**dvanced **W**hat-If **1**_Variable command to calculate the effect of different order quantities on cost. The /**A**dvanced **W**hat-If **2**_Variable command creates a more extensive table, as shown in the lower right portion of the figure. This table shows the effect on cost of both order point and order quantity. The result is a more complete analysis. This completeness is the advantage of the /**A**dvanced **W**hat-If **2**_Variable command.

To use the /**A**dvanced **W**hat-If **2**_Variable command, you enter the values for variable 2 (order quantity, in this example) in the row just above the first entry of variable 1 (order point). In the example, these values begin in cell F21. Notice also that you enter +N13, the address of the formula for Cost to Date, in the row directly above the first entry of variable 1, cell E21 in the example. Again, the Text format is used so that the cell displays +N13.

When you issue the /**A**dvanced **W**hat-If **2**_Variable command, Quattro calls for a table block and two input cells—for variables 1 and 2. You enter the following information for these parameters:

	A	B	C	D	E	F	G	H	I	J	K	L	M
1	Month	Jan	Feb	Mar	Apr	May	Jun	Jul	Aug	Sep	Oct	Nov	Dec
2	----------------------------	--------	--------	--------	--------	--------	--------	--------	--------	--------	--------	--------	--------
3	Beginning Inventory	43	15	39	28	10	38	18	45	21	11	39	20
4	Past Demand for Month	28	16	11	18	12	20	13	24	10	12	19	22
5	Ending Inventory	15	-1	28	10	-2	18	5	21	11	-1	20	-2
6	Quantity Ordered	0	40	0	0	40	0	40	0	0	40	0	40
7	Setup Costs ($10 per order)	$0.00	$10.00	$0.00	$0.00	$10.00	$0.00	$10.00	$0.00	$0.00	$10.00	$0.00	$10.00
8	Inventory Costs ($.2/unit)	$3.00	$0.00	$5.60	$2.00	$0.00	$3.60	$1.00	$4.20	$2.20	$0.00	$4.00	$0.00
9	Shortage Costs ($1/unit)	$0.00	$1.00	$0.00	$0.00	$2.00	$0.00	$0.00	$0.00	$0.00	$1.00	$0.00	$2.00
10	Total Costs for Month	$3.00	$11.00	$5.60	$2.00	$12.00	$3.60	$11.00	$4.20	$2.20	$11.00	$4.00	$12.00
11	Cum Cost from Last Month	$0.00	$3.00	$14.00	$19.60	$21.60	$33.60	$37.20	$48.20	$52.40	$54.60	$65.60	$65.60
12	Cumulative Costs to Date	$3.00	$14.00	$19.60	$21.60	$33.60	$37.20	$48.20	$52.40	$54.60	$65.60	$69.60	$77.60
13													
14													
15	Order Quantity Input Cell	40											
16	Order Point Input Cell	8											
17													
18		Order	Cumulative										
19	DATA TABLE 1 -->	Quant	Cost		DATA TABLE 2 -->			Order Quantity					
20		--------	--------			--------	--------	--------	--------	--------	--------	--------	
21			+014		+014	38	39	40	41	42	43	Average	
22		25	$104.00		1	$91.20	$103.80	$96.40	$96.00	$93.20	$91.60	$95.37	
23		26	$109.60		2	$91.20	$103.80	$96.40	$93.80	$93.20	$91.60	$95.00	
24		27	$106.40		3	$91.20	$86.40	$96.40	$93.80	$93.20	$91.60	$92.10	
25		28	$98.00		4	$91.20	$86.40	$96.40	$93.80	$93.20	$91.60	$92.10	
26		29	$99.60		5	$90.40	$86.40	$81.60	$93.80	$84.80	$91.60	$88.10	
27		30	$102.40		6	$90.40	$86.40	$81.60	$93.80	$94.80	$91.60	$89.77	
28		31	$95.20		7	$90.40	$86.40	$81.60	$81.60	$94.80	$91.60	$87.73	
29		32	$91.60		8	$93.20	$86.40	$81.60	$81.60	$94.80	$87.00	$87.43	
30		33	$94.60	o	9	$93.20	$93.60	$81.60	$81.60	$85.20	$87.00	$87.03	
31		34	$95.60	r	10	$93.20	$93.60	$87.20	$81.60	$85.20	$97.00	$89.63	
32		35	$86.60	d	11	$93.20	$93.60	$94.00	$88.60	$85.20	$90.00	$90.77	
33		36	$88.80	e	12	$88.80	$93.60	$94.00	$88.60	$93.60	$90.00	$91.43	
34		37	$84.60	r	13	$88.80	$93.60	$94.00	$88.60	$93.60	$98.60	$92.87	
35		38	$93.20		14	$96.40	$93.60	$94.00	$96.80	$93.60	$98.60	$95.50	
36		39	$93.60	p	15	$110.40	$100.20	$100.80	$103.80	$100.80	$106.00	$103.67	
37		40	$81.60	o	16	$110.40	$108.60	$100.80	$103.80	$100.80	$106.00	$105.07	
38		41	$81.60	i	17	$110.40	$108.60	$100.80	$103.80	$109.20	$106.00	$106.47	
39		42	$85.20	n	18	$110.40	$116.40	$108.80	$103.80	$109.20	$106.00	$109.10	
40		43	$87.00	t	19	$110.40	$116.40	$108.80	$103.80	$109.20	$106.00	$109.10	
41		44	$90.00		20	$110.40	$116.40	$114.40	$112.00	$109.20	$114.60	$112.83	
42		45	$88.40		21	$110.40	$116.40	$122.40	$112.00	$109.20	$114.60	$114.17	
43		46	$86.80		22	$110.40	$116.40	$122.40	$112.00	$117.60	$114.60	$115.57	
44		47	$86.40		23	$110.40	$116.40	$122.40	$112.00	$117.60	$114.60	$115.57	

Fig. 12.7. Using the /Advanced What-If command for inventory analysis.

Table Block	E21..K47
Input Cell Variable 1	B16
Input Cell Variable 2	B15

For /Advanced **W**hat-If **2**_Variables, the formula must be entered in the upper left corner of the table block.

After you enter this information, Quattro begins building the table of results. Although you may have to wait for the /Advanced **W**hat-If **2**_Variable command to work, the results are well worth your time. To duplicate manually what Quattro does would take much longer. If you plan to use the /**A**dvanced **W**hat-If command often, you may want to invest in an 8087, 80287 or 80387 coprocessor for your computer in order to speed calculations.

Note that you find no single correct answer concerning the effect of changes in order quantity and order point on total cost. Our limited analysis, however, shows that on average an order point of about 9 and an order quantity of about 41 are best (a combination of lowest cost and highest order point).

Advanced Database Output Using What-If Tables

The most powerful use of what-if tables is in combination with database statistical functions (described in Chapter 7 and in this chapter). If you use a database statistical function as the formula in a what-if table, you can create a complete statistical summary or cross referencing of your database. For example, you can cross reference a part-number column with a part-count column to generate a list of unique part numbers and the quantity on hand of each part.

When might you need this capability? Take an example of a personnel management system. One day your boss comes into your office and says that he needs to have total and average salaries for the entire company. You think that a few simple calculations will do the trick. So far, not very difficult. However, the boss goes on to ask for this information broken down by department. He also needs another report totaling and averaging salaries by employee classification. As soon as these reports are done, you need to generate few more of the same type.

What started out as a simple request has grown into a monster that will eat up much of your precious time . . . unless you use Quattro. Quattro can turn this reporting nightmare into a pleasant little data-processing interlude.

You can easily solve this problem by querying your database, using the @DSUM function, and then executing a **W**hat-If **1**_Variable command on the results.

Here are the major steps needed to compose the reports your box needs. These steps are explained and illustrated in the following paragraphs.

1. Do an /**A**dvanced **D**atabase **Q**uery **U**nique operation to create a unique list of departments.
2. Formulate an @DSUM function above and to the right of the department list.
3. Choose the correct criteria.

4. Set up a what-if table.
5. Issue the /**A**dvanced **W**hat-If table command.

In the examples that follow, you will create a statistical abstract of an employee database.

First, you need to set up an /**A**dvanced **D**atabase **Q**uery **U**nique operation in order to create a unique list of departments. This operation requires the creation of a copy of the Dept column header. The entry has been made in cell G1 as shown in figure 12.8.

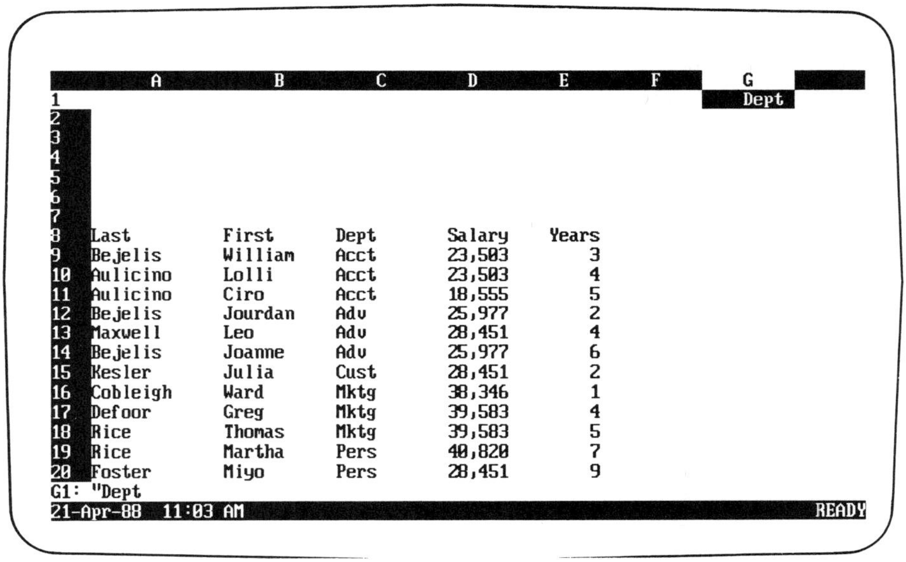

	A	B	C	D	E	F	G
1							Dept
2							
3							
4							
5							
6							
7							
8	Last	First	Dept	Salary	Years		
9	Bejelis	William	Acct	23,503	3		
10	Aulicino	Lolli	Acct	23,503	4		
11	Aulicino	Ciro	Acct	18,555	5		
12	Bejelis	Jourdan	Adv	25,977	2		
13	Maxwell	Leo	Adv	28,451	4		
14	Bejelis	Joanne	Adv	25,977	6		
15	Kesler	Julia	Cust	28,451	2		
16	Cobleigh	Ward	Mktg	38,346	1		
17	Defoor	Greg	Mktg	39,583	4		
18	Rice	Thomas	Mktg	39,583	5		
19	Rice	Martha	Pers	40,820	7		
20	Foster	Miyo	Pers	28,451	9		

G1: "Dept

21-Apr-88 11:03 AM READY

*Fig. 12.8. Preparing for the /**A**dvanced **D**atabase **Q**uery **U**nique command.*

The next step is to prepare the database for the Unique extract of department names. Figure 12.9 shows the blocks that have been entered to set up the query. Notice that the criteria table and the output block overlap. During normal database operations this overlap causes problems. Because this Unique extract is going to be used with what-if tables, the overlap actually proves to be a convenience. You do not need to enter separate criteria and output entries in cells. The result of the Unique operation is shown in figure 12.10.

Now that you have a list of the departments (column G), you can build the what-if table. As already explained, what-if tables are driven by a formula. The supplied variables are invisibly "plugged" into the input cell during the table

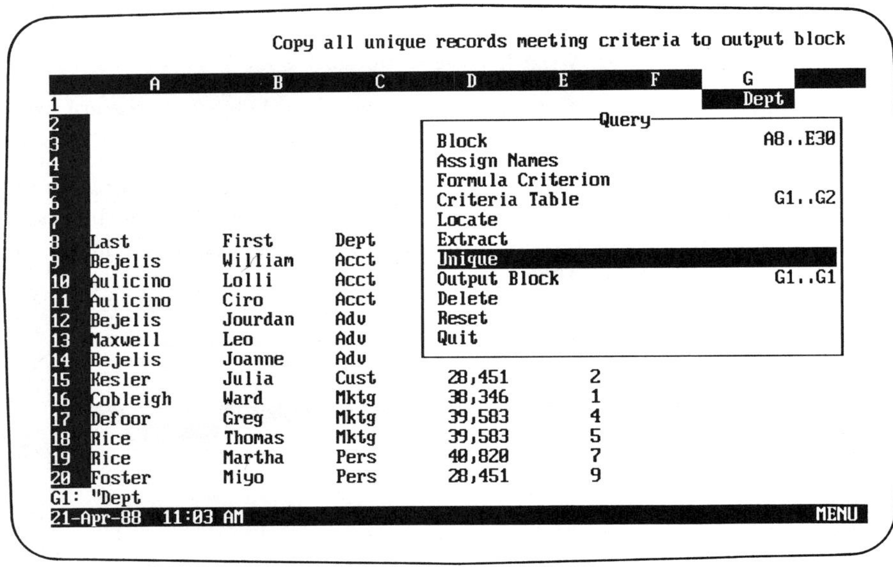

Fig. 12.9. Blocks specified for the query command.

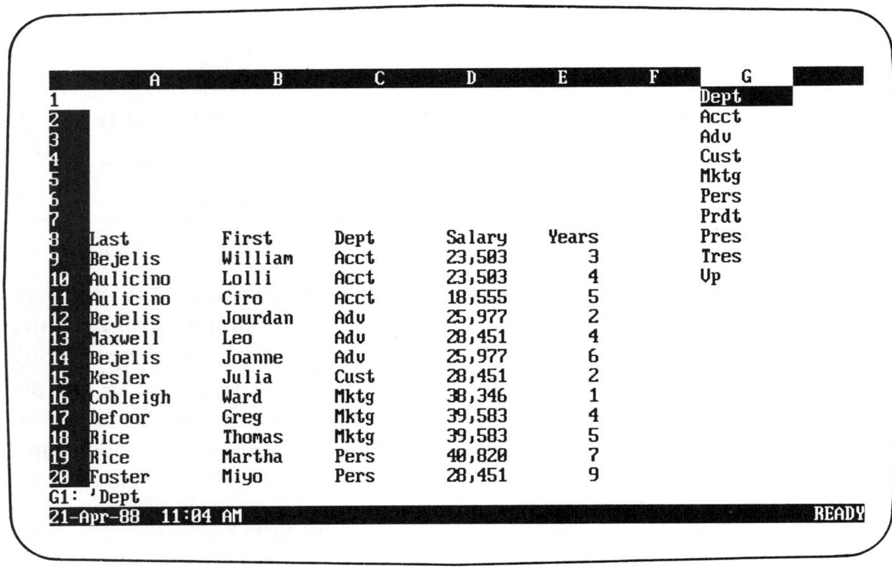

Fig. 12.10. Results of the Unique operation.

operation. In this case, you use a database statistical function. The input cell is the cell where the criterion normally is entered.

Figure 12.11 shows the database statistical formula in cell H1. The formula @DAVG(A8..E30,3,G1..G2) calculates the average salary for the Acct department in this example. The first argument of the formula is the input block; the second argument refers to the offset (Salary). The criteria block is G1..G2. When the /**A**dvanced **W**hat-If command is issued, the criterion ACCT is replaced by the other department names. In this way, the function generates the averages for all the other departments in the list in column G. The results are displayed in column H.

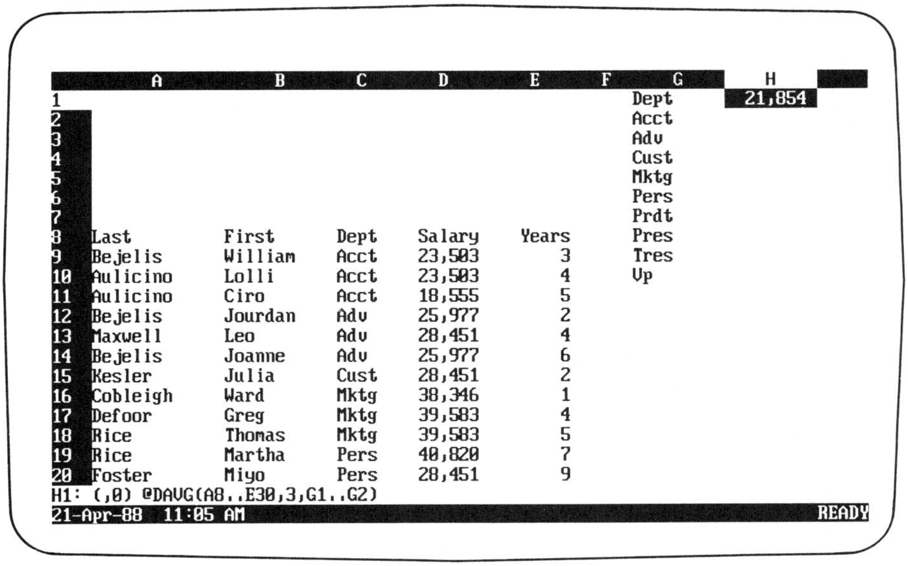

Fig. 12.11. Entering a database statistical function for calculating average salary by department.

Now you're ready to create the table. After you invoke the /**A**dvanced **W**hat-If **1**_Variable command, Quattro displays a prompt to identify the data table block. Figure 12.12 shows the block G1..H10 being highlighted.

As soon as the table block is entered, Quattro requests the input cell (see fig. 12.13). The input cell in the case of database cross referencing is always the criterion cell, G2 in this example. As a rule of thumb, the input cell is always the last cell referenced inside the function.

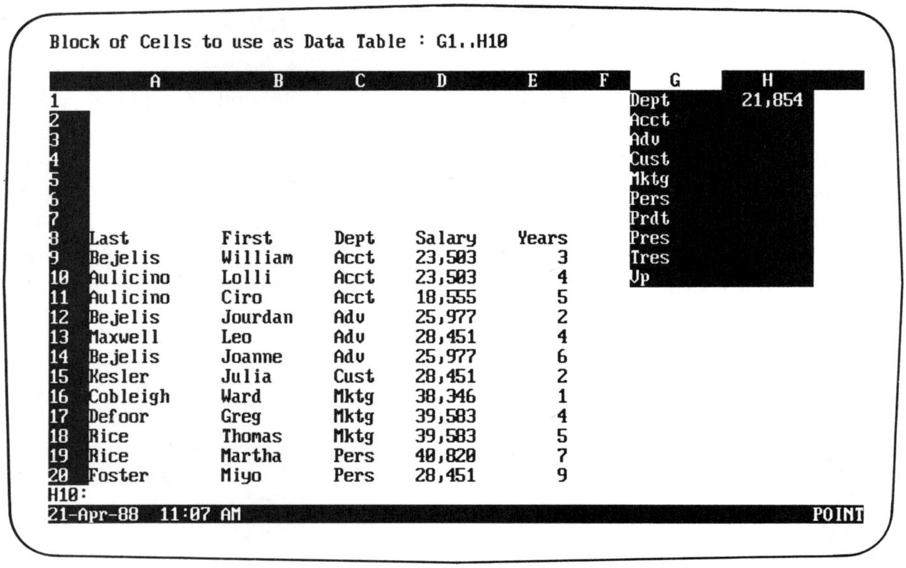

Block of Cells to use as Data Table : G1..H10

	A	B	C	D	E	F	G	H
1							Dept	21,854
2							Acct	
3							Adv	
4							Cust	
5							Mktg	
6							Pers	
7							Prdt	
8	Last	First	Dept	Salary	Years		Pres	
9	Bejelis	William	Acct	23,503	3		Tres	
10	Aulicino	Lolli	Acct	23,503	4		Vp	
11	Aulicino	Ciro	Acct	18,555	5			
12	Bejelis	Jourdan	Adv	25,977	2			
13	Maxwell	Leo	Adv	28,451	4			
14	Bejelis	Joanne	Adv	25,977	6			
15	Kesler	Julia	Cust	28,451	2			
16	Cobleigh	Ward	Mktg	38,346	1			
17	Defoor	Greg	Mktg	39,583	4			
18	Rice	Thomas	Mktg	39,583	5			
19	Rice	Martha	Pers	40,820	7			
20	Foster	Miyo	Pers	28,451	9			

H10:

21-Apr-88 11:07 AM POINT

Fig. 12.12. Specifying the data table block.

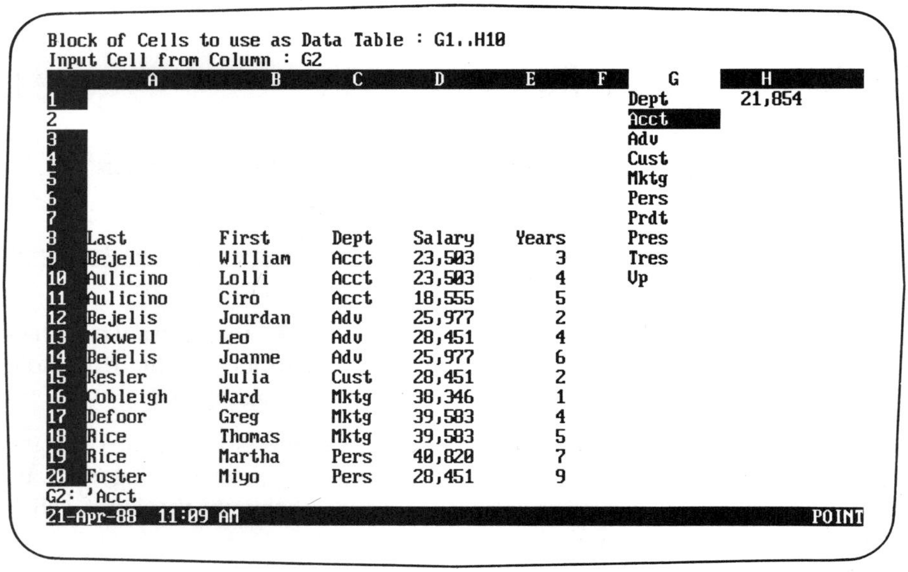

Block of Cells to use as Data Table : G1..H10
Input Cell from Column : G2

	A	B	C	D	E	F	G	H
1							Dept	21,854
2							Acct	
3							Adv	
4							Cust	
5							Mktg	
6							Pers	
7							Prdt	
8	Last	First	Dept	Salary	Years		Pres	
9	Bejelis	William	Acct	23,503	3		Tres	
10	Aulicino	Lolli	Acct	23,503	4		Vp	
11	Aulicino	Ciro	Acct	18,555	5			
12	Bejelis	Jourdan	Adv	25,977	2			
13	Maxwell	Leo	Adv	28,451	4			
14	Bejelis	Joanne	Adv	25,977	6			
15	Kesler	Julia	Cust	28,451	2			
16	Cobleigh	Ward	Mktg	38,346	1			
17	Defoor	Greg	Mktg	39,583	4			
18	Rice	Thomas	Mktg	39,583	5			
19	Rice	Martha	Pers	40,820	7			
20	Foster	Miyo	Pers	28,451	9			

G2: 'Acct

21-Apr-88 11:09 AM POINT

Fig. 12.13. Input cell prompt.

Figure 12.14 shows the result of the table operation after you finish the entries and press the Enter key; you now have a complete list of average salaries by department.

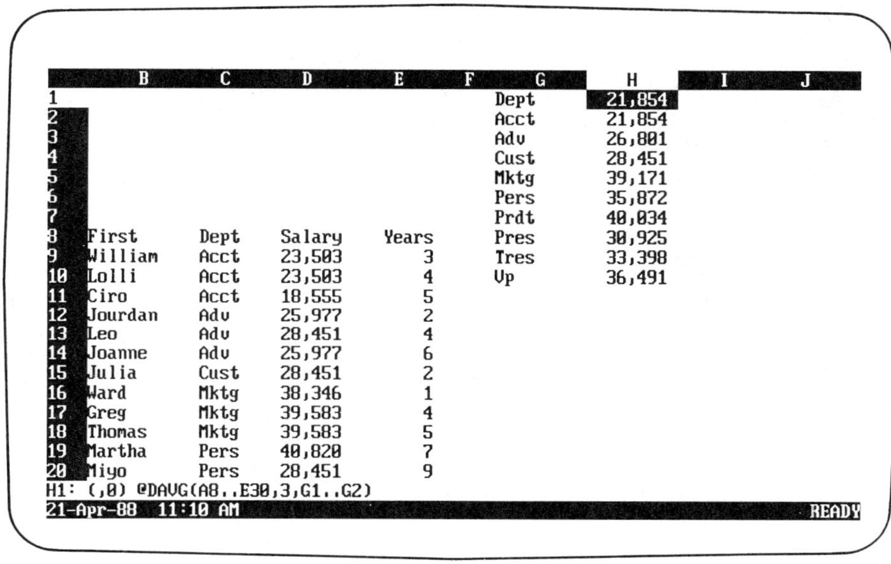

Fig. 12.14. Result of the what-if table operation.

Now that the averages have been calculated, sooner or later someone will ask for the totals by department. Figure 12.15 shows the results of a new @DSUM function in column I. The functions arguments are identical to the formula in H1. As the figure illustrates, all you need to do to include the new formula in the table operation is to widen the area of the data table. The input cell stays the same. Figure 12.16 shows the results.

The advantage of the /**A**dvanced **W**hat-If command is that it allows you to perform extensive sensitivity analysis and display the results in a tabular format. You can perform analyses that you might not otherwise perform because of the time required.

Frequency Distributions

The command for creating frequency distributions in Quattro is the /**A**dvanced **F**requency command. A *frequency distribution* describes the relationship between a set of classes and the frequency of occurrence of mem-

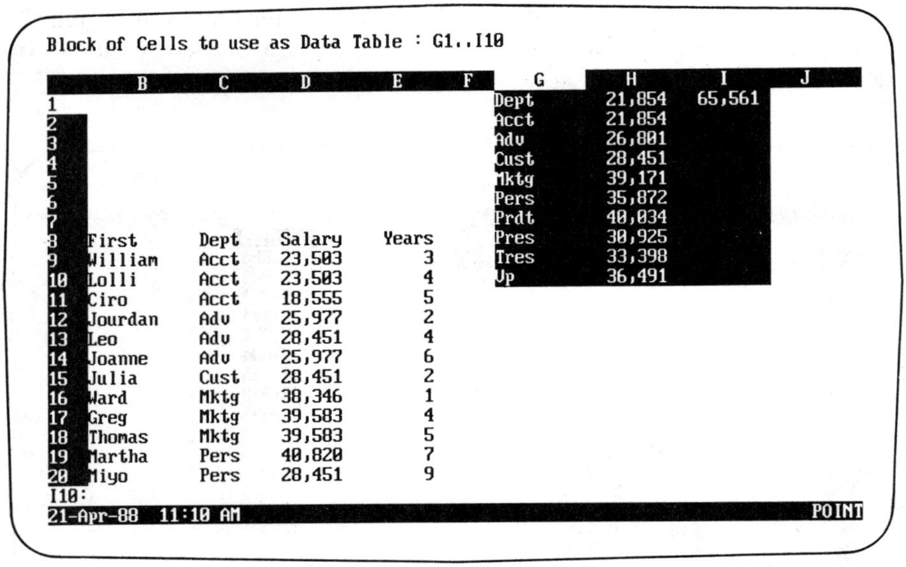

Fig. 12.15. Entering the @DSUM function in column I.

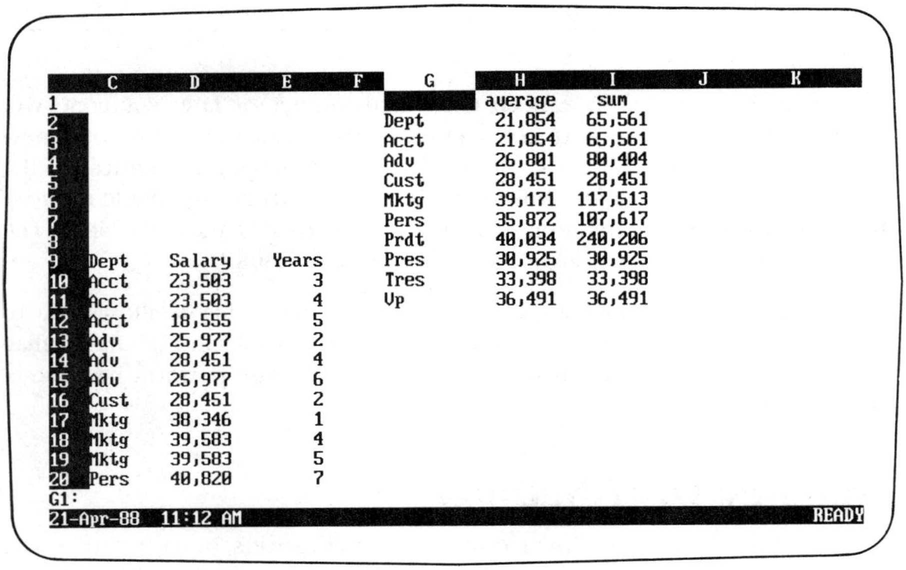

Fig. 12.16. Results of adding the @DSUM function.

bers of each class. A list of consumers with their product preferences illustrates use of the /**A**dvanced **F**requency command to produce a frequency distribution (see fig. 12.17).

	A	B	C	D	E	F	G
1		TASTE					
2	NAME	PREFERENCE		PREFERENCE	FREQUENCY		
3	Howard Perks	2		2	5		
4	Peter Arnold	7		4	1		
5	Chris Batts	8		6	4		
6	Patrick Campbell	8		8	5		
7	Robert Connery	7		10	1		
8	Louise Becker	2					
9	Nancy Deckard	6					
10	Richard Garber	5					
11	Gary Stokes	2					
12	Robert Fetzer	3					
13	Sue Johnson	7					
14	Kevin Kipp	6		2	Poor		
15	Edward Herman	9		4	Fair		
16	Michael Hasting	1		6	Good		
17	Daniel Lee	6		8	Very Good		
18	Kathy Woelfler	1		10	Excellent		
19							
20							

E3: [W11] 5

21-Apr-88 11:16 AM READY

Fig. 12.17. Using the /Advanced Frequency command.

To use the /**A**dvanced **F**requency command, you first specify a ***values block***, which corresponds to the block of Taste Preference numbers in this example. After specifying B3..B18 for the values block, you set up the ***block of intervals*** as D3..D7, in what Quattro calls the ***bins block***. You can think of intervals as numeric "pigeon holes." For instance, a postal sorter might have a series of pigeon holes, or bins, with a range of ZIP codes assigned to each. The first pigeon hole might have ZIPs ranging from 20000 to 20050, the next bin might go from 20051 through 21000, and so on. The count of the letters placed in each pigeon hole is analogous to the frequency number of each bin in the bins block. If you have evenly spaced intervals, you can use the /**B**lock **F**ill command to enter the values for the bins block. If the intervals are not evenly spaced, you cannot use the /**B**lock **F**ill command to fill the block. (/**B**lock **F**ill is discussed in Chapter 4.)

When you specify these blocks and issue the /**A**dvanced **F**requency command, Quattro creates the ***results column*** (E3..E8 in the example) to the right of the bins block (D3..D7). The results column, which shows the frequency distribution, is always in the column to the right of the bins block and always extends one row farther down.

The values in the results column represent the frequency of distribution of the numbers in the values block for each interval. The first interval in the bins block is for values greater than zero and less than or equal to two; the second, for values greater than two and less than or equal to four, and so on. The last value in the results column, in cell E8, shows the frequency of numbers that don't fit into any interval classification.

The /Advanced **F**requency command helps you create understandable results from a series of numbers. The results also are easily graphed.

The /Advanced Regression Command

The /Advanced **R**egression command gives you a multiple-regression analysis package within Quattro. Most people probably will never use this advanced feature. But if you need to use it, Quattro saves you the cost and inconvenience of buying a stand-alone statistical package for performing regression analysis.

You use /Advanced **R**egression when you want to determine the relationship between one set of values (the dependent variable) and one or more other sets of values (the independent variables). Regression analysis has a number of uses in a business setting, including relating sales to price, promotions, and other market factors; relating stock prices to earnings and interest rates; and relating production costs to production levels. Once you determine the relationship, you can use the trend of the relationship as an indicator of what may occur in the future.

Think of linear regression as a way of determining the "best" line through a series of data points. The more closely the data fits the line, the more useful the line is as a predictor of future events. Multiple regression does this operation for several variables simultaneously, determining the "best" line relating the dependent variable to the set of independent variables. As an example, you will use a data sample showing Annual Earnings versus Age. Figure 12.18 shows the data; figure 12.19 shows the data plotted as an XY graph.

The /Advanced **R**egression command can determine simultaneously both how to draw a line through these data points and how well the line fits the data. When you invoke the command, the following menu appears:

Independent [columns]
Dependent [columns]
Output
Y-intercept
Go
Reset

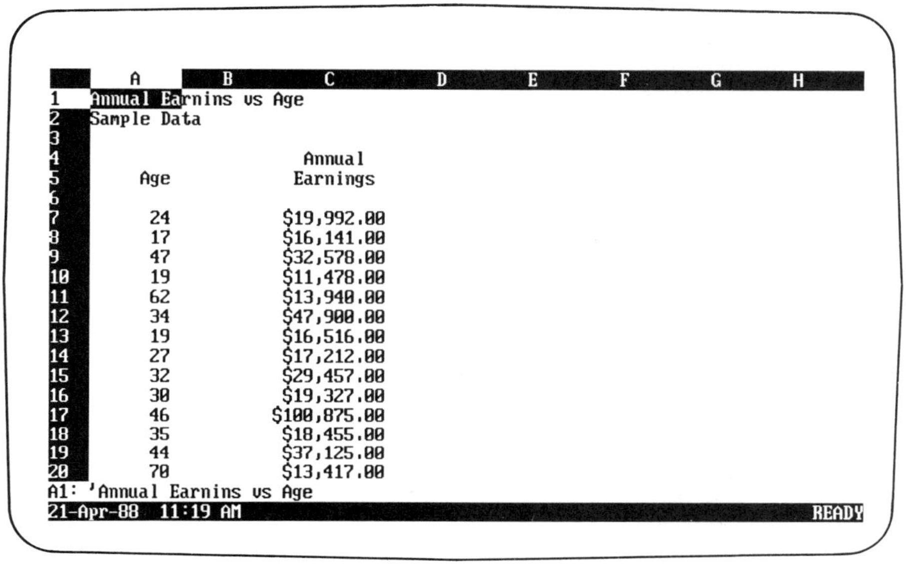

	A	B	C	D	E	F	G	H
1	Annual Earnins vs Age							
2	Sample Data							
3								
4			Annual					
5	Age		Earnings					
6								
7	24		$19,992.00					
8	17		$16,141.00					
9	47		$32,578.00					
10	19		$11,478.00					
11	62		$13,940.00					
12	34		$47,900.00					
13	19		$16,516.00					
14	27		$17,212.00					
15	32		$29,457.00					
16	30		$19,327.00					
17	46		$100,875.00					
18	35		$18,455.00					
19	44		$37,125.00					
20	70		$13,417.00					

A1: 'Annual Earnins vs Age
21-Apr-88 11:19 AM READY

Fig. 12.18. Data for use with the /Advanced Regression command.

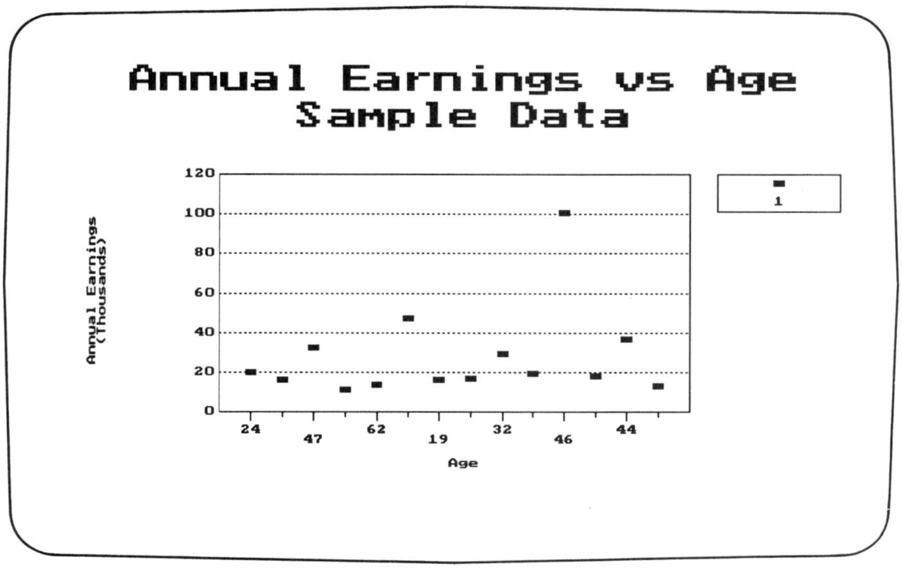

Fig. 12.19. XY graph of the results of the /Advanced Regression command.

You use the **I**ndependent option to select one or more independent variables for the regression. The /**A**dvanced **R**egression command can use as many as 16 independent variables. Because the variables in the regression are columns of values, any data in rows must be converted to columns with /**B**lock **A**dvanced **T**ranspose before the /**A**dvanced **R**egression command is issued (see Chapter 4). In this example, the Independent block is A7..A20.

The **D**ependent option specifies the dependent variable. The dependent block must be a single column; you therefore select C7..C20 for this example.

The **O**utput option specifies the upper left corner of the results block. This block should be an unused section of the worksheet, because the output is written over any existing cell contents.

The **Y**-intercept option lets you specify whether you want the regression to calculate a constant value. Calculating the constant is the default, but in some applications you may need to exclude a constant.

Figure 12.20 shows the results of using the /**A**dvanced **R**egression command in the Annual Earnings versus Age example. The results include the value of the constant and the coefficient of the single independent variable that you specified with the **I**ndependent option. The results also include a number of regression statistics that describe how well the regression line fits the data. In this case, the R-Squared value and the standard errors of the constant and the regression coefficient all indicate that the regression line does not explain much of the variation in the dependent variable.

The new formulas that the user has entered in column D compose the computed regression line. These values consist of the constant plus the coefficient of the independent variable times the independent variable for each row of the data. This line can be plotted against the original data.

The /Advanced Matrix Command

The /**A**dvanced **M**atrix command is a specialized mathematical command that lets you solve systems of simultaneous linear equations and manipulate the resulting solutions. This command is powerful but has limited application in a business setting. If you are using Quattro for certain types of economic analysis or for scientific or engineering calculations, you may find this command valuable.

The /**A**dvanced **M**atrix command has a menu with two options: **I**nvert and **M**ultiply. The **I**nvert option lets you invert a nonsingular square matrix of up to 90 rows and columns. Just select the **I**nvert option and highlight the block you want to invert. Then select an output block to hold the inverted solution

	A	B	C	D	E	F	G	H
1	Annual Earnings vs Age					Regression Output:		
2	Sample Data							
3								
4		Age X	Annual	Regression				
5	Age	Age	Earnings	Line	Constant			-56032.4
6					Std Err of Y Est			20621.69
7	17	289	$19,992	$5,456	R Squared			0.342581
8	19	361	$16,141	$10,789	No. of Observations			14
9	19	361	$32,578	$10,789	Degrees of Freedom			11
10	24	576	$11,478	$22,373				
11	27	729	$13,940	$28,123	X Coefficient(s)		4467.105	-50.0087
12	30	900	$47,900	$32,973	Std Err of Coef.		1881.828	22.01466
13	32	1024	$16,516	$35,706				
14	34	1156	$17,212	$38,039				
15	35	1225	$29,457	$39,056				
16	44	1936	$19,327	$43,703				
17	46	2116	$100,875	$43,636				
18	47	2209	$18,455	$43,452				
19	62	3844	$37,125	$28,695				
20	70	4900	$13,417	$11,622				

A1: [W6] 'Annual Earnings vs Age

21-Apr-88 01:06 PM READY

Fig. 12.20. Result of using the /Advanced Regression command.

matrix. You can place the output block anywhere in the worksheet, including on top of the matrix you are inverting.

The time required to invert a matrix is proportional to the cube of the number of rows and columns, so you may spend a great deal of time waiting. If you are going to use Quattro to invert matrixes, you may want to invest in a coprocessor appropriate for your computer.

The **M**ultiply option allows you to multiply two rectangular matrixes together in accordance with the rules of matrix algebra. The number of columns in the first matrix must equal the number of rows in the second matrix. The result matrix has the same number of rows as the first matrix and the same number of columns as the second.

When you select /**A**dvanced **M**atrix **M**ultiply, Quattro prompts you for three blocks: the first matrix, the second matrix, and the output block. **M**ultiply is fast compared to **I**nvert, but may still take some time if you multiply large matrixes.

Chapter Summary

This chapter shows you Quattro's advanced decision-support and data analysis commands. You have learned how to use database statistical functions, generate what-if analyses, and combine functions to create powerful database reporting capabilities. Finally, you have been introduced to the specialized frequency distribution, linear regression, and matrix commands.

The next section helps you customize Quattro by using add-in programs, creating macros, and changing Quattro's default settings.

Part IV

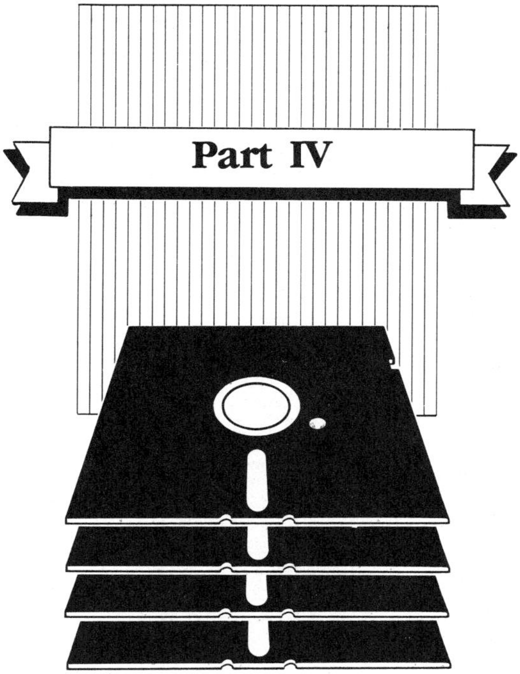

Customizing Quattro: Menus, Macros, and Add-In Programs

Includes

How To Make Quattro Look and Work
the Way You Want

Working with Add-In Programs

Using Macros in Quattro

Quattro Macro Command Reference

Making the Best Use of Quattro's Macro Debugger

CHAPTER

13

How To Make Quattro Look and Work the Way You Want

One of Quattro's most helpful characteristics is that you can change it to do almost anything you want. If you want different colors on the display, it's no problem for Quattro. If you want all new worksheets formatted in financial display format, you can do it. If you want Quattro to be able to run and create compatible macros, it's a breeze.

This chapter describes the many options you have in configuring Quattro to fit your personal needs and work habits. In this chapter you learn how to

- Change the way Quattro uses display hardware
- Modify the colors in the spreadsheet
- Set Quattro's International and Format options
- Establish default file directories
- Determine how Quattro recalculates formulas

- Customize Quattro's behavior when the program is started
- Make Quattro compatible with 1-2-3

Modifying Hardware-Related Defaults

When I first loaded Quattro on my system, I expected to be forced to go through the usual tedium of telling Quattro all about the hardware the program was going to be talking to. What a pleasure to discover that Quattro does a terrific job of getting that information without help from the user.

This automatic configuration is accomplished by using AUTODETECT drivers. Quattro uses these drivers to make what it considers the best use of your available hardware.

If you are responsible for installations and support for personal computer systems, the automatic installation feature of Quattro can save untold time and frustration. If you work with more than one computer, automatic installation is a boon because Quattro optimally configures itself every time you load it. You can work with a computer with a monochrome display at home and a computer with a VGA display at work, for instance, and Quattro handles the different details for you.

No matter how good Quattro is, though, some settings can't be determined by your hardware. The /**D**efault commands exist for these settings. This section describes how to make changes to hardware-related defaults. The following sections explain how to make changes to operational defaults.

One thing to keep in mind about many of the Default menus is that every default has a current setting. You need to know the current settings before you decide to change them. Information about the current defaults is given on the menus that control those settings. You can't see the current settings, however, unless the menus are expanded. So be sure to set your menus to this mode either by making it the default setting (described in the section on /**D**efault **S**tartup **C**ompatibility Options) or by pressing the plus (+) key on the numeric keyboard to expand menus as they appear.

Retaining Modifications to Defaults

If you are not careful, you may find that the changes you make to Quattro disappear after every work session. This disappearance occurs because all permanent changes must be stored in Quattro's configuration file, QUATTRO.DEF.

To add to this file the changes you make to default settings, choose the **U**pdate command from the Default menu. Most of the default settings and commands described in this chapter are made permanent by issuing this **U**pdate command.

After you make changes to default settings, you must leave the program and restart Quattro before the changes will take effect. This requirement is especially important for modifications to the/**D**efault **S**tartup and /**D**efault **F**ormats commands.

Modifying Hardware Screen Settings

To modify the way Quattro works with your hardware, you use the /**D**efault **H**ardware command. The resulting menu has two selections: **S**creen and **T**ext_Printer. The **S**creen selection is discussed in this chapter. The **T**ext_Printer options are described in detail in Chapter 9.

To change basic display settings, select /**D**efault **H**ardware **S**creen. The Screen menu is divided into two sections: Text Screen Option and Graph Screen Option. Figure 13.1 shows the Screen menu and the current settings for a system configured with an enhanced graphics adapter (EGA).

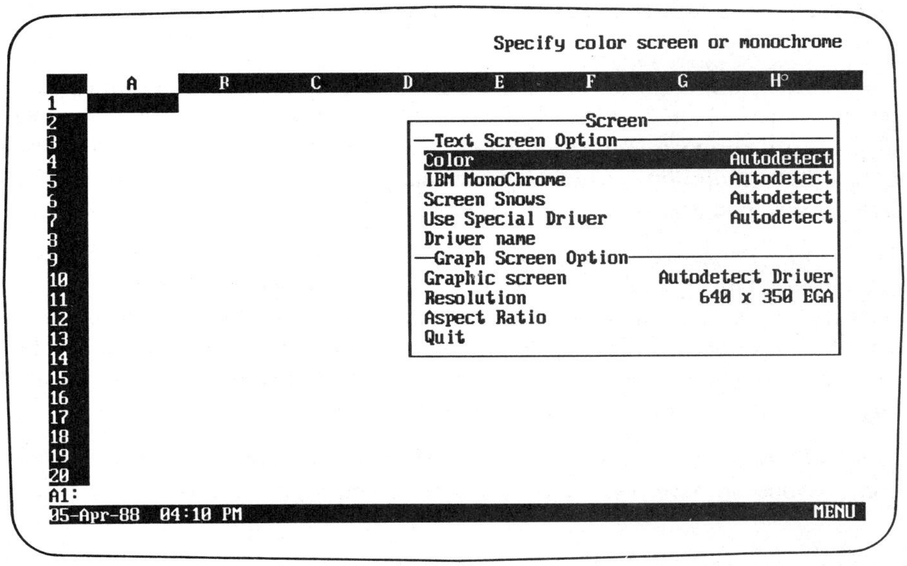

Fig. 13.1. Default Screen menu with settings for a system with an enhanced graphics adapter.

The Text Screen options determine the screen drivers Quattro uses to control the display of text. Normally, the choice of driver made by the Autodetect setting is what you need. If your computer does not respond properly to Quattro's automatic detection, you can change from Autodetect by specifying one of the following selections:

Color
IBM_Monochrome
Use_Special_Driver

Each selection has three menu choices: Yes, No, and Autodetect. If you set any of these three to Yes, the other two must be set to No. If you set **U**se_Special_Driver to Yes, you then need to specify the driver's name with the **D**river_name command.

The first Quattro packages included no special text drivers. Later versions support 35- and 43-line EGA displays for the spreadsheet.

The **S**creen_Snows option is used to suppress screen snowing or "flickering" during scrolling. Set this selection to Yes if snowing occurs.

Under Graph Screen Option, the **G**raphic_screen option selects the driver that provides access to the capabilities of your graphics card (if one is installed). Quattro supports an extensive list of graphics adapter cards, including Video Graphics Array and the IBM 8514/A high-speed, high-resolution display extender.

Use the **R**esolution option to set the display adapter to the resolution (pixels per inch) you want. Usually, the higher the resolution, the fewer colors the display card supports. With the EGA adapter, for example, if you select the 640_x_200 resolution, you can have as many as 16 colors. If you move up to 640_x_350, you are limited to 4 colors.

The **A**spect_Ratio option adjusts the roundness of pie graphs on-screen. When you choose **A**spect_Ratio, you see a crosshair displayed in a circle. Figure 13.2 illustrates an aspect ratio that produces "lemon" graphs rather than pie graphs. To widen the circle, press the down arrow. If you need to narrow the circle, press the up arrow. Figure 13.3 demonstrates that the circle becomes round after the down arrow is pressed several times.

Generally speaking, the more flexible your graphics adapter system, the more control you can have over color, resolution, and aspect ratio.

Modifying Default Color Choices

In some situations, you may need to modify Quattro's best guess as to your optimum configuration. For instance, Quattro can't tell what kind of monitor

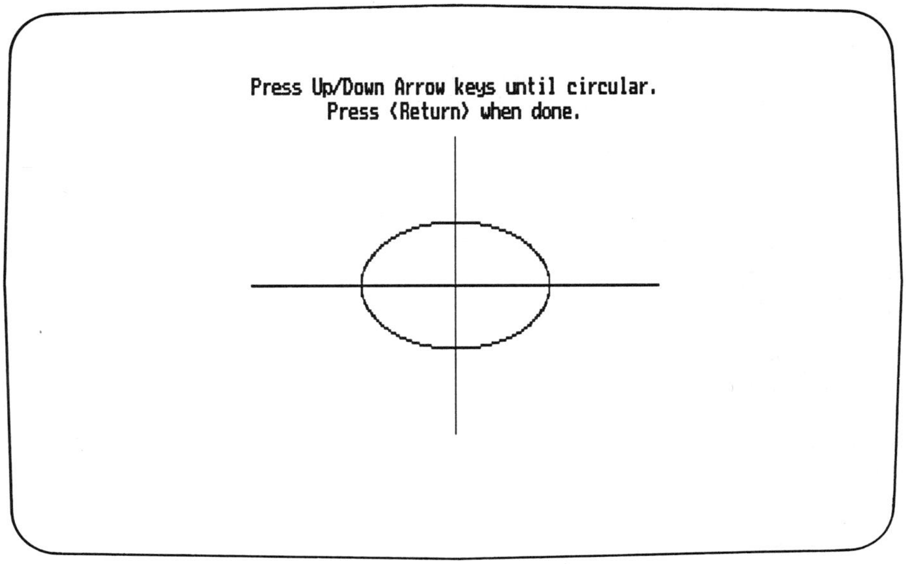

Fig. 13.2. Aspect ratio producing a "lemon" graph.

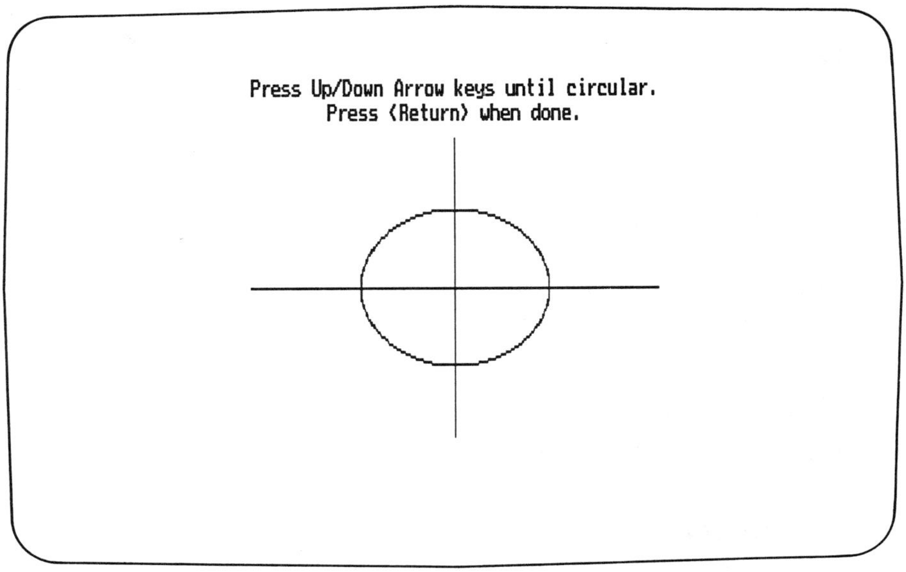

Fig. 13.3. Aspect ratio producing a round pie graph.

you are using. The program chooses its display characteristics based on the internal circuit card that works with your monitor, such as MDA, CGA, Hercules, EGA, or VGA adapters. If the monitor doesn't quite fit the display adapter card, Quattro may not choose a display that fits your needs.

For example, if you are using a portable computer that uses a graphics adapter, such as CGA or EGA, Quattro "assumes" that the display unit will produce color output. Yet few, if any, portable computers have a color display. When Quattro makes color choices for the spreadsheet, therefore, some of the colors, which appear as shades of green, will not be appealing visually. You can modify the choice of screen driver to alleviate confusing green tone displays.

The command that controls Quattro's colors is /**D**efault **C**olors. Options on the Colors menu give you complete control over the spreadsheet colors. From this menu you can control the colors available to Quattro overall and the individual color elements of the menu, spreadsheet, and help screens (see fig. 13.4).

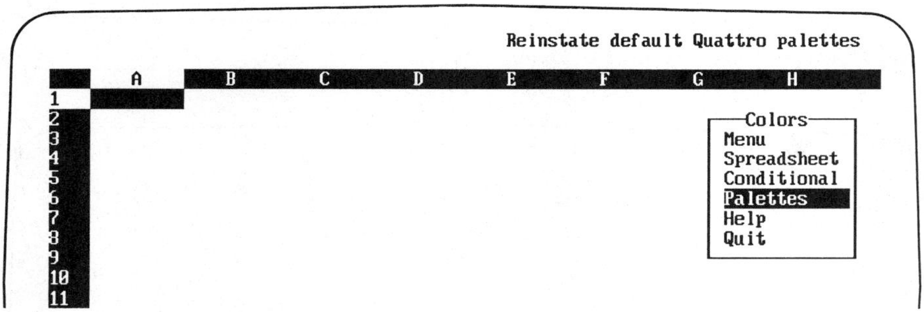

Fig. 13.4. The Default Colors menu.

I recommend some restraint in this area. Remember that a spreadsheet is usually considered a productivity tool. Noted *PC Magazine* columnist Stephen Manes has identified a class of software he calls "fritterware." In the same way, if you spend inordinate amounts of time playing around with colors, you will be frittering away precious time. To avoid this trap, remember that the most important of the color choices is the **P**alettes command.

Choosing Palettes

The **P**alettes command sets the palette of colors, which Quattro then makes available for the spreadsheet, menu, and help screens. The commands on the Palettes menu are shown in figure 13.5, which shows the display controlled by the **B**lack & White palette.

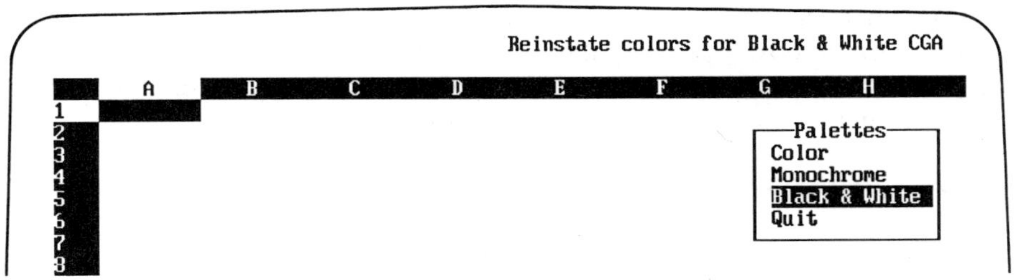

Fig. 13.5. The Palettes menu.

If you choose **C**olor, the full spectrum of colors available with your system is presented. The EGA system provides a palette of 128 colors. The menu, spreadsheet borders, cursor, and the spreadsheet itself all can be in different hues. Each screen element can be assigned any color on the Color palette. These options are detailed in the next section.

The **M**onochrome command sets up the palette for the display attributes that the monochrome display adapter can support, such as high-intensity displays and underlining. You can easily switch back and forth among the Color, Monochrome, and Black & White palettes.

The **B**lack & White option is used on a system where the display adapter supports color, but the monitor is a two-color system, such as black-and-white, amber, and green monitors. Users of portable and laptop computers will want to be aware of this selection.

The active palette determines the colors or screen attributes that can be chosen through the other /**D**efault **C**olors commands: **M**enu, **S**preadsheet, **C**onditional, and **H**elp.

When you select a new palette, you are effectively resetting any modifications to the default **C**olors settings for the **M**enu, **S**preadsheet, **C**onditional, and **H**elp settings. This fact is a good thing to know if your spreadsheet begins to look ghastly.

Selecting Menu Colors

The choices other than **P**alettes on the Colors menu present the palette chosen by the **P**alettes command. For instance, in the menu displayed by the /**D**efault **C**olors **M**enu command, you can move a cursor within the palette. When you press the Enter key, the new color is immediately used for the selected screen element.

The /**D**efault **C**olors **M**enu command controls the colors for the elements of the spreadsheet menu boxes, such as the menu frame, title, menu choices, and optional "drop shadows." When you are in an unfamiliar menu, you can access help screens by pressing the F1 key. Figure 13.6 shows the help screen that you access from the Menu Colors menu. The help screens provide a complete map of the menu elements and their purposes.

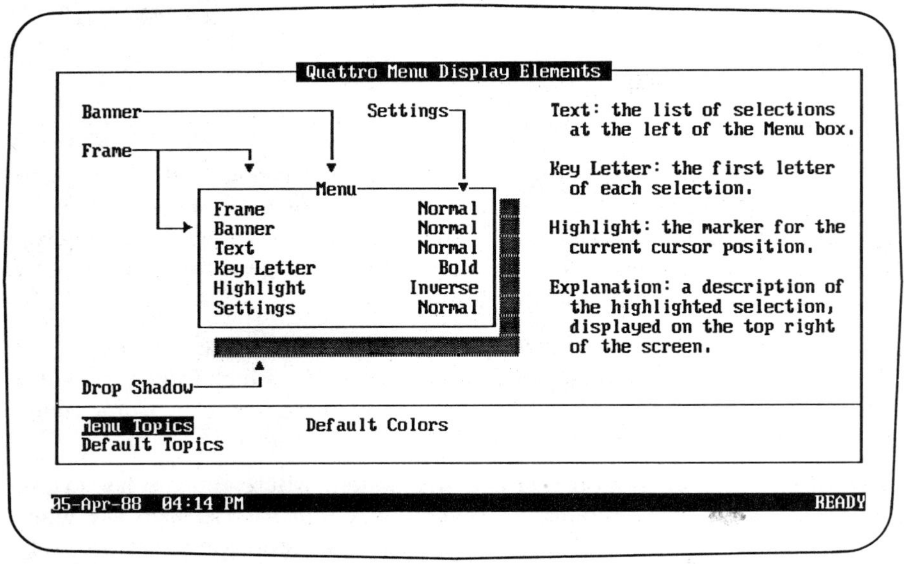

Fig. 13.6. The help screen for the Menu Colors menu.

Selecting Spreadsheet Colors

Each time you go to a menu that allows you to change colors, you see a color palette. Just as an artist selects colors for the canvas, you can choose from the palette colors for the elements in the display you choose.

Suppose that you issue the /**D**efault **C**olors **S**preadsheet command and then select **C**ells from the Spreadsheet menu. The palette is displayed automatically; each spot on the palette has a color combination, such as white on blue. When the palette is first displayed, the palette's cursor highlights the current colors for the selected element. To use the color palette, move the small square cursor to the spot on the palette that has the colors you want.

Be sure to avoid color combinations that cause the display to "wash out." To illustrate what I mean, take the extreme example of white on white. Because no contrast exists between white on white, the menu literally disappears.

If you have selected a Monochrome palette from the /**D**efault **C**olors **P**alettes command, the available palette is restricted to monochrome display attributes (see fig. 13.7). The elements that can be modified from the Spreadsheet colors menu are identified in the help screen shown in figure 13.8.

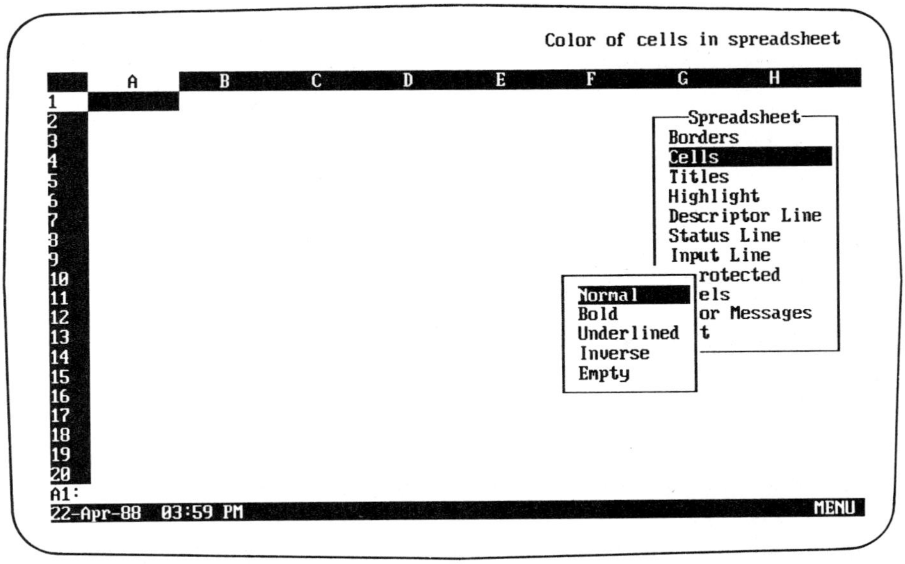

Fig. 13.7. Monochrome display attributes.

Setting Conditional Cell Colors

The main reason for using a spreadsheet is to help you make better decisions about business matters. Usually, Quattro does an exceptional job in supporting decisions. However, a spreadsheet can get so large or complex that you can't determine quickly which cells contain important or unusual data. Quattro has the capability to assign colors to cells that need to be highlighted more than usual. This feature is called conditional coloring.

The conditional coloring feature is on the /**D**efault **C**olors **C**onditional menu. Figure 13.9 shows the options available from the Conditional colors menu. From this menu, you can control the color of error cells and the appearance of exceptionally large or small numbers.

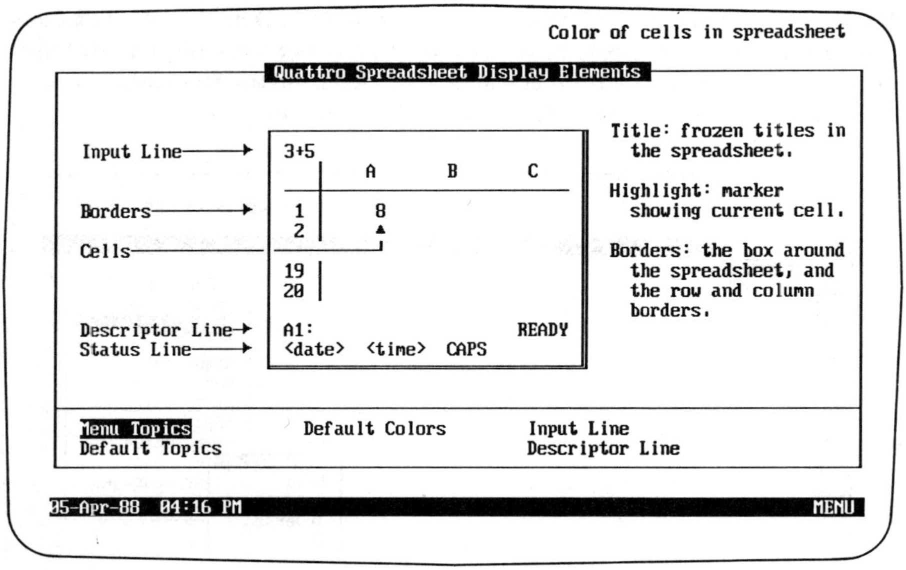

Fig. 13.8. Help screen for the Spreadsheet colors menu.

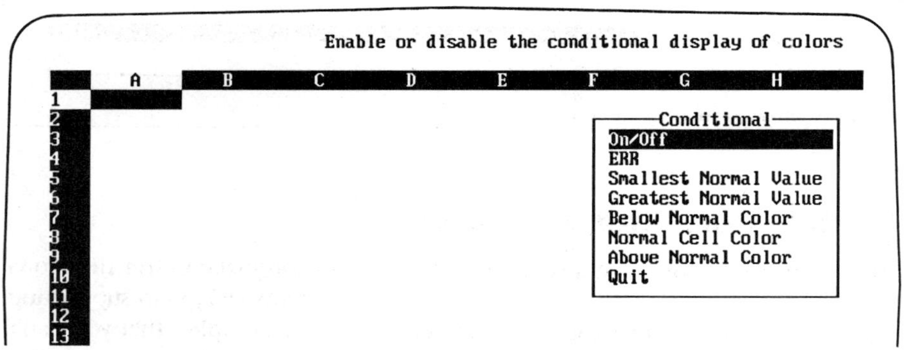

Fig. 13.9. The Conditional colors menu.

The example in figure 13.10 shows an invoice-age database, which is used to determine performance effectiveness of the person charged with collecting on accounts. Because the spreadsheet contains so many numbers, the model uses conditional coloring to highlight records that are unusually high or low.

Figure 13.10 shows the application with a **S**mallest_Normal_Value of 22 being entered. This value means that any number below 22 appears in the cell color assigned by the **B**elow_Normal_Color option. A **G**reatest_Normal_Value of

46.7 also is entered. As soon as the settings have been completed, the **O**n/Off menu choice is selected to enable conditional coloring. The different colors make seeing the unusual amounts much easier.

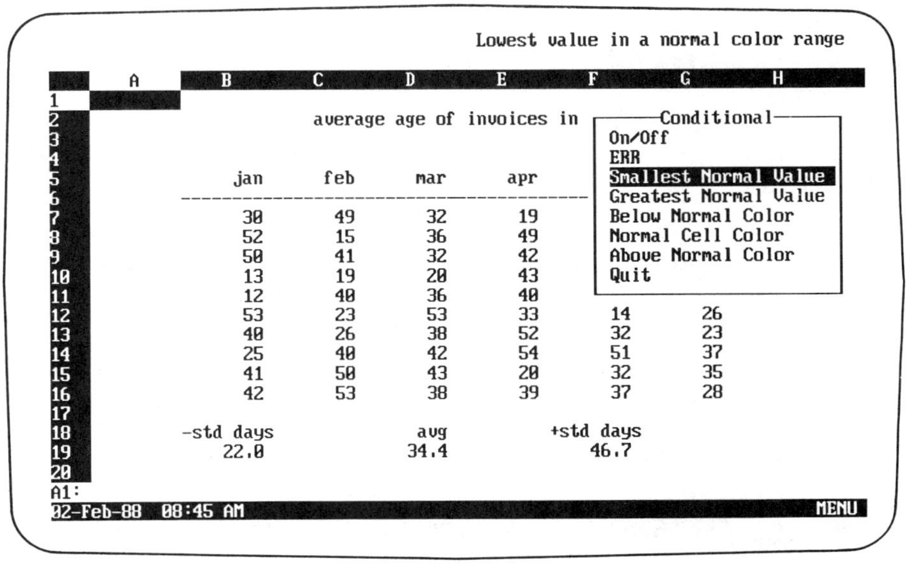

Fig. 13.10. The invoice-age database.

Changing the Help Screen Colors

The /**D**efault **C**olors **H**elp command gives you control over the appearance of the help screens. The help screens come with a simple scheme of two colors: black and white. I think this decision is good. You add only limited value by changing colors in the help screens. Figure 13.11 shows the Help colors menu.

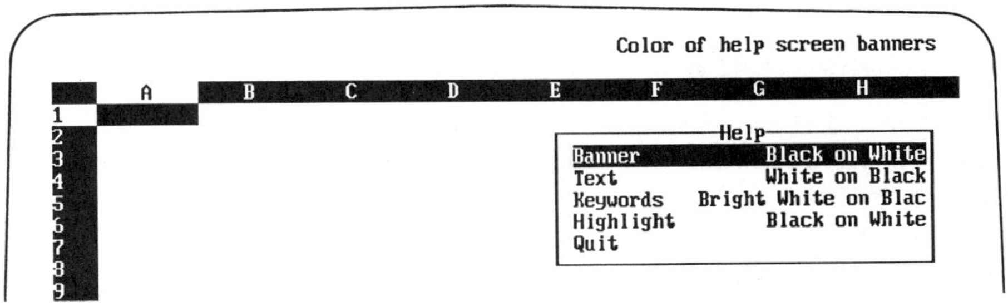

Fig. 13.11. The Help colors menu.

The **Banner** option on the Help colors menu selects the color for the titles of the help screens. **Text** obviously controls the color of the main text in the help screens. **Keywords** modifies the hues of menu choices within the help system, and **Highlight** determines the appearance of the Help menu cursor.

Internationalizing Quattro

If you need to use European or Asian time, date, currency, or punctuation conventions, the /**D**efault **I**nternational command provides the facilities for these changes.

Quattro allows you to specify the punctuation and currency sign displayed by Financial (,) and Currency formats and to control the way the date and time are displayed when you use the special International Date and Time formats.

To control these settings globally for the worksheet, use the /**D**efault **I**nternational command. Figure 13.12 shows the Default International menu.

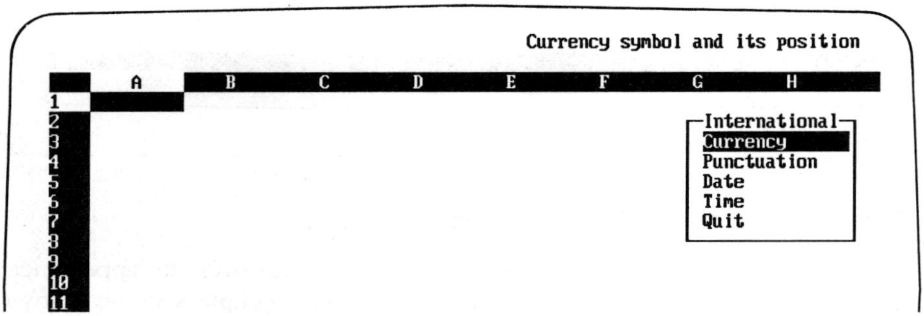

Fig. 13.12. The Default International menu.

With the **C**urrency option, you change the currency symbol displayed by Currency format and specify whether that symbol is a prefix or suffix. You can enter any character from the ASCII character set or a string of characters to be displayed (such as $US or $CAN).

The **D**ate and **T**ime options set the International Date and Time formats. You have four choices each for the date and time formats. The default format for dates is MM/DD/YY (01/16/88) and, for time, HH:MM:SS in 24-hour time (19:25:33).

The **P**unctuation option of the /**D**efault **I**nternational command gives you a choice of eight ways to punctuate numbers and to separate function arguments. The default is the standard American convention of a period between an integer and its fractional component, commas to separate thousands, and commas to separate function arguments. Seven other combinations are available for punctuating numbers; for example, you can use periods instead of commas to separate hundreds from thousands and so on.

Controlling Quattro's Formats

One of the nicer surprises in my explorations of Quattro was the discovery that I can modify basic format settings that other spreadsheet programs do not allow me to change. For instance, many financially oriented users of spreadsheets are irritated because the default display of numeric cells is General rather than Financial (,). Quattro lets you change display formats and other settings to whatever you want.

All the settings you make on the Default Formats menu can be made the standard default for all spreadsheets—with the odd exception of default column widths. The **Width_of_Col** command cannot be made to carry over to other spreadsheets. This exception is inconsistent with the rest of the options on the Default Formats menu and reduces the flexibility of the configuration routines.

Figures 13.13 and 13.14 show the Default Formats menu as it is distributed by Borland and after a user has customized it.

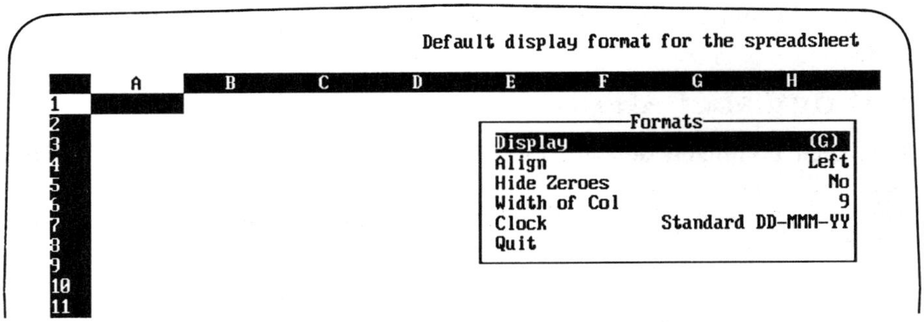

Fig. 13.13. The Default Formats menu as distributed.

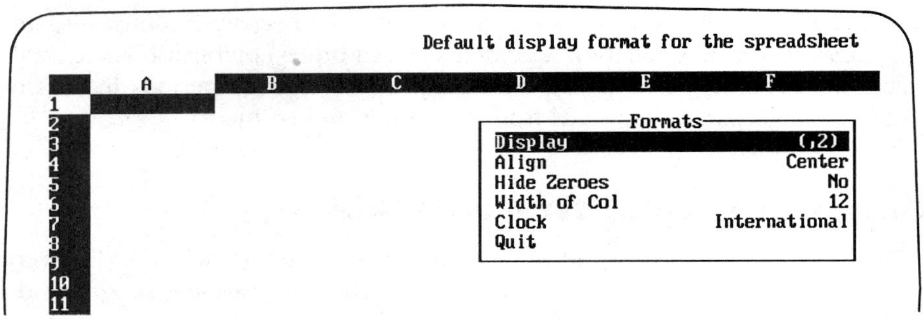

Fig. 13.14. A customized Default Formats menu.

Standardizing Display Formats

The **D**isplay option on the Default Formats menu sets the default or global cell format for the current session. The formats available are exactly the same as those you can choose from the /**B**lock **D**isplay_Format menu, including Fixed, Financial, Currency, Date, and so on.

To select a format other than General as the standard default format on new worksheets, use the /**D**efault **F**ormats **D**isplay command. Select the format and then press Esc twice to get to the main Default menu. Select **U**pdate from the Default menu to save the change to the QUATTRO.DEF definition file. The new default format takes effect after you leave and restart Quattro.

Setting Label Alignment

The **A**lign command determines the alignment of labels within cells. The default alignment is Left; all text entered into a cell aligns flush against the left edge of a cell. The other options are Right and Center. Changing the default alignment is not usually productive.

Suppressing the Display of Zeros

The /**D**efault **F**ormats **H**ide_Zeroes command suppresses the display of all the cells that have a numeric value of zero. This capability is often useful for preparing reports for presentation. You can enter formulas and values for all the items in the report, including the zero items, and then display the results with all the zeros removed.

If you use /**D**efault **F**ormats **H**ide_Zeroes, save the file, and then retrieve the file, the **H**ide_Zeroes command remains active. This feature is different from the equivalent command in 1-2-3, where zero suppression is disabled and the display of zeros is not suppressed when a file is retrieved.

The /**D**efault **F**ormats **H**ide_Zeroes command also has an option to reinstate the display of zero values.

Setting a Spreadsheet's Global Width of Column

The **W**idth_of_Col command gives you the option of determining the spreadsheet default for all column widths that have not been set individually with the /**C**olumn **W**idth command.

A good practice when designing a spreadsheet application is to determine that spreadsheet's overall optimum column width before you begin to create the worksheet. By presetting the spreadsheet default, you can save yourself much unnecessary work setting and resetting specific column widths.

Although the default column width is 9 characters wide, I find that a width of 10 characters is more efficient. One character may not seem like much of a difference until you realize that any cell with a full date format displays as asterisks in a 9-character column. In addition, if you use financial format with no decimal places as a default display format (my recommendation), you can't display a number larger than 999,999 without display overflow (*********).

Modifying the Clock's Look

The /**D**efault **F**ormats **C**lock command gives you control over the appearance of the date and time that appear in the lower left corner of the display. Usually the display shows date and time in the standard format of DD-MMM-YY and HH:MM AM/PM. The **C**lock option lets you choose from a submenu with the choices:

Standard
International
None

The **I**nternational choice changes the format of the date entry to the current international format, which is set through the /**D**efault **I**nternational **D**ate and **T**ime selections mentioned earlier in this chapter.

If you have not changed the default international date and time settings, when you select /**D**efault **F**ormats **C**lock **I**nternational, the clock appears in the format HH:MM where hours appear in 24-hour military time, such as 15:00.

Setting Default Directories

Each time you start Quattro, it must establish which disk drive(s) and directories will be searched when Quattro needs information. If you have not changed the default, Quattro "assumes" that the drive and directory from which you start the program also contain worksheet files and what Borland calls resource files. For instance, if you start Quattro from a directory named C:\QUATTRO, the program looks for all its files in this directory. Having both Quattro's program and worksheet files in the same directory is not the best way to have things organized, however. You end up with an overcrowded directory.

The /**D**efault **D**irectories command lets you specify where Quattro should look for files. The command has two choices: **R**esource and **D**ata (see fig. 13.15). The **R**esource choice refers to the directory that is designated to hold files Quattro needs in order to run properly, such as help files, menu files, and configuration files. Quattro program files with the extensions DEF, BGI, TRN, RSC, ALT, QAI, CHR, and OVL are special files that should be located in the current resource directory.

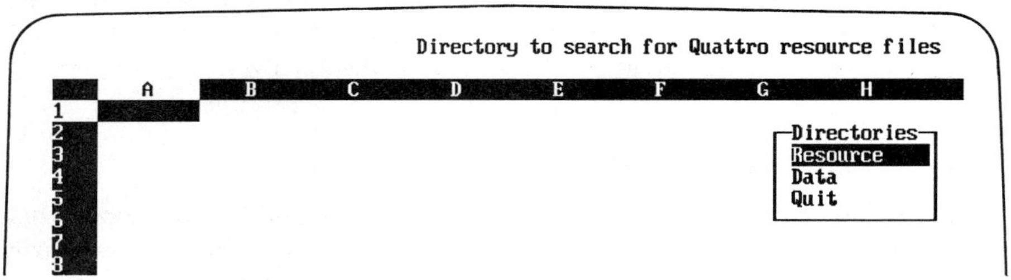

Fig. 13.15. The Default Directories menu.

If you find that Quattro has difficulty translating files, finding help files, or running add-in programs, your resource files are probably not in the directory Quattro is using as the resource directory.

The data directory holds data files created in Quattro. The data directory is the directory that Quattro automatically searches when you use the **S**ave, **R**etrieve, **I**mport, **C**ombine, **X**tract, and **P**rint commands.

If you decide to modify the default directories for more than the current session, you must remember to select the **U**pdate option from the Default menu.

Recalculating the Worksheet

One of the primary functions of a spreadsheet program is to recalculate all the cells in a worksheet when a value or a formula in one cell changes. This feature makes possible building a model—of sales projections, for example—and predicting the results of changes to various elements of the model. To see the effects of each change or set of changes, you need to recalculate the worksheet.

Most spreadsheets recalculate all cells whether they need recalculating or not. This practice can be a terrible waste of time. On several occasions when working with a large spreadsheet in 1-2-3, I have accidentally pressed the Calc (F9) key when working. This accident often resulted in several frustrating minutes of watching the WAIT indicator flash.

Quattro's powers of recalculation, however, go beyond the norm for spreadsheets. Quattro is "smart enough" to determine which cells in the spreadsheet need to be recalculated. If you accidentally press Calc when you do not need to recalculate, the READY mode indicator blinks once while Quattro determines that nothing needs to be done. This determination happens so fast that if you blink while the READY mode indicator blinks, you miss the whole thing.

Even though you have fewer reasons to use the Recalculation commands in Quattro than in other spreadsheets, you are given control over how recalculations are handled. You use another Default command, the /**D**efault **R**ecalculation command, to choose the method and order of recalculation.

Quattro provides two recalculation methods: automatic and manual. In automatic recalculation, which is the default, Quattro recalculates the cells that need updating whenever any cell in the worksheet changes. In manual recalculation, Quattro recalculates the worksheet only when the user requests recalculation from the keyboard or from a macro.

Quattro also provides three orders of recalculation: natural order and two linear orders—columnwise or rowwise. Natural order is the default, but you can choose any of the three orders.

You also can choose the number of times the spreadsheet is recalculated; because of circular references, which are explained in this section, the spreadsheet may need to be recalculated several times whenever you request recalculation.

You access all the recalculation options by using the /**D**efault **R**ecalculation command. Figure 13.16 shows the Recalculation menu and its options. Note that the **C**ircular_Cell entry in the menu is informational. This option shows which cells in a spreadsheet contain circular references. In most spreadsheets, a circular reference is unusual, and the entry usually (although not always) indicates a problem with the logic of the spreadsheet. More information on circular references and what they mean is given later in this section.

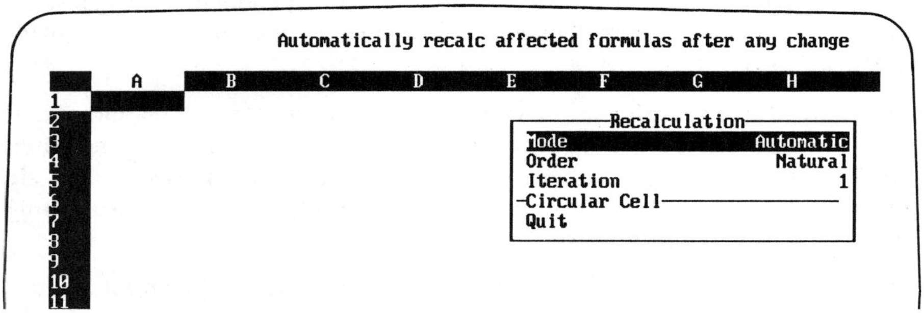

Fig. 13.16. The Default Recalculation menu.

Choosing a Recalculation Mode: Automatic or Manual

When you are working on a large worksheet that involves many formulas, worksheet recalculation may take some time. Recalculation occurs each time a value is changed or a new entry is made. One way to get around this problem is to change the default from automatic to manual recalculation. This change is done easily by executing the **/D**efault **R**ecalculation **M**ode command and then choosing **M**anual.

With manual recalculation, you can control Quattro so that it recalculates only when you press the F9 (Calc) key or when a macro invokes a recalculation. Manual recalculation is an advantage only with large worksheets in which you are changing many values—or if you have a slow computer. Otherwise, Quattro's speed is more than enough for recalculation to occur almost instantly.

The Edit and F9 (Calc) functions can be used together to convert to a simple number a formula stored in a cell. F9 is normally used for recalculating when **/D**efault **R**ecalculation **M**ode is set to Manual. When you are in EDIT mode, however, pressing F9 causes a formula to be converted to a number, the formula's current value.

For example, suppose that you want to use F9 to convert the formula +C4/H3*(Y5+4000) to its current value (which you may assume is 64,000), and store the result. Position the cell selector on the cell containing the formula and proceed as follows:

Key Pressed	*Descriptor Line Message*	*Explanation*
F2	+C4/H3*(Y5+4000)	Puts Quattro in EDIT mode
F9	64000	Converts the formula to its current value (64,000 picked at random)
Enter		Stores the entry in the current cell and shifts Quattro back to READY mode

Be careful when you use this technique. Converting the formula to a value in this way destroys the formula.

This trick also causes a cell address that refers to a label to convert to a label. For example, suppose that you have the label *Monthly Contributions* in cell B2 and you want to enter the same label elsewhere in your worksheet, say in cell AA25. You could enter +B2 into cell AA25 to cause *Monthly Contributions* to appear on the display in cell location AA25.

The problem is that cell AA25 still contains the entry +B2; if you ever copy the contents of the cell, relative addressing will cause the B2 to change to something else (see the "Relative Addressing" section in Chapter 4). You can solve the problem by using the F2 (Edit) and the F9 (Calc) keys. The sequence outlined previously converts +B2 to the label *Monthly Contributions*.

Choosing the Order of Recalculation: Columnwise or Rowwise

By default, Quattro uses the Natural order of recalculation; that is, the calculation proceeds from the cells that are least dependent on other cells to cells that depend most on other cells for their results. Explaining this order is difficult without having first explained the two linear orders: Columnwise and Rowwise.

In the columnwise procedure, recalculation begins at the entry in cell A1 and proceeds down column A, then continues at cell B1 and moves down column B, and so on. Similarly, Rowwise recalculation starts at cell A1 and proceeds across row 1, then moves down to cell A2 and across row 2, and so on.

These orders of recalculation can lead to the wrong answer unless you are careful about how you set up the worksheet. Forward and circular references are among the errors that can occur with linear recalculation.

A forward reference occurs when a cell refers to another cell that is lower in the worksheet. For example, imagine that you have created a worksheet with entries in four cells: A1, C1, C2, and C3. Suppose that those cells have the following contents:

A1 = +C3

C1 = 100

C2 = 200

C3 = +C1+C2

Both A1 and C3 have the value 300. Now suppose that the number in cell C2 is changed to 100. Let's step through the recalculation process. Because the recalculation begins at the upper left corner of the worksheet, cell A1 is evaluated first. Because the value of C3, 300, has not changed yet, A1 retains the value 300. The recalculation then proceeds either column by column or row by row across the worksheet until Quattro comes to cell C3. Because the value of cell C2 has changed, the value in C3 changes to 200.

Clearly, it does not make sense to have A1 and C3 contain different values when cell A1 is defined as equal to C3. Although recalculating the worksheet again eliminates the inequality, recalculation does not remove the basic problem. In large and complex models, you often intentionally build in forward references, but you also can easily build in undetected, and unwanted, forward references.

You select Columnwise or Rowwise recalculation in at least three situations:

1. You are importing a file that is built around the linear recalculation order.

2. You are solving intentional circular references (for example, to reflect the true algebraic relationship among the variables).

3. The same number of iterations is needed under both natural and linear orders. In this case, using one of the linear orders can be a bit faster than using the natural order. (For an explanation of iterations and circular references, see the "Using Iterative Recalculation" section of this chapter.)

If you want Quattro to recalculate in a linear fashion, override the default natural order setting by using /**D**efault **R**ecalculation **O**rder (**C**olumnwise or **R**owwise).

Recalculating the Worksheet in Natural Order

Quattro normally recalculates in a natural order. Because this order is the default, you do not have to issue a command for this option. If you have changed the default and want to change back to natural order, use the /**D**efault **R**ecalculation **O**rder **N**atural command.

Natural order recognizes that all the active cells in a worksheet are interrelated, and Quattro does not recalculate any given cell until after the cells that it depends on have been recalculated. Recalculation occurs in a topological fashion, starting at the lowest or easiest calculation level and working up.

C3
B1 B3 B4
A1 A2 A4 A7 A9

With natural recalculation, you do not have to worry about the order of recalculation or the problem of forward references. If you were to re-create the forward reference example in Quattro and use natural recalculation, cell C3—the most fundamental cell in the worksheet—is evaluated before cell A1, eliminating the forward reference.

Using Iterative Recalculation

In most cases, recalculating a worksheet takes only one pass. Recalculating only once is not satisfactory, however, when a worksheet contains a circular reference and also may be unsatisfactory when Columnwise or Rowwise recalculation is used, even if the spreadsheet has no circular reference.

A classic example of a circular reference is the problem of trying to determine the amount of a bonus to be paid to the executive of a corporation. Consider the following points in the process of performing the calculation:

1. The bonus is set at 10 percent of the after-tax profits of the corporation.
2. The bonus is a tax-deductible expense of the corporation and therefore must be known in order to calculate the after-tax profits.
3. The after-tax profits must be known in order to calculate the bonus.

You can see the circular pattern. When this kind of circular reference occurs, Quattro displays a CIRC indicator in the lower right corner of the screen. When you recalculate this type of worksheet using natural calculation, Quattro cannot accurately recompute all the values. Because each value in the circular set depends, directly or indirectly, on all the others, Quattro cannot find a "toehold"; that is, Quattro cannot find the most fundamental cell in the worksheet because no such cell exists. Iterative recalculation allows Quattro to overcome this problem.

Iterative recalculation overcomes a circular reference because each recalculative pass through the worksheet causes the actual values of the cells to approach more closely their correct values. For example, suppose that you build a worksheet with the following set of relationships:

A3 = .05*A5

A4 = 100

A5 = +A3+A4

When you first enter this formula, A3 has a value of 0, A4 equals 100, and A5 equals 100. Suppose that you recalculate the worksheet five times. Table 13.1 shows the values of each cell after each recalculative pass.

Table 13.1
Changing Values of Cells during Five Recalculations

Pass	Cell A3	Cell A4	Cell A5
1	5	100	105
2	5.25	100	105.25
3	5.2624	100	105.2625
3	5.263125	100	105.263125
5	5.26315625	100	105.26315625

Notice that on each pass, the difference between the preceding and the current values of cells A3 and A5 becomes smaller. After only five passes, the difference is too small to be significant. After nine passes, in fact, the difference becomes too small for Quattro to recognize. At that point, the problem with the circular reference is eliminated, although the circular reference remains (and the CIRC indicator remains on the screen).

You choose iterative recalculation with the **/Default Recalculation Iteration** command. The default number of iterations is 1, but you can specify as many as the maximum of 255.

When Quattro is in iterative mode, the worksheet recalculates a specified number of times each time you change cell contents for automatic recalculation or each time you press the F9 (Calc) key for manual recalculation. Normally, the worksheet recalculates only once for each F9 keystroke.

If your worksheet contains deliberate circular references, keep the number of recalculation passes high. Because Quattro does not recognize the iteration parameter when you're using natural order and the worksheet has no circular references, keeping the number of iterations high does not waste recalculation time.

The most efficient number of recalculations depends on the application; the only way to be sure is to experiment. Four points should be noted about iterative recalculation:

1. Suppose that you have the number of iterations set to a high figure (say 20), but Quattro encounters a set of circular references that is still too complicated to sort out. If this problem happens with one of your models, simply recalculate the worksheet twice. If, for example, the number of iterations is set to 20, pressing the Calc key twice is identical to setting the iteration count to 40.

2. Remember that recalculating a large worksheet as many as 20 times can take a long time. Be patient; control over Quattro will be returned to you.

3. You can enter circular references that cannot be solved by this iterative approach: for example, when a formula references the cell that contains that formula. One symptom of this problem is that values quickly grow larger after each iteration. Another symptom is that the output variables do not converge on the correct answer, but instead bounce around.

4. Some circular references are correct; that is, they describe true algebraic modeling relationships. You would ordinarily plan to build these references into your model. If you get unplanned circular references, chances are good that these circular references are incorrect.

You can widen the Default Recalculation menu to show the fields in the menu in order to check on the recalculation status of your worksheet. You simply press the plus (+) key on the numeric keypad. This command delivers, along with other information, the current recalculation method and order, the number of iterations in effect, and the location of a circular reference. Figure 13.17 shows a typical report from the Default Recalculation menu.

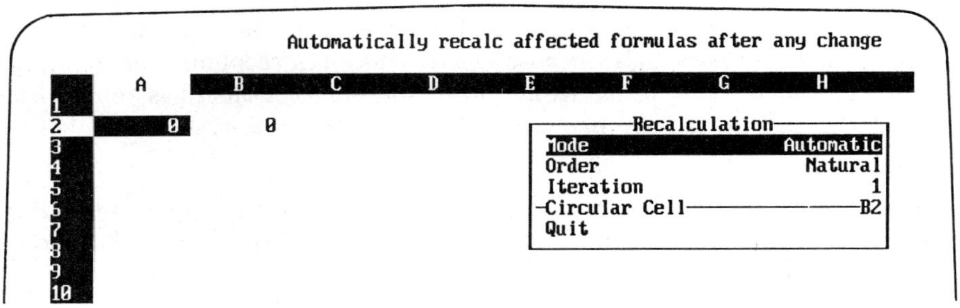

Fig. 13.17. A report from the Default Recalculation menu.

Protecting Your Spreadsheets

A great deal of time and thought goes into the creation of a spreadsheet application. Yet you can easily lose all this hard work by an inadvertent keystroke or command, such as issuing /**B**lock **E**rase on more cells than you intended. To protect your spreadsheet, you can use the cell-locking mechanism Quattro provides. Spreadsheet protection is found on the Default menu.

The Protection menu has two choices: **E**nable and **D**isable. The default setting is **P**rotection **D**isable. This setting means that cell protection is not normally active. To turn on protection for some or all cells in the spreadsheet, set **P**rotection to **E**nable. All cells that do not have a /**B**lock **A**dvanced **U**nprotect attribute (U) are secured from any modifications.

Not only are the cells themselves protected, but rows and columns are protected. You cannot insert or delete rows and columns in protected blocks. You are also restricted from copying and moving data into areas that are restricted by protection.

Defining Startup Defaults

What do you want Quattro to do when you first load it? Normally, Quattro displays a blank worksheet, ready to do your bidding. The /**D**efault **S**tartup commands give you control of Quattro so that you can make the program more convenient for your personal use. Options such as automatically loading a specified spreadsheet, starting a default macro you name, setting the default extension for saved files, and many others are yours.

This section shows you the changes you can make to startup defaults and tells you how to make them. Figure 13.18 shows the Default Startup menu and its standard settings. Keep this figure handy because you may want to refer to it later in the section.

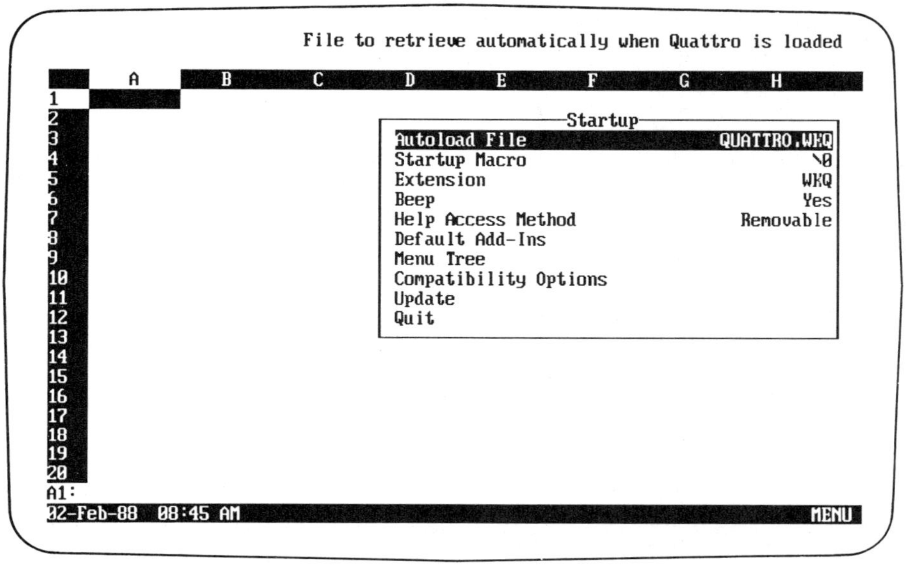

Fig. 13.18. The Default Startup menu.

The Autoload File and Auto-Execute Macros

The first option on the Default Startup menu is the **A**utoload_File command. This command specifies the name of the file Quattro retrieves automatically when you start the program. The default autoload file, QUATTRO.WKQ, is in the current Data directory.

An Autoload file is usually used to create a *turnkey system*, that is, a system that seems to start itself. A turnkey system can be implemented in Quattro through the use of macros, the Quattro command language, and spreadsheet templates (see Chapters 15, 16, and 17).

An example of a turnkey system is a simple accounting system. You have one file designated for accounts receivable, one for payables, another for payroll, and so on. The starting point for this kind of system is a file that loads automatically. You assign the name QUATTRO.WKQ to the starting file.

If you need to maintain compatibility with 1-2-3, the appropriate autoload file name is AUTO123.WK1. The /**D**efault **A**utoload command gives you the capability to change the default autoload name to another name. Thus, if you already have a turnkey 1-2-3 system, you can use it in Quattro by changing the Autoload file name. Inside the Autoload file is a macro that starts itself—an auto-execute macro that activates a custom menu for the accounting system.

The **Startup_Macro** command determines what block (macro) name Quattro looks for when a file is retrieved. If the block name in the Startup macro default is found, Quattro executes the macro automatically. Any file, however, can have an auto-execute macro.

The default auto-execute macro name is \0 (backslash zero). You can change the \0 name to something more descriptive, such as TOP or BEGIN. If you change the auto-execute macro name to TOP, every file that contains a TOP macro name starts automatically when that file is retrieved. You do not need to change the auto-execute macro name to have compatibility with 1-2-3 because it also uses \0 as the auto-execute macro name.

Consequences of Changing the Default Extension

Every spreadsheet you save to a file has a file name extension. Normally, this extension is WKQ for Quattro worksheet. The /**D**efault **S**tartup **E**xtension command allows you to specify any three characters for the default file name extension.

You can gain some interesting benefits by modifying this default. For instance, if you want to use the !SQZ! file compression utility, you normally must change the extension from WKQ to WKZ after you use the /**F**ile **S**ave command. If you want all your spreadsheets compressed automatically, simply change the default extension to WKZ. On my copy of Quattro, I have set the default extension to WKZ in order to compress all my files into the smallest space possible. This change saves at least 75 percent of the disk space that would normally be taken up by Quattro spreadsheets.

Another use of /**D**efault **S**tartup **E**xtension is in maintaining compatibility with a program for which Quattro does file translations. One of these programs, 1-2-3, uses a WK1 extension. If you want Quattro always to create 1-2-3-compatible files, set the extension to WK1.

The Beep Default

I don't have much to say about the /**D**efault **S**tartup **B**eep command other than "Thank Goodness!" Someone has finally given us the option to turn off that annoying beeping! The command takes a simple Yes or No answer.

You may not want beeping off if you are a new user; but as you gain experience, you probably will want the capability to turn off the beep.

Help Access Method

The /Default Startup Help_Access_Method command is designed to give the help screens the highest access speed consistent with the disk system you are using for Quattro. The two options for this command are Instant and Removable.

The default setting is Removable, which is best if you are using a floppy disk system. This option lets you remove the help system disk. When you press the Help key (F1), Quattro prompts you to reinsert the disk containing the help files.

The Instant setting is for hard disk systems. Instant means that the help files are always kept open by Quattro. When you press the Help key, you get instant access because the file is already open.

Even if you start Quattro from a hard disk, the default for Help_Access_Method remains Removable. I suggest that hard disk users change this setting to Instant. Be sure to choose Update from the Startup menu after you make your changes.

Default Add-Ins

The /Default Startup Default_Add-Ins command determines which add-in programs are automatically added to Quattro each time it is started. The command lists all the valid add-in program files in the program directory. Up to eight add-in programs can be added (limited by the amount of memory in your computer). The add-in program that is most useful as a default add-in is the Transcript program. Chapter 14, "Working with Add-In Programs," provides a complete description of how to work with add-in programs and what they can do for you.

The Menu Tree Defaults

Quattro is a unique software program in that its user interface, the menu tree, can be changed by the user. Borland calls this interface a *soft user interface.* The fact that the menu tree can be selected by the user means that you can make Quattro work the way you want instead of Quattro's forcing you to learn its ways of doing things.

No changes to menu tree defaults are put into effect until you first update the definition file with the /Default Startup Update command, leave Quattro, and then restart Quattro. You will avoid much frustration if you remember this rule.

Quattro can use two different classes of menus: resource menus and alternate menus. The resource menu is the menu that Quattro loads when the program is started. When you press the slash (/) key immediately after loading Quattro, you always see the resource menu selected by the **/D**efault **S**tartup **M**enu_Tree **M**ain_Menus command. Figure 13.19 shows the Menu Tree menu.

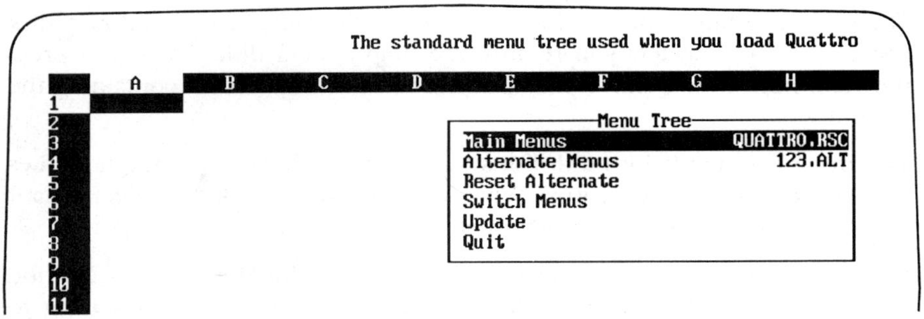

Fig. 13.19. Quattro's Menu Tree menu.

The default main menu is QUATTRO.RSC (RSC stands for resource). Two other main menus are supplied with Quattro. The first is called the novice menu (NOVICE.RSC). This menu eliminates many of the advanced commands that are on the standard Quattro menu so that a beginning user is not forced to choose from many unfamiliar and confusing commands. The other main menu option is 123.RSC. Select this menu if you want Quattro to use a Lotus-style menu as the standard menu system.

The **/D**efault **S**tartup **M**enu_Tree **A**lternate_Menus command gives you the option of having two menu systems resident and available in Quattro at any time. Alternate menus have the extension .ALT.

The only alternate menu shipped with Quattro is 123.ALT. This menu provides another way of gaining compatibility with 1-2-3. How is 123.ALT different than 123.RSC? If you use 123.RSC, the only menu you have available is the Lotus-style menu. If you enable 123.ALT as the alternate menu tree, you can toggle between the standard Quattro menu tree and the 1-2-3 menu system. Figure 13.19 shows the Menu Tree menu with its current settings: Quattro for the main menu and 1-2-3 as the alternate.

Before you can successfully use the main and alternate menu trees, you must issue the **U**pdate command and then quit and restart Quattro. The menu trees are "zippered" into Quattro when the program is first started.

After the new menus have been activated, use the **/D**efault **S**tartup **M**enu_Tree **S**witch_Menus command to toggle between the resource and alternate menu.

As a convenience, you may want to assign accelerator keys to switch between menus. I have set Ctrl-A to select the alternate menu and Ctrl-M to restore the main menu. For more information on accelerator keys, see Chapter 4, "Working with the Menu Commands."

You need about 20K additional bytes of memory to have the 123.ALT menu available. If you need to recover this memory to load a large spreadsheet, issue the **R**eset_Alternate command and then **U**pdate. After you quit and restart Quattro, you get the memory back.

The Compatibility Options

When writing Quattro, the programmers at Borland realized that Quattro would have to be compatible with other software if the program was going to be successful. The **/D**efault **S**tartup **C**ompatibility_Options command is part of the method Quattro uses to achieve compatibility.

On the Compatibility Options menu, you see a menu box divided into two sections. The top part of the box, Menus Option, provides options that control the way menus behave. The bottom of the box, Confirm Option, sets the behavior of macro recording, playback, and interaction with the menu system.

The first option in the Menus Option window is the **K**eep_Wide command. This command determines whether Quattro menus show the current status of commands that have settings. Figure 13.20 shows the Compatibility Options menu in a wide menu format.

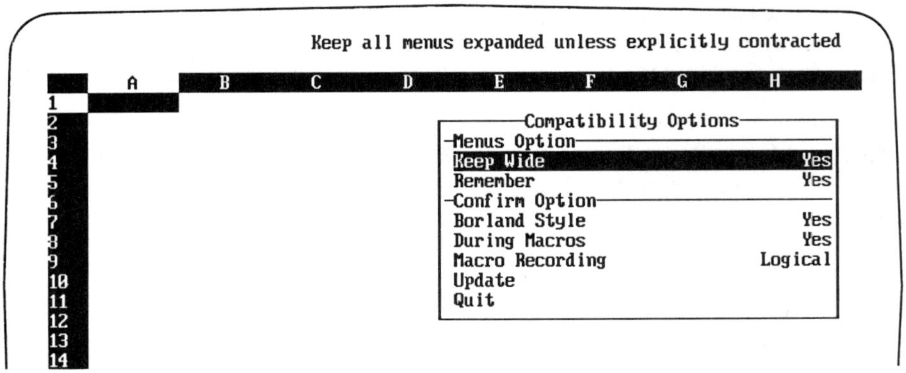

Fig. 13.20. Compatibility Options menu with Keep_Wide set to Yes.

As you can see, the **K**eep_Wide command status is currently set to Yes. Because I see little benefit in hiding important information, I recommend that you set your menus up so that they are always wide.

The next command in the Menus Option section of the Compatibility Options menu is **R**emember. The **R**emember option lets you set the menu system so that when you issue a command a second time, Quattro positions the menu bar on the most recent series of menu choices. This option is useful because menu operations tend to be repetitive. For instance, if you perform a /**B**lock **D**isplay_Format **F**ixed command once, you are likely to need it again. If you have turned on menu memory, the second time you go through the menu you need only press Enter three times, because the menu bar automatically highlights the previous choices in order.

The Confirm Option section of the menu tells Quattro how to treat the menu system if you want to maintain macro compatibility with 1-2-3. For instance, 1-2-3 always presents a Yes/No menu, which forces you to verify that you want to leave the program. The **B**orland_Style option sets things up so that confirmation menus appear only if they are needed. In Borland Style (the default), for instance, the Yes/No menu doesn't appear if the current file is saved when you select **Q**uit from the Main menu to leave Quattro. For macro compatibility, you can set this choice to No.

For complete macro compatibility with 1-2-3 during macro recording and playback, you should set the **D**uring_Macros and **M**acro_Recording choices to be compatible with 1-2-3.

The **M**acro_Recording command determines how macro commands are recorded. The two options are **L**ogical and **K**eystroke. The **L**ogical setting creates keyword menu commands such as {Block,Copy} instead of the equivalent /BC, which is entered in **K**eystroke mode, the other macro recording method.

If you plan to create Quattro macros that also run from within 1-2-3, you must set **M**acro_Recording to **K**eystroke and also use the 123.RSC menu system while macro recording is active. Figure 13.21 illustrates the appropriate choices for this menu if you want Quattro to be macro compatible with 1-2-3.

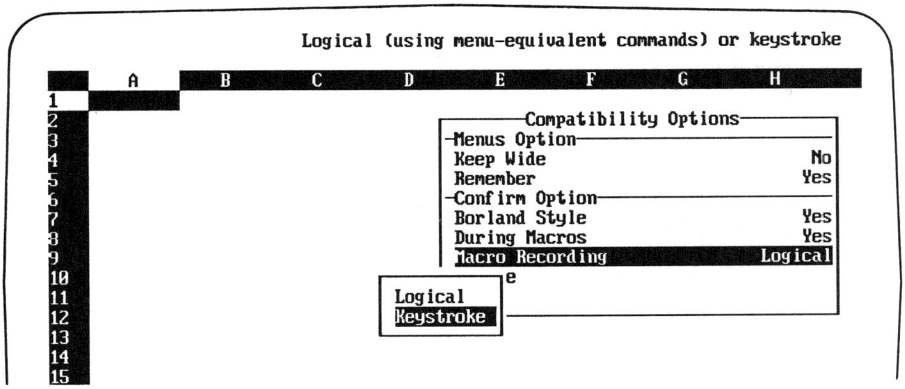

Fig. 13.21. Compatibility Options menu with choices appropriate for macros compatible with 1-2-3.

Be sure to choose **Update** to make the changes the new defaults.

Chapter Summary

By reading this chapter, you have learned how to make Quattro work the way you want it to. This information includes how to modify Quattro's hardware and software color settings, default formats, directories, recalculation, and protection.

You have also learned how flexible Quattro is; for example how it can modify basic defaults, such as file name extensions, and set default add-in programs. And you have seen how easily Quattro can be made to coexist with the rest of the spreadsheet world through compatible menus and macro systems.

The next chapter describes the open architecture of Quattro and shows you how to work with the add-in commands and programs like Transcript and the Menu Builder, which come with Quattro.

CHAPTER

14

Working with Add-In Programs

The Quattro program has the add-in capability to grow with you. In addition to its macro commands, Quattro can accept add-in programs. By supplying certain programs as add-ins, you can bring them into memory when you need them and remove them later, conserving memory.

An *add-in program* is a program that is loaded into random-access memory (RAM) and actually becomes a seamless part of Quattro. Two add-in programs currently are shipped with Quattro. One is a keystroke recorder called Transcript, and the other is a program that allows you to create and customize Quattro menus called, appropriately, Menu Builder. Eventually, a large number of add-ins will become available to Quattro users. No doubt they will include word processors, database managers, screen managers, and "post-it" style cell annotators, from Borland and other software companies.

This chapter describes how to load and run add-in programs, how to remove them when you no longer need them, and how to use Menu Builder and Transcript.

Using Add-In Programs

Add-in programs can be accessed in two ways. You can load an add-in manually when it is needed, or you can set up an add-in to automatically load and start when you start Quattro.

Up to eight add-in programs can be active in Quattro at any one time, as long as your computer has sufficient RAM memory. Unfortunately, computers never seem to have enough memory, so consider your needs carefully when you set up default add-ins. Because add-in programs occupy precious memory space, you should limit the number of add-ins that Quattro automatically loads.

The menu commands that allow you to work with add-ins are the /**D**efault **S**tartup **D**efault Add-Ins command, and the /**M**acro **L**oad, **R**un, and **U**nload commands. The first command is used to set up default add-in programs. The set of /**M**acro commands gives you control of whatever add-in programs you start during a Quattro session.

Of the two add-in programs supplied with Quattro, Transcript may be more useful as an automatically added program. The Transcript add-in is examined in detail later in this chapter.

Loading, Running, and Removing Add-Ins

After you start Quattro, running an add-in is simple. The Macro menu contains the commands that let you control add-ins: **L**oad, **R**un, and **U**nload.

Before you run an add-in, you must load it into memory. To load an add-in, choose the the /**M**acro **L**oad command. A menu of add-ins appears (files with the .QAI extension). You then can select the add-in you want to load, attaching it to the list of loaded add-ins.

After the add-in is loaded, it can be invoked by choosing /**M**acro **R**un. After an add-in completes its task, the Quattro spreadsheet returns to READY mode. The add-in is still loaded in RAM memory.

To restart the most recently used add-in, you do not need to go through the menus. Simply press the Shift-F8 key combination to restart that add-in.

If you don't need to use an active add-in, or if you need to increase the amount of memory available to your spreadsheet, you may want to remove an add-in program from memory. Issue /**M**acro **U**nload. Then select the add-in from the menu. Figure 14.1 shows the menu with the Transcript add-in about to be unloaded.

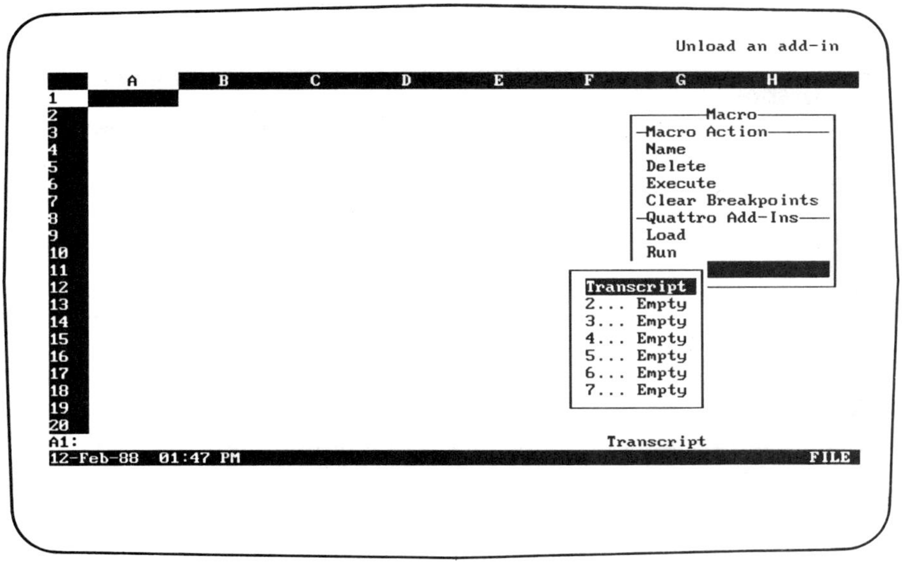

Fig. 14.1. Using the add-in menu to unload Transcript.

Setting Up a Default Add-In

When Quattro is loaded into memory, any default add-ins are activated automatically. The process of setting up a default add-in program to be automatically loaded is a straightforward one. Add-in programs must already be in the Quattro subdirectory for Quattro to find them automatically.

Default add-in programs are joined to Quattro through the Default menu. When you issue /**D**efault **S**tartup **D**efault Add-Ins, you see a menu for add-ins. Quattro has eight add-in slots available (see fig. 14.2).

Press Enter to display the available add-in programs that are in the subdirectory containing the Quattro program files (see fig. 14.3). Move the cell selector to the TRANS.QAI file and press Enter, placing it in the first add-in slot. The .QAI file extension is reserved for all Quattro add-in programs. After you have placed the add-in in the default add-ins list, select the **U**pdate option for the selection to be added to the file that defines how Quattro will start (QUATTRO.DEF).

After you have completed the menu selections and updated the QUATTRO.DEF file, you just need to issue **Q**uit and /**Q**uit again, quitting Quattro, for the changes to take effect. When you restart Quattro, the add-in will load automatically. Then issue /**M**acro **R**un to activate the add-in, and /**M**acro **U**nload to unload the add-in whenever needed.

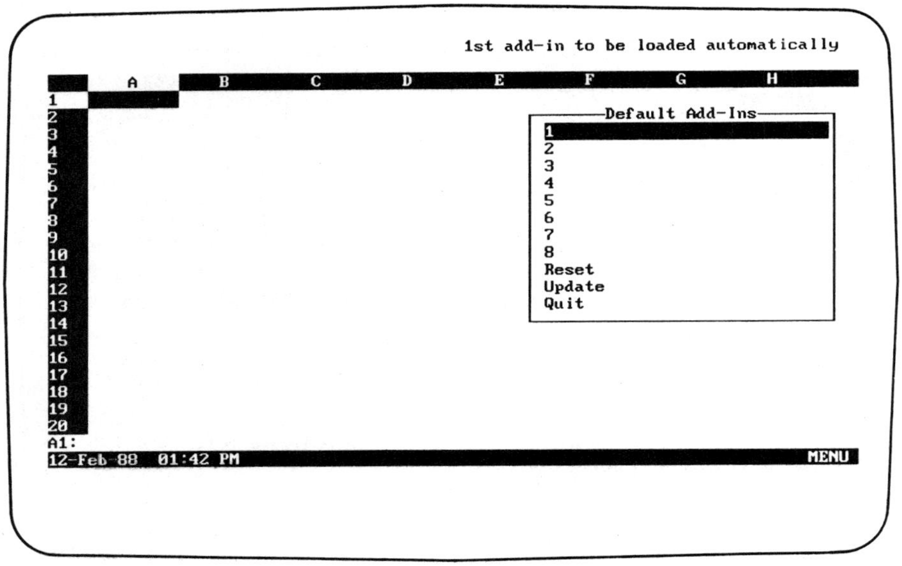

Fig. 14.2. Setting up a default add-in.

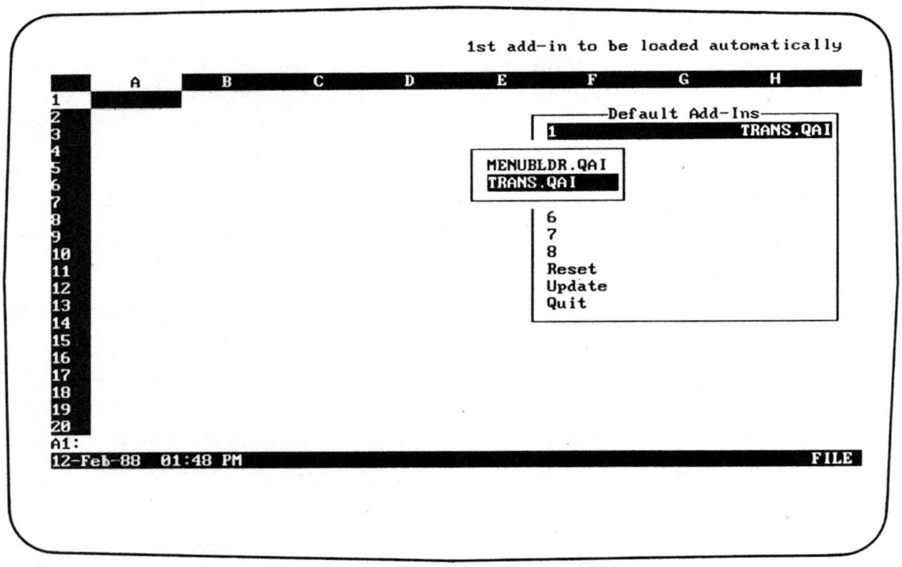

Fig. 14.3. "Plugging in" a default add-in.

Using the Menu Builder Add-In

Menu Builder, one of the two add-in programs that come with Quattro, allows you to modify the standard Quattro command menu or create your own menus that appear when a user presses the slash key (/).

Menu Builder gives you access to the *soft interface* capability of Quattro. This capability means that you have control over what the menu system will say, and to some degree, be able to do. Specifically, you can change the standard names, prompts, and actions of the Quattro menu. You also can modify the branching from higher-level menus (often called *parent menus*) to submenus (or *child menus*).

Three menu systems are supplied with the standard Quattro package. In addition to the default menu, you get a 1-2-3-compatible menu and a menu aimed at novice users. If part or all of these menus do not fit your needs, you can change them.

There are two classes of menus that can be created or modified with Menu Builder: main menus and alternate menus. *Main menus* are the default menus—that is, the menus that Quattro loads automatically at startup. *Alternate menus* are menus that you can switch to during a Quattro session. For example, to switch to a 1-2-3 menu, you would set up 123.ALT as the alternate menu.

You can have several main menus and several alternate menus. However, you can have only one main and one alternate menu active at any one time. To limit potential confusion, you should limit the number of main and alternate menus to just a few.

Adding a Macro to the Main Menu

One of the things I have always wanted to be able to do is make my macros available as menu choices on a standard spreadsheet menu. That way, a user would not need to be aware that anything out of the ordinary was going on. The Menu Builder program lets you add macros to the main menu or to alternate menus you might create.

The goal of using the Menu Builder add-in in this chapter is to graft a macro program to the Quattro's main menu structure. The macro to be added is called {SWAP}, which allows the user to point at any two cells so that they can switch places. This macro eliminates the irritating series of moves and copies that is usually involved in swapping two cells.

Figures 14.4 and 14.5 show the effect of the {SWAP} macro on the letters *a* and *b* in cells G1 and G2. The figures also supply you with the text for {SWAP}. You can use this macro in any spreadsheet; {SWAP} is designed so that it can be placed almost anywhere and still work reliably.

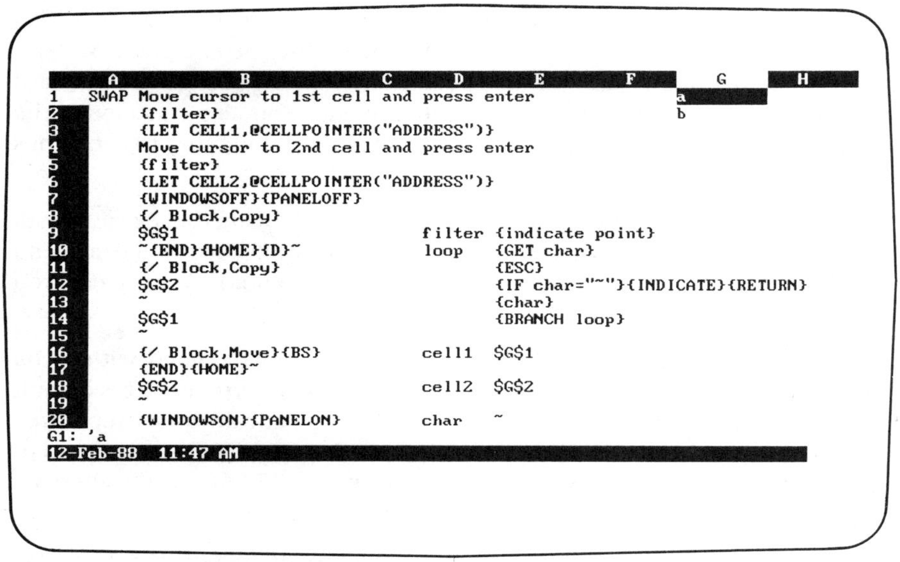

Fig. 14.4. The {SWAP} macro and the target cells before swapping.

After the macro has been thoroughly debugged, it is combined with the /**F**ile **C**ombine **C**opy command (discussed in Chapter 8) into a worksheet.

Invoke Menu Builder by loading it from Quattro with the /**M**acro **L**oad command, as shown in figure 14.6. Figure 14.6 shows a cash flow worksheet and the Macro menu before adding Menu Builder.

When you choose the **L**oad option, the prompt `Load a Quattro add-in` appears. Quattro searches the current resource directory for files with the extension .QAI (add-in programs) and displays them in a window. Choose MENUBLDR.QAI, loading Menu Builder into memory. Menu Builder is now available but is not active. To activate the add-in, select **R**un from the Macro menu, displaying a list of the currently loaded add-ins (see fig. 14.7). Any of the add-ins displayed in the list can be run. For the moment, only one add-in is available, Menu Builder. Select Menu Builder to run.

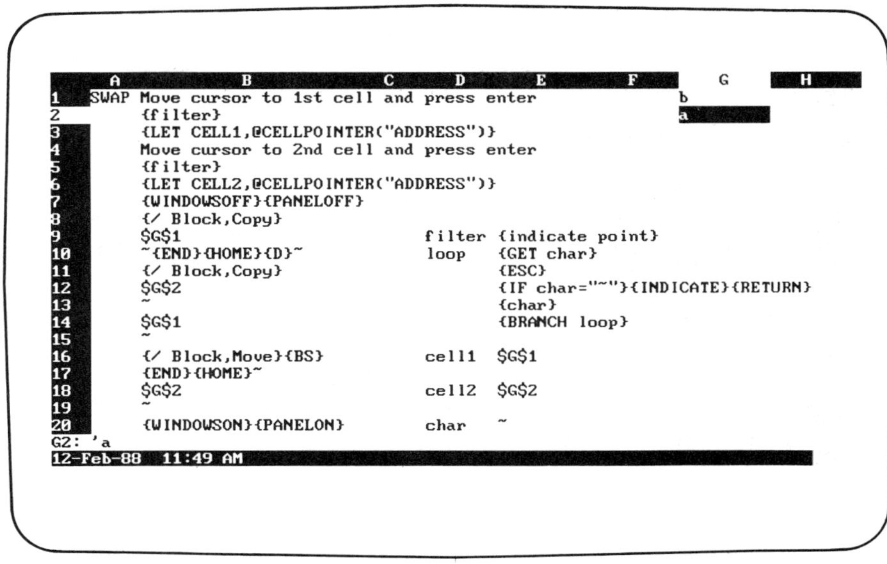

Fig. 14.5. The cells after swapping.

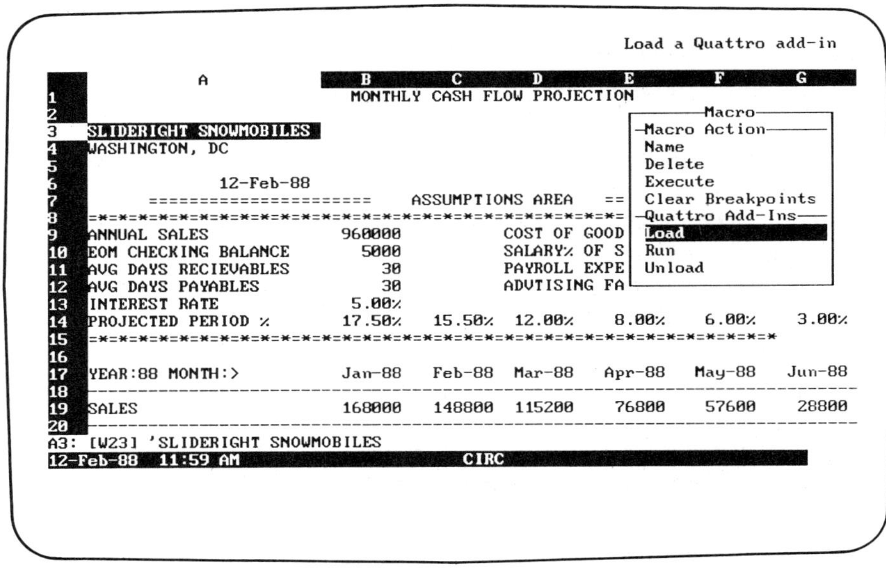

Fig. 14.6. Preparing to load an add-in program.

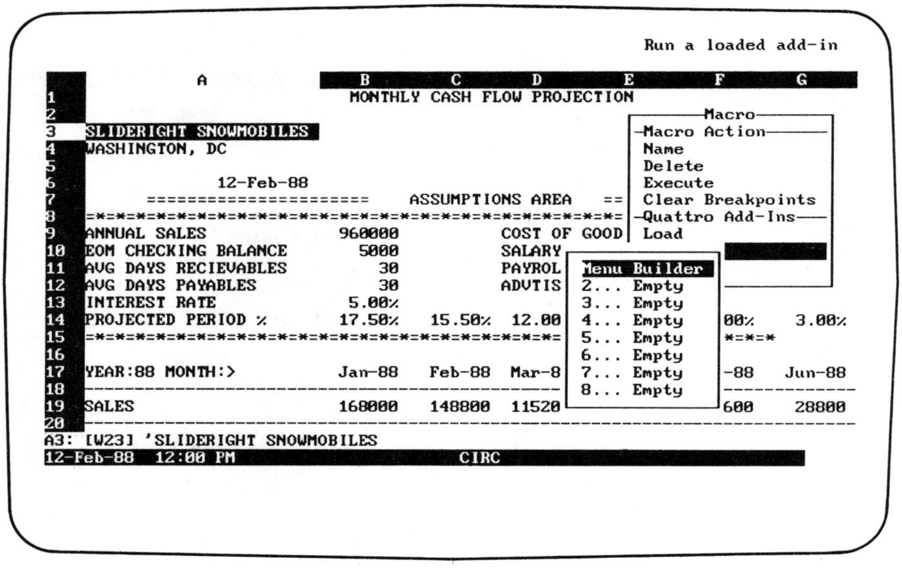

Fig. 14.7. Starting Menu Builder with the /**M**acro **R**un command.

When Menu Builder starts, the regular Quattro display disappears and is replaced by the menu building screen (see fig. 14.8). Menu Builder first needs to know what you want to do: **M**odify the Menus, or **S**ave Current Menu. Because you have not yet made any menu changes to save, select **M**odify the Menus from the menu shown in figure 14.8.

After choosing to modify a menu, you are presented with the main working area of Menu Builder, shown in figure 14.9. This work area is divided into two windows. The bottom window is used to select the choice or portion of the menu to modify. The top window is used to define changes to that menu selection. Press the F6 (Window) function key to move between the top and bottom windows. Also, you can press F1 (Help) at any time in Menu Builder for on-screen help.

When you are in Menu Builder, use the cursor-movement keys to move to the various menu locations in the bottom window. When you first enter Menu Builder, the cursor is located in the bottom window on the first menu choice of the first level of the current default main menu: usually /**B**lock **C**opy. Use the right-arrow key to move from the higher menu levels to the submenus, if any. Use the left-arrow key to move from a lower menu level to a higher one. Use the up- and down-arrow keys to move to a menu selection after you get to the appropriate menu. As you move left and right through the menu levels, the menus scroll as well, to keep your cursor near the middle of the screen.

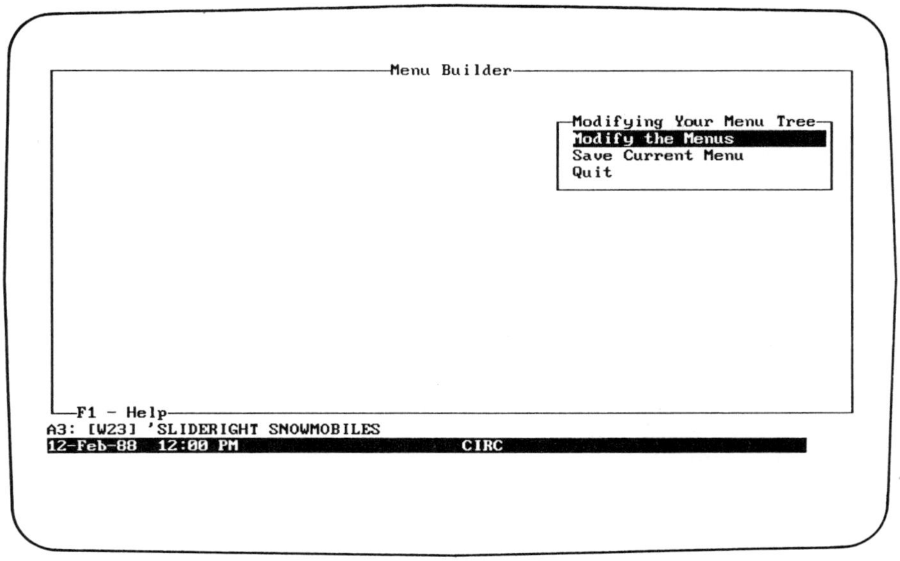

Fig. 14.8. Menu Builder's initial display to modify menus.

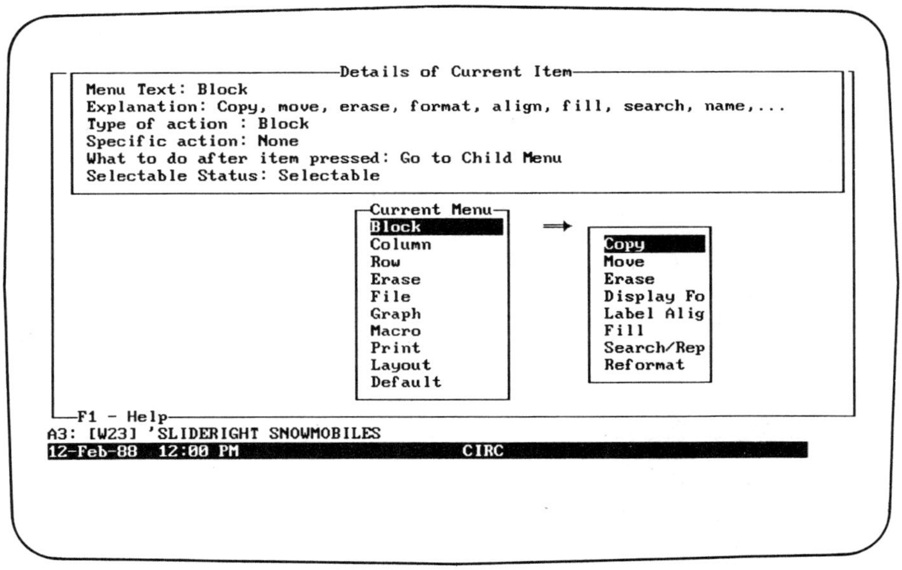

Fig. 14.9. The two windows of Menu Builder.

After you have moved the cursor to either the menu choice to change or the menu level to modify, press F6 to move to the top window to adjust that command's action. The fields in the top window define what the new menu choice will do and how it will appear. The fields are as follows:

Menu Text:	The label that will appear when the modified menu is invoked in Quattro
Explanation:	A description of what the menu choice will do, or a preview of the options on child menus
Type of action:	The overall kind of operation the menu choice will perform (for example, Block is a general action)
Specific action:	The specific action Quattro will take when you choose the menu selection (for example, Create)
What to do after item pressed:	How the menu will act when the choice is made: reappear, quit, proceed to a higher-level menu, or go down to a lower-level menu
Selectable Status:	Displays one of two options: **S**electable means that the choice will lead to some effect (as most menu choices do), and **D**isplay Only will show a menu choice but will not lead to any operation. This field is just for information.

Move to the field you want to edit by pressing Enter. Then press the F2 (Edit) key to edit the field. In some cases, pressing F2 opens a menu of options you can choose from. In other cases, you can change the entry by editing its contents directly. If the field does not have a menu, you can press the Esc key to clear a field entirely. Press Enter again to record your selection.

Inserting a New Command

The Ins key is used to add a new command to an existing menu. The spot just above the **Q**uit choice on the main Quattro menu is where you will add the **S**wap menu choice. Press F6 (Window) to move to the bottom window. Position the cursor to just below the area to modify (that is, on Quit), and press the Ins key. A prompt requesting the new command appears at the top left of the screen. Enter the word *Swap* as the response (see fig. 14.10).

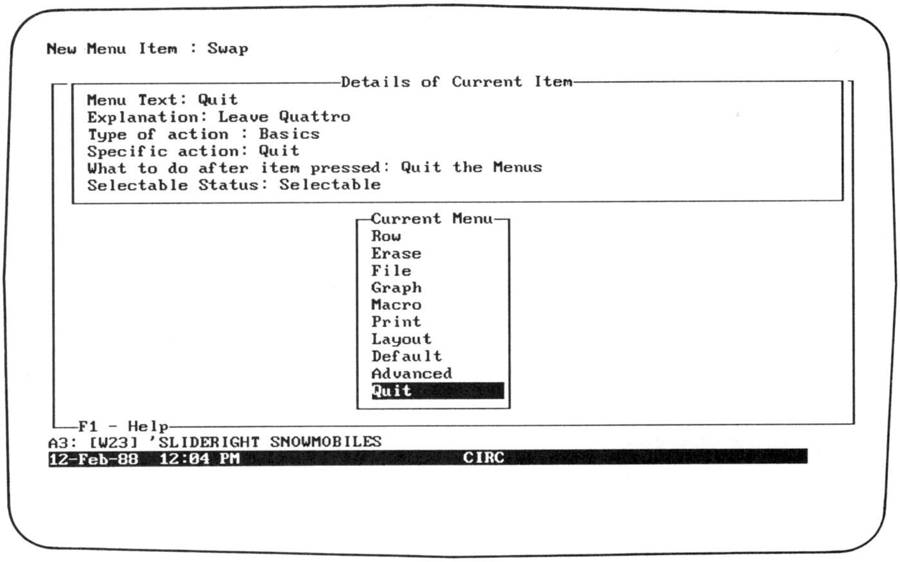

Fig. 14.10. Adding a new menu item.

Then press the Enter key. Menu Builder adds the new choice just above the choice on the menu that the cursor was highlighting (Quit).

Having added the new selection, press F6 (Window), moving to the Details of Current Item window to define the item's action. The cursor moves to the top window.

When adding a macro to a menu, the Menu Text and Explanation must be the same as the macro's name. This is because a macro is a single-action choice, as opposed to a command, such as /**B**lock, which has many subchoices. The entries for these fields were set to Swap, which is Quattro's automatic default action.

When the cursor switched to the top window, the cursor moved down to the "Type of action" field (see fig. 14.11). Press the F2 (Edit) or Enter key, opening a "drop-down" box that scrolls to show the various actions that the added menu selection might do. Note also that the lower right box holding the main menu now includes **S**wap. The selection from the "Type of action" menu to add to the macro must be **N**ame. By naming and associating the macro {SWAP} with the menu choice **S**wap, Quattro will be able to execute {SWAP} as a macro. Press Enter to record your choices.

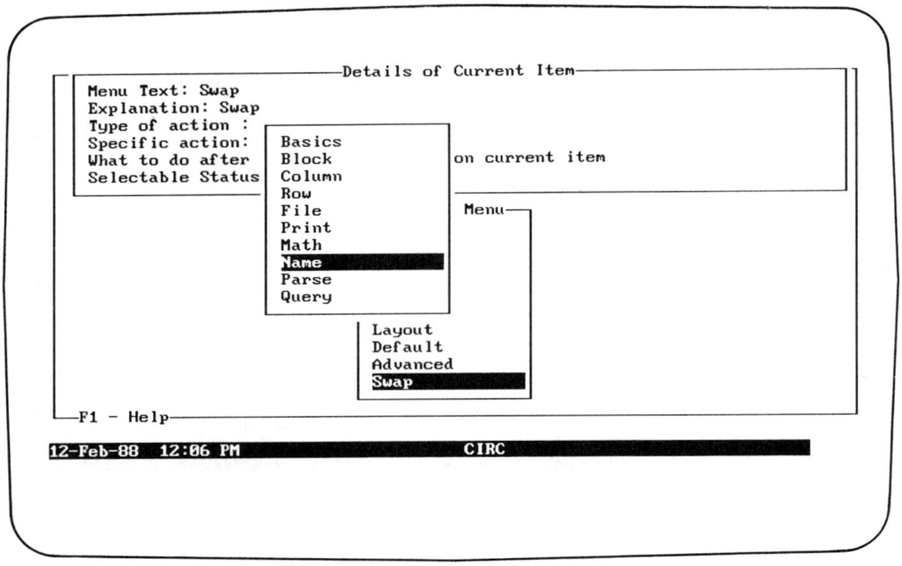

Fig. 14.11. Assigning a "Type of action" to Swap.

Next, define the "Specific action" field. When adding a macro to a menu, choose **Attach** from the "Specific action" options, as shown in figure 14.12. This option specifies that the block name SWAP will be attached to the menu choice **Swap**. Thus when you select **Swap** from the main menu, it will run a macro with the block name SWAP.

When a user calls a macro from a Quattro menu, the menu is always removed from the screen, so you do not need to specify what to do after the item is pressed or what its selectable status is.

When you have finished defining the menu, press the Esc key, removing the option boxes and presenting two choices in a menu. The selections determine whether the menu will be treated as a main (normal) menu option or an alternate menu structure. Select **Alternate Menu** and type the file name for this menu, *SWAP.ALT*, in the list of alternate menus (see fig. 14.13). You will use this file name when you want to activate the new menu during a Quattro session. The .ALT file extension is supplied automatically, as a default.

As soon as you assign a name to the menu, the Menu Builder program begins to process the menu structure. As it does, the messages `analyzing`, `compressing`, and `saving` appear, one after the other. These messages are simply for your information. The compression has nothing to do with the /**F**ile **!**SQZ! command discussed in Chapter 8. Select **Quit** (or Esc and **Quit**), quitting Menu Builder and returning to READY mode.

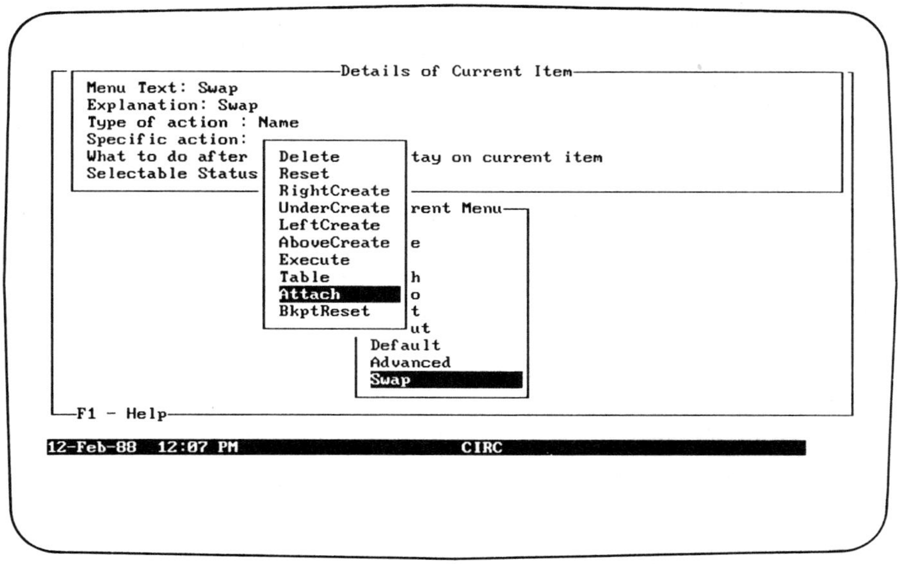

Fig. 14.12. Defining a specific action for the new menu choice.

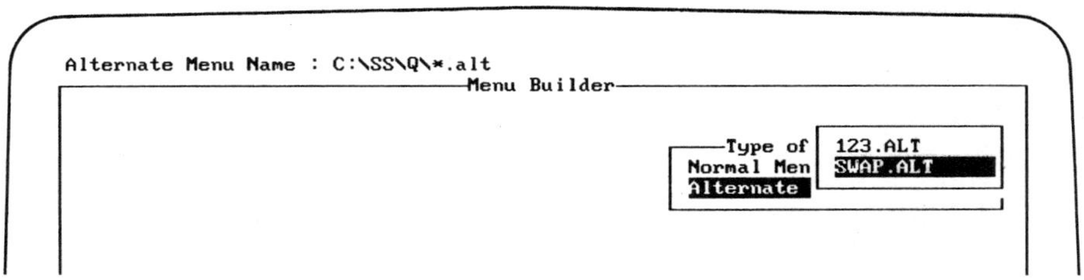

Fig. 14.13. Naming the new alternate menu file.

Now that you have created a new menu, you must make it available to the Quattro program. To do this, after quitting Menu Builder, invoke the /**D**efault **S**tartup **M**enu Tree **A**lternate Menus sequence. Choose the SWAP.ALT menu as the alternate menu from the list of alternate menus that appears. Only files with the .ALT extension can be used as alternate menu selections. The first (root) name of the alternate menu files should describe the kind of menu—SWAP.ALT for a menu with {SWAP}, for example.

In order for any modifications to the overall menus in Quattro to take effect, use the /**D**efault **U**pdate command to add the new settings to the default definitions file (QUATTRO.DEF), and **/Quit** Quattro completely. The changes do *not* take effect if you only temporarily exit to DOS with the **/File OS** command. You only need to exit Quattro once; the update is permanent.

After you have updated the defaults and left Quattro, you can restart the Quattro program. To work with the new menu for this work session, use the menu command **/Default Startup Menu** Tree **S**witch **M**enus. To make the new menu permanent, issue **/Default Startup Menu** Tree **U**pdate. Figure 14.14 shows the result of your labor: a menu that can execute a macro directly. The menu will only swap in spreadsheets that have the macro. In other spreadsheets, the **S**wap choice will be ignored unless you use the **/File Combine Copy** command to bring the macro in, and name the block as SWAP. (See Chapter 8 for more information on combining files.)

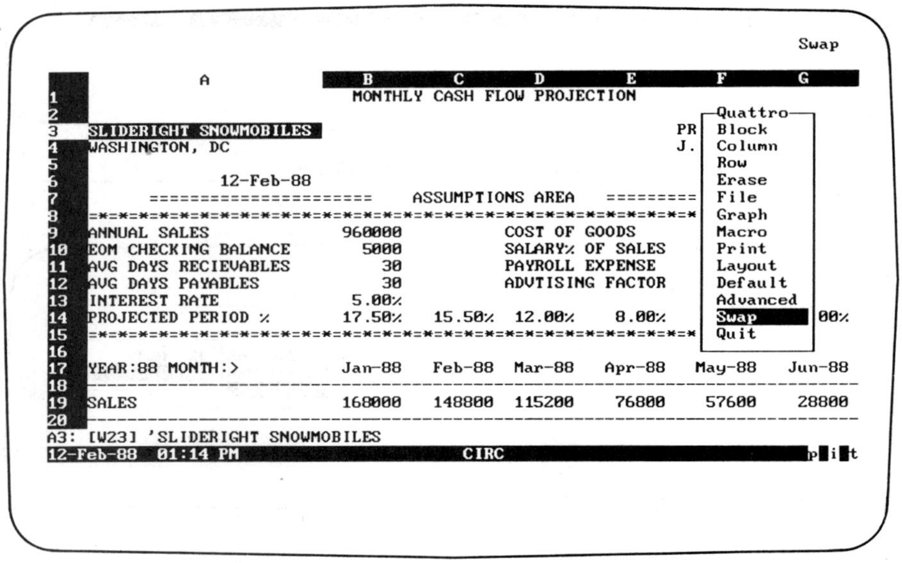

Fig. 14.14. The Swap *option in the alternate menu.*

Tip Removing and Moving Menu Commands

When you are in Menu Builder, you can use the minus key on the numeric keypad to remove a command from a menu entirely. Removing a command might be useful if you want to remove troublesome menu commands to prevent accidental access by new or unauthorized users.

To remove a menu command,

1. Use the cursor-movement keys to highlight the menu choice you want to relocate.
2. Press the minus key (-) on the numeric keypad, removing the menu choice and placing it in a memory buffer.

If you want to move the command to a new location in the menu, making the command a bit easier to access, follow the preceding steps. In addition,

3. Position the cursor just below where you want the choice moved to.
4. Press the plus key (+) on the numeric keypad.

Tip Creating a Submenu

You can use Menu Builder to add a new child menu (submenu) to an existing Quattro menu choice that does not already have a submenu:

1. Move the cursor to that menu choice.
2. Press the F6 (Window) key to move to the top window, and define the submenu.
3. Highlight the "What to do after item pressed" field, and press F2 (Edit) to make the options list appear.
4. Select the "Go to child menu" option.
5. Press the F6 key to return to the bottom area of Menu Builder. A new submenu will be attached, with a Quit option already created.
6. Move to the new submenu with the cursor-movement keys.
7. Press the Ins key to add menu choices.
8. Press F6 (Window) to define what each choice will do.

Using the Transcript Add-In

Remember *Perry Mason*? The show was as predictable as the sun rising in the morning. At least once every show, Perry would strenuously object to the way the district attorney was trying to get the jury to hang Perry's client. Just as predictably, the wizened old judge would sustain the objection and solemnly charge the jury to forget what was said. The he would look down and tell the court reporter to remove the remarks from the record. The court reporter would delete the record obediently.

Quattro has a similar "court reporter," Transcript. While you are using Quattro, the Transcript add-in can record your actions as you develop a spreadsheet. Transcript is so unobtrusive that you may even forget it's at work. But when you need to know exactly how you reached a point in working with Quattro, nothing beats having an exact transcript available.

The Transcript add-in has several uses. You can use it to reconstruct from scratch a damaged or lost spreadsheet by replaying the keystrokes the led to its creation. You also can "undo" any unfortunate actions by replaying the transcript with the exception of the last operation, thus effectively undoing the offensive operation. In addition, because transcripts are recorded in macro format, they can be used to assist in macro development.

Working with Transcript

As with other add-ins, you can work with Transcript in two ways. You can set up Transcript as a default add-in with the /**D**efault **S**tartup **D**efault Add-Ins menu sequence. Or, Transcript can be started at any time by using the /**M**acro **L**oad and **R**un commands. Unless you have limited memory available to your machine, loading Transcript as a default add-in is a good idea, because Transcript must be loaded and running to record commands.

If you decide to load Transcript as a default add-in, Transcript is automatically invoked every time you start Quattro. The benefit of this approach is that you will always have the transcript available to recover your spreadsheet from disasters. The negative side is that Transcript can slow down spreadsheet processing somewhat. The severity of this problem depends on your system. On a floppy disk drive system, for instance, Transcript may take so much time to do its job that it becomes more irritating than useful. On a hard disk drive IBM PC or PC XT™, the transcription process may delay processing occasionally, but it should be bearable. On a Personal Computer AT or PS/2 machine, the transcription process is hardly noticeable.

If you work with Transcript loaded, an indication is displayed at the bottom right of the screen, as shown in figure 14.15. You also will hear the disk activate after every several keystrokes. This sound is caused by the add-in appending the spreadsheet activity to a file that contains a log of your spreadsheet history. The file is named QUATTRO.LOG and is stored in the Quattro directory. Whenever you need the transcript history, you can open this LOG file, which is presented in the spreadsheet display.

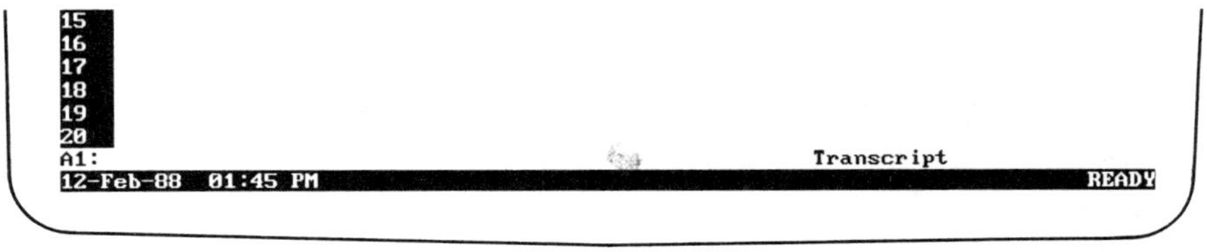

Fig. 14.15. The Transcript add-in indicator.

Every time the LOG file reaches a predefined maximum length (default is 2K bytes), the file's name is changed to QTROLOG.BAQ and a new QUATTRO.LOG file is started. If a QTROLOG.BAQ file already exists, it is overwritten. Transcript takes these actions to prevent a LOG file from growing larger and larger until it takes over your disk like some science-fiction runaway fungus.

You can set the amount of history retained in QUATTRO.LOG to be anywhere from 1 byte to 25,000 bytes. Issue the /**M**acro **R**un **M**ax History Length command to set the history amount. Good performance on an IBM Personal Computer AT or compatible is retained with a 10,000-byte LOG.

Running Transcript opens a Command History window (see fig. 14.16). The command history is a record of your actual keystrokes. Each line of the history holds a complete sequence of actions and usually ends with an Enter keystroke ({CR}) or some other action that completes an operation. This convention keeps the length of each history line down to a comprehensible number of characters.

Occasionally a line has more commands than can be displayed in the Command History window. To see all the commands on a long line, move the cursor in the window to that line; the full line will appear at the top left of the display, as in figure 14.16. You cannot use the F2 (Edit) key to directly modify commands in the Command History window.

At the bottom left of the Command History window is a line that seems to "bracket" several lines. The beginning of this line indicates the point where the last /**F**ile **S**ave, /**F**ile **R**etrieve, or /**E**rase occurred. Transcript uses these operations as *checkpoints*, which Quattro considers to be a milestone during your work session. You can easily recover your work from any one of these commands. The line on the left side of the Command History window thus brackets the commands from the last checkpoint to your most recent spreadsheet action.

You can use the checkpoint as a reference point for recovering from problems. For instance, if you have modified a macro that suddenly doesn't work any-

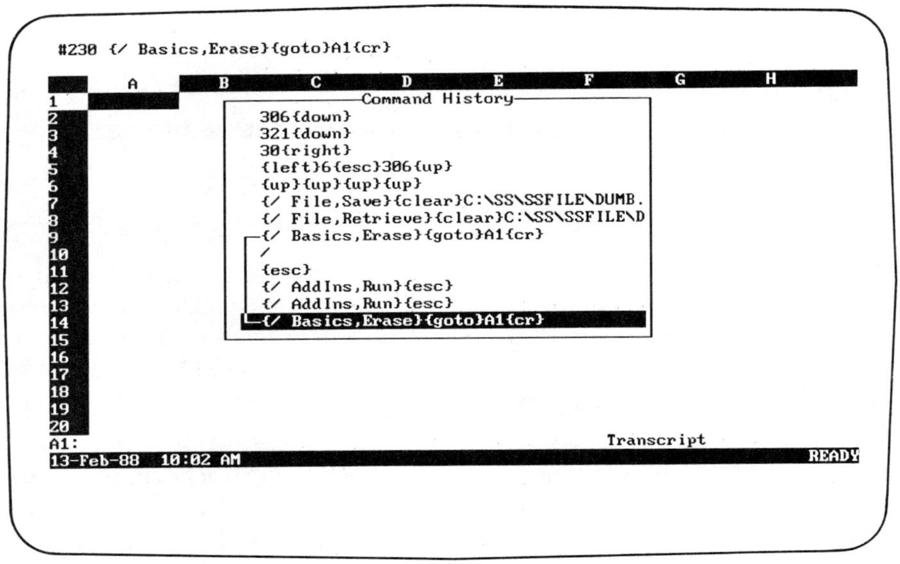

Fig. 14.16. The normal Command History window.

more, run Transcript to replay the keystrokes just prior to the last /**F**ile **S**ave command. You then will be able to recreate an earlier (working) version of the macro.

Recovering a Spreadsheet Block with Transcript

Even if you are the most cautious of users, you will inevitably make an error from time to time. One of my frequent mistakes is accidentally erasing the wrong part of a spreadsheet with the /**B**lock **E**rase command. However, you can use Transcript to restore the portion of the spreadsheet that was accidentally erased.

Suppose you belatedly notice that the top area of the spreadsheet has been erased. After realizing what went wrong, you can breathe a sigh of relief: the indicator at the bottom right of the spreadsheet shows that Transcript is active. You can restore the missing data by activating the Macro menu and choosing the **R**un option. **R**un is only used to start an add-in program that has already been loaded. Activate the Transcript program from the menu of loaded add-ins.

Running Transcript opens the Command History window. However, you need to restore the data you lost just before going on a coffee break. By pressing the plus and minus keys on the numeric keypad, you can expand and contract the width of the Command History window. Expanding the window displays the time and date when a particular set of operations occurred. In figure 14.17 you can see what you did just before your 9:45 break.

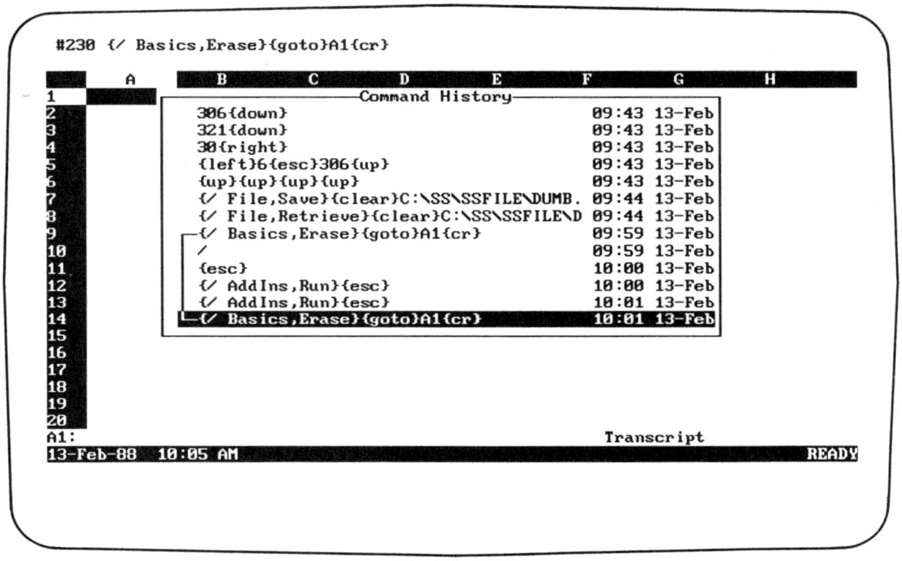

Fig. 14.17. The expanded Command History window.

Transcript is controlled through the Transcript menu. To run Transcript, issue the /**M**acro **R**un Transcript command and press the slash key (/). Once the Command History window is open, you can press the slash key again to bring up the Transcript menu with its options. The menu is divided into two areas. The options in the top part of the menu allow you to manipulate keystroke recordings, and those in the bottom part let you specify the settings for Transcript. The Transcript menu offers the following options:

Edit History

Undo Last Command	Resets the spreadsheet to its state just prior to the last checkpoint, and replays the history from the checkpoint to just before the last command
Restore To Here	Resets the spreadsheet to its state just prior to the last checkpoint, and replays the history from the checkpoint to the line highlighted by the cursor

Playback Block	Plays back the block of actions marked by **B**egin Block and **E**nd Block (no action occurs if no lines have been marked)
Copy Block	Copies to the spreadsheet the actions identified by **B**egin Block and **E**nd Block. Once you are in the sheet, the block can be edited.
Begin Block	Marks the starting point in history for the **P**layback Block and **C**opy Block options
End Block	Marks the ending point in history for the **P**layback Block and **C**opy Block options
Settings	
Max History Length	Determines how large in lines a transcript file will get before it is backed up and restarted
Single Step	Plays back the command history one command at a time (similar to DEBUG). Press the space bar to step.
Failure Protection	Determines how many command history lines will be stored in the protection buffer before actions are stored on disk. Lower numbers give greater protection to power failures but also can slow Quattro.

If you want to leave the Transcript environment, press the Esc key until you have returned to READY mode.

Now you need to tell the Transcript program where to start and stop its playback. Do this with the **B**egin Block and **E**nd Block menu options. After you select either option, you cannot move the cursor in the Command History window; therefore, always position the cursor in the window to the current line before bringing up the menu. Figure 14.18 shows the Transcript menu. The cursor in the Command History window highlights the line that holds the starting entries of the part of the spreadsheet that was accidentally erased.

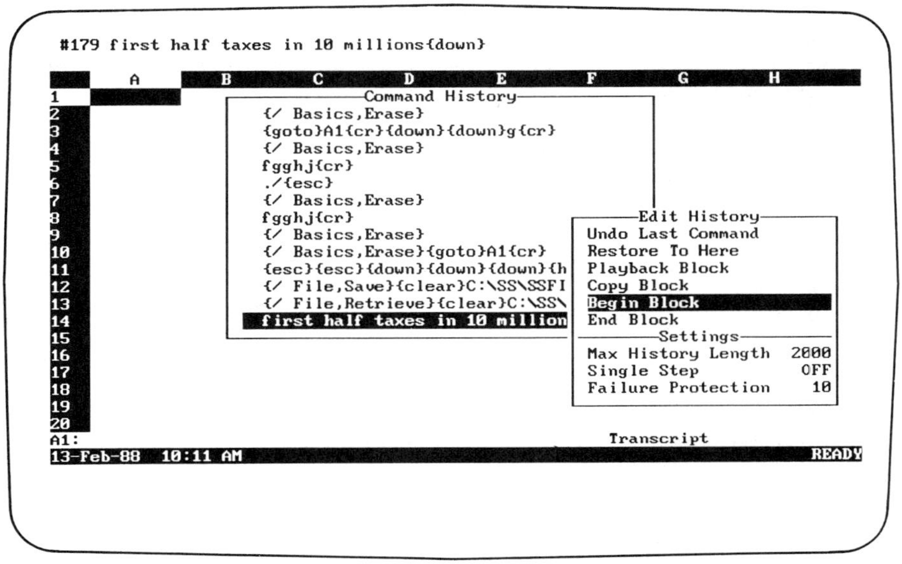

Fig. 14.18. Identifying the beginning line for spreadsheet recovery.

Using the **B**egin Block option marks the line in the Command History window with a right triangle, as shown in figure 14.19. Notice that the Transcript menu disappears after the **B**egin Block option has been executed. If you want to set an **E**nd Block, you must rerun the Transcript add-in from the Macro menu. You may find this procedure a bit tedious, and no doubt Borland will modify the menus in a future release so that they will remain on-screen.

Position the cursor in the Command History window to a line before the accidental erasure and issue the **E**nd Block option, marking the end of the block. All the history lines between the beginning and ending lines of the block are automatically marked with a right triangle.

Now that you have identified the block, use the **P**layback Block option. When you choose the playback option, you will see a `playback%` message on-screen that tells you how much of the playback has occurred (this message is just for your information). Figure 14.20 shows the result—the lost table successfully restored.

While the Transcript program is playing back keystrokes, you can press the Ctrl-Break key combination to stop the playback.

Use the same marking process to copy a portion of the command history into a section of the spreadsheet. After marking the lines, use the **C**opy Block option

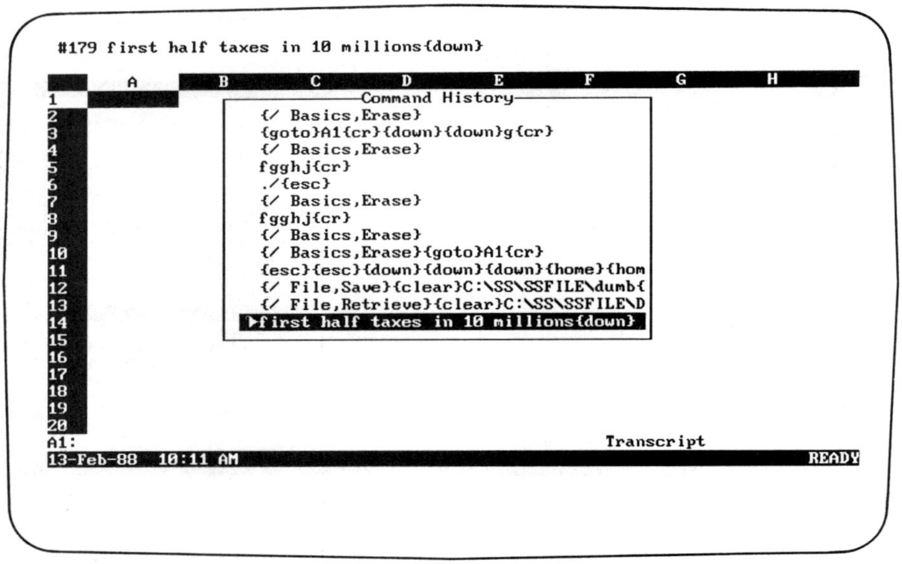

Fig. 14.19. The beginning of the block identified.

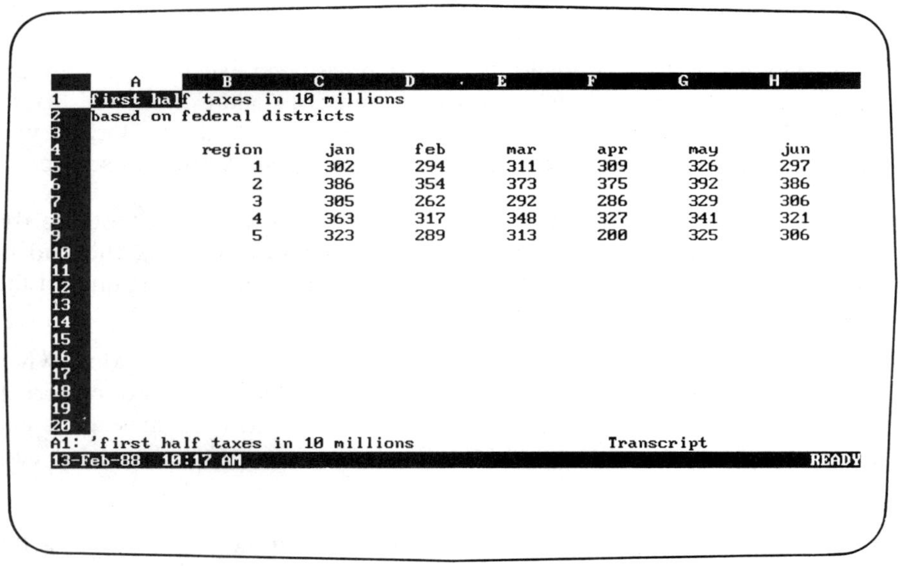

Fig. 14.20. The block restored.

to copy the command history. You will be prompted for the starting cell to use as the destination of the history. This technique is also useful for storing actions that would otherwise be lost as they went beyond the buffer limit of Transcript. But notice: The act of copying history to the spreadsheet can overwrite cells if they are in the way.

Using Transcript To Undo Errors

If any feature is really valuable to have in any software program, it is the ability to undo mistakes. They are as inevitable as human imperfection, and it is a wonder that users have let so many software developers get away with ignoring an undo function.

Fortunately, the people at Borland didn't commit this sin of omission. The Transcript add-in makes undoing the most recent command or entry easy, as long as the add-in is active when the problem occurred.

To undo an error, activate the /**M**acro **R**un menu to open the Command History window. Then press the slash key again to open the Transcript menu. At this point, simply select the Undo Last Command option. Your spreadsheet will return with the offensive command eliminated.

While the Transcript program is undoing a command, you can press Ctrl-Break to stop the undo process.

Chapter Summary

The standard add-ins that Borland ships with Quattro, Menu Builder and Transcript, let you add new functionality as your needs grow. The next chapter introduces the exciting capabilities of macros, which you can use to speed and simplify repetitive spreadsheet operations.

CHAPTER

15

Using Macros in Quattro

If you ask anyone experienced with spreadsheets to name the most exciting feature of spreadsheets, invariably the answer is "macros." Quattro's macro capabilities can be used to automate typing repetitive text, speed menu selections, or implement large applications. Powerful features, such as keystroke recording, instantly available macro command lists, and macro debugging tools—to name just a few—set Quattro's macro facilities head and shoulders above other programs' macro capabilities.

This chapter is an introduction to the concepts and use of macros. The text details the steps involved in planning, creating, and running macros. If you want to use macros to automate repetitive tasks in your worksheet files, you will find your answers here. This chapter suggests ways macros can be used and tells you how to create them. For information about how to test and correct macros, refer to Chapter 17.

Understanding Basic Macro Concepts

What are macros? No doubt, you are familiar with the process of recording and playing back speech on a tape recorder. You record the words once, and you can replay them as many times as you wish. Macros work in a similar fashion. Macros consist of keystrokes (labels) that are entered (recorded) into the spreadsheet for the purpose of playing them back later as a series of menu actions, text entries, or formula entries.

A working macro has only two necessary components: the name of the block that contains the starting point of the macro and the actual keystrokes, or instructions, that tell the macro what to do. Look at a macro that automatically enters a name and a department:

```
Adam Prime{RIGHT}
Accounting~
```

When this macro is run, it places the name *Adam Prime* in the current cursor location. After the name is entered, the key-equivalent command, {RIGHT}, both completes the entry and moves the cursor to the right. Then the label *Accounting* is entered on the edit line of the next cell. The character immediately after *Accounting* is called a tilde. The tilde is used to perform an ENTER command. That is, the tilde "presses" the Enter (Return) key for macros. Another way of emulating the Enter key with Quattro is the {CR}, carriage return, command. A tilde and {CR} have the same effect. The macro stops operating when the program comes to a blank cell in the macro.

In this example, you might use the block name \N to name the cell where the macro begins. Then when you want to run the macro, you can press and hold down the Alt key while you press the N key. This method is the fastest way to start a macro—"Wake it up by name." (Quattro's other ways to start a macro are discussed in later sections.)

Always use macro names that are easy to remember. For example, the preceding macro is named \N to help you remember the purpose of the macro (*N*aming macro), and \P and PRINT are good names for printing macros. Avoid using macro names that are reserved by Quattro. For example, Quattro reserves EDIT for the F2 function key. Using reserved words as macro names causes errors in the macros.

All macro instructions must be either labels or string formulas. If a macro reaches a macro cell that contains only a value or numeric formula, the macro stops. (See Chapters 6 and 7 for information about formulas and functions.)

In macros, some instructions are enclosed in braces: { and }. These commands are called key-equivalent commands because each command performs the operation of the key with that name. The braces are used by Quattro to differentiate the key-equivalent commands from simple labels, which Quattro enters automatically.

Some key-equivalent commands accept optional arguments. (Arguments in macros are essentially the same as arguments in functions.) For instance, suppose that you want to have a macro create a spreadsheet window with Quattro's window command. The first thing you might want to do is have the macro move the cursor down to the middle of the screen in preparation for the window's creation. One way to do this is illustrated in figure 15.1.

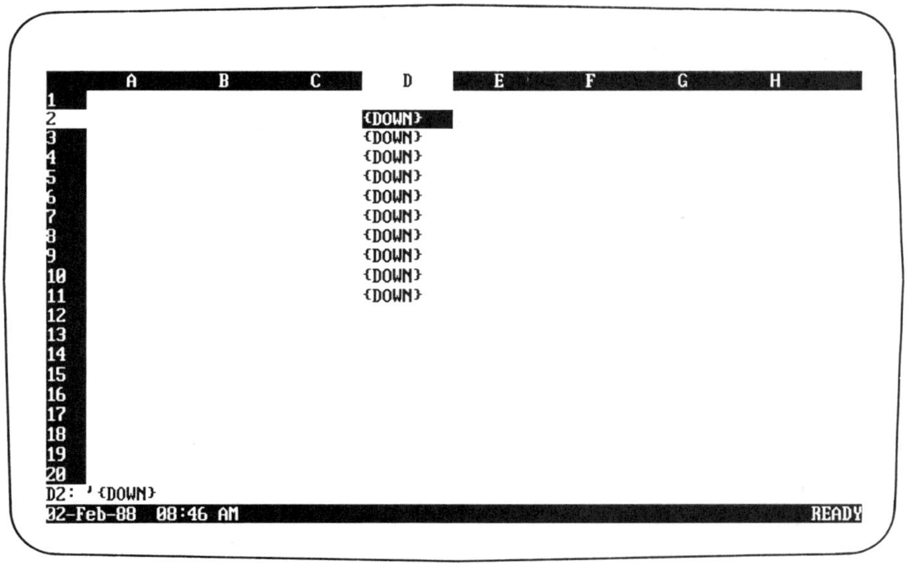

Fig. 15.1. An inefficient macro to move the cursor down.

By repeating the {DOWN} key-equivalent command 10 times, you get the job done. However, I'm sure you'll agree that this method is redundant. Using the same key-equivalent command with an optional repetition argument, such as {DOWN 10}, reduces the repetitiveness of cursor-movement macros.

An especially appealing aspect of the repeat factor is that it can be a reference to a value contained in a block name. Hypothetically, you could perform a {BACKSPACE} keystroke FRED number of times, where FRED is a block name containing a value. The macro would be written in this way:

{BACKSPACE FRED}

Key-equivalent commands are available for all function-key, cursor-movement, and alphabetic-key commands. Special keys such as Ctrl, Alt, Shift, NumLock, etc., are not supported. A special case might bear mentioning here. In the Quattro manual, reference is made to the {BIGLEFT} and {BIGRIGHT} keys. These commands are used to emulate the Tab and Shift-Tab keystrokes. Table 15.1 shows a complete list of the key-equivalent macro commands and their operations.

Table 15.1
The Key-Equivalent Macro Commands

Command	*Function*
{ABS}	Sets relative or absolute cell addresses (same as F4)
{ADDIN}	Brings up the Add-In command history box, from which you can select your most recent commands
{CALC}	Recalculates spreadsheet (same as F9)
{EDIT}	Puts content of current cell in EDIT mode so that it can be changed (same as F2)
{FUNCTIONS}	Presents list of @functions (same as Alt-F3)
{GOTO}	Moves cell selector to cell address supplied (same as F5)
{GRAPH}	Shows current graph, if any (same as F10)
{MACROS}	Presents list of macro commands (same as Shift-F3)
{NAME}	Displays list of current block names
{QUERY}	Repeats most recent database query (same as F7)
{TABLE}	Repeats most recent what-if operation (same as Alt-F7)
{WINDOW}	Moves cell selector to other window (same as F6)
{BACKSPACE},{BS}	Moves cursor (destructively) to one position to the left when program is in EDIT mode

Command	*Function*
{BIGLEFT}	Moves cell selector one full screen to the left (same as Shift-Tab and Ctrl-left arrow)
{BIGRIGHT}	Moves cell selector one full screen to the right (same as Tab or Ctrl-right arrow)
{DOWN}	Moves cell selector down one cell
{END}	Moves cell selector to next nonblank cell
{HOME}	Sends cell selector to top left of spreadsheet (cell A1)
{LEFT}	Moves cell selector one cell to the left
{PGDN}	Cell selector moves down one full screen
{PGUP}	Cell selector moves up one full screen
{RIGHT}	Moves cell selector one cell to the right
{UP}	Moves cell selector up one cell
{DELETE}, {DEL}	In READY mode, deletes current cell contents
	In EDIT mode, deletes character at current cursor location
{ESCAPE}, {ESC}	In EDIT mode, removes contents of edit line, preserving current contents of cell, if any
	In MENU mode, backs up one menu level
	When prompted, backs up to preceding step
{INSERT}, {INS}	In EDIT mode, overstrikes characters
{{}	Types literal opening brace as text
{}}	Types literal closing brace as text
{~}	Types literal tilde as text
{CR}, ~ (tilde)	Emulates Enter key
{DATE}	Enters a date

Any kind of data can be played back by a macro. For instance, to play back numbers or formulas from a macro, enter the numbers or formulas as labels in the macro. When the macro is run, the labels are entered correctly as numbers.

Creating Macros

Quattro has two ways to create macros. One is to type one instruction at a time. The other way is to use the macro learning mode, or the keystroke recorder, activated by pressing the Alt-F8 key. The typing method is discussed first. Then you learn how to use the automatic recorder. First, however, you need to decide where to put your macro and then you must plan it.

Locating Macros

Because macros must reside on the spreadsheets the macros are intended to work with, some thought must be given to where to put them. Otherwise, macros may be damaged because of column and row insertions or deletions or other spreadsheet operations. For instance, if you insert a row in a spreadsheet, that row may seem harmless enough. Unfortunately, you may find later that the same row also was inserted through the middle of the macro and that the blank row has stopped the macro's operation.

The best location for macros is well away from and below the main spreadsheet area. The graphing macro, recorded in a following section, is placed all the way down on row 5000 and in the far right of the spreadsheet at column IR. If anyone inserts, deletes, or moves rows or data in the main spreadsheet area, which begins in cell A1, any effect on the macro is extremely unlikely.

Generally speaking, if you lay out your application as in figure 15.2, you should experience few macro conflicts due to location.

You may think that having the macro so far to the bottom right of the spreadsheet will make the macro difficult to get to. As a matter of fact, this location makes the macro convenient to access. When you want to get to the macro area of the spreadsheet, you simply press End-Home. This key combination instantly moves the cursor to the macro because it is at the extreme bottom right of the sheet. You also can go to the macro by pressing F5 and typing the name of the macro.

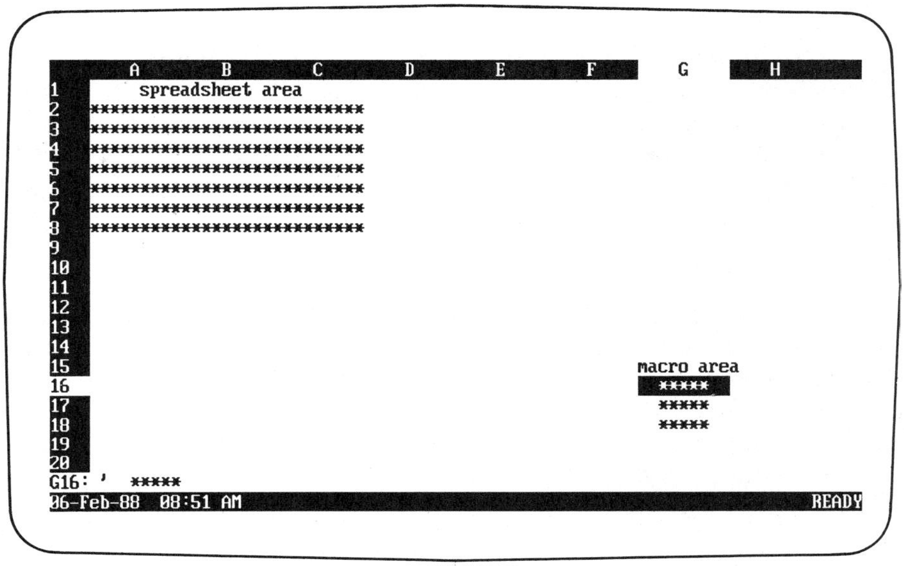

Fig. 15.2. Suggested spreadsheet layout for macros.

Planning and Typing Macros

Macros are used often to speed repetitive menu operations, such as printing or creating and displaying graphs. Creating macros that automate the use of Quattro menus is easy. You simply type an apostrophe before you type the slash key in the macro so that the slash character is entered into a cell. When the macro is run, the slash activates the Quattro menu. Look at a simple printing macro:

'/PG

This macro causes the printer to print the current print block by first activating the main menu (/), then the **Print** command, and finally, the **Go** option. No tildes are required here because the act of choosing **Go** performs the print operation.

You must try to think ahead when you create macros because they do exactly what you tell them to do—not necessarily what you want them to do. In the /PG macro, no thought has been given to what mode the spreadsheet will be in after printing. The user must leave the Print menu and advance the paper in the printer in order to get the report out. By thinking ahead, you can avoid these shortcomings by adding the menu commands. A more complete print macro might be as follows:

'/PGAF{ESCAPE}Q

This macro includes the **Adjust_Printer** and **Form_Feed** commands. After the printing is complete, the macro continues by adjusting the printer with a form feed to get the page to clear the printer. Next, the macro activates the Esc key to return to the main Print menu. The Q causes Quattro to quit the Print menu.

Recording Macros

The other way to create a Quattro macro is to use the RECORD mode, which records your keystrokes automatically for later playback. This convenient feature can be used to record frequently used operations in macro format. In fact, you don't need to know a great deal about writing macros to record and run macros. If you are new to macros, seeing the macros that Quattro creates when it is in RECORD mode is a good way to learn how to make your own macros.

The macro recorder is invoked by pressing Alt-F8. Once the recorder is invoked, a RECORD indicator appears in the status line just after the date and time. Turning off RECORD is accomplished by again pressing, or toggling, Alt-F8.

Tip At first, recording macros seems to require little effort on your part. However, just as a tape recorder records all sounds—even mistakes and coughing—the macro recorder records all your keystrokes—the good and the bad. You should always look ahead and plan the most efficient way to carry out the action you want to record, just as you plan what you dictate to a tape recorder before you begin talking. That way, you can avoid unnecessary and incorrect keystrokes.

The next series of figures (figs. 15.3 through 15.8) illustrates the use of the macro recorder. In this sequence, the recorder copies the keystrokes to a user-specified location. The purpose of this macro is to automate the process of creating a sales graph.

In figure 15.3, the spreadsheet is displayed with two windows set up. These windows are used so that you can see the area holding the data to be graphed in the top window and the recorded macro keystrokes in the bottom window.

Figure 15.3 shows what happens just after Alt-F8 (Record) is pressed. In order to begin recording, the recorder needs to know the block name and cell location you want to assign to the recorded macro. Both are entered in the input line. The macro is named \G and begins in cell IR5000.

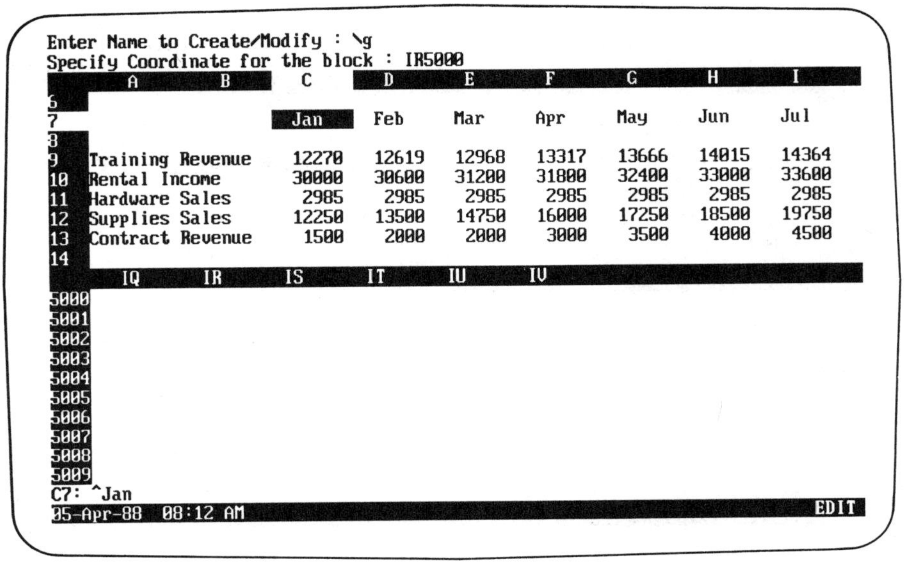

Fig. 15.3. Spreadsheet set up to begin recording a macro.

Notice also in the top window that the spreadsheet cursor is positioned on the first cell of the block to be graphed. This position prevents the recording of unnecessary cursor movements. Here is an example of thinking ahead before turning on the recorder.

After telling the recorder where to locate the macro, you can begin to record. If you need to access the Quattro menu, just press the slash key as you normally do. Unlike other spreadsheet recorders, Quattro does not record cursor movements, such as {UP} and {DOWN}, while you are making selections in the menu system. Other recorders also force you to press the first character of the appropriate choice. Quattro ignores cursor movements and records just the actual menu choices made. The macros that result are much faster and simpler to create and are more easily understood.

Figure 15.4 shows the screen as the /**G**raph **X**-axis_Values menu choice is about to be made. At this point, Quattro offers the options of pointing to the block to be displayed as the X series or typing the cell addresses (see the prompt in the input line).

Figure 15.5 shows the entered cell addresses. If you point to the cells by moving the cursor, the resulting macro would look like this:

{RIGHT}{RIGHT}{RIGHT}{RIGHT}{RIGHT}{RIGHT}{RIGHT} . . . etc.

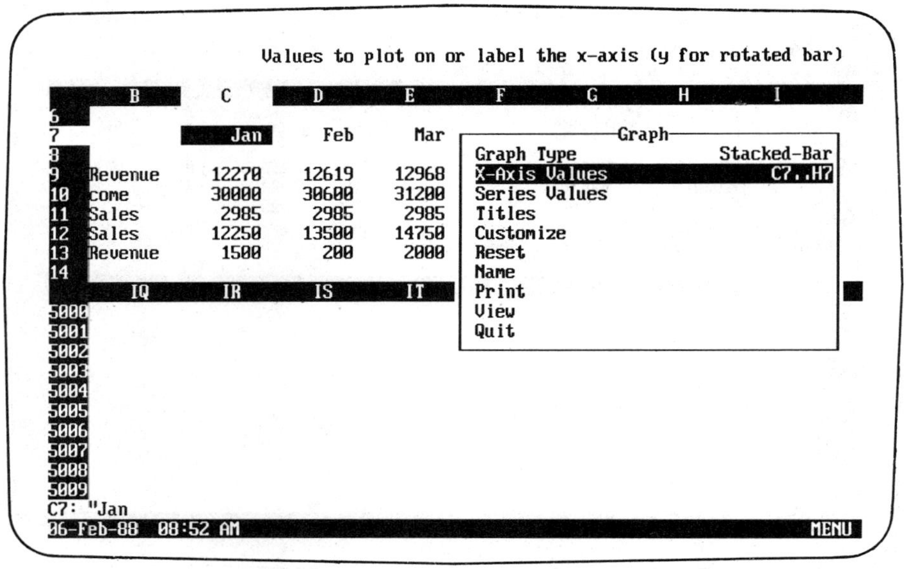

Fig. 15.4. Prompt for identifying values for graph.

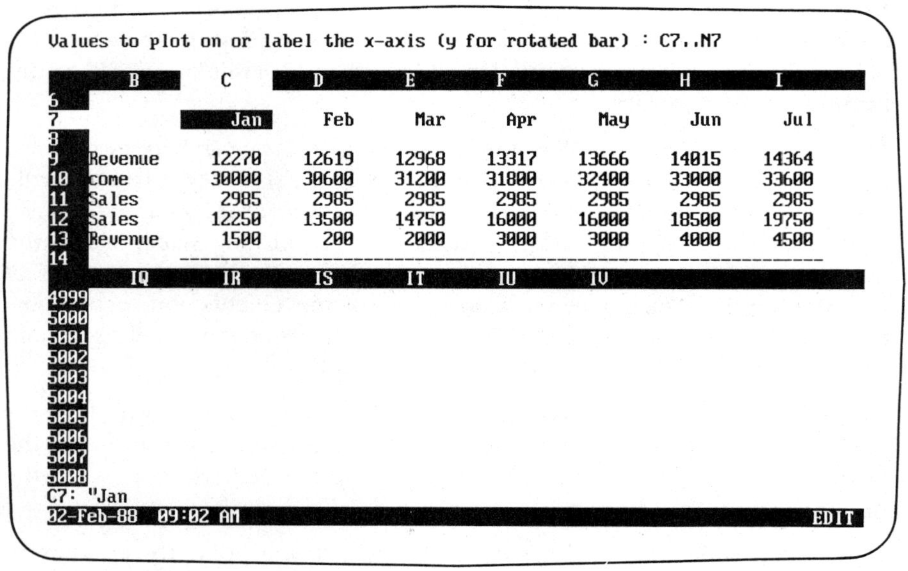

Fig. 15.5. Cell addresses entered for graph.

Although, as mentioned, when in RECORD mode, Quattro ignores cursor movements in menus, the program records all cursor movements in the spreadsheet. Pointing with the cursor while in RECORD mode results in an excessively long and confusing macro. Entering the cell addresses is more efficient.

After setting up the X-axis, you need to select a series value. Figure 15.6 shows the first series being selected. Take special note of the bottom window as you look at this figure. The recorder has started to display some of the keystrokes stored in its buffer. This macro is a form of a menu macro. Quattro has special macro commands that represent the menu functions. In this case, the first macro instruction does not include the first Graph choice from the menu. The instruction {/ XAxis,Labels} shows that the Graph menu was selected. This kind of macro statement, which results in shorter, more concise programs, is a special feature of Quattro.

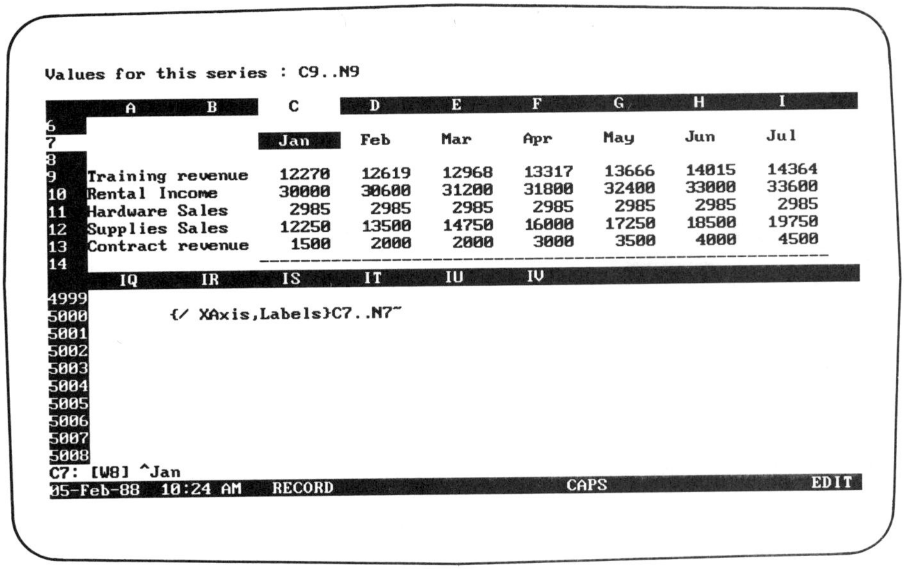

Fig. 15.6. Selecting series value; note first instruction line in the lower window.

After the series values have been specified, you can view the graph (see fig. 15.7). While the graph is displayed, the action of viewing the graph is being recorded.

After the graph is displayed, the Esc key-equivalent command returns you to the menu, and Quit returns you to the READY mode. The complete macro can be seen in figure 15.8. Remember that the first step of macro recording

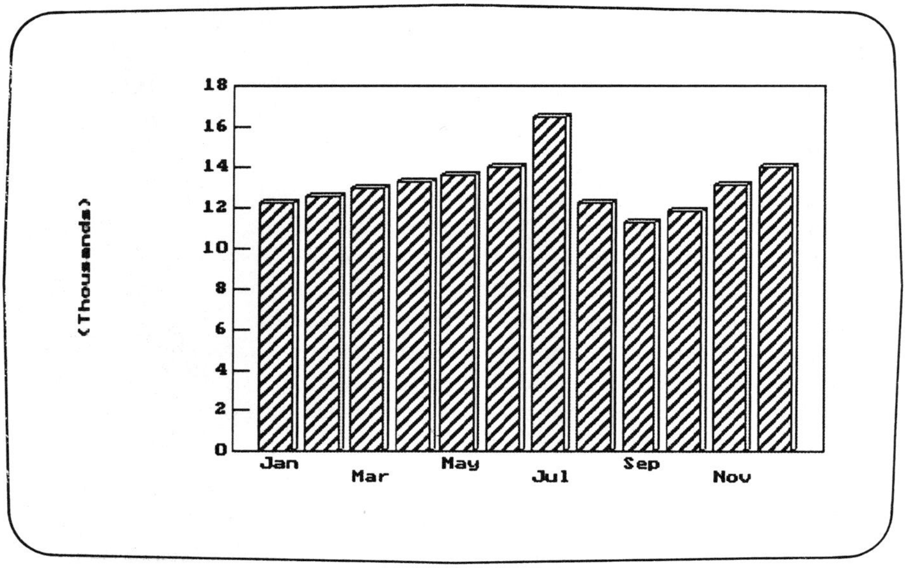

Fig. 15.7. Graph created while recording a macro.

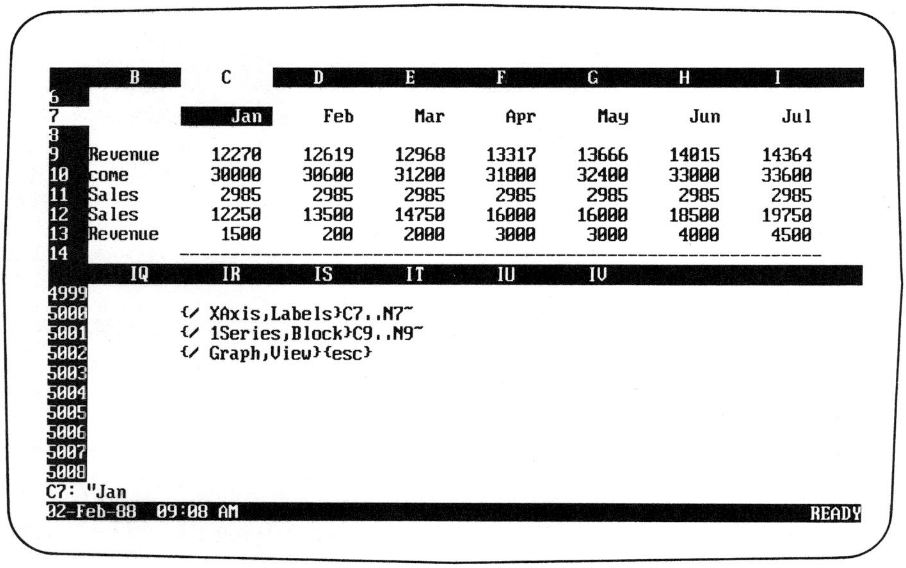

```
       B          C       D       E       F       G       H       I
6
7                Jan     Feb     Mar     Apr     May     Jun     Jul
8
9   Revenue     12270   12619   12968   13317   13666   14015   14364
10  come        30000   30600   31200   31800   32400   33000   33600
11  Sales        2985    2985    2985    2985    2985    2985    2985
12  Sales       12250   13500   14750   16000   16000   18500   19750
13  Revenue      1500     200    2000    3000    3000    4000    4500
14           ------------------------------------------------------------
       IQ        IR      IS      IT      IU      IV
4999
5000            {/ XAxis,Labels}C7..N7~
5001            {/ 1Series,Block}C9..N9~
5002            {/ Graph,View}{esc}
5003
5004
5005
5006
5007
5008
C7: "Jan
02-Feb-88  09:08 AM                                          READY
```

Fig. 15.8. The completed graphing macro.

is to name the macro. To run this macro, all you need to do is press Alt-G (\G is the name of this macro, defined when recording was being invoked [see fig. 15.3]), and the whole sequence plays back.

After grinning in satisfaction at the macro you have created, you may think you are finished. But wait! A very important step remains. Turn off RECORD by pressing Alt-F8. I have often forgotten this step and have ended up with huge macro recordings. Although this error is irritating, it is not fatal. If you forget to turn off RECORD, you can erase the extra instructions.

Starting Macros

Quattro provides three ways to start macros. The first, as you have seen, is to press the Alt key and an alphabet key to invoke a keyboard macro with a block name such as \P. You also can start macros by using the F8 (Macro) function key, or you can run a macro by making a selection from the special macro choice on the command menu.

The F8 (Macro) key gives you the capability to start any macro by simply pointing to its block name in a box that pressing the F8 key displays. Figure 15.9 shows the graphing macro that was recorded earlier. A small box near the top right of the screen has been opened. All block names for the current spreadsheet are displayed in this box. In this particular spreadsheet, only one block name exists. If at this point you press Enter, the \G macro will begin to run.

Figure 15.10 shows another spreadsheet after the Macro key has been pressed. The macro box displays several block names that can be selected. Only the \P and PRINT_IT block names are actually macro names, however. The other names refer to variable cells.

You need to know which names are macro names in order to use the Macro key effectively. You may want to reserve a certain prefix character for macro names, a pound sign (#), for instance. Using this example, the PRINT_IT macro name becomes #PRINT_IT. The # always causes the macro names to be placed at the top of the block name list. By using a special prefix, you can easily see the block names that start macros, as shown in figure 15.11.

Another way to start a macro is by using the /**M**acro **E**xecute menu command. When you access the Macro menu, you have four choices that relate directly to spreadsheet macros (see fig. 15.12). The first choice, **N**ame, provides an alternative method to create a block name for a macro. This method has the same effect as /**B**lock **A**dvanced **C**reate. The second choice, **D**elete, lets you delete a block name (see Chapter 4 for more information).

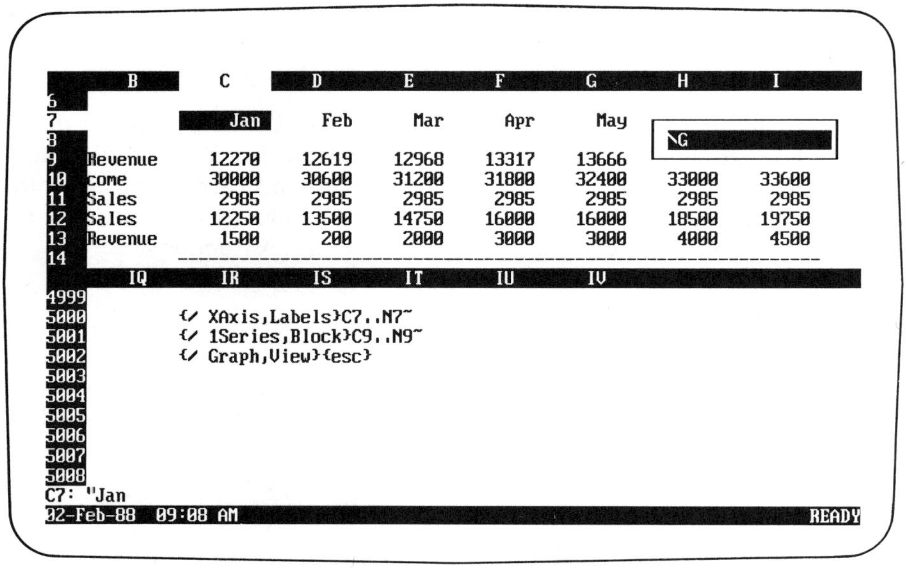

Fig. 15.9. Using the F8 (Macro) key to run a macro.

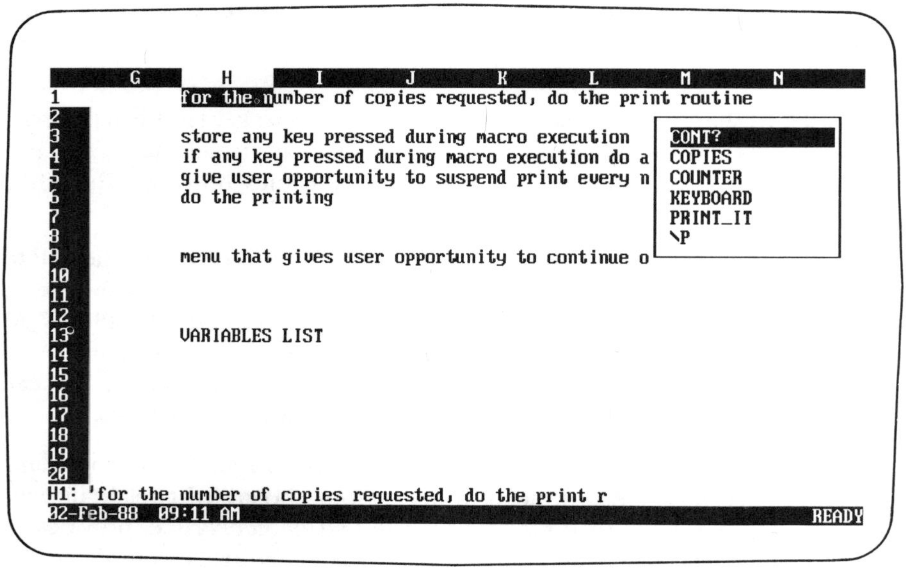

Fig. 15.10. Macro window displaying several block names.

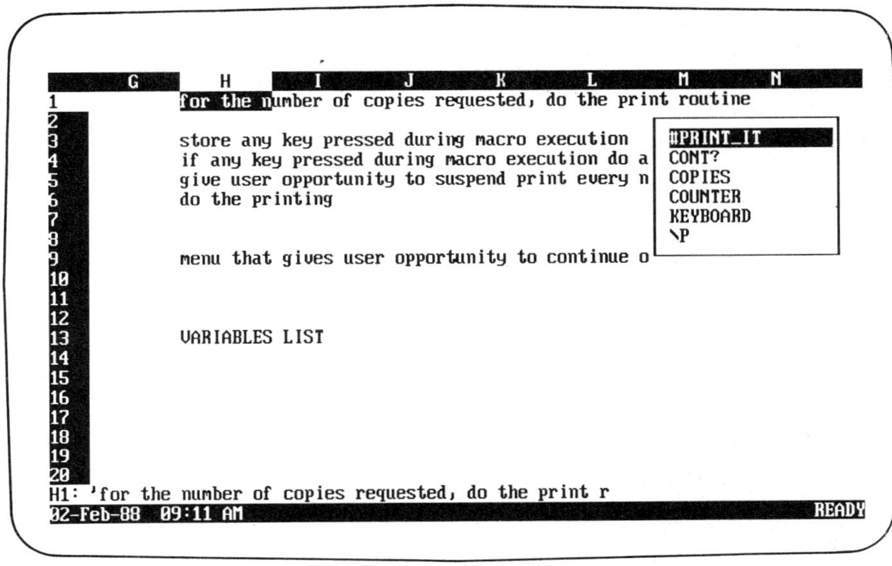

Fig. 15.11. Macro window with macro name identified by #.

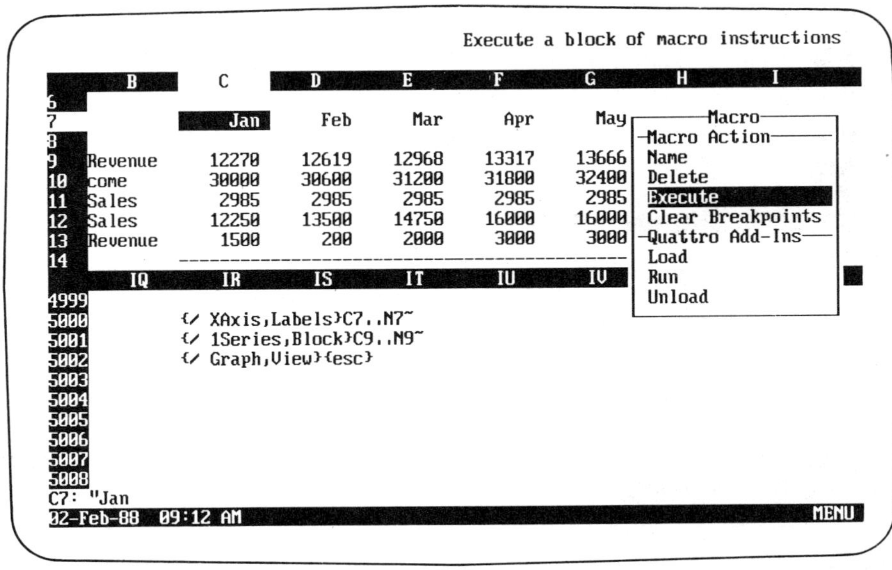

Fig. 15.12. The Macro menu.

The next menu selection is **Execute**. This option starts a macro. After choosing **Execute** from the menu, you are prompted for the cell address or block name of the macro to execute. With the **Execute** command, you can start the macro at any line; you don't have to run the entire macro. Figure 15.13 shows the graphing macro that was recorded earlier. The prompt at the top of the screen has been supplied: the cell address IR5002. When you press the Enter key, the macro instructions beginning at IR5002 are executed. Because you can choose individual starting points, the **Execute** command is helpful when you just want to determine whether a macro statement works or how it works without having to give the cell a block name.

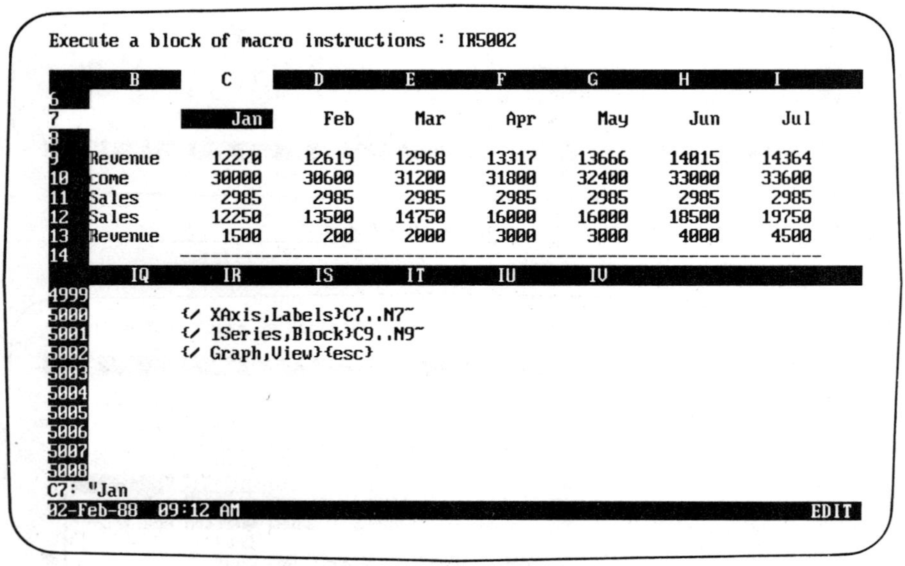

Fig. 15.13. Starting the macro at IR5002.

The final Macro menu choice, **Clear_Breakpoints**, is used to remove from a macro stopping points and to trace cells that were set from the macro debugging mode (Shift-F8). For more information on breakpoints, see the chapter on Quattro's debugging capabilities.

Pauses for Input

One of the special commands in Quattro's macro environment is the pause command, a question mark between braces {?}. The pause command is useful whenever you want a macro to allow input from the keyboard.

If you do not have a pause command, the macro will not stop until it has finished running. On many occasions, however, you need to interact with the macro. For example, a menu command requires your input to determine what to do next. Consider the macro command

{/ File,Save}

This macro instruction needs a name to give to the file being saved. If you can't pause, you have to use the same file name every time. This factor severely limits the flexibility and general usefulness of the macro. If you include a pause, the same macro can wait for you to enter a file name. Examine the example in figure 15.14. As you can see, the macro has paused allowing the /File Save command to display its standard prompt so that the user can enter a new file name. You respond to this prompt in the normal fashion (typing or pointing to a file name).

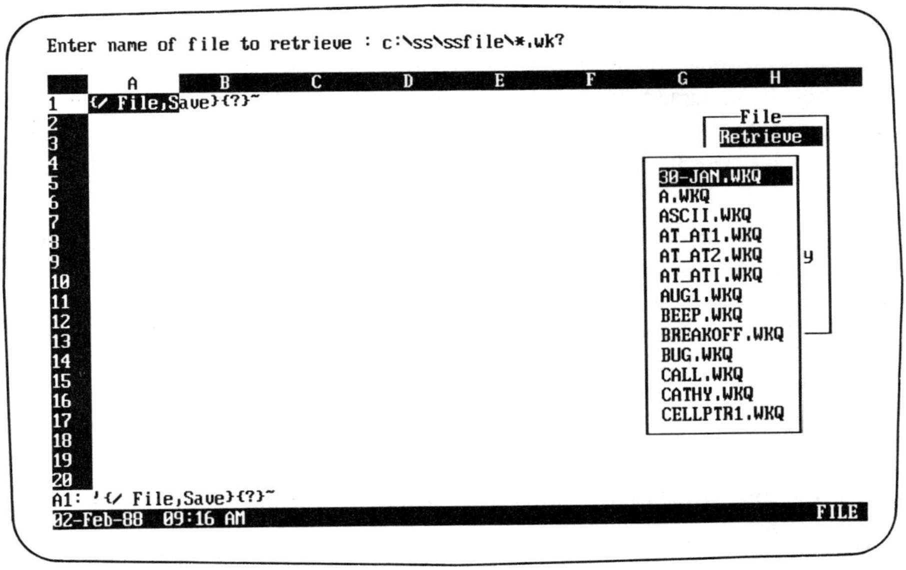

Fig. 15.14. Macro pausing for user input.

The macro resumes running when you press the Enter key. The {?} instruction uses the user's Enter keypress to signal the end of the pause. To complete the entry the user types during the pause, you ordinarily include a tilde or a {CR} command following the pause command.

Automatic Macro Execution

Quattro gives you the capability to create a macro that starts itself when a spreadsheet file is retrieved. The auto-execute macro feature makes possible the creation of an application that runs automatically. Each spreadsheet can have its own auto-execute macro. You might use this kind of macro to make working with a spreadsheet application easier for a new or inexperienced user or for temporary help.

Auto-execute macros are no different from other Quattro macros. The only difference lies in the block names the macros are given. Any macro named \0 starts itself when the spreadsheet on which it is defined is retrieved.

This kind of macro does have certain limitations. First, you can have only one \0 macro per spreadsheet. Second, you cannot start a \0 macro directly from the keyboard by pressing Alt-0. Of course, you can press the Macro (F8) key or issue the **M**acro **E**xecute command to start a macro with any block name.

If you want to develop a completely automated macro system, you should also learn about autoload files. An autoload file is a file that the program looks for when it is started. If the file is found in the current data file directory, Quattro loads the file instantly. If you have a \0 macro in the autoload file, the \0 macro starts. With this system, all the user needs to do is type *Q* to start Quattro; the autoload file is loaded and the auto-execute macro starts.

The default autoload file is QUATTRO.WKQ. If you want the program to use a different autoload file name, you can change the file name through the /**D**efault **S**tartup **A**utoload command. You also can instruct Quattro to use a block name other than \0 for auto-execute macros. Figure 15.15 shows the Default Startup menu.

If you are a couch potato like me, you should be aware of one more automatic feature. Normally, when you start Quattro, you type a *Q* at the DOS prompt. If you like, you have the option of specifying directly at the DOS prompt which file Quattro should load and what macro to run.

The command to start Quattro, load a file named PAYROLL, and run a macro named MONTHEND is

```
C:\Q>Q PAYROLL MONTHEND
```

Note that in order for this command to work, you must be in the Quattro directory.

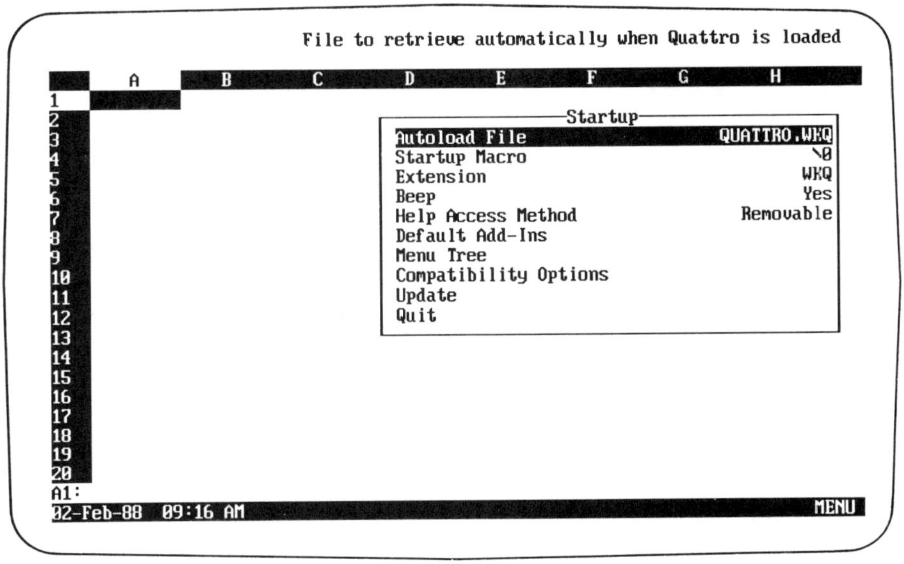

Fig. 15.15. The Default Startup menu.

Designing Reliable Macros

After you have worked with macros for a while, you may realize that they can be quite fragile. Unless you follow certain conventions, you will find that more and more of your time is spent fixing and maintaining macros rather than actually using them. In this section are some useful suggestions that make writing macros easier.

If you have developed several macros, you probably will have forgotten many of their names. Figure 15.16 shows beginning at IR5000 a macro that names a spreadsheet. Imagine that you created this macro a few weeks ago. Now you've retrieved the file and want to use the macro again. Unfortunately, you can't see block names and you have forgotten what the macro is named.

To prevent this problem, you should follow the practice of entering a label just to the left of the macro's named blocks. Figure 15.17 shows the label in cell IQ5000.

Now whenever you need to know what block names are used in macros, you can look at the labels in the column to the left of the macros. The macro examples that follow in this chapter use this convention.

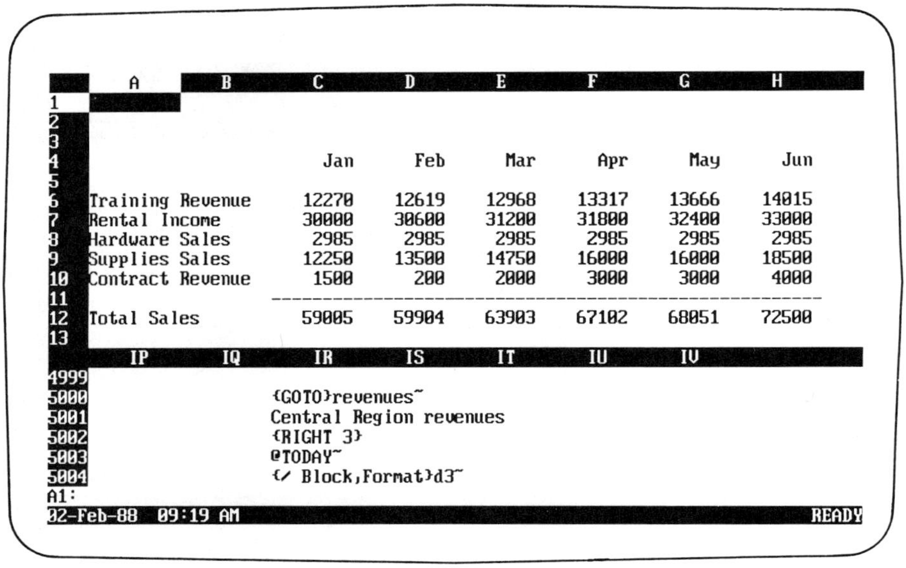

	A	B	C	D	E	F	G	H
1								
2								
3								
4			Jan	Feb	Mar	Apr	May	Jun
5								
6	Training Revenue		12270	12619	12968	13317	13666	14015
7	Rental Income		30000	30600	31200	31800	32400	33000
8	Hardware Sales		2985	2985	2985	2985	2985	2985
9	Supplies Sales		12250	13500	14750	16000	16000	18500
10	Contract Revenue		1500	200	2000	3000	3000	4000
11			-------	-------	-------	-------	-------	-------
12	Total Sales		59005	59904	63903	67102	68051	72500
13								

	IP	IQ	IR	IS	IT	IU	IV
4999							
5000			{GOTO}revenues~				
5001			Central Region revenues				
5002			{RIGHT 3}				
5003			@TODAY~				
5004			{/ Block,Format}d3~				

A1:

02-Feb-88 09:19 AM READY

Fig. 15.16. A macro to name a spreadsheet.

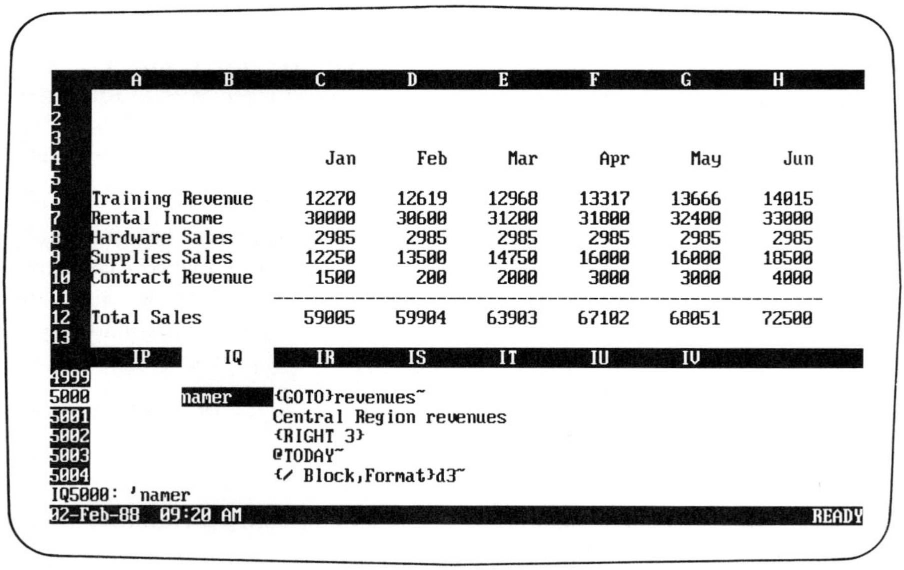

	A	B	C	D	E	F	G	H
1								
2								
3								
4			Jan	Feb	Mar	Apr	May	Jun
5								
6	Training Revenue		12270	12619	12968	13317	13666	14015
7	Rental Income		30000	30600	31200	31800	32400	33000
8	Hardware Sales		2985	2985	2985	2985	2985	2985
9	Supplies Sales		12250	13500	14750	16000	16000	18500
10	Contract Revenue		1500	200	2000	3000	3000	4000
11			-------	-------	-------	-------	-------	-------
12	Total Sales		59005	59904	63903	67102	68051	72500
13								

	IP	IQ	IR	IS	IT	IU	IV
4999							
5000		namer	{GOTO}revenues~				
5001			Central Region revenues				
5002			{RIGHT 3}				
5003			@TODAY~				
5004			{/ Block,Format}d3~				

IQ5000: 'namer

02-Feb-88 09:20 AM READY

Fig. 15.17. Macro with label entered in column to the left of the named blocks.

Placing labels for macro names to the left of the macro has another benefit. If you include labels, you can easily restore a macro's block names if they become lost or dislodged somehow. If you highlight the labels when using the /**B**lock **A**dvanced **L**abels **R**ight menu command, you can rename an entire macro with multiple block names in a single stroke.

Another aspect of a reliable macro is that it be easily understood. One way to achieve this clarity is for macros to have a series of comments in the column to the right of the macro. These comments describe why each instruction needs to be done or what the instruction is intended to do. The macro instructions themselves tell how to do something. Figure 15.18 shows the documentation column in the NAMER macro.

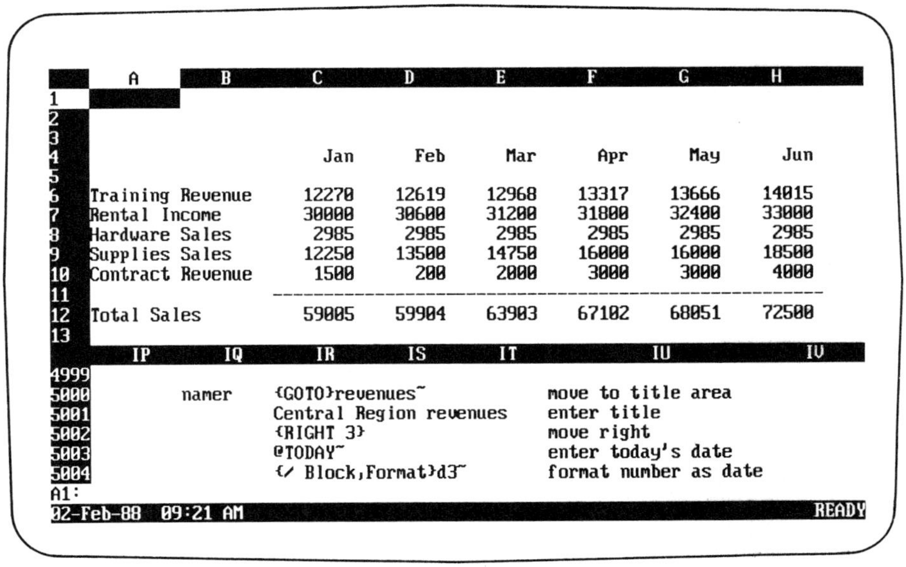

Fig. 15.18. Documenting a macro.

Tip The comments column should not be written when you can "get around to it." Do the comments column while you are writing the macro. Then if you have trouble, you won't get lost trying to remember why you did something.

If you like, you can use Quattro's reserved comment marker, a semicolon, {;}, to document your macros. The semicolon allows you to enter comments and documentation directly into a macro. The syntax for the comment line is

{;This is a comment}

The comment lines are ignored during macro execution.

Another special command similar to the comment marker is the blank command { }. This command does absolutely nothing but take up space. Why would you use this command? It can be used as a place holder during macro creation. As you develop the macro, put several blank commands on separate rows in the macro. Then when you need to add a command to the macro, you can place that command inside the empty braces without going through the trouble of moving or inserting rows in the macro.

A side benefit of the three-column macro structure is that the limitation of the screen's width helps you keep your macro instructions short. Macros with short instructions are much easier to edit. Copying these macros is a simple matter if you want to copy a single macro operation to another macro in the current or another spreadsheet. Finally, if the macro doesn't work, locating any problems is much easier because each line in the macro is next to its documentation line.

Don't wait until you finish a macro before you start documentation. You almost never have time to go back after the macro is finished. If you are not documenting macros as you go, it's just a matter of time before you can expect serious trouble. Unfortunately, some macro writers think of undocumented macros as job security. An undocumented macro program you've come to depend on is like a loaded gun. You may not know when it will go off; but when it does, somebody is going to get hurt.

Another efficient practice is to create reusable macros as often as possible. A reusable macro is one that works in a variety of situations without having to be rewritten. If you have worked with programs before, you may have noticed that much of what is written is quite similar. In fact, many programming operations are so generic that programmers put the code in library files. When these functions are needed in other programs, the program can "borrow" the code rather than the programmer's having to write the same codes again and again. The best way to illustrate the concept of reusability is to show a macro that is not reusable.

The NAMER macro could have been written more simply. The macro could have sent the cursor directly to the cell where the name and department are to be entered (cell A2). Figure 15.19 shows the macro after it has been modified.

This macro enters the name just like the longer macro. However, if the application is moved, the macro puts the name in the wrong place. This macro is too specific in that it depends on the spreadsheet's maintaining its current

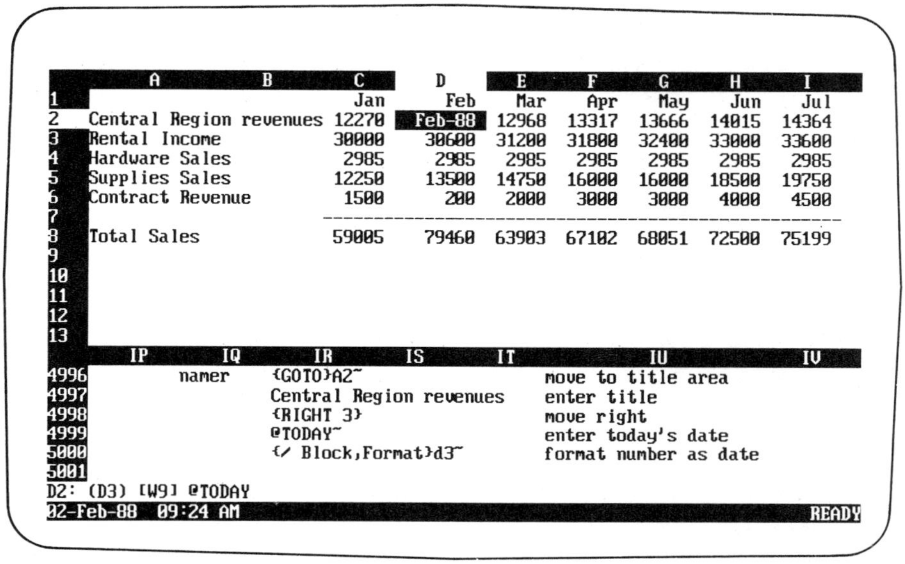

Fig. 15.19. NAMER macro that is not reusable.

size and layout. The earlier macro finds the REVENUES block name in the main application. No matter whether the spreadsheet shrinks or grows, the macro still works.

Tip The general rule to follow is always use block names rather than cell addresses to specify locations.

Reusable macros take a little longer to write, but it's a pay-me-now or pay-me-later proposition. If you don't take the time to make your macros generic when you first write them, you will surely have to make the time later.

As you use Quattro, you will come to appreciate the flexibility that macros provide. No doubt, you will use the macro recording feature to create many different macros that simplify your spreadsheet tasks. As you work with macros, you may find that some of the things you want to do are not possible with key-equivalent and menu-automating macros.

The next chapter takes you into the Quattro programming language. With the commands available in this special language, you can use Quattro as a complete development environment, creating programs that rival the power of dedicated languages like PASCAL and BASIC. Yet Quattro's command language is much friendlier, and because you have Quattro itself to build on, you can get significant results in very little time.

CHAPTER

16

Quattro Macro Command Reference

Quattro has a number of programming commands that supplement the keyboard and menu macros you have seen in earlier chapters. These powerful programming commands (also called *keywords*) give you extensive control over what your macros can do. With these commands, you can create complete applications. If you are somewhat familiar with BASIC, PASCAL, or 1-2-3's Command Language, these commands probably will seem familiar to you.

If you are new to programming languages, you will find this chapter to be a useful introduction to using Quattro's macro commands. In addition to showing how the various commands work, attention is paid to good programming style. If you follow the techniques described, you will find that your macros are flexible and perhaps significantly less frustrating to create than without these commands.

The Elements of Macro Commands

The commands discussed in this chapter are used most often with the keyboard macros discussed in Chapter 15. In the examples that follow, you will see how to use macros with the macro commands to produce complete, efficient programs that take Quattro's macro capability far beyond simply automating keystrokes.

Macro programs contain the macro commands and all the elements that can be included in macros. They can include

1. Keystrokes used for selecting Quattro commands (for example, /BDC0).
2. Block names and cell addresses.
3. Keynames for moving the cell selector (see Chapter 15 for a list of keynames).
4. Keynames for function keys (see Chapter 15).
5. Keynames for editing (see Chapter 15).
6. Key representation for Enter: the tilde (~) or {CR}.
7. Macro commands.

Macro Command Syntax

Like the keynames used in macros (discussed in Chapter 15), all macro commands are enclosed in braces. Just as you must represent the right-arrow key in a macro as {RIGHT}, you must enclose a command such as QUIT in braces:

{QUIT}

Many commands, however, require additional arguments within the boundaries of the braces. The arguments that follow commands have a grammar similar to the grammar used in Quattro @functions. The general format of commands that require arguments is

{COMMAND argument1,argument2,. . .,argumentN}

An argument can consist of numbers, strings, cell addresses, block names, formulas, and functions.

The commands and arguments are separated by a space and, for most commands, arguments are separated by commas (with no spaces). As you study the syntax for the specific commands described in this chapter, keep in mind the importance of following the conventions for spacing and punctuation. For example, when you use the BRANCH command to transfer program control to a specific location in the program, you must follow the word *BRANCH* with the cell address or block name indicating where the program should branch.

Flow Control Commands

As you continue working with macros, you will find that your macros start to get too long. In addition, they will seem impossible to enhance, because the macro cannot "jump" to a different location in the spreadsheet and process what it finds there. The flow control commands give you a comprehensive set of macro "directors" that greatly aid your ability to create more intelligently structured macros and that allow macro routines to be reused, instead of having to be continually reinvented.

The flow control commands let you create macros that reflect the best characteristics of a well-written story or article. That is, they have no run-on sentences, each paragraph has a concise theme, and each topic is sufficiently developed. Macros are much more efficient and easier to maintain if you appropriately use flow control macro commands such as BRANCH, IF, and FOR. The commands to control macro flow are listed in table 16.1.

Table 16.1
Flow Control Commands

Command	*Description*
{BRANCH}	Continues program at <location>
{DISPATCH}	Branches indirectly via <location>
{FOR}	Activates a loop a specified number of times
{FORBREAK}	Terminates a {FOR} loop
{IF}	Conditionally executes statements after IF
{ONERROR}	Traps errors, passing program control to <branchcell>
{QUIT}	Ends program execution
{subroutine}	Executes a group of commands
{RESTART}	Cancels a program subroutine
{RETURN}	Returns from a subroutine

Command	*Description*
{STEPON}	Opens the debugging window
{STEPOFF}	Closes the debugging window
{WAIT}	Waits until specified time

The BRANCH Command

The BRANCH command redirects processing of a macro to another cell location. Unlike the IF command, BRANCH performs this action unconditionally. Branching gives the macro writer the ability to reuse macro instructions instead of being forced to rewrite statements. Using BRANCH can help keep macros short, reusable, and efficient. The general form of the BRANCH command is

{BRANCH location}   Continues program at <location>

<Location> is usually a block name but can also be a cell reference.

Two macros are included in figure 16.1. Each of them sounds your computer's tone six times. The macro on the left can go back to its beginning to rebeep until it is done. Because the macro on the right has no branching statement, it must be as long as the number of beeps required, much longer than necessary. If 10 beeps were needed, the macro would be 10 cells long.

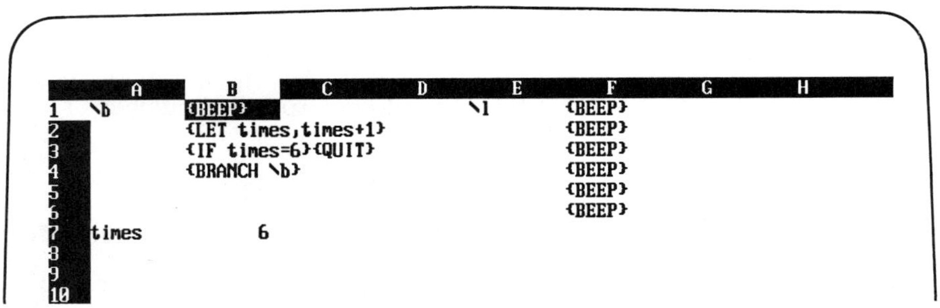

Fig. 16.1. Two macros for producing six tones.

The macro on the left uses a technique known as *looping*. A program "loops" back to replay an earlier series of instructions so that they don't need to be rewritten. A variable called "times" contains the number of times Quattro has traveled through the macro loop. Because times starts out blank, it is equal to zero. After the beeps are performed, a LET statement increases times by one. The LET command can be interpreted this way: "LET the value in times become the value in times plus one." Thus, every time the macro loops, the number in times grows by one.

The IF statement tests times to see if the loop has been performed six times. If not, the BRANCH statement in the cell below reroutes the macro to the beginning of the macro. This looping continues until times equals six. Then the IF statement detects that the macro should end, and the {QUIT} command to the right of the IF command is performed.

Although you must spend some time designing controls for the loop, this macro will not grow if more beeps are needed. In addition, notice that almost any action or command could replace the BEEP command easily. Thus the macro is reusable.

Tip Because nothing in the column to the right of a BRANCH statement is ever executed, the space following the BRANCH command can be used for program comments. Comments are especially useful if the block name argument of the branch statement is non-descriptive, such as this macro command:

{BRANCH routine_3} ---regular tone interval generator---

The DISPATCH Command

The DISPATCH statement allows for what is known as *indirect addressing*. In contrast to the BRANCH command, which directs processing to the block name specified, the DISPATCH keyword transfers flow of the macro to the block name that appears as a label in the argument cell. If you have a macro that needs to be told which way to go of several possible ways, you may need the DISPATCH command.

The syntax for DISPATCH is

{DISPATCH location}   Branches indirectly via <location>

where <location> is a cell that contains the name of another block in the macro.

Use the DISPATCH command when there is no way a macro can already know which path of execution to follow. The DISPATCH command tells the macro where to look for its routing instructions.

The following figure (fig. 16.2) shows a macro that requests a user's name (through the GETLABEL command). After the user enters the name, the macro sends the name to the cell named USER_NAME. The command on the next line uses the contents of the USER_NAME cell to determine where to go next:

{DISPATCH user_name}

After seeing the user's name, the macro branches to one of the blocks that brings up a particular user's menu.

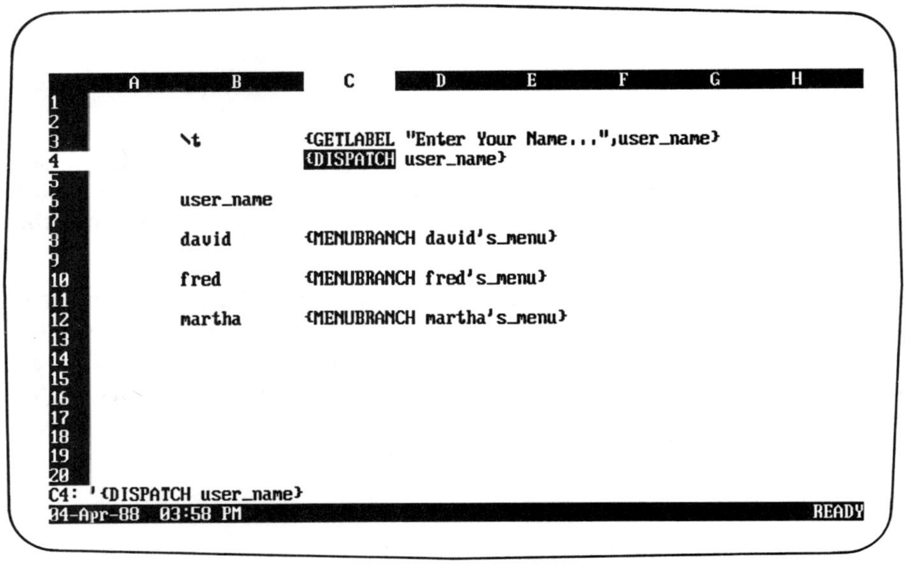

Fig. 16.2. Using the GETLABEL command to request a user's name.

The FOR Command

FOR is a powerful command that runs a subroutine a specified number of times automatically and then stops on its own when the specified number is met. One advantage of the FOR command is that no specific code must be created to reset the counter variable. The counter variable resets as soon as the FOR command begins. A further advantage is that no IF statement is needed to test for completion of the routine.

The syntax of the FOR command is somewhat complex:

{FOR counter,start#,stop#,step#,subroutine}	Activates a loop a specific number of times

The first argument of the FOR syntax is a block name that identifies the cell that will be used to record the number of times the FOR routine has repeated.

Next comes the number that the counter should start with, or <start#>. This number can be any number but will most often be 0 or 1.

The third argument, <stop#>, tells the FOR statement how many times it should repeat. When the number in the counter cell is one greater than the stop number, the FOR loop terminates. The stop number is usually a reference to a cell or block name.

The fourth argument, <step#>, determines the value the counter will use to increment, usually a 1.

After all the arguments that control looping have been specified, the block name of the subroutine that will run is specified.

The arguments of the FOR command can be actual numbers in the macro statement, formulas, block names, or even negative numbers. Only the subroutine argument must be either a block name or cell reference.

Figure 16.3 shows a macro that prompts the user to enter the number of needed copies of a printout. The number is then placed in the LAST_NUMBER block name and becomes the stop number. Then the FOR instruction clears the COUNTER block and fills it with the start number. The FOR command increases COUNTER by the step number (in this case 1). At this point, the subroutine call to run print_it is performed. When the subroutine is finished, the FOR command again executes the subroutine until the counter value is greater than the stop value (last_number).

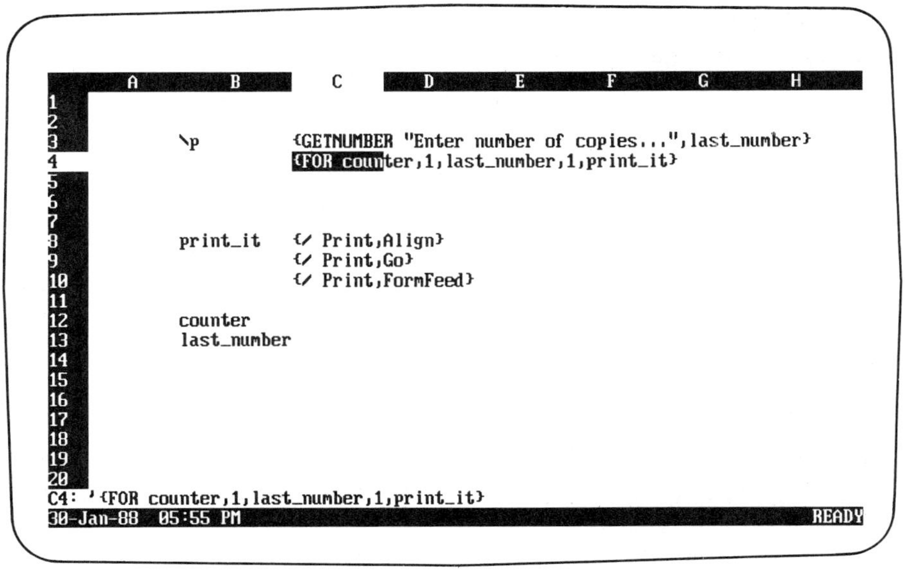

Fig. 16.3. Using FOR to control a printing loop.

The FOR statement also can be used to implement a countdown macro. Simply change the <step#> argument to -1 (negative one) and use <start#> as the number of loops desired. When this kind of FOR statement is executed, the macro places the <start#> in the counter, which is then reduced by 1 each time the FOR command executes. Because processing stops when the counter is less than the <stop#>, to prevent an extra operation, the <stop#> should be 1, not 0.

The only way to stop a FOR statement during execution is to execute a FORBREAK command in the subroutine after a conditional statement.

The FORBREAK Command

The FORBREAK statement is used to stop the operation of a FOR statement. When a FOR loop is in progress, the loop cannot be stopped by normal means, such as by using a QUIT command. If for some reason a FOR loop must be terminated prematurely, a FORBREAK command within the repeating subroutine can stop the processing of the FOR command. The FORBREAK command has no arguments; its format is simply

{FORBREAK}	Terminates a {FOR} loop

The following example shows a fragment of a printing macro that can print multiple copies of a report. If an unreasonable number of copies is requested (such as more than 25), the FORBREAK command in the printing subroutine will stop the excessive printing by stopping the FOR loop.

```
\t          {GETNUMBER "Enter number of copies to
            print",copies}
            {FOR counter,1,copies,1,print_it}

print_it    {IF counter>25}{FORBREAK}
            {/PRINT,GO}
```

The FORBREAK command has no effect unless it is present within the subroutine block.

The IF Command

A macro can use the IF statement to decide how to proceed at points where many options may be possible. The IF statement is the macro counterpart to a railroad switchman. A switchman has to make decisions about which tracks to use in order to route trains properly and prevent conflicts (derailments) and misroutings.

The syntax of IF is

{IF condition}	Conditionally executes statements after IF

where <condition> is any logical expression that can be true or false (one or zero). If the condition is equal to ERR, the IF statement is considered false. Numbers not equal to zero (0), including negative numbers, are considered to be true. A label also is considered true, as is the value NA. (See Chapter 6 for a discussion of ERR and NA).

When an IF expression is true, execution will continue on the same line. If the condition is false, processing will skip immediately to the next line:

```
{IF condition}{do true action}
{do false action}
```

All the spreadsheet's logical operators and functions are valid when defining the IF condition. The table below lists the logical operators and functions that can be used within the conditional argument of the {IF} keyword. In addition to these logical operators, the IF keyword can use any of the formulas and functions for conditional comparisons that are available in Quattro.

Table 16.2
Logical Operators and Functions for {IF}

Logical Operators	*Complex Logical Operators*	*Functions*
Equals (=)	#AND#	@TRUE
Not equals (<>)	#OR#	@FALSE
Greater than or equal (>=)	#NOT#	@ISERR
Greater than (>)		@ISNA
Less than (<)		@ISSTRING
Less than or equal (<=)		@ISNUMBER
		@FILEEXISTS
		@EXACT

For explanations of operators and functions, see Chapters 6 and 7 on spreadsheet functions.

The IF command has many uses. One simple use of IF is to test whether two cells are equal to each other. Figure 16.4 shows a macro that will stop if the cells are equal and continue execution if they are not equal.

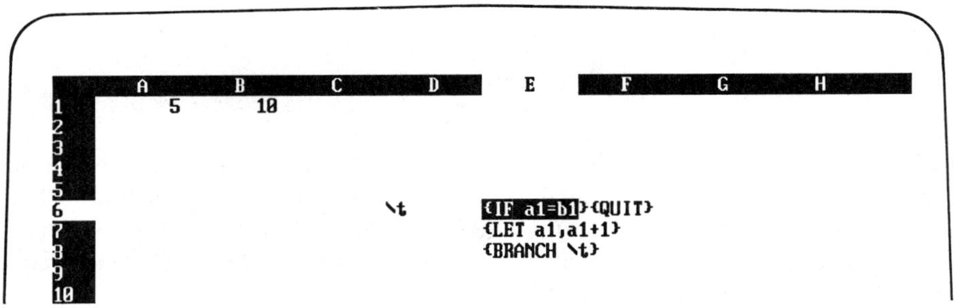

Fig. 16.4. IF can compare two cells.

Figure 16.4 uses actual cell references in the conditional comparison. Normally, block names would be used here to make the macro more flexible and maintainable. If you use cell references in macros, they are not adjusted when spreadsheet cells are moved or columns and rows are inserted, often resulting in bugs and frequent macro editing sessions.

In this case the IF statement could be rewritten to read generically or functionally. The first of the following equivalent commands is *generic*, meaning it can be combined easily into other spreadsheets (using /**F**ile **C**ombine) and reused. The second is *functional*, or relating to a particular spreadsheet, and is thus easier to understand:

{IF cell1=cell2}
{IF sales=quota}

IF statements also can be used to test variables that a user enters during the execution of a macro. For example, an IF statement can be used to ensure that a user has entered the correct kind of data. The macro in figure 16.5 asks a user for an employee number. If the user accidentally enters a name (a label), the GETNUMBER statement will place an ERR in the cell named ENTRY. The IF statement will trap the error when it occurs and will reroute the macro to the {BRANCH \t} statement, to ask the user again for the employee number.

The IF function's conditional argument can use the results of spreadsheet formulas and simply refer to them by block name. This method is better than having long formulas in the macro statement because it makes the macro simple and easy to read. In figure 16.6, for example, the IF command is the simple statement, {IF valid_zip_code}. What this command is testing for is clear because it can be read directly. The bulk of the comparative work is done by the formula in the block named VALID_ZIP_CODE. This formula will always evaluate to zero or one.

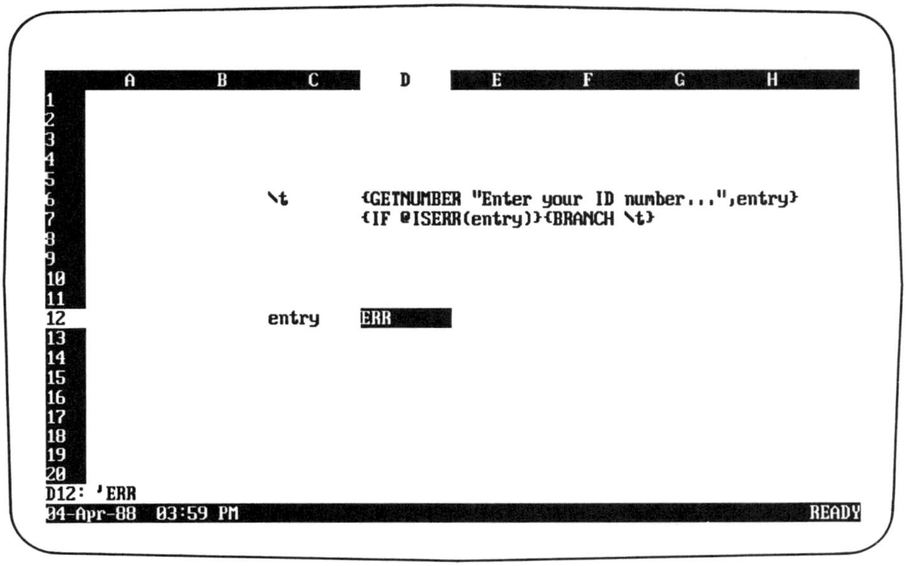

Fig. 16.5. IF can be used to obtain the correct kind of data.

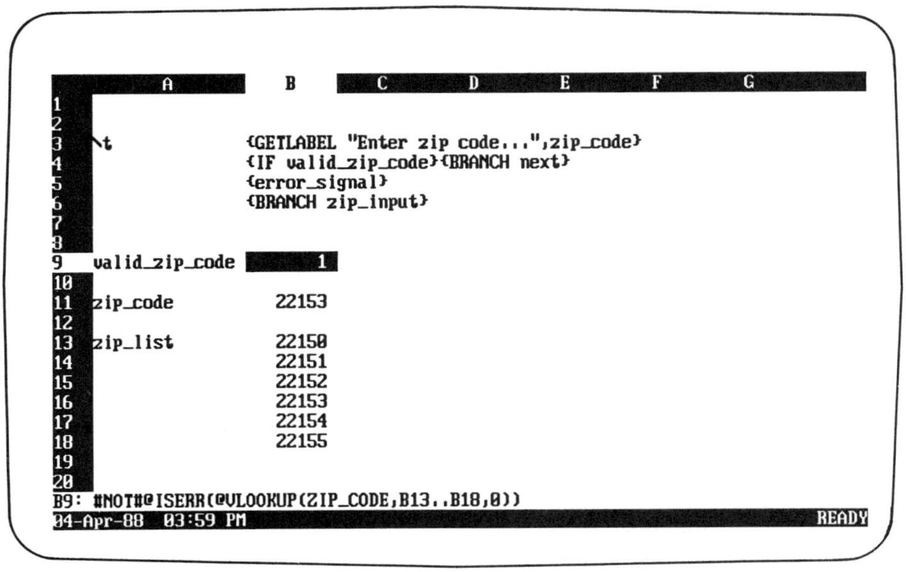

Fig. 16.6. The IF command can refer to a block name.

The @VLOOKUP function determines whether the zip_code entered is in the zip_list. If it is, then the function #NOT#@ISERR makes the result true (1). If the zip_code is not in the list, the @VLOOKUP function will be in error. The #NOT#@ISERR portion of the formula then will cause the macro to read a false result (0).

Sometimes you need to have several IF statements in sequence. Such a sequence is comparable to nested @IF functions. In this situation you may need to use logical conjunctions such as #AND# or #OR#. The following example, which offers some whimsical code to help you decide how to bet in a poker game, shows the use of nested IF macros.

```
{IF hand=terrific#AND#other_guy=bluffing#AND#pot=lotsa_money}{BETBIG}
{IF hand=ok#OR#you_can_bluff}{bet_a_few_$}
{IF not_sure}{call}
{fold}
```

This sequence starts with an expression that, if true, leads you to bet big. If false, the macro drops to the next IF, to determine if your position is just okay. This flow goes on until you bet big, bet a few dollars, call, or fold.

The same logic also can be written like this:

```
{IF hand=terrific}{IF other_guy=bluffing}{IF pot=lotsa_money}{BETBIG}
{IF hand=ok#OR#you_can_bluff}{bet_a_few_$}
{IF not_sure}{call}
{fold}
```

In this example, the #AND# conjunctions in the first line have been omitted, because IF statements following one another on the same line have the same effect as #AND#.

As a general rule, put the most likely conditions first in the order of execution. The macro in that order will run faster, because the system will rarely need to test all the conditions to find the correct path of execution.

The ONERROR Command

The ONERROR keyword is used to protect your macro from an error that would halt execution. Such an error is known as a *fatal* or *run-time error*. The syntax for ONERROR is

{ONERROR branchcell,displaycell}	Traps errors, passing program control to <branchcell>

The block name branchcell starts a macro designed to handle errors as they occur. The optional displaycell argument remains empty until an error occurs. Then the message normally seen at the lower left corner of the screen is pulled into the displaycell block. In effect, this traps the error. The ONERROR command is usually placed and executed near the beginning of a macro.

Figures 16.7 and 16.8 show a macro that uses ONERROR. This macro simply stores the error message to the DISPLAY_CELL block so that the user will be able to see the error message. Then the macro begins executing the instruction at the block named RESET. The first line of the macro moves the cursor to DISPLAY_CELL so that the user sees the error message. The {?} (pause) command, explained in Chapter 15, gives the user a chance to see the error display. Next, a subroutine (not shown in the figures) designed to reset the macro is run. Finally, the macro is restarted with a BRANCH command. Figure 16.7 shows the macro before an error occurs. Figure 16.8 shows the result after a command to retrieve a nonexistent file has failed. Only one ONERROR command can be active at a time.

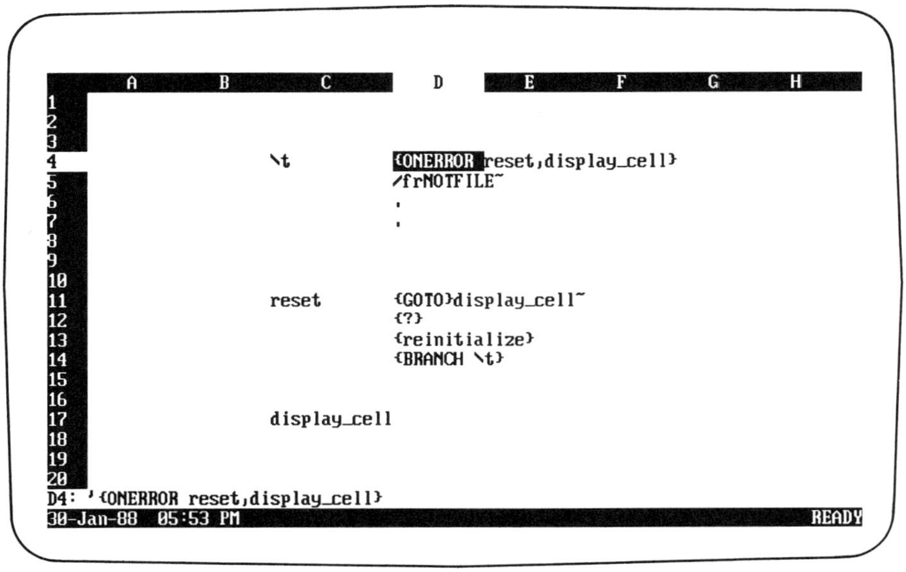

Fig. 16.7. Using ONERROR to trap an incorrect command.

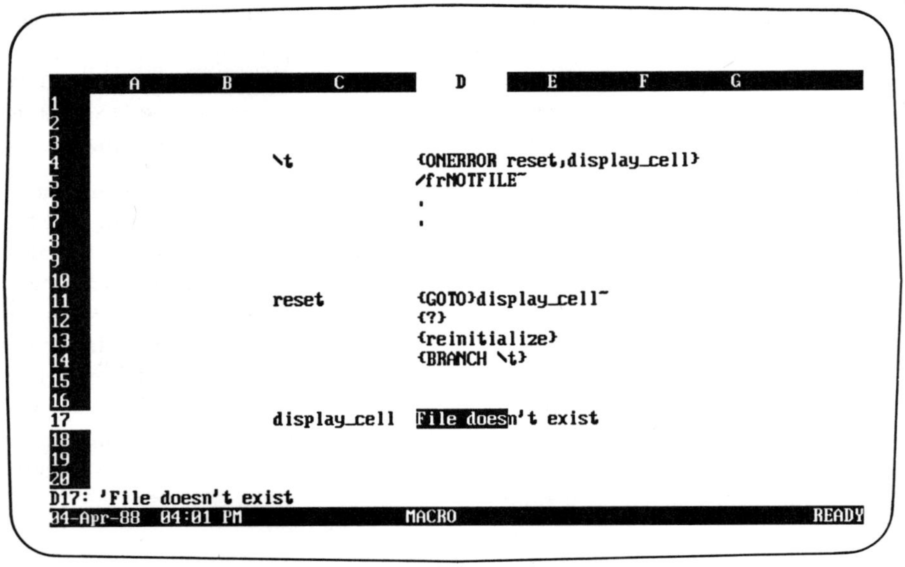

Fig. 16.8. The result of an incorrect command.

The QUIT Command

The QUIT command stops macro execution when encountered. The form of the QUIT command is

{QUIT} Ends program execution

Blank and numeric cells are also treated as an implied QUIT command unless a subroutine call is active. However, you must use a QUIT statement if you want to terminate the processing of a macro when an IF command is true. The following sample statements illustrate how to stop a macro on a true condition:

```
{IF finished}{QUIT}
{continue}
```

Subroutines

A *subroutine* is a specialized independent macro that other macros use as a helper or extender. Commonly used groups of functions thus can be grouped together and used as a subroutine.

The syntax for a subroutine is

{subroutine} Executes a group of commands

where <subroutine> is the block name for the subroutine. This command is the only macro statement that does not have a keyword at all. Use a {RETURN} at the end of a subroutine to return to the main or original macro.

Subroutines allow you to create specific macro tools or procedures that can be used over and over again. Without subroutines, these generic macro tools must be written repeatedly. This method is inefficient and results in

- Wasted computer memory
- Wasted time writing redundant macros
- Wasted time maintaining duplicate macros
- Inconvenience of having to keep track of several versions of nearly identical macros

The way a main macro program uses the subroutine is to "call" it by its block name. Thus a subroutine that is used by other parts of your macro as a counting device would be accessed by a call to {counter}.

Also, the user interface commands WINDOWSOFF, PANELOFF, and INDICATE are frequently used as a set. You can put them together as a subroutine and give them the name {screenoff}. This subroutine, along with its obvious counterpart {screenon}, will save many keystrokes for a programmer. Figure 16.9 illustrates the usefulness of subroutines; the main macro, \t, has no instructions other than to call subroutines.

If you have an especially complex macro to create, you might want to use this technique, making it easy to add functions to a macro. Simply add a row and enter an additional call to the new subroutine.

Avoid using reserved DOS and Quattro commands as subroutine names. For instance, if you give a subroutine the block name EDIT, a macro won't know what to do when it gets to an {EDIT} instruction: edit a cell, or call the routine named EDIT. By avoiding such words, you will avoid much confusion when it is time to debug your macro.

Subroutines have the optional capability to pass information or parameters to the called subroutine. This passing is accomplished by placing the parameters to the right of the block name. You must use the DEFINE command in order to pass parameters. See the section on the DEFINE command in this chapter for an explanation of parameter passing.

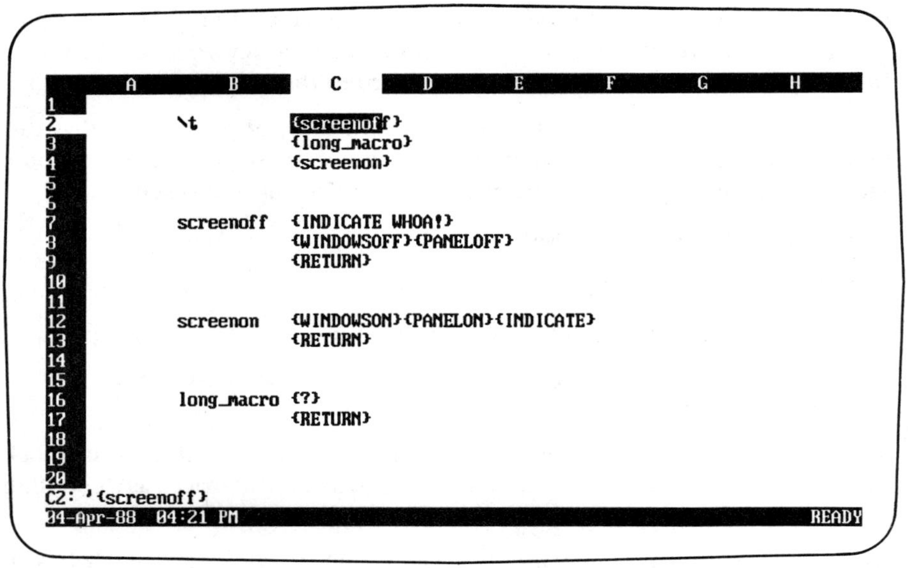

Fig. 16.9. Subroutines that call screen control commands.

The RESTART Command

As a program moves from subroutine to subroutine, the cell addresses are stored on a unit of memory called a *stack*. After several subroutines have been called, the stack collects several addresses. However, you may want to give the macro the capability to avoid returning along the path it originally followed. The RESTART command is used to clear the stack, preventing the retracing of the original execution path. It allows the macro to ignore the {RETURN} instruction and proceed on a new path of execution. In other words, the RESTART command allows a subroutine to be canceled at any time during execution. The RESTART command takes no arguments and is entered simply as

{RESTART}	Cancels a subroutine

Figure 16.10 shows a macro that asks the user to enter the hour and minute for an alarm to sound. The first line in the macro named waiter tests to see if the time requested for the alarm is earlier than the current time. If it is, then the macro presumes that an error has been made. The {RESTART} command to the right of the IF statement clears the subroutine stack; then the macro branches back to the beginning of the macro to give the user a chance to reenter the time.

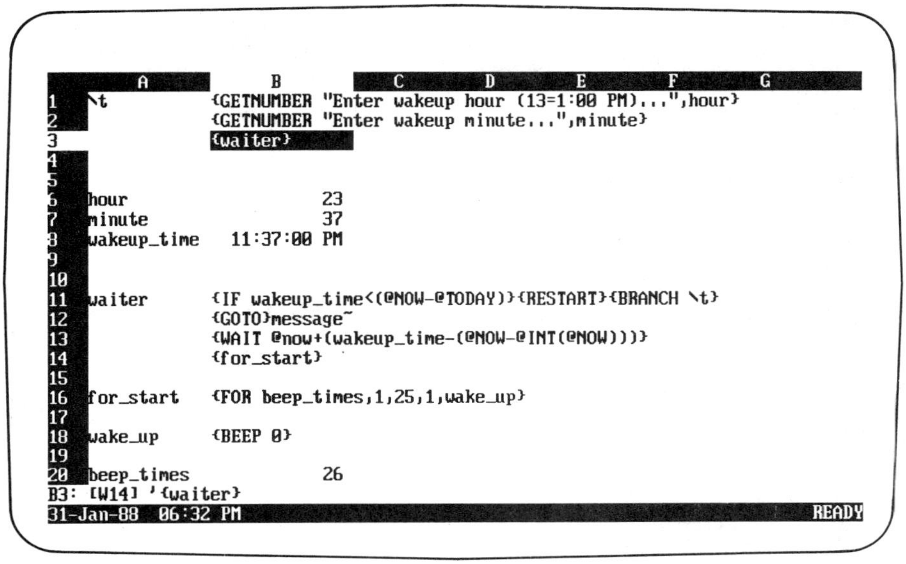

Fig. 16.10. Using the RESTART command to clear the stack.

You probably will not need to use this command until you have become an experienced Quattro macro command user. When you reach this point, though, RESTART can be quite helpful.

The RETURN Command

The RETURN command is used at the end of a subroutine, indicating that the subroutine is finished and returning the processing flow back to the point following the subroutine call in the original macro. The syntax for RETURN is simply

{RETURN} Returns from a program subroutine

The command is ignored unless the macro was called as a subroutine.

The RETURN command allows a macro application to exhibit a great deal of flexibility. It reminds me of what I always wanted my "Slinky" to do when it got to the bottom of the stairs—return back to the top automatically, so I wouldn't have to go down the steps to get it. The RETURN command gives macro calls a similar capability.

Figure 16.11 illustrates the use and effect of the RETURN command. The first macro routine (\t) starts by beeping a high tone. After the tone, the next routine (step1) is called, where a lower tone is sounded. Just as a person descends a flight of stairs, the macro descends the scale until it reaches the bottom. In the last step, a {?} (pause) instruction stops the macro. After the user presses the Enter key, a low tone sounds, and the {RETURN} command sends processing back up the "steps." The next command sounded is at cell C13, which is just after the step3 call. Immediately after this beep, the {RETURN} instruction sends the macro back up to cell C8.

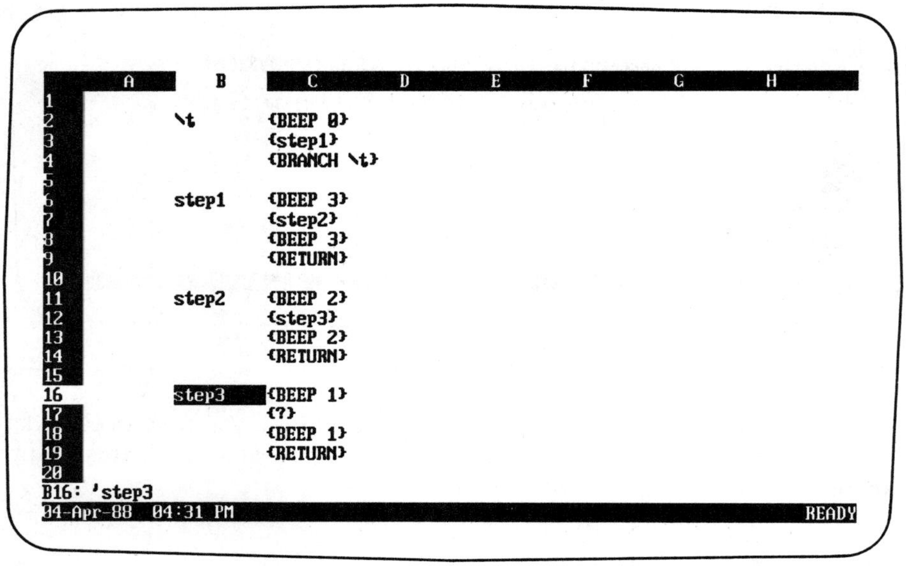

Fig. 16.11. Using RETURN to return from subroutines.

If you do not end a subroutine with a {RETURN} statement, Quattro will take one of two actions. If a {BRANCH} statement was used to run the subroutine, Quattro will consider a blank cell at the end of a subroutine to be a {QUIT}. If the subroutine was used as a called subroutine, then Quattro will interpret a blank cell as a {RETURN}.

The STEPON and STEPOFF Commands

The STEPON command gives a macro writer the ability to include debugging instructions within a macro. The STEPON and STEPOFF commands do not accept arguments. Their syntaxes are as follows:

{STEPON}	Opens the debugging window
{STEPOFF}	Closes the debugging window

If you are having a particularly difficult time debugging a section of a macro, put a {STEPON} command in the row just before where the problem seems to appear and a {STEPOFF} command at the point where the problem seems to end. When the macro is run, the macro goes into a "single-stepping" debugging mode where each instruction can be performed one line at a time. When Quattro encounters the STEPON command, Quattro opens the debugging window shown in figure 16.12. The STEPON and STEPOFF commands bound a problem macro.

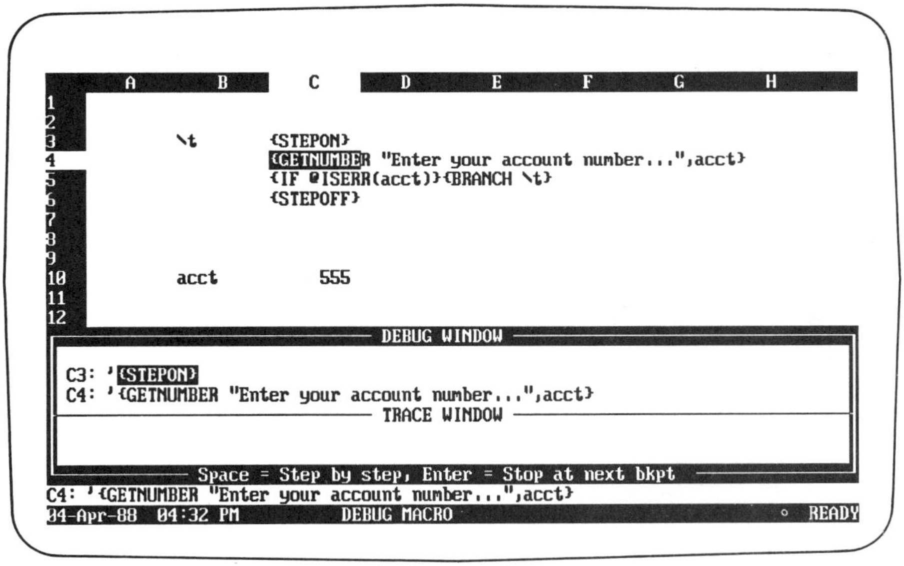

Fig. 16.12. The debugging window opened by STEPON.

Quattro's macro debugging environment is a useful tool for debugging macros quickly and easily. Using the debugging environment is explained in Chapter 17, "Making the Best Use of Quattro's Macro Debugger."

The WAIT Command

The WAIT keyword is used to stop macro operation for a specified period of time. The syntax for WAIT is

{WAIT value}   Waits until specified time

where <value> is the amount of time to wait. The standard use of WAIT is to wait from the current moment until a future moment. Thus the command {WAIT @NOW+time} is often used, where <time> is a time value such as 5 seconds.

There are various situations when you want to introduce a delay factor in a macro. This might be true when a message needs to be sent to the user. The macro

This is a message...{GET char}{ESC}

will display a message to the user, and the user must press a key to remove the message from the input line and continue. WAIT allows this process to be delayed for the period of time specified by the WAIT statement's argument.

The macro in figure 16.13 will wait 5 seconds from the time the WAIT command is started (based on the @NOW function) until the macro continues.

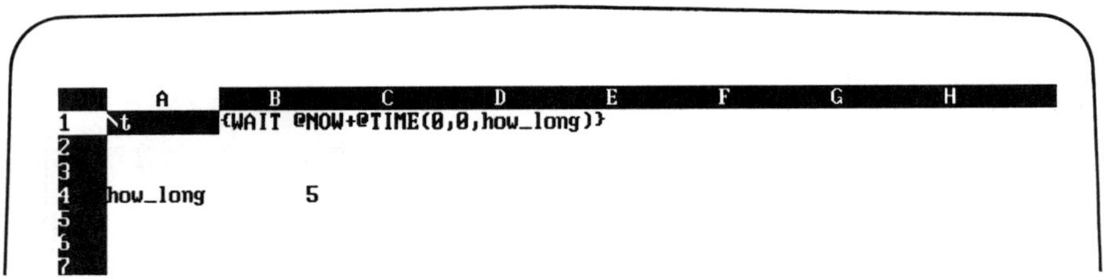

Fig. 16.13. Using WAIT to delay the processing of a macro.

WAIT also can reference a cell for its value argument. The following statement will wait the number of seconds found in the block named THIS_LONG:

{WAIT @NOW+@TIME(0,0,this_long)}

Variable Management Commands

Variable management macro commands give you comprehensive control over placing, calculating, and entering data in the spreadsheet. They allow for macro parameter passing, conversion of values to labels, automated database entry, and variable assignment control. These commands may seem to duplicate Quattro menu commands such as /**B**lock **E**rase, but in fact they operate much faster and more flexibly than their menu equivalents. The following table lists the variable management commands.

Table 16.3
Variable Management Commands

Command	*Description*
{BLANK}	Erases the cell or block
{CONTENTS}	Stores contents of <value_cell> to <label_cell>
{DEFINE}	Specifies cells for subroutine arguments
{LET}	Places value of <source> in <targetname>
{PUT}	Puts <source> into col, row within <table>
{RECALC}	Recalculates a specified portion of the worksheet row-by-row
{RECALCCOL}	Recalculates a specified portion of the worksheet column-by-column

The BLANK Command

The BLANK command is nearly the equivalent of the /**B**lock **E**rase menu command. BLANK directly erases the contents of a block without going through the /**B**lock **E**rase sequence. The blanking step is often used as an initialization step to return the variables in a macro to zero. The command uses the syntax

{BLANK location}   Erases specified cell or block

where <location> can be a single cell up to an entire spreadsheet.

The major differences between erasing cells and blanking them are that BLANK does not generate menu commands and therefore does not cause flickering on the prompt line during macro processing. And BLANK can erase a block's contents even while Quattro is in the middle of a menu command.

BLANK also is faster than the /**B**lock **E**rase menu command because BLANK removes data directly from memory. While this removal is occurring, the current display is not updated. Instead, any commands that reference the blanked cells use the contents of memory as the current variable. The display is updated when the macro is finished or a CALC is performed. If you need to get an accurate cell display prior to macro termination, the best method is to use a tilde, representing an Enter, just after the BLANK keyword: for example, {BLANK location}~.

The CONTENTS Command

The CONTENTS command converts a value in a specified source cell to a label in a specified target cell. For example, the CONTENTS command is useful for formatting numbers to appear exactly as you require, or for creating file names based on the contents of a block. The syntax for CONTENTS is

{CONTENTS label_cell,value_cell,width,format#}	Stores contents of <value_cell> to <label_cell>

<Value_cell> is a cell that contains a value, and <label_cell> is the cell that will hold the label that results from the converted value cell. Two optional arguments, <width> and <format#>, let you specify how many characters long <label_cell> will be and which display format will be used. The <format#> option, which gives you the ability to adjust the appearance of the label in <label_cell>, uses a code number from table 16.4.

Table 16.4
Numeric Format Codes for CONTENTS Command

Code	*Format*
0-15	Fixed, 0 to 15 decimal places
16-31	Scientific, 0 to 15 decimal places
32-47	Currency, 0 to 15 decimal places
48-63	Percent, 0 to 15 decimal places
64-79	Comma, 0 to 15 decimal places
112	+/- Bar Graph
113	General
114	D1 (DD-MMM-YY date format)
115	D2 (DD-MMM date format)
116	D3 (MMM-YY date format)
117	Text (formula shown)
118	Hidden
119	D6 (HH:MM:SS AM/PM time format)
120	D7 (HH:MM AM/PM time format)
121	D4 (Full International date format)
122	D5 (Partial International date format)
123	D8 (Full International time format)
124	D9 (Partial International time format)
127	Default display format

The example in figure 16.14 shows a practical way of using the CONTENTS command. You can use this "archiving" macro to automatically generate a file name based on today's date.

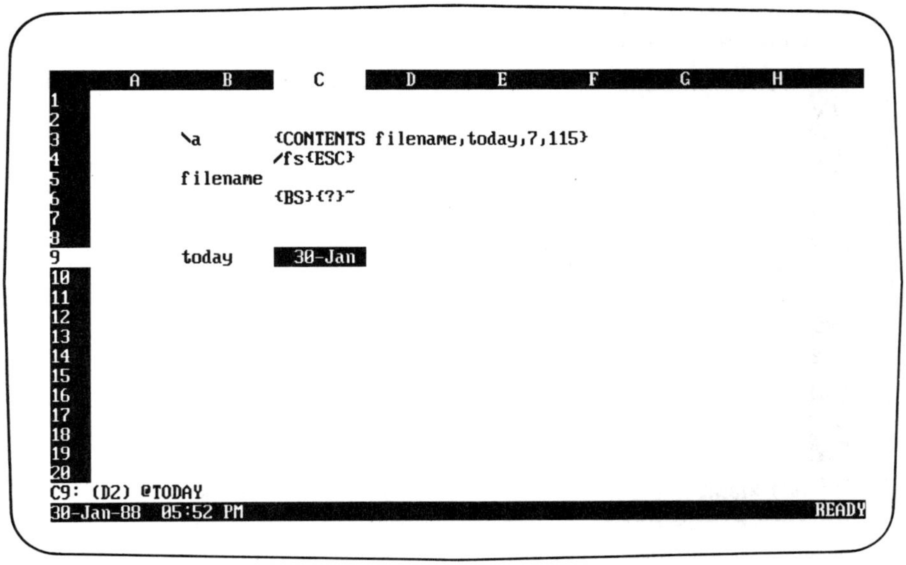

Fig. 16.14. Use of CONTENTS in an "archiving" macro.

The figure shows the macro before you execute it. The cursor is on the block named TODAY, where the @TODAY function is active. The CONTENTS command in the macro will take the contents of TODAY (a value) and, after converting it to a label, place the resulting string in the block named FILENAME. The width option sets the label at seven characters long. The format# option specifies that the results will be formatted as a DD-MMM date.

After running the CONTENTS command, invoke the /**F**ile **S**ave menu command. The {ESC} command then removes the current default file name from the menu. The macro continues to the FILENAME cell, where the date label is autotyped as the file name. The {BS} (BACKSPACE) command on the next line removes the space to the right of the label that always results when CONTENTS performs its conversion. The space occurs because all numbers are displayed with a space to their right for column separation. Figure 16.15 shows the macro at the {?} (pause) command just before the enter (~) is executed.

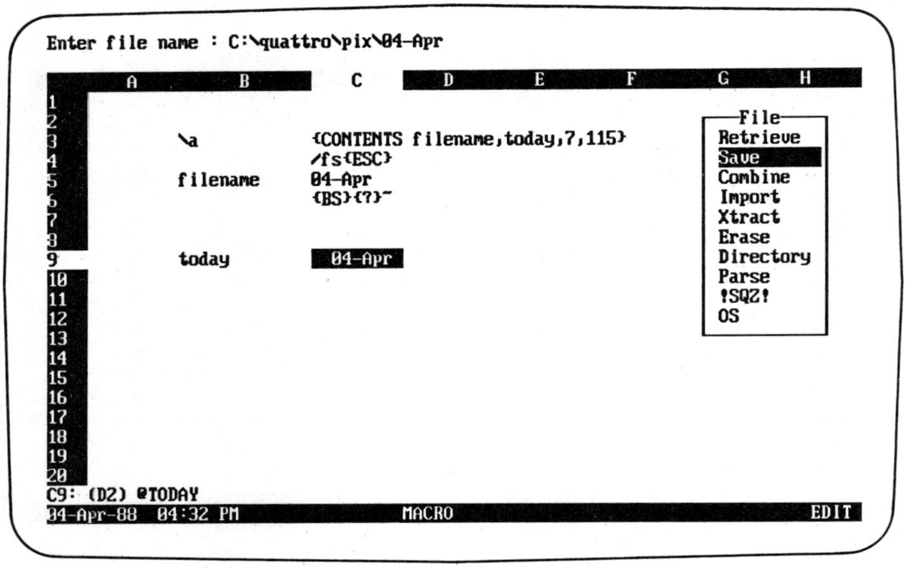

Fig. 16.15. Generating a file name based on the date with CONTENTS.

The DEFINE Command

With the DEFINE command your macros can accept arguments and variables passed from a subroutine. The syntax for DEFINE is

{DEFINE parameter1:type,parameterN:type,...}	Specifies cells for subroutine arguments

The parameter is a block name that a macro will use to store a parameter passed from a subroutine, and <type> is an optional argument that allows you to specify whether the data will be defined as a string (the default setting) or as a value.

To illustrate, let's compare a dry-cleaning establishment with subroutine variable passing. A dry cleaner performs a specific process, much like a subroutine. Many people use a single dry cleaner, just as many macros might use a single subroutine. Also, the dry cleaner needs certain information to process your clothes properly, and a subroutine also may need information to perform its process. Now let's consider this pseudo-macro:

```
{GOTO}coffee_klatch~
{IF coffee=spilled}{dry_clean}
{BRANCH gossip}
```

In this example, the dry cleaner has no information about the cleaning to be done. If we expect to get the clothes back in good shape, we need to pass some information to the dry-cleaning subroutine. The next section of macro illustrates how Quattro subroutine calls can send the information, or "pass the parameters," to the subroutine.

```
{GOTO}coffee_klatch~
{IF coffee=spilled}{dry_clean DAVE GOBEL,SHIRT,STARCH}
{BRANCH gossip}
```

Facts on the owner, clothing type, and processing are now added to the dry-cleaning subroutine. For the subroutine to use this crucial information, however, the subroutine must define the information through DEFINE.

Here is how this subroutine defines the variables. The macro must place the variables into the blocks named WHO, WHAT, and HOW, respectively. The subroutine must fill these block names with the passed variables. That is, it must DEFINE the variable block names with the following syntax:

```
{DEFINE who,what,how}
```

This statement fills the block names with the passed variables. WHO receives the variable DAVE GOBEL, WHAT receives SHIRT, and HOW receives STARCH. Now the dry cleaning macro will know whose clothes need which treatment without the blocks being predefined. Parameter passing with DEFINE thus permits creation of powerful and flexible subroutines.

One common practical type of subroutine is a printing subroutine. Instead of having several printing macros, DEFINE allows creation of one routine that does all the work. However, one occasional difficulty with report macros is providing the appropriate print block to the printing subroutine. The macro in figure 16.16 uses a menu to print several reports. Note how DEFINE sets the correct print blocks.

The LET Command

LET places an entry into a cell. This simple description, however, belies the power and versatility of the LET command.

The syntax for LET is

{LET targetname,source}	Places value of <source> in <targetname>

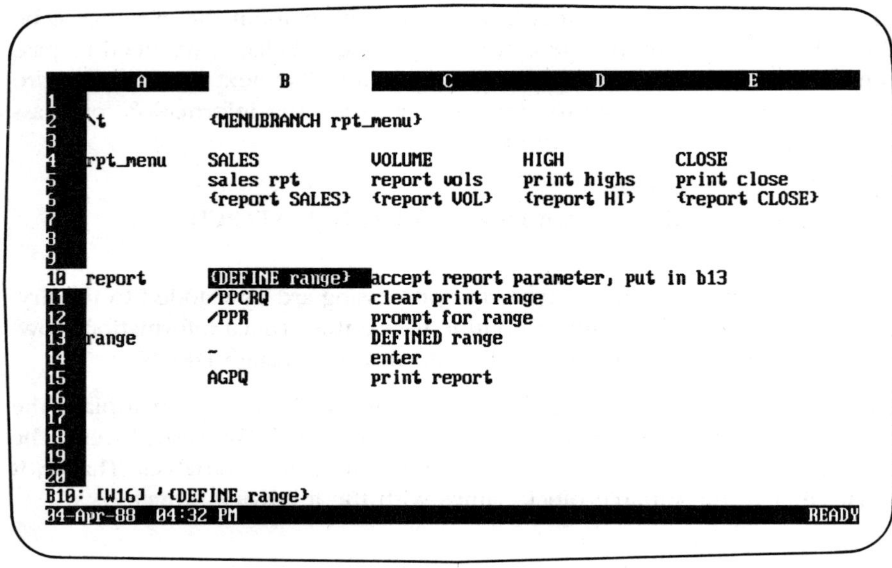

Fig. 16.16. Using DEFINE to set correct print blocks.

<Source> can be a reference to a cell containing the source information, or it can be a formula that creates a value. <Targetname> is the cell where the resulting entry will be placed. The LET command can be interpreted to read, "Let the targetname become the same as the source." Read the comma as *become*.

The source argument can be a string, value, formula, string expression, or mixed function (string and value). Any function or formula available to the spreadsheet will work as a source argument. The following examples show several ways you can use the LET command:

{LET number,5}
: Places the number 5 into the block named NUMBER

{LET price,cost*(required_margin+1)}
: Multiplies the value in the cell named COST by some percentage equal to or greater than 100%, and places the result into the cell named PRICE

{LET city,"NEW YORK"}
: Sends the character string NEW YORK into the block named CITY

{LET full_name,title&" "&first_name&" "&mi&" "&last_name}
Uses a string formula to combine title, first name, middle initial, last name, and spaces (the double quotation marks), and then to place the result into the block named FULL_NAME. The process of adding strings is known as *string concatenation.*

{LET counter,counter+step}
A special example of LET in that the cell to be modified may already contain a value. If it does, another number is added to it. That value then becomes the value of COUNTER, the target cell.

{LET target,@CELLPOINTER("CONTENTS")}
Places the contents of the current cell selector location into the target cell using the special @CELLPOINTER function

The power of the LET statement is limited only by your needs and imagination. For instance, look at the macro example in figure 16.17, which mixes string, date, math, and lookup table functions to determine the day name of a specified date and place that name into a block named DAY.

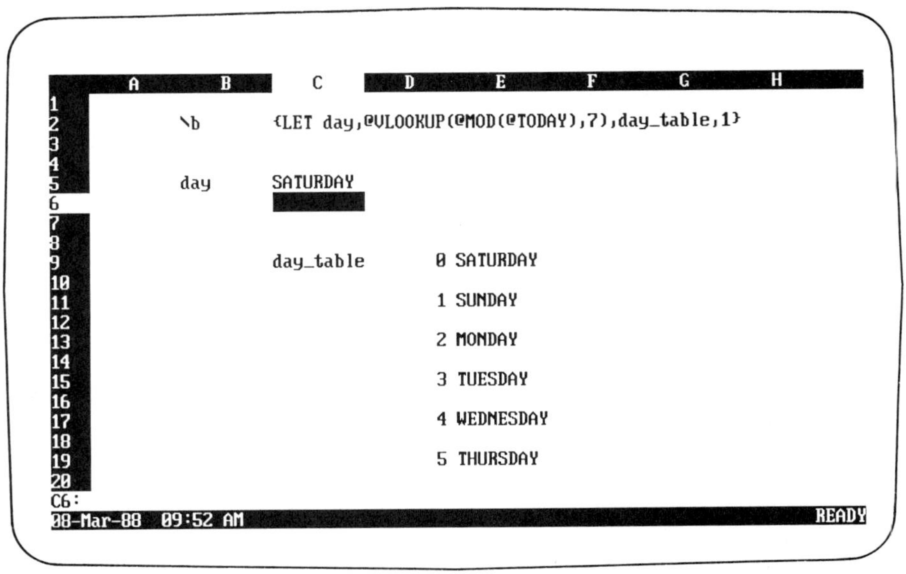

Fig. 16.17. Use of LET to place the day into a block.

Several cautions should be noted for using LET:

When working with string formulas, do not begin the formula with a double quotation mark. Doing so will produce a macro execution error. Instead, precede the string formula with the plus sign (+), which can be followed by the double quotation mark.

Also, when using a formula to produce a LET result, sometimes the formula itself will be placed in the target cell instead of the result of the evaluation of the formula. This bug usually means that the formula has a syntax error, and LET assumes that you meant a string argument. To correct this situation, place the formula equivalent in a spreadsheet cell and debug the formula as explained in Chapter 6, "Using Basic Spreadsheet Functions." After correcting the formula, make the correction to the LET command.

In addition, like the BLANK command, the LET command changes the contents of cells at the memory level without displaying the change on-screen until the cells are recalculated or the cursor is moved. Formulas or macros referring to the changed cells will read the contents of memory, not the display, for their arguments. By avoiding a display update operation, you can enhance macro execution speed significantly.

The PUT Command

The PUT command is deceptively similar to the LET command in that it places a value or a string in a target cell. Whereas LET is a general variable handling tool, PUT is designed to work with tables and databases. The syntax for the PUT statement is

{PUT table,col_offset#,row_offset#,source}	Puts <source> into col, row within <table>

The first argument, <table>, is a block name encompassing an entire table of cells. The <col_offset#> is a number describing which column the data should be placed into, and <row_offset#> indicates the row in the table where the source data (a string, cell reference, or block name) must go.

In figure 16.18 the command {PUT db,3,4,current_data} tells the macro to put the contents of the CURRENT_DATA cell into the third column offset and the fourth row offset in the DB block A1..D4. When thinking of <column_offset#>, think *over*, as in "Go over 3 columns from the left." Do the same when defining <row_offset#>, but think *down*: that is, "Go down 4." For the table in figure 16.18, the PUT command would place the current_data in the ZIPCODE column (3 columns over) and in row 5 (down 4).

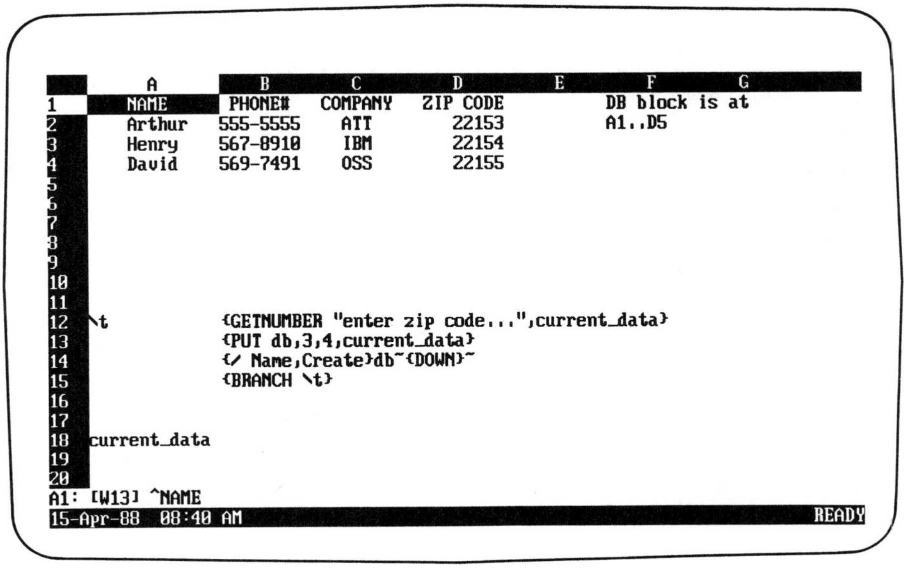

Fig. 16.18. The PUT command can place data into a table.

Using PUT in this manner can make writing data entry routines easier and more practical. Furthermore, if a function can be designed as a general purpose tool, you won't need to "reinvent the wheel." For example, one problem with the PUT command in figure 16.18 is that it can only put data into one row and column coordinate within the table, because the row and column offsets are unvarying column and row numbers within the table. The PUT command's offset arguments generally are produced through the use of functions such as @COLS and @ROWS.

For example, the PUT command in the macro in figure 16.19, when used with the table DB, will PUT the current entry of the current rightmost column into the bottom row of the DB table. The -1 information converts the results of the formulas to an offset number.

Figure 16.19 shows the state of the macro after the first ZIP code has been entered. The DB block has been expanded by one row so that the next operation of the PUT command will put the ZIP code in the next row down from the previous entry.

To use this PUT statement in a macro, you need to have a routine that will maintain the size of the DB block. The \t routine is powerful for database entry or spreadsheet table maintenance because the proper entry cell address can be derived from the @ROWS and @COLS functions.

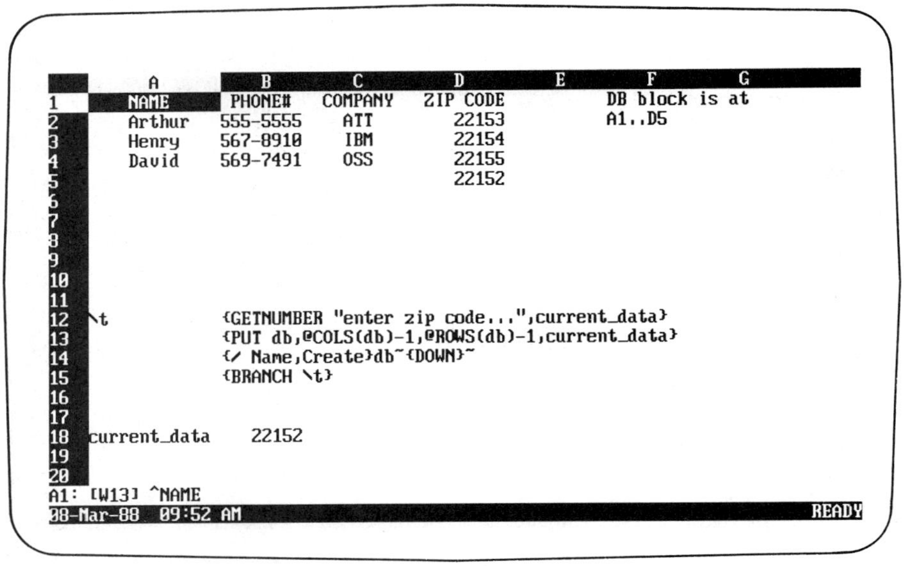

Fig. 16.19. Using PUT to place data into the bottom row of the right-most column.

The RECALC and RECALCCOL Commands

The RECALC and RECALCCOL commands recalculate single cells or groups of cells, by row and by column respectively, without invoking a full recalculation of the worksheet. The syntaxes for these commands are as follows:

{RECALC location,condition,iteration#}	Recalculates cells by row
{RECALCCOL location,condition,iteration#}	Recalculates cells by column

The location is a block of cells or a block name containing the formulas to be recalculated. The condition is an optional argument that stops the recalculating when the desired value is reached. (This capability can be useful if you have a goal-seeking calculation.) The iteration number is a number or a reference to a cell containing a number that limits the number of times RECALC or RECALCCOL will recalculate to satisfy the optional condition.

Because Quattro's method of calculation is already efficient, these two commands are available more to maintain macro compatibility with 1-2-3 than to improve macro recalculating in Quattro.

To get reliable results from recalculated macros, you must be sure that precedent cells for cells containing formulas are included in the RECALC location argument. *Precedent cells* are those cells that a formula depends on for proper evaluation.

User Interface Commands

The user interface commands provide you with a wide variety of ways to communicate with the user while a macro is running. They can be used to signal a user of various conditions, ask for data input, watch for user entry during macro execution, control the display update, and provide for user-friendly menu systems.

Table 16.5
User Interface Commands

Command	*Description*
{BEEP}	Sounds one of the computer's four beeps
{BREAKOFF}	Disables Ctrl-Break key sequence
{BREAKON}	Enables Ctrl-Break key sequence
{GET}	Accepts a single character into <location>
{GETLABEL}	Accepts a label into <location>
{GETNUMBER}	Accepts a number into <location>
{INDICATE}	Resets mode indicator to <string>
{LOOK}	Places first character from type-ahead buffer into <location>
{MENUBRANCH}	Prompts user with menu found at <location>
{MENUCALL}	Like MENUBRANCH except that control returns to the statement after the MENUCALL
{PANELOFF}	Suppresses control panel
{PANELON}	Displays control panel
{WINDOWSOFF}	Suppresses display of current window
{WINDOWSON}	Enables display of current window

The BEEP Command

You can implement BEEP whenever you want the macro to signal the user by a tone. The format for the BEEP command is

{BEEP number}	Sounds one of the computer's four beeps

or

{BEEP}

BEEP produces one of four tones. The argument can be 1-4, generating from a low to a high tone (also, {BEEP 0} has the same tone as {BEEP 4}). If no tone number is defined, the default tone is {BEEP 1}. As in many other commands, the argument may refer to a block name containing a variable, number, formula, and so on: for example, {BEEP alot}.

The BEEP command can have many uses:

{IF condition=error}{BEEP}
Signal error conditions

. . . {IF done=true}{BEEP}
Signal "process is complete" for long macros

{IF zip_code=#NOT#a_valid_zip}{BEEP}
Indicate an out of range or illogical input

The BREAKOFF and BREAKON Commands

The BREAKOFF and BREAKON commands allow the macro writer to disable the Ctrl-Break sequence, which normally halts macro execution when pressed. The ability to prevent "breaking" a macro can come in handy when a high level of macro or application security is required. BREAKOFF and BREAKON do not accept arguments. Their forms are as follows:

{BREAKOFF}	Disables the Ctrl-Break key sequence
{BREAKON}	Enables the Ctrl-Break key sequence

For example, if you want to create a macro that requires a user to enter a password in order to work in a spreadsheet, you need to use BREAKOFF. Otherwise, the user could bypass the macro entirely by pressing Ctrl-Break. After the user has entered the correct password, the macro can use the BREAKON keyword to enable the Ctrl-Break sequence.

The password macro shown in figure 16.20 first invokes {BREAKOFF}, which makes Ctrl-Break unavailable to the user until the correct password has been recognized. When the IF statement recognizes that the correct password has been entered, {BREAKON} restores the Ctrl-Break capability to the user.

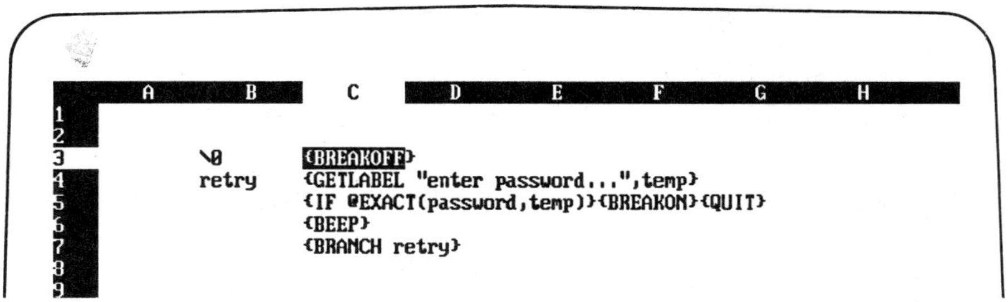

Fig. 16.20. Using BREAKOFF and BREAKON in a password macro.

Tip Use the BREAKOFF command with caution. It prevents anyone, including the macro writer, from using the Ctrl-Break sequence. Don't use BREAKOFF until a macro is fully developed and debugged!

Tip If a macro gets stuck because of BREAKOFF, you can use the /**F**ile **C**ombine **C**opy menu command to retrieve the file.

The GET Command

The GET command may become one of your favorite macro statements. The GET command intercepts the most recent keyboard entry and places it into a predefined block. The syntax for GET is

{GET location} Accepts a single character into <location>

where <location> is the name of the cell where the user's keystroke will be stored.

A key feature of this command is that the keystroke is *not* performed. Thus if the slash key is pressed, the macro statement {GET keystroke}, instead of bringing up the Quattro menu, will place a slash character in the cell named KEYSTROKE.

This feature permits the macro to assess all user inputs to determine *before* acting on the keystroke whether to take any exceptional action. This technique provides for macro processing in the background, which is similar in effect to the {?} (pause) command. The difference between them lies in the fact that the {?} command pauses until the user presses the Enter key; the GET command, however, can pause until the user presses any predefined key or keys.

Figure 16.21 shows the GET command used in a menu keystroke-filtering macro. The GET instruction places each keystroke in turn into the cell named KEYSTROKE. The IF statement compares the keystroke with the slash (/) character. If a slash was pressed, the macro proceeds to the MENUBRANCH command. Otherwise, the macro calls and performs the KEYSTROKE block as a subroutine. Finally, the macro branches back to the top of the loop to get the next keystroke.

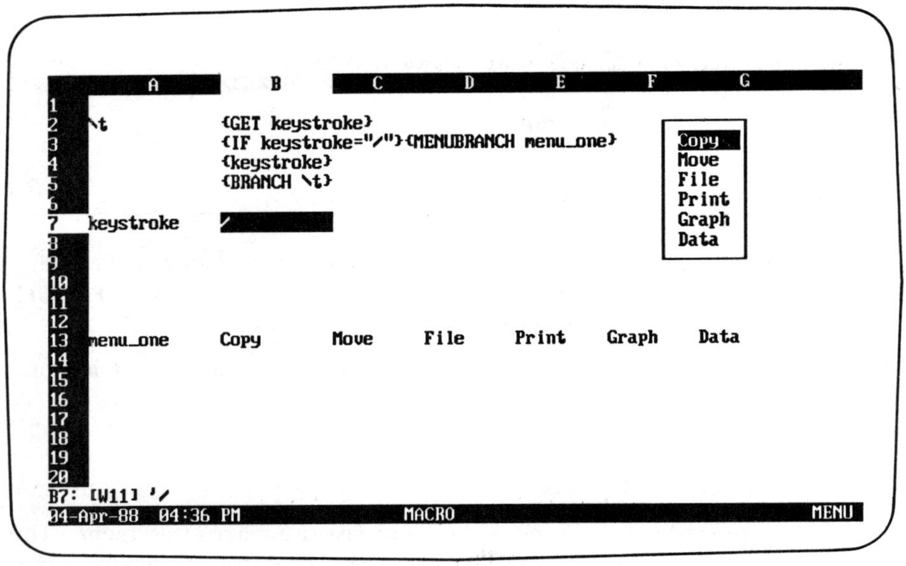

Fig. 16.21. Use of GET in a menu keystroke-filtering macro.

Any key you want to scan for can be placed in the IF statement in figure 16.21. The macro statement

Enter your choice now . . . {GET choice}{ESC}

will autotype a message to the user on the input line and will then wait for the user to press a key. The key pressed will be sent to the CHOICE block. Next, the ESC command will remove the message label from the input line.

This macro also demonstrates the ability of macro commands to execute even when the input line has data or when standard menus are active. If your macro needs to scan for a number of possible keystrokes, the structure in figure 16.22 will prove useful.

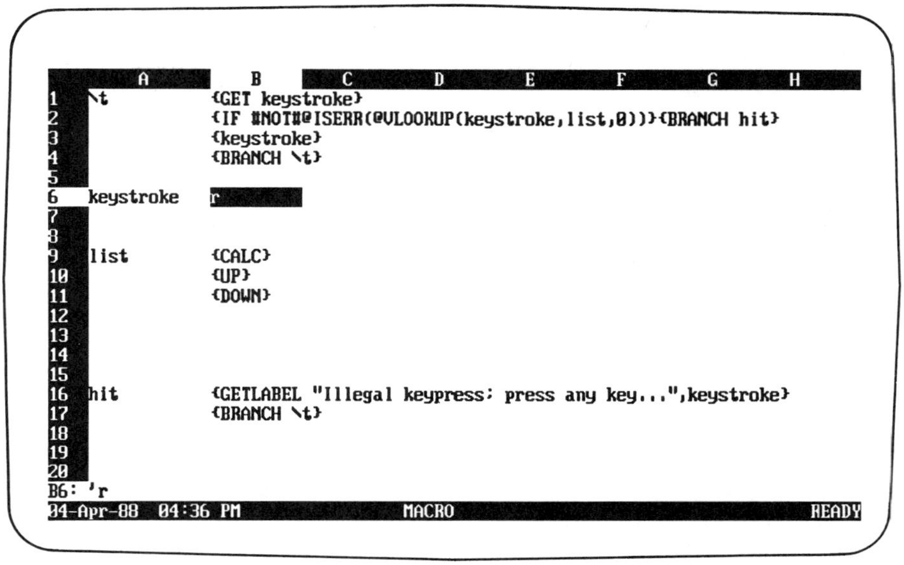

Fig. 16.22. Using GET in a macro that scans for several keystrokes.

If a key is typed that is in the list subroutine, the @VLOOKUP function will #NOT# be in error. Thus the IF command will be true, and the macro will BRANCH to the hit subroutine. Otherwise, the macro will perform the keystroke and loop back to the beginning. For the IF command to evaluate properly, the search list should be identical to the characters that GET would place into the KEYSTROKE block.

The GETLABEL Command

The GETLABEL command provides you with the ability to request interactive input from the user. The syntax for GETLABEL is

{GETLABEL "Prompt string",location}	Accepts a label into <location>

"Prompt string" is a short message telling the user what to enter, and <location> is a cell address or preferably a block name where the user's entry will be stored and evaluated.

The GETLABEL command pauses macro execution while displaying a prompt string at the top of the Quattro display. After the user responds to the prompt, the user entry is placed into a cell specified in the GETLABEL command. The

GETLABEL command in figure 16.23 displays a prompt in the input line. It is a good idea to finish a prompt with a space, an ellipsis (...), a colon (:), or an arrow (—>), to separate the prompt from the user's response.

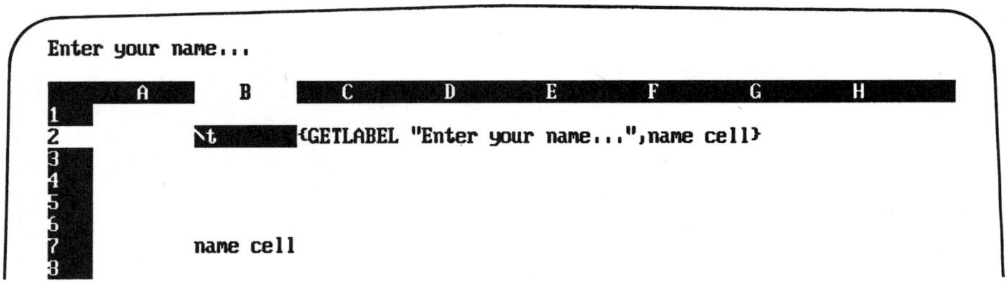

Fig. 16.23. Using GETLABEL to accept a label.

GETLABEL does not evaluate the user's response; it simply stores the entry as a string in the designated location. If the entry must be evaluated, another instruction, such as an IF command, is needed.

The GETNUMBER Command

The GETNUMBER command provides you with the ability to request numeric input from the user. It is different from GETLABEL in that all entries in response to a GETNUMBER are expected to be numeric. The syntax for GETNUMBER is

{GETNUMBER "Prompt string",location}	Accepts a number into <location>

"Prompt string" is a short message telling the user what to enter, and <location> is a cell address or preferably a block name where the user's entry will be stored. If a label is accidentally entered at the prompt, the macro will put an ERR into the location cell.

The GETNUMBER command pauses macro execution while displaying a prompt string in the input line of the Quattro display. After the prompt is responded to, GETNUMBER places the user entry into a cell specified in the GETNUMBER command. The GETNUMBER command in figure 16.24 displays a prompt in the input line. As with the GETLABEL command, you should finish a prompt with a space, an ellipsis (...), a colon (:), or an arrow (—>), to separate the prompt from the user's response.

Like GETLABEL, GETNUMBER does not evaluate the response. If the entry must be evaluated, another instruction, such as an IF command, is needed.

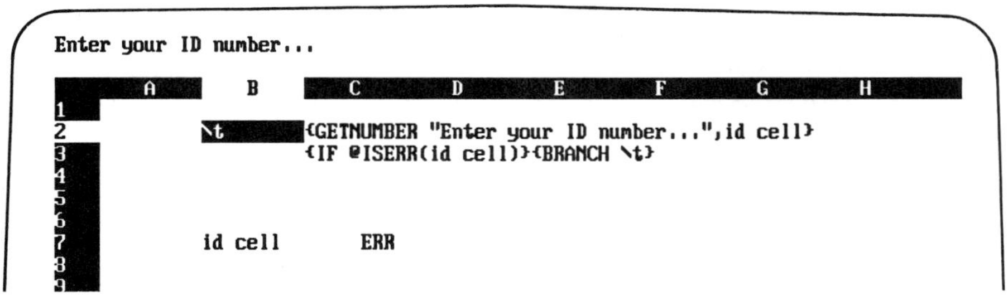

Fig. 16.24. Using GETNUMBER to accept a number.

The INDICATE Command

The mode indicator, at the bottom right of the Quattro screen, indicates Quattro's current operating mode. Quattro's available modes include READY, MENU, WAIT, EDIT, POINT, and so forth. The INDICATE command allows you to add a mode description, or name, of your choice.

The syntax for INDICATE is

{INDICATE string} Resets mode indicator to <string>

where <string> is up to 5 characters of text.

Generally, use this command in macros where you need to inform the user that there will be a delay, but where the WAIT display would not be supplied by the normal mode indicator. The following example shows a section of a macro for this type of need:

{BRANCH long_process}
{INDICATE "WAIT"}

Whatever indication you place in the mode indicator will remain there until you explicitly restore the indicator to the normal mode function, even if the macro has finished. To restore the normal mode function, use {INDICATE} (with no argument).

The LOOK Command

The LOOK statement seems the same as GET, but in fact it is much more specialized. Like GET, LOOK also reads a keystroke and places it in a location. Unlike GET, however, LOOK does not filter the keystroke. The syntax for LOOK is

{LOOK location} Places first character from type-ahead buffer into <location>

where <location> is the cell where the user's keystroke will be copied.

The LOOK statement is often used to check whether the user has typed a key since a macro began to run. Figure 16.25 illustrates a LOOK command in a macro that checks whether a key has been pressed.

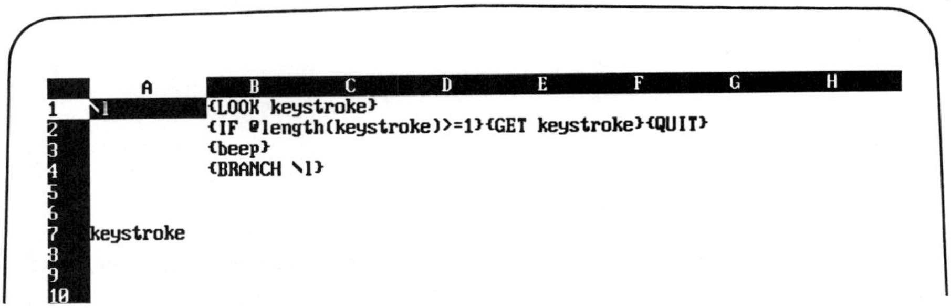

Fig. 16.25. Use of LOOK to check for a keystroke.

LOOK offers the macro writer other advantages. For one, the LOOK command can be used to implement a time-out routine. In a macro that expects the user to enter some kind of input, you might want to give the macro a maximum time to wait for the entry before the macro moves on. A LOOK statement can scan for a keystroke but if, after a certain number of passes through a loop no useful input has occurred, the macro can process along a different path.

The macro in figure 16.26 performs just such an action. If the user doesn't press a key before the time-out macro loops 33 times (MAXTRIES), the macro will request that the user press F1 (Help) and then will stop.

This macro can be used as an auto-executing macro for new users of Quattro. If the user hasn't pressed any keys for a period of time, the macro can prompt the user to get help.

The MENUBRANCH Command

If you develop an application with several macros that perform different tasks, you may want to put them under the control of a menu system similar to Quattro menus. The MENUBRANCH command gives you the ability to create a "point and shoot" menu, where your macros are started by making choices from the displayed macro menu.

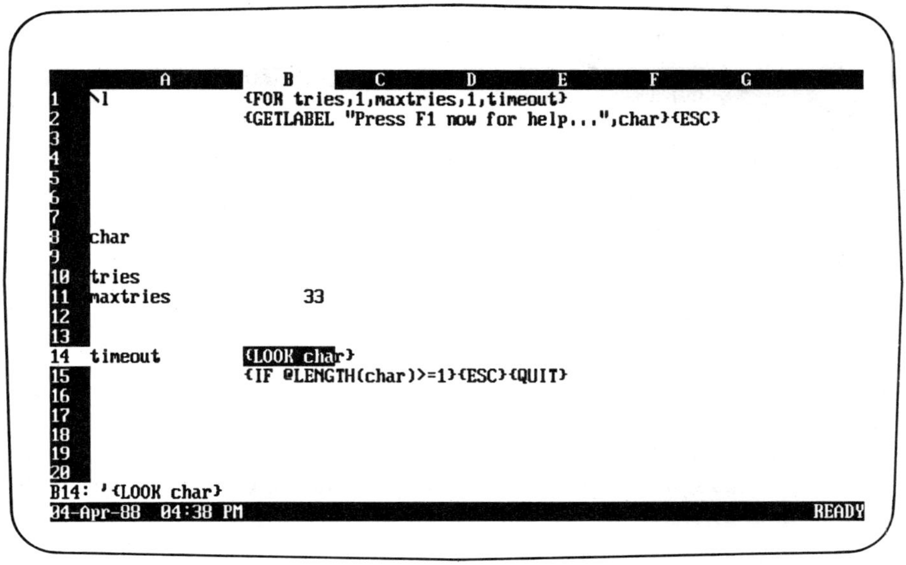

Fig. 16.26. Use of LOOK in a time-out macro.

The MENUBRANCH command takes the form

{MENUBRANCH location}	Prompts user with menu found at <location>

The location is the cell address or block name attached to the top left cell of the target menu structure.

The MENUBRANCH command is similar to a GOTO statement. When the macro encounters a MENUBRANCH statement, the flow of the program is transferred to the block specified in the macro statement. A menu structure is expected at that block. The first row of the menu structure is designed to hold the choices for the menu. Each choice must be entered into a separate adjacent column. The second row, directly under the menu choices, is reserved for prompts or choice descriptions. The third row of the menu contains the actual macro commands that process the menu choices in the first row.

Figure 16.27 illustrates the MENUBRANCH command. The macro starts by menubranching to the block named MENU_ONE. When it does, the menu window on the right of the figure is opened, and the preview is displayed in the input line. For the sake of clarity, the previews in row 5 for the other menu choices have not been entered.

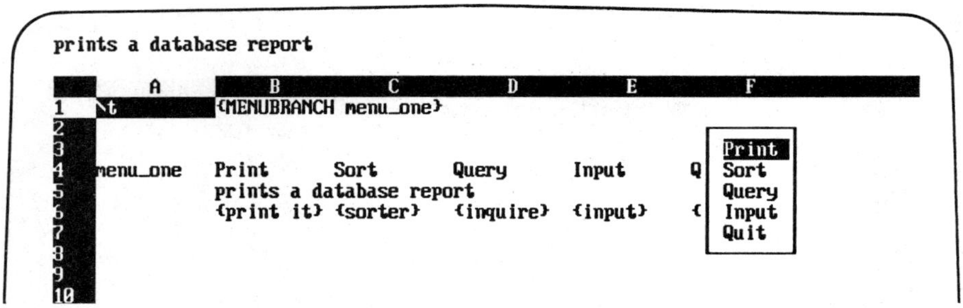

Fig. 16.27. MENUBRANCH calls up a menu and a preview.

This menu operates the same way as a normal Quattro menu. The user either points at the choice and presses Enter, or presses the first letter of the choice. Notice in figure 16.27 that the **Q**uery and **Q**uit menu choices begin with the same letter. This situation should be avoided by choosing menu choices with different first letters.

It is possible—in fact, likely—that the choices, prompts and menu macro commands will be overlapped by menu macros to their right. Although this overlapping may make reading and debugging your menu difficult, it does not harm the menu's operation.

The most efficient way for menus to process is to have a subroutine call the macro code that actually implements the menu choice's function. The menu structure then will rarely need to be deeper than four rows, making the menu easier to enhance, debug, and maintain. The menu in figure 16.28 shows this type of menu structure.

To branch to the escaping function, you may want to place the function to the right of the MENUBRANCH statement. Doing so would change the first line of the macro in figure 16.27 from

{MENUBRANCH menu_one}

to

{MENUBRANCH menu_one}{BRANCH \t}

as it is in figure 16.28. When the user presses the Esc key while this menu is displayed, processing of the MENUBRANCH command is terminated, and the routine to the immediate right, {BRANCH \t}, is performed. Thus the menu is re-executed every time the user presses the Esc key.

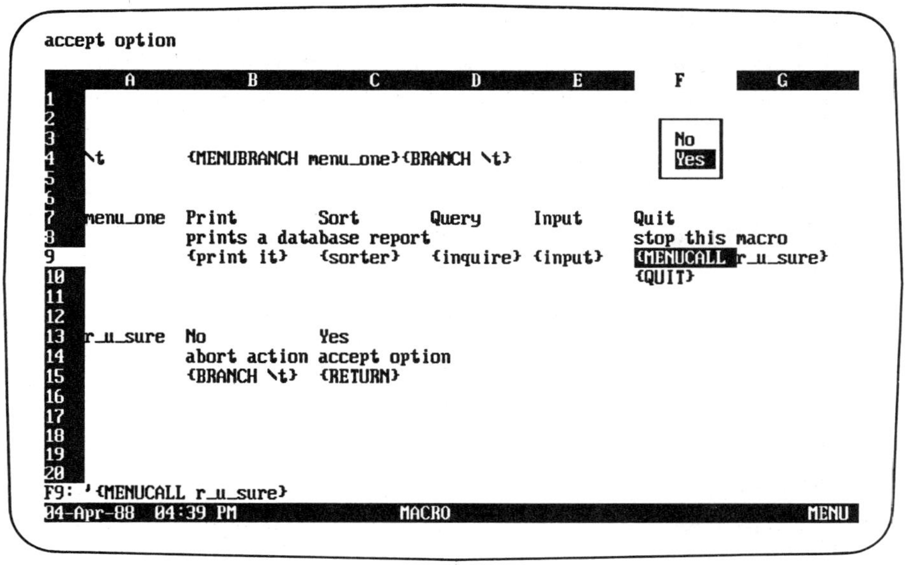

Fig. 16.28. Menu structure with subroutines that call macros.

The MENUCALL Command

The MENUCALL command is similar to a subroutine call. When the macro interpreter encounters a MENUCALL statement, flow of the program is temporarily transferred to the menu specified. When the menu choice is made, the flow can either return to the calling macro or branch to some other location. The MENUCALL command takes the form

{MENUCALL location}	Like MENUBRANCH except that control returns to the statement after the MENUCALL

The location is the cell address or block name attached to the top left cell of the target menu structure.

The menu in figure 16.28 calls another menu, named R_U_SURE. If the user chooses **N**o, the menu simply returns to the main macro, \t, with the {BRANCH \t} command. If the user chooses **Y**es, processing is returned to the last statement in the last row of MENU_ONE, where the macro quits. This kind of menu calling structure provides the macro writer with macros that are reusable, concise, and therefore significantly easier to maintain.

The PANELOFF and PANELON Commands

Usually when a macro is processing, a flickering effect is noticeable on the input line and menu boxes. This flickering is caused by the rapid succession of menu commands and macro statements that the macro interpreter is executing. To make a "clean" presentation to the user, use the PANELOFF command at the beginning of your macros to make this flickering invisible.

The PANELOFF statements do not accept an argument. Their forms are as follows:

{PANELOFF}	Suppresses display of control panel
{PANELON}	Redisplays control panel

To redisplay the control panel, the macro should execute a PANELON statement near its end and before macro completion:

```
{PANELOFF}
{action}
{PANELON}
```

The WINDOWSOFF and WINDOWSON Commands

The WINDOWSOFF AND WINDOWSON commands are similar to the control panel commands. Normally as a macro runs, various operations such as GOTO cause the screen display to move around repeatedly, perhaps confusing the user. To provide a stable screen presentation, use the WINDOWSOFF command. WINDOWSOFF does not blank the display. Rather, the screen (or window) is frozen and displays what was on-screen just before the WINDOWSOFF command executed. The forms of the commands are as follows:

{WINDOWSOFF}	Suppresses display of current window
{WINDOWSOFF}	Enables redisplay of current window

If you are working with a macro that is running slowly and moves the cursor a great deal, the WINDOWSOFF command can speed the macro by as much as 80%.

Use the PANELOFF and WINDOWSOFF commands together at the beginning of a macro, and PANELON and WINDOWSON at the end of a macro, for maximum control of your screen display:

```
{PANELOFF}
{WINDOWSOFF}
{action}
{WINDOWSON}
{PANELON}
```

File Manipulation Commands

Eight commands give Quattro the capability of opening, reading, writing, and closing a sequential data file containing ASCII text data. This capability allows Quattro applications to read and write files used by other business applications. Although the /**F**ile **I**mport and /**P**rint **D**estination **F**ile commands provide a limited capability to manipulate files foreign to Quattro, the file-manipulation commands shown in the table provide a capability equal to the sequential file commands in BASIC or other programming languages. The file manipulation commands are listed in table 16.6.

Table 16.6
File Manipulation Commands

Command	*Description*
{OPEN}	Opens file for reading, writing, or both
{CLOSE}	Closes a file opened with {OPEN}
{READ}	Copies specified characters to <location>
{READLN}	Copies next line from file to <location>
{WRITE}	Copies a string to the open file
{WRITELN}	Copies a string plus a carriage-return line-feed sequence to the open file
{SETPOS}	Sets a new position for the file pointer
{GETPOS}	Records the file pointer position in <location>
{FILESIZE}	Records size of the open file in <location>

Warning: To read from and write to foreign files successfully, you must understand exactly how these commands work and how the sequential files you are manipulating are organized. If you write to a file contained in another application, be sure to back up the file before trying to write to it from within Quattro. If you keep this warning in mind, this group of commands can open up the world of outside files to your Quattro applications. Should you need to process external data files, Quattro's commands make it possible to do so.

The OPEN Command

The OPEN command opens a disk file, providing access for you to write to or read from that file. The access-mode argument is a single character string that specifies whether you want to read only ("R"), write only ("W"), or both read from and write to the file ("M").

Note that Quattro will allow only one file to be open at a time. If you want to work with more than one file in your application, you will have to open each file before using it, and then close it again before opening and using the next file. Note also that the "M" (modify) argument cannot create a new file.

The form of the OPEN command is

{OPEN filename,file access mode}	Opens file for reading, writing, or both

The filename argument is a string, an expression with a string value, or a single-cell reference to a cell that contains a string or a string expression. The string must be a valid DOS file name or path name. A file in the current directory can be specified by its name and extension. A file in another directory may require a drive identification, a subdirectory path, or a complete DOS path in addition to the file name and extension.

The file access mode indicates how the macro will use the file. You have three access mode options:

"R" (Read)	Read opens an existing file and allows access with the READ and READLN commands. You cannot write to a file opened with Read access.
"W" (Write)	Write opens a new file with the specified name and allows access with the WRITE and WRITELN commands. Any existing file with the specified name will be erased and replaced by the new file.
"M" (Modify)	Modify opens an existing file with the specified name and allows both read (READ and READLN) and write (WRITE and WRITELN) commands.

The OPEN command succeeds if it is able to open the file with the access you requested. If the OPEN command succeeds, program execution continues with the cell below the OPEN. Any commands after the OPEN in the current cell are ignored.

The OPEN command will fail with an error message if the disk drive is not ready (for example, if the drive door is open). You should use an ONERROR command to handle this contingency.

If the access mode is Read or Modify but the file does not exist on the indicated directory, the OPEN command fails, and program execution continues with the commands after the OPEN command in the current cell. You can place one or more commands after the OPEN command in the same cell in order to deal with the failure. The most common practice is to place a BRANCH or a subroutine call after the OPEN to transfer to a macro that deals with the failure.

Here are some examples of the OPEN command:

{OPEN "PASTDUE","R"}{BRANCH FIXIT}
: Open the existing file named PASTDUE in the current directory for reading. If the file cannot be opened, branch to the routine FIXIT.

{OPEN "C:\DATA\CLIENTS.DAT",w}
: Open the new file named CLIENTS.DAT in drive C, subdirectory DATA, for writing.

{OPEN file,m}{BRANCH RETRY}
: Open the file whose name is in cell FILE for Modify access. If the file cannot be opened, branch to the routine RETRY.

Figure 16.29 shows an example of using all of the file commands except the READ and WRITE commands (which are similar to the READLN and WRITELN commands). The program named \0 uses the OPEN command to open a user-specified file. This program illustrates how to deal with `Disk drive not ready` and `File not found` errors. After prompting you for the file name, an ONERROR command sets the error jump to the routine that handles problems such as the drive not being ready.

The CLOSE Command

The CLOSE command closes a currently open file. If no file is open, the CLOSE command has no effect. CLOSE does not take an argument. This command is particularly important for files that you are writing or modifying. You can lose the data written to a file that you don't close. The form of the CLOSE command is

{CLOSE} Closes a file opened with OPEN

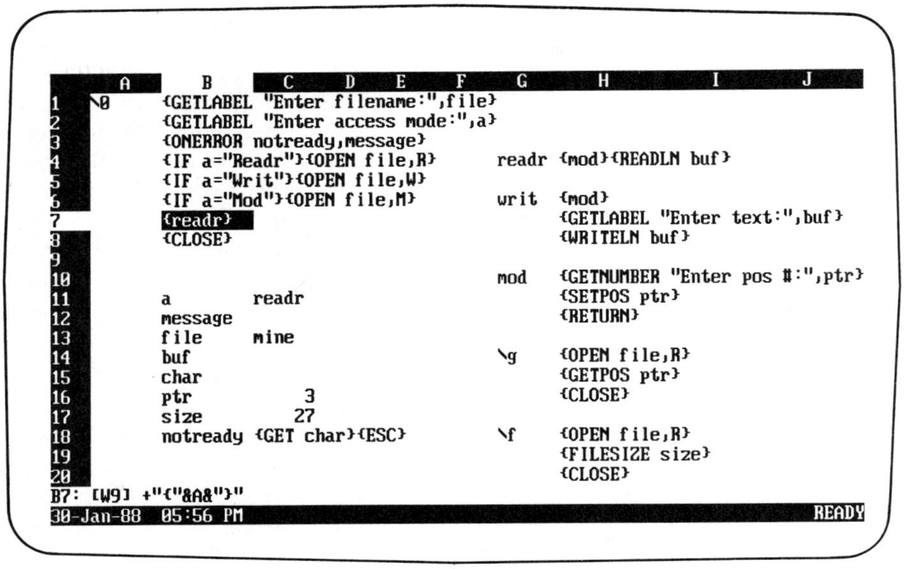

Fig. 16.29. A program that uses the file commands.

Although, under most circumstances, Quattro automatically takes care of a file that you do not close, you should make it a practice to use CLOSE when you are finished using any file opened with OPEN (better safe than sorry). Use of the CLOSE command is illustrated in several of the routines in figure 16.29.

The READ Command

The READ command reads a specified number of characters from the currently open file, beginning at the present file pointer location. The characters read from the file are placed in the spreadsheet at the cell <location> indicated. The form of the READ command is

{READ bytecount,location}	Copies specified number of characters from file to <location>

in which <bytecount> is the number of bytes to read, starting at the current position of the file pointer, and <location> is the cell to read into. READ places the specified number of characters from the file into the location cell as a label. The bytecount argument can be any number between 1 and 240, the maximum number of characters in a Quattro label. If the bytecount is greater than the number of characters remaining in the file, Quattro reads the remaining characters into the location. After the READ command finishes, the file pointer is positioned at the character following the last character read.

For example, the statement

{READ num,info}

transfers information from the open file into the cell location named INFO. The amount of information transferred is determined by the contents of the cell named NUM, which can contain either a value or a formula.

The READ command is useful primarily when you want to read a specific number of characters into the buffer. A data file that contains fixed-length records, for example, is read conveniently by the READ command with bytecount equal to the record length.

READ generally should not be used with ASCII text files from a word processor or text editor. Such files generally have variable-length lines terminated with a carriage-return line-feed sequence and are read better with the READLN command. Although figure 16.29 does not contain an example of the READ command, READ is used much like the READLN in the figure's readr program.

The READLN Command

The READLN command reads one line of information from the currently open file, beginning at the file pointer's current position. The characters read are placed in the cell <location> in the current spreadsheet. The READLN command form is

{READLN location}   Copies next line from file to <location>

For example, the statement

{READLN HERE}

will copy a line from an open file into the cell named HERE. The line read will be determined by the SETPOS command. (SETPOS is discussed later in this chapter.)

Use READLN to read a line of text from a file whose lines are delimited by a carriage-return, line-feed combination. You would, for example, use READLN to read the next line from an ASCII text file. ASCII text files are created with Quattro's /**P**rint **D**estination **F**ile command. Also referred to as print files, these files are assigned the .PRN file extension by Quattro. READLN is best suited to reading ASCII text files, otherwise known as print files. The program labeled readr in figure 16.29 illustrates the use of READLN.

Tip If you attempt to read past the end of the file, if no file is open, or if the file was opened with Write access, the READ or READLN command is ignored and program execution continues in the same cell. Otherwise, after the READ or READLN command is completed, program execution continues on the next line, which allows you to place a BRANCH or subroutine after the READ or READLN to handle the problem of an unexecuted READ or READLN statement.

The WRITE Command

The WRITE command writes a string of text to the currently open file. The WRITE command has the form

{WRITE string}	Copies a string to the open file

The argument string can be a literal string, a block name or cell reference to a single cell that contains a string, or a string expression. Because WRITE does not place a carriage-return, line-feed sequence at the end of the string, multiple WRITEs can be made to concatenate text on a single line. WRITE is well suited to creating or updating a file that contains fixed-length database records. Although there is no example of the WRITE command in figure 16.29, the WRITE command is used in much the same way as is the WRITELN command in the writ program.

If the file pointer is not at the end of the file, Quattro overwrites the existing characters in the file. If the file pointer is at the end of the file, Quattro extends the file by the number of characters written. And if the file pointer is past the end of the file (see discussion of the SETPOS command, later in this section), before writing the characters, Quattro extends the file by the amount indicated.

The WRITELN Command

The WRITELN command is identical to the WRITE command except that it places a carriage-return, line-feed sequence after the last character written from the string. The WRITELN command form is

{WRITELN string}	Copies a string plus a carriage-return line-feed sequence to the open file

WRITELN is useful when the file being written or updated uses the carriage-return line feed to mark the end of its lines or records. (The WRITE command is also useful.) In many applications, several WRITEs are used to write a line to the file; then a WRITELN is used to mark the end of the line. The WRITELN command is illustrated in the writ program in figure 16.29.

The SETPOS Command

The SETPOS command sets the position of the file pointer to a specified value. The form of the command is

{SETPOS file-position}   Sets a new position for the file pointer

<File-position> is a number, or an expression resulting in a number, that specifies the character at which you want to position the pointer. The first character in the file is at position 0, the second at position 1, and so on.

As an example, suppose that you have a database file with 100 records, which are each 20 bytes long. To access the first record, you can use the commands

```
{SETPOS 0}
{READ 20,buffer}
```

To read the 15th record, you can use the commands

```
{SETPOS (15-1)*20}
{READ 20,buffer}
```

Nothing prevents you from setting the file pointer past the end of the file. If the file pointer is set at or past the end and a READ or READLN command is executed, the command does nothing, and program execution continues with the next command on the same line (error branch). If the file pointer is set at or past the end and a WRITE or WRITELN command is executed, Quattro will first extend the file to the length specified by the file pointer and then, starting at the file pointer, write the characters.

Warning: If you inadvertently set the file pointer to a large number with SETPOS and write to the file, Quattro will attempt to expand the file and write the text at the end. If the file will not fit on the disk, the WRITE command does nothing, and program execution continues with the next command on the same line (error branch). If the file will fit on the disk, Quattro extends the file and writes the text at the end.

If a file is not currently open, SETPOS does nothing, and execution continues with the next command on the same line as the SETPOS command. Otherwise, when the SETPOS command is completed, execution continues on the next line of the program, which allows you to place a BRANCH command or a subroutine call after the SETPOS command to handle the problem of an unexecuted statement. SETPOS is illustrated in the mod program in figure 16.29.

The GETPOS Command

The GETPOS command allows you to record the file pointer's current position. The form of this command is

{GETPOS location}	Records the file pointer position in <location>

The current position of the file pointer is placed in the cell indicated by <location>, where <location> is either a cell reference or a block name. If <location> points to a multicell block, the value of the file pointer is placed in the upper left corner of the block.

The GETPOS command is useful if you record in the file the location of something you want to find again. You can use GETPOS to mark your current place in the file before you use SETPOS to move the file pointer to another position. You can use GETPOS to record the locations of important items in a quick-reference index. GETPOS is illustrated in the \g program in figure 16.29.

The FILESIZE Command

Another file-related command, FILESIZE, returns the length of the file in bytes. The form of the command is

{FILESIZE location}	Records size of the open file in <location>

The FILESIZE command determines the current length of the file and places this value in the cell referred to by <location>. The location can be a cell reference or block name. If the location refers to a multicell block, the file size is placed in the cell in the upper left corner of the block. FILESIZE is illustrated in the \f program in figure 16.29.

Chapter Summary

This chapter introduced you to Quattro's powerful macro commands. You learned about programming techniques such as looping, counting, branching, indirect addressing, managing variables, parameter passing, and how Quattro's macro commands perform these functions.

The next chapter details how to use Quattro's convenient and powerful debugging environment to tame the inevitable errors that crop up during macro development.

CHAPTER

17

Making the Best Use of Quattro's Macro Debugger

The most exciting and useful feature of Quattro's macro package is the macro debugger, a programming tool that helps you find and diagnose problems in your macros more easily. The Quattro debugger slows macro execution so that you can see what is happening. The debugger also allows you to specify points in a macro at which you want processing to stop temporarily. Then you can examine the state of the macro and spreadsheet while execution is suspended. You can even edit the macro while you are in the debugging environment.

Additionally, you can establish as many as four "trace" cells—cells that you want to track closely. The debugger can show you the contents of these cells during execution to help you determine whether, when, and how problems occur. Finally, you can use conditional formulas to pause the macro debugging session when certain conditions are met.

To illustrate how the macro debugger works, this chapter examines a simple macro and takes you step-by-step through the debugging procedure. You are shown how to use the Macro Debugging Menu, edit a macro in DEBUG mode, set macro breakpoints, specify conditional tests, and choose trace cells.

Stepping through a Macro

Whenever you have a macro with a problem that is difficult to track down, use the debugger. Press the Shift-F8 key combination to set the debugging environment. The DEBUG indicator then appears centered at the bottom of the screen. The DEBUG environment does not become active until you execute a macro.

Figure 17.1 shows a simple macro that was designed to eliminate unnecessary rows. The @CELLPOINTER functions test for the type of data in the cell selector's current location. If the macro finds that the cell contains a value, the macro moves the cell selector down one cell and checks again. If the current cell is blank (type="b"), however, the macro executes the /**R**ow **D**elete command. Let's examine this macro with Quattro's macro debugger. Note the DEBUG display at the bottom of the screen, which indicates that Shift-F8 has been pressed.

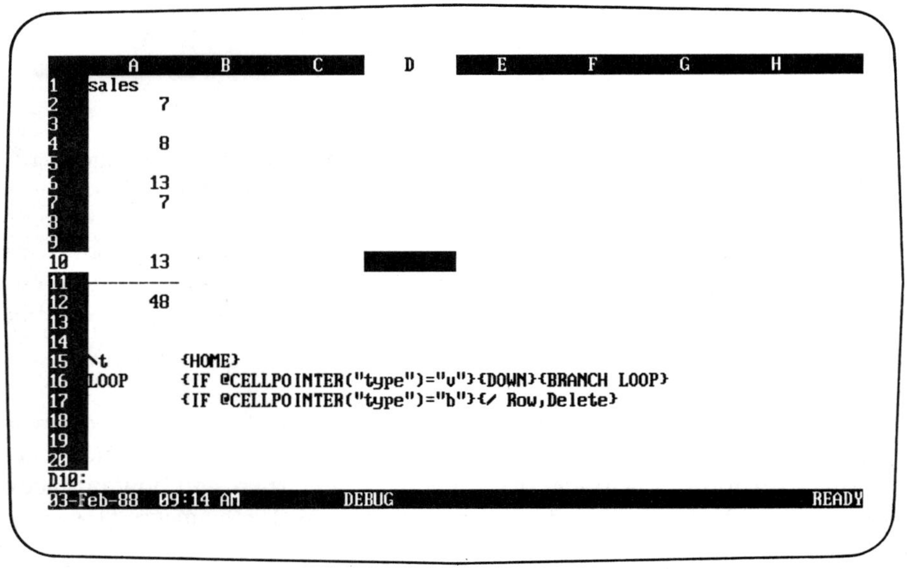

Fig. 17.1. A row-deleting macro.

Figure 17.2 shows what happens when you invoke the macro while DEBUG is set. A special debugging window is opened at the bottom of the screen. The debug window is composed of two parts. The top portion shows the macro instruction that is just about to execute, as well as the statements that surround the instruction. The debug cursor highlights the macro instruction that will run next. In the figure, note that this highlight is on the {HOME} command. The lower portion of the debugging window, the TRACE window, lets you watch the contents of certain cells as the macro runs. You choose these cells with tracing options, which are discussed later in the chapter.

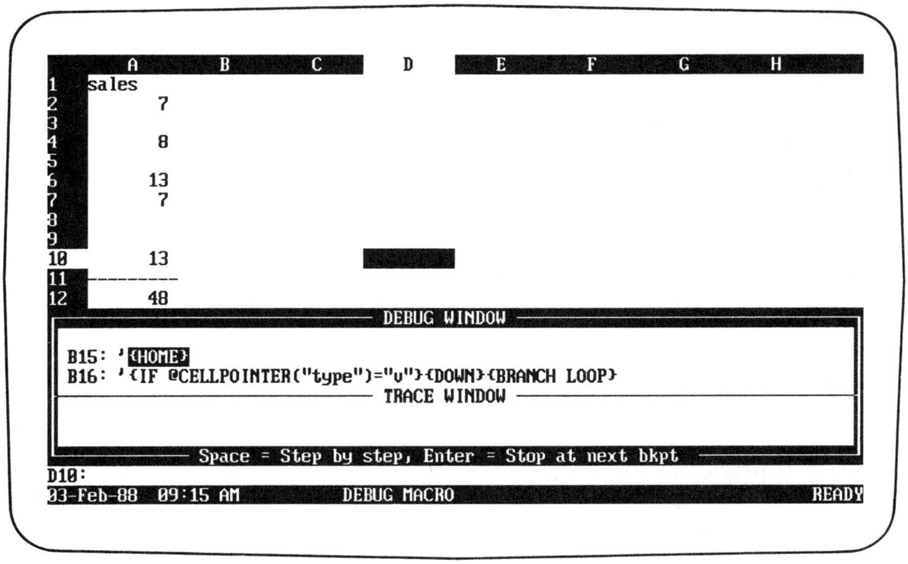

Fig. 17.2. The debug window.

The message at the bottom of the debug window tells you to press the space bar if you want to "single step," or step through the macro one command at a time. Single-step mode slows down macro execution so that you can get a "bird's eye view" of the macro's flow. The message also tells you to press the Enter key if you want to run the macro until a certain stopping point is encountered. Use this option when you either have set breakpoints (specific stopping points) or are satisfied with what you have seen and want the macro to proceed to the end at full speed.

In this example, suppose that you want to analyze the row-deleting macro one step at a time. Figure 17.3 shows the state of the system after you press the space bar once. Note that in the main window, the cell selector obeyed the macro command to move Home. In the debug window, the debug cursor has moved to the next instruction in preparation for that statement's execution.

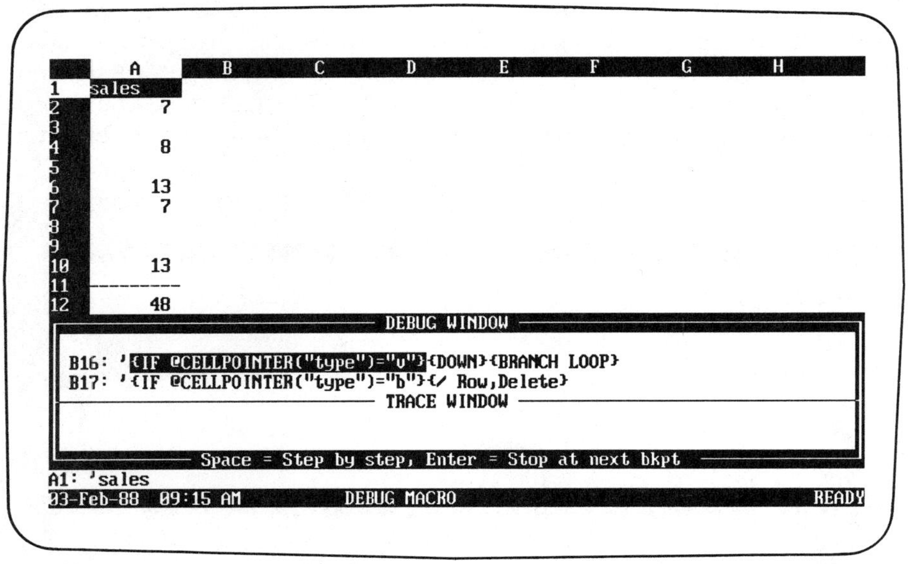

Fig. 17.3. After pressing the space bar once.

When you press the space bar again, a problem is revealed. Look at figure 17.4. The IF statement in line B16 in the debug window evaluated false (the current cell does not contain a value), so the {DOWN}{BRANCH LOOP} instructions on the same line were bypassed. (The cell selector is still on cell A1 in the spreadsheet.) But the next macro statement, the one highlighted, will also evaluate false, because the current cell is not empty. Obviously, this macro has not considered all the possible conditions that might exist.

The macro needs a command to handle labels, such as

{IF @CELLPOINTER("type")="l"}{DOWN}{BRANCH LOOP}

If you insert this line in the macro between the other two IF statements and then retest the macro in single-step mode, the debug cursor, when reaching this command, moves to the right and highlights the {DOWN} portion of the line (see fig. 17.5). This movement is visual proof that the IF function evaluated as true.

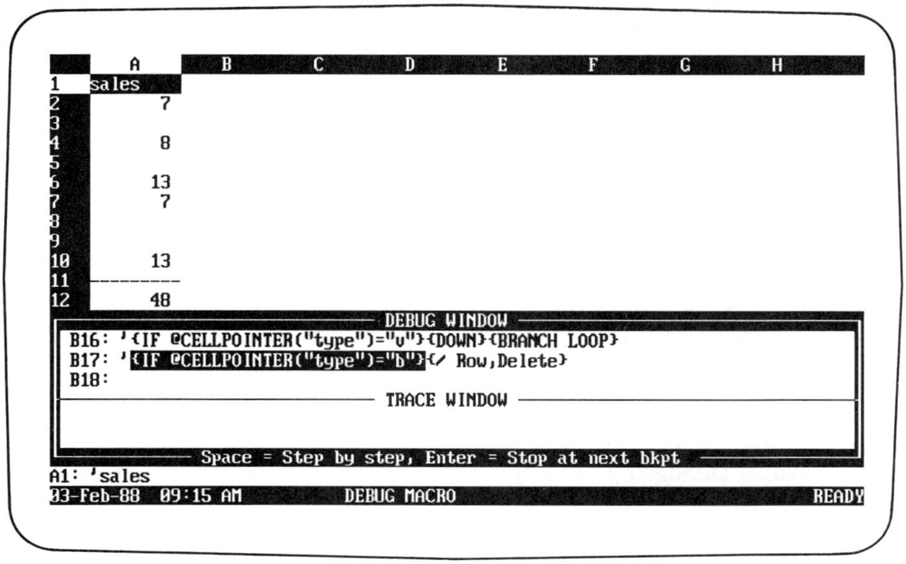

Fig. 17.4. The next step in macro execution.

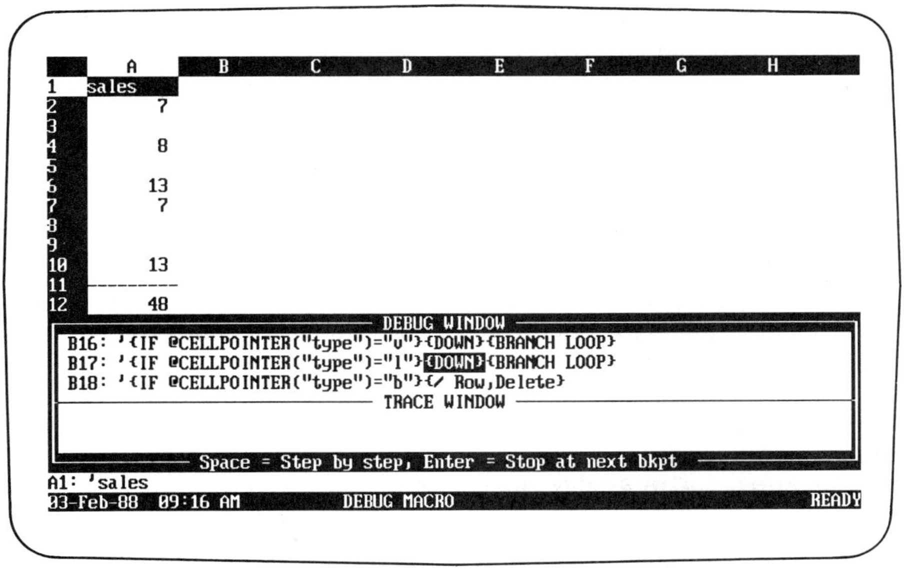

Fig. 17.5. Including a test for labels.

As soon as you press the space bar again, the spreadsheet's cell selector moves down to cell A2, and the debug cursor moves to the {BRANCH LOOP} instruction.

As the macro proceeds and the cell selector eventually moves to a blank cell, the first two IF statements evaluate as false, so the macro is single-stepped down to the third IF statement, which tests to see whether the cell is blank. The result of this evaluation is true, so the instruction to the immediate right of the IF statement ({/ Row,Delete}) should be performed. Unfortunately, the macro runs out of gas at this point, and no row is deleted. As the debugging session reveals, the Row Delete: prompt appears on-screen, but the **D**elete command is not executed because the line contains no tilde (~) or carriage-return command ({CR}) to complete the row deletion by indicating the current cell as the row to delete.

The next sections continue this macro example and show how the options on the Macro Debugging Menu can simplify the sometimes complex job of fixing macros.

Editing a Macro in DEBUG Mode

A major asset of Quattro is its capability to control and modify macro execution patterns on the fly. Instead of allowing a macro to run its course and then having to restart the macro, you can edit a macro while you are in DEBUG mode.

Suppose that you are debugging the row-deleting macro and have reached the point at which the debug cursor highlights the {/ Row,Delete} portion of the macro's fourth line. When you discover that something is wrong, you can bring up the Macro Debugging Menu by pressing the slash (/) key. Figure 17.6 shows the debugging menu with the Edit a cell selection highlighted.

You choose options from this menu just as you do any other Quattro menu—by typing the first letter of the option or by highlighting the option and pressing Enter. After you choose **E**dit a cell, a prompt appears at the top of the screen. Type the cell you want to repair; in this case, you would enter B18. The contents of that cell then display in the normal editing location at the top of the spreadsheet so that you can edit the macro command. Simply type a ~ at the end of the line to fix this sample macro.

As soon as you press Enter to signify the completion of editing, the macro single-steps to the added tilde in preparation for row deletion. Figure 17.7 shows the revised macro in the debug window, and figure 17.8 shows the results of the row deletion.

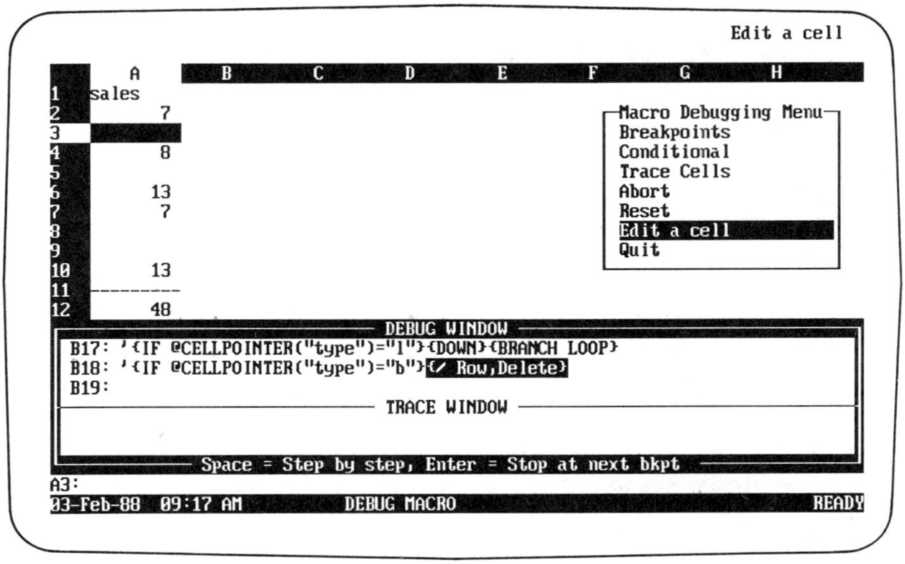

Fig. 17.6. The Macro Debugging Menu.

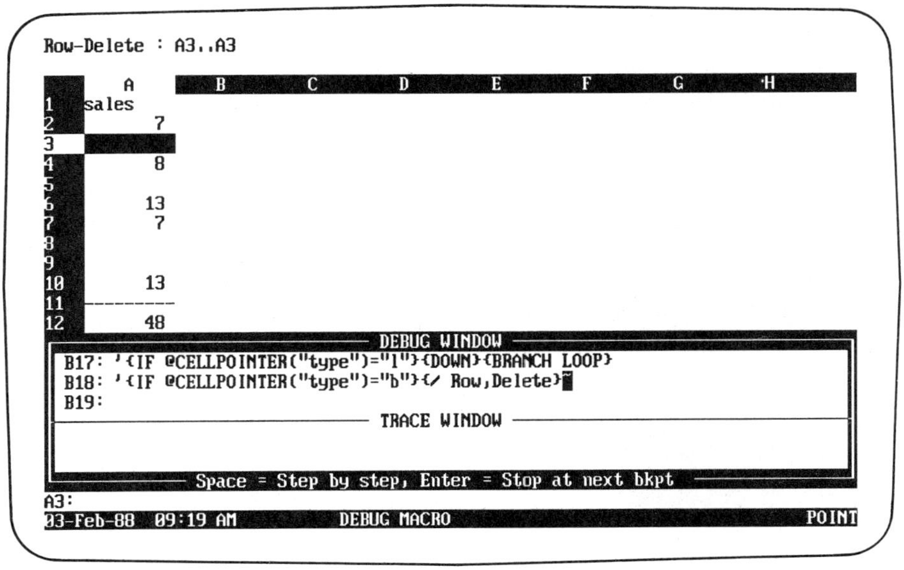

Fig. 17.7. The edited macro.

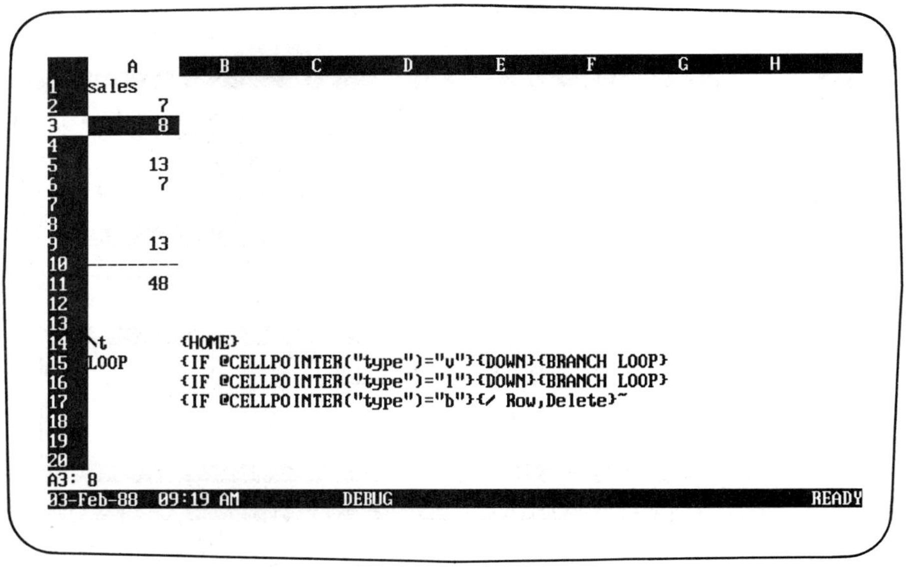

Fig. 17.8. After deleting a row.

The debug session continues to point out shortcomings in the macro. Although the macro successfully removed a blank row, execution stopped immediately after the deletion, leaving many blank rows intact. The solution is to add a BRANCH statement after the **/R**ow **D**elete command, as illustrated in figure 17.9, so that the macro loops back and begins testing the next cell.

Now the macro appears to be in good shape. When you retest the macro in single-step mode, all the empty rows are properly removed, as shown in figure 17.10. Unfortunately, however, the macro is preparing to remove row 11, which is outside the data area and is in fact part of the macro itself. To prevent the row deletion, you must press the slash (/) key to bring up the Macro Debugging Menu and then choose **A**bort.

Now the problem is that the macro doesn't stop when it should. Why isn't it stopping? Because you haven't told it how to quit. You need to provide a flag to signal the macro that the row-deletion process is completed. If you examine the layout of the data, you can see that the row of repeated dashes that precedes the total sales amount can serve as such a flag.

As shown in cell B17 of figure 17.11, you can use the command

{IF @S(@CELLPOINTER("contents"))="-"}

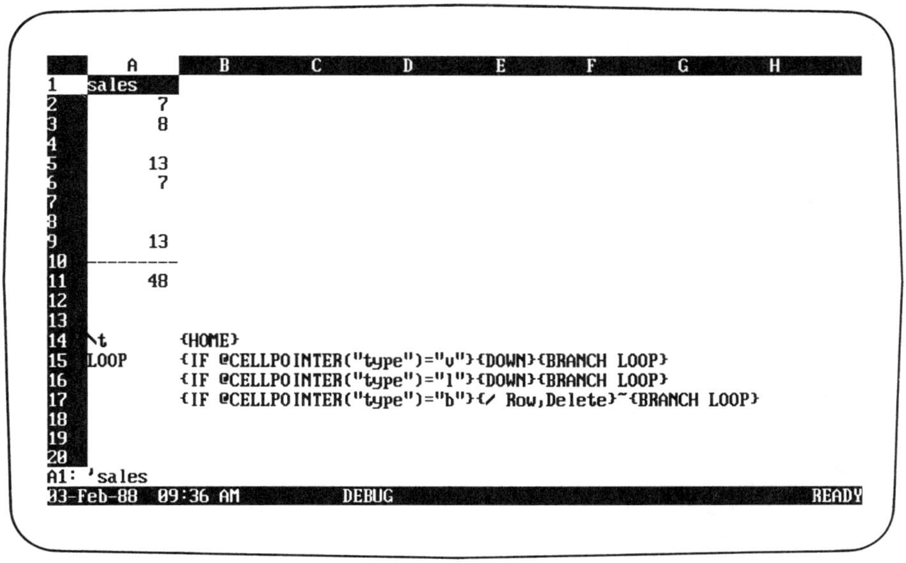

Fig. 17.9. Adding a BRANCH statement to the macro's last line.

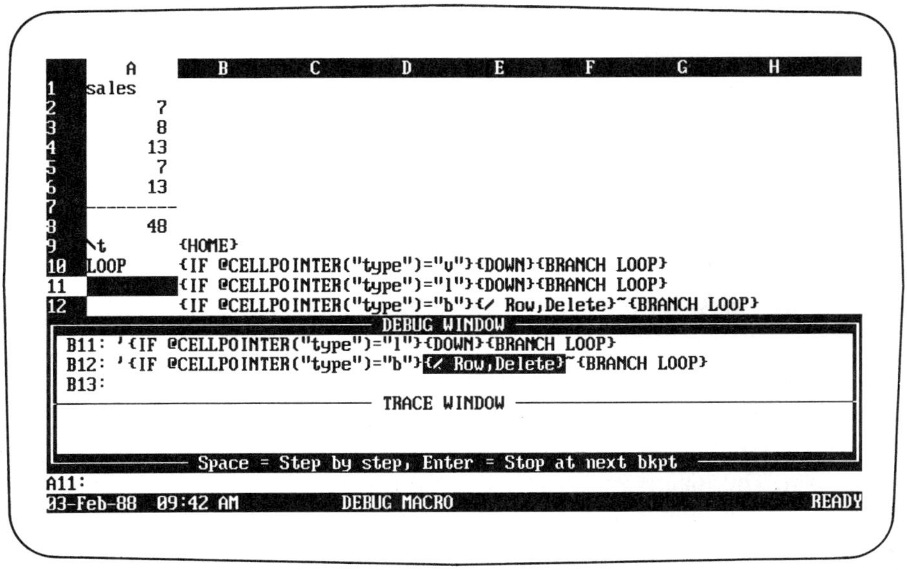

Fig. 17.10. Catching the macro before it destroys itself.

to check for the presence of the repeated dashes. The @S function causes all cells tested by this command to look as if they begin with an apostrophe. Thus even empty cells will be evaluated as text, not values.

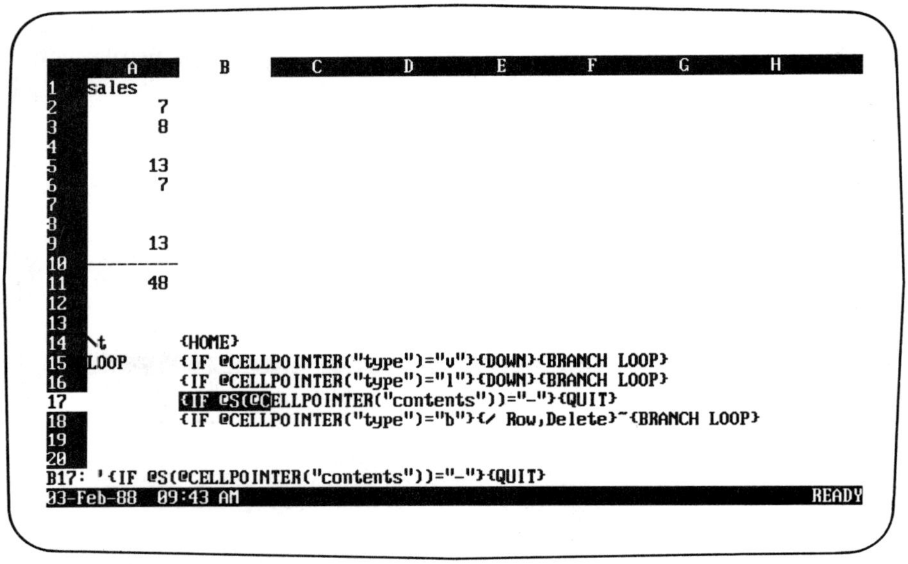

Fig. 17.11. A test for the dashed line to signify the end of the row-deletion process.

As this macro runs and loops, it gets more difficult to fix, because you must press the space bar numerous times to reach the points where problems occur. The next section shows you how to overcome this limitation by using macro breakpoints.

Inserting Macro Breakpoints

Quattro's debugging environment has some flexible methods of temporarily stopping a macro at selected points so that you can assess the macro after a specific condition occurs. For instance, you can tell the macro to pause when it reaches a certain cell. In a long macro, this "breakpoint" is something like a stop sign. The macro can proceed at full speed until it reaches a point at which you determine it needs closer scrutiny. In addition to stopping at cell locations, the debugger can also stop after a macro has looped through itself a specified number of times, called a "pass count."

The sample row-deletion macro is not lengthy, so setting a breakpoint at a particular cell seems unnecessary. Keeping track of the number of times the macro has looped would be more helpful. After the macro has completed a particular number of passes, you can have the macro switch to single-step mode so that you can see what has happened. To illustrate the breakpoint feature, let's set up a pass-count breakpoint for the row-deletion macro.

Suppose that you invoke the macro in DEBUG mode and then press / to call up the Macro Debugging Menu. The first option on this menu is **B**reakpoints. When you choose **B**reakpoints, the following options appear:

1st Breakpoint
2nd Breakpoint
3rd Breakpoint
4th Breakpoint
Quit

After you select **1**st Breakpoint, another menu appears. This menu lets you set the actual breakpoint. The first choice, **B**lock, allows you to specify a cell at which the macro should shift to single stepping. The second choice, **P**ass Count, is the one that you use to indicate how many loops you want the macro to execute before slowing down. When you select **P**ass Count, Quattro displays the prompt `Pass Count (1..240):`, and you must supply a number.

Once you have set a breakpoint (in this case, a pass count), you should press Enter to run the macro. The macro will execute at full speed until it has looped the specified number of times. Figure 17.12 shows the row-deletion macro after it has completed 8 loops (the pass count was set at 8). The macro has stopped just before executing its ninth loop with the {BRANCH LOOP} instruction. Notice that the spreadsheet cell selector is in cell A6, just above the dashes.

Now the macro reverts to single-step mode to allow you to examine the process. Look at figure 17.13. Does the macro work? The IF statement that tests for labels must have prematurely evaluated as true, causing the macro to move to the {DOWN} command. Obviously, the macro will loop before it ever reaches the line containing the {QUIT} command. By running the macro in single-step mode just before the macro was supposed to quit, you can determine that the macro will *never* quit. Instead, the macro is about to move the cell selector down to the next cell in the spreadsheet and begin a new loop.

The problem here is not the commands themselves but the order in which they are executed. As currently designed, the macro first tests for a value, then for a label, then for the dashes, and finally for a blank cell. But the macro statement to test for the series of dashes (and thus the conclusion of the macro) should precede the command that checks for the presence of labels, because a dash is a label and will thus satisfy the label test.

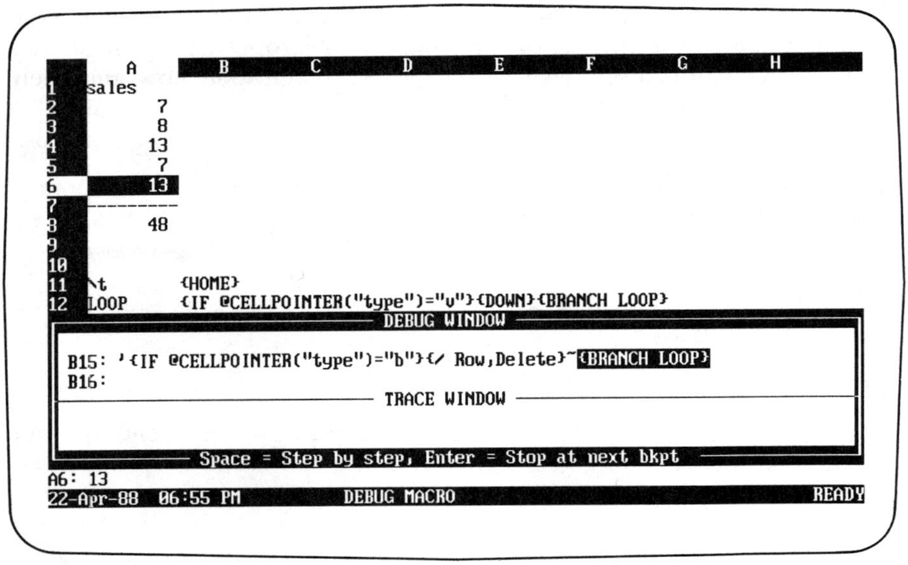

Fig. 17.12. The macro after completing eight loops.

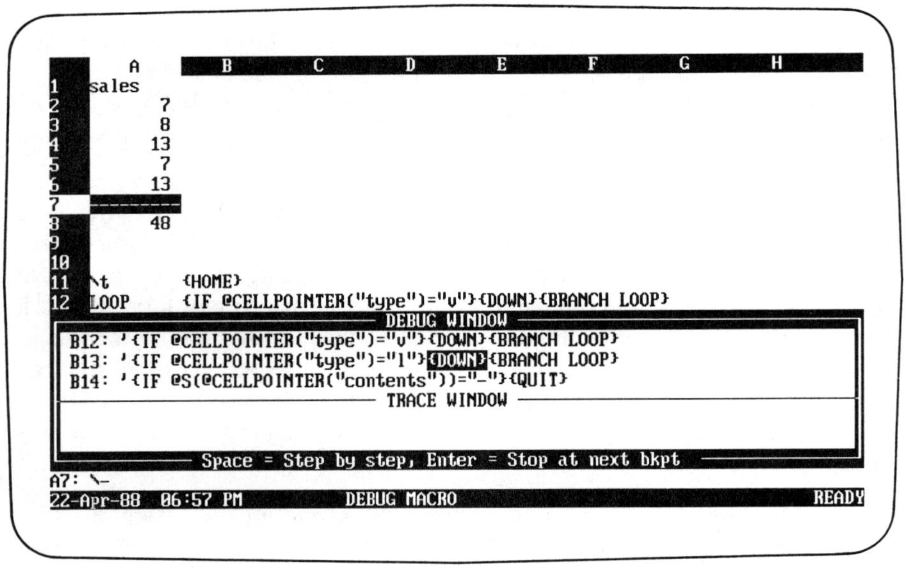

Fig. 17.13. Discovering that the macro will loop again and never quit.

You can fix the macro by simply swapping the two macro statements (the test for labels, and the test for dashes) into each other's cells. Figure 17.14 shows the macro in its final debugged state. The macro is now effectively testing to see whether it should quit. The pass-count capability makes practical and relatively painless the process of debugging long and complex macros.

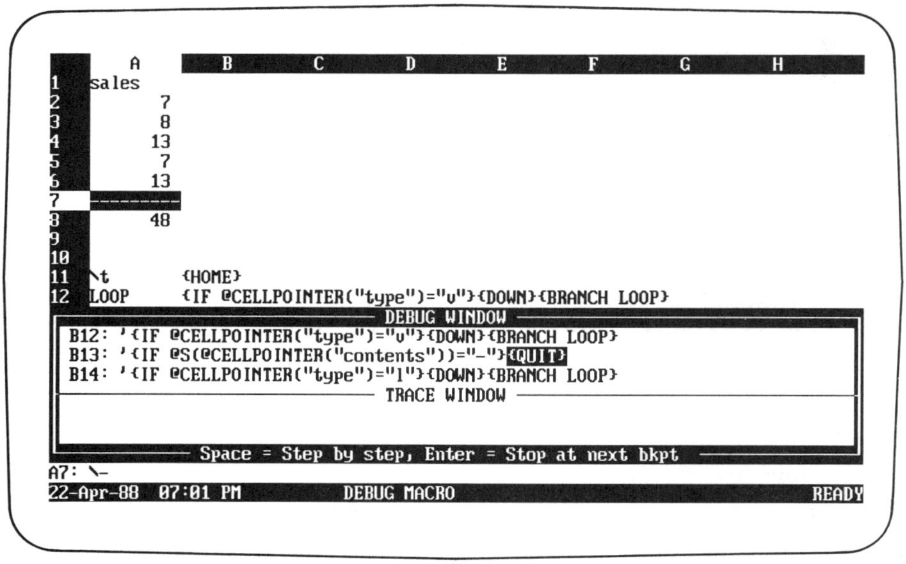

Fig. 17.14. Rearranging the macro commands to halt the macro appropriately.

Testing the Results of Conditional Formulas

Another asset of the macro debugger is its Conditional command, which you activate in DEBUG mode by pressing / and choosing Conditional. This command tests whether a formula in the spreadsheet evaluates as true. When a formula results as true, the debugger shunts the macro to single-step mode. The macro in figure 17.15 prints the number of copies specified by a user in response to the GETNUMBER command. Note that cell C17 contains a logical formula, +COUNTER=5. This formula is what the debug environment will use as its breakpoint. When the counter reaches 5, and the formula is thus true, the macro will slow to single-step.

To use the conditional-test feature of the macro debugger, select Conditional from the Macro Debugging Menu. A prompt then asks you which cell holds the conditional test. In this example, you would respond by typing C17.

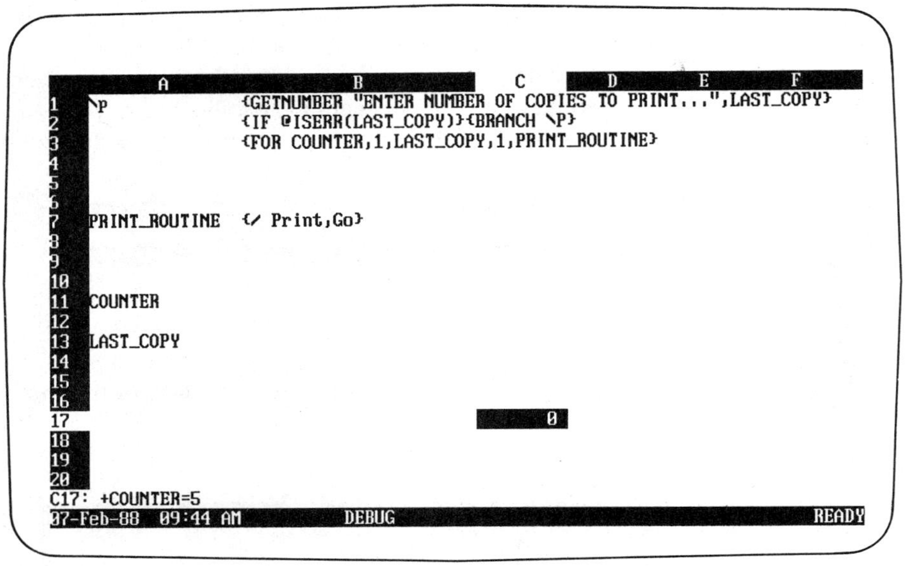

Fig. 17.15. A printing macro.

Keeping Track of Specific Cells

Quattro's debugger also lets you monitor specific cells, called trace cells. Trace cells are those cells that you need to keep an eye on but which may not normally display while the macro executes. For example, suppose that in addition to setting a conditional breakpoint, you want to be able to trace the value of C17 as the macro processes. The bottom half of the debug window is reserved to display trace cells. To set a trace cell, simply select **T**race Cells from the Macro Debugging Menu and indicate which cell you want to monitor (C17 in this case). When you step through the macro in DEBUG mode, the contents of this trace cell display in the bottom half of the debug window, showing what the cell contains at each step of the program.

Now you can run the macro at full speed by pressing Enter. As soon as the conditional cell C17 becomes true, the macro moves to single-step mode. Figure 17.16 shows the state of the spreadsheet and macro immediately after five copies of a report have been printed. Notice that the value of the trace cell in the TRACE window is 1, or true.

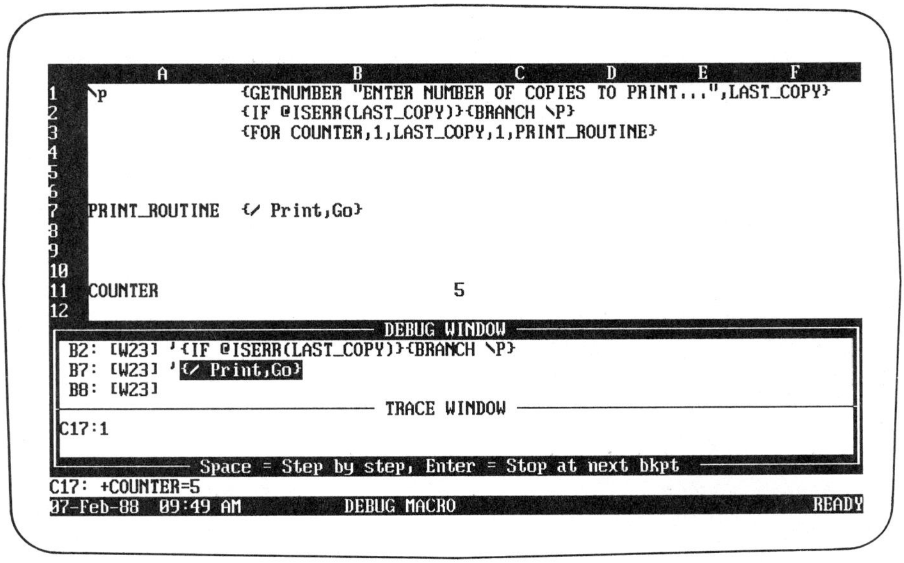

Fig. 17.16. After printing five copies.

You can clear the trace cells, conditional breakpoints, and other debug settings by selecting the **R**eset command from the Macro Debugging Menu, or by choosing /**M**acro **C**lear Breakpoints from the main Quattro menu. To remove individual settings, such as a conditional cell, select that setting from the Macro Debugging Menu and point to an empty cell in the worksheet.

Chapter Summary

In this chapter, you have seen practical examples of what Quattro's macro debugger can do. You have learned how to use the Macro Debugging Menu to edit a macro in DEBUG mode, abort a macro, select breakpoints at which you can halt a macro for a closer look, establish conditional stopping points that depend on the results of certain formulas, and set trace cells that you can monitor during macro execution. You can have as many as four conditional cells, four trace cells, and four breakpoints to assist you in monitoring and debugging macro processing. Quattro's macro debugger is one of the most effective spreadsheet development environments available. The more you use this handy feature, the more you will wonder how you ever got along without it.

APPENDIX

A

Command Reference Tables

In an earlier chapter, you learned about Quattro's menu commands, the tools Quattro provides for performing its tasks. This appendix is designed to help you follow the sequence of Quattro menu commands and to provide you with a complete picture of the complex command structure. Also, for 1-2-3 users converting to Quattro, this appendix will help you come up to speed quickly with Quattro.

Table A.1 lists Quattro's main menu command sequences and provides you with the corresponding 1-2-3 Release 2.0 commands.

Table A.1
Converting Quattro Commands to 1-2-3 2.0 Commands

Quattro Commands	*1-2-3 Commands*
/**B**lock **C**opy	/**C**opy
/**B**lock **M**ove	/**M**ove
/**B**lock **E**rase	/**R**ange **E**rase
/**B**lock **D**isplay_Format	/**R**ange **F**ormat
/**B**lock **L**abel_Align	/**R**ange **L**abel

Quattro Commands	*1-2-3 Commands*
/Block Fill	/Data Fill
/Block Search/Replace	NA
/Block Reformat	/Range Justify
/Block Advanced Values	/Range Value
/Block Advanced Transpose	/Range Transpose
/Block Advanced Protect	/Range Protect
/Block Advanced Unprotect	/Range Unprotect
/Block Advanced Create	/Range Name Create
/Block Advanced Delete	/Range Name Delete
/Block Advanced Labels	/Range Name Labels
/Block Advanced Reset	/Range Name Reset
/Block Advanced Make_Table	/Range Name Table
/Column Insert	/Worksheet Insert Column
/Column Delete	/Worksheet Delete Column
/Column Width	/Worksheet Column Set_Width
/Column Reset	/Worksheet Column Reset_Width
/Column Hide	/Worksheet Column Hide
/Column Expose	/Worksheet Column Display
/Column Set_Global	/Worksheet Global Column_Width
/Row Insert	/Worksheet Insert Row
/Row Delete	/Worksheet Delete Row
/Erase	/Worksheet Erase
/File Retrieve	/File Retrieve
/File Save	/File Save
/File Combine	/File Combine
/File Import ASCII	/File Import Text
/File Import Comma	/File Import Numbers
/File Xtract Formulas	/File Xtract Formulas
/File Xtract Values	/File Xtract Values
/File Erase	/File Erase
/File Directory	/File Directory
/File Parse Create	/Data Parse Format_Line Create
/File Parse Edit	/Data Parse Format Edit
/File Parse Input	/Data Parse Input_Column
/File Parse Output	/Data Parse Output_Range
/File Parse Go	/Data Parse Go
/File Parse Reset	/Data Parse Reset
/File OS	/System
/Graph Graph_Type Line	/Graph Type Line
/Graph Graph_Type Bar	/Graph Type Bar
/Graph Graph_Type XY	/Graph Type XY

Quattro Commands	*1-2-3 Commands*
/**G**raph **G**raph_Type **S**tacked_Bar	/**G**raph **T**ype **S**tacked_Bar
/**G**raph **G**raph_Type **P**ie	/**G**raph **T**ype **P**ie
/**G**raph **G**raph_Type **3**-D_Bar	NA
/**G**raph **G**raph_Type **A**rea	NA
/**G**raph **G**raph_Type **R**otated_Bar	NA
/**G**raph **G**raph_Type **M**arkers	NA
/**G**raph **G**raph_Type **C**ombined	NA
/**G**raph **X**-Axis_Values	/**G**raph **X**
/**G**raph **S**eries_Values	/**G**raph **A B C D E F**
/**G**raph **T**itles	/**G**raph **O**ptions **T**itles
/**G**raph **C**ustomize	/**G**raph **O**ptions
/**G**raph **R**eset	/**G**raph **R**eset
/**G**raph **N**ame	/**G**raph **N**ame
/**G**raph **P**rint **P**rinters	NA (Printgraph Program)
/**G**raph **P**rint **D**estination	/**G**raph **S**ave
/**G**raph **V**iew	/**G**raph **V**iew
/**M**acro **N**ame	/**R**ange **N**ame **C**reate
/**M**acro **D**elete	/**R**ange **N**ame **D**elete
/**M**acro **E**xecute	NA (Add-In Mgr)
/**M**acro **C**lear_Breakpoints	NA
/**M**acro **L**oad	NA (Add-In Mgr)
/**M**acro **R**un	NA (Add-In Mgr)
/**M**acro **U**nload	NA (Add-In Mgr)
/**P**rint **B**lock	/**P**rint **P**rinter **R**ange
/**P**rint **L**eft_Heading	/**P**rint **P**rinter **B**order **C**olumns
/**P**rint **T**op_Heading	/**P**rint **P**rinter **B**order **R**ows
/**P**rint **D**estination **F**ile	/**P**rint **F**ile
/**P**rint **D**estination **P**rinter	/**P**rint **P**rinter
/**P**rint **P**age_Layout **H**eader	/**P**rint **P**rinter **O**ptions **H**eader
/**P**rint **P**age_Layout **F**ooter	/**P**rint **P**rinter **O**ptions **F**ooter
/**P**rint **P**age_Layout **B**reak_Pages	/**P**rint **P**rinter **O**ptions **O**ther **U**nformatted
/**P**rint **P**age_Layout **M**argins	/**P**rint **P**rinter **O**ptions **M**argins
/**P**rint **P**age_Layout **C**reate_Break	/**W**orksheet **P**age
/**P**rint **P**age_Layout **S**etup_String	/**P**rint **P**rinter **O**ptions **S**etup
/**P**rint **P**age_Layout **U**pdate	/**F**ile **S**ave
/**P**rint **F**ormat	/**P**rint **P**rinter **O**ptions
/**P**rint **A**djust_Printer **S**kip_Line	/**P**rint **P**rinter **L**ine
/**P**rint **A**djust_Printer **F**orm_Feed	/**P**rint **P**rinter **P**age
/**P**rint **A**djust_Printer **A**lign	/**P**rint **P**rinter **A**lign

Quattro Commands	*1-2-3 Commands*
/Print Reset	/Print Printer Clear
/Print Go	/Print Printer Go
/Layout Titles	/Worksheet Titles
/Layout Windows	/Worksheet Window
/Layout Descriptor_Line	NA
/Default Hardware Text_Printer	/Worksheet Global Default Printer
/Default Hardware Screen	NA
/Default Colors	NA
/Default International	/Worksheet Global Default Other International
/Default Formats Display	/Worksheet Global Format
/Default Formats Align	/Worksheet Global Label_Prefix
/Default Formats Hide_Zeros	/Worksheet Global Zero No
/Default Formats Width_Of_Col	/Worksheet Global Column_Width
/Default Formats Clock	/Worksheet Global Default Other Clock
/Default Directories Resource	/Worksheet Global Default Resource_Directory
/Default Directories Data	/Worksheet Global Default Directory
/Default Recalculation	/Worksheet Global Recalculation
/Default Protection	/Worksheet Global Protection
/Default Startup	/Worksheet Global Default Other
/Default Update	/Worksheet Global Default Update
/Advanced Database Sort	/Data Sort
/Advanced Database Query	/Data Query
/Advanced Database Form_Input	/Range Input
/Advanced What-if	/Data Table
/Advanced Regression	/Data Regression
/Advanced Frequency	/Data Distribution
/Advanced Matrix	/Data Matrix

Table A.2 lists 1-2-3 Release 2.0 main menu command sequences and provides you with the corresponding Quattro commands.

Table A.2
Converting 1-2-3 2.0 Commands to Quattro Commands

1-2-3 Commands	*Quattro Commands*
/Worksheet Global Format	/Default Formats Display
/Worksheet Global Label_Prefix	/Default Formats Align

1-2-3 Commands	*Quattro Commands*
/Worksheet Global Column_Width	/Default Formats Width_Of_Col
/Worksheet Global Recalculation	/Default Recalculation
/Worksheet Global Protection	/Default Protection
/Worksheet Global Default Printer	/Default Hardware Text_Printer
/Worksheet Global Default Directory	/Default Directories Data
/Worksheet Global Default Resource_Directory	/Default Directories Resource
/Worksheet Global Default Status	/Default Startup
/Worksheet Global Default Update	/Default Update
/Worksheet Global Default Other	/Default
/Worksheet Global Zero	/Default Formats Hide_Zeros
/Worksheet Insert Column	/Column Insert
/Worksheet Insert Row	/Row Insert
/Worksheet Delete Column	/Column Delete
/Worksheet Delete Row	/Row Delete
/Worksheet Column Set_Width	/Column Width
/Worksheet Column Reset_Width	/Column Reset
/Worksheet Column Hide	/Column Hide
/Worksheet Column Display	/Column Expose
/Worksheet Erase	/Erase
/Worksheet Titles	/Layout Titles
/Worksheet Window	/Layout Windows
/Worksheet Status	/Default Hardware
/Worksheet Page	/Print Page_Layout Create_Break
/Range Format	/Block Display_Format
/Range Label	/Block Label_Align
/Range Erase	/Block Erase
/Range Name Create	/Block Advanced Create
/Range Name Delete	/Block Advanced Delete
/Range Name Labels	/Block Advanced Labels
/Range Name Reset	/Block Advanced Reset
/Range Name Table	/Block Advanced Make_Table
/Range Justify	/Block Reformat
/Range Protect	/Block Advanced Protect
/Range Unprotect	/Block Advanced Unprotect
/Range Input	/Advanced Database Form_Input
/Range Value	/Block Advanced Values
/Range Transpose	/Block Advanced Transpose
/Copy	/Block Copy
/Move	/Block Move

1-2-3 Commands	*Quattro Commands*
/File Retrieve	/File Retrieve
/File Save	/File Save
/File Combine	/File Combine
/File Xtract	/File Xtract
/File Erase	/File Erase
/File List	NA (automatic with /F choices)
/File Import Text	/File Import ASCII
/File Import Numbers	/File Import Comma
/File Directory	/Default Directories Data
/Print Printer Range	/Print Block
/Print Printer Line	/Print Adjust_Printer Skip_Line
/Print Printer Page	/Print Adjust_Printer Form_Feed
/Print Printer Options Header	/Print Page_Layout Header
/Print Printer Options Footer	/Print Page_Layout Footer
/Print Printer Options Margins	/Print Page_Layout Margins
/Print Printer Options Borders Columns	/Print Left_Heading
/Print Printer Options Borders Rows	/Print Top_Heading
/Print Printer Options Setup	/Print Page_Layout Setup_String
/Print Printer Options Pg_Length	/Print Page_Layout Margins Page_Length
/Print Printer Options Other Cell_Formulas	/Print Format Cell_Formulas
/Print Printer Options Other Unformatted	/Print Page_Layout Break_Pages No
/Print Printer Clear	/Print Reset
/Print Printer Align	/Print Adjust_Printer Align
/Print Printer Go	/Print Go
/Print File	/Print Destination File
/Graph Type	/Graph Graph_Type
/Graph X	/Graph X-Axis_Values
/Graph A	/Graph Series_Values 1st_Series
/Graph Reset	/Graph Reset
/Graph View	/Graph View
/Graph Save	/Graph Print Write_EPS/Pic
/Graph Options Legend	/Graph Customize Series Legends
/Graph Options Format	/Graph Customize
/Graph Options Titles	/Graph Titles
/Graph Options Grid	/Graph Customize Grids
/Graph Options Scale X_Scale	/Graph Customize X-Axis Scale

1-2-3 Commands	*Quattro Commands*
/**G**raph **O**ptions **C**olor	/**G**raph **C**ustomize **C**olors
/**G**raph **O**ptions **B**&W	/**G**raph **C**ustomize **C**olors
/**G**raph **O**ptions **D**ata_Labels	/**G**raph **C**ustomize **S**eries **I**nterior_Labels
/**G**raph **N**ame	/**G**raph **N**ame
/**D**ata **F**ill	/**B**lock **F**ill
/**D**ata **T**able	/**A**dvanced **W**hat-if
/**D**ata **S**ort	/**A**dvanced **D**atabase **S**ort
/**D**ata **Q**uery	/**A**dvanced **D**atabase **Q**uery
/**D**ata **D**istribution	/**A**dvanced **F**requency
/**D**ata **M**atrix	/**A**dvanced **M**atrix
/**D**ata **R**egression	/**A**dvanced **R**egression
/**D**ate **P**arse	/**F**ile **P**arse
/**S**ystem	/**F**ile **OS**

APPENDIX

B

Installation

Installing Quattro is an extremely easy process because most of the work is done automatically by the program. When you call up Quattro for the first time, the program configures itself to your computer system. Quattro determines and adjusts itself to your system's memory, screen display, and other components. You need only tell the program what printer you're using (see Chapter 9, "Printing Professional Reports").

This appendix presents the basic steps necessary to prepare to load and run Quattro, but does not discuss the default settings that Quattro makes automatically. To alter the default settings, see Chapter 13, "How To Make Quattro Look and Work the Way You Want."

Installing Quattro on a Hard Disk

To run Quattro from a hard disk system, simply copy the files from the four Quattro disks onto a subdirectory of your choice on your hard disk. For example, to install Quattro on a subdirectory named QUATTRO, type the following from the root directory of the C drive:

md quattro

Press Enter and then type

cd quattro

and press Enter again.

Insert the Quattro System Disk in drive A and type

copy a:.* c:*

Press Enter.

Repeat this procedure for the three remaining disks. To run Quattro, type *cd \quattro* and press Enter; then type *q* and press Enter again.

Installing Quattro on a Floppy Disk System

To install Quattro on a floppy disk system, you first prepare working copies of your Quattro disks, then copy the DOS file COMMAND.COM to the working copy of the Help disk, and finally proceed through the brief installation procedure.

Preparing Working Copies of the Quattro Disks

Working copies are disks that are duplicates of your original Quattro disks; you use the working copies and store your master disks in a safe place. If you intend to run Quattro on a floppy disk system, you should first make working copies of each of the four Quattro disks.

To make a working copy of your Quattro disks, first format four new disks. Insert a new disk in the A drive and then type the following at the A> prompt:

format a:

Press Enter.

Follow the screen prompts to format each of the four new disks.

To copy the Quattro program to your new working copies, put a Quattro disk in drive A and a newly-formatted disk in drive B and type

copy a:.* b:*

Press Enter.

Repeat this procedure for the other three disks. You can then use your copies to install and run Quattro.

To be able to access DOS from within the Quattro program, you need to copy COMMAND.COM from your DOS disk to the Quattro Help Disk. With your DOS disk in drive A and a backup copy of the Quattro Help Disk in drive B, type *a:* and press Enter. Then type

copy command.com b:

Press Enter. To access DOS from within Quattro, use the /**F**ile **OS** command while the Help disk containing COMMAND.COM is in drive A.

The Floppy Disk Installation Procedure

To install the Quattro program for use on your floppy disk drive system, put your backup Help Disk in drive A and your backup Resource Disk in drive B. At the A> prompt type

floppy

and press Enter.

Press any key to begin the installation procedure. Quattro will prompt you to approve screen and menu selections. After you press Y to confirm your selections, the setup procedure is complete. You are ready to run Quattro. Put your backup System Disk in drive A and your backup Resource disk in drive B; type *qf* and press Enter, and start working with Quattro.

Index

!SQZ!, 28, 321-323, 516
  Turner Hall Publishing, 322
  versions, 322
character in headers and footers, 349
* character, 304, 313
  in criteria table, 451-452
  in format lines, 327
  to mark hidden columns, 344
+/- format, 142
{ character macro command, 551
{} characters in macro commands, 548-549, 572
| character in headers and footers, 349
|| character, 342-343
  for printing, 355
} character macro command, 551
~ character
  in criteria table, 451-452
  in macros, 548, 572
  macro command, 551
1-2-3
  Command Language, 571
  files in Quattro, 298
  compatibility with Quattro, 8
  menu, 45
    switching with Quattro menu, 81
  Quattro acting like, 45-46
  Quattro compatibility with, 516
1-2-3.ALT file, 45
  menu, 518
123.RSC
  file, 45
  menu, 518
1st_Printer menu, 412
2nd_Printer menu, 412
3-dimensional-bar graph, 395,, 404
  selecting data series, 373
? character, 304, 313
  in criteria table, 451-452
? macro command, 562-563
@
  character in headers and footers, 349
  functions, 13, 55-56
@@ function, 240-242
  quick entry lister, 158

A

ABS
  function, 191
  macro command, 550
absolute references, 16, 97-105
  in extracting, 320
absolute value of number, 191
accelerator keys, 80-81
  Ctrl-A, 81
  Ctrl-M, 81
  Ctrl-Q, 81
  Ctrl-R, 81
  Ctrl-S, 81
ACOS function, 288-289
add (+) math operator, 159
add-in programs, 523-525
  Menu Builder, 523, 527-537
  Quattro menu commands for running, 524
  Transcript, 437, 523-545
add-in software, 29-30
  automatic customizing, 517
ADDIN macro command, 550
adding multiple cells, 171
Addition (+) mathematical operator, 53
addressing cells, 52, 72, 97-105
advanced commands, 21-23
Advanced Database command, 423
Advanced Database Form_Input command, 427-429
Advanced Database Query Assign_Names command, 452
Advanced Database Query Block command
  specifying search block, 442
Advanced Database Query
  command, 22, 41, 440-441
  menu, 440-441
Advanced Database Query Criteria_Table command, 443
Advanced Database Query Extract command, 447-450
  defining
    criteria table, 447-448
    output block, 447-448
  F7 shortcut, 454
  speeding execution, 449
Advanced Database Query Formula_Criterion command, 445, 460

Advanced Database Query Locate command, 22
Advanced Database Query Unique command, 22, 476-479
Advanced Database Sort Block command, 434
Advanced Database Sort
 command, 431-433
 menu, 434-436
Advanced Frequency command, 483-484
 bins block, 483-484
 block of intervals, 483-484
 values block, 483-484
advanced functions, *See advanced spreadsheet functions*
Advanced Matrix command, 23, 465, 486-487
Advanced Matrix Invert command, 486-487
 time required, 487
Advanced Matrix Multiply command, 487
Advanced menu, 423
Advanced Regression command, 23, 465, 484-486
advanced spreadsheet functions, 227-294, *See also spreadsheet functions, and Quattro functions*
 database statistical, 243-250
 engineering, 285-290
 programmers', 291-292
 statistical, 180-184
 special macro-related, 274-285
 table and array-handling, 227-242
 text, 250-274
 trigonometric, 285-290
Advanced What-If 1_Variable command, 471-473
 input cell, 479
Advanced What-If 2_Variables command, 471-476
Advanced What-If command, 23, 117, 471-481
alphanumeric keys, 35-36
Alt key, 24-25, 35
 to start macro, 559
Alt-F (Record), 554
Alt-F1 (Previous) key, 37
Alt-F3 (Functions) key, 38, 158
Alt-F7 (Table) key, 38
Alt-F8 (Record) key, 38
analysis
 what-if, 12, 20
annuity
 term of, 211-212
Apple LaserWriter printer, 412
area graph
 creating, 399-400
 selecting data series, 374
 uses, 395
arguments
 database functions, 466-467
 displaying necessary for functions, 158
 functions, 156-157
 in macro commands, 572-573
 in macro key-equivalent commands, 549
 separating, 502
ascending order database sorts, 433
ASCII
 printer codes, 353-356
 files
  importing to Quattro, 323-325
  macros to work with, 613-620
ASIN function, 288-289
ATAN function, 288-289
ATAN2 function, 288-289
auto-execute macro, 516, 564
AUTODETECT drivers, 492
autoload file
 changing name, 515
 QUATTRO.WKQ, 515
averaging numbers, 171-173
AVG function, 171-173

B

backslash (\) key, 58
BACKSPACE (BS) macro command, 550
Backspace key, 35, 113
bar graph, 386
 creating comparative, 400-402
 horizontal, 142
 negative scale values, 387
 selecting data series, 373
 uses, 394
BASIC, 571
 programs importing to Quattro, 323
baud rates
 choosing for printing graph, 412
 specifying, 362-363
beep turning off, 516
BEEP macro command, 601-602
Below_Normal_Color menu, 150
BIGLEFT macro command, 551
BIGRIGHT macro command, 551
bins block, *See also frequency distributions*
 Block Fill command to create, 483
blank cell in macro, 588
BLANK macro command, 591
Block Advanced Unprotect command, 127
Block Advanced Create command, 84-86
Block Advanced Labels command, 84-86
Block Advanced Labels Right command, 567
Block Advanced Make_Table command, 91
Block Advanced Protect command, 18, 118
Block Advanced Reset command, 89
Block Advanced Transpose command, 106, 108
Block Advanced Unprotect command, 118, 514
Block Advanced Values command, 106, 108, 189, 273, 450
Block Column Width command, 426
Block command, 16, 63
 menu, 58, 84
Block Copy command, 16-17, 27, 54, 58, 93-101, 106, 108, 120, 330, 448

Block Display Format Hidden command, 18
Block Display-Format Text command, 472
Block Display_Form command, 426
Block Display_Format command, 135-136, 139, 141, 153, 330
Block Display_Format Date command, 144
Block Display_Format Date Time command, 144
Block Display_Format Hidden command, 146, 344
Block Display_Format Reset command, 146, 344
Block Display_Format Text command, 453
Block Erase command, 16, 89, 113, 127, 450
- macro equivalent, 591
- recovering block with Transcript, 540-541

Block Fill command, 114, 116-118, 151
- creating bins block, 483
- table building, 471

block formats, 136
Block Label_Align command, 58-59, 138
Block Move command, 108-113, 120
- compared to File Xtract Formulas, 320

block names, 52, 72
- database searches, 441
- in database functions, 469
- in key-equivalent command arguments, 549
- in macros, 565-578, 583
  - DEFINE command, 595

block of cells
- assigning formats to, 16
- copying to another place on worksheet, 94-95
- hiding, 18

block of intervals, *See bins block*
Block Reformat command, 136, 147-150, 162-163, 165, 167, 169
Block Search/Replace menu, 62-63
blocks, 75, 82-91
- copying values from, 106-108
- creating table of names, 91
- defining, 82-83
- deleting names, 89
- destination, 93-94
- erasing, 89
- excluding from printing, 344
- filling with numbers, 114, 117-118
- hiding, 344
- listing names, 89, 91
- naming, 3, 16, 84-89, 91
  - with labels, 85
- pointing to
  - with End key, 113-116
  - with expanding cell selector, 111-113
- resetting to default setting, 146
- setup strings for, 355
- source, 93-94

borders printing on spreadsheet, 351
braces ({})in macro commands, 548-549
BRANCH macro command, 573-580, 583, 588
BREAKOFF macro command, 601-603
BREAKON macro command, 601-603
breakpoints in macros, 630-633
built-in subroutines, 155

C

CALC
- macro command, 550
- status indicator, 42

concatenation string in macro, 597
Caps Lock key, 41
CAPS status indicator, 42
cards, graphics, 26
cash flows, 201-203
CD command, 32
cell addresses, 72
- in macros, 572

cell attributes table, 276
cell contents, 357
CELL function, 276-278
cell pointer, *See cell selector*
cell references
- absolute, 16, 97-105
- mixed, 98-105
- relative, 16, 97-105

cell selector, 9, 69
- moving in macros, 572
- scrolling, 9

CELLINDEX function, 278-279
CELLPOINTER function, 276-278
cells, 9, 82-83
- addressing, 52, 97-105
- assign formats to block, 16
- block names, 52
- conditional colors, 150-151
- copying
  - to block of cells, 93
  - contents, 91-97
  - entries, 16-17
- current, 40
- formats global, 504
- formatting
  - contents, 135-153
  - problems, 151-153
- hiding contents, 146
- highlighting, 50, 82-83
- largest numerical value in given block, 176-180
- mathematical relationships between, 10, 12
- moving contents, 108-111
- printing list of contents, 357
- protecting, 18
  - contents, 118-119
- replicating, 58
- smallest numerical value in given block, 178-180
- tracing in macros, 634-635

centering text in headers and footers, 349
CHAR function, 272-273

characters
  label-prefix, 57-59
  special in headers and footers, 349
  wild-card, 22
checkpoints in Transcript Command History window, 539
child menus, 527
  creating with Menu Builder, 537
CHOOSE function, 228-229
CIRC status indicator, 42
circular references, 507-513
CLEAN function, 272
CLOSE macro command, 613-616
CODE function, 274
colors
  choosing for printed graphs, 414
  customizing, 494-502
    conditional cells, 499-501
    help screens, 501-502
    menu boxes, 497-498
    overall, 497-498
    palettes, 496-497
    spreadsheet, 498-499
  graphics display, 20
  legend, 20
Colors menu, 414
COLS function, 280
Column Delete command, 122, 125, 127, 343, 430
Column Expose command, 120, 344
column headings
  in translation, 307
  printing, 350-351
Column Hide command, 120-122, 146, 343
Column Insert command, 21, 122-123, 430
Column Reset command, 119-120
Column Set_Global command, 120
Column Width command, 119-120, 141
column width
  adjusting databases', 425
  overflow, 505
  setting, 119, 505
columns, 9, 119-127
  database functions, 466-467
  deleting, 122, 124-127
  excluding from printing, 343-344
  hiding, 120-122
  inserting, 122-124
  transposing, 106-108
columnwise recalculation, 507, 509-510
combined-lines-and-markers graph, *See lines & markers graph*
comma (,)
  format, 142
  function separator character, 156
  importing delimited files, 323-325
Command History window, 539-540
  checkpoints, 539
commands, *See also Quattro commands*
  advanced, 21-23
  database, 21-23
  file, 18
  inserting new in menu, 532-534
  macro, 23-24
  menu, 75-127
  multiple regression, 14
  pointing to, 76-77
  spreadsheet, 15-19, 82-134
  typing first letter of, 76-77
  undoing selection of, 78
comparison operators
  equal (=), 159
  greater than (>), 159
  greater than or equal to (>=), 159
  less than (<), 159
  less than or equal to (<=), 159
  logical AND (#AND#), 159, 193
  logical inclusive OR (#OR#), 159, 193
  logical NOT (#NOT#), 159, 193
  not equal (<>), 159
  spreadsheet functions, 159
Compatibility Options menu, 519-520
  Confirm Option window, 519-520
    Borland_Style, 520
    Macro_Recording, 520
  Menus Option window, 519-520
    Keep_Wide, 519, 520
    Remember, 520
compiling formulas, 162-165
compressing
  files, 321-323
  print, 354
concatenation with WRITE macro command, 618
conditional
  cell colors, 150-151
  formulas testing in macros, 633
Conditional colors menu, 499-501
CONTENTS macro command, 591-593
  numeric format codes, 592
continuous-feed paper, 345-346
copying
  block of cells to another place on worksheet, 94-95
  cell entries, 16-17
  cell to block of cells, 93
  contents of cells, 91-97
  values from one block to another, 106, 108
COS function, 287-288
COUNT function, 173-175
CR macro command, 548, 551, 572
  following pause command, 563
criteria table
  cell references in, 468
  changing, 469
  compound conditions, 454-460
  database functions, 466-467
  defining, 442-443
  field names in, 443
  formulas, 468

wild-card characters, 451-452
CTERM function, 211-212
Ctrl-*key* combinations, 80
Ctrl-A accelerator key, 81
Ctrl-Break
disabling in macro, 602-603
to stop printing, 338
Ctrl-D keys, 14, 143-144, 214-215, 424-425
Ctrl-M accelerator key, 81
Ctrl-Q accelerator key, 81
Ctrl-R accelerator key, 81
Ctrl-S accelerator key, 81
Currency format, 141
Currency international option, 502
current
ell, 40
graph setting for printing, 414-416
settings, 492
time and date, 221-223
cursor, 69
movement, 34-35
keys, 36-37, 69-72
table, 70
CURVALUE function, 281
customizing Quattro, 491-494
add-ins, 517
colors, 494-502
conditional cells, 499-501
help screens, 501-502
palettes, 496-497
column width, 505
default directories, 506
formats, 503-504
graph
colors, 398
display, 384-386
legends, 383
patterns, 398-399
hardware
defaults, 492
screen, 493-494
help access, 517
international conventions, 502
label alignment, 504
menu tree, 517-519
recalculation, 507-508
retaining changes, 492-493
screen, 493-494
resolution, 494
startup, 514-516
suppressing display of zeros, 504-505
user interface, 517-519

D

dangling space, 168
data
editing in worksheet, 59-62
entering
by pointing, 52
by typing, 52
in database, 426-427
in worksheet, 50-59
search and replace, 62-68
selecting for graphs, 370, 373-374
sorting, 21-23
data analysis commands
/Advanced Frequency, 483-484
/Advanced Matrix, 465, 486-487
/Advanced Matrix Invert, 486-487
/Advanced Matrix Multiply, 487
/Advanced Regression, 465, 484-486
/Advanced What-If, 471-481
/Advanced What-If 1_Variable, 471-473, 479
/Advanced What-If 2_Variables, 471, 473-476
data directories, 314, 506
database commands, 21-23
/Advanced Database, 423
/Advanced Database Form_Input, 427-429
/Advanced Database Query, 440-441
/Advanced Database Query Assign_Names, 452
/Advanced Database Query Block, 442
/Advanced Database Query command, 442
/Advanced Database Query Criteria_Table, 443
/Advanced Database Query Extract, 447-450
/Advanced Database Query Formula_Criterion, 445, 460
/Advanced Database Query Unique, 476-479
/Advanced Database Sort, 431-433
/Advanced Database Sort Block, 434
database functions, 22, 465
@DAVG, 468 478-481
@DCOUNT, 468-469
@DMAX, 468-469
@DMIN, 468-469
@DSTD, 468-469
@DSUM, 476, 481
@DVAR, 468-469
@PMT, 472-476
arguments, 466-467
average, 468
block names in, 469
column, 466-467
criteria, 469
criteria table, 466-468
format, 466-467
frequency distributions, 483-484
input block, 466-467
mean, 468
multiple regression, 484-486
offset, 479

preparing output block, 477
standard deviation, 468
statistical, 466-487
syntax, 466-467
table building, 470-481
what-if analysis, 470-481
Database Query command, 38
Database Sort menu, 431-432
database statistical
advanced spreadsheet functions, 243-250
functions table, 244
databases, 419-463
adding
fields, 430
rows, 429
cell selector
limiting movement of, 427-429
creating, 423-429
blank columns to avoid crowding, 426
column widths, 425
entering
data, 426-427
field names, 425-426
existing worksheet, 423
form-input area, 427-429
new worksheet, 423
planning, 424
setting display formats, 426
data retrieval, 439
data types, 425
defined, 420
deleting
fields, 430
rows, 430
editing, 429-431
entering data automatically with macro, 429
extracting
partial records, 450
records, 439
field names, 421
labels, 425
planning, 424
fields, 420
form-input area, 427-429
key fields, 420
labels, 421
limiting access, 427
macro to work with, 598-599
modifying, 429-431
records, 420
searching, 439-463
compound conditions, 454-460
criteria table, 442
defining criteria table, 442-443
deleting records, 462-463
formula criterion, 442
functions, 459
listing specified records, 447-450
minimum requirements, 440-442
numeric fields, 452-454
output block, 441-442
partial fields, 459
referencing cells outside database, 453
relational operators, 452
search block, 442
special operators, 459-460
unique records, 461
wild cards, 451-452
size limitations in Quattro, 421-422
sorting, 431-437
ascending order, 433
descending order, 433
field names, 432
keys, 432-437
one-key sort, 433-434
order, 432-434
primary key, 433-436
restoring presort order, 437
secondary keys, 435-436
sort block, 432
date and time function table, 215-216
Date format, 143-144
table, 144
DATE
function, 143, 216-217
macro command, 551
dates
calculations, 216-217
controlling display, 505
displaying, 144
entering with Ctrl-D, 424-425
from text, 217-218
functions, 14
including in headers and footers, 349
international conventions, 502
number, 220-221
spreadsheet function, 214-225
DATEVALUE function, 143, 217-218
DAVG function, 246-247, 468-469, 479-481
DAY function, 218-219
dBASE III Plus
translating files to Quattro, 306
DBF files, 306-307, 309
DCOUNT function, 248, 468-469
DDB function, 214
DEBUG mode, 622
editing macros in, 626-629
indicator, 41
debug window, 623-624
TRACE window, 623-624
debugger, *See macro debugger*, 621
debugging
formulas, 145, 160-169
functions, 160-169
STEPOFF macro command, 588-589
STEPON macro command, 588-589
decimal points
number of places displayed, 139-140

decompiling formulas, 162-165
Default Autoload command, 515
Default Colors command, 496-499
Default Colors Conditional
command, 499-501
menu, 150
Default Colors Help command, 501-502
Default Colors Menu command, 497-498
Default Colors Palettes command, 499
Default Colors Spreadsheet command, 498-499
Default Directories command, 305, 313-314, 506
default format, 136, 138-139
Default Formats Align command, 59
Default Formats Clock command, 505
Default Formats Clock International command, 505
Default Formats command, 493
Default Formats Display command, 135-136, 138, 140-141, 153, 387, 504
Default Formats Display Date command, 144
Default Formats Display Date Time command, 144
Default Formats Display Text command, 55
Default Formats Hide_Zeroes command, 333, 504-505
Default Hardware Screen command, 493-494
Default Hardware Text_Printer command, 337, 347-348, 364
checking printer settings, 360-361
Default Hardware Text_Printer menu, 333
Default International command, 16, 146-147, 502
Default International menu, 502
default label alignment, 57, 59
default menu, 45-46
add-in programs, 525
Default Protection command, 118
Default Protection Disable command, 119
Default Protection Enable command, 18, 118-119
Default Recalculation
command, 507-508
menu, 513
Default Recalculation Iteration command, 512-513
Default Recalculation Mode command, 508-509
Default Recalculation Order command, 510
Default Set Global Width command, 141
default setting resetting blocks to, 146
Default Startup Autoload command, 564
Default Startup Beep command, 516
Default Startup command, 493, 514-516
Default Startup Compatibility_Options command, 519-520
Default Startup Compatibility_Options Keep_Wide command, 79
Default Startup Default Add-Ins command, 517, 524-525, 538
Default Startup Extension command, 516
compatibility with 1-2-3, 516
Default Startup Help_Access_Method command, 517
for floppy disks, 517
for hard disk users, 517
Default Startup Menu-Tree Switch_Menus command, 81
Default Startup Menu_Tree Alternate_Menus command, 518, 535
Default Startup Menu_Tree Main_Menus command, 518
Default Startup Menu_Tree Switch_Menus Alternate_Menu command, 81
Default Startup Menu_Tree Switch_Menus command, 518-519, 536
Default Startup Menu_Tree Update command, 536
Default Startup Update command, 517-518
Default Update command, 80, 136, 314, 364, 535
defaults
add-in programs, 525
auto-execute macro, 516
autoload file, 515, 564
changing, 314
colors, 494-502
formats, 503-504
print settings, 347-348
printing, 364
checking, 337
customizing startup, 514-516
for 1-2-3, 515
directory, 313-314, 506
graph colors, 414
hardware customizing, 492
international conventions, 502
recalculation, 507-508
restoring
printing graphs, 411
printing, 359
retaining changes, 492-493
setup strings, 353-355
Transcript, 538
updating
for Graph Print, 411
menu changes, 536
Defaults Startup Menu_Tree Alternate_Menu command, 45
DEFINE macro command, 591, 594-595
in subroutine, 585
syntax, 594
defining blocks, 82-83
DEGREES function, 289
Del key, 25, 36
DELETE (DEL) macro command, 551
deleting
columns, 122-127
files, 313
rows, 122, 124-127
dependent variable
multiple regression, 484-486
XY graph, 406
descriptor line, 39-40
in screen dump, 336
destination block, 93-94
Details of Current Item Menu Builder, 533-534
Device menu, 362-363

directories
    changing default, 313-314
    data, 314, 506
    resource, 314, 506
    setting default, 506
    specifying
        for current session, 314
        for file retrieval, 304-306
    types in Quattro, 314
disk full error message, 320
DISPATCH macro command, 573, 575-576
displaying
    dates, 144
    formats setting in database, 426
    formulas, 145
    screen, 39-40
    times, 144
Display_Scaling No option, 388
Division (/) mathematical operator, 53, 159
DMAX function, 248, 468-469
DMIN function, 249, 468-469
DOS
    accessing from Quattro, 320, 321
    commands
        CD, 32
        CHKDSK, 320
        FORMAT, 320
double-declining-balance depreciation, 214
DOWN macro command, 551
draft-quality reports, 333, 337-338
drivers
    AUTODETECT, 492
    printer selecting for graph, 411
drives
    specifying
        for current session, 314
        for file retrieval, 305-306
DSTD function, 249-250, 468-469
DSUM function, 245-246, 476, 481
DVAR function, 250, 468-469

E

EDIT
    macro command, 550
    mode, 51, 54, 59-62, 69, 301, 305
        indicator, 40
        key actions, 59-60
editing
    data in worksheet, 59-62
    formulas, 160-169
    functions, 160-169
End key, 70-72, 77, 113-116
END
    macro command, 551
    status indicator, 42
End-Home keys for reaching macros, 552
end-of-file (EOF) marker, 359
Enhanced Keyboard, 25
Enter key, 43
ENTER macro command, 548
EPS files, 298
EPSON printer, 354
equal (=) comparison operator, 159
Erase command, 127-128
erasing
    blocks, 89
    entire worksheet, 127-128
ERR function, 279-280
error messages, 43
    disk full, 320
ERROR mode indicator, 41
errors
    correcting in formulas, 54-55
    fatal, 582-583
    finding in macros, 624
    run-time, 582-583
    suppressing, 199
    undoing with Transcript, 545
Esc key, 36, 43, 78, 305
    to leave Transcript, 542
ESCAPE (ESC) macro command, 551, 593
EXACT function, 258-259
exiting Quattro, 32
EXP function, 290
expanded
    menus, 78-80
    print, 355
Explanation field in Menu Builder, 532
exploding pie graph, 406
exponential scientific notation, 140
Exponentiation (^) mathematical operator, 53, 159
extensions, *See file extensions*

F

F1 (Help) key, 25, 37, 43, 498
F2 (Edit) key, 25, 37, 50-51, 59-61, 139, 157, 261
F3 (Names) key, 37, 52
F4 (Abs) key, 38, 103-104
F5 (GoTo) key, 38, 72, 84, 88, 91, 131
F6 (Window) key, 38, 132
F7 shortcut for extract operation, 454
F7 (Query) key, 38
F8 (Macro) key, 24, 38, 559
F9 (Calc) key, 17, 38, 139, 322, 508-509, 512
F10 (Graph) key, 25, 38
FALSE function, 198
fatal error
    protecting macro from, 582-583
field names
    database, 421, 432
    entering in database, 425-426
    in criteria table, 443
    in database labels, 425
    planning for database, 424

fields
  adding to database, 430
  database, 420
    searching partial, 459
  deleting from database, 430
  inserting, 21
File !SQZ! command, 321-323
File Combine Add command, 315-318
File Combine command, 315
File Combine Copy command, 315-318, 528
  to bring in macros, 536
  to retrieve macro file, 603
File Combine Subtract command, 315, 318
file commands, 18
File Directory command, 314
File Erase command, 313
file extensions, 298-307
  .DBF, 306-307, 309
  .EPS, 298
  .PIC, 18, 21, 298
  .PRN, 18, 298
  .WKQ, 18, 134, 298, 306
File Import command, 323-325
file manipulation commands, 613-620
  {CLOSE}, 613, 615-616
  {FILESIZE}, 613, 620
  {GETPOS}, 613, 620
  {OPEN}, 613-615
  {READLN}, 613, 617-618
  {READ}, 613, 616-617
  {SETPOS}, 613, 619
  {WRITELN}, 613, 618
  {WRITE}, 613, 618
FILE mode, 305
file names, 298-301
  blank space in, 298
  changing extension, 516
  display, 302
    list of, 299
  editing, 301
  extensions, *See file extensions*
  listed for File Retrieve command, 302
  period in, 298
  special characters in, 298
  wild cards in, 299
File OS commands, 320-321
File Parse command, 41, 325
  format lines, 327-328
    characters, 327
file pointer
  recording position with macro, 620
  setting with macro, 619
File Retrieve command, 81, 134, 299, 302, 304
  after File Xtract, 318-319
  passwords, 312
File Save command, 19, 81, 133, 299, 301, 306, 348, 392
  before deleting records, 463
  passwords, 310, 312
File Xtract command, 88, 307, 318-320
  cell references, 320
File Xtract Formulas command, 318-320
  compared to Block Move, 320
File Xtract Values command, 318-319
FILEEXISTS function, 282-283
files
  1-2-3
    translating to Quattro, 306
    in Quattro, 298
  1-2-3.ALT, 45
  123.RSC, 45
  ASCII importing to Quattro, 323-325
  autoload, 564
  backup copies, 301
  combining, 314-318
    File Combine, 315
  comma delimited, 323-325
  compressing, 321-323, 516
  dBASE translating to Quattro, 306-307, 309
  deleting, 313
  extracting, 318-320
    absolute references, 320
    relative references, 320
  importing, 323-325
    ASCII, 323-325
    BASIC, 323
    comma delimited, 323-325
    PRN, 323
    to Quattro, 18
  managing, 297-330
  naming, 298-301
    when saving, 301
  NOVICE.RSC, 45
  Paradox translating to Quattro, 310
  parsing, 325-330
  password-protected, 19
  PRN, 331, 359
    graphs, 416
  protecting with passwords, 18, 310, 312
  QUATTRO.DEF, 80, 314, 504
  QUATTRO.LOG, 538
  QUATTRO.RSC, 45
  QUATTRO.WKQ, 515
  Reflex translating to Quattro, 310
  retrieving, 299, 302, 304-306
  saving, 133-134, 299, 301
    on hard disk, 301
  Symphony in Quattro, 298
  TRANS.QAI, 525
  translating, 297, 306-307, 310
  translator files, 306
FILES mode indicator, 40
FILESIZE macro command, 613, 620
  syntax, 620
Financial format, 142
financial
  functions, 13, 199-214
    table, 200

FIND
function, 251, 253
mode indicator, 41
Fixed format, 139-140
flow control commands, 576-578
{BRANCH}, 573-575
{DISPATCH}, 573, 575
{FORBREAK}, 573, 578
{FOR}, 573, 576-578
{IF}, 573, 578-582
{ONERROR}, 573, 582-583
{QUIT}, 573, 584
{RESTART}, 573, 586
{RETURN}, 573, 587-588
{STEPOFF}, 574, 588-589
{STEPON}, 574, 588-589
{WAIT}, 574, 589-590
footers
centering text in, 349
including date, 349
justifying text in, 349
number of characters, 348-349
printing, 348-350
on last page of document, 346
page numbers, 349
restoring, 359
special characters, 349
suppressing, 356, 359
FOR macro command, 573, 576-578
syntax, 576-578
FORBREAK macro command, 573, 578
syntax, 578
form-input area in database, 427-429
Format command, 141
format lines characters, 327
for parsing files, 327-328
format options table, 137
formats
+/-, 142
block, 136
cell setting global, 504
comma (,), 142
Currency, 141
customizing, 503-504
display of zeros, 504-505
label alignment, 504
Date, 143-144
default, 136, 138-139
display setting in database, 426
Financial, 142
Fixed, 139-140
General, 138-139
Hidden, 146
international, 16, 146-147
Percent, 142-143
Scientific, 51, 140
Text, 145
Time, 143-145
formatting
cell contents, 135-153
problems, 151-153
graphs, 20
numbers macro, 592
text, 147-150
the worksheet, 15
formulas, 10, 12
compiling, 162-165
converting to values, 106-108, 508-509
correcting errors, 54-55
debugging, 145, 160-169
decompiling, 162-165
displaying, 145
editing, 160-169
entering, 51-55
in database searches, 452-454
operators in, 53-54
precedence in operators, 160
string in macro, 598
freezing titles on-screen, 128-131
frequency distributions, 481-484
bins block, 483-484
block of intervals, 483-484
intervals, 483-484
results column, 483
values block, 483-484
FRMT mode indicator, 41
function keys, 37-38, *See also keys*
Alt-F (Record), 554
F1 (Help), 498
F9 (Calc), 322, 508-509, 512
F10 (Graph), 376
function syntax, 156-157
functions
advanced spreadsheet, 227-294
arguments, 156-157
separating, 502
comma (,) separator character, 156
debugging, 160-169
displaying arguments necessary for, 158
editing, 160-169
IF macro command, 579
in database search, 459
in macro, 599
list of, 158
spreadsheet, 155-226
true and false, 193-195
functions key
FUNCTIONS macro command, 550
future value, 206
FV function, 206

G

General format, 138-139
general mathematical functions table, 185

GET macro command, 601, 603-605
compared to pause command, 603
syntax, 603
GETLABEL macro command, 575, 601, 605-606
syntax, 605
GETNUMBER macro command, 580, 601, 606
syntax, 606
GETPOS macro command, 613, 620
syntax, 620
global replace operation, 65-66
Go command, 63-66
GOTO macro command, 550
compared to MENUBRANCH, 609
Graph
command, 19, 370, 374
menu, 369-371, 374-376, 379-382, 398, 402, 405-406
pie graphs, 381-382
XY graph, 382
Graph Customize Colors command, 398
Graph Customize Colors Series command, 383
Graph Customize Grids command, 385-386
Line_Type, 385-386
Graph Customize menu, 392-393
Graph Customize Pies command, 405
Graph Customize Pies Explode command, 406
Graph Customize Pies Label_Format None command, 405
Graph Customize Series Interior_Labels command, 376, 379
Graph Customize Series Legends command, 383-384
labeling graphs, 376
Graph Customize Series Markers command, 383, 397
Graph Customize Series Override_Type command, 390-391
Graph Customize Series Patterns command, 383
Graph Customize X-Axis Alternate_Ticks command, 389-390
Graph Customize X-Axis command, 389
Graph Customize X-Axis Title command, 376
Graph Customize Y-Axis Display_Scaling No command, 387
Graph Customize Y-Axis Display_Scaling Yes command, 389
Graph Customize Y-Axis Format_of_Ticks command, 387
Graph Customize Y-Axis Scale command, 386-388
Graph Customize Y-Axis Title command, 388
Graph Graph_Type command, 370
Graph Graph_Type Pie View command, 405
GRAPH macro command, 550
Graph Name command, 391-392
Graph Name Display command, 20, 392
Graph Name Erase command, 392
Graph Name Reset command, 392
Graph Name Store command, 391-392
Graph Print Colors command, 414
Graph Print Colors Copy_the_Screen's command, 414
Graph Print command, 369, 41, 1416
Graph Print Destination command, 416
Graph Print Destination Name command, 416
Graph Print Layout command, 413-414
Graph Print Name command, 414-416
Graph Print Printers command, 411-412
Graph Reset command, 393
Graph Reset X-Axis command, 382
Graph Series Patterns command, 398
Graph Series_Values command, 370, 372-373
graph stack, 391
Graph Titles 1st_Line command, 378
Graph Titles 2nd_Line command, 378, 383
Graph Titles command, 376-377
Graph Titles Font command, 377
Graph Titles menu, 376-377
Graph Titles Size command, 377-378
Graph Titles X command, 376
graph types, 372-374
3-dimensional-bar, 395-404
area, 395, 399-400
bar, 372, 386, 394
choosing among, 393
line, 368-373, 372, 386, 394
lines & markers, 374-397
markers, 372, 395
mixing in one graph, 390-391
overriding, 390-391
pie, 372, 394, 405-406
rotated-bar, 372, 395-404
stacked-bar, 372, 386, 394, 397-399
XY, 372, 386, 394, 406-407
Graph X-Axis_Values command, 370, 376
Graph Customize X-Axis No_of_Minor_Ticks command, 389
graphics, 19-21
displaying color, 20
printing, 20-21
graphics adapter cards supported by Quattro, 494
graphing capabilities of Quattro, 367-368
graphs, 368-375
altering y-axis title, 388
axes tick marks, 371
changing
colors, 398
default colors, 414
display scale format, 388-389
some items, 392-393
colors
CGA color display, 405
EGA color display, 405
monochrome displays, 405
VGA color display, 405
current graph, 391
printing, 411, 414-416
default type, 374
deleting
all, 392
selected, 392
displaying compared information, 401

editing titles, 379
eliminating crowding on x-axis, 389-390
exiting display, 376
formatting, 20
graph stack, 391
grid lines, 385-386
improving appearance, 375-390
  deleting x-axis labels, 382
  display, 384-386
  editing
    interior labels, 380
    legends, 384
    titles, 379
  grid lines, 385-386
  labeling, 376, 379-380
    x-axis, 381-382
  legends, 382-384
  reducing, 381
  scale values, 387-389
  size and font of titles, 377
  skip factor, 387
  skipping x-axis labels, 389
  staggering x-axis labels, 389-390
  suppress indicator display, 387
  titles, 376
interior labels
  deleting, 380-381
  editing, 380
labeling, 376, 379-380
  more than one series, 380
legends, 382-384
  customizing, 383
  editing, 384
naming, 20, 391-392, 416
origin, 371
performing what-if, 20
printers, 378
printing, 410-414, 416
  adjusting on page, 413-414
  baud rate, 412
  current graph, 411
  hardware requirements, 369
  Lotus format, 416
  margin adjustments, 413
  naming, 416
  orientation, 413
  parity, 412
  PIC files, 416
  PostScript format, 416
  print files, 416
  PRN files, 416
  Quattro-supported printers, 412
  restoring default settings, 411
  selecting
    device, 411-412
    printer driver, 411
    resolution, 412
  setting
    colors, 414
    current graph, 414-416
  stop bits, 412
  to file, 416
  to plotter, 412
reducing size, 381
retrieving, 392
saving, 391-392, 416
scale values
  altering, 386-387
  changing increments, 387
  negative numbers, 387
selecting type, 371-372
settings
  saving, 391-392
  storing with worksheet, 392
skip factor, 387
tick marks changing display format, 387
titles, 376
  controlling size and font, 377
viewing, 19, 375-376
  F10 (Graph) key, 376
  hardware requirements, 369
  lines & markers, 375
working with multiple, 391
x-axis, 371, 376
  altering scale values, 386-387
  deleting labels, 382
  labeling, 381-382
XY, 370
y-axis, 371
  altering scale values, 386-387
  indicator suppressing display, 387
graphs improving appearance
  display scale format, 389
Graph_Type menu, 374
greater than (>) comparison operator, 159
greater than or equal to (>=) comparison operator, 159

H

hard disks starting Quattro, 32
hardware
  configuring Quattro for, 492
  required for graphing, 369
  requirements, 10, 12, 24-29
hardware settings
  default, 337
  printers, 360-364
headers, 348-349
  centering text in, 349
  including date, 349
  justifying text in, 349
  number of characters in, 348-349
  printing, 348-350
  restoring to print, 359
  special characters, 349

suppressing, 356, 359
Help colors menu, 502
HELP mode indicator, 41
Help screens, 43-45
accessing
customizing, 517
with F1, 498
customizing colors, 501-502
Help Topics screen, 43
HEXTONUM function, 291-292
Hidden format, 146
hiding
blocks of cells, 18
cell contents, 146
columns, 120-122
highlighting cells, 50, 82-83
HLOOKUP function, 232-238
Home key, 25, 54, 77
HOME macro command, 551
horizontal bar graph, 142
HOUR function, 225
hours portion of time, 225

I

IBM 8514/A display extender, 494
IBM PC, 25
IBM ProPrinter, 412
IBM PS/2, 25
IF function, 191-196
nested, 193-195
testing conditions with, 195-196
IF macro command, 573, 575, 578-582, 603
importing files, 323-325
ASCII, 323
BASIC, 323
comma delimited, 323-325
macros to work with, 613-620
independent variable
multiple regression, 484-486
XY graph, 406
INDEX function, 238-240
INDICATE macro command, 601, 607
syntax, 607
indirect addressing in macros, 575-576
input block database functions, 466-467
input cell in what-if analysis, 472-473, 479
input line, 39-40
INSERT (INS) macro command, 551
INSERT mode, 60
inserting
columns, 122-124
fields, 21
records, 21
rows, 122-124
installing Quattro, 645
INT function, 185-186
integers from numbers, 185-186
interactive macros, 562-563
interest rate, 207-210
internal rate of return, 203-204
international conventions
configuring Quattro for, 502
international formats, 16, 146-147
investment terms, 210-211
IRR function, 203-204
ISERR function, 198-199
ISNA function, 198
ISNUMBER function, 197
ISSTRING function, 197
iteration
changing number of, 512
in recalculation, 511-513
in what-if analysis, 471

J-K

justifying text in headers and footers, 349
key fields in database, 420
key-equivalent commands, 548, 549, *See also keynames*
keyboards, 25, 33-35
keynames, 572
keypads, 34-37
keys
Abs (F4), 38, 103-104
accelerator, 80-81
actions in EDIT mode, 59-60
Add-in (Shift-F7), 38
alphanumeric, 35-36
Alt, 24-25, 35
backslash (\), 58
Backspace, 35, 113
Calc (F9), 17, 38, 139, 322
Caps Lock, 41
Ctrl-D, 14, 143-144, 214-215
cursor-movement, 36-37, 69-72
Debug (Shift-F8), 38
Del, 25, 36
Edit (F2), 25, 37, 50-51, 59-61, 139, 157, 261
End, 70-72, 77, 113-116
Enter, 43
equivalent commands in macros, 548-550
Esc, 36, 43, 78
F9, 322
function, 37-38
Functions (Alt-F3), 38, 158
GoTo (F5), 38, 72, 84, 88, 91, 131
Graph (F10), 25, 38
Help (F1), 25, 37, 43
Home, 25, 54, 77
Macro (F8), 24, 38
Macros (Shift-F3), 38
minus (-), 138
Names (F3), 37, 52, 89, 91
Num Lock, 36, 41
Period (.), 36, 111-113
PgDn, 25, 69

PgUp, 25, 45, 69
plus (+), 138
Previous (Alt-F1), 37
PrtSc, 91, 336
Query (F7), 38
Record (Alt-F8), 38
Scroll Lock/Break, 36
Shift, 35
Shift-PrtSc, 336
Shift-Tab, 69
slash (/), 15, 32, 35, 58, 76
sorting databases, 432-433
Tab, 35, 69
Table (Alt-F7), 38
Window (F6), 38, 132
keystrokes
in macros, 572
recording, 24
keywords, *See also Quattro macro commands*
DISPATCH, 575-576
ONERROR, 582

L

LABEL mode, 56
indicator, 40
labels, 16, 50
adding to graphs, 376
database, 421
default alignment, 57, 59
entering, 56-59
naming blocks with, 85
prefix character, 57-59
setting alignment, 504
laying out spreadsheet, 128-134
Layout menu, 413-414
Layout Titles command, 128-129
Layout Windows command, 128, 132-133
learn mode macros, 24
LEFT
function, 257-258
macro command, 551
Left_Heading command, 350-351
LENGTH function, 259-263
less than (<) comparison operator, 159
less than or equal to (<=) comparison operator, 159
LET macro command, 575, 591, 595-598
line graph, 369-373, 386, 394
scale values
negative, 387
selecting data series, 373
y-axis indicator
suppressing display, 387
lines & markers graph, 395
adding titles, 378
creating, 374, 396-397
choosing series values, 375
selecting type, 374
selecting
data series, 374
type, 374
viewing, 375
list of
block names, 89, 91
functions, 158
numbers variability, 184
lists
counting number of elements in, 173-175
LN function, 290
lock key indicator, 39
LOG function, 290
logical functions table, 192
logical operators
#AND#, 159, 193, 579
#NOT#, 159, 193, 579
#OR#, 159, 193, 579
IF macro command, 579
in macros, 582
logical spreadsheet functions, 191-199
LOOK macro command, 601, 607-608
looping, 574-578, 604
stopping, 578
Lotus 1-2-3, *See 1-2-3*
LOWER function, 263

M

Macro Clear Breakpoints command, 635
macro commands, 23-24, 572-620
arguments, 572-573
string concatenation, 597
string formulas, 598
block names in, 576-578
call menu, 611
controlling menus, 610
erasing block, 591
file manipulation, 613-620
flow control, 573-590
functional, 580
generic, 580
looping, 608
menu functions, 557
numeric input from user, 606
recalculating, 600-601
request user input numeric, 606
reset mode indicator, 607
syntax, 572-573
user interface, 601-612
variable management, 590-601
working with imported files, 613-620
macro debugger, 621-635
Conditional command, 633
conditional formulas in, 621
debugging window, 623
inserting breakpoints in macros, 630-633
Shift-F8, 622
single-step mode, 623
trace cells, 621, 634-635
TRACE window, 634-635
Macro Debugging menu, 635

displaying, 626
Macro Execute command, 261, 559-562
Macro Load command, 29, 524
Transcript, 538
to load Menu Builder, 528
Macro menu, 559-562
macro recorder, 554, 559
Macro Run command, 29, 524
to activate add-ins, 525
Macro Run Max_History_Length command, 539
Macro Run Transcript command, 541
Macro Unload command, 524-525
macro-related special advanced spreadsheet functions, 274-285
macros, 547-620
auto-execute, 516, 564
automatic execution, 564
basic concepts, 548-550
basic elements, 572
blank cell in, 588
blank command, 568
block names in, 569, 572, 575, 583, 595
braces
use of in commands, 548-549, 572
carriage return, 548
cell addresses, 572
combining with spreadsheets, 536
commands, 551, 572
comments
column, 567-568
marker, 567-568
syntax, 567-568
compatibility with 1-2-3, 520
creating, 552-559
invoking recorder, 554
macro learning mode, 552
naming, 554, 559
recording, 554-559
typing, 552-554
debugging, 621, *See also macro debugger*
designing reliable, 565-568
disabling Ctrl-Break, 602-603
documenting, 565-568
editing, 626-629
errors finding, 624
flow control commands, 576-578
functions in, 590
indirect addressing, 575-576
inserting breakpoints, 630-633
instructions, 548-549
interactive, 562-563
invoking recorder, 554
key-equivalent commands, 548-550
keyboard, 23-24
keynames, 572
keystrokes, 572
labeling, 567-568
learn mode, 24
locations, 552
looping, 574-575, 577-578, 604
stopping, 578
menu commands in, 590
moving cell selector, 572
names, 548, 559
identifying in list, 559
\0, 564
passwords, 602-603
pause command, 583
pause for input, 562-563
planning, 553-554
reaching with End-Home, 552
recording, 552, 554
cursor movements, 555, 557
menu selections, 555
naming, 554
redirecting processing in, 574-575, 578-583, 587-588, 609-610
reusable, 568-569, 574-575, 580-582
block names, 569
speeding processing with WINDOWSOFF macro command, 612
stopping execution, 584
subroutines, 584-588, 604
block names, 585
cancelling, 586
DEFINE command, 585, 595
naming, 585
passing information, 585
RESTART macro command, 586
RETURN macro command, 585
returning to main macro, 587-588
stack, 586
syntax, 584
testing conditional formulas, 633
tilde (~) in, 548
turning off recorder, 554, 559
typing, 553-554
VLOOKUP function in, 582
\0, 516
MACROS macro command, 550
main command menu, 32-33, 58
managing
columns, 119-127
database, 21-23
rows, 119-127
manual recalculation, 508-509
margins
on printed graph, 413
setting for printing, 356
suppressing, 356
markers graph
selecting data series, 374
uses, 395
math operators in spreadsheet functions, 159
mathematical functions, 13
mathematical operators
Addition (+), 53, 159
Division (/), 53, 159
Exponentiation (^), 53, 159
Multiplication (*), 53, 159
Negative (-), 53, 159
order of precedence, 53, 159

Positive (+), 53, 159
Subtraction (-), 53, 159
text (string) addition (&), 159
mathematical spreadsheet functions, 184-191
matrix
inverting, 486-487
multiplying two, 487
MAX function, 174, 176-180
mean, 181-184
finding, 468
MEM status indicator, 42
MEMAVAIL function, 284-285
MEMEMSAVAIL function, 284-285
memory
limitations, 9
requirements, 27-29
Menu Builder, 30, 523
activating, 528
adding macros to menus, 527-530
adding menu to Quattro, 535-536
creating submenus, 537
fields, 532
inserting new menu command, 532-534
loading, 528
modifying menus, 530-534
moving menu commands, 537
removing menu commands, 536-537
soft interface, 527-530
windows, 530-532
Details of Current Item, 533-534
using cursor, 530-532
menu commands, 75-127
assigning accelerator keys, 80
in macros, 590
MENU mode indicator, 41
Menu Text field in Menu Builder, 532
menu tree customizing, 517-519
Menu Tree menu, 518
MENUBRANCH macro command, 601, 604, 608-610
syntax, 609-610
MENUCALL macro command, 601, 611
syntax, 611
menus
1-2-3, 45
123.RSC, 518
1st_Printer, 412
2nd_Printer, 412
adding
macros to, 527-530
new to Quattro with Menu Builder, 535-536
Advanced, 423
Advanced Database Query, 440-441
Advanced Database Sort, 434-436
alternate, 518, 527-530
123.ALT, 518
assigning name with Menu Builder, 534
Below_Normal_Color, 150
Block, 58, 84
Block Search/Replace, 62-63
called by macro, 611
changing defaults, 518
changing through Menu Builder, 527
child, 527
creating with Menu Builder, 537
Colors, 414
command, 76-78
Compatibility Options, 519-520
Conditional colors, 499-501
current settings, 492
Database Sort, 431-432
default, 45-46, 504
add-in programs, 525
Default Colors Conditional, 150
Default Formats, 503-504
Default Formats Display, 387
Default Hardware Test_Printer, 333
Default International, 502
Default Recalculation, 513
Default Startup, 514-516
Device, 362-363
expanded, 78-80, 387, 492
File Parse, 326
Graph, 369-370, 374-376, 379-382, 398, 402, 405-406
Graph Customize, 392-393
Graph Customize Grids, 385-386
Graph Customize X-Axis, 389
Graph Name, 391-392
Graph Print, 411, 416
Graph Series_Values, 372-373
Graph Titles, 376-377
Graph Titles Size, 377-378
Graph_Type, 374
Help colors, 502
Layout, 413
Macro, 559-562
Macro Debugging, 626, 628, 635
macro directed, 610
main, 527-530
1-2-3, 518
command, 32-33, 58
default, 518
novice, 518
Menu Tree, 518
modifying with Menu Builder, 530-534
assigning name, 534
inserting new command, 532-534
moving commands in Menu Builder, 537
NOVICE.RSC, 518
optional, 45-46
Page Layout, 348-349, 353-356, 359, 363-364
Palettes, 496-497
parent, 527
Print, 333, 337-340
Print Destination, 416
Print Destination File, 359
Print Reset, 359
Protection, 514
QUATTRO.RSC, 518
Query, 443-444, 462-463
Recalculation, 507-508
removing commands in Menu Builder, 536-537

Replace, 67
Series_Values, 375
Sort Order, 432-433
Spreadsheet Colors, 498-499
Transcript, 541-542
wide, 519-520
Y-Axis, 387
message area, 39
MID function, 254-257
MIN function, 178-180
minimal recalculation, 17
minus (-) key, 138
MINUTE function, 224-225
mixed cell address, 98-105
MOD function, 186-187
mode indicators, 39-41
DEBUG, 41, 622, 626,629
EDIT, 40, 51, 54, 59-69, 301, 305
ERROR, 41
FILES, 40, 305
FIND, 41
FRMT, 41
HELP, 41
INSERT, 60
LABEL, 40
MENU, 41
NAMES, 41
OVERTYPE, 60-61
POINT, 40, 52, 69, 91, 131
READY, 40, 56, 59, 61, 69, 76, 91, 301
RECORD, 554
REP, 41
VALUE, 40, 52
WAIT, 41
modulus, 186-187
MONTH function, 219-220
moving
around spreadsheet, 67, 69-72
contents of cells, 108-111
cursor, 34-35
multiple regression, 23, 484-486
multiple-key sort, 436
databases, 435-437
Multiplication (*) mathematical operator, 53, 159

N

N function, 267-269
NA function, 279-280
NAME macro command, 550
named blocks, 3, 72
names
macro, 554, 559
\0, 564
Names (F3) key, 89, 91
NAMES mode indicator, 41
naming
a new file, 299-301
blocks, 16, 84-89, 91
graphs, 20
natural recalculation, 17, 507, 509-511
Negative (-) mathematical operator, 53, 159
nested IF functions, 193-195
not equal (<>) comparison operator, 159
novice menu, 518
NOVICE.RSC
file, 45
menu, 518
NOW function, 143-144, 221-223
in macro, 590
NPV function, 201-203
Num Lock key, 36, 41
NUM status indicator, 42
number generator random, 187-191
number of decimal points displayed, 139-140
number of elements in list
counting, 173-175
numerical values smallest in block of cells, 178-180
numbers
absolute value of, 191
averaging, 171-173
entering, 50-51
filling blocks with, 114, 117-118
formatting with macro, 592
integers from, 186
making integers out of, 185
punctuating, 502
rounding, 184-185
variability of list of, 184
numeric
type in databases, 425
form of time, 223
keypad, 34-37
numerical values
largest in block of cells, 176-180
NUMTOHEX function, 291-292

O

offset database functions, 479
one-key sort in databases, 433-434
ONERROR macro command, 573, 582-583
in OPEN macro command, 615
syntax, 582
OPEN macro command, 613-615
access-mode argument, 614
ONERROR command in, 615
syntax, 614
operators, *See also mathematical operators and logical operators*
comparison, 159
in formulas, 53-54
math, 159
precedence in formulas, 160
optional menus, 45-46
order of precedence of mathematical operators, 53
output graphs, 410-414
output block
database searches, 441

preparing for database functions, 477
OVERTYPE mode, 60-61
overview of Quattro, 7-30
overwriting when combining files, 316
OVR status indicator, 42

P

page breaks
removing from spreadsheet, 347
restoring to print, 359
setting within spreadsheet, 346-347
suppressing, 356, 359
page layout
changing temporarily, 356
margins, 363-364
printing options, 363-364
Page Layout menu, 348-349, 353-356, 359, 363-364
page numbers printed in headers and footers, 349
page-break character
inserting, 346, 356
removing, 347
Page_Layout Margins Right command, 354
Palettes menu, 496-497
PANELOFF macro command, 601, 612
syntax, 612
PANELON macro command, 601, 612
syntax, 612
Paradox, 297
translating files to Quattro, 310
parameters passing through macro subroutines, 585
parent menus, 527
parity
choosing for printing graph, 412
setting, 363
parsing files, 325-330
format lines, 327-328
PASCAL, 571
password, 310, 312
protected file, 19
with macros, 602-603
path name
specifying for file retrieval, 305-306
pause command in macros, 583
Percent format, 142-143
percent sign (%), 51
Period (.) key, 36, 111-113
PgDn key, 25, 69
PGDN macro command, 551
PgUp key, 25, 45, 69
PGUP macro command, 551
PI function, 287
PIC files, 298, 416
for graphs, 411
pie graph, 405-406
adjusting roundness on-screen, 494
exploding, 406
selecting data series, 373
suppressing percentage display, 405
uses, 394, 405
plotter
selecting for graph, 412
plus (+) key, 138
PMT function, 207-208, 472-476
POINT mode, 52, 69, 91, 131
indicator, 40
pointing
to blocks, 111-116
to commands, 76-77
to enter data, 52
Positive (+) mathematical operator, 53, 159
PostScript, 378, 411-412
presort order restoring in database, 437
Print Adjust_Printer Align command, 340, 346
Print Adjust_Printer Form_Feed command, 346
Print Adjust_Printer Skip_Line command, 346
print block
hiding segments in, 342-344
Print Block command, 332, 337-338
Print command, 331, 337-344
menu, 333, 337, 338, 339, 340
Print Destination File
command, 331, 359
menu, 359
Print Destination menu, 416
Print Destination Printer command, 331
Print Format Cell-Formulas command, 55, 357
Print Left_Heading command, 340, 351
Print Page_Layout Break_Pages No command, 348, 356
Print Page_Layout Break_Pages Yes command, 359
Print Page_Layout command, 337
Print Page_Layout Create_Break command, 346-347, 356
Print Page_Layout Header command, 349
Print Reset All command, 337, 355, 359
Print Reset Borders command, 351
Print Reset
command, 358-359
menu, 359
print settings
clearing, 337
Print Top_Heading command, 338-340
printer
adjusting paper in, 340
baud rates, 362
connecting to computer, 361-362
printer codes
ASCII, 353-356
setup strings, 353-356
using from printer manual, 356
printer changing device, 361-362
printer driver
selecting for graph, 411
printer port
parallel, 361-362
serial, 361-362
specifying, 361-362
printer settings, 360-364
printers
Apple LaserWriter, 412

continuous-feed paper, 345-346
controlling the paper, 345-346
EPSON, 354
for graphs, 412
IBM Page Printer, 363
IBM ProPrinter, 412
laser, 363
PostScript language, 378
PostScript laser, 412
specifying ports, 361-362
printing
adjusting paper in printer, 340
ASCII printer codes, 353-356
blocks, 342-344
borders, 351
calculating
page length, 364
print width, 364
cell contents, 357
changing
baud rate, 362-363
page layout, 356
print options, 347-348
printer device, 361-362
settings temporarily, 360-361
column headings, 350-351
combining codes in setup strings, 355
compressed print, 354
continuous-feed paper, 345-346
controlling the paper, 345-346
draft-quality reports, 333, 337-338
excluding
blocks, 344
columns, 343-344
rows, 342-343
expanded print, 355
footers, 346-350
graphs, 20-21, 410-414, 416
headers, 348-350
inserting page breaks, 356
margins setting, 356
on other programs, 359
creating PRN file, 359
one screenful, 336
one-page reports, 337-338
page-breaks
characters, 356
for numeric data, 339
for text data, 339
page-layout setup strings, 364
planning reports, 332-333
printer
codes, 353-356
computer connections, 361-362
manual codes, 356
settings, 360-364
removing setup strings, 355
resetting print options, 358-359
row headings, 350-351
setting page breaks, 346-347
setup strings for blocks, 355
stopping with Ctrl-Break, 338
to PRN file, 359
updating defaults, 364
using setup strings, 353-356
without leaving the program, 19
worksheet, 19
PRN files, 298, 331, 359
for graphs, 416
insert EOF marker, 359
importing to Quattro, 323
printing to, 359
programmers' advanced spreadsheet functions, 291-292
programming commands, 571
programs
Menu Builder, 30
printing without leaving, 19
Transcript, 29-30
PROPER function, 263-264
protecting
cells, 18, 118-119
files, 18
password, 602-603
spreadsheets, 514
worksheet, 18, 118-119
Protection menu, 514
PrtSc key, 91, 336
PUT macro command, 591, 598-599
functions used with, 599
syntax, 598
PV function, 205

Q

QAI files, 524
Quattro
acting like 1-2-3, 45-46
compatibility, 519-520
compatibility with 1-2-3, 8
customizing, 491-494, 505
add-ins, 517
colors, 494-497
default directories, 506
hardware, 492
help access, 517
menu tree, 517-519
recalculation, 507, 508
retaining changes, 492-493
screen, 493-494
screen resolution, 494
startup, 514-516
user interface, 517-519
exiting, 32
getting started, 32-48
importing files, 18
installing, 645
overview, 7-30
starting
on hard disk, 32
on two floppy drive system, 32

Quattro commands
/Advanced Database, 423
/Advanced Database Form_Input, 427-429
/Advanced Database Query, 22, 41, 440-442
/Advanced Database Query Assign_Names, 452
/Advanced Database Query Block, 442
/Advanced Database Query Criteria_Table, 443
/Advanced Database Query Extract, 447-450
/Advanced Database Query Formula_Criterion, 445, 460
/Advanced Database Query Locate, 22
/Advanced Database Query Unique, 22, 476-479
/Advanced Database Sort, 431-433
/Advanced Database Sort Block, 434
/Advanced Frequency, 483-484
/Advanced Matrix, 23, 465-487
/Advanced Matrix Invert, 486-487
/Advanced Matrix Multiply, 487
/Advanced Regression, 23, 465, 484-486
/Advanced What-If, 23, 117, 471-481
/Advanced What-If 1_Variable, 471-473, 479
/Advanced What-If 2_Variables, 471, 473-476
/Block, 16, 63
/Block Advanced Unprotect, 127
/Block Advanced Create, 84-86
/Block Advanced Labels, 84-86
/Block Advanced Labels Right, 567
/Block Advanced Make_Table, 91
/Block Advanced Protect, 18, 118
/Block Advanced Reset, 89
/Block Advanced Transpose, 106, 108
/Block Advanced Unprotect, 118, 427, 514
/Block Advanced Values, 106, 108, 189, 273, 450
/Block Column Width, 426
/Block Copy, 16-17, 27, 54, 58, 93-108, 120, 330, 448
/Block Display_Format, 135-141, 153, 330, 426
/Block Display_Format Date, 144
/Block Display_Format Date Time, 144
/Block Display_Format Hidden, 18, 146, 344
/Block Display_Format Reset, 146, 344
/Block Display_Format Text, 453, 472
/Block Erase, 16, 89, 113, 127, 450, 540-541
/Block Fill, 114, 116-118, 151, 471
/Block Label_Align, 58-59, 138
/Block Move, 108-111, 113, 120, 320
/Block Reformat, 136, 147-150, 162-169
/Column Delete, 122, 125, 127, 343, 430
/Column Expose, 120, 344
/Column Hide, 120-122, 146, 343
/Column Insert, 21, 122-123, 430
/Column Reset, 119-120
/Column Set_Global, 120
/Column Width, 119-120, 141
/Database Query, 38
/Default Autoload, 515
/Default Colors, 496-499
/Default Colors Help, 501-502
/Default Colors Menu, 497-498
/Default Colors Palettes, 499
/Default Colors Spreadsheet, 498-499
/Default Directories, 305, 313-314, 506
/Default Formats, 493
/Default Formats Align, 59
/Default Formats Clock, 505
/Default Formats Clock International, 505
/Default Formats Display, 135-136, 138, 140-141, 153, 504
/Default Formats Display Date, 144
/Default Formats Display Date Time, 144
/Default Formats Display Text, 55
/Default Formats Hide_Zeroes, 333, 504-505
/Default Hardware Screen, 493-494
/Default Hardware Text_Printer, 337, 347-348, 360-361, 364
/Default International, 16, 146-147, 502
/Default Protection, 118
/Default Protection Disable, 119
/Default Protection Enable, 18, 118-119
/Default Recalculation, 507-508
/Default Recalculation Iteration, 512-513
/Default Recalculation Mode, 508-509
/Default Recalculation Order, 510
/Default Set Global Width, 141
/Default Startup, 493, 514-516
/Default Startup Autoload, 564
/Default Startup Beep, 516
/Default Startup Compatibility_Options, 519-520
/Default Startup Compatibility_Options Keep_Wide, 79
/Default Startup Default Add_Ins, 517, 524-525, 538
/Default Startup Help_Access_Method, 517
/Default Startup Menu_Tree Alternate_Menus, 518, 535
/Default Startup Menu_Tree Main_Menus, 518
/Default Startup Menu_Tree Switch_Menus, 81, 518-519, 536
/Default Startup Menu_Tree Switch_Menus Alternate_Menu, 81
/Default Startup Menu_Tree Update, 536
/Default Startup Update, 517-518
/Default Update, 80, 136, 314, 364, 535
/Default Colors Conditional, 499-501
/Erase, 127-128
/File !SQZ!, 321-323
/File Combine, 315
/File Combine Add, 315-318
/File Combine Copy, 315-318, 528, 536, 603
/File Combine Subtract, 315, 318
/File Directory, 314
/File Erase, 313
/File Import, 323-325
/File OS, 320-321
/File Parse, 41, 325-330
/File Parse Create, 326
/File Parse Edit, 326
/File Parse Go, 326
/File Parse Input, 326, 328
/File Parse Output, 326, 328
/File Parse Quit, 326
/File Parse Reset, 326

/File Retrieve, 81, 134, 299-319
/File Save, 19, 81, 133, 299-312, 348, 392, 463
/File Xtract, 88, 307, 318-320
/File Xtract Formulas, 318-320
/File Xtract Values, 318-319
/Format, 141
/Go, 63-64, 66
/Graph, 19, 370, 374
/Graph Customize Colors, 398
/Graph Customize Colors Series, 383
/Graph Customize Grids, 385-386
/Graph Customize Pies, 405
/Graph Customize Pies Explode, 406
/Graph Customize Pies Label_Format None, 405
/Graph Customize Series Interior_Labels, 376, 379
/Graph Customize Series Legends, 376, 383-384
/Graph Customize Series Markers, 383, 397
/Graph Customize Series Override_Type, 390-391
/Graph Customize Series Patterns, 383
/Graph Customize X-Axis, 389
/Graph Customize X-Axis Alternate_Ticks, 389-390
/Graph Customize X-Axis No_of_Minor_Ticks, 389
/Graph Customize X-Axis Title, 376
/Graph Customize Y-Axis Display_Scaling No, 387
/Graph Customize Y-Axis Display_Scaling Yes, 389
/Graph Customize Y-Axis Format_of_Ticks, 387
/Graph Customize Y-Axis Scale, 386-387
/Graph Customize Y-Axis Scale Manual, 388
/Graph Customize Y-Axis Title, 388
/Graph Graph_Type, 370
/Graph Graph_Type Pie View, 405
/Graph Name, 391-392
/Graph Name Display, 20, 392
/Graph Name Erase, 392
/Graph Name Reset, 392
/Graph Name Store, 391-392
/Graph Print, 369, 411
/Graph Print Colors, 414
/Graph Print Colors Copy_the_Screen's, 414
/Graph Print Destination, 416
/Graph Print Destination Name, 416
/Graph Print Layout, 413-414
/Graph Print Name, 414-416
/Graph Print Printers, 411-412
/Graph Reset, 393
/Graph Reset X-Axis, 382
/Graph Series Patterns, 398
/Graph Series_Values, 370
/Graph Titles, 376-377
/Graph Titles 1st_Line, 378
/Graph Titles 2nd_Line, 378, 383
/Graph Titles Font, 377
/Graph Titles Size, 377-378
/Graph Titles X, 376
/Graph X-Axis_Values, 370, 376
/Layout Titles, 128-129
/Layout Windows, 128, 132-133
/Macro Clear Breakpoints, 635
/Macro Execute, 261, 559-562
/Macro Load, 29, 524, 528, 538
/Macro Run, 29, 524-525, 538
/Macro Run Max_History_Length, 539
/Macro Run Transcript, 541
/Macro Unload, 524-525
/Print, 331, 337-340, 342-344
/Print Adjust_Printer Align, 340, 346
/Print Adjust_Printer Form_Feed, 346
/Print Adjust_Printer Skip_Line, 346
/Print Block, 332, 337-338
/Print Destination File, 331, 359
/Print Destination Printer, 331
/Print Format Cell-Formulas, 55, 357
/Print Left_Heading, 340, 351
/Print Page_Layout, 337
/Print Page_Layout Break_Pages No, 348, 356
/Print Page_Layout Break_Pages Yes, 359
/Print Page_Layout Create_Break, 346-347, 356
/Print Page_Layout Header, 349
/Print Reset, 358-359
/Print Reset All, 337, 355, 359
/Print Reset Borders, 351
/Print Top_Heading, 338-340
/Quit, 32, 81, 133
/Replace String, 63
/Row Delete, 122-127, 347, 430
/Row Insert, 21, 122-123, 429
/Search String, 63
Default Startup Extension, 516
Quattro disks, 25
Quattro functions, 13-15
@, 13, 55-56
@@, 240-242
@ABS, 191
@ACOS, 288-289
@ASIN, 288-289
@ATAN, 288-289
@ATAN2, 288-289
@AVG, 171-173
@CELL, 276-278
@CELLINDEX, 278-279
@CELLPOINTER, 276-278
@CHAR, 272-273
@CHOOSE, 228-229
@CLEAN, 272
@CODE, 274
@COLS, 280
@COS, 287-288
@COUNT, 173-175
@CTERM, 211-212
@CURVALUE, 281
@DATE, 143, 216-217
@DATEVALUE, 143, 217-218
@DAVG, 246-247, 468-469, 479-481
@DAY, 218-219
@DCOUNT, 248, 468-469
@DDB, 214
@DEGREES, 289
@DMAX, 248, 468-469
@DMIN, 249, 468-469
@DSTD, 249-250, 468-469
@DSUM, 245-246, 476, 481

@DVAR, 250, 468-469
@ERR, 279-280
@EXACT, 258-259, 579
@EXP, 290
@FALSE, 198, 579
@FILEEXISTS, 282-283, 579
@FIND, 251, 253
@FV, 206
@HEXTONUM, 291-292
@HLOOKUP, 232-238
@HOUR, 225
@IF, 191-196
@INDEX, 238-240
@INT, 185-186
@IRR, 203-204
@ISERR, 198-199, 579
@ISNA, 198, 579
@ISNUMBER, 197, 579
@ISSTRING, 197, 579
@LEFT, 257-258
@LENGTH, 259-263
@LN, 290
@LOG, 290
@LOWER, 263
@MAX, 174, 176-180
@MEMAVAIL, 284-285
@MEMEMSAVAIL, 284-285
@MID, 254-257
@MIN, 178-180
@MINUTE, 224-225
@MOD, 186-187
@MONTH, 219-220
@N, 267-269
@NA, 279-280
@NOW, 143-144, 221-223
@NPV, 201-203
@NUMTOHEX, 291-292
@PI, 287
@PMT, 207-208, 472-476
@PROPER, 263-264
@PV, 205
@RADIANS, 289
@RAND, 187-191
@RATE, 209-210
@REPEAT, 264-267
@REPLACE, 259
@RIGHT, 257-258
@ROUND, 184-185
@ROWS, 280
@S, 267-269
@SECOND, 224
@SIN, 287-288
@SLN, 212-213
@SQRT, 285-286
@STD, 180-184
@STRING, 269-270
@SUM, 55-56, 155, 171, 465
@SYD, 213-214
@TAN, 287-288
@TERM, 210-211
@TIME, 144, 223
@TIMEVALUE, 144, 223-224
@TODAY, 220-221
@TRIM, 271-272
@TRUE, 197, 579
@UPPER, 263
@VALUE, 270-271
@VAR, 184
@VLOOKUP, 230-232, 235-238, 582
@YEAR, 220
Quattro macro commands
{?}, 562-563
{ABS}, 550
{ADDIN}, 550
{BACKSPACE} {BS}, 550
{BEEP}, 601-602
{BIGLEFT}, 551
{BIGRIGHT}, 551
{BLANK}, 591
{BRANCH}, 573-575
{BREAKOFF}, 601-603
{BREAKON}, 601-603
{CALC}, 550
{CLOSE}, 613, 615-616
{CONTENTS}, 591-593
{CR}, 548, 551, 563, 572
{DATE}, 551
{DEFINE}, 591, 594-595
{DELETE} {DEL}, 551
{DISPATCH}, 573, 575-576
{DOWN}, 551
{EDIT}, 550
{END}, 551
{ESCAPE} {ESC}, 551, 593
{FILESIZE}, 613, 620
{FORBREAK}, 573, 578
{FOR}, 573, 576-578
{FUNCTIONS}, 550
{GETLABEL}, 601, 605-606
{GETNUMBER}, 601, 606
{GETPOS}, 613, 620
{GET}, 601, 603-605
{GOTO}, 550
{GRAPH}, 550
{HOME}, 551
{IF}, 573, 578-582
{INDICATE}, 601, 607
{INSERT} {INS}, 551
{LEFT}, 551
{LET}, 591, 595-598
{LOOK}, 601, 607-608
{MACROS}, 550
{MENUBRANCH}, 601, 608-610
{MENUCALL}, 601, 611
{NAME}, 550
{ONERROR}, 573, 582-583
{OPEN}, 613-615
{PANELOFF}, 601, 612
{PANELON}, 601, 612
{PDUP}, 551
{PGDN}, 551
{PUT}, 591, 598-599

{QUERY}, 550
{QUIT}, 573, 584
{READLN}, 613, 617-618
{READ}, 613, 616-617
{RECALCCOL}, 591, 600-601
{RECALC}, 591, 600-601
{RESTART}, 573, 586
{RETURN}, 573, 587-588
{RIGHT}, 551
{SETPOS}, 613, 619
{STEPOFF}, 574, 588-589
{STEPON}, 574, 588-589
{TABLE}, 550
{UP}, 551
{WAIT}, 574, 589-590
{WINDOWSOFF}, 601, 612
{WINDOWSON}, 601, 612
{WINDOW}, 550
{WRITELN}, 613, 618
{WRITE}, 613, 618
{{}, 551
{}}, 551
{~}, 551
Quattro
menu switching with 1-2-3 menu, 81
tutorial, 47
database capabilities, 419
QUATTRO.DEF file, 80, 314, 492-493, 504
QUATTRO.LOG, 538-539
QUATTRO.RSC
file, 45
menu, 518
QUATTRO.WKQ file, 515
Query command, 439
QUERY macro command, 550
Query menu, 443
deleting records, 462-463
Locate command, 443-444
query operations, 439, *See also searching database*
Quit command, 32, 81, 133
QUIT macro command, 573, 584

R

RADIANS function, 289
RAM, 26
RAND function, 187-191
random
access memory (RAM), 26
number generator, 187-191
ranges, 3, *See also blocks*
RATE function, 209-210
READ macro command, 613, 616-617
READLN macro command, 613, 617-618
READY mode, 56, 59, 61, 69, 76, 91, 301
indicator, 40
RECALC macro command, 591, 600-601
RECALCCOL macro command, 591, 600-601
recalculation, 17-18, 507-508
automatic, 508
checking status, 513
circular references, 507-513
iteration, 511-513
manual, 508-509
order 507-511
setting defaults, 507-508
with macros, 600-601
Recalculation menu, 507-508
RECORD mode, 554, 559
recording
keystrokes, 24
macros, 554-559
cursor movements, 555, 557
menu selections, 555
records
database, 420
deleting, 462, 463
sorting, 431-437
extracting from database, 439, 450
inserting, 21
Reflex
translating files to Quattro, 310
reformatting text, 136
regression
analysis, 484-486
multiple, 23
relational operators in database searches, 452
relative cell references, 16, 97-105
in extracting, 320
remainder, 186-187
REP mode indicator, 41
REPEAT function, 264-267
REPLACE function, 259
Replace menu, 67
replace operation global, 65-66
Replace String command, 63
replicating cells, 58
requirements
hardware, 10, 12, 24-29
memory, 27-29
software, 24-25
Reset_Alternate , 519
resolution command, 494
choosing for printing graph, 412
resource directories, 314, 506
RESTART macro command, 573, 586
syntax, 586
results column, 483
retrieving files, 302, 304-306
RETURN macro command, 573, 587-588
RIGHT
function, 257-258
macro command, 551
rotated bar graph, 395, 404
ROUND function, 184-185
Row Delete command, 122, 125, 127, 347, 430
row headings printing, 350-351
Row Insert command, 21, 122-123, 429
rows, 9, 119-127
deleting, 122, 124-127

excluding from printing, 342-343
inserting, 122-124
transposing, 106, 108
ROWS function, 280
rowwise recalculation, 507, 509-510
run-time error
protecting macro from, 582-583

S

S function, 267-269
saving files, 133-134, 299, 301
scatter plot see XY graph, 406
Scientific format, 51, 140
scientific notation, 51, 140
screen
customizing, 493-494
descriptor line, 39-40
display, 39-40
input line, 39-40
lock key indicator, 39
message area, 39
mode indicator, 39-41
splitting, 131-133
status line, 39-40
worksheet area, 39-40
Scroll Lock/Break key, 36
scrolling
cell selector, 9
worksheet, 69
search and replace data, 62-68
search block defining, 442
Search String command, 63
searching database, 22, 439-463
combining fields, 459-460
criteria of cells outside database, 453
criteria table, 442
compound conditions, 454-460
defining, 442-443, 447-448
field names in, 443
deleting records, 462-463
Extract command, 447-450
formula criterion, 442
functions, 459
listing specified records, 447-450
minimum requirements, 440-442
numeric fields , 452-454
output block, 441-442, 447-448
partial fields, 459
relational operators, 452
search block, 442
special operators, 459-460
unique records, 461
wild cards, 451-452
SECOND function, 224
seconds in portion of time, 224
Selectable Status field in Menu Builder, 532
series labeling, 376
Series_Values menu, 375
SETPOS macro command, 613, 617, 619
setup strings
combining codes, 355
default, 353-354
for blocks, 355
in printing, 353-356
page-layout, 364
removing, 355
restoring to default, 355
temporary, 353-354
Shift key, 35
Shift-F3 (Macros) key, 38
Shift-F7 (Add-in) keys, 38
Shift-F8 (Debug) key, 38, 524, 622
Shift-PrtSc, 336
Shift-Tab key, 69
simultaneous equations, 23
SIN function, 287-288
skip factor graphs, 387
slash (/) key, 15, 32, 35, 58, 76
SLN function, 212-213
soft user interface, 517-519
accessing through Menu Builder, 527-530
software
add-in, 29-30
requirements, 24-25
sort block in database, 432
Sort Order menu, 432-433
sorting 435-437
order, 432-433
data, 21-23
records, 431-433
Sort_Order command in databases, 432-433
source block, 93-94
spaces dangling, 168
special
functions, 14-15
operators in database searches, 459-460
Specific action field in Menu Builder, 532
speed of operating, 29
splitting the screen, 131-133
spreadsheet
basics, 49-73
colors
conditional cells, 499-501
customizing, 498-499
menu, 498-499
commands, 15-19
functions, 155-226
@@, 240-242
@ABS, 191
@ACOS, 288-289
@ASIN, 288-289
@ATAN, 288-289
@ATAN2, 288-289
@AVG, 171-173
@CELL, 276-278
@CELLINDEX, 278-279
@CELLPOINTER, 276-278
@CHAR, 272-273
@CHOOSE, 228-229

@CLEAN, 272
@CODE, 274
@COLS, 280
@COS, 287-288
@COUNT, 173-175
@CTERM, 211-212
@CURVALUE, 281
@DATE, 216-217
@DATEVALUE, 217-218
@DAVG, 246-247
@DAY, 218-219
@DCOUNT, 248
@DDB, 214
@DEGREES, 289
@DMAX, 248
@DMIN, 249
@DSTD, 249-250
@DSUM, 245-246
@DVAR, 250
@ERR, 279-280
@EXACT, 258-259
@EXP, 290
@FALSE, 198
@FILEEXISTS, 282-283
@FIND, 251, 253
@FV, 206
@HEXTONUM, 291-292
@HLOOKUP, 232-238
@HOUR, 225
@IF, 191-196
@INDEX, 238-240
@INT, 185-186
@IRR, 203-204
@ISERR, 198-199
@ISNA, 198
@ISNUMBER, 197
@ISSTRING, 197
@LEFT, 257-258
@LENGTH, 259-263
@LN, 290
@LOG, 290
@LOWER, 263
@MAX, 174, 176-180
@MEMAVAIL, 284-285
@MEMEMSAVAIL, 284-285
@MID, 254-257
@MIN, 178-180
@MINUTE, 224-225
@MOD, 186-187
@MONTH, 219-220
@N, 267-269
@NA, 279-280
@NOW, 221-223
@NPV, 201-203
@NUMTOHEX, 291-292
@PI, 287
@PMT, 207-208
@PROPER, 263-264
@PV, 205
@RADIANS, 289
@RAND, 187-191
@RATE, 209-210
@REPEAT, 264-267
@REPLACE, 259
@RIGHT, 257-258
@ROUND, 184-185
@ROWS, 280
@S, 267-269
@SECOND, 224
@SIN, 287-288
@SLN, 212-213
@SQRT, 285-286
@STD, 180-184
@STRING, 269-270
@SUM, 155, 171
@SYD, 213-214
@TAN, 287-288
@TERM, 210-211
@TIME, 223
@TIMEVALUE, 223-224
@TODAY, 220-221
@TRIM, 271-272
@TRUE, 197
@UPPER, 263
@VALUE, 270-271
@VAR, 184
@VLOOKUP, 230-238
@YEAR, 220
recalculating, 507-508
template, 315
spreadsheets
laying out, 128-134
moving around, 67-72
primary commands, 82-134
protecting, 514
SQRT function, 285-286
stack, 586
stacked-bar graph, 386
creating, 397-399
selecting series values, 398
customizing, 398-399
selecting data series, 373
uses, 394
y-axis indicator
suppressing display of, 387
standard deviation, 180-184, 468
startup procedures, 31-32
customizing, 514-516
statistical spreadsheet functions, 13-14, 169-180
status indicators, 42
status line, 39-40
in screen dump, 336
STD function, 180-184
STEPOFF macro command, 574, 588-589
syntax, 588
STEPON macro command, 574, 588-589
syntax, 588
sticky menus, 434
stop bits
choosing for printing graph, 412
setting, 363
stopping macro execution, 584
straight-line depreciation, 212-213
string concatenation in macro, 597

string data type in databases, 425
string formulas in macro, 598
STRING function, 14, 269-270
subdirectories, 32
  and file retrieval, 304-306
subroutines built-in, 155
Subtraction (-) mathematical operator, 53, 159
SUM function, 55-56, 155, 171, 465
sum-of-the-years'-depreciation, 213-214
switching back and forth between Quattro menu and 1-2-3 menu, 81
SYD function, 213-214
Symphony files in Quattro, 298
syntax functions, 156-157

T

Tab key, 35, 69
Table and array-handling advanced spreadsheet functions, 227-242
table building
  Block Fill command, 471
  database functions, 470-481
TABLE macro command, 550
tables
  cell attributes, 276
  creating of block names, 91
  cursor-movement key, 70
  database statistical functions, 244
  date and time functions, 215-216
  date formats, 144
  File Manipulation Commands, 613
  financial spreadsheet functions, 200
  general mathematical functions, 185
  Key-Equivalent Macro Commands, 550
  logical functions, 192
  macro to work with, 598-599
  macro-related special advanced spreadsheet functions, 275
  Numeric Format Codes for CONTENTS Command, 592
  Quattro format options, 137
  Search Options, 441
  statistical spreadsheet functions, 170
  text functions, 252-253
  time formats, 145
  User Interface Commands, 601
  Using Wild Cards in Search Operations, 452
  Variable Management Commands, 591
TAN function, 287-288
template for spreadsheet, 315
TERM function, 210-211
term
  annuity, 211-212
  investment, 210-211
testing
  conditions with IF functions, 195-196
  for more than one condition, 193-195
text
  advanced spreadsheet functions, 250-274
  drivers special with Quattro, 494
  formatting, 147-150
  functions table, 252-253
  lookups, 235-238
  reformatting, 136
  (string) addition (&) math operator, 159
Text format, 145
time display, 144
  controlling, 505
  international conventions, 502
Time format, 143-145
  table, 145
time from string of text, 223-224
time function, 14, 144, 214-225
TIMEVALUE function, 144, 223-224
titles freezing on-screen, 128-131
TODAY function, 220-221
top of page, 345
Top_Heading command, 350-351
trace cells, 621
  in macro debugging, 634-635
TRACE window, 624
  debug window, 623
TRANS.QAI, 525
Transcript, 29-30, 523-524, 537-545
  checkpoints, 539
  Command History window, 539-540
  history retained, 539
  leaving, 542
  menu options, 541-542
  QUATTRO.LOG file, 538
  recovering erased block, 540-545
  setting up as default, 538
  stopping playback, 543-545
  time required to run, 538
  to restore presort order, 437
  using to undo errors, 545
translating files, 306-310
  1-2-3, 306
  column headings, 307
  dBASE, 306-307, 309
  dBASE III Plus, 306
  Paradox, 310
  Reflex, 310
  TRN extension, 306
transposing
  columns, 106, 108
  rows, 106, 108
trigonometric advanced spreadsheet functions, 285-290
TRIM function, 271-272
true and false function, 193-195
true cost of loan, 205
TRUE function, 197
Turner Hall Publishing, 322
turnkey system, 515
tutorial Quattro, 47
two floppy drive system starting Quattro, 32
typing
  data, 52
  first letter of command, 76-77
  macros, 552-554

U

undoing selection of command, 78
Undo_Last_Command Transcript, 545
uneven cash flows, 201-203
unique records searching database for, 461
UP macro command, 551
UPPER function, 263
user interface
  customizing, 517-519
user interface commands, 601-612
  {BEEP}, 601-602
  {BREAKOFF}, 601-603
  {BREAKON}, 601-603
  {GETLABEL}, 601, 605-606
  {GETNUMBER}, 601, 606
  {GET}, 601, 603-605
  {INDICATE}, 601, 607
  {LOOK}, 601, 607-608
  {MENUBRANCH}, 601, 608-610
  {MENUCALL}, 601, 611
  {PANELOFF}, 601, 612
  {PANELON}, 601, 612
  {WINDOWSOFF}, 601, 612
  {WINDOWSON}, 601, 612
utilities
  !SQZ!, 28, 321-323, 516

V

value future, 206
VALUE
  function, 270-271
  mode, 52
    indicator, 40
values, 50
  block, 483-484
  from formulas, 106-108
VAR function, 184
variable management commands, 590-601
  {BLANK}, 591
  {CONTENTS}, 591-593
  {DEFINE}, 591, 594-595
  {LET}, 591, 595-598
  {PUT}, 591, 598-599
  {RECALC}, 591
  {RECALCCOL}, 591, 600-601
  {RECALC}, 600-601
variance, 180
Video Graphics Array, 494
View Structure command, 307
viewing graphs, 19
VLOOKUP function, 230-232, 235-238

W

WAIT macro command, 574, 589-590
  syntax, 589
WAIT mode indicator, 41
What to do field in Menu Builder, 532
what-if analysis, 12, 20, 470-481
  coprocessors for, 476
  input cell, 472-473, 479
  iteration, 471
  two variables, 473-476
what-if graphs, 20
wild cards
  *, 304, 313
  ?, 304, 313
  characters, 22
  database searches, 451-452
  in deleting files, 313
  in file names, 299
  retrieving files from subdirectories, 304-306
WINDOW macro command, 550
windows, 10-11
  debug, 623
WINDOWSOFF macro command, 601, 612
  syntax, 612
WINDOWSON macro command, 601, 612
  syntax, 612
WK1 files, 298
WKQ files, 298, 306
worksheet
  area, 39-40
  entering
    data, 50-59
    formulas, 51-55
    numbers, 50-51
  erasing entire, 127-128
  formatting, 15
  printing, 19
  protecting, 18
  protecting areas, 118-119
  recalculating, 17-18, 507-508
  scrolling, 69
WRITE macro command, 613, 618
WRITELN macro command, 613, 618

X-Y-Z

x-axis, 371, 376
  changing, 376
  deleting labels, 382
  labeling, 381-382, 389-390
XY graph, 386
  adjusting scaling, 389
  creating, 406-410
  dependent variable, 406
  independent variable, 406
  scale values
    changing, 409
    negative, 387
  selecting data series, 373
  y-axis indicator
    suppressing display of, 387
Y-Axis menu, 371, 387-388
  setting numeric limits, 387
YEAR function, 220
zero
  suppressing display , 504-505

More Computer Knowledge from Que

LOTUS SOFTWARE TITLES

1-2-3 QueCards	21.95
1-2-3 for Business, 2nd Edition	19.95
1-2-3 Business Formula Handbook	19.95
1-2-3 Command Language	21.95
1-2-3 Macro Library, 2nd Edition	21.95
1-2-3 Tips, Tricks, and Traps, 2nd Edition	19.95
Using 1-2-3, Special Edition	24.95
Using 1-2-3 Workbook and Disk, 2nd Edition	29.95
Using Lotus HAL	19.95
Using Symphony, 2nd Edition	24.95

DATABASE TITLES

dBASE III Plus Applications Library	21.95
dBASE III Plus Handbook, 2nd Edition	21.95
dBASE III Plus Advanced Programming, 2nd Edition	22.95
dBASE III Plus Tips, Tricks, and Traps	19.95
R:BASE Solutions: Applications and Resources	19.95
R:BASE System V Techniques and Applications	21.95
R:BASE System V User's Guide, 2nd Edition	19.95
Using Reflex	19.95
Using Paradox	21.95
Using Q & A	19.95

MACINTOSH AND APPLE II TITLES

HyperCard QuickStart: A Graphics Approach	21.95
Using AppleWorks, 2nd Edition	19.95
Using dBASE Mac	19.95
Using Dollars and Sense	18.95
Using Excel	19.95
Using Microsoft Word: Macintosh Version	19.95
Using Microsoft Works	18.95
Using WordPerfect: Macintosh Version	19.95

APPLICATIONS SOFTWARE TITLES

Smart Tips, Tricks, and Traps	23.95
Using Dollars and Sense on the IBM	18.95
Using Enable, 2nd Edition	22.95
Using Excel: IBM Version	19.95
Using Managing Your Money	18.95
Using Quattro	21.95
Using Smart	22.95
Using SuperCalc4	19.95

WORD-PROCESSING AND DESKTOP PUBLISHING TITLES

Microsoft Word Tips, Tricks, and Traps	19.95
Using DisplayWrite 4	19.95
Using Microsoft Word, 2nd Edition	19.95
Using MultiMate Advantage, 2nd Edition	19.95
Using PageMaker on the IBM	24.95
Using WordPerfect, 3rd Edition	19.95
Using WordPerfect 5	21.95
Using WordPerfect Workbook and Disk	29.95
Using WordStar	18.95
WordPerfect Tips, Tricks, and Traps	19.95
WordPerfect Advanced Techniques	19.95

HARDWARE AND SYSTEMS TITLES

DOS Programmer's Reference	22.95
DOS QueCards	21.95
DOS Workbook and Disk	29.95
IBM PS/2 Handbook	19.95
Managing Your Hard Disk	19.95
MS-DOS User's Guide, 2nd Edition	21.95
Networking IBM PCs, 2nd Edition	19.95
Programming with Windows	22.95
Understanding UNIX: A Conceptual Guide, 2nd Edition	21.95
Using Microsoft Windows	19.95
Using PC DOS, 2nd Edition	22.95

PROGRAMMING AND TECHNICAL TITLES

Advanced C: Techniques and Applications	21.95
C Programmer's Library	21.95
C Programming Guide, 2nd Edition	19.95
C Self-Study Guide	16.95
C Standard Library	21.95
Debugging C	19.95
Turbo Pascal for BASIC Programmers	18.95
Turbo Pascal Program Library	19.95
Turbo Pascal Tips, Tricks, and Traps	19.95
Using Assembly Language	22.95
Using Turbo Prolog	19.95

QUE™

Que Order Line: **1-800-428-5331**

All prices subject to change without notice. Prices and charges are for domestic orders only.
Non-U.S. prices might be higher.

SELECT QUE BOOKS TO INCREASE YOUR PERSONAL COMPUTER PRODUCTIVITY

Using PC DOS, 2nd Edition

by Chris DeVoney

The best-selling guide to PC DOS is now even better! DOS master Chris DeVoney has updated *Using PC DOS*—the Que classic that covers every aspect of the IBM operating system. Critically acclaimed, *Using PC DOS* is a combination of beginning tutorial and lasting reference, now covering PC DOS through version 3.3. This new 2nd Edition adds up-to-date information on IBM's PS/2 computers and shows how to work with 3 1/2-inch disks. Also featured is a comprehensive beginning tutorial and the popular Command Reference, an easy-to-use consolidation of essential DOS commands. No IBM microcomputer user should be without a copy of *Using PC DOS*, 2nd Edition!

Managing Your Hard Disk

by Don Berliner

Que's *Managing Your Hard Disk* introduces innovative techniques to bring your hard disk to peak performance. Storing and retrieving "libraries" of information is simple when you follow this book's easy-to-understand instructions. *Managing Your Hard Disk* will show you proper backup procedures, ways to activate menu programs, and strategies for using programs that normally won't run on a hard disk. If your personal computer utilizes a hard disk, you need Que's *Managing Your Hard Disk*!

Using WordPerfect 5

by Charles O. Stewart III, et al

WordPerfect 5 is the latest version of the popular word processor and Que's new *Using WordPerfect 5* is the perfect WordPerfect guide. This comprehensive text introduces you to WordPerfect basics; helps you learn to use macros, Styles, and other advanced features; presents information on outlining, referencing, and text columns; and shows you how to use WordPerfect for desktop publishing. Also included are numerous **Quick Start** tutorials, a tear-out command reference card, and an introduction to WordPerfect 5 for 4.2 users. Become a WordPerfect expert with *Using WordPerfect 5*!

IBM PS/2 Handbook

by Richard Dalton

The hot new book on IBM's hot new microcomputers! Richard Dalton, founding editor of The Whole Earth Software Catalog, presents an overview of Personal System/2 hardware, including technical information on each model, tips on integrating PS/2 with other machines, and discussions of PS/2 software. This book helps you understand the differences between PS/2 models, decide which machines best suit your needs, and get the most out of your hardware investment. IBM Personal System/2 is the new standard in microcomputers, and Que's *IBM PS/2 Handbook* will help you with your hardware purchasing decisions!

REGISTRATION CARD

Register your copy of *Using Quattro* and receive information about Que's newest products. Complete this registration card and return it to Que Corporation, P.O. Box 90, Carmel, IN 46032.

Name ____________________ Phone __________

Company __________________ Title __________

Address ______________________________

City ______________ State _______ ZIP _______

Please check the appropriate answers:

Where did you buy *Using Quattro*?
- ☐ Bookstore (name: ____________________)
- ☐ Computer store (name: ________________)
- ☐ Catalog (name: ______________________)
- ☐ Direct from Que ______________________
- ☐ Other: _____________________________

How many computer books do you buy a year?
- ☐ 1 or less
- ☐ 2-5
- ☐ 6-10
- ☐ More than 10

How many Que books do you own?
- ☐ 1
- ☐ 2-5
- ☐ 6-10
- ☐ More than 10

How long have you been using Quattro?
- ☐ Less than 6 months
- ☐ 6 months to 1 year
- ☐ 1-2 years
- ☐ More than 2 years

What influenced your purchase of *Using Quattro*?
- ☐ Personal recommendation
- ☐ Advertisement
- ☐ In-store display
- ☐ Price
- ☐ Que catalog
- ☐ Que mailing
- ☐ Que reputation
- ☐ Other: _____________________________

How would you rate the overall content of *Using Quattro*?
- ☐ Very good
- ☐ Good
- ☐ Satisfactory
- ☐ Poor

COMMENTS: _________________________

How would you rate the *1-2-3 to Quattro reference tables*?
- ☐ Very good
- ☐ Good
- ☐ Satisfactory
- ☐ Poor

COMMENTS: _________________________

How would you rate the *Command Reference Map*?
- ☐ Very good
- ☐ Good
- ☐ Satisfactory
- ☐ Poor

COMMENTS: _________________________

How would you rate *Section IV: Customizing Quattro*?
- ☐ Very good
- ☐ Satisfactory
- ☐ Good
- ☐ Poor

What do you like *best* about *Using Quattro*?

What do you like *least* about *Using Quattro*?

How do you use *Using Quattro*?

What other Que products do you own?

For what other programs would a Que book be helpful?

Please feel free to list any other comments you may have about *Using Quattro*.

____

____

____

____

____

____

____

FOLD HERE

Place
Stamp
Here

Que Corporation
P.O. Box 90
Carmel, IN 46032

FOLD HERE

Place
Stamp
Here

Que Corporation
P.O. Box 90
Carmel, IN 46032